Concurrences Books

Tributes

Herbert Hovenkamp – The Dean of American Antitrust Law, 2021

Frédéric Jenny – Standing Up for Convergence and Relevance in Antitrust, (Vol. I & II), 2019 & 2021

Albert Foer – A Consumer Voice in the Antitrust Arena, 2020

Richard Whish – Taking Competition Law Outside the Box, 2020

Douglas H. Ginsburg – An Antitrust Professor on the Bench (Vol. I & II), 2018 & 2020

Wang Xiaoye – The Pioneer of Competition Law in China, A. Emch, W. Ng (eds.), 2019

Ian S. Forrester – A Scot without Borders (Vol. I & II), A. Komninos (eds.), 2015

William E. Kovacic – An Antitrust Tribute (Vol. I & II), 2013 & 2014

Practical Books

Global Dictionary of Competition Law, D. Healey, W. Kovacic, P. Trevisan, R. Whish, Forthcoming 2022

Antitrust in the Pharmaceutical Sector, M. Cowie, G. Gordon M. Thill-Tayara, Forthcoming 2022

Competition Law Treatment of Joint Ventures, B. Bleicher, N. Campbell, A. Hamilton, N. Hukkinen, P. Khan, Forthcoming 2022 (in collaboration with the IBA)

State Aid & National Enforcement, J. Derenne, D. Jouve, C. Lemaire, F. Martucci (eds.), Forthcoming 2022

Competition Digest – A Synthesis of EU and National Leading Cases, 5th edition, F. Jenny N. Charbit, (eds.) Forthcoming 2022

Information Exchange and Related Risks – A Practical Guide, Z. Marosi & M. Soares (eds.), Forthcoming 2021 (in collaboration with the IBA)

Perspectives on Antitrust Compliance, A. Riley, A. Stephan, A. Tubbs (eds.), Forthcoming 2021 (in collaboration with the ICC)

Turkish Competition Law, G. Gürkaynak, Forthcoming 2021

Competition Law – Climate Change & Environmental Sustainability, S. Holmes, D. Middelschulte, M. Snoep (eds.), 2021

Merger Control in Latin America – A Jurisdictional Guide, P. Burnier da Silveira, P. Sittenfeld, 2020

Competition Inspections under EU Law – A Practitioner's Guide, N. Jalabert-Doury, 2020

Gun Jumping in Merger Control – A Jurisdictional Guide, C. Hatton, Y. Comtois, A. Hamilton (eds.), 2019 (in collaboration with the IBA)

Choice – A New Standard for Competition Analysis? P. Nihoul, 2016

PhD Theses

Essays in Competition Economics, T. Klein (Forthcoming 2022)

Competition & Regulation in Network Industries – Essays in Industrial Organization, J-M. Zogheib, 2021

The Role of Media Pluralism in the Enforcement of EU Competition Law, Konstantina Bania, 2019

Buyer Power, Ignacio Herrera Anchustegui, 2017

General Interest

Women and Antitrust – Voices from the Field (Vol I & II), E. Kurgonaite & K. Nordlander, 2020

Conference Proceedings

Antitrust in Emerging and Developing Countries – (Vol I & II), E. Fox, H. First, 2015 & 2016

Global Antitrust Law – Current Issues in Antitrust Law and Economics, D. Ginsburg, J. Wright, (eds.) 2015

Competition Law on the Global Stage – David Gerber's Global Competition Law in Perspective, D. Gerber, 2014

e-Book versions available for **Concurrences+** subscribers

ELEANOR M. FOX

Liber Amicorum

All rights reserved. No photocopying: copyright licences do not apply. The information provided in this publication is general and may not apply in a specific situation. Legal advice should always be sought before taking any legal action based on the information provided. The publisher accepts no responsibility for any acts or omissions contained herein. Enquiries concerning reproduction should be sent to the Institute of Competition Law, at the address below.

Copyright © 2021 by Institute of Competition Law
106 West 32nd Street, Suite 144 New York, NY, 10001, USA
www.concurrences.com
book@concurrences.com

First Printing, October 2021
978-1-939007-97-1 (Hardcover)
Library of Congress Control Number: 2021920072

Cover Design: Yves Buliard, www.yvesbuliard.fr
Book Design and Layout implementation: Nord Compo

ELEANOR M. FOX
Antitrust Ambassador to the World

Liber Amicorum

Foreword by Maria Coppola and David Lewis
Introduction by Ilene Knable Gotts

Editors
Nicolas Charbit
Sébastien Gachot

Foreword

MARIA COPPOLA AND DAVID LEWIS
US Federal Trade Commission | Corruption Watch South Africa

Times have changed, and questioning antitrust orthodoxy was not always popular as it is today. Looking outside the US borders for inspiration was perhaps even less popular. And yet this book honors someone who has done both for decades and is unequivocally one of the most beloved and vibrant figures in the international competition community. An intellectual vanguard and a treasured friend.

When we think of avant-garde and an octogenarian, the assumption is that person was a pioneer in his or her "day". Eleanor was indeed a pioneer as a young woman in law school, one of eight females in her graduating class. When she became the first female partner at her white-shoe law firm in 1970, only two other women were or had ever been partners in major Wall Street law firms. In the early 1980s, as the Chicago School began to dominate thinking, she questioned the efficiency narrative and argued for antitrust to encompass not only consumer interests, but others as well, such as dispersion of economic power and protection of the competitive process as market governor. In 1986, long before international antitrust was even a concept, she was writing comparisons of US and EU approaches to single firm conduct. When market reform and the Washington consensus began to gain traction in the early 1990s, Eleanor was already in Central Europe, working on a book about how competition law was changing economies, asking why central European nations need to adopt EU competition law instead of one more adapted to their needs? At the turn of this century, when the US, EU, and others realized there was a need for a new international approach to competition policy, Eleanor was busy drawing up plans for the Global Competition Initiative, an enterprise that later materialized as the International Competition Network, today the preeminent multilateral competition body. And in 2007, the so-called high-water mark of consensus that antitrust was on the right course, Eleanor was writing articles that eschewed consideration only of aggregate consumer or total wealth and advocating for an analytical standard that opens paths of mobility and access to markets so critical for economic success, particularly in developing countries. These days, she writes about how competition agencies in developing nations can use their public interest standard to address the economic strains imposed by the coronavirus, and what an international framework for addressing competition concerns of digital platforms might look like. Her "day" encompasses more than sixty years.

Eleanor's scholarly work spans a broad array of subjects, but it is her comparative work, particularly in regard to the US and the EU, that is the most celebrated. Her work is regularly consulted by scholars, practitioners, and agency officials, and has shaped profoundly how we approach and think about these two systems. Her work offers deep insight into ways the transatlantic titans could learn not only from one another but also from younger agencies, including those in the developing world. While others pressed for convergence and harmonization, Eleanor recognized that those pursuits needed to be complemented by understanding and respecting differences, and successfully advocated for informed divergence to be part of the ICN's mission, alongside convergence.

Eleanor's written contributions are testament to the pioneer she is. Her legacy, however, will be in her human interactions. While others with unorthodox views might run for cover, time and again Eleanor has raised her hand to participate, often the only female in the room and even more often, the only one with a different viewpoint. For decades Eleanor has espoused her views on a stage physically and metaphorically full of traditionalists, engaging them with grace. Indeed, Eleanor's intellectual curiosity and fairmindedness leads her to *seek out* people with different views, an exercise in pluralism, as she seeks to understand diverse views and how they relate to her own. From the earliest days of her career, she has been a mentor and friend not only to her students but to agency officials, fellow academics, and others. How typical that, during the pandemic lockdowns, while others secluded themselves from social engagements Eleanor was reaching out to friends, colleagues, and students – offering kindness, sympathy, and words of positivity.

It is fitting that Eleanor received a lifetime achievement award for her "substantial, lasting, and transformational impact on competition policy and/or practice" in 2011: she was a transformationalist before transformationalism was in vogue. Today's advocates for change may be unaware of the debt they owe to this remarkable woman, but this volume is one of many testaments to the decades Eleanor has spent defying gravity.

Introduction

ILENE KNABLE GOTTS
Wachtell, Lipton, Rosen & Katz

It is my great honor to provide this introduction for Eleanor Fox's Liber Amicorum.

I met Eleanor for the first time in the Spring of 1984. As a graduating law student heading to the FTC to begin my antitrust career, I decided to attend the Antitrust Section's Spring Meeting. Scanning the large banquet room, I saw a sea of over 1,000 men in dark suits talking and engaged with each other–and seated in the front row, a sole woman reviewing the program materials. I worked my way over to that woman and saw an empty seat next to her. Not sure what to do, I shyly asked whether that seat was available; the woman looked up, immediately smiled, and said enthusiastically "Yes, I am Eleanor, nice to meet you." Little did I know at the time, that as Humphrey Bogart said in Casablanca, this was "the beginning of a beautiful friendship."

Fast forward three years. I decided to go to the Fordham Law conference in New York City, which at that time focused only on European Commission and US law. I, who up to that time had been a student and practitioner only of US competition law–with a focus on economics and the developing Chicago School principals–was intrigued by the discussions about a different approach to some of the basic principles of competition law and policy. And who on the panel opened my eyes to the possibilities that we, in the US, might not necessarily have it "all right," or perhaps not right for all economies and circumstances: no one other than Eleanor Fox.

We stayed in touch after that conference, and I followed Eleanor's prolific writings, and her unfashionable call for the human aspects of competitive policy. By the late 1990s, Eleanor's reach had extended beyond the US, Europe, and the "developed" economies, to the developing world, including Africa.

Eleanor has been a trail blazer throughout her career. In doing so, she has been a mentor and role model for me, multiple generations of US lawyers, and, as evidenced by this liber, throughout the world.

Eleanor joined the New York law firm of Simpson Thacher & Bartlett as an associate in 1962–right after the birth of her first child (she ultimately had three children while continuing to work at the firm). Her talents were immediately recognized by one of the finest antitrust litigators in the country at that time– Whitney North Seymour, Sr. – and under his tutelage she developed a love for antitrust law. Eleanor became the firm's first female partner in 1970 and remained a partner at Simpson until 1976, when she embarked on her full-time academic career at NYU, while still remaining affiliated with Simpson in a counsel role.

Forty-five years later, Eleanor is the Walter J. Derenberg Professor of Trade Regulation at the NYU School of Law, where she continues to teach, both inside and outside the classroom, the next generation of competition lawyers.

When I was the International Officer of the ABA's Antitrust Section (2013-2016), I affectionately referred to Eleanor as the "Competition Ambassador to the World." If you went to the NYU website around that time, you would have seen the usual materials that you would expect for a Professor of Eleanor's high stature–a bio with a long list of articles, prestigious positions, etc. But, if you searched the NYU website more broadly, you would find under "news" a story that really provides some insight into the fervor with which Eleanor has undertaken her role. The title of the article is "Eleanor Fox goes on global tour" and states with respect to Eleanor's upcoming summer plans, "Don't look for Eleanor Fox at the beach in coming weeks. Instead, Fox ... will be crisscrossing the globe." The site then provides an interactive map, which, if you click on any of the pins, provides a summary of the competition authorities and topics she covered at each site during her summer break. Of course, Eleanor's role as "Competition Ambassador to the World" has been much more pervasive than a single summer hiatus.

Eleanor has never seen antitrust as confined to narrow concerns and has constantly reminded us of the importance of the social and political concerns that have historically been part of the fabric of antitrust. Eleanor's 1987 article on "The Battle for the Soul of Antitrust" epitomizes this philosophy. So, too, does her 1987 article co-written with Larry Sullivan, "Antitrust-Retrospective and Prospective: Where Are We Coming From? Where Are We Going?", which notes that legacies of the antipower, prodiversity era remain as the historical preference for pluralism, freedom of trade, access to markets, and freedom of choice. In these and subsequent articles, Eleanor challenges us to see the basis for recognizing the human aspects of competition and industrial policy–the potential to create a regime that will best incentivize firms to be, using Eleanor's words, "lively, creative, innovative, and responsive; to produce and invent what people want."

These articles also reflect another part of Eleanor's enduring character, her optimism. Eleanor identified herself as "an optimist" in her 1989 Fordham Law Review article "Being a Woman, Being a Lawyer and Being a Human Being." As she further recognizes, part of being an optimist is recognizing that success can be slow to achieve.

Eleanor's successes in broadening the role of antitrust outside of the US have been well-recognized and noted but have been slow to gain broad acceptance here in the US. For much of the last four decades, her views were a departure from mainstream economic thinking. Eleanor's patience, however, may finally be paying off. Today's debate on US competition policy in the halls of Congress, Presidential campaigns, and among Neo-Brandeisian enforcers suggests that Eleanor's harkening back to the principles and objectives that formed the basis of our federal antitrust laws is not so much sentimental, but rather, as with a good vintage wine, may be just now coming into their peak time. In fact, her unabated focus on equality and fairness as part of the antitrust law mandate has been prescient and may more accurately reflect the reach of the antitrust laws in the emerging new world order than the narrower Chicago School approach, she began questioning decades ago.

In sum, Eleanor has made a difference with her optimism and compassion for all of us who have been fortunate enough to know her, to count her as a friend, and to have witnessed all that she has achieved in the United States and globally to make the world a better place.

Contributors

Skaidrīte Ābrama
Competition Council of Latvia (Ex)

Berfu Akgün
*ELIG Gürkaynak
Attorneys-at-Law*

Giuliano Amato
Italian Constitutional Court

Donald I. Baker
Baker & Miller

Maciej Bernatt
University of Warsaw

Darryl Biggar
*Australian Competition
Commission*

Tembinkosi Bonakele
*Competition Commission
of South Africa*

Dennis M. Davis
*Competition Appeal Court
of South Africa*

Lisl J. Dunlop
Axinn, Veltrop & Harkrider

Adrian Emch
Hogan Lovells

Allan Fels
University of Melbourne

Harry First
New York University School of Law

Owen Fiss
Yale University

Albert A. Foer
American Antitrust Institute

Michal S. Gal
University of Haifa

Damien Gerard
*College of Europe and University
of Louvain*

David J. Gerber
Chicago-Kent College of Law

Bulut Girgin
*ELIG Gürkaynak
Attorneys-at-Law*

Gönenç Gürkaynak
*ELIG Gürkaynak
Attorneys-at-Law*

Deborah Healey
University of New South Wales

Andrew Heimert
Federal Trade Commission

Alberto Heimler
*Italian National School
of Government*

Edward Iacobucci
University of Toronto

Jonathan Klaaren
University of the Witwatersrand

Assimakis P. Komninos
White & Case

Ujjwal Kumar
CUTS International

Pradeep S. Mehta
CUTS International

Giorgio Monti
*Tilburg Law and Economics
Center*

Wendy Ng
University of Melbourne

Sibusiso Radebe
University of the Witwatersrand

Albie Sachs
*Constitutional Court
of South Africa (Ex)*

Taimoon Stewart
University of the West Indies

Michael Trebilcock
University of Toronto

Xiaoye Wang
Shenzhen University

Joseph Wilson
McGill University

Koren W. Wong-Ervin
Axinn, Veltrop & Harkrider

Table of Contents

Foreword I

Introduction.. III

Contributors VII

Table of Contents IX

Eleanor M. Fox Biography and Publications......................... XIII

Introduction: In Her Own Words

Words of Wisdom: Interview with Eleanor M. Fox............................ 3
Michal S. Gal

Part I: The Eleanor Effect: Scholarship and Influence in South Africa and Beyond

My Secret Weapon 13
Albie Sachs

A New Competition Law Paradigm: The Influence of Eleanor Fox 25
Dennis M. Davis

Tracing Professor Fox in South Africa's Competition Jurisprudence...... 33
Jonathan Klaaren and Sibusiso Radebe

Professor Eleanor Fox: Making Markets Work for the People –
A View from South Africa 51
Tembinkosi Bonakele

A Few Snapshots of Professor Eleanor Fox 73
Skaidrīte Ābrama

Part II: Competition Policy: Foundations and Development

Neo-Antitrust, Machiavelli and the Rule of Law 91
Giuliano Amato

The American Antitrust Counter-Revolutionaries:
A European Perspective 103
Giorgio Monti

In Antitrust We Trust.. 129
Damien Gerard

The Goals of Competition Law Debate and Competition Policy
for Labor Markets 139
Darryl Biggar, Allan Fels and Alberto Heimler

The Vision for One Antitrust World... 163
Joseph Wilson

Part III: Emerging Economies: Challenges and Opportunities

The Quest for Relevant and Inclusive Competition Laws
in Small Vulnerable Economies.. 187
Taimoon Stewart

After Convergence: Competition Law in Emerging Markets................ 243
David J. Gerber

Digital Platforms and Competition Policy in Developing Countries.... 253
Harry First

Part IV: Intersection with Social Policies: Race, Inequality, and Fairness

Reasonable Expectations 275
Owen Fiss

Competition Policy and Access to Healthcare...................................... 285
Pradeep S. Mehta and Ujjwal Kumar

Antitrust and Healthcare Inequity 295
Lisl J. Dunlop

Fairness as a Counterpoint to Efficiency in Competition Policy? 307
Edward Iacobucci and Michael Trebilcock

A Perspective on Privatization: Whatever Happened
to the 1960s New Towns Movement? 321
Albert A. Foer

Part V: Agency Actions: Mandate, Cooperation, and External Pressures

The Antitrust Agencies' Successful System
of International Cooperation Being Tested in the Digital Age 361
Donald I. Baker

Mandate of Competition Agency in Populist Times 391
Maciej Bernatt

Part VI: Enforcement and Judicial Review: Current Issues

Extraterritoriality: Approaches Around the World
and Model Analysis 405
Koren W. Wong-Ervin and Andrew Heimert

The Digital Markets Act and Private Enforcement:
Proposals for an Optimal System of Enforcement 425
Assimakis P. Komninos

Still Hanging in the Balance – Judicial Assessments
of Authorities' Merger Decisions 445
Gönenç Gürkaynak, Berfu Akgün and Bulut Girgin

Part VII: Reform: Focus on China

Competition Law 2.0: Amending China's Anti-Monopoly Law 467
Wang Xiaoye and Adrian Emch

The Antimonopoly Law of China: Prospects for Change 485
Deborah Healey

Unpacking the Personal Information Protection Regime
and its Potential Implications for Competition Law in China 507
Wendy Ng

Eleanor M. Fox

Biography & Publications

Biography

Eleanor M. Fox is a professor of law and is the Walter J. Derenberg Professor of Trade Regulation at New York University School of Law. She teaches, writes, lectures, and advises on antitrust law, competition policy, and globalization, and has a special interest in developing countries and the interrelationship between equality and efficiency.

Eleanor was a partner at the New York law firm Simpson Thacher & Bartlett. She served as a member of the International Competition Policy Advisory Committee to the Attorney General of the US Department of Justice (1997–2000) (President Clinton) and as a Commissioner on President Carter's National Commission for the Review of Antitrust Laws and Procedures (1978–79). She has advised numerous younger antitrust jurisdictions including South Africa, Egypt, Kenya, Tanzania, The Gambia, Indonesia, Russia, Poland, and Hungary, and the common market COMESA. Eleanor received an honorary doctorate degree from the University of Paris-Dauphine (2009). She was awarded an inaugural Lifetime Achievement Award in 2011 by *Global Competition Review* for "substantial, lasting and transformational impact on competition policy and/or practice" and lifetime, inaugural, or other achievement awards from ASCOLA, AALS Antitrust Section, New York State Bar Antitrust Association, and the American Antitrust Institute. With Mor Bakhoum, she wrote *Making Markets Work For Africa* (2019). Her other books include US and EU competition casebooks (with Dan Crane and Damien Gerard, respectively), *Global Issues in Antitrust and Competition Law* with Dan Crane, and readings on developing countries and competition with Abel Mateus.

Publications
(as of September 2021)

Books

Case and Materials on US Antitrust in Global Context (with Daniel Crane). West Academic Press, 4th ed., 2020.

Making Markets Work For Africa: Markets, Development, and Competition Law in Sub-Saharan Africa (with Mor Bakhoum). Oxford University Press, 2019.

EU Competition Law: Cases, Texts, and Context (with Damien Gerard). Edward Elgar, 2017.

Global Issues in Antitrust and Competition Law (with Daniel Crane). West Academic Press, 2d ed., 2017.

The Design of Competition Law Institutions: Global Norms, Local Choices (ed., with Michael J. Trebilcock). Oxford University Press, 2013.

Antitrust Stories (ed., with Daniel Crane). Foundation Press, 2007.

Articles, Essays and Chapters in Collection

"Mergers, Antitrust, and the China Card." In *Research Handbook on Global Merger Control*, edited by Nicholas Levy & Ioannis Kokkoris (forthcoming).

"Antitrust and Inequality: The History of (In)Equality in Competition Law and Its Guide to the Future" (with Philipp Bazenov). In *Competition Law and Economic Inequality*, edited by Jan Broulik & Kati Cseres (forthcoming).

"Integrating Africa by Competition and Market Policy" Rev. Indus. Org., special issue on Africa edited by T. Ross & Liberty Mncube (2021) (forthcoming).

"The new US antitrust administration" (with Alden F. Abbott, Robin Adelstein, Megan Browdie, Michael A. Carrier, Peter C. Carstensen, Samuel Clark, Lisl J. Dunlop, Harry First, Albert A. Foer, Eleanor M. Fox, Jacqueline Grise, Ryan Kantor, Donald C. Klawiter, John Kwoka, James Langenfeld, Tad Lipsky, Alessandro Massolo, Howard Morse, Gabriella Muscolo, James Bo Pearl, Noah Pinegar, Chris Ring, Christopher Sagers, Richard S. Taffet, Willard K. Tom, Eliot Turner, Doug Tween, Tommaso Valletti and Michael L. Weiner) 1-2021 Concurrences (2021).

"We Need Rules to Rein in Big Tech" (with Harry First), special edition of the CPI Antitrust Chron. (Oct. 2020).

"Competition Law In Sub-Saharan Africa: The Market Solution Or A Faustian Pact?" (with Mor Bakhoum) in Competition law and developing countries: Overarching themes from Africa, cartels and corruption, and mergers, 2-2020 Concurrences (2020).

"Antitrust and the clash of sovereigns – Bringing under one roof: Extraterritoriality, industrial policy, foreign sovereign compulsion, and (bad) applications of law against "my country's" firms" 4-2019 Concurrences (2019).

"Antitrust: Updating Extraterritoriality" 0/2019 (inaugural issue) Antitrust & Pub. Policies Rev. (2019) (published by the Italian Competition Authority) (Concurrences Best Antitrust Academic Cross-border Article, 2020).

"Platforms, Power and the Antitrust Challenge: A Modest Proposal to Narrow the US–Europe Divide" 98(2) Neb. L. Rev. 297 (2019).

"Extraterritorial Jurisdiction, Antitrust, and the EU Intel Case: Implementation, Qualified Effects, and the Third Kind" 42 Fordham Int'l L.J. 981 (2019).

"China, Export Cartels, and Vitamin C: America Second?" CPI's North America Column (March 2018).

"Outsider Antitrust: 'Making Markets Work for People' as a Post-Millennium Development Goal." In *Competition Policy For The New Era: Insights from the BRICS Countries*, edited by Tembinkosi Bonakele, Eleanor Fox, & Liberty Mncube. Oxford University Press, 2017.

"Antitrust Without Borders: From Roots to Codes to Networks." In *Cooperation, Comity, and Competition Policy*, edited by Andrew T. Guzman. Oxford University Press, 2015.

"Monopolization and Abuse of Dominance: Why Europe is Different" 59 Antitrust Bull. 129 (2014).

"When the State Harms Competition – The Role for Competition Law" (with Deborah Healey) 79 Antitrust L.J. 769 (2014).

"China, the WTO, and State-sponsored export cartels: Where trade and competition ought to meet" (with Merit E. Janow) 4-2012 Concurrences (2012).

"The law and economics of resale price maintenance: A comparative perspective" (with Jérôme Philippe, Philippe Nasse, Lucas Peeperkorn, and Anne Perrot) 4-2008 Concurrences (2008).

"The Efficiency Paradox." In *How The Chicago School Overshot The Mark: The Effect of Conservative Economic Analysis on US Antitrust*, edited by Robert Pitofsky. Oxford University Press, 2008.

"An antitrust fable – A tale of predation" 3-2008 Concurrences (2008).

"International Antitrust and the Doha Dome" 43 Va. J. Int'l L. 911 (2003).

"Toward World Antitrust and Market Access" 91 Am. J. Int'l L. 1 (1997).

"Being a Woman, Being a Lawyer and Being a Human Being" 57 Fordham L. Rev. 955 (1989).

"The Battle for the Soul of Antitrust" 75 Cal. L. Rev 917 (1987).

"Modernization of Antitrust: A New Equilibrium" 66 Cornell L. Rev. 1140 (1981).

INTRODUCTION
In Her Own Words

Words of Wisdom: Interview with Eleanor M. Fox

MICHAL S. GAL*
University of Haifa

Abstract

This part includes an interview with Professor Eleanor Fox, conducted by Professor Michal Gal, which was first published in Women & Antitrust[1]: Voices from the Field. It provides a unique glance into the perspective of the woman whose stellar career and numerous achievements are celebrated in this book. The interview touches upon many issues, including Professor Fox's personal story and how she broke the glass ceiling; the reason she chose to specialize in competition law; why she was interested in competition law enforcement outside her own jurisdiction, at a time when such enforcement was not common; the basis of the divergence between competition law in the EU and in the US; her view on the proposed break-up of large technology firms; the relationship between competition law and international trade law; her experience in writing a book focusing on competition law in Africa; whether the state of development should affect equality and inclusiveness goals; what excites her most about her career; and her advice for young people in the field.

---

* Michal Gal (LLB, LLM, SJD) is professor and director of the Center for Law and Technology at the Faculty of Law, University of Haifa, Israel, and the elected president of ASCOLA, the international organization of competition law scholars. Professor Gal is the author of several books, including *Competition Policy for Small Market Economies* (Harvard University Press 2003). She has also published numerous articles in leading journals, and has won prizes for her research and her teaching.

1 Women & Antitrust: Voices from the Field, Vol. II (edited by Kristina Nordlander), Concurrences, 2021.

You started your career as an antitrust lawyer in 1962. Antitrust used to be a man's world. Yet you broke many glass ceilings that existed for women, including becoming the first female partner in a major New York firm. Can you share with us some of your experiences and takeaways from this period in your life?

Let me start with law school. I went to New York University School of Law, entering in 1958. Many law schools did not all admit women then, on the grounds that women would take the place of male students and male students were serious about becoming lawyers. I was grateful that NYU Law School admitted women. For students in the first year, NYU had two sections of about 100 students each. There was one other woman in my section. One of my professors did not call on women, but he made an exception. One day a semester he would have "Ladies Day." On Ladies Day he would call on me and my female classmate. Everyone thought it was a big joke and laughed. So I laughed too.

For my second summer I looked for a law job. At that time you just walked into a firm and left your résumé at the front desk, and someone would come to interview you (at least if you had an excellent academic record and were on law review, and I did and was). Being in New York, I went to the Wall Street law firms. Everywhere I went they said that they were not hiring women. Some said, we tried it once and it did not work out. She got married (or pregnant) and left. I heard that the US Attorney's Office in the Southern District of New York would hire women in the Civil Division (not in the Criminal Division, because women were not fit to deal with blood or murder). I went for an interview and was hired. I had a great summer and I was grateful.

In 1961 when I graduated from law school, I was pregnant with my first child. For the summer and fall, I worked for professors at the law school. My son Doug was born in November. In January I was ready to look for a job. I knew that most firms were not hiring women. Simpson Thacher and Bartlett offered me a job to do a document search to answer a document request in a large antitrust case. I was grateful and I accepted. The firm liked my work. It hired me as an associate, and, eight years later, in January 1970, I became their first female partner. I believe I was the first female partner in the top 10 or so Wall Street law firms as measured by size of firm. I was in the litigation department. Antitrust was placed in the litigation department. There was a merger wave, and I advised on scores of mergers, handicapping them for investment banking firms such as Lehman Brothers. Also, I handled major monopoly litigation for plaintiff corporations. For mergers, much of the litigation was under the antitrust and securities laws to fend off takeovers. We often went to court for preliminary injunctions, which often were granted.

Was there a glass ceiling? The expression had not even been invented. But that was the theme of the novel I wrote as I was leaving the firm. The novel is entitled *WL, Esquire*. WL stood for Wendy Lieberman, the main character; also for Women's Liberation. Esquire means gentleman. Until about the mid-1970s, lawyers were addressed, on letters and in formal writing, with the honorific "Esq." following their names. Wendy Lieberman, Esq. could not rise in her profession without being a gentleman. So she was one of the boys, and she rose. But she could never rise to the top, because she was, after all, not a gentleman.

Despite your meteoric success in practice, you decided to become an academic. Can you share with us the reasons for this choice? Also–why did you choose competition law as your specialism and would you make the same choice today?

The women's movement began and blossomed in the 1960s. By the early 1970s I began to understand a lot of things. I had always assumed that the place of women was a given; things were the way they were. If there was a Ladies Day in class and everyone laughed, maybe I should laugh too. The converse was much worse. Not laughing meant accepting humiliation. But by the early 1970s I began to take a broader view, including on what I wanted to do in life and whom I wanted to help. I always wanted to be a writer and scholar. I wanted also to be a teacher. And I wanted an environment where I could choose my own agenda for thinking and writing.

For my area of specialty, I did not *choose* antitrust; it chose me. But it was a happy choice that fit me. It has been fascinating for me to see antitrust policy move from a major tool to constrain the power of business, to microeconomics and freeing up business in the name of efficiency, and now, at least in the rhetoric and debate, a symbiosis.

You were one of the first Americans to study European Union competition law. In fact, when you started writing about the subject, there was not much interest in the US about competition law enforcement outside the US. What was the trigger for this decision, and what are the most important insights you gained from such a study?

The European Community began seriously enforcing its competition law in the mid-1960s and 1970s. At about the time that I moved from Simpson Thacher to NYU (1976), officials of the European Community began to ask me to lecture there so that they could better understand US law. Barry Hawk, who was then a professor at Fordham, took his sabbatical at the European Commission and convinced me that on my first sabbatical I must go to Brussels, which I did. A few years later US colleagues who were experts in European law asked me to join their casebook, which I did. From the start, European law fascinated me. Just at a time when US law was being magnetically drawn to the Chicago school, I saw European competition law blossom in the context of the European treaties, with no semblance of Chicago school presumptions, and with a major mission to create community.

There seems to be an apparent divergence between the way EU and US authorities currently treat the large digital platforms, although recently it seems to have narrowed. In light of your long-standing study of EU and US competition laws, what do you think stands at the basis of such divergence, can it be overcome, and do you foresee that it will increase or decrease?

US and EU competition laws are from different roots. They have a huge amount of convergence. But on monopolization/abuse of dominance, some differences seem essential. US law assumes that single-firm conduct is efficient and that freedom of even dominant firms to act is the right prescription for inducing competitive and inventive behavior. Firms have almost no antitrust duties to deal, and certainly no duties to deal fairly. EU competition law is greatly influenced by its place in the European treaties, which create open markets and limit discrimination and privilege. Under EU law, dominant firms have the duty not to foreclose competition on the merits. Both dominance and its abuse are easier to prove. The large digital platforms, their conduct, and the attempt to make them accountable, may fall precisely in the divide.

In both jurisdictions, as well as in other parts of the world, we hear increasing numbers of voices calling for the break-up of the large technology giants, given their significant market power. There is even a branding of such voices, including as neo-Brandeisians and hipsters. What is your take on such views?

I do not use the word hipster. It was invented to belittle a point of view.

We do not hear much call for break-up outside of the United States, except to the extent of calling attention to anticompetitive mergers that should have gotten a closer look on day one.

Within the United States, the neo-Brandeisians have helpfully called attention to the great power of the big data platforms, and to the general problem of increasing concentration and inequality. They want to return to roots, when US antitrust did not isolate antitrust from political economy. The neo-Brandeisians have given voice to a debate that had to happen. They touch concerns of the people. While they are criticized for importing non-competition values into the debate on antitrust, in fact, if you look at it closely, at least 95% of their critiques and proposals map entirely on to the question of how to improve competition in America. They would improve competition with more inclusiveness and less indulgence for incumbent firms. They would topple the traditional high burdens for proving monopoly power, which, according to conservative analysts, would require proof of power to reduce output in a market. They would topple the requirement that no conduct of a monopolist is anticompetitive unless it increases the power to reduce output in the same or an adjacent market. Their approach would make it possible to call big data platforms to account.

Whether break-up is the right solution is a different question. But it is the call for break-up that has galvanized the debate.

Your expertise reaches well beyond these two jurisdictions. In fact, much of your work focuses on international and comparative competition law. You have also taken an active part in some of the US endeavors to determine, inter alia, the relationship between trade and competition law, and in particular the role that the World Trade Organization (WTO) should play in competition law enforcement. Could you describe some of your experiences in the field? Do you think that there

is a chance that international cooperation endeavors can go one step further, toward joint enforcement?

I was very much part of the debate in the 1990s when experts were taking seriously the observation that transactions are global and law should be commensurate with their effects. I proposed a world framework in the WTO, which basically would adopt cosmopolitan (or community-regarding) principles, prohibit beggar-thy-neighbor restraints, and look at transactions from a community-wide view, much as Europe does for the European Union, but with national enforcement. Many Europeans were sympathetic (and they had their own proposal). Americans were not. And, of course, all such proposals are off the table now, and the WTO and internationalism in general are under intense stress.

International cooperation on a horizontal level is not a complete substitute, for it leaves lots of room for nationalism. But it should go further. Take, for example, the global mega-mergers such as Holcim/Lafarge, the biggest cement companies in the world in the most cartel-prone business in the world. It is astounding that the major enforcers all cleared the merger, with spinoffs that would (might) protect their countries' consumers, while leaving developing countries–the most vulnerable victims–to fend for themselves. That merger should not have been allowed. If affected jurisdictions collaborated in their merger reviews, they might have mutually gained the courage of convictions to prohibit the merger.

Recently you have published an important book, with Mor Bakhoum, on competition and markets in sub-Saharan Africa, and you have done a book tour in Africa. Can you tell us about the book, about the experience writing it, and why you decided to study the competition laws of the African nations?

Mor and I wrote the book, *Making Markets Work for Africa*. Mor (from Senegal) had just completed an assignment to review and write a report on all of the competition authorities in French West Africa. I had been doing work in South Africa and wanted to expand my scope; to learn about other African countries. For one thing, I was interested in the fit of Western law with developing country markets, and if not the Western standard, what standards? So, we undertook this project–to study jurisdictions in sub-Saharan Africa that already had competition laws, to find out what the authorities were doing, what were they doing well, what could they do better, what challenges they faced. We knew that their markets were different, they often hardly functioned, and in many areas the people were not sympathetic to markets. We had a hugely interesting time exploring the facts, discerning the narrative they told, and thus creating the book. We–or at least I–gained a new appreciation for the tasks of the competition authorities of sub-Saharan Africa. They have so many tasks to accomplish for progress in their work. They have a different balance of advocacy and enforcement, for they must be able to tear down some barriers before competition can function at all. For example, where governments are autocracies and leaders lavish the best market opportunities on their cronies, the space for competition is squeezed.

The nations we studied ranged from those that still clung to colonial traditions of socialism with suspicion for markets, to those that had freed themselves from their colonial heritage and were working hard and wisely to open up the markets for their people. We also studied the regional free trade agreements and common markets in Africa and, while observing their drawbacks and dysfunctionalities, we still concluded that collaboration among the African nations is needed for effective cross-border enforcement and a voice of Africa.

You are a leading voice on the proposition that equality of opportunity is and should be a value of antitrust in the context of developing jurisdictions. Would you also recommend that developed jurisdictions take this path?

The growing literature on inclusiveness as a value in the competition laws of developing countries should have a positive spillover effect in the developed world. The antitrust law of the United States, for example, needs to absorb these lessons in the law of exclusionary practices. Currently, US law weighs heavily on the side of dominant firms in having freedom to take strategies with exclusionary effects. It gives little regard to the exclusionary effects if the dominant firm tells a story about how it does not have the power to limit output, and how its conduct is efficient and will enhance its incentives to invest and invent. This is the wrong emphasis for an antitrust law. The literature on inclusiveness–empirical, anecdotal, and conceptual–shows how dominant firms erect and constantly reinforce barriers that protect them from competition and that keep at bay feisty and potentially efficient competitors with better ideas.

In light of your experience, how do you suggest framing the relationship between antitrust law and economics?

Antitrust and economics are and should be deeply linked. The problem is not that economics is deeply embedded in antitrust. The problem is with assumptions of some economists and assumptions of one very important school of economics (e.g. that markets almost always work if left alone, and economic power is hard to get and will be punished by the market if exercised). For antitrust *law*, the law part of the equation must be superior, for the law part sets the norms and generalizes economics into rules and standards that are judicially administrable and easily enough understood for compliance. Economics should be in service of the norms.

I know you love being an academic. You were also a partner in private practice. Could you compare academia to practice and do you have advice for young women lawyers making the choice? What excites you most about your career?

I have been very fortunate in my career, and I love and have loved my career. It was of course beyond all of my expectations when I entered law school in 1958, because, as a woman, I had none. As a member of a law faculty, I am excited to interact with my colleagues and my students, to learn from them, and to help them. When they tell me I have made an impact on them, that is a great gift. My time for scholarship is a gift.

My practice was also very satisfying. I am always fascinated by the law, analysis of it and applications of it. As a practitioner, I loved the teamwork, and loved learning new markets (and people) with each new case. As an academic I have more space to contemplate what I think the law should be, and thus to think about the values of law. Academia has also given me a platform for lecturing and giving technical assistance in all parts of the world, and thus for developing an amazing network of friends and acquaintances, globally.

What (other) advice do you have for young people considering a career in antitrust law?

Antitrust is a great field. It is multifaceted, for it spans law, political economy, economics, and even foreign relations. It offers opportunity for all of the practice skills, as well as scholarship and teaching. It is a very interpersonal field, for it exposes you both to teamwork at home and new acquaintances abroad. Follow your star. Follow the path that suits you and excites you. And if you devote yourself to the task, you will be richly rewarded by the personal satisfactions that it brings.

PART I
The Eleanor Effect: Scholarship and Influence in South Africa and Beyond

My Secret Weapon

ALBIE SACHS[*]

Former Justice of the Constitutional Court of South Africa

Abstract

Albie Sachs was recently asked to moderate a panel of experts at a conference in Pretoria on the constitutional dimensions of competition law. Experienced in constitutional law but knowing very little about competition law, he reached out by email to Eleanor Fox, who had visited South Africa's Constitutional Court, for guidance. In return he not only received a short email course on competition law with special relevance to South Africa: he learned how North–South dialogue could be conducted in a dignified and mutually enriching way; how important context always was for understanding and applying principles of law; and how personally generous, focused, thoughtful, creative, and helpful a colleague could be.

---

[*] Albie Sachs was a Justice of South Africa's first Constitutional Court (1994 to 2009).

My Secret Weapon

Eleanor Fox was my secret weapon. I owe her.

I was in a crisis. I had accepted an invitation from the organizers of a conference to be held in Pretoria to discuss the implications of the amendments that had been made in 2019 to South Africa's Competition Act.[1] They asked me if I would chair the first plenary panel brought together to speak about the constitutional implications of the amendments to the Act. I had immediately accepted. The four panelists, about whom I will say more a little later, were all brilliant. It would be an exciting occasion and I wanted to be in the mix.

The easy part was saying something about the constitution. Since my 15-year term on the Constitutional Court had come to an end in 2009, I had never missed an opportunity to speak about the constitution. I had been involved in its early conceptualization and the negotiations that led to its adoption. As a judge on the Constitutional Court, I had taken part in the process of certifying that it complied with certain principles, which had been agreed to in advance. Finally, I had adjudicated on its implementation. I felt completely comfortable as far as the constitutionalism dimension of the upcoming discussion was concerned.

The problem was that I knew that I knew nothing about competition law. No, even worse, I had a little knowledge, which, as we are reminded, is a dangerous thing. In all my years on the Court we had had only one case dealing with competition law. The facts and the legal issues have receded completely from my mind. I don't even remember its name. I recall only that it didn't go to the heart of competition law; it dealt with an attempt based on tenuous technical grounds by a supplier of fertilizer to delay implementation of a ruling by the Competition Tribunal against it. Our Court upheld the decision that had been made by Judge Dennis Davis, who, as it happened, was now going to be one of the panelists. But the conference was a long way ahead and, as we South Africans say, I would *make a plan* as far as the competition law dimension was concerned. So, I penciled the dates of the conference into my diary, noted that I'd have to fly up from Cape Town to Pretoria the day before, and duly forgot all about it. The months sped by and suddenly I received an email giving me details of my plane tickets and accommodation. I hadn't made a plan and was hit by doubt.

What to do? I wanted to be there. I wanted to stimulate a lively and meaningful discussion. A lot of work had been put into organizing discussion on a theme that was clearly important for the country. From a purely personal point of view, I wanted to show the wisdom expected of a former Constitutional Court judge. More importantly, the delegates who would be coming from all parts of the country would be filled with expectation. It would be great if they could leave feeling they had taken part in memorable discussions. But the fact was that I was completely out of my depth. I hated the idea of simply being a timekeeper, telling speakers when to start and stop, and not a moderator helping the discussion

---

1   Competition Act, 1998 (Act No. 89 of 1998).

along. The potential shallowness of my participation would only be highlighted by the fact that the four panelists all happened to be brilliant.

Dennis Davis was the Judge President of the Competition Appeal Court. One of the sharpest legal minds in a country filled with sharp legal minds, he had expertise in labor law, constitutional law, taxation and competition law. What was remarkable about him was that he had become a true expert in each of these different fields. The government had called upon him to head a commission of inquiry to recommend the development of tax policy for South Africa, which came be known as the Davis Commission. He had written extensively on a number of topics, hosted several popular television shows dealing with the law and, as a guest speaker, never failed to provoke, amuse, stimulate, and educate an audience.

I had first come to know Tembeka Ngcukaitobi, the second panelist, when he had been a standout law clerk in the chambers of Chief Justice Arthur Chaskalson at the Constitutional Court. Born into a poor, rural family, he had grasped education opportunities with both hands, earning law degrees first at the University of Transkei and then at the London School of Economics. As a young advocate, he had achieved fame for the extraordinary forensic poise he had displayed when leading a successful legal charge in the Constitutional Court to compel President Jacob Zuma to pay back the substantial sum of money that had been overspent on security upgrades to his private home. He had acted as a judge in the Land Claims Court and, an accomplished legal historian, had written a bestseller on early Black lawyers in South Africa, entitled *This Land Is Ours*. He and I were planning to write a book together on Mandela, the lawyer. People were speaking about him being a future incumbent of the chambers in which he had clerked.

In terms of manner, style and demeanor, the third panelist, Jonathan Klaaren, Professor of Law at the University of the Witwatersrand, could not have been more different. Forgoing all oratorical fireworks, he would get audiences eating out of his hand with the sheer rationality and rigor of his arguments. Super erudite, he had a BA from Harvard, an MA from the University of Cape Town, a JD from Columbia, an LLB from Witwatersrand and a PhD from Yale. But unlike many other extremely learned scholars, he was able to express profound and complex ideas in clear and accessible language. He had been a law clerk for United States Judge Leon Higginbotham, an African American leader who had visited South Africa to give great support to the Black Lawyers Association, and whose son Michael happened to be a colleague of Eleanor's at New York University (N.Y.U.). His capacity to get an audience to stop and think again about received truths would be particularly valuable.

Tembinkosi Bonakele, the fourth member of the quartet, was the Commissioner of South African Competition Commission and the principal organizer of the conference. He had been a student activist at Fort Hare University before qualifying as an attorney. After working with Cheadle, Thompson and Haysom, specializing in torrid labor law disputes, he had gone from the fire into the frying pan, and spent a year working in corporate finance and antitrust groups at Clifford Chance in New York. All the time he was obtaining law degrees from different universities, ending up with an MBA from the Gordon Institute of Business Science at the University of Pretoria. He went on to serve as the chairperson of the African Competition Forum, and became a member of the BRICS Competition Forum and of the International Competition Network Steering Group. Despite having to function as a well-organized powerhouse at the heart of the machinery created to implement the Competition Act, he managed to maintain some of the charisma of a successful student activist.

The more excited I became thinking about the quality of the panelists, the more undone I felt by my total lack of preparedness for my role as moderator. My stomach started to flinch. What to do? The answer was instant: get Eleanor!

I think when she and I had first met, Eleanor was *getting* me. I was sitting in my chambers in the Constitutional Court–it was in the late 1990s–when my colleague Richard Goldstone told me that Professor Eleanor Fox from N.Y.U. was visiting, and would like to put a few questions to me. I walked over to Richard's chambers, expecting to be quizzed by an overtly gregarious and notably emphatic American professor. Eleanor turned out to be quite different to many of the sharp-shooting American legal scholars with whom I'd enjoyed rich discussions. I was surprised and intrigued by her capacity to deliver insightful thoughts in a quiet manner with soft speech, as well as by the fact that she was more of a listener than a talker. It was these subtle qualities that gave her composure and gravitas. I answered a number of well-focused questions she put to me about the South African Constitution and the Constitutional Court. Before I returned to my chambers, she said that when I next traveled to New York I should be sure to drop in to her office at N.Y.U.

A year or so later, that is exactly what I did. I don't know why, but I was surprised by how tidy and unassuming her office was. My chambers were on the flamboyant side–with a large pot plant, a vivid vase, a number of contemporary art works by Dumile Feni and Bill Ainslie on the walls, and open books and papers spread out everywhere. She didn't have the plaques, certificates and photographs of herself with celebrities that I frequently found in the offices of American lawyers. It was as though the thought and the conversation were everything. What mattered was the idea itself, not the trappings. And the concepts in which she was immersed were particularly attractive to me because they were so mysterious and recondite. I had had wonderful conversations with American lawyers about constitutional rights and racism in the law. I had even co-authored with an American feminist scholar a book called *Sexism and the Law*, which I believe was the first book anywhere in the English language on that topic. I had had discussions on children's law, freedom of speech, property law, family law, labor law, and poverty law, but I had never spoken about competition law.

To me, competition law belonged to realms of corporate law that I simply left to others. And here was Eleanor–progressive-minded, empathetic, and thoughtful, for whom competition law was the center of her working life. What struck me profoundly from the beginning of our intellectual osmosis was the coherence, forcefulness, rigor, and social significance of her thoughts on the subject.

Clearly, she was the person to whom I should turn at this precipitous moment. I sat down at my computer and sent out my cry for help. I wrote that I was sure she was aware of the changes being made to competition law in South Africa and asked if she could offer me any guidance on what the pressing themes were. The result was spectacular–a short course in competition law with special reference to South Africa. I had asked for a lifebelt to save me from drowning and received a helicopter to lift me right out of the water. Our correspondence follows.

> Hi Albie,
>
> Did my book come? If not, I want my assistant to track it. [Eleanor M. Fox and Mor Bakhoum, *Making Markets Work for Africa: Markets, Development and Competition Law in Sub-Saharan Africa* (2019).]
>
> Here is the note I promised you [for your role as chair of the high-level panel on the constitutional dimensions of South Africa's Competition Act].
>
> In *United States v. Topco Associates, Inc.*, Justice Thurgood Marshall proclaimed: "Antitrust laws in general, and the Sherman Act in particular, are the Magna Carta of free enterprise." United States v. Topco Assocs., Inc., 405 U.S. 596, 610 (1972). Marshall popularized the constitutional dimension of the antitrust laws.
>
> This was the early 1970s, before United States antitrust got taken over by Chicago School and libertarian premises, and was made over to protect incumbent firms and their merger partners, so today in the United States one has to recognize the irony.
>
> But in South Africa, there is no irony. The idea of markets that work for the people, and of competition law that helps the markets work for the people and cares about inclusiveness, is constitutional in the sense of the basic values on which the society is built and to which it aspires. This is not in the book [which focuses on competition law in sub-Saharan Africa].
>
> Here are some themes from the book–also drawing from the amendments [made in 2019 to South Africa's Competition Act], which were pending but only passed after the book went to press. The book has both big ideas and a lot of details that form the basis for the

big conclusions. Markets can do a lot to help people help themselves. If there is freedom and real ability to enter and succeed on merits, this empowers people, and at the same time it delivers to people as buyers the goods and services they need. But markets are often co-opted, both by big business with power and by governments and their cronies.

For developing countries, these are multinationals from outside, as well as privileged enterprises on the inside, often state-owned enterprises, that want to preserve the status quo and keep outsiders out–even if they produce the latest "new thing" and claim that there is so much competition between them and their cohorts. This means there is a two-tiered system of competition–a top tier that you see in the Fortune 500–and the rest, who are systematically kept down and out. There is actually a systematic campaign against inclusiveness, and you cannot see it unless you are steeped in lots of facts, stories and law across disciplines of competition, trade, investment, and how international bodies work in formulating what they call "international standards" – which they try to sell to the world.

So the book is a story both of what competition authorities do and what they can possibly do, what the West does to them, and how they can overcome the barriers and at least try to get more of a level playing field.

The amendments are one piece of the story. Vulnerable people and countries are constantly being exploited. HDIs [historically disadvantaged individuals–that is, those who did not have the vote under apartheid] are not only a prime example but are people who are owed something for the outrageous past. Focusing on HDIs and SMMEs [small, medium, and micro enterprises], we have a good laboratory for thinking about what must be done to advance inclusiveness and what can be done within the confines of the competition law. The drafters of the amendments say: at least we can use the competition laws to stop the exploitation when it is done either on the buying or on the selling side. On the buying side, when there is buying power of a dominant firm, that is called "monopsony power." The dominant firm underpays the small farmer just because it has the bargaining power and can get away with it. Or it puts all risk of crop loss from rains, flooding or drought, on the farmer. On the selling side, the problem is addressed in the area of price discrimination. This was the problem of Mr. Foot. See my book–pages 110–112. [Mr. Foot, a small producer of poles for grape vines, which were weatherproofed by wood preservatives, was charged by integrated energy and chemical company Sasol a significantly higher price for creosote than big buyers were charged. The Competition Tribunal upheld his complaint that this constituted price discrimination.] The seller sells to the big guys at a competitive price and to the powerless little guys at an elevated price, and the little guys cannot compete in the market. We will see how the amendments work. They can definitely achieve some equity, but I am afraid that what they will be able to do is limited.

But there is a larger story, a bigger canvas, and this is one of themes of my book. The West has developed notions about antitrust law that are not right for everyone. In some respects, the notions are wrong and poisonous for developing countries, but this is not obvious on the surface because the Western experts have such good-sounding arguments with premises that are not transparent. They have established international institutions to set notional international standards. The institutions and their working groups are open to the world, and developing countries are warmly invited to participate, but the developing countries' competition agencies do not have the same capacities, expertise, and time, and as you can imagine and expect, the first drafts are always written by the Western experts. The West may have monopolized the word and concept "efficiency," arguing that antitrust law must above all be efficient, and that if it is not efficient it will shrink the size of the pie and make everyone worse off because everyone's slice of the pie will be smaller. The weightiest premise/presumption, at least of the US, is that markets generally work; that markets have a "pure" job to do based on efficiency and consumer welfare (which is a proxy); if you add anything else such as public interest values of workers, HDIs and SMMEs, and particularly distributive values such as alleviating poverty and inequality, you are undermining efficiency and shrinking the pie (and, ironically especially for South Africa, harming the value of freedom).

Western law, particularly United States law, is built on these presumptions and premises, and advocates try to "sell" this formulation of law to developing countries on grounds that it is good for them! This is not sinister aforethought. I think most of the Western experts believe it.

This phenomenon shows itself most prominently in the law on exclusionary practices of dominant firms. The law of the US is libertarian. It assumes that what a firm does unilaterally (meaning not in conspiracy with competitors) is efficient and pro-consumer. A dominant firm can do almost no antitrust wrong, after a famous decision in 2004 called *Trinko*. "Handicapping" the dominant firm with antitrust duties is thought to interfere with efficiency and inventiveness.

My point is: a society like South Africa, with a horribly excluded majority, can never fulfill its promise of efficiency without inclusion. Strategies of dominant firms that tend to exclude outsiders are presumptively inefficient. I want to reclaim the efficiency territory and then think roots up about what is good for South Africa, etc., in terms of generalizable principles of rules of law of when a firm abuses dominance.

David Lewis was doing this when he was chair of the South African Competition Tribunal. He always incorporated the values of section 2 of the Competition Act in interpreting the prohibitory provisions. I think he got it exactly right. His decisions were often overturned by Dennis [Davis], the good (indeed extraordinary) lawyer, [then President of the Competition Appeal Court] who found that the technical language of the prohibitions did not allow the elasticity and presumption in favor of equality of opportunity that David read into the law. See the South Africa chapter in the book ["South Africa: Leaning in toward inclusive development," pages 89–120].

I was somewhat disappointed in the amendments. I wanted the law to incorporate the value of inclusivity as a matter of interpretation of all prohibitory sections. It took a different tack, which is ad hoc, tweaking particular sections and giving special privileges to HDIs and SMMEs. Of course, having been so pushed back, HDIs deserve a boost, to say the least. But for amending a body of law I would have preferred a rule-of-law approach rather than ad hoc affirmative action. I would have preferred inclusion as a universal principle. HDIs are naturally well represented in the population empowered by the principle.

What do you think? I do not know if I am right or wrong.

But I do hope that, since the whole impetus for the amendments is inclusiveness as an antitrust value, the effect of the spirit of the amendments can be to reinstate the jurisprudence of David Lewis, whether or not the issue before the court specifically involves amended language.

Other themes: the competition agencies of Africa cannot do their job alone. They need alliances both for a stronger voice and for a better understanding of the facts on the ground and powers to match the problems. If Africa only had a stronger, coherent voice, if "it" got out in front of the big international cement merger Holcim/LaFarge, or the big chemical and seed merger Bayer/Monsanto, it probably could have convinced the developed world to enjoin the merger. These mergers were clearly anticompetitive and should have been stopped, but the developed countries simply required fixes for themselves, and left the problem to the powerless developing countries who were the most harmed and the least able to protect themselves.

As for understanding facts: many of the antitrust restraints are cross-border. They include cartels that divide national markets, such as the cement companies do. They include lobbying governments to get anticompetitive border restraints, as the cement companies also do. In a common market context, these cross-border restraints and protective state restraints can be torn down (as is done in the EU). This is an aspiration. There are regional systems developing in Africa. The aspiration is hard to reach.

***

Eleanor ... I opened your book as soon as it arrived and got so engrossed in it that I forgot to say thanks! So I'm saying it now.

This is an amazingly rich email ... In response, let me start with a point made to me by my son Michael, who resigned from Treasury [where he was Director of the Budget] in reaction to a demand made on it by Jacob Zuma towards the end of his [Zuma's] office, and who is now a Prof. at Wits [University]. Michael said that until now, competition law had focused on dealing with collusion to produce monopoly pricing and dealing; it didn't deal with situations where economic actors already had monopoly control ... An example would have been South African Breweries that produced and sold 95% of beer in South Africa. The amendment, he said, could have been intended to give the minister powers to break up such monopolies to allow for new entrants. If the minister then chose to exercise power in that way, this might raise constitutional questions.

It struck me that in that event the "as applied" doctrine [developed by the US Supreme Court in relation to restrictions on free speech that served a legitimate purpose but were overbroad in their potential reach] might be relevant ... The empowering provisions could not be challenged as such on the grounds of their potential overbreadth, but would have to be read down to prevent ministerial interventions that might be seen as being constitutionally over-robust.

A question from me re your email: do you think the amending Act facilitates interpretations that accord with David Lewis' approach, but with a stronger textual foundation to make Dennis feel happier? Or do you think they just have different philosophies?

***

Hi Albie,

Maybe [as chair of the panel] you are supposed to deal with potential real constitutional issues. My long email did not address real constitutional issues; just control of power in the market as having a constitutional dimension. Maybe that is not what you will talk about at all.

Very interesting about your son Michael. I did not know he was at Wits. I would have looked him up when I was there.

The competition law did always deal with abuse of dominance (monopolies), and the Tribunal always had the power to stop anticompetitive mergers. (It let SAB Miller through as not anticompetitive. Apparently, Miller was not yet doing competing business in South Africa.)

But until now the law did not give power to break up business (apart from anticompetitive mergers). The new market inquiry provisions (Chapter 43) give a lot more powers regarding market inquiries. They give a lot more powers to the minister, who can require a market inquiry. Breakup is not out of the question. But the law says that the Commission must consider less restrictive remedies to cure any anticompetitive effect. Regarding market inquiries, mergers, and exemptions, the amendments give the minister much more power. Parties may go the minister to bless the deal, and the minister may do so on various conditions, such as giving up a share of the deal to HDIs and setting up well-funded projects for capacity building. On the one hand, this sounds great for more equity and justice. But on the other hand, it removes a chunk of the inquiries from the rule-of-law channel to ministerial discretion. Fortunately, the current minister is wonderful, smart, honest and devoted, but there is some concern with unpredictability in the future and undermining the rule of law.

Your question–David and Dennis–I think the answer is yes; the law affords a stronger basis for David's interpretations. Dennis shares most of David's philosophy.

***

Eleanor, I'm learning all the time!

Indeed, I was learning all the time–and not only about competition law. I was discovering how dialogue between North and South could take place in a way that was both dignified and mutually enriching. I was also finding out how important context always is for the way principles of law must be understood and applied in practice. And finally, I was learning how personally generous a colleague could be. Greater love hath no scholar than to give up her time to enable a colleague to shine. And I knew that her gift wasn't just for me. It was for a country she had grown to admire and for competition lawyers in that country she had come to love.

Others can say whether or not I did shine when I acted as moderator. What I can state is that the panel discussion was rollicking. The panelists were scintillating. Each in his own very distinctive way spoke with intelligence, warmth, eloquence and edge. Competition law was taken seriously, but with lots of humor and abundant personality. The audience responded enthusiastically.

If it was evident from the start that there were only men on the podium, it was notable by the end that each and every panelist, as well as the moderator, had brought the voice of Professor Eleanor Fox onto the stage, citing her as *the* authority in support of their propositions. None of the panelists knew, though, of her secret missives to me.

Whether or not Eleanor is a prophet honored at home, she is certainly a prophet honored abroad.

A New Competition Law Paradigm: The Influence of Eleanor Fox

DENNIS M. DAVIS[*]

Competition Appeal Court of South Africa

Abstract

Eleanor Fox has been a pioneer of a coherent set of competition law and policy principles designed to promote markets that work in favor of inclusivity, and to ensure economic development that reduces unequal access to markets. In particular, she has argued consistently against the monastic vision for the field that began to dominate with the rise of Chicago economics. This tribute examines the challenges posed to competition policy–and thus competition law–through the prism of current forms of economic globalization that have exacerbated inequality and accelerated a concentration of economic power that makes the pathology that gave rise to the Sherman Act at the turn of the twentieth century pale almost into insignificance. In particular, the South African experience over the past three decades is, in this contribution, employed to examine the scale of the present challenges for competition policy and law, as well as the possibility for the acceptance of a new paradigm.

---

[*] Judge President, Competition Appeal Court of South Africa.

Writing recently of the importance of competition law and policy for developing countries, Professor Eleanor Fox and Mor Bakhoum argue as follows:

> There is a pro-poorer/pro-development perspective on competition law, procedurally and substantively. It would require the competition agency to: (1) target state and hybrid restraints that create a stranglehold on markets, and draft the law with these targets in minds; (2) assure procedural vehicles to make the justice system accessible to the poorer and outsider populations; (3) adopt simpler but sound rules, lest were create a paradox that antitrust is a luxury for the well-off; and (4) within the range of possibilities for efficient and dynamic markets, lean pro-outsider.
>
> There is a pro-poorer/pro-development perspective on competition policy. It would require the agency to: (1) develop programs to identify and advocate against excessive and unnecessary anticompetitive state restraints, especially those that create a stranglehold on economic opportunity; (2) advocate for world norms to oblige nations to stern and rectify the antitrust harms they cause; and, of course, (3) prioritize restraints in markets most essential to the daily lives, health, and well-being of the poorer populations.[1]

This is the latest of many contributions in which Eleanor Fox has consistently argued for a competition law that works inclusively for the entire population, promoting efficiency, equity, and development.[2] Once a lonely voice, Professor Fox now finds an intellectual wind blowing at her back. Neoliberal economics that resisted her plea for a competitive paradigm that transcended the narrow strictures of efficiency is no longer hegemonic. In 2017, for example, the International Monetary Fund explored the relationship between income inequality and economic growth in a large number of countries. It concluded that, on average, countries grow faster when inequality is reduced. It also found that redistribution policies do not necessarily inhibit growth.[3] In turn the pattern of inequality continues to increase focused attention generally on the role of law in the market, and on competition law policy in particular.[4]

---

[1] ELEANOR M. FOX & MOR BAKHOUM, MAKING MARKETS WORK FOR AFRICA: MARKETS, DEVELOPMENT, AND COMPETITION LAW IN SUB-SAHARAN AFRICA 198 (2019).

[2] *See, e.g.*, Eleanor M. Fox and Abel Moreira Mateus(eds), *Economic Development: The Critical EEI Role of Competition Law and Policy Edward Elgar.* (2011); Eleanor M. Fox, *"We Protect Competition, You Protect Competitors"*, 26(2) WORLD COMPETITION 149 (2003).

[3] *See* PAUL DE GRAUWE, THE LIMITS OF THE MARKER: THE PENDULUM BETWEEN GOVERNMENT AND MARKET 21–73 (2017).

[4] IMF, *Market, Power, Growth and Inclusion: The South African Experience* (IMF Working Paper, WP/30/206, Sept. 2020).

In a recent book, Katharina Pistor[5] has argued that capital is created and fashioned by law. If law plays an important role in the construction of capital, as well as the identity of those who have access and those denied access thereto, it stands to reason that anyone concerned with increasing levels of inequality and poverty needs to interrogate the role of law, in particular the role of law in the construction of the market.

Markets do not lift themselves unaided into reality; in particular, private law empowers some actors while disempowering and subordinating others. For example, private law establishes ground rules that govern assets acquired and how a person may use their assets and legal endowments in any interaction with others. Thus, a landowner, P, negatively affects the interest of Q, a malnourished, homeless person, when P denies Q's request for rent-free access to a property and/or edible yield. Though grievous harm or even death may result to Q, P is nonetheless privileged to refuse Q's request pursuant to the public policy decisions embodied in the rules of the common law of property, namely that an owner can prevent strangers from entering on its land and, if necessary, the owner can call upon the local authority, which may use force, if necessary, to uphold the owner's privilege to exclude others.

Markets are constructed by law. It follows that the interrogation of this construction is relevant to questions that concerns development, poverty, and inequality, and making markets work inclusively. Pistor summarizes the importance of law in the construction and preservation of capital thus:

> [Capital] owes its capacity to create wealth to the modules of a legal code that is backed by state power; and its resilience in times of crisis can be attributed to a combination of legal asset-shielding devices and the state's willingness to extend a helping hand to capital to preserve not only capitalism but social stability, and by implication, the state itself. In short, capital is inextricably linked to law and state power, because in its absence the legal privileges capital enjoys would not be respected by others.

In turn, this focus on the role of law in the construction of markets calls into question the manner in which antitrust competition law has changed over the past 125 years. There has been a massive ideological distance traveled by the field since the introduction of the Sherman Act. Recall the statement of Senator Sherman, when he introduced his bill: "If we will not endure a king as a political power, we should not endure a king over the production, transportation, and sale of any of the necessities of life. If we would not submit to an emperor, we should not submit to an autocrat of trade, with power to prevent competition and to fix the price of any commodity."[6]

---

5   Katharina Pistor, The Code of Capital: How the Law Creates Wealth and Inequality (2019).

6   *Cited by* Barry Lynn, Liberty from all Masters: The New American Autocracy vs. the Will of the People 143 (2020).

A school of economics that prioritizes lowest consumer prices as a signal of allocative efficiency, and then embraced what become known as the consumer welfare standard, replaced the earlier objectives attributed by Sherman, in particular the protecting of independent businesses and the reduction of wealth transfers from consumers to producers. Prior to 1980, consumer welfare as the standard for competition law was but a proverbial blink in Milton Friedman's and Robert Bork's eye. With the publication of Robert Bork's *The Antitrust Paradox* in 1978, the idea that markets were self-correcting, and that free entry is but a natural condition of the operation of a market that will inexorably erode the concentration of market power, became hegemonic in the field.

But as we move into this third decade of the twenty-first century, this seismic shift in antitrust/competition law, which occurred more than 40 years ago, has increasingly been called into question. In particular, serious questions arise about the dependence of antitrust upon conservative economists who have demanded economic quantification and complex forms of economic proof and levels of statistical significance in order for any case to pass legal muster. The rules of the game shifted toward avoiding false positives and over-deterrence. Ironically these moves may well have led to false negatives and under-deterrence.

The adverse political implications of this conservative competition law presided over by courts for the past 30 years have come back to haunt the paradigm, in particular because of the implications of dominant Internet platforms. The dominance of Google, Apple, Amazon, and Facebook, in particular, coupled with the disastrous economic consequences caused by COVID-19, present an inflection point for competition lawyers and policymakers.

It is not particularly surprising that the uncritical commitment to consumer welfare has left competition authorities rather powerless to respond to the twenty-first century economy. A number of scholars, including Eleanor Fox, have called the strictures of the dominant standard into critical question. Already, in 1998, Eleanor Fox wrote the following about US antitrust:

> In the 1960s US law was construed to prohibit restraints that foreclosed less well situated firms from a significant share of the market even if the exclusion resulted from strong preferences for dealing with one's friends (reciprocity). The United States has abandoned this construction of law in favor of permissive legal principle that value the freedom of firms to impose vertical restraints unilaterally. Plaintiffs challenging vertical restraint under US law today must normally prove the restraint will limit output and harm consumers; it is not enough to show that the restraint merely block competitors unreasonably.[7]

---

7   Eleanor M. Fox, *International Antitrust: Against Minimum Rules; for Cosmopolitan Principles*, 43(1) ANTITRUST BULL. 5, 11–12 (1998).

Over the past 40 years, this approach to competition law has harmed consumers and workers, and contributed to the stifling of innovation. The plasticity of the standard and its scope for opportunistic interpretation has been an obstacle against the development of global convergence and, as I shall argue, the development of an appropriate jurisprudence for developing countries. In summary, its use has hardly curbed the unbridled economic power of the few.[8]

The arguments advanced by Professor Fox over almost five decades have thus have moved from the periphery of concern in the field to the center. Given her magnificent role in the development of the South African competition law of 1998, the balance of this tribute focuses on how the South African Act sought to the embrace a competition jurisprudence and policy that rises to the challenge of inclusivity, reduction of inequality, and economic democracy.

I. South Africa

In short, when the South African Act of 1998 was passed, the indigenous conditions that the country inherited from the apartheid regime meant that the early history of American antitrust had considerable traction among the drafters of the South African Act. In particular, the animating idea of the liberty of individual citizens to engage freely in whatever line of business they wished was an anathema to the racist policies of the apartheid regime. The concern to preserve democracy that could resist the potential danger presented by a concentration of economic power, which, in turn, creates at best a democracy for elites as opposed to the entire nation, were fundamental objectives of the South African political enterprise.

In the balance of this paper I shall argue that in 1998 some of the content of the South African Competition Act was at that outlier line when judged against the dominant approach to competition law. But that is no longer the case.[9] But, as ambitious as the Act was in its desire to break with the dominant paradigm, it has still proved inadequate. As a result, the 1998 Act has recently been amended significantly, in the view of the legislature, to reinforce the initial objectives of the Act as set out in the original. Hence, the record of the South African Act focuses attention on whether it is possible to conceive of a competition law that embraces economic freedom, democracy, and a greater level of inequality. It is these objectives and the consequent record to which I now turn.

---

8   *See, e.g.,* Marshall Steinbaum & Maurice E. Stucke, *The Effective Competition Standard: A New Standard for Antitrust*, 87(2) U. CHI. L. REV. 595 (2020).

9   *See, e.g.*, OECD, *Working Paper No. 3 on Co-Operation and Enforcement: Public Interest Considerations in Merger Control* (DAF/COMP/WP3(2016)3, June 14, 2016); In more general terms regarding the broader debate prompted by neo-Brandeisians, *see* Florian Kraffert, *Should EU Competition Law Move Toward a Neo-Brandeis Approach?*, 16(1) EUR. COMPETITION J. 55 (2020).

II. The Objective of the 1998 Act

The preamble to the 1998 Act expressly recognized the effect of apartheid history on the nature of the economy, stating:

> The people of South Africa recognize:
>
> > That apartheid and other discriminatory laws and practices of the past resulted in excessive concentrations of ownership and control within the national economy. Inadequate restraints against anti-competitive trade practices, and unjust restrictions on full and free participation in the economy by all South Africans.

It was for this reason that section 2 of the Act, apart from claiming that the purpose was to promote the efficiency and adaptability in the development of the South African economy, and to provide consumers with competitive prices and greater choice, stated that one of its purposes was "to promote a greater spread of ownership"; in particular to increase the ownership stakes of historically disadvantaged persons.

At the time, the Act introduced public interest considerations in terms of section 12A(3), so that the competition authorities, in determining whether a merger can or cannot be justified on public interest grounds, had to consider the effect that the merger would have, inter alia, on employment and the ability of small businesses or firms controlled or owned by historically disadvantaged persons who become competitors.

As indicated, these provisions were deeply influenced by Eleanor Fox, in her role as an adviser to the drafters of the Competition Act of 1998. They were predicated on the sound economic footing that, when the market is characterized by highly concentrated barriers to entry, and the power of a few large firms owned by white shareholders prevent new competitors from building businesses, South African consumers would be faced with fewer choices. Employees would receive lower wages, which in turn would slow overall economic growth and thus the welfare of society. In addition, the dominance of white-owned capital would, if it remained unfettered, subvert the objective of constructing a non-racial society, and hence the expansion of an economy open to all participants.

These were clearly uppermost concerns of the legislature when the 1998 Act was passed. As South Africa became less of an outlier in the competition world for promoting public interest considerations in its merger enquiries, so did the broader objectives of its legislation find themselves at the center of the debate about the future of competition law in the global context. In a recent report by Steinbaum and others,[10] the point is made that a 40-year assault on antitrust

---

10 MARSHALL STEINBAUM ET AL., POWERLESS: HOW LAX ANTITRUST AND CONCENTRATED MARKET POWER RIG THE ECONOMY AGAINST AMERICAN WORKERS, CONSUMERS, AND COMMUNITIES (Roosevelt Institute, 2018).

and competition policy, as well as on the applicable law and regulations meant to safeguard against the concentration of power in a few private firms, has tipped the economy in favor of powerful corporations under the false pretense that the incumbent ambitions of private business will align with the public good.

The authors argue further that the single biggest problem underlying antitrust has been a simplistic view of free markets that ignores the power dynamics of the market and implies the existence of some natural state in which markets flourish without regulatory oversight. As indicated, this argument supports the view that there is no state of natural market equilibrium. Markets depend on rules to create a balance of market power between workers, consumers, and businesses. It is a necessary, although admittedly not a sufficient, condition that the outcome of this balance is determined by the applicable legal regime. But the importance of law in achieving the existing balance means that the development of antitrust law over the past 30 years has helped produce the skewed outcomes that haunt the global economy today. This paradigm has been at war with the attempt by South Africa, in particular, the objective of developing an alternative normative vision for competition law and policy.

That the first 20 years of South African jurisprudence did not fully promote these objectives meant that, as noted, in 2019 a series of further amendments to the Act were introduced. In welcoming these legislative initiatives, Professor Fox noted that the goals of an equitable and efficient competition law overlap in a significant space. Maximizing this space requires a finer appreciation of the harmful effects of a range of exclusionary conduct, which creates blockages to the equitable functioning of the market system. By refocusing on achieving a balance between equity and efficiency, the law could be both distributive to historically disadvantaged people as well as beneficial for consumers and the general state of competition.

Professor Fox has been consistent in her advocacy of a normative framework for the South African Act from the moment she played so a significant a role in its drafting. Competition law and policy cannot unaided lift a society into improved levels of equality, economic democracy, and inclusive growth. But if the nature of a market and the manner in which conduct and rules prevent inclusivity and skew allocation and distribution in favor of the advantaged few, then it has a significant role to play, far beyond the limited constraints of the traditional concept of efficiency. Some might call this the promotion of social justice, and to that objective, even if partial implementation is achieved, it would be a fitting tribute to the sustained, imaginative, and courageous contribution that Professor Fox has made to our overall knowledge of the subject.

This tribute has focused upon the influence of Professor Fox. Regrettably, this influence has not sufficiently percolated into the law firms, barristers' chambers, and offices of those economists who regularly advise and testify in competition disputes before the South African competition authorities. Of course, there are some exceptions to this assertion but, in the main, an uncritical borrowing from US jurisprudence, and somewhat more rarely from the EU, by the lawyers who appear before the Competition Tribunal and Competition Appeal Court, as well as an almost rigid adherence to conservative economics, has bedeviled the development of a jurisprudence that more fully aligns with the objectives of the Act. A combination of a conservative legal culture and economists who merely repeat economic shibboleths has contributed to the Tribunal and Court aligning their jurisprudence with the objectives of the Act. One can only express the hope that the intellectual influence of Professor Fox and those who follow in her wake will grow, as South African law develops in the future.

Tracing Professor Fox in South Africa's Competition Jurisprudence

JONATHAN KLAAREN[*] AND SIBUSISO RADEBE[**]
University of the Witwatersrand

Abstract

This paper identifies several locations where one might look to trace how Professor Eleanor Fox has contributed to the South African competition regime. Choosing one of those, her contributions to its published jurisprudence, we survey decisions of the competition authorities to find those referring to Professor Fox and her work. Those decisions include ones in the areas of extraterritorial jurisdiction and anticompetitive exclusionary practices. Discussing several prominent cases in those areas, we observe that Professor Fox has been part of the debates within South African jurisprudence from their beginnings, and that her work is considered highly and cited effectively as authority in itself. We argue that, while she has never held the formal position of a litigant or an adjudicator, South Africa's competition regime is the richer for Professor Fox's participation and engagement.

---

[*] Professor of Law and Sociology, University of the Witwatersrand; former director of the Mandela Institute at the School of Law.

[**] PhD student, School of Law, University of the Witwatersrand; research associate at the Mandela Institute.

At an online event on November 3, 2020, paying tribute to Dennis Davis, the South African legal scholar and outgoing Judge President of the Competition Appeal Court (CAC), it was hardly a surprise when Tembinkosi Bonakele, the Commissioner of the Competition Commission (CC) of South Africa, cited Eleanor Fox twice as authority for his words. Those two institutions, the CAC and the CC, together with the Competition Tribunal constitute the full set of what are colloquially known as the South African competition authorities. In his own address, Davis J.P. also referred to Eleanor as collecting and shepherding him and others in a hotel in the 1990s to draft South Africa's post-apartheid Competition Act, and referenced her continuing assistance to the CAC and to the competition authorities more generally.[1] While the legislative history of the Act at its most significant deliberative forum, NEDLAC, is no longer available, Fox's part in the formulation of the South African regime is clear and significant. As authoritative as the authorities themselves have become and as capable as they have become as institutions, it is nonetheless remarkable that their leaders should routinely refer to a white female former corporate lawyer from America to ground their normative judgments and nuanced communications among each other. The remarkable Eleanor Fox has been there from the beginning of the democratic competition regime in South Africa.

These genuine and high-profile references show that Eleanor has had a deep and lasting influence on the South African competition regime. So, to quote the meme, where's Eleanor? Where–apart from online farewell events for veterans of the competition authorities–might one look for Eleanor's South African traces? We would argue that there are three particular places where one might look.

One place is, of course, her extraordinary devotion and ability to engage in what is often called capacity-building. Understanding that people form the raw material out of which institutions are built, Eleanor has engaged in this sort of activity with grace, goodwill, and energy. This story is told well in this volume by Commissioner Bonakele.[2] This is exactly the space in which Davis J.P.'s November 2020 farewell event occurred.

A second particular area to examine, in order to trace Eleanor's impact, is perhaps judicial education, emphatically understanding this to include dialogues with the adjudicative members of the authorities, a number of whom are, of course, economists rather than lawyers by training. This too is noted in the Commissioner's paper, although the stories that undoubtedly exist and could be unearthed are

---

1   Davis J.P. noted Eleanor in longstanding and continual support of judicial education in the field in South Africa, among other respected international competition scholars including Harry First and Richard Whish.

2   *See also* Jonathan Klaaren, *Laying the Table: The Role of Business in Establishing Competition Law and Policy in South Africa*, 33(1) INT'L REV. OF APPLIED ECON. 119–33 (Jan. 2, 2019), https://doi.org/10.1080/02692171.2019.1524034.

not fully told there. Nor will they be told here. It will remain for another occasion to track the years and the events of judicial education in the authorities and in the field's conferences in South and Southern Africa in which Eleanor has participated.

A third place where Eleanor's traces may be seen is in jurisprudence, narrowly understood as the writings of the adjudications of the competition authorities under the Competition Act. This is the place we focus on in this commemorative paper. Our method uses the free access website, SAFLII (www.saflii.org). A search on SAFLII conducted in December 2020 using the term "fox" in three databases (the Competition Tribunal, the CAC, and the Constitutional Court) yielded an initial list of 22 cases.[3] Discarding the cases not having anything to do with Eleanor left us with a list of nine. These cases are: *Competition Commission v. American Natural Soda Ash CHG Global (Pty) Ltd*;[4] *Competition Commission of South Africa v. Bank of America Merrill Lynch International Limited and Others*;[5] *Competition Commission v. Bank of America Merrill Lynch International Limited and Others*;[6] *Competition Commission v. South African Airways (Pty) Ltd*;[7] *Venter v. Law Society of the Cape of Good Hope and Others*;[8] *Competition Commission v. Pioneer Foods (Pty) Ltd*;[9] *Sasol Oil (Pty) Ltd v. Nationwide Poles CC*;[10] *Minister of Economic Development and Others v. Competition Tribunal and Others, South African Commercial, Catering and Allied Workers Union (SACCAWU) v. Wal-Mart Stores Inc and Another*;[11] and *South African Airways (Pty) Ltd v. Comair Ltd and Another*.[12] In the remainder of this paper, we refer to each of these nine cases and discuss in detail the four most significant.

---

3   The search yielded 14 cases from the Competition Tribunal. 4 cases from the CAC, and 5 cases from the Constitutional Court of South Africa.

4   *Competition Commission v. American Natural Soda Ash CHG Global (Pty) Ltd* (49/CR/Apr00) [2006] ZACT 75 [hereinafter *Competition Commission v. American Natural Soda Ash (CT)*].

5   *Competition Commission v. Bank of America Merrill Lynch International Limited and Others* (CR121Feb17) [2019] ZACT 50 [hereinafter *Competition Commission v. Bank of America Merrill Lynch (CT)*].

6   *Competition Commission v. Bank of America Merrill Lynch International Limited and Others* (175/CAC/Jul19) [2020] ZACAC 1; 2020 (4) SA 105 (CAC) [hereinafter *Competition Commission v. Bank of America Merrill Lynch (CAC)*].

7   *Competition Commission v. South African Airways (Pty) Ltd* (18/CR/Mar01) [2005] ZACT 50 [hereinafter *Competition Commission v. South African Airways*].

8   *Venter v. Law Society of the Cape of Good Hope and Others* (014688) [2013] ZACT 103 [hereinafter *Venter v. Law Society of the Cape of Good Hope*].

9   *Competition Commission v. Pioneer Foods (Pty) Ltd* (15/CR/Feb07, 50/CR/May08) [2010] ZACT 9.

10 *Sasol Oil (Pty) Ltd v. Nationwide Poles CC* (49/CAC/Apr05) [2005] ZACAC 5 [hereinafter *Sasol Oil v. Nationwide Poles*].

11 *Minister of Economic Development and Others v. Competition Tribunal and Others, South African Commercial, Catering and Allied Workers Union (SACCAWU) v. Wal-Mart Stores Inc and Another* (110/CAC/Jul11, 111/CAC/Jun11) [2012] ZACAC 2 [hereinafter *Wal-Mart Stores*].

12 *South African Airways (Pty) Ltd v. Comair Ltd and Another* (92/CAC/MAR10) [2011] ZACAC 3; 2012 (1) SA 20 (CAC).

I. Professor Eleanor Fox's Work on Extraterritoriality

1. *Competition Commission v. American Natural Soda Ash*[13]

The series of cases concerning American Natural Soda Ash Corporation (ANSAC) came about following a complaint referral filed by the CC with the Tribunal on 23 March 2000. The complaint referral alleged that ANSAC, an association of soda ash producers from the United States, was operating in South Africa in contravention of section 4(1)(*b*)(*i*) and (*ii*) of the Competition Act. The case before the Tribunal in *Competition Commission v. American Natural Soda Ash*, however, did not directly concern the interpretation of section 4(1)(*b*) or its application to the facts, instead it came about as a result of ANSAC having lost its bid to get the Tribunal to interpret section 4(1)(*b*) of the Competition Act as, first, requiring the complainant to prove that the horizontal agreement that formed the basis of the section 4(1)(*b*) charge produced anticompetitive effects; and second, permitting the defendant to prove that its conduct produced efficiency gains that outweighed the anticompetitive consequences caused by the said conduct.[14] The panel that heard the application, however, rejected ANSAC's argument and concluded that: "section 4(1)(*b*) required no showing of anticompetitive effect and that it permitted of no efficiency defence– the mere fact of the agreement was sufficient to condemn it."[15]

In an attempt to avoid the harshness of the per se rule, it appears ANSAC sought thus to have the effects of its conduct, both anticompetitive and procompetitive, considered and weighed under the section 3(1) jurisdiction enquiry. The hope here was, so it appears, to get the Tribunal to assess subject-matter jurisdiction using an effects-based test for jurisdiction that only confers subject-matter jurisdiction where it is demonstrated that the anticompetitive effects caused by the conduct outweigh the procompetitive effects or efficiency gains produced by the said conduct.[16] If such a test were to be adopted, ANSAC believed that no subject-matter jurisdiction would be established over it as it opined that its conduct produced efficiency gains that outweighed the anticompetitive effects caused by its conduct; if no subject-matter jurisdiction could be established over it, ANSAC would be able to avoid conviction under the section 4(1) per se rule.

The issue before the Tribunal, thus, concerned the interpretation of the word "effects" as it appears in section 3(1) of the Competition Act.[17] ANSAC argued that:

> A threshold requirement or a jurisdictional prerequisite is that a complainant in a competition matter, in order to invoke the

---

13 *Supra* note 4. The page references for this case are taken from the PDF version provided on SAFLII; available at www.saflii.org/za/cases/ZACT/2006/75.pdf.

14 *Competition Commission v. American Natural Soda Ash (CT)*, supra note 4, at 6.

15 *Id.* at 3.

16 *Id.* at 6.

17 *Id.* at 5–7.

> provisions of the Competition Act, must establish that the act complained of impacts negatively upon competition. This presupposes a balance between anti- and procompetitive effect, with the onus, presumably, on the complainant to introduce evidence establishing the anti-competitive consequences of the act complained of and the onus, presumably, on the defendant to introduce evidence of procompetitive gains attributable to the conduct in question. The adjudicator would then, in order to determine jurisdiction, balance the evidence of anti- and procompetitive effect and would only accept jurisdiction if the net balance proved to be deleterious in its consequence.[18]

The Tribunal framed this to be an "ambitious" reading of the word "effects,"[19] but nevertheless considered all three arguments advanced by ANSAC on this point. One of the arguments in question was an international law argument, the crux of which was that "in international law ... harm is an essential element of what is termed the 'effects doctrine',"[20] and thus the Tribunal must adopt an effects-based test for establishing subject-matter jurisdiction that confers subject-matter jurisdiction if the net balance of effects proved to be deleterious.[21] The CC, in response, argued that, inter alia, ANSAC had not established a customary international law practice that met the requirements for recognition as such.[22] In an attempt to establish a customary international law practice that met the requirements of recognition, ANSAC urged the Tribunal to consider case law from the United States on this point as international customary law and hence more authoritative and binding upon us than comparative law might otherwise be.[23] After considering a number of cases from the United States on the point of extraterritorial jurisdiction, the Tribunal considered that the case that came closest to the approach contended for by ANSAC was the decision of the Ninth Circuit in *Metro Industries v. Sammi*.[24] The Tribunal summed up the *Metro Industries v. Sammi* case as follows:[25]

> the court [in *Metro Industries v. Sammi*] was faced with considering whether a practice among Korean firms, constituting a private system of mutual intellectual property recognition which firms were bound by commercial practice to accept, amounted to a system

---

18   *Id.* at 6.
19   *Id.* at 6.
20   *Id.* at 7.
21   *Id.* at 6.
22   *Id.* at 14.
23   *Id.* at 16–17.
24   Metro Industries v. Sammi Corporation, 82 F.3d 839 (9th Circuit) (1996).
25   *Competition Commission v. American Natural Soda Ash (CT)*, *supra* note 4, at 22.

of market division which although occurring in the Korean market should be treated as a naked market division agreement and hence to be treated as a per se restraint under US law in terms of the Sherman Act. The court held:

> "Because conduct occurring outside the United States is only a violation of the Sherman Act, if it has a sufficient negative impact on commerce in the United States, per se analysis, is not appropriate. Indeed, when the alleged illegal conduct occurred in a foreign country, we must examine the impact on commerce in the United States before we can determine that we have subject-matter jurisdiction over the claim."

Later on the court went on to conclude that:

> "Foreign conduct cannot be examined under a per se rule ... Application of the per se rule is not appropriate where the conduct in question occurred in another country."

ANSAC argued that this case was authority for three propositions regarding the establishment of subject-matter jurisdiction over conduct that takes place outside of a court's jurisdiction, two of which being that the complainant must, first, show a negative impact and, second, that the said impact is a sufficiently negative impact.[26]

The Tribunal refused to follow the *Metro Industries v. Sammi* decision by reason that, first, the case reflected the views of merely one Circuit Court, with no indication it had been followed by other courts within the United States and abroad; secondly, and more importantly according to the Tribunal, the approach taken by the court in *Metro Industries v. Sammi* was conceptually flawed as the court had "muddled comity (an international law issue) with substantive issues (the content of which is the subject for the domestic law of the state asserting its jurisdiction)";[27] thirdly, the court in *Metro Industries v. Sammi* created a distinction between foreign-based and domestic cartels without providing any principle to justify the distinction;[28] and fourthly, the decision had not received much support from leading commentators, particular reference being made to Professor Fox, and a remark made by her, citing *Metro Industries v. Sammi*, to the effect that:[29]

> Some jurists feeling bound to apply Hartford but sensing an illegitimacy in American condemnation of certain acts abroad,

---

26   *Id.* at 22–23.
27   *Id.* at 23.
28   *Id.*
29   *Id.*

have shifted to second-best grounds, perversely creating a different substantive standard for foreign defendants and US defendants.

Here, the Tribunal is using Professor Fox in a conventional albeit quite strong manner, both as an individual expert commentator in her own right and as a trusted guide to the overall weight of academic expert authority on the particular question. The Tribunal, in essence, used, inter alia, Professor Fox's analysis of the case law to expose the weakness of a case which a party sought to rely on as authority for an argument or a point sought to be made by the said party. This is evidence that Professor Fox's work has been highly influential and closely followed by South African competition authorities. The Tribunal went on to conclude, on this point, that "the case law and literature offer no support for ANSAC's view that 'effects' must be interpreted as negative effects to comply with international law"; and ultimately concluded that:

> We utilize section 3(1) to establish whether the conduct is economic activity having an "effect" within the territory. Once we establish evidence of "effect" we do not inquire into its nature, as that is a substantive issue that takes place when we evaluate whether a prohibited practice has been established. The issue of harm is dealt with in the substantive provisions of the Act. This is the logical place for it to be addressed since one does not stand convicted simply because a tribunal assumes jurisdiction. That being the case the foreign respondent is in the same position as the domestic one.[30]

Dissatisfied with the decision of the Tribunal, ANSAC took the Tribunal's decision on appeal to the CAC. In the CAC, ANSAC persisted with the argument that it advanced in the Tribunal, i.e. that the word or term "effect" in section 3(1) of the Competition Act refers to a "negative or deleterious effect on competition within South Africa."[31] Furthermore, according to ANSAC, a "negative or deleterious effect" was one that was anticompetitive, as understood in competition law, meaning that section 3(1) had to be interpreted in a manner that would limit the Act's application to "to all economic activity within, or having an anticompetitive effect within, the Republic."[32] The CAC upheld the Tribunal's decision and held that:

> The question is not whether the consequences of the conduct is criminal or, for that matter, anticompetitive, but whether the conduct complained of has "direct and foreseeable" substantial consequences within the regulating country. In other words,

---

30 *Id.*

31 *American Soda Ash Corporation CHC Global (Pty) Ltd v. Competition Commission and Others* (12/CAC/Dec01) [2003] ZACAC 6 [hereinafter *American Soda Ash Corporation v. Competition Commission*], para 8.

32 *Id.*

the "effects" in the present case must be such that they fall within the regulatory framework of the Act, whether they are anticompetitive or not ... This inquiry does not involve a consideration of the positive or negative effects on competition in the regulating country but merely whether there are sufficient jurisdictional links between the conduct and the consequences.[33]

The above holding by the CAC, on the interpretation of section 3(1) of the Competition Act, and accordingly the application of the Competition Act, became and stood as final authority on this matter, until the matter was brought up again in *Competition Commission v. Bank of America Merrill Lynch (CT)* and *Competition Commission v. Bank of America Merrill Lynch (CAC)*.

2. *Competition Commission v. Bank of America Merrill Lynch (CT)* and *Competition Commission v. Bank of America Merrill Lynch (CAC)*

The case before the Competition Tribunal in *Competition Commission v. Bank of America Merrill Lynch (CT)*[34] concerned 23 banks–some local, some foreign– which had been charged by the CC under section 4(1)(*b*)(*i*) and (*ii*) of the Competition Act for fixing the rand–dollar exchange rate.[35] While the charge against the banks in question, that led to the present matter, was a section 4(1) charge, the present matter did not directly concern section 4(1), instead it concerned, inter alia, the CC's and the Competition Tribunal's jurisdiction over, first, firms that were not domiciled in and that did not carry on business in the Republic, so-called pure *peregrini*; and second, foreign firms that had some presence in the republic, so-called local *peregrini*.[36]

In the Tribunal, the respondents argued that in order for the Commission and the Tribunal to have jurisdiction over any of the respondents, there had to be both personal jurisdiction and subject-matter jurisdiction.[37] Personal jurisdiction, so the argument went, was regulated by the common-law principles concerning *peregrini*, and subject-matter jurisdiction was regulated by section 3[38] of the Competition Act.[39]

---

33   *Id.*, para 18.

34   *Supra* note 5.

35   Section 4 of the Competition Act 89 of 1998 states that: "Restrictive horizontal practices prohibited–
(1) An agreement between, or concerted practice by, firms, or a decision by an association of firms, is prohibited if it is between parties in a horizontal relationship and if–
(*b*) it involves any of the following restrictive horizontal practices:
(*i*) directly or indirectly fixing a purchase or selling price or any other trading condition;
(*ii*) dividing markets by allocating customers, suppliers, territories, or specific types of goods or services."

36   *Competition Commission v. Bank of America Merrill Lynch (CT)*, *supra* note 5, paras 30–34.

37   *Id.*, para 34.

38   Section 3 of the Competition Act 89 of 1998 provides that the Competition Act and its provisions apply "to all economic activity within, or having an effect within, the Republic."

39   *Competition Commission v. Bank of America Merrill Lynch (CT)*, *supra* note 5, para 35–36, 53.

After concluding that personal jurisdiction was established over the local *peregrini* but not over the pure *peregrini*, the only issue that the Tribunal was left to decide was thus that of subject-matter jurisdiction over the local *peregrini*.[40] The Tribunal articulated the issue at hand as follows: "If two foreign-based traders are involved in a cartel, the Tribunal will only have subject-matter jurisdiction if the cartel has, in the language of section 3(1), an economic effect in South Africa."[41] The Tribunal considered that section 3 of the Competition Act established what is commonly referred to as effects-based subject-matter jurisdiction.[42] Furthermore, the Tribunal considered that, while establishing jurisdiction on this basis may be unpleasantly received by, inter alia, foreign-based firms, for its perceived violation of the international law presumption against extraterritoriality, this approach was not uncommon.[43] The Tribunal remarked that:

> Effects-based jurisdiction is not a new problem for courts grappling with jurisdiction in competition law cases to decide. The dilemma is best summed up in a quote from American academic Professor Eleanor Fox who stated: "Competition law is national, markets are global, there is the rub." Put differently what is being said is that cartel effects may spill over borders, but competition enforcement is limited by borders. Nevertheless, courts in competition cases have applied the effects doctrine to address these problems.[44]

The Tribunal, in this instance, appears to have quoted Professor Eleanor Fox to a certain extent for rhetorical effect. Her analysis of the tension between the effects-based approach and the principle of extraterritoriality, in her work titled *National Law, Global Markets, and Hartford: Eyes Wide Shut*,[45] is not employed to address the specific issue of the potential distinction between local and foreign *peregrini* but rather to gloss the underlying problematic of extraterritorial jurisdiction. The relatively ambitious assertion of extraterritorial jurisdiction is a distinguishing feature of South African competition policy, a feature not paralleled in an otherwise comparable jurisdiction such as India.[46]

After a discussion of case law from the United States and the European Union concerning effects-based subject-matter jurisdiction, the Tribunal considered that:

> our law follows the same approach as does US law and European law to subject-matter jurisdiction for competition law cases.

---

40   *Id.*, para 85.
41   *Id.*, para 87.
42   *Id.*, para 87–88.
43   *Id.*
44   *Id.*, para 88–91.
45   Eleanor M. Fox, *National Law, Global Markets, and Hartford: Eyes Wide Shut* 68 ANTITRUST L.J. 73 (2000).
46   Marek Martyniszyn, *Export Cartels: Is It Legal to Target Your Neighbour? Analysis in Light of Recent Case Law*, 15 J. INT'L ECON. L. 181 (2012).

More specifically that through the lens of section 3(1) we adopt an effects-based test that is qualified. Perhaps the clearest formulation to adopt is that of the EU in *Intel* viz. that it is *foreseeable that the conduct will have a direct or immediate, and substantial effect in the Republic*. (Note we have used both the words "direct" as does the [CAC] in *ANSAC* and "immediate" as is used in the EU. While there is some overlap in the language, there are some cases in which the facts fit the one concept better than the other. We explain this more fully below when we consider the pleadings in this case). We will refer to this formulation from now on as the "qualified effects" test.[47]

The Tribunal's consideration of section 3(1) of the Competition Act–and its apparent reformulation or reinterpretation of the effects-based test under section 3(1) – comes against a jurisprudential background in which the CAC, a forum of a higher status that the Tribunal, in *American Soda Ash Corporation v. Competition Commission*, had already arguably fully considered the parameters of this provision.[48] Nonetheless, following its assessment of the facts, the Tribunal concluded that the CC had not pleaded sufficient facts to meet the threshold for establishing subject-matter jurisdiction in terms of the effects-based test envisaged under section 3(1) of the Competition Act,[49] and it accordingly dismissed the CC's application.

Dissatisfied with the Tribunal's interpretation of section 3(1) of the Competition Act and that authority's assessment of the facts and application of the law thereto, the CC took the decision on appeal to the CAC. The appeal, in *Competition Commission v. Bank of America Merrill Lynch International Limited and Others (CAC)*, turned on two main issues, namely: "whether the Act could apply extraterritorially in the light of a presumption against extraterritoriality, and whether there was a requirement for personal jurisdiction to be established prior to the assumption of any powers possessed by the Tribunal."[50]

These issues, it was agreed, concerned the parameters of section 3(1) of the Competition Act, particularly the meaning of all economic activity within, or having an effect within, the Republic. While the CC was of the view that the section 3(1) of the Competition Act conferred extraterritorial jurisdiction, the respondents' argued that: "the presumption against extraterritoriality always

---

47 *Competition Commission v. Bank of America Merrill Lynch (CT)*, supra note 5, para 100.

48 *Competition Commission v. Bank of America Merrill Lynch (CAC)*, supra note 6, para 36, where the court remarked that: "In *American Natural Soda Corporation v. Competition Commission* 2003 (5) SA 633 (CAC) this Court carefully examined the parameters of s 3(1) of the Act. Writing for a unanimous court, Malan AJA (as he then was) exhaustively examined the implications of the section in respect of its potential extraterritorial application."

49 *Competition Commission v. Bank of America Merrill Lynch (CT)*, supra note 5, para 112.

50 *Competition Commission v. Bank of America Merrill Lynch (CAC)*, supra note 6, para 35.

trumps wording such as that contained in section 3(1) ... such that the presumption overrides any possible application of extraterritorial jurisdiction of the competition authorities."[51]

In the first of four references to Eleanor Fox's work in this case, the CAC preliminarily responded to the respondents' argument and simultaneously foreshadowed the position that it would later adopt regarding the two main issues stated above, by quoting a passage from Professor Eleanor Fox's article, *Extraterritorial jurisdiction, antitrust and the European Union Intel case*.[52] This quotation was to the effect that:

> in this altered world market place the presumption against extra territoriality for economic law in defense of markets is no longer appropriate. We need to deal with the reason behind the presumption to prevent clashes caused by one sovereign's unreasonable intrusion on another sovereign's legitimate interest, and to tailor the law of restraint to the reason for it. Since general retreat and withdrawal from antitrust enforcement against non-nationals and foreign-based acts would deeply undermine the global and national competition systems, it is fitting to stress modes for accommodation more than rules for retreat.[53]

In our reading, the above-quoted passage by Professor Fox cautions against a strict, rigid "trump all other principles" presumption against extraterritoriality, as such a presumption would deeply undermine the global and national competition systems.

The CAC appears to have drawn upon Professor Fox's scholarly authority to do two things. In the first instance, it used Professor Fox's work substantively to highlight the policy dangers of the argument contend for by the respondents. The CAC did so in the context of the global economy of the twenty-first century where, first, anticompetitive conduct can detrimentally affect the national economy in circumstances where the conduct takes place on foreign soil or on the Internet; and secondly, multinational corporations are able to, and do in fact, configure their economic behavior to avoid national regulation. In the second instance, the CAC uses Professor Fox's work to argue, more indirectly as an interpretative matter, that in the context of global markets, arguments such as that advanced by the respondents should be discounted in favor of questions and enquiries that seek to establish whether provisions such as section 3(1) of the Competition Act appropriately rise to the challenge of the global economy.[54]

---

51   *Id.*, para 43.

52   Eleanor M. Fox, *Extraterritorial Jurisdiction, Antitrust, and the EU Intel Case: Implementation, Qualified Effects, and the Third Kind*, 42(3) FORDHAM INT'L L.J. 980 (2017).

53   *Competition Commission v. Bank of America Merrill Lynch (CAC)*, *supra* note 6, para 6.

54   *Id.*, para 7.

Following an analysis of the domestic and foreign judgments that have dealt with this issue, along with academic writings by, inter alia, Professor Fox, the CAC concluded that: "there is no merit in the argument that the presumption against extraterritoriality always trumps wording such as that contained in section 3(1) ... such that the presumption overrides any possible application of extraterritorial jurisdiction of the competition authorities,"[55] and stated that the Competition Act applies "to all economic activity that was located outside of South Africa but where the conduct complained of had direct and foreseeable substantial consequences in South Africa,"[56] thus averting the policy dangers of retreat alluded to by Professor Fox. It is worth stating here that the CAC's statement of the position under section 3(1) of the Competition Act in this case was (as noted above) a restatement of the same court's statement in *American Soda Ash Corporation v. Competition Commission*, and thus one could argue that the CAC used Professor Fox's work to emphasize the continued relevance of its earlier statement.

The CAC's second reference to Fox came in the framework of a debate[57] in the CAC as to whether section 3(1) of the Competition Act applies or ought to apply the "qualified effects" test as applied by the European Court of Justice (ECJ) in *Intel Corporation v. European Commission*.[58] The CAC was considering whether any reliance could be placed on the ECJ's *Intel* decision as authority for the "qualified effects" test. It decided not as, according to the CAC, Professor Fox

> [threw] doubt upon whether the Court of Justice did apply a test of foreseeable, immediate and substantial effects in the EU economic area. As she notes at 992:
>
>> There seemed to have been no fact-finding to support a conclusion that Intel's agreements with Lenovo had foreseeable immediate and substantial effects in the EEA. The hidden holding of the case is: where offshore conduct not directly implemented in the EEA and potentially although not immediately affecting the EEA is an integral part of a strategy covered by the EU law. EU law covers the conduct.[59]

Thereafter, essentially using Prof Fox's analysis–and her identification of the "hidden holding" of such a case–as a mechanism for filtering out comparative

---

55 *Id.*, para 43.

56 *Id.*, para 54.

57 Note that the debate is not fully recorded in the judgment but rather referred to in a footnote of the judgment. See *Competition Commission v. Bank of America Merrill Lynch (CAC), supra* note 6, fn 8.

58 Case C–413/14 P Intel Corporation v. European Commission EU:C:2017:632.

59 *Competition Commission v. Bank of America Merrill Lynch (CAC), supra* note 6, fn 8. See Fox, *supra* note 52, at 992.

European case law with inadequate factual foundations, the CAC went on to conclude that: "there does not appear to be any substantial reason as to why the approach adopted by this Court in *ANSAC* should now be disturbed nor does a different test really affect the approach which this Court seeks to adopt,"[60] viz. that the Competition Act "applied to all economic activity that was located outside of South Africa but where the conduct complained of had direct and foreseeable substantial consequences in South Africa."[61] Evidently, the CAC was persuaded by Professor Fox's analysis and conclusions regarding the *Intel* decision to the extent of using her analysis and conclusions, without more, as a premise against placing reliance on the said decision. High praise indeed.

On a slightly different note, the CAC cited two separate works by Professor Fox,[62] at two separate places in its judgment, as authority for the proposition that "cartel activity is the most egregious form of anticompetitive conduct."[63] It is interesting to note the difference between these two citations–one cite is to a coauthored textbook and the other is to a scholarly article. Citing to both demonstrates that the South African competition authorities are comfortable in relying even upon Fox's non-peer-reviewed work.

II. Professor Fox's Work on Anticompetitive Exclusionary Practices and Effects

1. *Competition Commission v. South African Airways*

A key case in South African competition jurisprudence, the proceedings against South African Airways (Pty) Ltd (SAA) in *Competition Commission v. South African Airways (Pty) Ltd* concerned certain loyalty reward agreements concluded by SAA with various travel agents in South Africa from late 1999 to mid-2001. Briefly, in terms of the agreements, SAA offered to pay travel agents a certain amount of money for a certain number of SAA domestic flight tickets sold. SAA had been concluding loyalty reward agreements with travel agents since the 1980s, and had had them in place prior to the subject agreements. These agreements were being challenged, however, because the threshold for obtaining the reward promised under these agreements was significantly higher than that under the pre-1999 agreements and, in addition, the reward promised under the agreements was more lucrative than that offered under the pre-1999 agreements. This meant, first, that travel agents had to sell more SAA tickets to obtain the promised reward and, second, notwithstanding the difficulty of selling more SAA tickets, travel agents had a strong enough financial incentive to conclude

---

60 *Competition Commission v. Bank of America Merrill Lynch (CAC)*, *supra* note 6, fn 8.

61 *Id.*, para 54.

62 The CAC cited Fox, *Extraterritorial jurisdiction, antitrust and the European Union Intel case*, *supra* note 52, at 990, and Eleanor Fox and Damien Gerard, EU Competition Law: Cases, Texts and Context 33 (2017).

63 *Competition Commission v. Bank of America Merrill Lynch (CAC)*, *supra* note 6, paras 61, 78.

these agreements with SAA and to work toward obtaining the rewards promised under the agreements.

One of the issues that the Tribunal had to decide in this case was the meaning that was to be ascribed to the word "anticompetitive," as it appears in section 8(1)(*d*) of the Competition Act, and the appropriate approach for establishing "anticompetitive effects."[64] The Tribunal began its discussion of the concept of "anticompetitive" by asking the question: "Should an abuse of dominance provision that seeks to proscribe exclusionary behavior require there to be evidence of each part of a chain of causation establishing the links from the act of exclusion to the loss of consumer welfare?"[65]

Thereafter, the Tribunal noted that this question, and thus the question of what constitutes "anticompetitive," was still an area of controversy even in mature competition law jurisdictions such as the United States, and noted that two positions have emerged in US case law on this point.[66] In the Tribunal's understanding, the first position required the complainant to demonstrate harm to consumer welfare in order to for the conduct to be considered anticompetitive and, therefore, unlawful, and the second position only required evidence that the exclusionary practice was or would lead to substantial market foreclosure. This gaze toward the US provided the occasion for a further reference to Eleanor's work. Perceiving a degree of eclecticism in the various American judgments, the Tribunal noted that:[67]

> Sometimes this eclecticism manifests itself in the approach taken in the same decision. Fox notes in her gloss on the Court of Appeals decision in *Microsoft* that: "While it may be sui generis in many respects, it is typical in its ambivalence regarding seriously exclusionary practices that may not have output effects." And later Fox asks rhetorically: "What did the court mean by "anticompetitive" and did it use that word consistently."

The Tribunal, thus, relied on Professor Fox's analysis of the *Microsoft* case, with little more, as support for its proposition to the effect that the concept of "anticompetitive" was still a matter of controversy even in the United States. The Tribunal thus subtly suggests that the issue before the Tribunal should come as no surprise to litigants in exclusionary abuse cases and that there should be no expectation of a hard and fast rule or approach on this point. That the only authority cited for the Tribunal's proposition to the effect that the concept of "anticompetitive" was still a matter of controversy in the United States is the

---

64 *Competition Commission v. South African Airways, supra* note 7, at 112.

65 *Id.* at 115.

66 *Id.* at 116.

67 *Id.*

Microsoft decision, not as read by the Tribunal, but rather as analyzed by Professor Fox, demonstrates, once again, the level of confidence that the South African competition authorities have in Professor Fox.

Later in the same matter, the Tribunal again cites Fox and appears to have considered the matter less controversial in the European Union, coming to that conclusion on the basis of Professor Fox's study and analysis of the ECJ cases. The Tribunal states that Professor Fox argues that in ECJ cases it is clear that:[68] "harm to competition is a wider concept than the result-oriented output limitation. Use of dominant power to procure significant advantages not on competitive merits, thereby pre-empting competitors' opportunities, is a harm to competition under Article 82."

On this point, the Tribunal did not engage in a lengthy discussion of ECJ cases, as it did with the US case law. The Tribunal accepted Professor Fox's analysis and conclusions and concurred without more, once again demonstrating the confidence that the South African competition authorities have in Professor Fox and her reputation in the competition law space.[69]

In this foundational *SAA* case, after discussing the US and the EU position on the concept of "anticompetitive," the Tribunal remarked that:[70]

> What are courts doing when they find behavior to be anticompetitive in the absence of evidence of harm to the consumer? Essentially they are consciously, or sometimes unconsciously as Fox suggests, making inferences of fact and law and sometimes, mixed fact and law, to arrive at findings of competitive harm by way of proxy. Courts may find that, as a matter of fact, a particular business practice is exclusionary. As a matter of fact, a court may also find that the practice has the potential to foreclose the market for competitors of the dominant firm. As a matter of inference on the facts the court may find that this is likely to foreclose competition. As a matter of inference the court may determine that if competition is foreclosed, there will be an adverse impact on competition. This latter type of inference, as Fox has pointed out, is not factual, but legal. It is based on an assumption that: "… markets are more likely to reward merit if they are not clogged by substantial unjustified exclusions."

---

68 *Id.* at 126.

69 This is not to say that the competition authorities blindly adopt her analysis and conclusions. What instead appears from the Tribunal's decision, albeit not explicitly, is that it read the cases analyzed by Professor Fox alongside her analysis and conclusions of the said cases, and was convinced by her analysis and conclusion, and consequently adopted her conclusions. This is particularly true for the *Microsoft* case, and less clear with regard to the ECJ decisions.

70 *Competition Commission v. South African Airways, supra* note 7, para 128.

The Tribunal went on to assess the SAA's conduct using the abovementioned approach, an approach that was, according to the Tribunal, "informed to some extent by Fox ... and Areeda and Hovenkamp in their treatise."[71] It is worth noting here that the Tribunal's decision in *Competition Commission v. South African Airways* is considered to be the *locus classicus* when it comes to the assessment of exclusionary acts and anticompetitive exclusionary acts,[72] which status thus further engraves Professor Fox's legacy into the very fabric of South African competition law.

III. Conclusion on the South African Competition Authorities' Use of Professor Fox's Work

The cases that we have selected for detailed discussion in order to demonstrate and investigate the traces Eleanor Fox has left within South African competition jurisprudence are by no means a few isolated instances. The South African competition authorities' use of Professor Fox's work in this manner is not uncommon. The CAC used her work in a similar manner in *Sasol Oil v. Nationwide Poles*.[73] The CAC there endorsed Professor Fox's analysis and conclusions regarding the objectives of European competition law, without more.[74] The story of this case and particularly its oral argument (where Eleanor's work was referred to by opposing counsel, each for their own argument) has become part of the lore of South African competition law and policy, well told in other contributions to this volume.[75]

Likewise, the Tribunal in *Venter v. Law Society of the Cape of Good Hope* considered Professor Fox's statement on the US law pertaining to horizontal restraints and its potential application to the rules of professional association to be convincing and worthy of endorsement, again, without more.[76]

Beyond the judges and adjudicators, those litigating in front of South Africa's courts and authorities have also drawn upon Professor Fox's authority. For instance, in *Wal-Mart Stores*, in support of its argument that the South African Act was to be interpreted beyond a narrow consumer welfare standard,

---

71 *Id.*, fn 75.

72 Philip Sutherland & Katharine Kemp, Competition Law of South Africa para 7.11.3.3 (2020); *Computicket (Pty) Ltd v. Competition Commission* (170/CAC/Feb19) [2019] ZACAC 4, para 16; *Competition Commission v. Media 24 (Pty) Limited* (CCT90/18) [2019] ZACC 26, para 76. *See also* Helen Jenkins et al., *The South African Airways Cases: Blazing a Trail for Europe to Follow?* (Paper prepared for the Third Annual Competition Conference, Pretoria, Aug. 14, 2009).

73 *Supra* note 10. The page references for this case are taken from the PDF version provided on SAFLII; available at *www.saflii.org/za/cases/ZACAC/2005/5.pdf*.

74 *Sasol Oil v. Nationwide Poles*, *supra* note 10, at 18.

75 *See* the Bonakele paper elsewhere in this volume.

76 *Venter v. Law Society of the Cape of Good Hope*, *supra* note 8, para 59 and associated note.

the trade union SACCAWU referenced several sources including David Lewis's *Global Competition: Law Makers and Globalisation* (2011) and Professor Fox's *Poverty and Markets* (March 2009).[77] While most citations made by litigants do not survive into the written opinion justifying the forum's order, these ones did. What is also interesting to note, at least for the purposes of this discussion, is that Professor Fox's work, in this case, is being cited by parties directly in aid of articulating their interests, rather than exclusively supporting their legal interpretations. In light of the manner in which SACCAWU used, inter alia, Professor Fox's work, the CAC opined that it did not take SACCAWU, in citing the aforementioned authorities, "to be arguing in favor of a total welfare standard which would take account only of consumer and producer surplus, but rather that the Act supported a more nuanced test than that of a consumer welfare standard."[78]

While she has never held the formal position of a litigant or an adjudicator, South Africa's competition regime is the richer for Eleanor Fox's participation and engagement.

---

77 *Wal-Mart Stores*, *supra* note 11, para 92.

78 *Id.*

Professor Eleanor Fox: Making Markets Work for the People – A View from South Africa

TEMBINKOSI BONAKELE*

Competition Commission of South Africa

Abstract

Professor Eleanor Fox has made an immense contribution to the development of competition law in South Africa and throughout Africa as a whole. Every conversation with Eleanor's friends, when writing this paper, led to another and yet another person who was keen to honor her in this publication. In observing Eleanor over the years I have known her, I have been profoundly touched by her humility, friendliness, accessibility, sincerity, empathy, honesty, humor, strong work ethic, and her obvious love for teaching. She broke the mold with her views on the purpose of competition law and the resulting framework that competition agencies should adopt in pursuing their goals. Using her extensive platform, she elevated the voice of developing nations in competition dialogue. She unapologetically pursued fairness and equality amidst voices calling for a more traditional approach to administering competition law. All this while making significant substantive contributions to the development of the law which scholars, practitioners, and the judiciary still consult

---

* Tembinkosi Bonakele has been the Commissioner of South Africa's Competition Commission since 2013. He is an admitted attorney and holds a BJuris and an LLB from the University of Fort Hare, and an MBA from Gordon Institute of Business Science, University of Pretoria. He is an adjunct visiting professor of law at Wits Law School, an adjunct professor in the Business School of Nelson Mandela University, an associate of the European Summer School and Conference in Competition and Regulation of Athens University of Economics and Business, a fellow of the University of Johannesburg's Centre for Competition, Regulation and Economic Development, a board member of the University of Stellenbosch's Centre for Competition Law and Economics, and a member of the University of Fort Hare Council. He has published widely in academic journals, and writes for newspapers and business magazines on competition matters.
The author would like to thank Nandi Mokoena for research assistance and Dikeledi Raboroko for her editorial assistance. The author is responsible for all errors.

Professor Eleanor Fox: Making Markets Work for the People – A View from South Africa

today. Her latest contribution to our continent–Making Markets Work for Africa– is a book she wrote with one of our own, Prof. Mor Bakhoum. Eleanor may have considered the name of this book to be just another convenient title but I would argue that this title is in fact her lasting legacy: she has spent much of her life making markets work for Africa. And we are deeply grateful.

I. Introduction

I have known Eleanor for more than a decade and a half, but her intellectual engagement with South Africa predates that by at least another decade. My first encounter with her was while working as legal counsel to the Competition Commission of South Africa; by then she had established herself as a long-standing friend and trusted adviser of the competition authorities of South Africa–the Competition Commission; our court of first instance, the Competition Tribunal; and the Competition Appeal Court. Before then, she had worked as part of the core team that authored South Africa's post-apartheid competition law.

It is for this reason that I undertook the mammoth task to sum up her immense contribution with a mixture of trepidation, excitement, and humility. What counts in my favor is that I credit Eleanor with my own development in the area of competition law. I have been in many ways her student for more than 15 years. I have collaborated with her more than any other international law expert I can think of: we co-edited a book on competition law in BRICS countries; I have done a review of her book on competition law and policy in Africa; I been a guest lecturer in her N.Y.U. Masters class; featured regularly as a speaker in her developing country–focused N.Y.U. annual conference; I have been a co-panelist with her exploring competition law in developing countries; I and my colleagues in South Africa have benefited from her generous support in reviewing and discussing our cases and law, and have imbibed her prolific writings. How then can I, to whom so much has been given, have nothing to say about so generous a giver?

To counter limitations that I may have to cover the breadth and depth of Eleanor's contribution, my reflections have benefited from interviews conducted with–and sometimes direct passages of reflections from–some of Eleanor's friends and colleagues from South Africa. Of course, it would be impossible to cover everything and everyone: I apologize in advance for any limitations occasioned by space, time, and loss of memory on my part. I hope this contribution will give readers a sense of the significant role she played in crafting and shaping the current state of South Africa's competition regime.

Whether observing her from a distance or working with her closely, I've been profoundly touched by Eleanor's vast knowledge of competition law and policy, generously shared with humility, friendliness, sincerity, empathy, honesty, and humor. I have been inspired by her work ethic as well as her determination to ensure that competition law is a weapon and a shield for the poor of the world, as opposed to–in a Marxist sense–an exercise in *management of the affairs of the bourgeoisie*.

Before I delve deep into my tribute, I would like to explain why I chose to structure this paper as I did. I wanted to honor the person that Eleanor is through the lens of her work and her very focused contribution to the South African competition regime. There are two reasons for this approach.

First, as I wrote, I realized there is no separation between Eleanor, her personality traits, and her life's work. The themes she has focused on, the audience she has targeted and the opinions she has adopted over the years have fused the person and the professional. From her work emerges a portrait of a fine and powerful activist, armed with a pen and paper. She is what she does. Unlike traditional academic works, Eleanor's writings always reveal the person holding the pen. And so, anyone who really wants to know what kind of person Eleanor is need only pick up "The Comparative Advantage of Developing Countries,"[1] or another of her articles on competition regulation for developing countries, to know that she writes with sincere respect–even for those she disagrees with–and to confirm that all the traits I described above come through in her work. From reading just one of her articles you will know where she stands.

Second, as tempting as it was to speak only of the friend I have come to love and respect in Eleanor, I felt it would be a pity to leave readers unfamiliar with Eleanor's concrete opinions and thoughts, as expressed through her many books, speeches, chapters, and articles. This collection of literary works has been a source of great inspiration in designing an enforcement culture that is aligned and relevant to South Africa's unique need for a growing and inclusive economy, rather than one based solely on a traditional Western idea of what competition enforcement should look like. Therefore, shaping this chapter along Eleanor's big personality and her work at the same time is my way of creating a reference piece for any competition practitioner looking to explore the broader policy choices South Africa's competition regime has faced over the years, and to understand the pivotal role that Eleanor's work has played in deciding which path we took.

> I was first introduced to Eleanor Fox, a professor from New York University and a massive contributor to antitrust scholarship. Her combination of extraordinary generosity, boundless intellectual curiosity and an unceasing quest to establish a link between competition and poverty alleviation ensured that she became, and has remained, a beacon for me and many others grappling with the special problems confronting competition law and policy in developing countries. While she is not the only one who

---

[1] Eleanor Fox, *Competition Policy: The Comparative Advantage of Developing Countries*, 79(69) LAW & CONTEMP. PROBS. (2016).

> fits that description, there is something particularly striking about Eleanor's willingness to elevate intellectual rigor above political calculation and personal ambition.
>
> Extract from *Thieves at the Dinner Table: Enforcing the Competition Act: a personal account* (2012), David Lewis, former chairperson of the Competition Tribunal of South Africa

II. Eleanor Broke the Mold

Anyone who has encountered South African competition law enforcers will tell you that those guys have a blend of competition law and social policy–and they all seem quite passionate about both. Many are struck by the objectives of South African competition law, which transcend efficiency notions so favored by mainstream academia to infusing public interest and equity considerations. Initially I was somewhat surprised by Eleanor's willingness–to the point of encouragement–to accept our view that an African brand of competition law need not resemble an American or European one. In a world so dominated by the Chicago school of thought, I initially put Eleanor's willingness down to professional courtesy–perhaps she respected without necessarily agreeing, or she just did not want to come across as offensive. But I soon came to know that Eleanor's views on competition enforcement stemmed from long-established liberal roots.

Her writings are consistent in this regard. In "The Battle for the Soul of Antitrust" – written in 1987, more than 10 years before South Africa's competition agency came into existence–Eleanor already showed her strong partiality to the "new coalition" which represented those who distanced themselves from the traditional Chicago school of thought on competition policy.[2] In it she described members of the Chicago school as those who commonly asserted their preference for freedom from government interference in the economy:

> They assume that competition in markets untouched by positive law is robust, that the natural tendency of firms is to be efficient and that the progressive, industrious entrepreneur is likely to succeed. Members of the New Coalition ... worry about private as well as government power, the coercion and exclusion of the weak by the powerful and the distribution of power and opportunity. They take seriously the imperfections of free market competition.

Eleanor ended her piece with a strong endorsement for the new coalition's way of thinking and a prediction that their approach would more likely be the blueprint for the second century of antitrust that was to come. What I suspect Eleanor didn't know at the time was that she would play a central role in realizing

---

2   Eleanor Fox, *The Battle for the Soul of Antitrust*, 75 Calif. L. Rev. 917 (1987).

the future that she imagined, at least in South Africa and many countries in Africa that followed its example.

Closer to home, Eleanor's article "Equality, Discrimination and Competition Law: Lessons from and for South Africa and Indonesia"[3] – written as early as 2000, when South Africa was itself trying to carve out the role that competition law would play in its fledgling democracy–showed Eleanor's sincere belief in the views she boldly professed in every forum where she appeared. "The experience of mature market economies is highly useful," she said in the article, "but may not be wholly transferable. While the American determination not to mix equality with efficiency may work for the United States in the year 2000, it may not be an obvious truth for the world."

Eleanor's views were particularly empowering for our newly established competition agencies. At the time, the South African's post-apartheid government under Nelson Mandela passed a package of legislation to transform the economy. Competition law was viewed as a tool for inclusion–prescribing rules to allow the broadest participation in the economy and protecting consumers from monopolies. The government had passed the Competition Act in 1998, winning both praise and admonishment, depending on which side the commentator came from.

Big business had a reason to be concerned. Nelson Mandela, after his release from jail, had vowed that "the excessive concentration of power in a few white hands had to change."[4] To place Mandela's remarks in context: at the time it was reported that fewer than 10 corporate conglomerates controlled almost 90% of the shares listed on the Johannesburg Stock Exchange. Anglo American, a global mining company then headed by Gavin Relly, was among these. Relly reacted to the circulating idea that Anglo American might be broken up by way of the competition law under discussion. "I think the idea perfectly foolish," he had said. Relly added that he did not think that South Africans were "stupid enough to kill the goose that lays the golden egg."[5]

Internationally, the newly established competition agencies often had to defend the policy decision to include public interest criteria in the assessment of mergers and acquisitions. Norman Manoim, who chaired the Competition Tribunal for a decade, still remembers being "lynched" at international conferences for South Africa's approach to public interest considerations in mergers. He recalls that Eleanor always defended our position, reminding the audience, tactfully but emphatically, that what worked for America would not necessarily work for South Africa.

---

3   Eleanor Fox, *Equality, Discrimination and Competition Law: Lessons from and for South Africa and Indonesia*, 41 Harv Int'l L.J. 579 (2000).

4   Reg Rumney, *Is big also bad? ANC and industry agree to differ*, Report from undated media archives.

5   *Id*.

Professor Eleanor Fox: Making Markets Work for the People – A View from South Africa

While the inclusion of public interest criteria was not altogether uncommon in foreign competition regimes, South Africa's Competition Act elevated public interest factors to the point where they alone–to the exclusion of traditional competition factors–could determine whether a merger was approved or prohibited. In his 2002 speech to the International Competition Network (ICN) Dave Lewis, who was then the chairperson of the Competition Tribunal, defended this unique position and ultimately warned that South Africa's competition agencies would soon lose relevance in their jurisdiction if they ignored the impact of competition policy on the most pressing concerns of the day.

> I readily concede that public interest considerations weigh more heavily in developing countries than they do in developed countries. The reasons for this are instructive: first, it is widely accepted that there is a greater role for industrial policy, for targeting support at strategically selected sectors or interest groups, in developing than in developed countries; secondly, developing country competition authorities are still engaged in a very basic struggle to achieve credibility and legitimacy in their countries. While credibility will certainly not be achieved by bending to the whim of every interest group, nor will it be secured by a competition authority that refuses to take direct account of major national economic problems and aspirations. Hence, in a country like South Africa, while we in the competition authorities may well understand the pitfalls in balancing competition and public interest, we equally recognize that a competition statute that simply ignored the impact of its decisions on employment or on securing a greater spread of black ownership, would consign the act and the authorities to the scrap heap.[6]

Eleanor remains relevant in the COVID-19 crisis

Looking back, I would say that one of Eleanor's greatest contributions to South Africa was that she brought an enormous amount of experience, having practiced in a jurisdiction that had competition laws for over 100 years. Added to that, she had an incredible ability to understand South Africa's economic context as a developing country, along with its historical imbalances.

From the onset South Africa didn't take the conventional approach to competition law that the United States did yet Eleanor remained a proponent of our unique position. While others wavered, Eleanor could see competition policy as an effective instrument to address poverty and inequality. In that respect Eleanor has proven to be a "how can we do it?" kind of person, eager to use competition policy to achieve fairness in the economic landscape. And her tireless efforts are yielding global results. Now, more than ever before, I encounter competition agencies in developed countries exploring the idea of public interest considerations in competition enforcement or looking at other

---

6 David Lewis, The Role of Public Interest in Merger Evaluation, ICN Merger Working Group (Sept. 28–29, 2002).

ways to align their work with broader industrial policy or national priorities, which shows that Eleanor was ahead of the curve when she contributed to South Africa's approach more than 20 years ago.

Now, with the global onset of the COVID-19 pandemic, Eleanor has continued her efforts to highlight the plight of developing countries and to urge more developed nations to distribute resources fairly. In her thought-provoking article "Developing countries, markets, and the coronavirus: two challenges,"[7] Eleanor reflects on the tendency of developed nations to self-protect and self-prioritize when disaster strikes. While acknowledging that a global crisis presents difficult choices for countries to make, Eleanor calls on developed nations to consider the impact of their choices on the developing world. "First, developed countries, which have overwhelming advantages and constantly use them to steer the economic ship to their advantage, should not do market harm to developing countries. Nationalistic trade restraints set the developing countries back unfairly and inefficiently in their constant efforts to bridge the divide." In this she also highlights the comparative, though narrow, advantage of developing nations to make use of transparent public interest provisions to achieve desired outcomes during the COVID-19 crisis and in its aftermath. In a second article on the subject, Eleanor advises competition agencies to intervene with circumspection because, in the long run, competition must be preserved for the benefit of the economy.

On a more personal note, I've found Eleanor to be highly responsive and generous with her knowledge and time. Extreme differences in time zones don't seem to matter as she answers any question asked ever so promptly.

Still keeping with my personal observations, I cannot end my tribute without admiring Eleanor's vast knowledge and boundless energy. Eleanor is a library of information on competition issues, traveling the world to share invaluable insights. Her energy to travel, to learn, to teach, to listen, to advise, and to dance, beats even that of younger practitioners in the field. I should know because I retired from the dance floor in Cape Town late one night, leaving Eleanor to close the party in the early hours of the morning, I'm told.

Mondo Mazwai, Chairperson of the Competition Tribunal of South Africa

III. Elevating the Voice of Developing Countries

In all the years I've observed her, Eleanor has used her high platform to elevate developing countries and to garner support for their independent thinking and tailored characterization of competition law. "The key point is knowledgeable choice," she wrote in her 2012 research paper on "Competition, Development and Regional Integration,"[8] referring to the right of developing countries to charter their own path in developing their respective competition laws.

---

7   Eleanor M. Fox, *Developing countries, markets, and the coronavirus: two challenges*, 8(2) J. ANTITRUST ENFORCEMENT 276 (2020), https://doi.org/10.1093/jaenfo/jnaa018.

8   Eleanor M. Fox, *Competition, Development and Regional Integration: In Search of a Competition Law Fit for Developing Countries*, in COMPETITION POLICY AND REGIONAL INTEGRATION IN DEVELOPING COUNTRIES (Josef Drexl, Mor Bakhoum, Eleanor M. Fox, Michal Gal, & David Gerber eds., 2012).

Professor Eleanor Fox: Making Markets Work for the People – A View from South Africa

In 2013 I had the privilege to listen to Eleanor giving a talk to the Global Forum on Competition of the Organisation for Economic Cooperation and Development (OECD), where she brought to light, on a global stage, the challenges of developing nations in drafting competition laws that helped to address the developmental challenges they face. In her thought-provoking address – "Imagine pro-poor(er) competition law"[9] – Eleanor challenged the audience to look at the antitrust world through the eyes of lower and lowest income people, those without connections and power, and to ask themselves what they would then choose as key antitrust initiatives. She implored the audience to consider creating a competition system that was more sympathetic to people without power than to people with power; more sympathetic to outsiders than to incumbents, especially incumbents upon whom privilege had long been showered.

Eleanor's address made concrete suggestions for ways in which competition laws designed to protect the vulnerable could be approached. One approach was to apply competition law as usual but with a distinct priority for those restraints that harmed the poor the most. These would be restraints in industries covering the necessities of life such as infrastructure, food, cement, and healthcare. Not one to show blind affinity, Eleanor also called out state acts in developing countries for their propensity to harm the most vulnerable in society and went on to suggest six principles for drafting competition laws that could target state acts, as well as state officials who facilitated anticompetitive conduct such as bid-rigging. She recommended that defenses allowed for state acts and exemptions should be narrowly drawn to enable maximum effectiveness.

Wendy Ndlovu, who was the chief legal counsel of the Commission, appreciated Eleanor's balanced approach to South Africa's competition law developments. Although Eleanor was certainly sympathetic to the challenges developing countries faced in defining a suitable enforcement model, she also favored intellectual soundness and would call out any decisions she felt were lacking in legal or economic rigor. Eleanor was also an objective commentator. As Wendy tells it, when consulting on competition issues, Eleanor would always refer her to local case precedent. "She would always ground me back into our jurisprudence and not try to sell me ideas that were applicable in the US."

It wasn't only her excellent intellectual contribution to this less-researched area of law that stood out for me when Eleanor addressed the OECD. It was the way she shared her views with such a personal knowledge of the circumstances of each country that I appreciated. Eleanor drew on examples from several jurisdictions, displaying a deep and personal knowledge of the issues emerging and the actors involved–invoking cases and experiences from Mexico, Kenya, India, Tanzania, Senegal, Pakistan, South Africa, and many more. This on-the-ground research in developing countries is confirmed by Francis W. Kariuki, director

---

9   Eleanor Fox, Address to OECD (2013).

general of the Competition Authority of Kenya, who revealed the source of her vast knowledge as being personal conversations, alongside the desktop research academics were accustomed to.

Another one of Eleanor's contributions to competition law development was her insistence on accommodating and encouraging diversity in the formulation and application of competition law. Almost any writing by Eleanor on the subject of competition and developing countries would confirm this observation, but she left no doubt on this point in her 2012 research paper on "Competition, Development and Regional Integration,"[10] when she framed her objective in this way: "The essay argues that developing countries must develop their own brand of competition law, resisting pressures to copy 'international standards' without regard to fit."

Perhaps developing countries would in any event have achieved the same prominence they now enjoy on the global competition stage, but there is no doubt that Eleanor's influence has catapulted us forward, and her continued research in this area has given developing nations the kind of momentum we may not have had without her efforts.

Her 2016 paper: "Competition Policy: The Comparative Advantage of Developing Countries"[11] urged developing countries to consider their advantageous position as later entrants into the competition field, prompting us to see our delayed entry as an opportunity rather than a setback.

> Developing countries are encumbered by countless disadvantages. In the midst of all of their sometimes insurmountable challenges, this article has uncovered two bright but hidden truths. First, path dependence. Mature competition jurisdictions have the baggage of an entrenched path, which is sometimes inflexible even in times of global change. New competition jurisdictions do not have this baggage. Developing jurisdictions with unformed competition law are well positioned to take advantage of this insight. They are free to address their own needs and need not be seduced to transplant law tailored to markets very different from their own.

> …Second, the trade-and-competition interface. Developed economies with large markets, in particular the United States, have little interest in connecting the world by a coherent trade-and-competition system. The system as it is, with the division between trade and competition, and with national-only law that is indifferent to external harms, suits them. But developing countries, especially small developing countries, are harmed every day by a

---

10 Fox, *supra* note 8.

11 Fox, *supra* note 1.

poisonous mix of cross-border state and private restraints. Moreover, developing countries are the usual victims of foreign-originating anticompetitive acts. Finally, regional agreements among similarly situated neighbors can offer something especially important to developing countries–a trade-and-competition community that would break down barriers and significantly increase competitiveness, without the worry of exploitation by an over-sized partner.

Eleanor brings both heart and mind to work

I met Eleanor for the first time in London many years ago at a meeting of competition law experts. She had a striking and eccentric personality, which is probably what made me pay attention to her in the first place. From the bold views she expressed on the subject I learned she was a maverick and outlier in her field. They were views we South Africans could not ignore. Eleanor was as steeped in knowledge as any paid-up member of the antitrust orthodoxy but, at the same time, displayed a progressive ideology. She never lost sight of the fact that antitrust, or competition law as we call it in South Africa, was first and foremost about ensuring market access.

This is probably why Eleanor was so interested in the *Nationwide Poles* case that the Competition Tribunal heard in 2005. The case was brought by a small producer of wooden poles against a South African oil giant, Sasol Oil (Pty) Ltd. Mr. Jim Foot, who owned the wooden poles business and appeared before us without legal representation, complained that Sasol charged his ailing business considerably more than his competitors for a wood preservative called creosote. It turned out that Sasol's discriminatory pricing was based on volume discounts and Jim Foot's business wasn't able to purchase in the kind of volumes that would enable him to compete effectively with others who bought creosote from Sasol in larger volumes. This matter had all the makings of a David and Goliath story, and Eleanor felt it represented precisely the type of case that should occupy competition law practitioners' time. She has since covered the case and its relevance for competition in developing countries in many of her publications.

Eleanor's humanism is another unique characteristic of hers–both in her work and in her personal life. This is not to say other competition practitioners are less so but rarely have I seen such activism and compassion come through in their professional work as it does in Eleanor's work. In the developed world there is nobody quite as concerned with developing world aspects of competition law. From her very first engagements with South Africa, more than 20 years ago, she embraced us and we embraced her. I also think she has remained highly relevant and engaged over all these years because of her intellectual curiosity. Even with all the knowledge she has gained over time, Eleanor is still a very curious human being.

David Lewis, executive director of Corruption Watch and former chairperson of the Competition Tribunal of South Africa

IV. In Pursuit of Fairness and Equality

> Fairness in antitrust has been a relentless bone of contention. In 1987, Eleanor Fox already described an ongoing battle for the soul of antitrust between those who defend that the markets work more efficiently when (almost entirely) unconstrained by regulation, and those for whom economics is just "one of the tools used to carry out the spirit of the law."
>
> Sandra Marco Colino, *The Antitrust F Word: Fairness Considerations in Competition Law* (2019)

I have said before that Eleanor's approach to regulating competition stood in contrast to the more traditional views the Commission was increasingly exposed to in its interactions with international counterparts. In many ways, her thinking had evolved beyond what our fledgling competition regime could accommodate in its early years. Through her writing she identified, supported, and thus legitimized the virtues that she believed competition laws in developing countries ought to pursue. Chief among them were fairness and equality. Her extensive research on competition systems in developing markets consolidated the experience of competition agencies the world over and became a helpful resource to me and undoubtedly to other agencies interested in learning about the interface between competition and the development agenda.

Eleanor summed up the global "fairness" debate aptly when she said:

> In the United States, fairness is neither a recognized goal nor a permissible consideration of the antitrust law. Rather, the law is about efficiency. Application of elements of fairness, it is feared, will protect inefficient small business and raise prices to consumers. Thus, fairness is at war with antitrust. To many developing countries the deep problem of fairness cannot be avoided. Business, society, and the law have been unfair to the poor and to the left-out and unconnected majority for many years. Injustices need to be righted, for efficiency and for humanity. Competition law cannot do everything, but at least it can provide an environment in which the left-out population has a fair chance to compete and smaller producers are not exploited by exercises of market power. Developing countries are looking for ways to make their law responsive to and alleviative of poverty, inequality, and past injustices of exclusion from economic life. Whereas US antitrust law leans toward protecting the dominant firms and their strategies on the assumption that intervention is inefficient, developing countries may prefer a strategy of keeping a clear path for the outsider–a route that has strong efficiency properties and is fair as well.[12]

---

12 *Id.*

Unsurprisingly Eleanor shared the same view on equality as a goal of competition policy, particularly for developing countries. In "Competition, Development, and Regional Integration: In Search of a Competition Law Fit for Developing Countries,"[13] she suggests that a competition policy that seeks to foster equality of opportunity to partake in the market and share in its benefits must include measures to overcome inequality, or at least its effects.

In the same spirit, Eleanor promoted the achievement of inclusive economic growth–as opposed to economic growth in and of itself–in much of her work. In 2012 she cited favorably the 2008 Spence Growth Report, which identified the characteristics necessary and important for growth designed to lift the peoples of developing countries out of poverty: "[The Spence Growth Report] concludes that not only does growth critically matter, but inclusive growth critically matters. Distribution counts. And distribution of wealth and, more important for our purposes, of opportunity and the chance for mobility, was deeply skewed." Eleanor campaigned for the adoption of a competition policy, in developing countries, more aligned to the conclusions in the Spence Growth Report than to the prevailing consensus in more developed nations at that time.

Eleanor has strongly endorsed the idea that both fairness and equality should be recognized as legitimate goals of competition policy in so many of her writings. The fact that she has devoted so much of her life's work to this subject is, in itself, testimony to the value she places on the debate concerning the goals of competition policy. Yet Eleanor by no means left her contribution at the level of academic debate. She has, in fact, repeatedly traveled to South Africa and many developing countries to share her knowledge and to assist in crafting competition laws that take account of the developmental needs of emerging economies. In that sense Eleanor has earned her stripes as a credible commentator on this important subject, and got her hands dirty along with the lawmakers who had difficult policy choices to make in the process of drafting legislation. Norman Manoim was part of the team that drafted the Competition Act of South Africa, and he recalls that Eleanor actually drafted parts of the law on abuse of dominance, with some reworking from the appointed committees, and she was very influential in how the law was finally formulated. This part of the law is among the more interventionist in the world of antitrust, protecting consumers from exploitative abuse while constraining market exclusion. What impressed Norman at the time was that Eleanor borrowed insights from several jurisdictions, not just her home jurisdiction, when drafting, because "she had very good sense of what was going on around the world."

Eleanor has also contributed at every major amendment to the competition statute of South Africa. In the latest amendments, where the competition authorities' powers were extended in order to address excessive concentration in the economy, Eleanor

---

13 Fox, *supra* note 8, at 273, 275, 281–83, 285.

was the preeminent academic who served as a sounding board to the ministry that was driving the process. The process of amending our Competition Act offered an opportunity to delve deeper into some of the areas Eleanor had covered in her life's work of using competition policy to achieve more equitable outcomes for society.

V. Institutions Matter

It isn't only the substantive elements that Eleanor finds relevant to attaining the goals South Africa seeks from its competition regime. She believes that institutional design is just as important to achieve the required end. She argues for "the importance of an independent competition authority, trustworthy institutions, judicial review, and an advocacy role for the authority."[14] She has advocated for simpler form of advocacy, such videos, to *take down knowledge from books and make it real*.

She has also supported regional and continental cooperation institutional mechanisms in Africa. Eleanor has always believed that regional arrangements contribute economies of scale in enforcement, increase the voice of developing nations on the global stage, and assist in detecting cross-border cartels. Eleanor was even instrumental in establishing the African Competition Forum (ACF) in 2011. She helped to set up an important cross-country study among ACF members, believing these to have tremendous value in the sharing of knowledge and expertise.

The lasting legacy of Eleanor Fox

If I had to highlight just three of Eleanor's greatest contributions to South Africa they would be (1) her pivotal role in conceptualizing South Africa's competition law; (2) capacitating the bodies set up to administer the Competition Act; and (3) her ongoing role as a sounding board for the development of competition policy, draft legislation and case law.

Developing the concept

In 1992 Nelson Mandela, who was then President of the ANC, returned from the World Economic Forum annual meeting in Davos with a clear vision of the economic policies that were likely to attract foreign investors to South Africa. In his address to the gathering of more than 1,000 delegates, Mandela urged the nations in attendance to lift economic sanctions and assured them of South Africa's determination "to move forward as speedily as possible to establish the political and social climate which [was] necessary to ensure business confidence and create the possibility for all investors to make long-term commitments to help develop the South African economy."[15]

---

14 *Id.*

15 *Nelson Mandela's 1992 Davos address*, WORLD ECONOMIC FORUM (Dec. 6, 2013), www.weforum.org/agenda/2013/12/nelson-mandelas-address-to-davos-1992/.

Professor Eleanor Fox: Making Markets Work for the People – A View from South Africa

This context set the backdrop for the development of a more robust and focused competition policy than had been the case until that point. Alistair Ruiters, who was the director general in the Department of Trade and Industry, assembled a small team comprising himself, Eleanor Fox, David Lewis and I to devise a framework for a new competition regime. All credit should go to David Lewis–later to be the formidably brilliant chair of the Competition Tribunal–whom I believe enticed Eleanor to join the team, having previously been exposed to her work. What followed were three days of intense conversation among the team as to what form the new competition law would take. At times, it seemed to me that Alistair, David and especially myself seemed like babes in the woods while Eleanor spoke, given that we had such limited knowledge of the subject. Eleanor, on the other hand, had an incredible grasp of the law from both an American and European perspective, which was hugely beneficial. She was also genuinely sympathetic to the historical context with which we were engaged which made her uniquely suited to the task at hand.

Out of those initial deliberations a Competition Act emerged that is now widely seen as a successful piece of legislation. Looking back, I can confidently say we would not have had such a statute without Eleanor.

Building our capacity

Having passed the law and established the three bodies that would administer the Competition Act, early training was critical in capacitating these institutions to deliver effectively against their respective mandates. In the early days the Competition Appeal Court, which I headed, and the Competition Tribunal, under the leadership of David Lewis, conducted their training sessions together. Eleanor Fox was always available to teach our judiciary and impart her skills during these training sessions. Even now, 21 years later, she continues to do the same. But our connection to Eleanor has yielded added benefits because, through her, we have received training from other distinguished competition scholars, such as Professor Harry First from New York University School of Law. To my knowledge no South African court outside the Competition Appeal Court receives this level of training.

Knowledgeable sounding board

I mentioned that Eleanor had the unique advantage of being an expert in both the European and American competition regimes from which other competition systems have derived precedent. Although they cover similar concepts, these jurisdictions have different ideologies that inform the outcomes of their respective competition cases, with the Europeans generally adopting a more interventionist approach. Given her knowledge, coupled with her extensive work in developing countries all over the world, Eleanor has been the ideal sounding board for competition practitioners in developing nations. She fulfills this role generously in her training sessions but also informally, through conversations and in the course of her other work, such as sharing her insights in the formulation of the recent amendments to the Competition Act. We benefited from her well-educated perspective in the early days and we continue to do so today.

Judge President Dennis Davis, Competition Appeal Court

VI. Substantively Speaking

Eleanor believes that the substantive rules of competition regulation, as applied in developing countries, have to correlate to development goals if they are to be effective or, at least, contribute to development goals such as fairness and equality. She observed that the attitude some developed nations had cultivated over time to market abuses like "predatory pricing" or "refusal to supply a scarce resource" was informed by a market philosophy that was too permissive. Cases against such abuses had become virtually impossible to win in some developed countries. Eleanor found this approach unsuited to the needs of developing countries.

> In societies long dominated by state-owned firms and their privileged successors, however, in which capital markets work poorly, barriers to entry are high, problems of capture are great, and social ties breed collusion and discourage detection, dominant firm predation and exclusion are rampant and harmful. They are major forces in keeping markets closed and uncompetitive. In developing countries, the costs of antitrust non-intervention in many circumstances are likely to be higher than the costs of intervention.[16]

While the more developed jurisdictions had a tendency to focus competition outcomes on improving consumer welfare, Eleanor has always believed buyer power should receive consideration in developing jurisdictions. In her chapter "Drafting Competition Law for Developing Jurisdictions,"[17] which she wrote in collaboration with Gal, Bakhoum, Drexl and Gerber, Eleanor found that suppliers in poor developing countries were more likely to be victims of exploitative buyer power than were suppliers in developed countries. Developed countries could adopt consumer welfare as their goal but poor developing countries could prefer to take account of all market harms, not just consumer welfare harms. Small farmers, for instance, were particularly vulnerable to harm from monopsonic purchase and distribution practices, and mergers creating buyer power. In this regard she cited examples from Zambia and Côte d'Ivoire. The authors suggested finally that jurisdictions with most jobs and businesses in the agricultural sector may need to take serious account of buyer power.

Over and above the adoption of robust rules against abuse of dominance, Eleanor put forward the EU approach–which had special regard for openness and access but also took a suspicious stance toward competition restricting state action and rules against discrimination in state procurement–as an additional consideration for establishing competition rules in developing countries.

---

16 Fox, *supra* note 8.

17 *In* THE ECONOMIC CHARACTERISTICS OF DEVELOPING JURISDICTIONS: THEIR IMPLICATIONS FOR COMPETITION LAW (Michal S. Gal, Mor Bakhoum, Josef Drexl, Eleanor M. Fox, & David J. Gerber eds., 2015).

Eleanor also believes that the design of competition rules around the burden of proof could help or hinder the goal of achieving fairness and equality, and thus inclusive growth. She has argued that shifting this burden to the typically well-resourced incumbents, upon a minimal showing of dominance and abuse conduct by the competition agency–coupled with an effective system of judicial review–could assist a competition agency in a developing country to achieve its broad goals.

Another model offered by Eleanor was to explicitly introduce values of fairness and other development objectives in developing countries' competition rules. This would be particularly relevant to countries wary of the deep pockets and leverage of powerful corporations in the market.

All this being said, Eleanor has never been one to discount lessons from any jurisdiction or legal system, even if she did not agree with it. In this regard I have found Eleanor to be a consummate scholar on all things. In her writings and in our personal discussions, she has always encouraged readers to draw what they can from US and EU competition law–using the lessons most relevant to them and discarding what may not fit or apply.

Unsurprisingly, Eleanor has also advocated for simplicity in rulemaking: "For poor developing countries, human resources and capital resources are extremely scarce. The competition authorities do not have teams of lawyers and economists ready to identify and analyze reams of documents and construct scores of models and studies."[18] For this reason Eleanor has argued that the simplest form of rules against anticompetitive conduct should be adopted in developing countries. These would include prohibitions like resale price maintenance or product bundling by dominant firms. These could be presumed illegal unless justified, as in Europe and other parts of the world.

VII. Both a Teacher and a Scholar

> Eleanor Fox has become a mentor for a generation of younger scholars spread around the world, who strive to emulate her concern to account for the complexity of the forces at play in the field of antitrust as a mirror of social tensions, traditions and evolutions.
>
> Damien Gerard, College of Europe (Belgium), May 2016

Eleanor is extremely generous with time, except that she will never give you her students' time. Eleanor's life is surrounded by students–she is a much-loved professor in her university, but has a following reaching far and beyond. What makes her a fantastic teacher is her genuine interest in what each person, each

---

18   *Id.*

student, thinks. When you meet Eleanor, she would want to know a lot about what you have been up to, and how you think about current issues.

Over the years Eleanor has shown much support to young researchers in South Africa and other developing countries as well. She has also supported the work of CCRED (the Centre for Competition Regulation and Economic Development, which is a university-based research group) in east Africa and other parts of southern Africa.

VIII. Making Markets Work for Africa

Perhaps Eleanor's most comprehensive written contribution to competition law development on the African continent is her book *Making Markets Work for Africa*,[19] which she authored with Mor Bakhoum. There is generally limited literature on competition law in developing countries. Africa, especially, has largely been ignored, despite a growing number of countries that have adopted competition laws in this vast continent. The lack of scholarship focusing on developing countries in general and Africa in particular leads to greater focus on the West, predominantly the US and Europe. The consequence of this is that most literature hardly addresses the challenges of competition policy and enforcement from a developing country's perspective. This, in turn, means that there are few books one can consult for guidance when enforcing competition law in a developing country. The authors therefore fill a big gap in the literature on competition law and policy in Africa. The book, however, holds lessons for developing countries more generally, and even those in developed countries interested in a progressive understanding of competition policies. In their tour-de-force study of the continent of Africa, the authors expand the frontiers of competition law without sacrificing its core value.

The book is a rich source of knowledge and research in understanding how competition law and policy has been adopted and is enforced in selected countries in sub-Saharan Africa. It provides the sociopolitical context and challenges for competition policy in Africa. The central thesis posited in the book is that competition law and policy can contribute toward making markets work for development–creating pro-development markets. In this sense, the book is also a critic of the approach followed in the US, which departed from the original view of competition policy as a tool for the downtrodden, giving opportunity to the marginalized to constrain corporate market power. It calls for a fundamental departure from the narrow focus of the Chicago school of competition economics, which it traces from the Reagan years in the US.

---

19 ELEANOR M. FOX & MOR BAKHOUM, MAKING MARKETS WORK FOR AFRICA: MARKETS, DEVELOPMENTS, AND COMPETITION LAW IN SUB-SAHARAN AFRICA (2019).

Professor Eleanor Fox: Making Markets Work for the People – A View from South Africa

The book provides illuminating insights on the contrasting historical and economic imperatives that drove the development of competition law and policy in the US, post–World War II Europe, and in selected countries on the African continent. The authors explain that in the US antitrust law was a response to the Industrial Revolution and, in its wake, large enterprises. For almost a century, the US courts interpreted antitrust law "to protect the weak from the strong." There was a significant shift in US antitrust law under the Reagan administration "away from economic democracy and toward efficiency," as the US focused on global competitiveness and economic power. Post–World War II Europe adopted competition law "as a necessary underpinning of the common market," and as a part of the package of initiatives to support peace and economic integration after the after the ravages of World War II.

The evolution of competition law is different in Africa. Competition law in several African countries was largely adopted in the period following the collapse of the Berlin Wall, as a prescription of the Washington Consensus. The authors point out that a number of important historical events combined to trigger the adoption of competition law in several African countries. These included the conclusion of the Uruguay trade round in 1994 and the Asian financial flu of 1998, which devastated a number of developing economies. These countries were forced to turn to the IMF and World Bank for financial assistance, who insisted on loan conditions that included the adoption of competition law. In addition, the US and the EU require partners in trade agreements to adopt competition laws.

The book closely examines how selected countries in western, eastern and southern Africa have crafted the transition from colonial economies to economic-liberalizing reforms, including competition law and policy, as a result of influence from the World Bank and IMF as part of structural adjustment programs, with varying degrees of success. The outcomes are interesting and varied. The authors point out that in French West Africa, which is characterized by a history of dirigiste (state-controlled) economic systems, the patterns and trends of competition law and policy still reflect vestiges of state intervention, particularly on pricing. Competition law enforcement in West Africa is limited and there is no merger control law.

In contrast, eastern and southern Africa did not inherit a dirigiste economic system, and were better positioned to adjust to market-oriented reforms. The book gives a glimpse of the institutional makeup and challenges of enforcement in various regions of the continent. It observes that some agencies have done very well, even as they are confronted with various challenges, including lack of adequate resources.

Their take on South Africa is both encouraging and courageous. They observe that the system has matured into one of the most outstanding and even pathbreaking in the developing world. While they commend the work of the authorities, they nevertheless point to some challenges. For example, they decry a tendency by courts toward "a more technical judicial path, often on grounds that the language of the law does not permit the social policy overlay." They equally credit South African jurisprudence for introducing values of inclusiveness and reasonable simplicity. They also touch briefly on the proposed amendments to the South African competition legislation, which address the inclusivity issues more robustly.

The book examines in greater detail regional arrangements which occupy a greater part of African competition policy. Most regional organizations are motivated by benefits in trade, not competition. The competition project must fit within the trade mandate. The authors argue that the ACF has strong potential to provide a base of collaboration and coordination of competition law and policy across Africa and to support a competition voice for Africa in the world.

The book also examines an appropriate framework for competition law nationally and internationally. The authors highlight that significant qualitative differences in economies and needs and capabilities may call for different laws and policies. Lastly, the book examines how markets can be made to work for developing countries.

The strength of this book lies in the authors' freedom from any competition law ideological stranglehold, which allows them to explore beyond its often-unnecessary limits. For this, it is essential reading for any policymakers, enforcers, practitioners, and students wanting an outside-the-box view of competition policy. In many ways, they remind us of the original idea behind competition law, which idea finds resonance in the African continent.

IX. A Lasting Friendship

My predecessor, Shan Ramburuth, attributes Eleanor's credibility and longevity to both her personality and her status as an "outsider." Eleanor was not attached to any competition agency and not beholden to any institutional ideology. As a result, she listened without judgment and advised impartially.

Yasmin Carrim, who has served as an adjudicating member of the Competition Tribunal for more than 15 years, remembered Eleanor's generosity when the Tribunal asked her to cast an eye over their thinking on a competition-related subject. The next morning Eleanor sent back an extensively researched and well considered response that went far beyond their expectations, leaving them with the impression that she must have worked through the night to respond so thoroughly on short notice. In fact everyone interviewed mentioned that Eleanor mentioned often went beyond the call of duty to assist wherever she could. I had a similar experience with Eleanor when she and I edited a book – along with Dr Liberty Mncube – *Competition Policy for the New Era: Insights from the BRICS Countries* (2018). Eleanor pulled much more than her weight when editing the various contributions. She pulled ours too. I remember that she worked tirelessly, with great enthusiasm from start to finish. And she gave of her time unselfishly throughout the whole project, putting younger colleagues like Liberty and me to shame with her boundless energy.

Our book contributors included an A-list of competition experts from practice and academia, notably the Nobel prize–winning Professor Joseph E. Stiglitz. It was always going to be difficult to edit such eminent contributions. It would have been tempting to accept them as is. But Eleanor would not compromise on the academic rigor, and gently and confidently debated and, where necessary, corrected contributors on case law and other sources. It was her labor of love, and pure joy to all of us involved.

X. Conclusion

Even though Eleanor's contribution to South Africa seems to have been achieved with ease, one must not underestimate the enormous effort it took. Eleanor laboriously worked on submissions for legislative development of our competition statues, and diligently reviewed tribunal and court decisions. Competition law, by its nature, is a highly contested area. It is a remarkable achievement that she, as an American, won the trust of policymakers, practitioners, and adjudicators in South Africa. She often had to deal with heated disagreements even among us, who worked in the agencies, many of whom are her friends and acquaintances. She brought to these discussions amazing patience, sympathy, and critical insights that recognized everyone's bona fides. The reason for this, I hope, is clear from these reflections.

Eleanor brought intellectual rigor and passion in advocating a different path for competition policy; one more suitable for developing countries, but one that is for the people everywhere. She is a believer in markets as creating a great potential to empower people, and antitrust as tool to make markets work for the outsider– the marginalized. In many ways, South Africa became a canvas for her ideas, and, in turn, she became a lodestar of our system.

Hiding in plain sight

In 2005 I remember co-lecturing students in the Masters program at the University of Cape Town with Eleanor. At the same time, the Competition Tribunal had just handed down its judgment in their first case concerning price discrimination–*Nationwide Poles CC v. Sasol (Oil) (Pty) Ltd*[20]–and I was set to preside at this appeal shortly thereafter. I invited Eleanor to talk to the students about the *Nationwide Poles* case, but told her I would not be present. I also invited her to bring the students to the hearing in order for them to get exposure, which she subsequently did.

---

20   [2005] ZACT 17.

> When the hearing started, Justice David Unterhalter, who was then a prominent senior counsel acting for the appellant in the case, opened his argument by quoting Professor Eleanor Fox from a publication she had written. Perhaps owing to the large body of credible work she had produced on the subject, the respondent quoted the same Professor Fox in his opening address but with a very different interpretation to that of counsel for the appellant. The debate went back and forth about the real meaning we should attach to Professor Fox's words until my colleague Judge Selikowitz, out of sheer frustration, quietly said to me "Oh for goodness sake why don't you just ask her, she's right here in the room!"
>
> As told by Judge President Dennis Davis, Competition Appeal Court

A Few Snapshots of Professor Eleanor Fox

SKAIDRĪTE ĀBRAMA[*]

Former Chairperson of the Competition Council of Latvia

Abstract

In this paper, the author outlines through brief snapshots the most essential moments of accomplishment of Professor Eleanor Fox, which have affected the development of the idea of competition, especially in the Competition Council of Latvia. This means independence and accountability of competition authorities; competition law and its applicability to anticompetitive acts or actions created by the state or local governments; or, in other words, competition policy for safeguarding the competitive neutrality. At the same time, the author addresses Eleanor's personal qualities, which she has highly appreciated during personal contacts–simplicity, sincerity, and empathy to colleagues and friends. Having assessed the thematically and geographically broad scope of the research carried out by Professor Fox, in correlation with her personal features, the author has concluded that the accomplishments of Professor Fox are able to destroy borders and bring nations, markets, jurisdictions, and experts closer together.

---

[*] Skaidrīte Ābrama was the chairwoman of the Competition Council of Latvia and the Head of the Board of the decision-making body from 2012 to 2020. She holds an MBA from the University of Latvia. At the Competition Council, she worked as a board member (2004–2009) and later as a chief economist (2009–2011). Before joining the Competition Council, she gained extensive business experience working in leading positions for the private sector, and she has also managed a research project ordered by the Ministry of Economy of Austria, analysing investment opportunities in the area of transport and logistics of Latvia and Lithuania (2011–2012). In 2016 included in the prestige survey *Women in Antitrust* issued by *Global Competition Review* thus ranking among the world's leading women in the field of competition law protection and enforcement. 2019-2020 Member of the Office of the OECD Competition Committee, thus becoming the first Eastern European representative who participate in developing OECD competition policy program and agenda. She actively promotes competition culture and competition advocacy not only in Latvia but also in other countries, especially focusing on supporting young competition authorities.

Preface

How could I briefly characterize what Professor Eleanor Fox means to me?

The first thing I consider important to say–she is one of my greatest authorities of the competition law in the world. I admire Professor Fox's research scope, which is very broad and incredibly diverse–antitrust, convergence and divergence of economic law globally, impact of globalization on economies, European Union law, US competition law, developments of markets and competition thinking in different jurisdictions, and more.

Secondly, several basic topics of research by Professor Fox deeply resonate with the questions to which I have looked for solutions since starting managing the Competition Council of Latvia in June 2012. These issues are – independence and accountability of competition authorities; competition law and its applicability to anticompetitive acts or actions created by the state or local governments or, in other words, competition policy for safeguarding competitive neutrality. In Latvia, where the open market and competition culture formed only in the early 1990s, and a high proportion of enterprises are still state and municipally owned, these issues were, are, and will remain topical in the near future. For us competition practitioners from Eastern European countries, the contribution and conclusions of Professor Fox, which are based on her studies on problems and possible solutions of the competition law in different jurisdictions, including young competition regime countries, serve as an invaluable guide.

Professor Eleanor Fox is not only a globally highly appreciated and erudite researcher, but also quite simply and amazing person. One can learn a lot for one's own professional life from her rich knowledge. However, even more than that–she is able to inspire and motivate her colleagues and friends with her sincerity, simplicity, openness to new things and huge positivism. I think that Professor Fox is one of the most prominent academics of modern competition law, from whom each person can learn something professionally or humanly.

I. Snapshot I: Personal Motive

I personally met Professor Eleanor Fox relatively recently–in July 2014, in Geneva–when I participated in the multi-day work session of the Intergovernmental Group of Experts on Competition Law and Policy (IGE), organized by the Competition and Consumer Policies Branch of the UN Conference on Trade and Development (UNCTAD). For the first time in the history of IGE, a very significant task–managing this annual multi-day conference–was entrusted to me, a representative from one of the new EU Member States. I will not deny that for me as a chairperson of a small, although very active–not only on a Latvian scale, but also internationally–competition authority, that was huge honor and responsibility. It was also an excellent opportunity to say for the first time to representatives of approximately 120 UNCTAD Member States: we have a considerable practice in Latvia, and we wish to share it internationally.

I have to say that, for us, members of national competition authorities, international forums serve as an important opportunity for exchange of our experience and adoption of best practices from other countries. Each year we use the opportunity to gather in such significant and valuable events dedicated to competition law as forums and regular expert meetings organized by the European Competition Network (ECN), the Organisation for Economic Co-operation and Development (OECD) Competition Committee's working parties and annual global forums, the International Competition Network's (ICN's) annual forums, the spring meetings organized by American Bar Association Section of Antitrust Law, the annual conferences on international antitrust law and policy organized by Fordham Competition Law Institute, the already-mentioned conferences organized by UNCTAD. These are the places where not only national enforcement practitioners but also academics, researchers, and developers of new competition policy ideas meet in one place. At these gatherings, we draw new ideas and gain approval for our own ideas and activities, which are frequently not accepted with too much enthusiasm and approval in our countries, especially among policymakers of certain sectors, ministries, or local governments. And this is particularly important for representatives of competition authorities of all those countries that face similar competition enforcement problems. In short, these gatherings are places where one can find inspiration and feel the supporting shoulder of similarly thinking "competition family" members.

At the UNCTAD forum, I had the honor to meet and listen to a speech by Professor Eleanor Fox in person for the first time. Before that, I had already several times indirectly become acquainted with her extensive range of work materials included in publications or events–articles, video presentations, etc. However, I had never met her in person before. And there she was–as a living legend in my perception, holding a very impressive list of positions, titles of honor, and research publications. I carefully listened to her during a workshop, where participants discussed a topic that, in my opinion, is significant for any competition authority, including my own–independence and accountability.[1]

Some say that the first impression is misleading, but this was not the case. The first thing that particularly surprised me was the huge energy and enthusiasm that radiated from each sentence. She was seemingly a very fragile woman, naturally youthful, despite her quite respectful age, but endowed with such huge vigor and a strong spirit. Usually, these qualities are inherent to those people who are deeply confident in what they are doing and, importantly, willingly share their knowledge with others. Later, when we became more acquainted, I realized

---

1   UNCTAD, *Independence and accountability of competition authorities: Note by the UNCTAD secretariat* (TD/B/COM.2/CLP/67, May 14, 2008), https://unctad.org/en/Docs/c2clpd67_en.pdf.

that she combines everything that may characterize a guru in a specific field, , but precisely in the case with Professor Fox. These qualities involve generosity and simplicity, true interest in peers and processes, and, at the same time, constant desire to learn, discover new things, and support others generously.

And here I move to the next snapshots–generous guiding of and support to others. I personally and, I believe, many others from the large competition community, have benefited from Professor Fox's invaluable base of knowledge.

Two topics from the contribution of Professor Eleanor Fox that have been particularly important for my authority in general, are independence of competition authorities and competitive neutrality.

II. Snapshot II: Competition Authority and its Independence

Returning to our first meeting at the UNCTAD workshop on independence and accountability of competition authorities, I remember listening to Professor Fox and thinking: this is all precisely what is important for my authority.

In this and also other international events, Professor Fox defended in a reasoned way the idea that independence and accountability of competition authorities are and have to be closely related in the future, that is to say, they have direct interdependency. It is impossible to reason ideas in a more substantiated manner than is done by Professor Fox, and I completely agree with her. Namely, competition authorities have to be independent in order to be able to address any competition distortion impartially and objectively, including instances when such distortions have been caused by the state, local government, or laws and decisions adopted by them. Otherwise, if a competition authority is dependent on the executive power, this may largely hamper its capacity to act. Moreover, if decisions are adopted that adversely affect certain groups of economic interests or carriers of public power, a competition authority can be influenced in various ways, for example, by the threat of budget cuts. In addition, according to Professor Fox, every competition authority should be accountable to all stakeholders, whether they are parliamentarians, consumers, private sector, or the judiciary.

This issue was not yet topical for me, at the time, when I was a board member of the CC from 2004 until 2009. However, we specifically focused on it in 2012,[2] when I started to manage the authority. Since establishment of the CC in 1992, it has been subordinate to the Ministry of Economics (the MoE), implemented in the form of supervision. This concerns both budget allocation and spending control, and nomination and possible removal of the chairperson and board

---

2   I held the position of the chief economist of the Competition Council from 2019 to 2011.

members of the council. These are quite critical issues. Admittedly, it has to be noted that the CC is independent in terms of investigation and decision-making, and it is stipulated by the Competition Law of Latvia, stating that "directions regarding the commencement of an investigation of a case ... as well as regarding the manner in which the investigation shall be conducted or a decision taken, may not be given to the Chair and members of the Competition Council by the Cabinet, the Minister for Economics or other persons. The Competition Council shall not coordinate the ascertainment with a higher institution."[3]

But, even more important, in this small authority,[4] from the outset a subordinated authority with chronically insufficient financing, the authority management–the council and chief executive staff–strongly protect and advocate the authority's independence, and have ensured that it is respected by the government, politicians, and other public administrative bodies, as well as NGOs and undertakings.

It may raise a question–why is the independence issue so important for the CC?

Among other things, the answer corresponds to the statement by Professor Fox that national competition authorities should be aware of "the need to tackle government interference with NCAs' decisions by way of planning ahead strategies on how to handle such situations."[5]

First of all–and that is my strongest position–an authority should have all powers to take action, in the enforcement context, against public administrative bodies including ministries and other state or local government institutions.

Secondly, in my opinion, huge risks for decision-making independence of competition authorities are now more than ever caused by the increasing protectionism in Europe and the idea of favoring national champions, which, paradoxically, serves as a response to market globalization. In Latvia, there is high proportion of state-owned enterprises, and the CC supervisory MoE and other ministries are shareholders in such powerful dominant players. Such examples may lead to new endurance tests and challenges for competition authorities and, especially, their heads, be it decision-making on admissibility, or prohibition of merger of national large enterprises, or in antitrust cases.

And exactly in this regard I, as a competition enforcement and advocacy practitioner, completely agree with the opinion advocated by Professor Fox in that

---

3   Latvian Competition Law with amendments of May 12, 2016, www.kp.gov.lv/en/normativie-akti/latvijas-konkurences-normativie-akti.

4   The LCC is a single administrative authority, 50 persons, consisting of two bodies–investigative and decision-making body or the Board. The Board is comprised of three members, including the chair. The investigative body has two investigation departments–the Cartel Department, which deals with verticals and horizontals, and the Analytical Department, which investigates abuse cases, reviews mergers, and conducts market inquiries. In addition, there is the Chief Economist Unit, Legal and Litigation Department, Competition Advocacy Division, Communication Unit, and Administrative Division. The Board is entitled to establish infringements and impose fines by a decision, and there is strong separation between fact-finding and decision-making.

5   UNCTAD, *supra* note 1.

forum and at other events: in order to be able to properly protect competition and enjoy the trust of all stakeholders, competition authorities require full independence, especially from the executive power.

Speaking about the difficult path of the CC of Latvia to full independence, international organizations have repeatedly drawn the attention of our government to the necessity for full independence of the CC–such as the OECD, which examined the state of play of competition policy in Latvia in 2014 and, consequently, the readiness of the state and the CC for joining this organization,[6] as well as the European Commission in its recommendations. Unfortunately, the CC still has not managed to achieve full independence, despite the drafted amendments to the Competition Law, prepared a long time ago, and multiple attempts to convince the supervisory MoE first of all.

Now we have great expectations of the so-called EU Competition Directive,[7] in connection with which we have prepared a package of proposals for amendments to the Competition Law, to ensure, inter alia, full independence and sufficient financial, technological, and human resources.

But, as I outlined before, the topic of independence of competition authorities, accented by Professor Fox, is linked to another issue topical for the CC–ensuring the competitive neutrality in actions of public administrative bodies. It seems, that I will not be wrong in stating that the honorable Professor Fox is one of the most prominent advocates of the idea[8] that this is the task of the competition policy and competition authorities.

III. Snapshot III: Competition Authority and Competitive Neutrality

In 2012, the CC started to receive increasingly more complaints from private companies that state and local government authorities or their owned companies are destroying the level playing field. To establish the reasons and circumstances of spreading of this trend, we carried out a market study on engagement of public administrative bodies in commercial activity. The results surprised us, not in a positive way. The obtained data revealed that the negative trend of establishment of local government companies has increased in recent years, instead creating an investment-promoting environment, moreover, on markets not related to performance of public autonomous functions: medical services,

---

6   From July 1, 2016, Latvia has been a full-fledged member state of the OECD.

7   Directive (EU) 2019/1 to empower the competition authorities of the Member States to be more effective enforcers and to ensure the proper functioning of the internal market, 2019 O.J. (L 11) 3, https://eur-lex.europa.eu/legal-content/EN/TXT/?uri=CELEX%3A32019L0001.

8   I wish to emphasize the significance of accomplishments by both great competition–Professor Eleanor Fox and Professor Deborah Healey–both separately and in collaboration, studying the role of the legal framework of competition and taking action against acts or measures of the state that significantly harm competition.

funeral services, engineering services, installation of public transport stops and placement of advertisements in them, publishing of municipal newspapers, bottling of drinking water, management of household waste, tourism information services, public procurements, house management. Besides, it was only one aspect of the markets, where municipally owned companies were established.

Alongside this problem, it frequently stood out that a desire of public administrative bodies to support with their adopted decisions the economic activities of companies owned by them has emerged, discriminating private competitors over publicly owned ones.

How should a competition authority act, if the Competition Law grants the powers to eliminate antitrust infringements–abuse of dominance and cartels– caused by companies, whereas when public administrative bodies act harmfully toward competition the CC is allowed only to assess, make proposals, or express objections, which only have recommendatory nature? On top of that, when there is an adverse effect on competition, these recommendations or objections are not taken into consideration, because the aim is to create advantages and guaranteed income for municipally owned companies.

Thus, the only tool that we had in Latvia was competition advocacy. First, we monitored all draft legislation amendments, and, if competitive neutrality might be affected, we provided our objections to the respective local government, ministry or to the parliament. We closely cooperated with other state institutions as well as with NGOs, trying to establish that our opinion prevents administrative competition distortions.

Our experience shows that advocacy helps less, if there is no strong enforcement. Quoting Professor Fox, "the hand of the law strengthens the hand of advocacy."[9] Moreover, studies of public opinion, conducted by the CC once every two years, confirmed that the most disciplinary measures for motivating elimination of infringement are severe fines. Unfortunately, under the Competition Law, we did not have stronger enforcement powers against public administrative bodies.

In this regard, I wish to look in particular at the article "When the State Harms Competition–the Role for Competition Law,"[10] by Eleanor Fox and Deborah Healey. In my view, it is very significant for each competition authority, especially those that do not have the power to take action against competition restrictions caused by the state and local government, except by suggestions of recommendatory nature. The analysis of legal frameworks of competition and most specific anticompetitive cases carried out by the authors, involving 35 countries, provides valuable information in helping to understand at what level the respective national

---

9   Eleanor Fox, *ICN Training on Demand: State Restraints on Competition* (Jan 12, 2018), www.youtube.com/watch?time_continue=523&v=wBqN5VciLSM&feature=emb_logo.

10 79 ANTITRUST L.J. 3 (2014).

legal framework is, and what is the case practice of other states in terms of addressing infringements caused by state or local government. Tis article may even encourage improvement of the national competition law.

The authors precisely classify the competition restrictions made by state-owned enterprises (SOEs) and which, most likely, can be found in every jurisdiction. Many of the described groups of restrictions are identified also in Latvia. Namely, these are: a) infringements committed by SOEs having a dominant position, to which special or exclusive rights or privileges are granted (in Latvia, infringements are most frequently detected in activities of providers of postal services, port administrations, etc.); b) the state or its officials complicit in bid-rigging and preferences in awarding state contracts;[11] c) discriminatory state or local government measures that block markets; d) abuse of administrative power of public administrative bodies. In each of these groups the CC has adopted infringement decisions, imposed fines or given warnings as a stringent tool of advocacy. The article also recounts stories of success and frustration revealed by the study, told by 35 competition authorities, among them: SOE liability for organizing cartels, for monopolizing adjacent markets, and for tipping procurement bids to cronies, and calling to account local governments for blocking markets and discrimination against outsiders.

In the conclusion, Professor Fox and Professor Healey give recommendations for convergence, indicating that the competition regulatory frameworks harmonization projects implemented so far "have thus far ignored the critical area of the state, the market, and the scope of competition law to reach anticompetitive acts of the state."[12]

In my opinion, the most important value of this article, especially during my practice, are the main basic principles suggested by the authors, which should be included in the legal framework of competition in order to ensure balance between the interests of private and public law subjects. These are:

1. Competition law should apply to SOEs, in law and in fact, derogations should be narrow;

2. Competition law should apply to state officials who join and facilitate illegal private conspiracies and bid-rigging;

3. Competition law should apply to enterprises with exclusive privileges and special obligations, except as necessary to carry out a public

---

[11] The CC frequently receives complaints from entrepreneurs that requirements that can be fulfilled only by a specific company are integrated in the procurement conditions; in such cases we inform the Procurement Monitoring Bureau, as well as the procurement organizer itself, calling to rectify the procurement requirements and specification. In 2019, the CC adopted an infringement decision on bid-rigging facilitated by the municipally owned passenger transportation company SIA Rīgas satiksme and implemented by six applicants on supply of nanotechnology chemicals. The municipal company SIA Rīgas Satiksme was also fined €2.4 million.

[12] Fox & Healey, *supra* note 10, at 813.

mandate–EU law is a guide to the scope of the "public mandate" defense;

4. A state action or no-autonomy defense to charges of private anti-competitive conduct should be narrowly limited;

5. Federal systems with principles of federal supremacy should consider robust doctrines of preemption of excessively and unnecessarily anti-competitive state measures by federal competition law where the measure is incompatible with competition law;

6. In common markets, the law should integrate free movement, state restraint and competition principles along lines drawn by the European Union.

And, although the authors of the article have put more emphasis on state-created restraints, it can also be fully applied to restraints created by local governments as public administrative bodies.

The CC did not participate in this study, but we would express frustration regarding anticompetitive activities of local administrative bodies back then, similar as specific member states included in the study. As I already mentioned, we had authority to provide our opinions regarding certain anticompetitive measures, but the Competition Law did not require public administrative bodies to take our opinion into account. Simply, the Latvian Competition Law was not well equipped to deal with all aspects of inefficient competition between public and private sector entities or monopolization of market power stemming from decisions or actions of public authorities, in raw local governments. Competitive neutrality issues could not be reached by competition law, either because the government or municipal businesses do not have market power, or the advantages they receive from their public owners do not qualify as abuses covered by competition law.[13]

After the study on engagement of public administrative bodies in commercial activity, conducted in 2012, the CC increased its focus on the assessment of activities of public administrative bodies that distort competition. At the same time, we started to prepare proposals for amendments to the Competition Law to gain enforcement powers, thus preventing public administrative bodies–both state and local government–from committing infringements.

Professor Fox has helped us a lot along the way.

---

13 Otherwise, regarding enforcement powers against antitrust infringements, such as abuse of market power, cartels, non-notified mergers, none of the sectors in Latvia is excluded from application of competition rules and both state and local government enterprises are treated just as any other market players, subject to competition law. By now, the CC has addressed nearly all largest state-owned enterprises–either through enforcement, sector inquiries, or competition advocacy. There have been cases on abuse of dominant position, or soft law enforcement in various significant regulated, public utilities sectors, against powerful market players in railway, freeport authorities, airport, telecommunication, gas or electricity supply, postal services markets, etc.

On May 5, 2015, in Riga, the capital of Latvia, the CC organized the 30th European Competition Day within the framework of the Latvian Presidency of the Council of the European Union.[14] The motto of the conference was "Broadening borders for more effective competition protection." For one of the panel sessions we had chosen a topic that is extremely topical for the development of economy and competition in Latvia–ensuring a level playing field between public- and private-owned business.[15] One of the key speakers in this session was Professor Eleanor Fox.[16]

Undoubtedly, among experts and lawyers in competition law from different states, who attended the European Competition Day in Riga, the presence of recognizable speakers significantly extended the limits for the vision as to what is the role of competition authority, if local governments engage in economic activity by establishing their own companies and favoring them over private players. Professor Fox, who has researched competition law around the world on how legal frameworks of different states tackle restraints to competition created by state, gave a summarizing overview on what harm is done to states by unequal game rules and engagement of public administrative bodies in commercial activity. It is interesting that she–a professor from the USA–had mainly focused her research area on Europe, and had studied before the conference the situation in Latvia concerning the possibilities of the CC to address competition distortions caused by public administrative bodies.

Professor Fox indicated to the conference participants, many of whom were representatives of public administrative bodies, the information given in the Annual Report of the CC: "we have faced the bitter truth that not only the risks of violations of the competition laws arise out of irresponsible or incompetent actions of private entrepreneurs but they also arise out of increasing intention of public persons to establish capital companies in order to enter markets with guaranteed sales without any need for strategic investments or innovative solutions."[17]

Both in her speech in Riga and in other addresses and private discussions, Professor Fox tends to ask a question: why is it so difficult to draw a line when the public power intervenes in competition? Also, in countries where laws have been adopted that provide for intervention against the state legislation that prevents development of open market, why are there still decisions or actions

---

14 Competition Council, Republic of Latvia, *European Competition Day: Broadening Borders for More Effective Competition Protection* (Riga, May 7, 2015), www.kp.gov.lv/en/european-competition-day.

15 European Competition Day Conference in Riga, Panel 1 (May 7, 2015), www.youtube.com/watch?v=caumgXa6ib4.

16 Eleanor Fox, Address at the European Competition Day Conference, State and State-Sanctioned Bodies: When Their Acts Are Caught By Competition Laws (May 7, 2015), https://lemumi.kp.gov.lv/oldfiles/23/competitionday%2Fe_fox.pdf

17 Competition Council, Republic of Latvia, Annual Report 2013 (2013) https://lemumi.kp.gov.lv/oldfiles/38/citi%2Fkp_2013_en.pdf.

implemented by public administrative bodies that undermine the markets? Probably, as indicated by Professor Fox, because "competition law coverage of law and local restraints is an under-explored area."[18]

My response is: allowing exceptions for own companies, while others have to overpay considerably for such decisions, mere lack of competition morals and understanding of regularities of market development, which can turn out to be very costly to the national economy.

On the European Competition Day in Riga, Professor Fox emphasized that state restraints are some of the worst competition restraints, and drawing lines between permissible and impermissible restraints by the state can sometimes be hard, as the Baltic states are acutely aware. At the same time, she proposed to raise the issue globally, for example, at the level of ICN, solving this problem for development of international standards, using the EU as a guide.[19]

As I mentioned before, such international meetings and exchanges of opinions make the goal to be achieved clearer and motivate us for further work.

After the European Competition Day in Riga, the CC reinforced advocacy against competition distortions caused by public administrative bodies, organizing various events, publishing articles, explaining the negative impact of such restrictions on the development of entrepreneurship, attraction of investment, and the national economy in general. By establishing closer contact with Eleanor, I felt entitled to quote and use statements from her publications in my speeches more often, using the conclusions drawn in her studies as the main idea: support by state or local government makes companies inefficient, and it is delusion that a national champion can be created by doing so. We truly followed the suggestion given by Professor Fox, "to the extent that good competition law can be developed with a sharper eye on the public channel, this should be a priority project."[20]

Thanks to Professor Fox's initiative, I had an opportunity to participate in ICN video module on "State Restraints on Competition: When Competition Law Applies"[21] in 2016. The produced video, which is a very valuable reference material, was "a start for cross-fertilization for rules, standards and strategies in the use of competition law tools in the fight against excessive state and local restraints."[22] I presented the experience of the CC of Latvia in fighting against competition distortions caused by the state and local government, emphasizing that strong and reliable competition policy is an integral part of the Latvian

---

18 Fox, *supra* note 9.

19 Fox, *supra* note 16.

20 Fox & Healey, *supra* note 10, at 814.

21 It "addresses the use of competition law to push back excessive state and local restraints on competition and explains how authorities make strategic decisions about when to use advocacy, when to use the law, and how to use the two together for mutual reinforcement." Fox, *supra* note 9.

22 Fox, *supra* note 9.

economy, and that the CC is very active both in enforcement and competition advocacy. However, the most problematic area in Latvia, as in all Baltic states, is of competition restraints created by SOEs and public administrative bodies, especially local government. I stressed that local governments that ignore the principle of competitive neutrality jeopardize favorable investment climate, and the bottom line is the damage that is done to consumers and the welfare of society. Hence, Professor Fox and us other participants of the ICN module, emphasized the need for providing more extensive powers and more efficient tools in the national legal frameworks of competition to eradicate competition infringements caused by the state and local government.

I think that our activities resulted in the business environment in Latvia gradually becoming increasingly more encouraged, and entrepreneurs started to point out various problems more often. Among these problems are–adoption of discriminatory legal frameworks, binding regulations, and decisions, which create unjustified barriers for entrepreneurs; establishment of municipally owned companies and such companies entering the markets, where private companies already operate successfully, thus administratively creating competition advantages for own companies; refusal to organize public procurement tenders or organization of such tenders in bad faith; when the rights to provide the required services are exclusively granted to firms selected without clear grounds or to *in-house* service providers.

As a result of this, responding to alarm signals by the CC and NGOs, with the purpose of restricting the desire and possibilities of public administrative bodies to establish own capital companies on competition markets groundlessly, the parliament adopted amendments to the State Administration Structure Law in late 2015. These amendments stipulate three instances when public authorities or local governments in Latvia are permitted to establish capital companies or extend their operation. These cases are as follows: a) if it is necessary for compensation of market deficiencies; b) for management of properties that are strategically significant for development of state or local government administrative territory or state security; c) for ensuring strategic products or services. Now, before engaging in commercial activities, public administrative bodies are obliged to consider the impact of such engagement on competition, consulting with the CC and respective associations. However, it has to be said that these opinions are also non-binding, and the law does not provide a mechanism as to what happens if the opinion of the CC and the NGO has not been taken into account.

Speaking with the words of Professor Fox and Professor Healey, these developments brought us "to the cusp of our challenge: rethinking the relationship between competition law and significant unjustified anticompetitive acts and measures of the state [and local governments] that might appropriately be brought under the wing of antitrust law."[23]

---

23 Fox & Healey, *supra* note 10, at 774.

After more than five years since we started the discussion with the state and local government authorities on the need to take action against public administrative bodies that infringe competitive neutrality, a positive turn is finally achieved. On March 28, 2019, Parliament finally adopted amendments to the Competition Law, which grant the CC power to address competition distortions caused by public administrative bodies, local governments, and their owned undertakings.[24] The new provision entered into force on January 1, 2020.

Undoubtedly, certain credit in this entire process has to be given to Professor Eleanor Fox, who supported us and gave confidence that we are on the right path.

IV. To Conclude: Breaking Stereotypes and Crossing Borders

About 20 years ago, I traveled around the USA for quite a long time. Most of the people I met did not know where Latvia is located, nor what other European countries that are larger than Latvia stand out for. A stereotype developed in my mind that at least part of Americans are geographically and culturally self-sufficient, and their interests do not extend beyond their own borders.

It is different with Eleanor Fox. In international meetings of competition experts, she is always surrounded by many people, representatives of various nationalities, whom she, it seems, has met in her foreign projects, and they have a friendly chat, competently discussing what new thing has happened in their authorities, countries, markets. And these conversations reveal that she has excellent knowledge of the competition situation in many economies around the world, not only the USA. During our meetings, Eleanor told me multiple times that she will go to or has already returned from Africa. I see that these visits have already transformed into a certain result–in early 2019, she published a new book, *Making Markets Work for Africa*, in cooperation with Mor Bakhoum.[25] I have not read this book yet, but I can conclude from the table of contents that a broad geography is chosen for it, covering market developments and competition in countries of Sub-Saharan Africa. The book also includes the topic, closely studied by Professor Fox, of challenges of the competition authorities when the state harms competition. In another research it turns out that also

---

[24] The amendments to the Competition Law stipulate that public administrative bodies will be prohibited from a) discriminating against market participants, b) creating advantages to undertakings controlled by public administrative bodies, and c) carrying out any other activities, which exclude new market participants from the market or prevent them from entering the market. To prevent competition distortions caused by state and local governments, the CC will be able to carry out negotiations with the particular public administrative body or its undertaking. If competition distortions are not eliminated through mutual negotiations, the authority will be entitled to impose on an undertaking controlled by the state or local government a legal obligation to change its conduct, and to impose a fine up to 3% of the net turnover of the company in the last financial year, but not less than €250. Competition Law, No 795 (Sept. 21, 2020) www.kp.gov.lv/en/normativie-akti/latvijas-konkurences-normativie-akti.

[25] Eleanor M. Fox & Mor Bakhoum, Making Markets Work for Africa: Markets, Development, and Competition Law in Sub-Saharan Africa (2019).

BRICS countries have been studied,[26] because a collaborative work on competition, antitrust law and government policy in these countries has been carried out. I really admire Eleanor's professional curiosity, even bravery, to cross the borders. And, what is no less important, the ability to combine these qualities in order to create useful writings, which help practitioners and academics of competition law around the world in their everyday work.

In the CC, one of the recent accomplishments of Eleanor in the field of the competition law is very popular, created in collaboration with Professor Damien Gerard. It is the case book *EU Competition Law*, issued in 2017.[27] In my opinion, a very successful format has been found for this work–briefly and understandably explained aspects of EU competition policy and main topics of application of competition law, illustrated with most essential case descriptions and excerpts from decisions, judgments, even speeches. Another approach worth highlighting is asking several proactive questions for understanding the topic of each section, thus stimulating critical thinking and promoting discussion. While watching development of young experts of the CC, I have concluded that this is a way to help new employees entering the work of the competition authority efficiently. I assume that it can be used equally efficiently for preparation of students at universities, where competition law is studied.

But, from my point of view, a very significant statement is given in the preface. As stated by the authors, Professor Fox and Professor Gerard, "that original endeavor reflected more than two decades of continuous study of the EU enforcement practice as part of an effort to promote transatlantic cooperation and convergence in the field of competition policy."[28]

To promote transatlantic cooperation and convergence, in addition to the statements I have highlighted previously, this conclusion is what I have learned about Eleanor and which breaks this old stereotype in my mind. And this is the issue that gives huge value to Eleanor's deeds.

Indeed, the international scope of competition enforcement gives us, practitioners of national competition authorities, both opportunities and challenges. Because no competition authority in the world would be able to operate separately and isolated. Markets are globalizing, and competition enforcers across the world are dealing with similar problems. Infringements and cases are getting more complex, while mergers more frequently appear among strong competitors, including cross-border. Also, market developments require a more coherent approach in procedural rules and remedies applied among jurisdictions if the merger filing is made in several jurisdictions. Being aware of each other's

---

26 COMPETITION POLICY FOR THE NEW ERA: INSIGHTS FROM THE BRICS COUNTRIES (Tembinkosi Bonakele, Eleanor M. Fox, & Liberty Mncube eds., 2017).

27 ELEANOR M. FOX & DAMIEN GERARD, EU COMPETITION LAW, CASES, TEXTS AND CONTEXT (2017).

28 *Id.* at xiv.

competition legislation and practice, we gain a better insight of competition challenges and can use the opportunity to improve ours, as well.

In my opinion, Professor Fox's scope of research is capable of destroying borders and bringing nations, markets, jurisdictions, and experts closer together. This makes her unique–with her impressive experience and knowledge, at the same time, enriching anyone who wants to use it.

As I mentioned at the beginning, I know Eleanor for at least seven years. It seems that we have good mutual understanding, not only of the application of competition law, but also on a purely personal level, regardless of the fact that we do not meet each other too often. One of my warmest memories is that during my visit to New York, Eleanor took me to an unusual place on a cool, rainy day–a picturesque garden, hidden from view, not far from the Central Park, which I would never notice while passing by to the venue of the Fordham conference. That's what she is–a careful and very sincere person. I suppose that many people from our broad global competition community think the same, because it seems that Eleanor can easily find a common language with anyone and, also, find time for a kind conversation during short breaks of the intense conferences.

I know that in 2011 Global Competition Review awarded to Professor Fox a lifetime achievement award for "substantial, lasting and transformational impact on competition policy and practice." And it is fully deserved. With her knowledge and research work, crossing continents and exploring competition in national economies, she proves continuously that she is worthy of this award. She is a true reformer–I wish her to stay the same also in the future, continuing to promote the idea of free and fair competition without borders with the same confidence.

***

Eleanor, you are a great person, and it is real pleasure to know you. I bow my head before you in admiration and respect. Thank you for your invaluable contribution to the global competition law!

PART II
Competition Policy: Foundations and Development

Neo-Antitrust, Machiavelli and the Rule of Law

GIULIANO AMATO[*]
Italian Constitutional Court

Abstract

How far can antitrust go in the digital world? Vigorously calling our antitrust family to exercise its own responsibilities in this new world of increased and wide-ranging private powers is not a heresy. However, antitrust is just a component of the legal order and we cannot rely only on its rules and tools to reach all the types of conduct by which such powers erode the rights of consumers. Nor are administrative and judicial authorities allowed to freely expand the means they are supplied with by the law, in order to better pursue the ends they read in it. The Machiavellian principle "the end justifies the means" has not entered into our rule of law.

---

[*] Professor Emeritus, Treasury Minister, Minister of Interior, and twice Prime Minister of Italy, he also was Vice President of the Convention on the Future of Europe. Honorary Fellow of the American Academy of Arts and Sciences, he is currently Justice of the Italian Constitutional Court. He has written on antitrust, personal liberties, government, European integration and humanities.

I.

It is undeniable that the political reason for the US Congress to unanimously approve the Sherman Act was the defense of small producers against the "exploitation" by big trusts. It is equally undeniable that such defense can be interpreted as a natural precedent for the populist mood of our time.[1] However, reading the Sherman Act as the manifestation of a populist policy is, to say the least, too narrow, for there is much more in a statute that regulates and curbs the exercise of private power in the economy of the American society of the late nineteenth century. There is the Madisonian principle of the diffusion of power, which applies to the public sphere but extends its reach also to the private one. There is the consequent repudiation of powers devoid of legitimacy and yet exercised toward others. More broadly, there is the Jeffersonian view of a society in which anyone has the right to build his own life and to support his family, without depending on others. Therefore the heading "populism" is not at all appropriate to express the full sense of these principles and values. Actually, they represent the ideal texture upon which first of all the US Constitution, but more generally the constitutions of liberal democracies, are grounded.[2]

We could not explain otherwise the interpretation of the Sherman Act, that not only initially but for several decades treated those very principles and values as the aims of its enforcement. As Judge Learned Hand wrote in *Alcoa*, "it is possible, because of its indirect social and moral effect, to prefer a system of small producers, each depending for his success on his own skill and character, to one in which the great mass must accept the direction of the few." The Supreme Court itself argued that the rationale of antitrust was not to pursue economic efficiency as such, but to provide checks to restrain economic power and therefore protect–as much as possible–open and plural markets. In *Brown Shoes* the Court wrote:

> Of course, some of the results of large integrated or chain operations are beneficial to consumers ... But we cannot fail to recognize Congress' desire to promote competition through the protection of viable, small, locally owned business. Congress appreciated that occasional higher costs and prices might result from the maintenance of fragmented industries and markets. It resolved these competing considerations in favor of decentralization. We must give effct to that decision.[3]

---

[1] Joshua D. Wright et al., *Requiem For A Paradox, The Dubious Rise and Inevitable Fall of Hipster Antitrust*, 51 ARIZ. ST. L.J. 293 (2019); R. Pardolesi, *Hipster antitrust e sconvolgimenti tettonici:back to the future?* MERCATO CONCORRENZA REGOLE 81 (2019).

[2] GIULIANO AMATO, ANTITRUST AND THE BOUNDS OF POWER (1997).

[3] United States v. Alcoa, 148 F. 2d 416 (1945). Brown Shoe Co. v. United States, 370 U.S. 294 (1962). On this initial but long-standing interpretation see A.D. NEALE, THE ANTITRUST LAWS OF THE UNITED STATES OF AMERICA (1962).

In the seventies–as we all know–things changed profoundly. The *Sylvania* case, decided by the Supreme Court in 1977, was the turning point. Justice Lewis Powell wrote in the opinion of the Court that a restriction (in a franchise agreement) of the locations where retailers could sell the manufacturer's products was not to be prohibited per se, as it had been done in the past. To the contrary, the rule of reason should apply, considering whether a franchise agreement had any redeeming virtue.[4] Politically the change was due to the new, aggressive (and mostly Japanese) competition US companies had to face both in the international market and in the domestic one. This renewed context was ideal for promoting less severe doctrines in defining as "restraints" of competition conduct that economic analysis could evaluate differently. It was the right moment for the Chicago school, that already had specialized in economic analysis of antitrust rules and their implementation, to conquer the center of the scene.

Undoubtedly, the antitrust doctrine promoted by the Chicago scholars was more minimalist than the previous ones. Its guiding rule was and still is an error-cost framework aimed at protecting the "false positive," in order not to "chill" conducts that may make markets more competitive. However, what this school has produced is much more than the bias toward (more) *laissez-faire*. We owe to it a rigorous economic analysis, due to which several principles and rules have been revisited and given a new and frequently undisputable interpretation. Restraint of competition does not necessarily follow any restraint of contractual freedom. Per se prohibitions are based on presumptions that in several cases are not confirmed by actual restraints and should therefore be abandoned on behalf of the rule of reason. There are vertical and sometimes horizontal restraints that do not limit but rather foster competition among different producers. Finally, but much less undisputably, efficiency and consumer welfare are the real aims of antitrust.

This new set of assumptions has led antitrust actions toward outcomes quite different from the previous ones. Not surprisingly the doctrinal and political positions in relation to these new outcomes have been sharply divergent from each other. On the one side are those who see the post-*Sylvania* antitrust as a loss that, despite undeniable technical improvements, no longer safeguards the openness of markets.[5] On the other side are those who define it as a coherent, principled and workable system of law that replaces the confused doctrines and populist notions of the past (that is, the best of all possible worlds).[6]

The first of these two positions has remained in the minority throughout recent decades, despite the excellent scholars, first of all Eleanor Fox, who have given

---

4   Continental Television v. GTE Sylvania, 433 U.S. 36 (1977).

5   Eleanor Fox & Lawrence A. Sullivan, *Antitrust–Retrospective and Prospective: Where Are We Coming From? Where Are We Going?*, 62 N.Y.L. Rev. 936 (1987).

6   Seth B. Sacher & John M. Yun, *Twelve Fallacies of the "Neo-Antitrust" Movement*, 26 Geo. Mason L. Rev. 1491 (2019).

voice to it. Here, I do not want to enter into this dispute. What I intend to investigate in this paper is whether the recent wave that has led to hipster antitrust is simply aimed at restoring the "old" antitrust, or whether it has ambitions far beyond the limits of it. Such wave is moved by the demand of an antitrust actively contributing to the reduction of the increased inequalities of our times.[7] It is nurtured by a strong and heavy criticism toward the "neoliberal" Chicago doctrines.[8] Where does it go from here?

Something that is rarely noticed is that, due to the transition initiated in *Sylvania*, a new reading of the antitrust rules has supervened, yet none of these rules have actually been removed or replaced, nor have the tools in the hands of antitrust authorities been renewed. Whatever the aim–to reduce power or create efficiency, to protect competitors or competition, to guarantee an open market or consumer welfare–the rules and the tools of antitrust authorities have never been modified. What those rules were meant to do, and what they still do, is to prescribe criteria to assess whether a specific behavior restrains competition in its given market, whether there are barriers to entry in that market, whether a foreclosure is reasonably foreseeable and the like. This is why the most perplexing issue raised by neo-antitrust is whether it only implies a return to the initial reading of the rules–mostly as far as the aims are concerned–without affecting the content of the toolbox and thus leaving the area of possible prohibitions untouched. Is it so, or does "neo-antitrust" also aim to go beyond the settled rules and tools of our discipline?

I consider this a crucial issue, due to the impact it has on the very notion of antitrust. Since the beginning, and in the broadest sense, antitrust has always been applied to market power, exercised through typified behavior in restraint not just of the rights of others, but ultimately of competition. Now, several demands of neo-antitrust supporters remain within the borders of this notion, for they only plead for a more stringent use (objectionable as it might be) of the existing tools. Yet, are we still speaking of antitrust when the power of Big Tech companies is challenged over the sale of their costumers' data? Or, even more, when those companies are challenged over their right to subject customers to surveillance, in order to collect tradable data regarding their activities and tastes?

These are the demands and the problems we should deal with, in any discussion of neo-antitrust. Too frequently (and mostly in the United States), debate seems very general and unspecific. For sure, assuming we are dealing with monopolies that have been abusively and deceptively built is not sufficient to justify a wider (and indefinite) antitrust. At the same time, disqualifying such ambitious expectations, both in legal and economic terms, does not solve by itself the issues the new antitrust is raising (whatever the figures and the tables that are used against it).

---

7   Jonathan B. Baker & Steven C. Salop, *Antitrust, Competition Policy and Inequality*, 104 Geo. L.J. 1–28 (2013).

8   Lina M. Khan, *The Amazon Antitrust Paradox*, 126(3) Yale L.J. 564 (2017). See also the debate that followed that article in the same journal in 2018.

What I intend to do here is to test the potential and the limits of the antitrust tools vis-à-vis the new demands, moving from a very firm principle: namely, the ends we read in antitrust (whatever they are, as long as they respond to a legitimate interpretation) cannot change the means established by the law to pursue them. Of course, the means–the tools at our disposal–can be adapted over time, something that has occurred repeatedly over the years. But stepping out of antitrust in the name of antitrust is a different thing altogether, and would demand envisaging something else entirely.

II.

Let us now examine, upon these simple premises, the conducts at which neo-antitrust is aimed. Some of them, such as self-preference and refusal of data (that are very frequent in the digital world) fall into the restraints and exclusionary conducts, traditionally included in the usual antitrust categories. Nor does the well-known dispute on how to treat "refusal to deal" change the picture. Indeed, any proposed solution of the said dispute lies within the established boundaries of antitrust.

More problematic are the expectations of neo-antitrust supporters in the area of agreements (horizontal as well as vertical) and of mergers and acquisitions. Here too they advocate the use of traditional tools; however, some of these tools have been abandoned by the post-*Sylvania* antitrust. Take per se prohibitions, based on presumptions, for example. Let us assume that not only efficiency, not only consumer welfare, but also (indeed, first and foremost) combating power is restored as a legitimate end of antitrust. Does it justify the return to per se prohibitions?

The original rationale of per se prohibitions was the evidence offered by previous cases, in which the prohibited conduct had always been adopted to restrain competition: the case of price-fixing is the prime example. Being it so, why waste time assessing the same restraint in the case to be decided? The prohibition per se offered a much simpler solution than any further investigation. However, over time, we could avail ourselves of a more sophisticated analysis of the facts, and economic analysis has indisputably demonstrated that even price-fixing can be used not to reduce but to foster competition. This is what happens when the producer sets a maximum price for the sale of his product by the distributor to the final consumer. Here, both the intent and the outcome are the reduction of the distributor's margin in order to increase the competitiveness of that product in the relevant market.

As expounded by the Chicago school and its followers, the economic analysis in the interpretation of antitrust rules has been criticized from several angles. The priority of efficiency over competition is the paramount reason behind criticism, which others have consequentially followed. According to these critics, the notion of consumer welfare is unilateral: consumers may be satisfied by walking from one shop to another and making their own choice, more than by finding the product they need at a low price in one or two shops only. Furthermore, the error-cost framework is too generous in respecting the false positive, which generates a somewhat reversed per se rule to the damage of competition.

Now, I may also agree with these objections, but can they be a sufficient reason to dismantle the sound economic analysis that has greatly improved the interpretation and enforcement of antitrust laws? Something can certainly be rescued of the old antitrust: not, however, the legalistic formalities and the approximate common sense of the lawyers that economic analysis has replaced. Furthermore, and going back to per se prohibitions, not only economic analysis objects to them. Even from a legal angle, there are solid reasons against such prohibitions. The principle of legality–which is implicitly or explicitly adopted by most of the liberal democratic constitutions of our time–does not allow afflictive measures to be based on presumptions automatically applied by the courts. A case-by-case assessment of the facts is a constitutional prerequisite that economic analysis allows us to satisfy with appropriate methodologies.

III.

What about the attention required upon mergers and acquisitions? In recent years the presumed leniency of US antitrust authorities has been criticized not only by the supporters of the hipster antitrust, but also by a liberal–conservative journal such as *The Economist* or by liberal–conservative journalists such as Martin Wolf.[9] Conversely, others have denied both such leniency and the reduction of competition (plus anomalous increase of profits) it had allegedly produced. Even if we set aside this dispute on the past, for the future we cannot ignore the largely new problem that we have to face, mostly in the innovative sectors; namely, successive acquisitions of minor companies by big ones, that produce no immediate effect of foreclosure at each step, but may eventually lessen competition to a significant degree. This is precisely what happens in the specific area of promising start-ups in technological sectors, when they fall in the hands of Big Tech. There is no actual foreclosure here. Indeed, frequently, the start-up's production continues, greatly aided by the fact it has entered into the solid frame of a Big Tech company. But what about the future, is it not a pre-emption of future competition?

We all remember the past contrasts between US and European antitrust agencies upon the relevance of future foreclosure. In the well-known case of *General Electric Honeywell*, at the turn of this century, opposite decisions

---

9   See the issue of *The Economist* of Jan. 20, 2018 and the article by Martin Wolf, *Why Rigged Capitalism is Damaging Liberal Democracy*, Financial Times, Sep. 18, 2019.

were adopted on the two sides of the ocean. Therefore we might deduce from them that no antitrust intervention would be admissible in the US, while in Europe–at least in principle–future foreclosure would be debatable. Actually, for the GE–Honeywell merger, the European Commission had explicitly admitted the benefits for the consumer in the short run, but it deemed the ensuing advantages over competitors would be such that competition would become impossible in the future. The reaction from the US was: "We are more humble in assessing the future."[10] So they preferred to stick to the immediate advantages for the consumers.

Undoubtedly, the conflicting views expressed on that case were rooted in different notions of consumer welfare. However–and this too demands notice–such differences were and remain well within the boundaries of traditional antitrust cultures and of the different use these cultures imply of the antitrust weaponry.

Let us now go back to the cases we may presently face, such as the innovative start-ups acquired one after the other by Big Tech. Despite its longstanding care for the future lessening of competition, not even the European Union would have an immediate, positive solution. Actually, the existing turnover thresholds are too high to allow investigations on mergers between big and small companies or between Big Tech and a promising start-up. However, it is noticeable that this point already is under scrutiny to the end of removing such obstacle without touching the basic antitrust rules, and simply modifying the regulation on mergers, as has been done repeatedly in the past. Indeed, a proposal in this sense has been advanced by three professors: Jacques Crémer, Yves-Alexandre de Montjoye and Heike Schweitzer, appointed by the EU Commission to produce a report on "competition law for the digital era."[11] The three professors drafted a prudent paper, in which they did not suggest an immediate modification of the thresholds. However, as they put it: "where a dominant platform and/or ecosystem which benefits from strong network effects and data access, which acts as a significant barrier to entry, acquires a target with a currently low turnover but a large and/or fast-growing user base and a high future market potential, the case would deserve attention." To this end, a new threshold based on transaction value could be introduced.

Of course, adapting the threshold would not solve the problem. It would simply allow the antitrust agencies to investigate on it and several not-easy questions should be answered: whether the acquirer would avail itself of barriers to entry due to network effects; whether the smaller target would come to represent a competitive constraint; whether the acquisition would increase the barriers to entry and therefore the acquirer's market power. As already said, these are all

---

10   Eleanor Fox, *Diritto della concorrenza, mercati globali e il caso General Electric Honeywell*, Mercato Concorrenza Regole 347 (2002).

11   Jacques Crémer, et al., *Competition Law for the Digital Era* (2019), https://ec.europa.eu/competition/publications/reports/kd0419345enn.pdf.

very difficult questions indeed, and they carry the risk of answers surrounded by the uncertainties of an unknown future. However, humble as we want to be in relation to the future, we cannot ignore that economic analysis and its sophisticated models can lend a powerful hand in reducing those uncertainties and in clarifying the scenarios that most likely would stem from action or inaction in individual cases. Above all, what is most important for the specific inquiry of this paper, even accepting this widening of the relevant acquisitions, we would remain within the boundaries of traditional antitrust rules and of previously experienced divergence in their interpretation.

IV.

The boundaries themselves are at stake when the tech giants are challenged regarding the power they hold over their frequently unaware costumers. The list of the conducts by which such power is exercised is not at all short: it includes the power to extract data from customers, whatever site they access; the power to sell that data to third parties, for whatever use they want to make of it; and the power to impose innovations upon users, creating situations in which the only practical way for them is to accept.

In all the listed cases what we are facing here is power, beyond any reasonable doubt. Our question is whether it is a power that can always be fought by using antitrust tools. In the *Facebook* case, the German antitrust agency, the Bundeskartellamt (BKartA) has clearly admitted that, first of all, here we have violations of the privacy rights of costumers. However–it has argued–such violations are abuses that also violate antitrust rules. To say the least, this is a very controversial solution, for it has already been reversed on appeal by the Düsseldorf Oberlandesgericht, according to which for a violation to be caught under antitrust rules it has be in restraint of competition, and this is not the case here. Subsequently the Bundesgerichtshof has reversed this decision and restored the abuse. However, in the reasoning of the Court the abuse is based on strictly antitrust grounds (the costumers either accept the use of their data or have no access to the platform), not on the violation of privacy rights.[12] Others propose to treat all these violations as self-evident symptoms of monopoly power, which can be neutralized by dismantling the monopoly. However, even the author of this proposal[13] is forced to admit that the monopoly is just a dominant position. Also dominant companies have power, but how that power can be reached and curbed has to be seen.

---

12 The (monumental) decision delivered by the BKartA on February 6, 2019 can be read at bundeskartellamt.de. The decision of August 26, 2019 of the Düsseldorf Court can be read at olg-duesseldorf.nrw.de. The decision of June 23, 2020 of the Bundesgerichtshof can be read at bundesgerichtshof.de.

13 Dina Srinivasan, *The Antitrust Case Against Facebook. A Monopoly Journey Towards Pervasive Surveillance in Spite of Consumers' Preference for Privacy,* 16(1) Berkeley Business L.J. 39 (2019).

It has to be seen in a context in which the answer "never mind, the market will take of itself" is less and less credible. In the last years few objections were raised to the remarkable self-restraint of our antitrust agencies that has accompanied the growth of the giants of the digital sector. The antitrust agencies used to explain such an approach not for the sake of leniency and *laissez-faire,* but by constantly using the argument that innovation in this sector is rapid, frequently unexpected and–as such–can subvert the existing order of the market much more easily than could any antitrust action. This argument was supported by convincing evidence: in the early years of the sector, dominant companies were regularly and quickly superseded by newcomers. Nowadays, however, that golden age is over. A few giants seem solidly stable in their dominant positions. Therefore, the initial caution shown by antitrust agencies is no longer justified. It is a fact that, today, massive actions are being brought against Big Tech, both in Europe and in the US. Due to this reinvigorated attention, most of these actions put under scrutiny behavior that falls into an area usually investigated in antitrust: namely, where others are excluded or discriminated against, or where, in one way or another, competition is reduced. Nor is the return to a more zealous antitrust limited to the digital world. It is worth noting here the attention that has been paid to excessive pricing, at least in Europe, where the EU Treaty explicitly mentions it as an abuse. Excessive pricing is a behavior that, in the past, antitrust authorities had ignored, mostly because, in several cases, it seemed to be an issue better dealt with by regulatory agencies. For sure, excessive pricing is a restriction of competition when a vertically integrated company practices it toward competitors in its own market. When excessive prices fall upon consumers directly, they are not restrictions of competition, and their being "excessive" vis-à-vis the relevant costs much more appropriately falls under the attention of the competent regulatory agencies (in the sectors where such agencies exist).

However, it has to be admitted that excessive pricing, which necessarily is the consequence of previous restrictions of competition, does precisely what competition intends to avoid, namely depriving the consumer of the margin above costs; a sufficient reason for antitrust agencies not to feel totally foreign to the scrutiny that might be promoted. Having said so, we cannot forget that companies that hold dominant or monopolistic positions may harm consumers in a variety of ways, yet such behavior does not fall under the jurisdiction of antitrust just because it is, or may be, the consequence of restrictions of competition.

Let us return to the so-called monopoly power of Big Tech. The problem is that such power is exercised upon the costumers not by raising prices or reducing output, but by subjecting them to treatment that violates their rights, which is something that does not necessarily break antitrust rules. On what legal basis could antitrust authorities exercise their jurisdiction on such behavior? Is rejecting efficiency and restoring the fight against abusive powers a sufficient legal basis for antitrust action? Personally, I have never abandoned the original antitrust meaning of antitrust, but whether such meaning provides sufficient grounds for antitrust authorities to punish behavior that lies beyond the restraints foreseen by our laws is another matter.

V.

The authors of the EU report on competition law for the digital era have rightly underlined the flexibility of antitrust law. That flexibility gives the law a particular strength and allows it to address new phenomena, such as novel positions of power. However, they themselves also admit such flexibility meets limits. More precisely they write that not even the "broad, open and general rules" of competition law can be interpreted so widely as to include all behavior by which a paramount power can be exercised. Were it so, we would not have consumer protection laws, unfair trading laws or data protection laws. To the contrary, the General Data Protection Regulation (GDPR) – adopted by the European Union in 2016–offers eloquent evidence that specific rules are needed–and specific rules are actually applied–to counter a substantial part of the actions that neo-antitrust supporters suggest should be incorporated into the antitrust jurisdiction.

Of course, there are no barriers between different areas of law; new rules in one of them can have an impact in others. In Europe we have article 102 of the Treating on the Functioning of the EU, in which abuses are listed, but the list is not exhaustive, so other behavior could still fall under this open notion. Let us take the case of some behavior that violates the GDPR or other specific new regulations. Should it be brought under the attention of an antitrust authority, there might be room for that behavior to be scrutinized as an abuse. This is what the BKartA has done in the *Facebook* case, mentioned above, even though, as we have seen, the Düsseldorf Oberlandesgericht subsequently denied the abuse, for, in its view, the conduct was not anticompetitive, while the Bundesgrichtshof has admitted the abuse on different grounds. Nonetheless, in principle, the two areas of regulation and the consequent jurisdictions are not mutually exclusive.

In conclusion: in the digital world private power has enormously increased and has eroded the space and rights of consumers in previously unimaginable ways. Therefore, vigorously calling our antitrust family to exercise its own responsibilities vis-à-vis such a new world is not at all a heresy. All of us are aware that for the digital market to take care of itself is not as easy as it had been in its initial years: according to several members of the family, the border between sound economic analysis and *laissez-faire* was very thin and frequently invisible; now it is very much visible and therefore undisputable.

There are limits, however. I cannot imagine a liberal democracy, the core of which is offering protection to rights and liberties against abusive powers (private or public as they may be), without a robust antitrust legislation, enforced by independent authorities. Nevertheless antitrust, though essential, is just a component of such a legal order. I may agree on fighting power as its first and foremost mission, but such mission is not a sufficient legal basis for us to use it as a universal shield against any possible manifestation of private power. Let us be clear: administrative and judicial authorities are not allowed to freely expand the means, or the reach of the means, they are supplied with by the law in order to better pursue the goals the law itself bestows upon them. It would be against the rule of law.

Several historians consider it doubtful that Niccolò Machiavelli ever enunciated his most famous principle by using the words "the end justifies the means." Whatever the truth to this, it is certain that such principle has not entered into the rule of law of liberal democracies.

The American Antitrust Counter-Revolutionaries: A European Perspective

GIORGIO MONTI[*]
Tilburg Law and Economics Center

Abstract

Professor Fox's work of the 1980s set the framework for debating the shape of antitrust law. She was prescient in noting the practical and political salience of the Chicago school's approach. This paper offers a European perspective on US debates since that time. It examines why the dominant paradigm has been successful and how it has been challenged. It examines three approaches: tinkering with the burden of proof, focusing on the competitive process and legislating away uncomfortable precedent. Each of these asks for a rethinking of our assumptions and perspectives about what it means to say that antitrust safeguards well-functioning markets.

---

[*] Professor of Competition Law, Tilburg Law and Economics Center.

I. Introduction

As a student of what was then EEC competition law in the early 1990s, I was taught to be excited about the European Court of Justice's (ECJ's) 1991 *Delimitis* judgment.¹ It was considered as significant as the US Supreme Court's judgment in *Sylvania*.² Finally, so the seminar discussions went, the ECJ had shown a willingness to adopt a more economics-oriented approach to antitrust and to focus on the effects of the agreement as opposed to its form.³

The judgment probably also resonated in the minds of Americans: as the internal market project neared completion, US commentators had begun to participate in debates in Brussels to hasten the shift toward a more permissive approach in EEC competition law.⁴ The US antitrust revolution, which the European Commission was being asked to follow by these lawyers, began to be felt in the Supreme Court in the 1970s.⁵ Intellectually, it was inspired by a distinctive, simple and intuitive law and economics paradigm.⁶ Politically, it succeeded because its prescriptions chimed with concerns that aggressive regulation (including antitrust) was seen as stifling US industry.⁷ To US lawyers that had begun to build their practices in Brussels the *Delimitis* judgment provided a hope that EU competition law would be as accommodating as US antitrust. This inevitably led to considerations of how much of the Chicago school's antitrust revolution would percolate into the Commission's enforcement practices.⁸

As someone skeptical of this antitrust revolution (it looked too easy!) the scholarship of Professor Eleanor Fox in the 1980s provided a much-needed tonic. In her rich writings of this decade, which form the motivation for this paper, she identified a key set of concerns about the Chicago approach to antitrust. First, she observed how this method of analysis would work: courts and agencies would

---

1   Case C-234/89 Stergios Delimitis v. Henninger Bräu AG, EU:C:1991:91. RICHARD WHISH & BRENDA SUFRIN, COMPETITION LAW 204–205 (3d ed. 1993), noting that the significance of the judgment lay in its unprecedentedly detailed examination of the effects of distribution agreements.

2   Continental Television v. GTE Sylvania, 433 U.S. 36 (1977).

3   However, in academic writings authors were more cautious. Valentine Korah, *The Judgment in* Delimitis– *A Milestone towards a Realistic Assessment of the Effects of an Agreement–Or a Damp Squib?*, 8 TUL. EUR. & CIV. L.F. 17, 51 (1993). This well-known advocate for the more economics approach suggested that "a substantial change in attitude will be required of many officials if the judgment is to bear its full fruit."

4   Most notably *see* Barry E. Hawk, *The American (Anti-trust) Revolution: Lessons for the EEC?*, 9 EUR. COMPETITION L. REV. 53 (1988).

5   A book exploring the leading cases that embody this approach has been published since 1989, with an unchanged title: LAWRENCE J. WHITE & JOHN E. KWOKA, THE ANTITRUST REVOLUTION (7th ed. 2018). In contrast, Richard Posner changed the title of his classic work. In its first edition (published in 1976) it carried a subtitle "(An Economic Approach)," but the second edition omitted the subtitle because the author took the view that there was no need to convince readers of the economic approach now. RICHARD A. POSNER, ANTITRUST LAW (2001).

6   ROBERT BORK, THE ANTITRUST PARADOX (1978).

7   LESTER C. THUROW, THE ZERO-SUM SOCIETY: DISTRIBUTION AND THE POSSIBILITIES FOR ECONOMIC CHANGE (1980).

8   ANNE C. WITT, THE MORE ECONOMIC APPROACH TO EU ANTITRUST LAW (2016).

inquire whether the conduct in question was likely to restrict output thereby reducing short-run aggregate welfare. The key result of this was that "this conception of antitrust would prohibit almost nothing at all."[9] Second, she explained that this method of applying antitrust law was not a technocratic fix to a system that was not working. On the contrary it was deeply political. In commenting specifically on the influential work of Frank Easterbrook, she explained that a "call for application of an efficiency principle as the guide to the law, plus an insistence on nonintervention whenever economics is indeterminate, is a way of stating the case for laissez-faire. The case is not based on economics. It is based on a social-political preference."[10]

Professor Fox saw the 1980s as an era where, in the US, there was a "battle for the soul of antitrust."[11] Against the Chicagoan antitrust revolutionaries she identified a "New Coalition" of scholars who took the view that economics was just one of the tools by which to apply antitrust law, and that one should also remain faithful to the statutory text, its legislative history and judicial construction.[12] By 1987, in what is one of the finest antitrust articles of all time (and which has been on all my reading lists since I started teaching competition law in 1993) Professors Fox and Sullivan were optimistic that the realist/traditionalist approach to antitrust they championed would prevail: "the courts will slay the paper dragon from Chicago."[13] As we now know, this was an overly-optimistic prediction: courts have increasingly supported a non-interventionist approach championed by the Chicago school and its supporters.[14]

Since the 1990s generations of scholars have bemoaned the disappearance of antitrust enforcement. Professor Fox's prediction of reduced enforcement proved prescient. However, while we have had plenty of counter-revolutionaries, there has been no counter-revolution. Post-Chicago economics made modest contributions to widening the scope of antitrust.[15] Behavioral economics has had no visible impact on antitrust doctrine. Those working outside the Chicagoan economics paradigm kept criticizing the Chicago school for overshooting the mark and wished for revitalized antitrust, but their pleas led

---

9   Eleanor M. Fox, *Modernization of Antitrust: A New Equilibrium*, 66 Cornell L. Rev. 1140, 1145 (1981).

10 Eleanor M. Fox, *The Politics of Law and Economics in Judicial Decision Making: Antitrust as a Window*, 61 N.Y.U. L. Rev. 554, 576 (1986).

11 Eleanor M. Fox, *The Battle for the Soul of Antitrust*, 75 Cal. L. Rev. 917 (1987).

12 *Id.*, referring to the work of the late Lawrence Sullivan, in particular *The Viability of the Current Law on Horizontal Restraints*, 75 Cal. L. Rev. 835 (1987).

13 Eleanor M. Fox & Lawrence A. Sullivan, *Antitrust–Retrospective and Prospective: Where Are We Coming from–Where Are We Going*, 62 N.Y.U. L. Rev. 936, 968 (1987).

14 Warren S. Grimes, *Fifteen Years of Supreme Court Antitrust Jurisprudence: The Defendant Always Wins*, in The Development of Competition Law: Global Perspectives (Roger Zäch et al. eds., 2010).

15 United States v. AMR Corporation, 335 F.3d 1109 (10th Cir 2003) is an instance where the Department of Justice ran a more adventurous theory of predatory pricing which left the court unconvinced. But *see* Christopher S. Yoo, *The Post-Chicago Antitrust Revolution: A Retrospective* 168 U. Penn. L. Rev. 2145, 2165 (2020), noting a few more cases where post-Chicago was successful, as well as the position on unilateral conduct in the Horizontal Merger Guidelines.

to no counter-revolution.[16] The Obama administration did not appear to yield the paradigm-shift some hoped for.[17] In the last five years or so, the clamor for a recalibration of US antitrust has grown considerably: increasing economic inequality and a financial crisis that led many to question economic orthodoxy more generally, providing added ammunition for a new antitrust revolution. The so-called GAFAM firms have served up a visible target for counter-revolutionaries and a symbol of what is wrong with antitrust non-enforcement.[18] The ranks of the counter-revolutionaries have grown considerably and a neo-Brandeisian approach to antitrust has emerged.[19] This new writing is rich and inspiring, like that of its precursors, and its policy recommendations very radical.

In all of the antitrust battles of the past 40 years, Professor Fox's original concerns have remained. The increased use and sophistication of economics in determining whether there is an antitrust infringement have served to raise agencies' costs considerably. The choice of grounding antitrust in a particular economic vision remains one that is rooted in a political choice about the nature of markets.[20] And yet the use of economics is now inevitable; reorientation of antitrust will necessarily reflect a particular vision about markets. Markets are social constructs, not autonomous entities: our choices as to which activities are opened to markets (by the generation of property rights and contract rules) reflect our beliefs about the proper scope of markets, and our choices to regulate them via antitrust or sector-specific regulation reveal our beliefs about what good market performance is. We might prefer markets that are open to rivals at the expense of efficiency, for example.

If devising antitrust requires us to construct an economic and political ecosystem within which to apply the rules, what prospects are there to depart from today's dominant paradigm? And why is it that all the antitrust counter-revolutionaries of the past 40 years have failed? These are the questions we pursue here by examining three ways through which one might reset antitrust. In section II we attempt to explain the enduring success of the dominant antitrust paradigm. We suggest that in addition to the valid observations about this paradigm being based on a given ideology about how markets work and a narrow technique for identifying anticompetitive effects, there is one more ingredient that accounts for its success: the convergence between the error–cost framework that

---

16   How the Chicago School Overshot the Mark (Robert Pitofsky ed., 2008).

17   For an optimistic assessment, see David A. Balto, *Reinvigorating Antitrust Enforcement: The Obama Administration's Progressive Direction on Competition Law and Policy in Challenging Economic Times*, Ctr. for Am. Progress (July 2011) https://cdn.americanprogress.org/wp-content/uploads/issues/2011/07/pdf/antitrust_enforcement.pdf.

18   Lina Khan, *Amazon's Antitrust Paradox*, 126 Yale L.J. 710 (2017).

19   Tim Wu, The Curse of Bigness: Antitrust in the New Gilded Age (2018).

20   Eleanor M. Fox, *Against Goals*, 81(5) Fordham L. Rev. 2157 (2015) labels these perspectives and assumptions, which are developed further in this paper.

Chicagoans introduced and the legal standard. We then explore how this might be overcome. In section III, we turn to the more ambitious approaches to change the direction of antitrust and focus our discussion on scholars who wish to see antitrust geared to protect the competitive process. In examining this paradigm, we show two reasons why approaches such as these are unlikely to gain much traction. The first is that, paradoxically, the system already seems to contain some of the ingredients that are being advocated. The second is that the proponents of this approach have some work to do to explain what their approach signifies. Finally, in section IV, we turn to some recent legislative initiatives: if the common law cannot change quickly enough, might a new statute fill the antitrust enforcement gap?

In examining these three attempts at a counter-revolution, a comparative account of developments in EU competition law furnishes a helpful lens through which to view US developments. All these three pathways have their roots in Professor Fox's scholarship, which has furnished us with the keys to debate antitrust for generations.

II. Tweaking the Balance in Favor of Plaintiffs
1. Chicago's convergence with legal standards

The most prosaic, but as I will suggest the most effective, tool used by the dominant paradigm to render antitrust enforcement difficult is to insist on the risk of Type 1 errors (false positives). Much of the literature critical of this focuses on explanations about why it is wrong to believe that Type 1 errors are more costly than Type 2 errors (false negatives).[21] While this literature is important in elucidating the superior approach to error–cost analysis, it does not observe a more obvious, but more problematic, effect that using the error–cost framework has on judges. In law, it is always necessary, if faced with a risk of Type 1 error, not to condemn: *in dubio pro reo* is a maxim that no judge would likely forget.

To put this more bluntly: from the perspective of a legislator, the error–cost framework could prove useful. The legislator can discuss whether it is better for a rule to be under-inclusive (so prone to Type 2 errors) or whether there is a risk of a rule which is over-inclusive (a Type 1 error). For example: should there be a law to ban resale price maintenance (RPM) all the time (prone to Type 1 errors) or should the legislator allow RPM (a rule prone to Type 2 errors)? The legislator then can weigh up the costs of both kinds of error and make a choice based on this by considering both the likelihood and magnitude of each error. Or the legislator can be biased in believing that Type 2 errors are always less significant because the market will correct them. The legislator can legitimately use the error–cost framework when designing laws, and we can legitimately be critical if it is used poorly.

---

21 Thomas A. Lambert, *The Limits of Antitrust in the 21st Century* (Univ. Mo. Sch. of Law, Legal Studies Research Paper Series, Research Paper No. 2020-06).

However, a judge is in a different position when faced with the argument that applying a per se illegality rule risks Type 1 errors. The problem for the judge is not that they are blinded by Chicago to ignore the risks of Type 2 errors or ideologically fixated in the belief that markets solve all problems. Granted, some judges may be so minded, but a more fundamental matter is that the judge is concerned about making an erroneous conviction, irrespective of the economic consequences. A judge cannot convict if, applying the relevant standard of proof, there is a risk of condemning a practice that is lawful. A judge is much more willing, given the legal canons, to authorize conduct that may be harmful in a situation of uncertainty. The judge prefers a Type 2 error not because of any economic assumption, but because, unless relevant proof is available, the better mistake is not to condemn.

In sum: legislators may be happy to choose a rule which over-enforces the law for they are sovereign. Conversely, judges cannot deliberately issue a rule that is over-inclusive and penalizes the innocent. On the other hand, judges are willing to under-enforce the law and allow some guilty parties to go free. This, in my view, is the somewhat unexciting reason why the Chicago-inspired antitrust paradigm has gained so much traction: all it takes is to sow some doubt in the minds of the judges and they will respond by crafting rules that raise the burdens on plaintiffs, to avoid convicting the innocent. The emergence of pro-defendant rules is not just premised on an ideology that is unique to Chicago, but on a fortunate convergence between this ideology and a judge's training: both are wary of false convictions. But for different reasons: the Chicagoans because false convictions chill the very conduct that antitrust protects, the judge because false convictions penalize the innocent. But the outcome is the same, which explains why, as two scholars have concluded, "plaintiffs continue to face arguments about conduct, institutions, and market structure to persuade courts to impose overly demanding burdens of production and proof."[22]

Consider the *Matsushita* judgment, where the allegation was that Japanese firms had conspired to engage in a predatory pricing campaign in the US market for color TVs. On the one hand, those critical of the judgment focus on the manner in which the majority focused on Chicago school literature, doubting the rationality of predatory pricing, and the Court's conclusion that "predatory pricing schemes are rarely tried, and even more rarely successful."[23] Criticism of this posture is right: predation is more prevalent than the Supreme Court believes.[24] However, the justices went on to explain that their skepticism was further justified by a finding that while this conspiracy had been going on for some time, the expected effects had not yet materialized: the market share of US color TV

---

22 Andrew I. Gavil and Steven C. Salop, *Probability, Presumptions and Evidentiary Burdens in Antitrust Analysis: Revitalizing the Rule of Reason for Exclusionary Conduct*, 168(7) U. Penn. L. Rev. 2107, 2130 (2020).

23 Matsushita v. Zenith Radio Corp., 475 U.S. 574, 579 (1986).

24 Christopher R. Leslie, *Predatory Pricing and Recoupment*, 113(7) Colum. L. Rev. 1695 (2013).

manufacturers had grown, rather than shrunk.²⁵ In other words, the reason for dismissing this claim was not only ideological but pragmatic too: if 20 years of price cuts don't yield an increase in the predators' market share, then the risk of convicting innocent parties is high. One can understand a judge's reluctance to allow this case to proceed to trial.

From this perspective, the counter-revolutionaries asking for a change of perspective from the courts face a formidable task: it is not just that judges rely on a simplistic, possibly outdated, economic paradigm. They are also fearful of convicting the innocent. However, this does not mean that a counter-revolution is impossible. It just requires the right strategy.

2. Recalibrating burdens

In a recent illuminating paper, Professors Gavil and Salop go some way to explaining how the current biases in the antitrust standards can be corrected. The particular value of their suggestion rests in the fact that they are grounded in legal territory, which is likely to be more appealing to judges. The first and second of their principles are particularly important. The first is that judges applying the rule of reason should be neutral about the competitive effects of the conduct under scrutiny. To European ears this resonates as the most sensible starting point. The issue was discussed in the context of the merger rules, and the ECJ explained that there is not general presumption that a notified merger is pro- or anticompetitive. It is for the Commission to assess whether the merger substantially impedes effective competition.²⁶ This neutrality means that in a dispute about predatory pricing the starting point is not that low prices are presumptively beneficial but whether the plaintiff has evidence to satisfy the legal standard.

The second principle is that the plaintiff should prove probable anticompetitive effects, not actual effects. Furthermore, the harm should not be quantified. As the authors note, this is already the law, but it is worth explaining why these principles need restatement. In *McWane*, FTC Commissioner Wright had issued a dissenting opinion, which is representative of the more skeptical approach to antitrust: he began by suggesting that exclusive dealing agreements were likely procompetitive and therefore clear evidence of anticompetitive effects was required.²⁷ This approach violates both of the principles set out by Gavil and Salop: it starts with a presumption of legality and uses this to justify a higher standard of proof

---

25 *Matsushita*, 475 U.S. at 591–92.

26 Case C-413/06 P Bertelsmann AG & Sony Corp. of Am. v. Independent Music Publishers and Labels Ass'n (Impala), EU:C:2008:392, para. 48. *See also* Jérôme Philippe & Aude Guyon, *Standard of proof–Annulment: The ECJ confirms the CFI ruling having annuled the EC merger clearance Sony-BMG and rules on the standard of proofs in merger proceedings (*Bertelsman–Sony/Impala*)*, Concurrences N° 4–2008, Art. N° 22257 (2008).

27 Dissenting Statement of Commissioner Joshua D. Wright, *In re* McWane et al., FTC No. 9351 (Jan. 30, 2014).

for the plaintiff. Indeed, on appeal the court recalled that the correct legal standard is probable effect, but it balanced this by being clear that the FTC could only win if its findings were "supported by substantial evidence."[28]

Another recommendation made by Professors Gavil and Salop proves more debatable, however. This is the suggestion that there should be a lower burden on the plaintiff in exclusionary conduct cases when the defendant has substantial market power. There are good reasons for this, and indeed US antitrust already reflects this in one way. Even Justice Scalia (no friend of progressive antitrust) noted this: "Behavior that might otherwise not be of concern to the antitrust laws ... can take on exclusionary connotations when practiced by a monopolist."[29] But this much is obvious: a small firm's pricing below marginal cost will not have the same exclusionary potency as the same conduct engaged in by a monopolist trying to exclude a new entrant. What is needed to make the suggestion workable is an explanation of what level of market power the authors have and a granular explanation of what a lower burden means.

For example, would the authors treat the approach in *Le Page's Incorporated v. 3M* as one where the Third Circuit has implemented this suggestion? The monopolist, 3M, had a 90% share of the transparent tape market. This would easily confer on it substantial market power. The question on appeal was whether in penalizing a policy of bundled rebates the plaintiff had to show that prices were below cost. The Third Circuit held that this was unnecessary because the effect of the bundled rebates was to foreclose the market.[30] Conversely some other circuits have taken the view that in cases of bundled rebates an assessment akin to that found in predatory pricing should be undertaken.[31] Thus the judgment in *Le Page's* might embody the kind of policy prescription the authors have in mind, but it is imperative that this is spelled out so that it is clear what sort of legal standards are taken to be appropriate. The example selected here is done purposefully because in the EU the Commission has recently elected to move in the opposite direction: while the early case law penalized a range of discounting practices by monopolists, the Commission aspired to narrow the focus of its enforcement to instances where it could be shown that the dominant firm's prices were below cost for the contestable share of the market.[32] Is this an example where the Europeans are more Chicagoan than some US courts?

---

28 McWane Inc v. Fed. Trade Comm'n, 783 F.3d 814, 837 (11th Cir. 2015). *See also* Helen Cho Eckert & David R. Garcia, *The US Court of Appeals for the 11th Circuit holds that a rebate program requiring exclusivity from distributors was unlawful maintenance of monopoly power (*McWane*)*, e-Competitions April 2015, Art. N° 72658 (Apr. 15, 2015).

29 Eastman Kodak Co. v. Image Tech. Servs., Inc., 504 U.S. 451 at 488 (1992) (Scalia, J., dissenting).

30 LePage's Incorporated v. 3M, 324 F.3d 141 (3d Cir. 2003).

31 Cascade Health v. Peacehealth, 515 F.3d 883 (9th Cir. 2007).

32 European Commission, Guidance on the Commission's enforcement priorities in applying Article 82 of the EC Treaty to abusive exclusionary conduct by dominant undertakings, 2009 O.J. (C 45) 7.

3. Burden recalibration from an EU perspective

The debate on the burden of proof has some resonance with recent ECJ case law, which has struggled with a similar issue. In the EU, much like the US antitrust rules of the 1960s, there has been a tendency to convict defendants too quickly. In Article 101 TFEU this is achieved by a wide reading of the concept of restrictions by object, and in Article 102 TFEU this is achieved by focusing on the way conduct harms rivals. This allows courts to bypass an effects-based analysis. The *Delimitis* judgment has not gained the following that many expected, but matters may have recently turned. This is so in particular if we study three recent judgments: *Cartes Bancaires*, *Generics*, and *Intel*. We argue that these three judgments adjust the burden of proof in a manner that balances the rights of plaintiffs and defendants in a promising manner.

Cartes Bancaires is a judgment whose tone fits well with judgments of the Supreme Court in the 1970s, a time when the categories of conduct that fell into the per se rule began to be reduced. For example, in *Sylvania* the Court recalled that the default analytical framework under the Sherman Act is the rule of reason and the application of a per se rule "must be based upon demonstrable economic effect, rather than ... upon formalistic line drawing."[33] The ECJ, in its conceptual discussion of restrictions by object, inserts a new reflection that echoes these sentiments:

> it is established that certain collusive behavior, such as that leading to horizontal price-fixing by cartels, may be considered *so likely to have negative effects*, in particular on the price, quantity or quality of the goods and services, that it may be considered redundant, for the purposes of applying Article [101(1) TFEU], to prove that they have actual effects on the market. *Experience shows* that such behavior leads to falls in production and price increases, resulting in poor allocation of resources to the detriment, in particular, of consumers.[34]

On the facts of the case, a decision by an association of banks that agreed a membership fee whereby banks who only issued bank cards without investing in developing acquiring services were asked to pay more than banks who invested in developing the acquiring side of the market, was not the kind of practice that is so likely to have anticompetitive effects as to qualify as a restriction by object. Having regard to the two-sided nature of the market, and the importance for consumers that the bank cards they have can be used in a large number of shops, the measure was designed to create incentives for member banks to invest

---

33 Continental T.V., Inc. v. GTE Sylvania, Inc., 433 U.S. 36, 59 (1977).

34 Case C-67/13 P Groupement des Cartes Bancaires (CB) v. Commission, EU:C:2014:2204, para. 51 (emphasis added). The reference to experience echoes the position taken by Justice Scalia in his dissenting opinion in Eastman Kodak Co. v. Image Tech. Servs., Inc., 504 U.S. 451, 486 (1992).

in developing the acquisition network. Here, the efficiencies appeared more obvious than the restraint, this indicates that an effects analysis is required. The Commission went on to win anyway, for it showed that the conduct was likely to exclude new entrants, and the efficiencies pleaded by the firms were not credible.[35]

However, not all restrictions by object are as clear-cut as price-fixing cartels. Sometimes the Commission will need to dig a little deeper to deliver a convincing argument that a practice is restrictive by object. This is the lesson that emerges from the judgment in *Generics*, where a reverse payment settlement agreement may be found restrictive of competition by object if the following conditions are met: we are dealing with a process patent, the payment made to the would-be entrant has "no other explanation than the commercial interest of the parties to the agreement not to engage in competition on the merits," and there are no procompetitive effects that cast doubt as to the agreement's harm to competition.[36]

Bringing the approaches in these two cases together, we can suggest that there will be object cases which can be condemned fairly easily, while others will require a closer look at the legal and economic context before being clear that the agreement is restrictive by object. The two different definitions of restrictions by object in the case law might then best be read as alternatives rather than as mutually exclusive options.

Even if a restriction seems clearly anticompetitive under either standard, the defendant may succeed in requesting an effects analysis. This is clear from the judgment in *Generics*: if the defendant brings evidence that a reverse-patent settlement is procompetitive they "justify a reasonable doubt" about the object of the agreement,[37] and will require the Commission to demonstrate anticompetitive effects. This echoes the approach in *Cartes Bancaires*.

Another way for the defendant to require that the plaintiff carries out an effects analysis is found in *Intel*. The case concerns a dominant undertaking granting rebates to its clients, which the Commission considered unlawful because they were awarded on the condition that the customers bought the dominant firm's chips exclusively from it and as such foreclosed market access to rivals. The ECJ began by making a reference to the foundational judgment, *Hoffman-La Roche*, which provides that "loyalty rebates, that is to say, discounts conditional on the

---

[35] Case T-491/07 RENV *Cartes Bancaires v. Commission*, EU:T:2016:379. *See also* Daniel Muheme & Greta Juknaite, *The EU Court of Justice annuls a judgment of the General Court which held that certain pricing measures adopted restricted competition "by object" (*Groupement des Cartes Bancaires*)*, e-Competitions September 2014, Art. N° 72930 (Sept. 11, 2004).

[36] Case C-307/18 Generics (UK) Ltd and others v. Competition and Markets Authority, EU:C:2020:52, para. 111. *See also* Sandrine Mathieu & Amélie Lamarcq, *The EU Court of Justice clarifies the conditions under which pay-for-delay agreements preventing generic versions of a patented medicine from entering the market or delaying such entry may constitute a restriction of competition 'by object' or 'by effect" as well as an abuse of dominant position (*Generics–UK/GlaxoSmithKline/Actavis/Xellia Pharmaceuticals/Merck/Alpharma*)*, e-Competitions January 2020, Art. N° 94657 (Jan. 30, 2020).

[37] *Id.*, para. 107.

customer's obtaining all or most of its requirements–whether the quantity of its purchases be large or small–from the undertaking in a dominant position" constitute an abuse of a dominant position.[38] But it immediately followed this restatement of the law with this caveat: "However, that case law must be further clarified in the case where the undertaking concerned submits, during the administrative procedure, on the basis of supporting evidence, that its conduct was not capable of restricting competition and, in particular, of producing the alleged foreclosure effects."[39]

In these cases, the Commission is obliged to study the effects of the rebate as well as any possible efficiency claim.[40] The approach in *Generics* and *Intel* is largely consistent with the quick look/rule-of-reason framework we find in US antitrust: a plaintiff may argue that the conduct at hand is obviously anticompetitive such that a quick look suffices to shift the burden on the defendant to justify the conduct, but the court might conclude that the facts at hand "raise sufficient doubt about the anticompetitive nature of the agreement such that detailed scrutiny is required to understand its effects."[41] The ECJ's judgment in *Intel* is thus significant for indicating that a similar option exists for defendants in the EU.

This trilogy of judgments reveal two significant reconfigurations of the analytical framework in the EU. First, the case law identifies three kinds of cases: (i) a category of practices whose anticompetitive nature is so obvious that the Commission can safely condemn them by object; (ii) other agreements that, after a review of the relevant economic context, are also clearly anticompetitive, and which may be deemed restrictive of competition by object; (iii) agreements where the impact on competition is ambiguous so that the Commission must examine the likelihood that the agreement will have anticompetitive effects.

The second reconfiguration is that when the Commission opts for an object assessment under the first or second type of case mentioned above, the defendant can bring up evidence to show that the harm to competition is not as obvious as one might think. There are two ways for the defendant to challenge the Commission. One is to establish that the agreement may be efficient. This approach is described well by A.G. Kokott: an effects analysis is needed when the facts "reveal a complex arrangement with pro- and anticompetitive components, from which it would be impossible to determine whether, overall, it has an anticompetitive object."[42] The second is to bring up evidence that the

---

38   Case 85/76 Hoffmann-La Roche v. Commission, EU:C:1979:36, para. 89.

39   Case C-413/14 *P Intel v. Commission*, EU:C:2017:632, para. 138. *See also* Anne-Lise Sibony, *Economic analysis: The EU Court of Justice embraces the effects-based approach in a fidelity rebates case (*Intel*)*, Concurrences N° 4–2017, Art. N° 85211 (2017).

40   *Id.*, paras. 139–40.

41   California *Ex Rel.* Harris v. Safeway, 651 F.3d 1118, 1138 (2011).

42   *Generics*, *supra* note 36, para. 171.

agreement is not capable of harming competition, as intimated in *Intel*. Either of these, if demonstrated, forces the Commission to explore whether the practice has anticompetitive effects. This is very similar to the opportunities open to defendants in the US when the plaintiff opts for a quick-look analysis: in most cases we see that the defendant tries to give an efficiency rationale for its conduct, but there are also cases where the defendant questions the anticompetitive nature of the agreement.[43]

From a comparative law perspective we can make the following observations: first the ECJ in *Generics* is right to insist that the approach it prescribes is not a rule of reason when this is defined as a standard for balancing pro- and anticompetitive effects; but when we observe that the rule of reason is about requiring the plaintiff to bring up sufficient evidence to meet its case then the affinities between the EU and US courts are much easier to see. More specifically, it is interesting to compare how the two jurisdictions handle similar cases, for instance reverse payment settlements. As we noted above in *Generics*, the ECJ held that such settlements may be restrictive by object when the size of the payment leaves no doubt that it is a payment designed to share profits between the originator and the would-be entrant. The US Supreme Court in a similar dispute (*FTC v. Actavis*) held that these cases were not suitable for a quick-look analysis, but required a comprehensive analysis. However the court also found that the criteria to assess the legality of these agreements are linked to the payment's "size, its scale in relation to the payor's anticipated future litigation costs, its independence from other services for which it might represent payment, and the lack of any other convincing justification."[44] In other words, rather than fixating on the precise label (object v. effect, or quick look v. rule of reason) one had better study the degree of proof the court requires before the burden shifts to the other side. Viewed from this perspective we see that the two courts converge on the evidence required to examine reverse-patent settlements, even if they label these in ways that appear to suggest divergent approaches.

For the purposes of this paper, this comparative account reveals how vital the allocation of the burden of proof is to managing cases, so that the plaintiff's burden is not incapacitated when they have a strong case, while more may legitimately be asked of the plaintiff when the welfare effects are more ambiguous. The EU, coming to this debate rather late in the day, appears to have taken advantage of the discussion in the US courts, and to have come up with an approach that balances the two sides: on the one hand the plaintiff is entitled to benefit from a relatively lighter burden of proof when they are able to rely on economic evidence that suggests a high risk of harm is likely. On the other hand, the defendant is afforded two chances to defend its practices. First, by countering

---

43   *E.g., Safeway*, 651 F.3d, California Dental Association v. Fed. Trade Comm'n 526 U.S. 756 (1999).

44   FTC v. Actavis, Inc., 570 U.S. 136 (2013). *See also* Michael A. Carrier, The US Supreme Court issues first ruling on antitrust legality of reverse-payment drug patent settlements (Actavis), e-Competitions June 2013, Art. N° 53120 (June 17, 2013).

the economic evidence and requesting a closer analysis of conduct, secondly by the ability to plead an efficiency defense. This method of analysis can serve to revitalize antitrust by giving the Commission/plaintiff a greater likelihood of shifting the burden of proof to the defendant. This should make judges less concerned about Type 1 errors: finding in the Commission's favor does not mean that the conduct is condemned, it requires the defendant to bring forward evidence and arguments. In this manner the decision-maker can safely condemn without fear of a Type 1 error for they have afforded the defendant opportunities to rebut the plaintiff's case.

4. Is burden recalibration enough?

While recalibrating burdens is a valuable approach to facilitate effective antitrust enforcement, it will not suffice if it is accompanied by a continued reliance on economics that is no longer mainstream. For instance, it is argued that the position on predatory pricing taken by the Supreme Court according to which recoupment in cases of predation in an oligopoly is difficult to execute underplays the economic findings that were available at the time of the judgment.[45] From this perspective, the problem with US antitrust is not so much the use of Chicago school ideology. Indeed, the more extreme positions taken by this school have normally not been implemented: e.g. RPM is subject to a rule of reason, it is not per se legal;[46] predatory pricing remains an antitrust offense; it is not presumed that all price cuts are lawful. Indeed, when we look at US antitrust today, it is not a replica of a Chicago school approach that anyone would recognize.[47] The concern is that courts ask too much of plaintiffs. And from this perspective, the approach suggested above is likely to have a limited impact for some.

III. The Competitive Process

Other scholars have been bolder, and suggested that there needs to be a reconfiguration of antitrust whereby the theory of harm is based not on whether conduct risks harming consumer welfare, but on whether conduct distorts the competitive process. Different reasons motivate this move: nearly everyone agrees that the phrase "consumer welfare" has been misused.[48] This departure thus signals a rhetorical shift away from a concept that is politically charged with many of the assumptions underpinning the Chicago approach. Abandoning it is

---

45 Brooke Group Ltd. v. Brown & Williamson Tobacco Corp., 509 U.S. 209 (1993). Herbert Hovenkamp & Fiona Scott Morton, *Framing the Chicago School of Antitrust Analysis*, 168 U. PENN. L. REV. 1843, 1850–51 (2020).

46 Richard A. Posner, *The Next Step in the Antitrust Treatment of Restricted Distribution: Per Se Legality*, 48 U. CHI. L. REV. 6 (1981).

47 Yoo, *supra* note 15, at 2158–59, noting that the mixed results in part have to do with the fact that Chicagoans were not unanimous about what should replace the existing antitrust standards.

48 In brief, the confusion is that one oft-cited work used consumer welfare to mean total welfare. BORK, *supra* note 6.

a signal for more aggressive antitrust enforcement. But there are some substantive reasons too: for some, it is that the consumer welfare standard is too static and does not capture wider economic gains; for some, its focus on consumers is misleading as other actors' welfare matters as well; for others, the emphasis on welfare is problematic for this is hard to measure. Finally, it is claimed that the use of the consumer welfare standard has led to a period of under-enforcement that has served to increase concentration and harm consumers.[49] The suggestion, which also harks back to the work of Professor Fox, is to focus on determining whether conduct harms the competitive process. However, this phrase appears as hard to understand or operationalize as consumer welfare.

1. General standards of assessment

Some of the scholars suggesting a change in standard admit that more work is needed to develop this fully, but a recent paper by Professors Steinbaum and Stucke provides us with a clearly articulated explanation of what an effective competition standard would look like. At a high level, the standard is defined thus:

> Agencies and courts shall use the preservation of competitive market structures that protect individuals, purchasers, consumers, and producers; preserve opportunities for competitors; promote individual autonomy and wellbeing; and disperse private power as the principal objective of the federal antitrust laws.[50]

This vision is very close to the concept of competition as a process that Professor Fox had in 1981, whose running themes were: distrust of power, concern for consumers, and commitment to opportunity for entrepreneurs. By dispersing power, she argued, opportunities and incentives for smaller rivals would be increased. A byproduct of this, in her view, would be an increase in efficiency, but the standard for legality would focus on the competitive process.[51]

While this sounds appealing at first blush, two concerns arise. The first is that, given that there are multiple beneficiaries of competitive market structures, is the proposal to design enforcement so as to protect each in the most effective manner? If so, then this sounds like a total welfare standard, but it is clear that this is not what the authors want or we would be back to the analysis in Bork's work, which is precisely that which these authors are arguing against. However, it is important to consider how conduct that affects different groups differently is assessed (e.g. a distribution agreement that squeezes suppliers but benefits consumers). For some this scenario is one where the competitive process

---

49   On the economic effects generally, *see* THOMAS PHILIPPON, THE GREAT REVERSAL: HOW AMERICA GAVE UP ON FREE MARKETS (2019), attributing this to more than just lax antitrust enforcement.

50   Marshall Steinbaum & Maurice E. Stucke, *The Effective Competition Standard: A New Standard for Antitrust*, 85 CHI. U. L. REV., 595, 602 (2020).

51   Fox, *supra* note 9, at 1154.

is damaged as soon as the suppliers are squeezed, for this is an indication that the middleman has market power.[52] If this is so then it means that competition enforcement prioritizes the competitive process, even when this leads to inefficient results.[53] This comes very close to the ordoliberal understanding of the role of competition law for which the competitive process matters more than the results.

Second, and relatedly, it seems like the basis upon which beneficial effects occur is a competitive market structure. Some might say brings us back to the SCP paradigm that still to some extent continues to inform merger policy, by which analysis begins by asking if the merger increases concentration above a certain degree and what presumptions of harm arise when a given concentration threshold is met.[54] The concern of the authors with current merger policy is that the market power thresholds set by the Horizontal Merger Guidelines are too high.[55] However, it raises the more general question as to whether the effective competition standard is then only about having a lower threshold for market power, and whether this should be used as a basis for enforcement of all the antitrust prohibitions. Unfortunately, the degree of market power that would suffice to raise concerns is not clearly articulated by those proposing this approach. For example, Steinbaum and Stucke limit themselves to suggesting that direct evidence of market power can be as valuable as indirect evidence but without offering a threshold. From an EU perspective, one of the concerns with the application of the monopolization offense found in section 2 of the Sherman Act is that courts appear to require very high market shares before intervening; the ECJ has held that, under the comparable provision in Article 102 TFEU, a firm is dominant when the market share is 50%, which is at the lower end of what is sufficient in the US to apply the prohibition against monopolization.[56]

A lower threshold for market power would help make the notion of competitive process more concrete in two ways. First, those proposing it would be able to say what real difference there is between their approach and the consumer welfare standard. Second, a lower threshold may be justified by an emphasis on the competitive process without slipping back to an era where agreements between firms with no market power are penalized. This may be illustrated by the *Sylvania* judgment. Here, a producer of TVs whose market share was at 1–2% entered into franchise agreements by which it "limited the number of franchises granted for any given area and required each franchisee to sell his Sylvania products only

---

52 Warren Grimes, *Breaking Out of Consumer Welfare Jail: Addressing the Supreme Court's Failure to Protect the Competitive Process*, 15 Rutgers Bus. L. Rev. 49 (Fall 2020).

53 Steinbaum & Stucke, *supra* note 50, at 604: "substantial lessening of competition suffices for liability. Enforcers and courts need not … balance the harms to one set of stakeholders against the supposed benefits for another."

54 The best account of this paradigm is found in F.M. Scherer & David Ross, Industrial Market Structure and Economic Performance (3d ed. 1990), ch. 1.

55 Steinbaum & Stucke, *supra* note 50, footnote 46.

56 Giorgio Monti, *The Concept of Dominance in Article 82 EC*, 2 Eur. Competition J. 31 (Special Issue) (2006) giving a comparative account on market power thresholds in the EU and US.

from the location or locations at which he was franchised."⁵⁷ A literal reading of the competitive process would condemn this because it hampers intra-brand competition and prevents the entry of additional retailers. However, if those supporting the competitive process approach were to make this claim, then it is unlikely that any policymaker or court would take their claim seriously: surely a firm so small can hardly harm the competitive process in any meaningful way. A market power threshold would however serve to distinguish those vertical restrains that we should be concerned about, and those where we would consider the market power of the manufacturer sufficiently high to warrant scrutiny.

However, if we agree that market power can serve as a first screen to identify possible sources of anticompetitive risk, we should acknowledge that for vertical restraints in the US this is already the law, so supporters of a wider liability rule would have to explain whether they would apply a lower threshold. Would supporters of the competition as a process approach, for example, consider that the *Schwinn* case should not have been overruled? Schwinn had market power as the leading bicycle producer (market share of 22%) and a brand name that "enjoyed superior consumer acceptance and commanded a premium price."⁵⁸ I hope that the answer that supporters of the competition as process would not wish to go this low, but it is something that needs to be explored more fully by its proponents.

To develop this further, consider the discussion about the *Leegin* judgment. As is well-known, the Supreme Court held that minimum RPM agreements should be assessed using the rule of reason. Those championing a recalibration of the antitrust rules discussed in section II above view this as a reasonable judgment.⁵⁹ However this judgment is viewed as flawed by Professor Grimes, for placing the focus on consumer welfare and ignoring "upstream power abuses."⁶⁰ However, when the case returned to the lower courts the plaintiffs were unable to define a market where the manufacturer held market power.⁶¹ Absent such power, it is hard to see how there can be any abuse.

One might agree that the Supreme Court defers too much to the business judgment of the manufacturer, but the question then remains: do the proponents of a competitive process approach propose to condemn all vertical restraints? This seems to be the position taken by Professor Grimes, who suggests that the justification for this is that distributors are a source of innovation and therefore any restraint that stifles their economic freedom should be condemned.⁶²

---

57   Continental T.V., Inc. v. GTE Sylvania, Inc., 433 U.S. 36, 38 (1977).

58   *Id.* at 63, White J concurring and referring to United States v. Arnold, Schwinn & Co., 388 U.S. 365 (1967), which the majority in *Sylvania* overruled.

59   *E.g.*, Gavil & Salop, *supra* note 22.

60   Grimes, *supra* note 52, at 87.

61   PSKS, Inc. v. Leegin Creative Leather Products, 615 F.3d 412 (5th Cir. 2010).

62   Grimes, *supra* note 52, at 87.

This is intriguing: on the one hand, the advantage of giving the retailer greater freedom is that this enhances efficiency, presumably to the benefit of consumers, so that the economic consequences continue to matter. And yet the competitive process approach appeared to be interested in safeguarding the process irrespective, it seemed, of the economic effects. A similar question may be asked of the suggestion that for vertical price and non-price restraints the effective competition standard should opt for a "strong presumption" against these. If there is a presumption, however, we need to have further discussion on what factors may be used to rebut this: is it a showing of overall efficiency?[63] Both of these suggestions on how to reform the law of vertical restraints raise a general question as to whether the difference of view between Chicago and its opponents is between two visions of how efficiency is attained: by allowing manufacturers the freedom to design their distribution agreements or by allowing retailers the freedom to do as they please.

At a high level, the idea of focusing on the competitive process appears inviting. However, unless some limiting principles are built in, it risks forbidding everything. As noted by Justice Brandeis, over a century ago, every contract restrains trade in some way.[64] Analogously, every contract will restrain the competitive process in one way or another: the challenge is to draw a line between restrictions we allow and those we do not. It seems obvious that proponents of the competitive process approach want more aggressive antitrust, but it is not always clear what principles would be used to draw the line between lawful and unlawful restraints.

2. Unilateral conduct and the competitive process standard

The major modern concern in antitrust is in policing the extreme powers held by certain firms, particularly in digital markets. It is therefore useful to see how the proponents of the competitive process approach would recalibrate the regulation of anticompetitive conduct. Here too, the approach taken by Professors Steinbaum and Stucke proves inspiring, for they suggest an application of standards that draws from EU law. As others have noted, for certain forms of monopolization conduct US standards, once seen as the global best practice, are now only applied by the US; the rest of the world has migrated to standards used in the EU.[65]

When it comes to refusals to deal, for example, the proposal is to align the US with the approach taken in the EU. As a result, a refusal to deal by a dominant firm is treated as an abuse if the goods or services are indispensable, the refusal results in the elimination of competition, the refusal prevents the emergence

---

63   Steinbaum & Stucke, *supra* note 50, at 611, footnote 49.

64   Chicago Board of Trade v. United States, 246 U.S. 231, 238 (1918): "Every agreement concerning trade, every regulation of trade, restrains. To bind, to restrain, is of their very essence."

65   Spencer Weber Waller, *Harmonizing Essential Facilities* (2010) 76(3) Antitrust L.J. 741.

of a new product or the improvement of an existing product, and there is no objective justification for the refusal.⁶⁶ While this is definitely more aggressive than the limited scope of the refusal to deal case law in the US, the experience of the European Commission has revealed that even this standard may not go far enough. In the telecommunications sector, for example, the notion of indispensability has been qualified.⁶⁷ And more notably in the *Google Shopping* decision, the Commission was unable to rely on the case law on refusals to deal to handle the competition concern that it had. It will be recalled that the Commission decided that Google gave preference to its vertical search engines at the expense of other rivals offering competing services. Arguably this abuse could have been made to fit the refusals to deal category by indicating that the general search engine was the indispensable service and the denial of fair access to that service was an abuse of dominance. However, the Commission designed a new theory of harm to address this conduct.⁶⁸ The takeaway for the purposes of this paper is that while EU standards may be perceived to be closely aligned to the competitive process standard of antitrust analysis, even some of the wide standards designed by the case law are not capacious enough to address all forms of conduct. The proponents of protecting the competitive process thus need to advocate for something wider if antitrust is to have the impact sought.

On the other hand, the EU standards can at times prove overly aggressive. A good example is found in the judgment in *Post Danmark 2*. The Danish competition authority took issue with a retroactive rebate scheme implemented by Post Danmark in respect of bulk advertising mail. The rebates were offered in response to the entry of competition in that market from postal operators established overseas. The ECJ explained that the test was whether the rebates:

> can produce an exclusionary effect, that is to say whether they are capable, first, of making market entry very difficult or impossible for competitors of the undertaking in a dominant position and, secondly, of making it more difficult or impossible for the co-contractors of that undertaking to choose between various sources of supply or commercial partners.⁶⁹

This dictum is very much in line with the competitive process: note how the ECJ protects both would-be entrants and the customers of the dominant firm.

---

66   Steinbaum & Stucke, *supra* note 50, at 608. This standard is an elegant mix of the rulings on *Oscar Bronner* and *Microsoft*.

67   Niamh Dunne, *Dispensing with Indispensability* (LSE Legal Studies Working Paper No. 15/2019, 2019).

68   Case AT.39740–*Google Search (Shopping)* (Dec. 18, 2017). *See also* Thomas Höppner, *The EU Commission fines a search engine for market dominance by promoting its comparison shopping service (*Google shopping*)*, e-Competitions June 2017, Art. N° 96502 (June 27, 2017).

69   Case C-23/14 Post Danmark A/S v. Konkurrencerådet, EU:C:2015:651, 2 para. 31. *See also* Daniel Muheme & Maria Tsoukala, *The EU Court of Justice rules on issues concerning retroactive rebates and the procedures through which these rebates can be characterized as abusive (*Post Danmark II*)*, e-Competitions October 2015, Art. N° 76553 (Oct. 6, 2015).

On the facts, the ECJ noted that Post Danmark held 95% of the relevant market and that these rebates were likely to make it hard for rivals to outbid it by offering discounts. However, the ECJ then discussed whether the likely anticompetitive effects should be serious or appreciable before condemnation: it held that this was an unnecessary requirement. It reasoned that since the dominant firm already weakened the structure of competition, "any further weakening of the structure of competition may constitute an abuse of a dominant position."[70] This is somewhat concerning, for it risks making dominant firms liable even if the adverse impact on the market is minimal. The question for the supporters of the competitive process is whether this is also the sort of conduct that they would wish to prohibit.

From an EU perspective, some US case law on this issue provides a preferable standard. It is helpful for the purposes of this paper to contrast *Post Danmark 2* with the judgment in *FTC v. McWane*.[71] This judgment is instructive for the present discussion for two reasons: first it suggests that the EU approach is overly broad, and second it reveals that US antitrust already embodies a competitive process standard, at least for some exclusionary conduct. The facts, briefly, were that the dominant producer of domestic pipe fittings required that its distributors buy pipe fittings exclusively from it. This served to exclude smaller manufacturers, many of whom were unable to produce the entire range of pipe fittings that the distributors required.

In setting out the standard by which to test for the legality of these agreements, i.e. determining if the agreement caused anticompetitive harm, the court cited the Microsoft judgment, which held that conduct: "must harm the competitive *process*, and thereby harm consumers. In contrast, harm to one or more *competitors* will not suffice."[72] This statement is problematic for the supporters of the competitive process approach, for it seems that at least some appellate circuits apply this standard rather than a consumer welfare standard. What are supporters of the competitive process are offering as new, if this is already in the case law?

More specifically, the court in *McWane* explained that to satisfy this standard there had to be proof that the contracts served to cause significant foreclosure, and that this harmed competition. The notion of significant foreclosure is one that is missing in the EU approach to similar issues, but which serves to make sense of the competitive process standard. As shown in *McWane*, the exclusivity agreements meant that rivals were unable to make sales to the two largest distributors (who controlled 50–60% of the distribution channels) and were also unable to sell to the third largest. By excluding key dealers, the FTC had

---

70   *Id.*, para. 72.

71   McWane Inc v. Fed. Trade Comm'n, 783 F.3d 814 (11th Cir. 2015).

72   United States v. Microsoft, 253 F.3d 34, 58 (D.C. Cir. 2001), emphasis in the original.

demonstrated that the agreement's foreclosure was significant.[73] In discussing harm to competition, the court focused on the impact that this had on Star, an emerging rival who was unable to grow as a result of the conduct of the defendant. The court did not explore whether the effect of this was to harm consumer welfare.

3. The competitive process: lessons from Professor Fox

We have suggested that those pleading for the use of the competitive process as a standard for diagnosing antitrust infringements have some work to do before the approach is fully convincing: criteria are needed to identify when conduct harms such process. We have suggested that a market power screen may be helpful, but that since this is often already part of the legal assessment, perhaps the threshold could be lower. Furthermore, the question arises whether any harm to any one actor suffices to trigger liability. More generally, those supporting this approach have to explain whether the competitive process is protected, even at the expense of efficiency. This is not to criticize the approach on the merits, but to explain what must be articulated for the proposal to be understood on its terms, and to gauge how significant a difference it would make to the current enforcement paradigm.

In the 1980s, Professor Fox had also sympathized with the competitive process. However, her analysis was more nuanced than that presented above. In brief, there are two steps in her approach. The first is to identify categories of settings where conduct is prohibited (often per se) where there is no clear connection to consumer welfare. The list includes: tying, collective boycotts of a single dealer, RPM, and market divisions among small firms. "The bases of these rights are varied. They reflect concerns for fairness, opportunity, and autonomy for sellers without power. They reflect also the concern that individuals in a democratic society should be relatively free from great aggregations of power, lest those centers of power, however benign and progressive today, exploit them economically or control them politically tomorrow."[74] Furthermore, she claimed that using these rules to keep markets open would afford the possibility of mavericks entering and revolutionizing the industry. Her approach was to base these per se prohibitions on what the Supreme Court had banned in the preceding years. This may be criticized as a somewhat haphazard selection of prohibitions.

The second step was to note that often the competitive process and consumer interests would go hand in hand. However, there may be settings where antitrust may clash with consumer interests. In these contexts, "efficiency should serve as a limiting principle, in the sense that antitrust law should never be applied in a manner that threatens to hurt consumers over the long run."[75] This is an

---

73 *McWane*, 783 F.3d at 837–38.

74 Fox, *supra* note 9, at 1181.

75 *Id.* at 1191.

important qualification, for it recognizes that there are inevitable trade-offs to be made when applying antitrust. The Chicago school viewed these trade-offs as a simple utilitarian calculus, even if this stage is never reached in concrete cases. Professor Fox places the interests of consumers above other aspects of the competitive process. Today's supporters of the economic process approach must also make a policy choice here.

IV. The Inevitability of Legislation

Some, faced with a Supreme Court that continuously sides with defendants, are suggesting new rules, in particular when dealing with firms dominating digital markets.[76] Others consider redrafting the antitrust statutes. For example, a bill in the state of New York, proposing a "Twenty-First Century Anti-Trust Act," contains two provisions to regulate monopoly power. One replicates section 2 of the Sherman Act, while the other draws on Article 102 TFEU, making in unlawful "for any person or persons with a dominant position in the conduct of any business, trade or commerce or in the furnishing of any service in this state to abuse that dominant position."[77] As the brief account in this paper of some EU case law suggests, simply replicating EU standards may not suffice to make the concerns over under-enforcement go away, and may recreate the concerns about over-enforcement. More generally, legislative intervention has been a regular feature of US antitrust history: when faced with gaps in coverage, several statutes have been added to the Sherman Act.[78]

A more precisely framed bill to "reform the antitrust laws to better protect competition in the American economy" has been introduced by Senator Klobuchar; it is worth examining this in some detail, for it echoes the concerns of the counter-revolutionaries and seeks to create statutory language to deliver that which the courts have stifled.[79] We focus here on the way the bill proposes to strengthen enforcement of unilateral conduct, which allows us to see the differences between it and the previous two reform models.

The preamble essentially echoes the position that Professor Fox took in the 1980s:

> antitrust enforcement against anticompetitive exclusionary conduct has been impeded when courts have declined to rigorously examine the facts in favor of relying on inaccurate economic assumptions

---

76   Lina Khan, *The Separation of Platforms and Commerce,* 119(4) COLUMBIA L. REV. 973 (2019), where of the five case studies on structural separation only one draws on an antitrust precedent. Likewise a number of expert reports produced in 2019 advocated legislative intervention. For discussion, *see, Special Advice on Competition Policy for the Digital Era*, 57(2) COMMON MKT. L. REV. 315 (2020).

77   Senate Bill S8700A (N.Y. July 8, 2020), www.nysenate.gov/legislation/bills/2019/s8700/amendment/a; https://legislation.nysenate.gov/pdf/bills/2019/S8700A.

78   Steven C. Salop, *Dominant Digital Platforms: Is Antitrust Up to the Task?*, 130 YALE L. J. F. 563, 586 (2021).

79   The text used here is the first draft of the bill: SIL21191 6C1, 117th Cong. (2021).

that are inconsistent with contemporary economic learning, such as presuming that market power is not durable and can be expected to self-correct, that monopolies can drive as much or more innovation than a competitive market, that above-cost pricing cannot harm competition, and other flawed assumptions.[80]

In addition, and probably equally remarkable, is another passage in the preamble which provides that "nascent or potential rivals–even those that are unprofitable or inefficient–can be an important source of competitive discipline for dominant firms."[81] This statement appears to run counter to the rhetoric of the Supreme Court about the importance of protecting competition and not competitors. In the EU, the Commission had also observed that in certain market contexts unilateral conduct should be prohibited, even when rivals are not as efficient as the dominant undertaking.[82]

The bill then moves on to propose an amendment to the Clayton Act by adding a section on exclusionary conduct. This contains a general standard couched in fairly broad terms (making it unlawful to "engage in exclusionary conduct that presents an appreciable risk of harming competition").[83] What is remarkable, however, are the interpretative subsections that purport to create statutory language to overturn much of the existing antitrust rules.[84] It provides that a finding of a violation may include but does not require that the defendant terminated or altered an existing course of dealing (which eliminates the obstacle that *Trinko* put in place in claims of refusals to deal);[85] that a price was below cost (which eliminates a requirement that sometimes makes rebate cases difficult to bring); that the firm is likely to recoup losses incurred from below-cost pricing (overruling *Brooke Group*); that the conduct of the defendant makes no economic sense apart from its tendency to do harm (eliminating a test that some have proposed is perceived to narrow down the scope of liability considerably); that the risk of harm should be quantified; and that when a defendant operates a multi-sided platform business, the conduct of the defendant presents an appreciable risk of harming competition on more than one side of the multisided platform (thereby quashing the approach in *Amex*).[86] All of these indications

---

80   *Id.*, § 2 (findings and purposes), ¶ 21.

81   *Id.*, ¶ 20.

82   Case C-307/18 Generics (UK) Ltd and others v. Competition and Markets Authority, EU:C:2020:52, para 24. The Commission probably had in mind technology markets where economies of scale and scope make new entry more tricky.

83   Bill SIL21191 6C1, *supra* note 79, § 9.

84   *Id.*, § 9(e).

85   *Verizon v. Trinko*, 540 U.S. 398 (2004). *See also* Frédérique Daudret-John & François Souty, *United States of America: The US Supreme Court rules on the current relationhip between antitrust law and sectoral regulation in the telecommunications sector* (Trinko), CONCURRENCES N° 1–2004, ART. N° 1603 (2004).

86   *Ohio v. American Express Co.*, 138 S.Ct. 2274 (2018). *See also* Irving Scher, *The US Supreme Court rules that "anti-steering" clauses are not anti-competitive on the two-sided credit card market* (American Express), E-COMPETITIONS JUNE 2018, ART. N° 96404 (June 25, 2018).

bring US antitrust into alignment with the approach found in the EU, and more generally in alignment with global standards elsewhere.[87]

As if these major steps were not enough, the bill also proposes inserting a presumption that such a violation takes place when the firm has a market share of 50% or above.[88] Again, this echoes the dominance threshold found in the EU and it adopts the kind of risk-based approach to finding abuse that some of the EU case law has also embraced.[89] This is balanced by allowing the defendant to plead either an efficiency defense or show that, notwithstanding exclusionary conduct on its part, one or more firms have entered the market, thereby eliminating the risk of anticompetitive exclusion. This also echoes the two counter-arguments that the ECJ has constructed in the *Intel* judgment for dominant undertakings.[90]

The bill suggests a skepticism that the common law can evolve gradually away from the current dominant paradigm by seeking to reverse what the counter-revolutionaries see as the excessively lenient approach of the past 40 years. One wonders, however, whether even on the terms proposed by the bill, this will satisfy all antitrust critics. In the EU, following frustration at the slow pace of competition law enforcement in the big tech sector, the Commission has tabled a draft Digital Markets Act in order to have a regulatory tool that allows for speedier and more effective intervention in some digital markets.[91] If the antitrust counter-revolution commences in the US, more radical reforms such as this one might be perceived to be necessary.

V. Conclusion

The purpose of this paper was to discuss what accounts for the inability of US antitrust to reverse course after the Chicago school's revolution. Three factors emerge. The first is that in addition to the factors identified by Professor Fox about the key elements of the Chicago approach (narrow economics and a political vision that trusts markets) the success of the dominant paradigm has been to create reasonable doubt about conviction. The ever more detailed consideration of economic theory in courts makes it easy for defendants to make the judge fearful of wrongful conviction. This, in my view, more that the faith in markets, animates an approach that is friendly to defendants. The second is that the counter-revolutionaries do not present a clear narrative, in particular

---

87   Spencer Weber Waller, *The Omega Man or the Isolation of U.S. Antitrust Law*, 52 CONN. L REV 127 (2020).

88   Bill SIL21191 6C1, *supra* note 79, § 9(c).

89   Case C-23/14 Post Danmark A/S v. Konkurrencerådet, EU:C:2015:651.

90   See discussion in section II above, and more fully in Giorgio Monti, *EU Competition Law and the Rule of Reason Revisited* (TILEC Discussion Paper DP 2020-021).

91   European Commission, Proposal for a Regulation on contestable and fair markets in the digital sector (Digital Markets Act) COM (2020) 842 final.

in wishing to shift from protecting consumer welfare to safeguarding the competitive process, more work is needed to establish criteria by which one can determine what conduct harms this process and what conduct restricts trade but is not harmful. Furthermore, a clear stance should be taken on whether safeguarding the competitive process always has priority over the efficient working of markets: in instances where a balance is to be struck, how is it to be done? A third reflection is that the record in the US courts is not all pro-defendant. There are some judgments where the courts do appear to lean in favor of a more pro-plaintiff antitrust stance. Again, those favoring more aggressive enforcement should examine whether these more progressive judgments (e.g. *3M* and *McWane*) are aligned with their policy prescriptions. These questions have, to some extent, been addressed by the Klobuchar Bill discussed in section IV.

A comparative perspective suggests that tinkering with the standard of proof may prove an appealing strategy to convince courts to move away from existing frameworks, because the choice for judges is no longer between a rule of reason approach where everything matters and doubts can be cast, or a per se approach with the risk of false positives. Rather, contemporary EU case law shows that allocation of the burden of proof can serve to ease the burden on the Commission, while still affording defendants a chance to explain their conduct. In this way, the risk of wrongful conviction can be attenuated by affording the defendant a chance to explain their conduct. On the other hand, a comparative perspective suggests that placing faith in the competitive process may be too hopeful: not only is the notion somewhat fuzzy, but the EU experience also shows that it may not be broad enough to satisfy those demanding more aggressive antitrust. Finally, legislation might prove more decisive in changing the shape of US antitrust, but this might not suffice to address the concerns some have about digital markets, for which the EU is moving beyond antitrust.

By these three pathways for reform (tinkering with burdens of proof, safeguarding the competitive process, legislating undesirable precedent away), we observe that those proposing them are, in Professor Fox's words, seeking to change the perspective and assumptions that shape our thinking about how to preserve well-functioning markets.[92] Let us take these in turn. Perspective is about whether we focus on outcomes or whether we are also concerned about the competitive process. We suggest, however, that this divide is not so much about economic philosophy, but about the basis for liability. In other words: in most settings protecting the competitive process yields the same antitrust outcome as if we were protecting an outcome (consumer or total welfare).[93] The emphasis on process is thus largely about saying that plaintiffs should be entitled to win as soon as they show that the competitive process is harmed, there is no need

---

[92] Fox, *supra* note 20, at 2160.

[93] POSNER *supra* note 5, who also notes that often protecting the competitive process yields positive welfare results.

to require them to show how welfare is reduced. Assumptions are about whether markets work well, whether government antitrust intervention is undesirable and whether Type 2 errors are unproblematic. These are political assumptions, which modern economics has called into question. Shaking free of them, however, calls for a reflection on our social preferences when regulating markets: this is today's major challenge, even beyond antitrust.

In Antitrust We Trust

DAMIEN GERARD[*]
College of Europe and University of Louvain

Abstract

Triggered by references to trust and distrust in private market power and/or government as epistemological devices to rationalize evolving trends in antitrust enforcement, this short paper inquires tentatively into the relationship between antitrust and trust as a social arrangement and the "prime currency of liberal societies." In doing so, it maps the case for a contribution of competition law enforcement to trust in market outcomes and liberal institutions at large and presents supporting considerations drawn from the social sciences literature on the function of trust as a governing mechanism of complex organizations. From there, it questions the distinctiveness of any such contribution and reflects on its potential significance, including in terms of the overall welfare effects of competition law enforcement and its role as part of the social compact. As such, it explores an uncommon facet of the social embeddedness of competition policy.

---

[*] Adjunct Professor, College of Europe and University of Louvain. All views are personal.

Almost 20 years ago, a (very) junior lawyer in the Brussels-based antitrust practice of a prominent US law firm enrolled in what was then known as the "Trade Regulation" program (now "Competition, Innovation, and Information Law Program") at New York University School of Law–the only one of its kind at the time–and was hired as research assistant by Professor Fox while taking part in her seminar. The 10 bucks an hour spent researching footnotes, updating casebooks and proofreading papers were quickly spent at Ben's Pizza or the local Gristedes, but the perk laid of course elsewhere, and the stimulating conversations filling the weekly meetings in Vanderbilt Hall resonate until today.

If the aim of the process of education is to create autonomous learners, Eleanor Fox has been the one enabling me, and many others, to discover or rediscover the language of antitrust, to understand its relationship to social welfare, but also, and more fundamentally, to get confronted with a particular way to articulate ideas and to challenge the rationales behind legal rules and policy assumptions and evolutions, thereby opening up a wider range of possibilities in producing knowledge. For that, I will be forever grateful, as I told her when in June 2016, Ioannis Lianos and I organized a symposium in Brussels honoring Eleanor Fox the scholar: the resilient producer of original knowledge for half a century.

To do so, we invited colleagues from around the world to reengage with specific strands of Professor Fox's body of work from their own vantage point in an attempt to assess its distinctiveness, to distill its essence, to uncover its underlying trends both from a substantive and methodological point of view. In laying the ground for this exercise, five overall themes were identified as cutting across that body of work: (i) the role of antitrust in making markets work for people by curbing inequality, discrimination, and barriers, and promoting development; (ii) the governance of antitrust enforcement in a global world; (iii) the ideological premises of normative prescriptions about antitrust enforcement; (iv) the promotion of comparative competition law analysis with a view to fostering understanding and achieving convergence; and (v) the texture of antitrust as a set of norms enforced in particular institutional contexts and integrating the teachings of economics.

Together, these topics offer a roadmap into the most intricate issues and most relevant questions debated in the field of antitrust enforcement over the past 50 years. Yet, each of them also encapsulates a particular dimension of the trade-off between equity and efficiency that lies at the core of the social arrangements governing liberal democracies–hence the focus of the volume published as a result of the symposium on the intellectual underpinnings of the interactions between "equity" and "efficiency" as they materialize in the context of competition policy.[1]

---

1   RECONCILING EFFICIENCY AND EQUITY: A GLOBAL CHALLENGE FOR COMPETITION POLICY 462 (Damien Gerard & Ioannis Lianos eds., 2019).

The unusual and very tentative focus of this short paper lies elsewhere, however, on the interplay between competition policy and trust as a social arrangement, i.e., not the particular legal construct that gave its name to the discipline of antitrust.

I. Power, Trust, and Antitrust

The intuition behind the present contribution originates in a recent short piece by Eleanor Fox entitled "Power: Trust and Distrust," which reviews the history of antitrust enforcement in the US, with reference to the European Union, through the lens of the dynamic relationships between three inflection perspectives:

> 1) a pervasive concern with the economic power of corporations and a strong policy goal to harness their power for the good of the people; 2) a commitment to laissez-faire; keeping government out of the business of business; a belief that the free market unhampered by governments (apart from cartels, even antitrust) will deliver the most welfare to people; and 3) (for which we stare the coronavirus in the face) industrial policy: a belief or acceptance of government's ascendant role, which it may fulfill in the form of government/big business partnerships, removal of antitrust constraints, commands to produce, commands to price low, commands to stop competing; a skepticism that the market, even with antitrust and a social welfare net, can deliver what the people need.[2]

In essence, this crisp analysis captures a tale of trust and distrust of private economic power as "a narrative of history repeating itself with a difference," illustrated by the direction of antitrust enforcement. It concludes with a word of faith and caution, namely that competition policy is "one of the best tools for delivery" when it comes to containing power over markets, but that competition agencies worldwide "may or may not prevail on their governments" to recognize the virtues of antitrust enforcement.[3]

Beyond the arguments developed in that paper, personal research interests prompted a–still nascent–reflection on the potential role of antitrust as a discipline, in arbitrating between reliance on power and trust as ways to structure market-based interactions (and, by extension, to govern society). That attraction was fueled by frequent references in speeches by EU Commissioner for Competition Margrethe Vestager to competition policy as a vehicle to safeguard

---

2 Eleanor M. Fox, *Power: Trust and Distrust*, Concurrentialiste, Apr. 6, 2020.

3 At the end, Fox advises wisely to "read again Giuliano Amato's book, *Antitrust and the Bounds of Power: The Dilemma of Liberal Democracy in the History of the Market* (1997), and Mario Monti's keynote speech at the American Antitrust Institute in June 2009, 'Competition Authorities of the World, Unite!'."

trust in markets and society as a whole, particularly by ensuring fair outcomes. The most notable of such speeches is entitled "How Competition Can Build Trust in Our Societies" and articulates the following reasoning:[4]

1. Trust is "the most important currency our societies have" for "without trust, everything we do becomes harder" (so that "we can't live our lives today without trusting in strangers"), whereas "as our societies grow, trust gets more important than ever–and harder to achieve" ("especially when new technologies change the way we interact");

2. Naturally "our societies are much more than the market–but lack of trust in the market can rub off on the society as such–so we lose trust in our society." This is notably because "we do have to deal with the market every single day" and if "we feel cheated, ignored, taken for granted by the market," i.e., "not treated fairly," "that undermines our trust in the society around us" and "can give people a sense that the world isn't fair" (and "when people have the sense that markets aren't listening to their needs, then we shouldn't be surprised if they start to look for radical alternatives");

3. In turn, "real and fair competition has a vital role to play in building the trust we need to make the best of our societies" and "that starts with enforcing our competition rules" because "sometimes, for business, competition can be inconvenient" or, put otherwise, "the temptation to avoid competition is powerful" whereas "competition rules mean that companies can't misuse their power to undermine competition" thereby "making sure that greed and fear don't overcome fairness" (for "when greed and fear are linked to power, they create a dangerous mix");

4. Moreover, "together with regulation, competition rules … can help to make sure that new technologies treat people fairly and that everyone can compete on a level playing field," which "can help us build the trust we need so real innovation can flourish."[5]

In a nutshell, Vestager put forward that competition as policed by competition law enforcement enables fair market outcomes and thereby, given the ubiquitous nature of the market and associated interactions, contributes to nurture trust in the institutions of liberal societies inasmuch as they rely on trust as their prime currency. These are bold and candid claims, yet they resonate with sophisticated arguments developed some time ago in the realm of social sciences on the function of power and trust.

---

4   Margrethe Vestager, How Competition can Build Trust in our Societies, TED Talk, New York (Sept. 20, 2017). For an earlier version of the argument, *see* Margrethe Vestager, Restoring Trust in our Economy, Speech in Copenhagen (Jan. 27, 2017). *See also* M. Vestager, Fairness and Competition, Speech at GCLC Annual Conference, Brussels (Jan. 25, 2018).

5   For more recent iterations of that part of the argument, *see* Margrethe Vestager, Building trust in technology, EPC Webinar, Digital Clearinghouse, (Oct. 29, 2020); and Margrethe Vestager, Trust in the Digital Decade, Speech at Euractiv event (June 21, 2021).

II. Trust as a Social Arrangement

In one of the most well-known monographs in the field, Niklas Luhmann presented trust and power as ways of addressing conditions of social complexity.[6] Yet Luhmann's core claim is that "trust constitutes a more effective form of complexity reduction" than power, notably because "where there is trust there are increased possibilities for experience and action,"[7] and thus forms of cooperation. Put otherwise, "trust, by the reduction of complexity, discloses possibilities for action which would have remained improbable and unattractive without trust–which would not, in other words, have been pursued."[8] However, whereas it allows consolidating expectations and lowering the unpredictability of change, trust "remains a risk undertaking" that therefore has to be "learned,"[9] i.e., it is more likely to emerge when certain preconditions are met. Among these conditions, Luhmann refers to the familiarity of the trustee, vital in situations of interpersonal trust, knowledge of partners' motivational structures and related incentives, but also legal arrangements inasmuch as they "lend special assurance to particular expectations."[10] All these clues employed to form trust do not eliminate risk but make it manageable and "serve as a springboard for the leap into uncertainty, although bounded and structured."[11]

Interestingly, on the relation between trust and law, Luhmann considers that "various legal regulations can be subsumed under the notion of 'safeguard of trust'," because "trust can only come about thanks to the limitations of risk afforded by the law," yet also "the notion of trust lies at the basis of law as a whole" as a form of social framework organizing the reliance on other men.[12] Eventually, Luhmann recognizes that trust finds fertile ground in relations characterized by a relative persistence and reciprocal dependencies for the "overriding consideration is that one is going to meet again" and, in that regard, finds that the possibility of hierarchical intervention and sanction is capable of stabilizing interactions "also of those between equals."[13]

---

6 NIKLAS LUHMANN, TRUST & POWER 208 (1979).

7 *Id.* at 8. Conceptually, Luhmann's argument is that by increasing possibilities for experience and action, trust increases the complexity of the social system in question, thereby enabling it to more closely match the complexity of its underlying environment and thereby strengthen its ability to manage/simplify that complexity without being overwhelmed by it or sacrificing it. Moreover, for Luhmann, the benefits of trust have increased with modernity "as the world becomes more complex and uncertain–a risk society" (as discussed by John Braithwaite, *Institutionalizing Distrust, Enculturating Trust in* TRUST AND GOVERNANCE 350 (Valerie Braithwaite & Margaret Levi eds., 1998).

8 *Id.* at 25.

9 *Id.* at 27.

10 *Id.* at 33.

11 *Id.*

12 *Id.* at 35.

13 *Id.* at 37. On the value of norms and sanctions to stabilize trust, *see also* RUSSELL HARDIN, TRUST & TRUSTWORTHINESS 30, 40, 46 (2002).

Building on these considerations, Luhmann then introduces a distinction between "personal trust" and "system trust."[14] Personal trust corresponds to personal interactions and amounts to a "generalized expectation that the other will handle his freedom, his disturbing potential for diverse action, in keeping with his personality which he has presented and made socially visible."[15] System trust, on the other hand, relates to trust in social systems designed to manage highly differentiated interactions; it relies on continuous experience with functional processes that are also "generalized media of communication" (such as money).[16] In turn, system trust is deemed to be more diffuse but also more resilient because it "does not always have to be learned anew from scratch,"[17] even though it increases the difficulty of control, which "demands increasing expert knowledge" and "must be built [internally] into the systems which require trust."[18] While trust generally "accumulates as a kind of capital which opens up more opportunities for more extensive action but which must be continually used and tended,"[19] system trust is also inherently reflexive for it "builds upon the fact that others also trust and that this common possession of trust becomes conscious" or, in other words, its rational basis lies "in the trust placed in the trust of other people."[20]

However, if trust is self-reinforcing, so is distrust, and social systems therefore need to set up mechanisms to prevent distrust from gaining the upper hand and escalade into a destructive force.[21] Though the multitude of possibilities "makes it fruitless to search for general formulae," these "safeguards against the breakdown of trust" should essentially be designed to stabilize expectations for only once that stability is structurally guaranteed is it possible to "do away with the safety precautions for particular actions in specific situations."[22] In turn, trust is also reliant on "inner resources available [to the truster] which are not structurally tied up" to the system and which "in the case of a disappointment of trust" can be put into action and "take over the burden of the reduction of complexity and the solving of problems."[23] Along these lines, others have

---

14 In later works, Luhmann also uses the term "confidence" to refer to "system trust" (*see, e.g.*, Niklas Luhmann, "Familiarities, Confidence, Trust: Problems and Alternatives" *in* TRUST: MAKING AND BREAKING COOPERATIVE RELATIONS 94 (Diego Gambetta ed., 1988). In that regard, though wary of an "easy analogy from individual to institutional issues that abstracts from the differences in individual-level and institutional-level constraints and possibilities," Hardin also supports conceptual relations between individual-level and institutional-level trust "even though different kinds of data or evidence are commonly relevant at different levels" (HARDIN, *supra* note 13, at 22).

15 Luhmann, *supra* note 6, at 39.

16 *Id.* at 55.

17 *Id.* at 57.

18 *Id.*

19 *Id.* at 64.

20 *Id.* at 69.

21 *Id.* at 75.

22 *Id.* at 83–84.

23 *Id.* at 80.

explained how "system power" in the form of collectively binding arrangements constraining the temptation of opportunistic behavior can assist in generating "system trust," that is "to encourage social actors to trust each other on the grounds of collectively binding rules which reduce the risk of trust," while these arrangements can be enforced through institutionalized threats of collective sanctions or more informal mechanisms, including reputation costs.[24]

III. Antitrust Pro-Trust?

However succinct, the above summary of Luhmann's account of the social function and requirements of trust appears to give some theoretical support to an argument presenting antitrust enforcement as a trust-building endeavor contributing to the strengthening of the inner fabric of liberal societies, notably as a form of economic regulation aimed at limiting risk and stabilizing expectations on the outcomes of market-based interactions, against the background of institutionalized threats of collective sanctions. In turn, the ubiquity of competition laws, their transversal nature, open texture, default application, far-reaching sanctions, and political salience can probably distinguish them from other forms of economic regulation in terms of overall social impact, relevance, and therefore trust-building potential. Subsequently, any distinct ability of "trust-busters" to act as "trust-builders" may add to the range of diffuse "welfare" effects more traditionally associated with antitrust enforcement.

In that respect, when contemplating potentially unaccounted yet socially desirable effects of competition law enforcement, stimulating thoughts arise from the unmistakable connection between trust and cooperation, which lies at the basis of numerous discussions of trust in organizations and the relation between trust and governance.[25] For example, echoing considerations formulated in Section II, Kramer, Brewer, and Hanna underline how "trust lubricates cooperation" and how "cooperation breeds trust," i.e., the existence of a mutually reinforcing relation between trust and cooperation at the level of complex organizations.[26] Hence, when considered through the medium of trust, the pervasive opposition between competition and cooperation would seem worthwhile revisiting inasmuch as competition law enforcement may rather be conceived as part of the core tenets enabling–rather than hindering–cooperative social interactions to unfold at system level. Conversely, attempts to limit the reach of competition or to interfere with competitive outcomes in the name of cooperation or by

---

24 Christel Lane & Reinhard Bachmann, *Co-operation in Inter-Firm Relations in Britain and Germany: The Role of Social Institutions*, 48 BRIT. J. OF SOC. 232 (1997).

25 *See, e.g.*, numerous accounts included in TRUST IN ORGANIZATIONS–FRONTIERS OF THEORY AND RESEARCH 429 (Roderick M. Kramer & Tom R. Tyler eds., 1996), and TRUST AND GOVERNANCE 386 (Valerie Braithwaite & Margaret Levi eds., 1998).

26 Roderick M. Kramer, Marilynn B. Brewer and Benjamin A. Hanna, "Collective Trust and Collective Action–The Decision to Trust as a Social Decision" *in* Kramer & Tyler *supra* note 25, at 379.

"commands" rooted in some distrust of–even policed by–market outcomes, as Fox put it in the piece referred to in Section I, may well have consequences beyond their direct impact on supply and demand or innovation dynamics, thus increasing the social costs of such disruptions.

Trust as a prime currency of complex, multi-layered, liberal societies also sheds a specific light on the role of competition policy as part of the core social compact governing these societies. In the European Union, competition law has long been considered part and parcel of economic constitution, i.e. the body of "legal rules that are essential for establishing the preferred economic system," one of economic freedom, and it is viewed historically in certain Member States as an essential and integral part of the welfare state.[27] However, the evolution toward a "more economics-based" interpretation of competition law in the European economic constitution has recently been criticized, in particular from the perspective of an economic constitution serving a social market economy.[28] A trust-enabling approach to competition policy may further enrich that perspective while building on the original role ascribed to competition rules as part of the market integration enterprise, including as a "safeguard of trust" between Member States.[29] However, the connection between trust, antitrust and the fabric of liberal societies is likely to resonate beyond the EU and may serve to enrich the (albeit contested) discourse surrounding the benefits of competition policy.

Finally, but by no means exhaustively, exploring the relationship between trust and antitrust naturally invites reconsideration of the meaning and reach of fairness, for it is by achieving fair market outcomes that competition law enforcement would contribute to safeguarding trust in society, according to Vestager's views summarized in Section I.[30] Notably, for Vestager, anticompetitive effects are unfair because they ultimately deprive consumers of the power to arbitrate the marketplace.[31] By extension, competition law enforcement as governed by established substantive standards and procedural rules contributes to ensuring faith in the allocative functions of free markets, conceived as institutions of liberal societies. In that sense, fairness is not conceived as an operational principle capable of determining the outcome of individual enforcement actions, but as an expression of confidence in the outcome of competitive market interactions. As such, it endows competition law enforcement with the preservation of a social commitment to free markets by reconciling individual and collective

---

27 For a discussion *see, e.g.,* Josef Drexl, *The European Economic Constitution and Its Relevance to the Ordo-Liberal Model*, 25(4) REV. INTL. DE DROIT. ÉCON. 419 (2011).

28 *See, e.g.,* Anna Gerbrandy, *Rethinking Competition Law within the European Economic Constitution* 51(1) J. COMMON MKT. STUD. 127 (2019).

29 *See* SPAAK REPORT (Apr. 21, 1956). For a general conceptualisation of the European integration process as an exercise of trust-building and nurturing of cooperative interactions in international relations, *see, e.g.,* ANDREW H. KYDD, TRUST AND MISTRUST IN INTERNATIONAL RELATIONS, 304 (2005).

30 For a collection of essays discussing the resurgence of references to fairness in competition policy discourses, see DAMIEN GERARD ET AL., FAIRNESS IN EU COMPETITION POLICY : SIGNIFICANCE AND IMPLICATIONS 184 (2020).

31 See Vestager, Fairness and Competition, *supra* note 4.

rationality, i.e., each entrepreneur's efforts to maximize profits, on the one hand, and the welfare of society at large, on the other hand. To that extent, fair competition may entail boundaries to profit maximization strategies beyond which these are considered socially unacceptable by reference to certain standards of justice, as articulated in antitrust principles and applied by means of an array of legal tests and enforcement rules. In turn, the social embeddedness of competition law enforcement may explain and justify the particular sensitivity of cases involving the ownership and use of specific rights and resources granted by society (such as statutory monopolies, IP rights, or public compensation in general) or dealings by market players, having achieved levels of prominence making them socially unavoidable within the boundaries of justiciable competition law principles.

*

Triggered by references to trust and distrust in private market power and/or government as epistemological devices to rationalize evolving trends in antitrust enforcement, this short paper has tentatively inquired into the relationship between antitrust and trust as a social arrangement and the prime currency of liberal societies. In doing so, it first sought to map the case for a contribution of competition law enforcement to trust in market outcomes and liberal institutions at large by structuring various statements originating in speeches by EU Commissioner for Competition, Margrethe Vestager. It subsequently attempted to relate that case to considerations drawn from the social sciences literature on the function of trust as a governing mechanism of complex organizations, by relying on the work of Niklas Luhmann. From there, the paper questioned the distinctiveness of any contribution of antitrust to fostering or safeguarding "system trust" and reflected on its potential significance, including in terms of overall welfare effects of antitrust enforcement and its role as part of the social compact. As such, it carried no other ambition than to advance the author's own intellectual curiosity into the social embeddedness and relevance of competition policy, as initially and continuously nourished over the years by the scholarship of a formidable mentor in the person of Eleanor Fox.

The Goals of Competition Law Debate and Competition Policy for Labor Markets

DARRYL BIGGAR,[*] ALLAN FELS,[**] ALBERTO HEIMLER[***]
Australian Competition Commission | University of Melbourne
Italian National School of Government

Abstract

In recent years, both academics and competition enforcers have addressed emerging anticompetitive practices in labor markets. But, the development of a coherent competition policy in this area requires us to confront an old debate: What is the economic foundation of competition law? We argue that the consumer welfare standard is unable to provide a rationale for most enforcement actions in labor markets, since consumers typically benefit from any reduction in labor costs. An often-proposed alternative (the "protection of the competitive process standard") lacks a foundation in economic welfare principles and is unable to provide a guide for solving possible trade-offs among alternative objectives that often arise in this area. We suggest that a newly emerging approach, known as the transactions cost approach to competition law offers promise as a credible alternative foundation for competition policy in labour markets and other antitrust markets more generally.

---

[*] Special Economic Adviser, Australian Competition and Consumer Commission (ACCC). The views expressed here are those of the authors and not those of the ACCC.

[**] Professorial Fellow, University of Melbourne and former Chairman, ACCC.

[***] Professor of Economics, Italian National School of Government (Scuola Nazionale dell'Amministrazione), Rome, Italy, and Chairman, Working Party 2 of the OECD Competition Committee.

I. Introduction

In recent years there has been a dramatic increase in interest in the application of competition law to labor markets.[1] This is a positive development. For too long, labor markets have been seen as "off-limits" to competition enforcers. The exercise of market power in labor markets has significant potential to harm workers, to discourage investment in education and innovation, and to discourage labor market mobility. Reinvigoration of competition enforcement in labor markets is being seen as a tool for addressing declining wages and increasing inequality. We are sure that Eleanor Fox would approve.

The first step in the reinvigoration of antitrust enforcement in the context of labor markets is the articulation of a clear competition policy for labor markets. Several recent papers have sought to do just that.[2] However, in developing a competition policy for labor markets, antitrust economists must confront, once again, the question of the economic goals of competition policy. These issues, which are always present in competition policy analysis, particularly come to the fore when considering competition policy in input markets. The renewed interest in competition policy in labor markets re-opens old debates–debates to which Eleanor Fox herself has contributed.

Until recently, the conventional wisdom among most competition scholars was that competition law and policy seeks to promote some form of "consumer welfare." The term is usually understood to refer to the welfare of the buyer side of the market. The consumer welfare standard has served the antitrust community well for several decades, but in recent years has come under sustained attack.[3] This loss of confidence has arisen, in part, from concerns that an exclusive focus on the downstream or buyer side of the market has the potential to overlook severe anticompetitive harm in upstream or seller markets[4]–precisely

---

1 See, e.g., OECD, *Competition Concerns in Labour Markets–Background Note* (DAF/COMP(2019)2, 2019); Herbert J. Hovenkamp, *Competition Policy for Labour Markets* (Faculty Scholarship at Penn Law 2090, 2019), https://scholarship.law.upenn.edu/faculty_scholarship/2090; Célia Baye & Francesca Arduini, *Labour markets: a blind spot for merger control?* OXERA (Sept. 30, 2019), www.oxera.com/agenda/labour-markets-a-blind-spot-for-merger-control/; Ioannis Lianos, et al., *Re-thinking the competition law/labour law interaction: Promoting a fairer labour market*, 10(3) EUR. LAB. L.J. 291 (2019); Cristina Volpin, *Competition enforcement could help labour markets function better*, OECD ON THE LEVEL (Nov. 26, 2019), https://oecdonthelevel.com/2019/11/26/competition-enforcement-could-help-labour-markets-function-better/.

2 See, e.g., Eric A. Posner et al., *Antitrust Remedies for Labor Markets*, 132 HARV. L. REV. 536. (2018); José Azar et al., *Antitrust and Labor Market Power*, ECONOMICS FOR INCLUSIVE PROSPERITY (May 2019) https://econfip.org/policy-brief/antitrust-and-labor-market-power/.

3 See, e.g., Lina M. Khan, *Amazon's Antitrust Paradox* 126(3) YALE L.J. 564, 710 (2017); Prof. Carl Shapiro, Opening Statement to the Senate Judiciary Committee, Subcommittee on Antitrust, Consumer Protection and Consumer Rights: The Consumer Welfare Standard in Antitrust: Outdated, or a Harbor in a Sea of Doubt? (Dec. 13, 2017), https://faculty.haas.berkeley.edu/shapiro/consumerwelfarestandard.pdf; Renata Hesse, Acting Asst. Att'y Gen., Antitrust Division, Opening Remarks at 2016 Global Antitrust Enforcement Symposium: And Never the Twain Shall Meet? Connecting Popular and Professional Visions for Antitrust Enforcement (Sept. 20, 2016), www.justice.gov/opa/speech/acting-assistant-attorney-general-renata-hesse-antitrust-division-delivers-opening; Tim Wu, *The "Protection of the Competitive Process" Standard* (Columbia Pub. Law Research Paper No. 14-612, 2018), https://scholarship.law.columbia.edu/faculty_scholarship/2290.

4 Unless, that is, those harms lead to anticompetitive effects downstream.

the domain in which labor markets fall. It does not seem right to begin our analysis of competition policy in labor markets by applying an economic standard that essentially neglects the economic consequences of anticompetitive actions in input markets upstream.

To many economists, it seems more natural to conduct competition policy analysis using the same concept of total welfare or total surplus that applies throughout the economic analysis of public policy. This approach identifies the key economic harm from the exercise of market power as the loss in welfare known as deadweight loss. Over the years, many highly regarded economists have argued that competition decision-makers should seek to apply a concept of total economic welfare in all areas of competition policy analysis.[5] All of the recent academic papers exploring the application of competition policy to labor markets implicitly or explicitly adopt a "total welfare" approach.[6]

However, there is a fundamental problem: competition scholars recognize that competition authorities do not behave as though the promotion of total economic welfare is their primary concern.[7] In part, this is because the law itself prevents them from doing so: especially in the context of the EU, the wording of the competition law is not able to interpreted as though the promotion of total welfare is the fundamental goal. If competition agencies do not pursue total economic welfare in their other enforcement activities, why should we expect them to do so in the context of labor markets?

Perhaps there is another way. Eleanor Fox, in her own contribution to the goals of competition law debate, argued that there is a substantial consensus around the view that we want competition law to deliver "robust markets." Eleanor seems to have favored an objective similar to the "protection-of-the-competitive-process" standard.[8]

But, as a goal for competition law, the objective of "protecting the competitive process" leaves most economists uneasy. In the conventional welfarist approach to public policy, competition is not an end in itself; it is a means to an end. That end is the promotion of some concept of economic welfare. By abandoning a total welfare framework, the protection-of-the-competitive-process standard eschews any ability to make trade-offs between competing objectives. In our view, these flaws are material.

---

5   *See, e.g.*, Joseph Farrell & Michael L. Katz, *The Economics of Welfare Standards in Antitrust*, 2(3) COMPETITION POL'Y INT'L 3 (2006); Dennis W. Carlton, *Does Antitrust Need to be Modernized?*, 21(3) J. ECON. PERSPECTIVES, 155 (2007).

6   *See*, Posner et al., *supra* note 2; Hovenkamp, *supra* note 1.

7   Kenneth Heyer (2012) *Welfare Standards and Merger Analysis: Why Not The Best?*, 8 COMPETITION POL'Y INT'L, 146; Farrell & Katz, *supra* note 5.

8   *See* Eleanor M. Fox (2012) *Against Goals*, 81(5) FORDHAM L. REV. 2157.

How should we as economists proceed? In our view, there is a resolution to this quandary. For the reasons set out, we believe that a newly emerging approach–known as the transactions cost approach to competition law–offers promise as a credible economic foundation for competition law.

This paper does not seek a full elaboration of competition policy for labor markets based in the transaction cost approach–such an elaboration is beyond its scope. Instead, we merely seek to turn a spotlight on the economic foundation for competition policy, particularly in the context of labor markets. The objective is merely to highlight the issues that must be resolved if we are to place a competition policy for labor markets on a sound footing, and suggest how the transactions cost approach to competition law can resolve those issues.

II. An Economic Foundation for Competition Policy in Labor Markets

What, exactly, is the economic foundation for competition policy? This question is, of course, fundamental to all competition policy analysis. As Bork has observed: "Antitrust policy cannot be made rational until we are able to give a firm answer to one question: What is the point of the law–what are its goals? Everything else follows from the answer we give ... Only when the issue of goals has been settled is it possible to frame a coherent body of substantive rules."[9] As we will see, this question is particularly important in the context of competition policy in input markets.

1. Consumer welfare and input markets

Until relatively recently there was widespread acceptance among antitrust scholars that competition policy sought to promote some concept of "consumer welfare." This view, which dates back to the work of Robert Bork, argues that the consumer interest (or, at least, the interest of the buyer side of the market) should be the ultimate arbiter of anticompetitive behavior.[10]

More formally, the consumer welfare standard asserts that, in assessing whether or not a particular action is anticompetitive (i.e., in breach of competition law), attention should be paid to the impact on downstream consumers. If consumers are not left worse off, the practice is deemed to be benign, if not actually efficient or procompetitive. Heyer's so-called First Theorem of Antitrust is summarized as follows: "If consumers are hurt by the merger, it is anticompetitive and should

---

9 ROBERT H. BORK, THE ANTITRUST PARADOX (1978).

10 In practice there is considerable debate over what exactly Bork intended by the term consumer welfare, and, more importantly, how we should interpret the term today.

be blocked. If consumers benefit, the merger is procompetitive and should be allowed."[11] Hovenkamp introduces the consumer welfare standard as follows:

> Antitrust law in many jurisdictions defines its consumer welfare goal in terms of low consumer prices. For example, mergers are challenged when they threaten to cause a price increase from reduced competition in the post-merger market. While the consumer welfare goal is under attack in some circles, it remains the most widely expressed goal of antitrust policy in the United States.[12]

The consumer welfare standard provided a valuable organizing principle for what was previously seen by many economists as a jumble of potentially contradictory legal decisions. Following its advocacy by Bork, the concept of consumer welfare gained widespread favor, especially in the later part of the twentieth century.

Despite its popularity, the consumer welfare standard has several fundamental flaws. First, and perhaps foremost, the consumer welfare standard, with its exclusive focus on the buyer side of the market, seems particularly ill-suited to analysis of competition issues in input (or supplier) markets. On a strict consumer welfare standard, market power exercised by dominant buyers in labor markets (or other input markets) is at worst benign, and is possibly beneficial, for downstream consumers.[13] This is particularly a problem for scholars who seek to develop competition principles in labor markets.

This problem with the consumer welfare has been a central focus of the critiques by advocates of the "hipster antitrust" movement. That movement argues that the consumer welfare standard potentially blinds competition enforcers to harmful anticompetitive action by dominant buyers against the suppliers of inputs. Central to their concern is the alleged actions of dominant online platforms, such as Amazon, against their suppliers.[14]

Indeed, as Posner, Weyl and Naidu point out, the exercise of market power by a dominant buyer in labor markets might be considered procompetitive: "wage suppression even as it hurts workers, at least benefits consumers."[15] Azar, Marinescu and Steinbaum emphasize that the focus on the consumer welfare standard "has overlooked harm to workers and monopsony power in labor

---

11 Heyer, *supra* note 7.

12 Hovenkamp, *supra* note 1.

13 *E.g.*, "Buyer power may have procompetitive benefits. For example, buyer power may place a firm in a better negotiating position, incentivizes supplier firms to be more competitive, which in turn may result in lower prices and other benefits for consumers," Andries Le Grange & Nabeela Edris, *Competition authorities seek to regulate "buyer power"* (Apr. 25, 2018), www.lexology.com/library/detail.aspx?g=d4e6cc7a-e686-4bc6-89bc-b317fda0f3c5 (2018).

14 Khan, *supra* note 3.

15 Posner et al., *supra* note 2.

markets." These authors conclude: "The existing antitrust enforcement regime, based as it is on the consumer welfare standard, is inadequate to the question of policing anticompetitive structure and conduct in labour markets."[16]

Hovenkamp makes the same point. Anticompetitive restraints in labor markets might result in *lower* prices to consumers, which should be promoted under the consumer welfare standard.

> Focusing entirely on [output] price makes it awkward to work the supply side of markets into debates about consumer welfare. Labor markets are a notable example. Labor appears in the market as suppliers, not as purchasers. While consumers-as-consumers benefit from lower prices, combating restraints in labor markets generally focuses on wage suppression. That is, today the principal problem of competition policy in labor markets is wages that are too low, not those that are too high.[17]

In seeking to develop a sound competition policy for an input market–in this case, the labor market–the consumer welfare standard is, at best, out of place. We cannot develop sound competition principles for labor markets by starting with an economic approach that asserts that the exercise of market power by a dominant firm in labor markets is benign or even procompetitive.

There are other fundamental problems with the consumer welfare standard: Perhaps most troubling for economists, the consumer welfare standard is inconsistent with conventional economic welfare concepts. According to standard textbook analysis, economic policy should seek to promote some concept of *total* economic welfare, such as the conventional economic notion of total surplus (the sum of producers' surplus and consumers' surplus). The consumer welfare concept, to the extent that it neglects the welfare of the seller side of the market, is inconsistent with these conventional welfare principles.

Moreover, competition enforcers do not, in practice, behave as though "consumer welfare" is their primary concern. Many antitrust scholars have pointed out that a literal application of the consumer welfare standard would exempt anticompetitive practices on the buyer side of the market, such as merger to monopsony, as long as those practices did not result in harm to consumers.[18] This is inconsistent with the way that the majority of competition enforcers around the world behave. As the OECD observes, competition enforcement in practice is consistent with the view that competition law "is applicable to monopsony

---

16   Azar, et al., *supra* note 2, at 3.

17   Hovenkamp, *supra* note 1.

18   Carlton, *supra* note 5, at 158: "if only consumers matter, then a buying cartel should be perfectly legal and indeed should be encouraged." Louis Kaplow & Carl Shapiro, *Antitrust*, *in* HANDBOOK OF LAW AND ECONOMICS 1168 (A. Mitchell Polinsky & Steve Shavell eds., 2007): "If only consumer welfare mattered, increases in buyer power through horizontal mergers and otherwise might be praised, not condemned."

power even where there is no harm to consumers downstream, under analogous legal standards as those of product markets."[19] In any case, as with the total welfare standard, the competition laws themselves, especially in the EU, do not admit an interpretation that promoting consumer welfare is their primary goal.

In our view, the flaws in the consumer welfare standard set out above are serious. These flaws have increasingly been highlighted by the hipster antitrust movement. As Tim Wu has observed: "The good faith version of the consumer welfare standard in antitrust has been ... an ambitious and even worthy experiment, but ultimately a project that has failed on its own terms."[20] If we are to argue for enhanced competition law enforcement in labor markets, we must replace the consumer welfare standard. But, with what should we replace it?

2. Total welfare as the foundation of competition policy

As economists, the most natural economic foundation for competition policy is the same welfarist foundation that is used throughout all of public policy analysis–the concept of total welfare. Many highly respected economists have argued that, when it comes to competition policy, governments and courts should seek to maximize a concept of total economic welfare, usually reflected in the sum of producers' surplus and consumers' surplus.[21]

Importantly, this approach is adopted in all the recent papers arguing for stricter competition law enforcement in labor markets. For example, Posner, Weyl and Naidu argue that the exercise of market power by a monopsonistic labor-hirer leads to a reduction in the wage, and a reduction in the volume of labor hired, leading to a reduction in welfare in form of the deadweight loss.[22] The implicit (if not explicit) position of Posner et al. is that competition enforcers should seek to promote the textbook concept of total economic welfare, by minimizing the harm known as deadweight loss.

Similarly, Hovenkamp argues that competition policy should focus exclusively on output, not price.

> We would do better ... to define [the goal of competition law] in terms of output rather than price. Competition policy should strive

---

19 OECD, *supra* note 1, at 34. Hovenkamp, *supra* note 1, at 6, emphasizes that the merger provisions of the Clayton Act "apply to any merger whose effects may be substantially to lessen competition or create a monopoly in any line of commerce, not distinguishing buyer from seller effects." Similarly, the EU Merger Regulation refers to both (upstream) suppliers and (downstream) users.

20 Wu, *supra* note 3.

21 Some authors argue that Robert Bork, while using the term "consumer welfare," was actually referring to total welfare. For example, Hovenkamp, *supra* note 1: "In the late 1970s Robert H. Bork used the term 'consumer welfare' to describe the *sum* of producer profits and consumer gains." But, he acknowledges that this is not common practice: "Today's understanding of consumer welfare looks only at the welfare of the consumers as consumers."

22 Posner et al., *supra* note 2.

to facilitate the highest output in any market that is consistent with sustainable competition ... When "consumer welfare" is defined in terms of output it becomes much easier to articulate a defensible competition policy that does everything that antitrust can properly do to ensure a healthy economy, reflecting both the buy and sell sides of the market.[23]

Although he doesn't use the term, Hovenkamp's focus on output, rather than price, is consistent with reliance on the total welfare standard. Under a total welfare standard, there is no clear relationship between total welfare and prices. For example, an increase in price discrimination may result in higher prices to some customers and lower prices to other customers. The overall impact on economic welfare is ambiguous, as it depends on the changes in the deadweight loss to both groups of customers. In contrast, under the total welfare standard there is a clear relationship between welfare and sales *volumes*. Price discrimination enhances economic welfare if and only if total sales volumes increase. If competition authorities are serious about pursuing a total welfare standard, they should focus exclusively on sales volumes (as advocated by Hovenkamp) and not on price.

But, is the total welfare standard a sound foundation for competition policy in labor markets? There are two reasons to be concerned:

- First, due to a low elasticity of labor supply and the ability of labor-hirers to engage in wage discrimination, the economic welfare loss arising from the exercise of market power in the labor market will often be small. If we adopt a total welfare standard, the role for competition law enforcement in labor markets may be limited or non-existent.

- Second, despite years of exhortation by economists, competition law enforcers and policymakers do not, in practice, behave as though the promotion of total economic welfare is their primary concern. It seems troubling to adopt as a standard for competition policy an economic framework whose prescriptions are systematically ignored by decision-makers in practice (where those prescriptions are not directly ruled out by the competition law themselves).

A. *Is the deadweight loss large enough to justify intervention?*

The conventional economic model shows that a dominant firm in a labor market exercises market power by reducing the wage below the competitive level, resulting in a reduction in the labor supply. Under the conventional application of the total welfare standard, the resulting economic harm is known as the deadweight

---

23   Hovenkamp, *supra* note 1.

loss. The magnitude of the deadweight loss depends on the size of the reduction in labor supply. If there is little or no reduction in labor supply, there is no economic harm from the exercise of market power in the labor market, regardless of any change in the wage.

However, several authors have observed that the responsiveness of labor supply to a change in the wage may be small, for two reasons: (a) the overall elasticity of labor supply is quite small; and (b) most labor-hirers can effectively price-discriminate between workers. If the responsiveness of labor supply to a change in the wage is small, the exercise of market power in the labor market would have little or no effect on total welfare. In other words, under the conventional total welfare standard, there may arise very little justification for enhanced antitrust enforcement in labor markets. For those who believe in the need for reinvigoration of antitrust enforcement in labor markets, this is a serious intellectual hurdle to overcome.

This point is emphasized, for example, by Krueger. He points out that the overall elasticity of labor supply is very low–any given change in wages results in a very small change in employment. As a consequence, the deadweight loss from a reduction in wages is likely to be small:

> Most estimates in the voluminous literature indicate that aggregate labor supply is fairly inelastic, especially for men .... The aggregate labor supply elasticity is probably on the order of only 0.1 or 0.2.
>
> ... To be clear, I am not arguing that aggregate labor supply is perfectly inelastic. There is some responsiveness to wages and working conditions, and this is especially the case for the most disadvantaged workers in society. On balance, however, I would argue that the main effects of the increase in monopsony power and decline in worker bargaining power over the last few decades have been to shrink the slice of the pie going to workers and increase the slice going to employers, *not to reduce the size of the pie overall.* (emphasis added).[24]

Even if the elasticity of labor supply is material, the impact of market power on employment levels may be insignificant if the labor-hirer is able to price-discriminate. Importantly, the potential for price discrimination is far greater in labor markets than in most product markets.

---

24   Alan B. Krueger, Luncheon address at the Jackson Hole Economic Symposium: Reflections on Dwindling Worker Bargaining Power and Monetary Policy. (Aug. 24, 2018). *See also* OECD, *supra* note 1, at 5: "Studies also estimate that the level of responsiveness of workers to wage decreases is overall low in Europe, the United States, Canada and Australia," *citing* Anna Sokolova & Todd Sorensen, *Monopsony in Labor Markets: A Meta-Analysis* (IZA Institute of Labor Economics, Discussion Paper Series No. 1196, 2018), http://ftp.iza.org/dp11966.pdf; Boris Hirsch et al., *Differences in Labour Supply to Monopsonistic Firms and the Gender Pay Gap: An Empirical Analysis Using Linked Employer-Employee Data from Germany*, 28(2) J. Lab. Econ. 291 (2010).

In most consumer-product markets, prices are public and posted before the seller knows anything about the identity of the buyer.[25] In contrast, wages and salaries are typically highly confidential information. Individual workers may have an idea of the range of salaries for work of a particular category, but workplace taboos make it difficult to know exactly what other workers are paid. This materially increases the scope for the labor-hirer to engage in wage discrimination.

In addition, the repeated nature of labor market transactions mean that the employer has significant opportunity to learn about an employee's willingness to accept a lower wage–such as information about their risk aversion, willingness and ability to tolerate a period of unemployment, willingness to commute, willingness of their spouse to relocate, or any special needs of their family. The employer can, in principle, take this information into account when making wage adjustments over time.

Furthermore, many employers pursue a practice of not revising wages until the employee expresses a willingness to take up an outside offer. At this point, the employer may match the outside offer. This practice ensures that each employee is paid just enough to keep them in the present employment–a form of "perfect wage discrimination."[26]

The ability to discriminate on wages paid can significantly reduce the risk that a change in the wage will lead to any reduction in the volume of labor supplied. In other words, in the presence of wage discrimination, any economic harm from the exercise of market power in the labor market may be small. But, if the economic harm from market power in labor markets is small, why bother to intervene at all? The total welfare foundation, with its primary focus on deadweight loss, provides, at best, mediocre grounds for intervention in labor markets.

B. *Total welfare is not the primary concern of competition enforcers*

In our view, there is an even more fundamental problem with the total welfare standard: Competition economists generally agree that competition enforcers *do not* pursue the textbook concept of total economic welfare. For example, it is widely recognized that competition enforcers will block a merger that raises prices even if the merger, say, allows for enhanced price discrimination, reducing deadweight loss and thereby *increasing* overall economic welfare. This fact has

---

25 The rapid growth in online transactions has increased the information a seller may have about a buyer (such as the history of past purchases), but also increases the ability to shop around, to potentially identify when that information is being used to price-discriminate.

26 "if employers with monopsony power are able to differentiate among workers' reservation wages, then they can also set wages that discriminate among their own employees. In the extreme case of 'perfect' wage discrimination, firms can pay each worker the minimum he or she is willing to accept, regardless of the worker's skills or productivity." Council of Economic Advisers, *Labor Market Monopsony: Trends, Consequences, and Policy Responses* (Council of Economic Advisers Issues Brief, Oct. 2016) https://obamawhitehouse.archives.gov/sites/default/files/page/files/20161025_monopsony_labor_mrkt_cea.pdf .

long been pointed out by economists. For example, Heyer concludes: "Neither the US competition authorities, nor competition authorities in most other economies, appear willing to adopt explicitly and unambiguously a total welfare standard for merger enforcement."[27] Kirkwood is even more strident: "no court has ever applied a total welfare test. No judge has ever concluded that a merger or other challenged practice that is likely to raise prices to consumers should be allowed because it would increase total welfare."[28] Farrell and Katz argue that competition authorities routinely ignore the total welfare implications of the economic models they use.[29] They conclude: "Evidently, either we don't trust those models, or we don't believe in a purely welfarist total surplus standard."[30]

Many economists assume that this lack of willingness to pursue the textbook welfare concept simply reflects the lack of economic understanding by competition enforcers, or their desire to pursue other political objectives. In our view, this belief does not stand up to scrutiny. Competition enforcers around the world treat similar cases in a similar manner. If competition enforcers were all departing from economic purity, why do they not depart in their own idiosyncratic or parochial manner? The fact that competition enforcers depart from textbook welfare prescriptions in a broadly similar manner is a key fact to be explained.

In any case, the competition laws of many countries cannot easily be reconciled with a total welfare objective. This is particularly the case in the EU. As a consequence, enforcers have developed categories that lack an economic welfare basis or, in some cases, seem contrary to standard economic principles.

In the context of competition policy for labor markets, Posner, Weyl and Naidu seem to want to have a bet each way: although their paper is explicitly based in the conventional economic notion of total economic welfare, they abandon this approach at a key point, arguing that a merger that lowers wages to workers should be prevented, regardless of the impact on total economic welfare:

> By analogy to the "consumer welfare" standard, we believe that mergers that trigger scrutiny by reducing labor market competition should be subject to a "worker welfare" standard. The fact that the

---

27 Heyer, *supra* note 7, at 154. *See also* Robert H. Lande, *Chicago's False Foundation: Wealth Transfers (Not Just Efficiency) Should Guide Antitrust*, 58(2) ANTITRUST L.J., 631 (1989); ICN, *Competition Enforcement and Consumer Welfare: Setting the Agenda*, International Competition Network, 10th Annual Conference (2011), www.internationalcompetitionnetwork.org/wp-content/uploads/2019/11/SP_CWelfare2011.pdf.

28 John B. Kirkwood, *Tech Giant Exclusion,* SSRN 3761448 (2021).

29 Farrell & Katz, *supra* note 5: "For example, the models of medium-term effects that antitrust economists tend to use predict that entry into an oligopolistic market by an inefficient producer or in an industry with large economies of scale may well reduce total surplus. But we would be surprised if any court ruled that stand-alone entry harmed competition. Similarly, a claim of excessive competition is unlikely to be a winning defense of price fixing ..."

30 A few countries, including Australia, have provisions in their competition law, which, under certain conditions, allow balancing of "public benefits" against "competition detriments." This has been interpreted by many economists as explicitly requiring a consideration of total economic welfare. However, even in these cases the courts and competition authorities have been reluctant to interpret these provisions as equivalent to total economic welfare. A full discussion of these issues takes us beyond the central concern of this paper.

merger might raise firm profits more than it harms workers *should not* be sufficient to excuse the merger. Instead, the merger would be permitted [only] if … harms from reduced competition are more than fully offset and therefore workers' wages, benefits, or conditions will improve because of the merger.[31]

But this just raises further questions. Why do these authors, who base their analysis on a total welfare standard, abandon the total welfare standard at this key point? In any given competition case how do we know whether to focus on the welfare of consumers (downstream buyers) or the welfare of workers (upstream suppliers)? The extension proposed by Posner et al. is ad hoc and unexplained.

In our view, these objections to the total welfare standard are serious. Competition authorities around the world reject the total welfare standard as the economic foundation for competition law. How then, can we expect to reintroduce the total welfare standard specifically for the purposes of labor markets? If we do so, how do we overcome the concern that, in many industries, labor-suppliers are simply not that responsive to the wage paid, so perhaps there is very little need for competition enforcement in labor markets at all?

3. The protection of the competitive process

In recent years, there has been increasing support for the proposition that the primary purpose of competition law is the protection of the *process of competition* (see, for example, Khan[32] and Wu[33]). This approach has a long historical tradition. In Europe, the "ordoliberal school" views competition law as part of an economic constitution designed to protect economic freedom, "by ensuring that the competitive process and market structure are not distorted."[34]

This view (that competition law should seek to protect and promote the competitive process) has recently received surprising support from such distinguished authorities as Carl Shapiro[35] and Gregory Werden.[36] Even the US Department of Justice (DOJ)

---

31   Posner et al., *supra* note 2, at 37.

32   Khan, *supra* note 3, at 803: "Antitrust law and competition policy should promote not welfare but competitive markets. By refocusing attention back on process and structure, this approach would be faithful to the legislative history of major antitrust laws. It would also promote actual competition–unlike the present framework, which is overseeing concentrations of power that risk precluding real competition … [W]e should replace the consumer welfare framework with an approach oriented around preserving a competitive process and market structure."

33   Wu, *supra* note 3: "[The protection of the competitive process standard] takes the antitrust laws as I believe they were intended: As a statement of faith in the virtues of competitive systems, and a quasi-constitutional commitment to preserving a competitive as opposed to a trustified or monopolized economy … I want to suggest that the standards for merger review … have drifted too far from an emphasis on economic structure as a means of protecting the competitive process."

34   Ignacio Herrera Anchustegui, *Competition Law Through an Ordoliberal Lens*, 2(2) Oslo L. Rev., 139 (2015).

35   Shapiro, *supra* note 3: "As I use the term, applying the 'consumer welfare' standard means that a business practice is judged to be anticompetitive if it disrupts the competitive process and harms trading parties on the other side of the market."

36   Gregory J. Werden, *Antitrust's Rule of Reason: Only Competition Matters*, 79(2) Antitrust L.J. 713 (2014).

itself has called for a return to a "protection-of-the-competitive-process standard." In a speech, Renata Hesse, Acting Assistant Attorney General of the Antitrust Division of the DOJ, argued that, in accordance with what the original drafters intended, the DOJ looks at harm to competition wherever it occurs: "upstream, downstream, midstream. The antitrust laws protect competition throughout."[37]

Eleanor Fox, in her own contribution to the goals of competition law debate, seems to have been an advocate for the protection of the competitive process. She seems to argue for promoting "the process of rivalry, relatively open access, and contestability of markets by entrepreneurs and firms without market power."[38]

We are sympathetic to, and respect, those who advocate for the protection-of-the-competitive-process standard. We acknowledge that much of the day-to-day work of competition law enforcers can loosely be described as "protecting the competitive process." This approach is therefore arguably consistent with the decisions of competition authorities in practice.

But, as economists, we find this approach unsatisfactory. Consistent with the economic analysis of public policy, we would prefer a foundation for competition law based in conventional welfarist principles. In the conventional economic approach to public policy, competition is not an end in itself, it is a means to an end. That end is the promotion of some concept of overall economic welfare.[39]

This is important because, in the absence of a central notion of economic welfare, the protection-of-the-competitive-process cannot make clear predictions in circumstances where competing economic objectives are placed in conflict. Intervening in a market will often involve trade-offs between the interests of different market participants, or between conflicting objectives, such as trade-offs between innovation and productive efficiency, or between incentives for upstream innovation and downstream investment. The competitive process standard is silent on such trade-offs: For example:

- Does protecting the process of competition imply that a competition authority should prohibit or promote price discrimination?

- Does protecting the process of competition imply that we should force the owner of a bottleneck facility to sell to rivals at cost? Or is it better for competition to allow a firm to decide with whom and on what terms to deal?

---

37 Hesse, *supra* note 3: "Some commentators have ... suggested that the antitrust laws should judge all practices by their impact on the welfare of downstream consumers, as measured by price and output effects in downstream markets. But, although we believe competition maximizes consumer welfare, the ultimate standard by which we judge practices is their effect on competition, not on consumer welfare ... [W]e are just as concerned with lost competition among upstream input suppliers as we are with lost competition among sellers of finished goods downstream."

38 Fox, *supra* note 8.

39 Anchustegui, *supra* note 34, points out that advocates of ordoliberalism assert that promoting the competitive process will promote economic efficiency (although the mechanism remains unspecified). But ordoliberalism is not consistent with a welfarist approach.

- Is it better for the process of competition to allow a merger with substantial cost efficiencies regardless of the impact on prices, or is it better to prevent a firm from exploiting such cost efficiencies?
- Is it better for competition to allow a dominant buyer of farm products to cut the prices it offers to farmers, if it passes some of those price cuts on downstream, or is it better to prevent it from doing so?

Although superficially attractive, the protection-of-the-competitive-process objective provides little guidance as to how competition authorities should find a way through a forest of discretion. Conventional textbook economic analysis resolves such dilemmas by appealing to the concept of overall welfare. But, advocates of the protection of the process of competition standard are at best silent on the connection with economic welfare. As Federal Trade Commissioner Caroline Wilson has pointed out, this leads to the risk of unpredictability and inconsistency:

> The pursuit of multiple goals necessarily requires trade-offs among the different goals, a difficult task when there is ambiguity regarding the list of goals to be pursued. Moreover, once the list of goals is defined, advocates of this approach do not explain how to weight them. The assignment of weights necessarily makes enforcement subjective. Consequently, even if the combination of goals is the same, it is likely that different weights will be applied in different cases, by different agencies, and at different times. If the list of goals and the weights assigned to each is indeterminate, then firms contemplating particular conduct will not be able to predict reliably whether antitrust enforcement is likely in a particular case. Without such predictability, we will unwittingly chill procompetitive transactions and conduct. Equally important, indeterminate rules are more prone to capture by rent seekers. Moreover, the indeterminacy of the goals and weights would make antitrust enforcement more susceptible to political whims and influence.[40]

In summary, the protection-of-the-competitive-process standard is superficially attractive, but lacks a welfarist foundation. Advocates of this approach have not articulated how protecting the competitive process promotes economic welfare, or how to solve trade-offs when they emerge.

Where does this leave us? The textbook welfare standard is the standard approach to public policy, but is not used by competition enforcers around the world. Moreover, there are good reasons for the concern that, in many sectors, the deadweight loss from market power in labor markets may be small. The consumer

---

40 Caroline S. Wilson, Luncheon Keynote Address at George Mason Law Review 22nd Annual Antitrust Symposium: Welfare Standards Underlying Antitrust Enforcement: What You Measure is What You Get (Feb. 15, 2019), www.ftc.gov/public-statements/2019/02/welfare-standards-underlying-antitrust-enforcement-what-you-measure-what.

welfare standard is more consistent with the patterns of decisions made by competition enforcers around the world when dealing with market power exercised upstream against downstream buyers. But, the consumer welfare standard seems to fail entirely when applied to the exercise of market power by a dominant buyer against upstream sellers–precisely the context in which we might be concerned about the exercise of market power in labor markets. Are we left with no economic foundation on which to base our analysis?

In our view, there is a suitable economic foundation for competition, which comes out of transactions cost economics.

III. The Transaction Cost Approach to Competition Law

Recently, an alternative economic foundation for competition law has been proposed.[41] This approach, known as the transaction cost approach to competition law, argues that competition law exists to protect, and thereby promote, sunk, relationship-specific investments in the economy. We consider that this alternative approach offers promise as an economic foundation for competition law in that:

(a) The approach is soundly based in the conventional economic concepts of total welfare–the key difference is the economic model within which these concepts are applied, which places the focus on a more dynamic rather than static analysis;

(b) This approach yields policy predictions that seem broadly consistent with the decisions of competition authorities around the world–including decisions related to buyer power or monopsony in labor markets–and which seem broadly consistent with the prohibition examples set out in the antitrust law of many jurisdictions.

The transactions cost approach to competition law starts from the observation that nearly all ongoing economic relationships–including labor market relationships–will require some form of sunk investment by one or both of the transacting parties. Such sunk investments are well known in labor markets. Most workers spend years developing generic human capital (e.g., a general education) together with a wide range of special skills (e.g., as a chef, carpenter, or economist). These investments are made in the expectation that they will raise the wage of the labor-supplier in the long run.

But, the sunk investment of labor-suppliers is not limited to human capital. In most cases, the supply of labor requires the physical presence of the labor-supplier. As a result, most labor markets are strictly local (within commuting

---

41   *See* Darryl Biggar & Alberto Heimler, *Is Protecting Sunk Investments a Primary Economic Rationale for Antitrust Law?*, J. ANTITRUST ENFORCEMENT (2020); Darryl Biggar & Alberto Heimler, *Digital Platforms and the Transactions Cost Approach to Competition law*, IND. AND CORP. CHANGE (2020).

distance). Most workers will therefore make a sunk investment in a location. For example, a worker may choose to relocate their family to find a job in a small town. The worker and their family take some time to get established in the community–to find a job for their spouse, to establish relationships with neighbors, to develop local service relationships (e.g., a local doctor or dentist), to get the kids set up in schools and so on. The time and cost required to establish these arrangements is a form of sunk investment in reliance on the expectation of employment, at reasonable terms and conditions, in the town.

In addition, labor supply inevitably involves a range of personal interactions with other workers, colleagues, suppliers, and customers. Labor-suppliers make sunk investments in developing and maintaining these relationships.[42]

Like all sunk investments, these sunk investments face the threat of hold-up–the threat that, once sunk, the other party to the transaction will seek to change the terms and conditions of trade.[43] In the context of labor markets, the threat of hold-up is the threat that once the worker has become established in a job the labor-hirer will cut the wages (or, equivalently, refuse a promised increase in wages).

Fortunately, competitive markets offer some protection against the threat of hold-up. In a competitive market, the investment by one side of the market is not specific to one particular trading partner. In the event of an attempt at hold-up, the party who has made the sunk investment can switch to another trading partner. If there is more than one suitable potential employer within commuting distance, a worker faces at least some protection against hold-up: In the event of a threat to cut wages the worker can, in principle, switch to an alternative employer. If a labor force can easily be replaced, an employer can make valuable investments without the fear of having to share the upside of those investments with the workers.

In addition, there are private arrangements that can offer some protection against the threat of hold-up. The most common example is a simple contract. A contract allows the contracting parties to make a formal, enforceable commitment to not engage in hold-up. The producer of, say, a play, who must make a substantial sunk investment in marketing, is likely to seek a formal contract with the actors rather than risk a last-minute attempt by key actors to seek an increase in their pay.

---

42   In addition, of course, on the other side of the market, labor-hirers make a substantial sunk investment in equipment, plant, processes, and products in reliance on an ongoing supply of labor.

43   The role of sunk investments in labor markets is highlighted in a number of papers. E.g., Michael L. Wachter and George M. Cohen. *Law and Economics of Collective Bargaining: An Introduction and Application to the Problems of Subcontracting, Partial Closure, and Relocation*, 136 U. PA. L. REV. 1349, 1360-61 (1987): "Workers make sunk investments in their jobs by agreeing to long-term implicit contracts that provide for 'deferred compensation,' that is, below-market wages at early stages of employment and above-market wages at later stages ... workers invest in job-specific training and deferred compensation represents the quasi-rents earned on this training ... Once workers make a sunk investment in monitoring or job-specific training the firm acquires bargaining power over them because it can strategically force the workers to suffer a sunk cost loss by misrepresenting product market conditions, thereby expropriating the workers' expected return."

A worker who must make a substantial sunk investment in relocating their family may seek a long-term employment contract, rather than risk that, after relocating, a promised pay rise will not materialize.

Another possible mechanism for protecting against hold-up is vertical integration. Labor market vertical integration is reflected in, among other things, worker-owned cooperatives, in which labor (acting collectively) owns the capital equipment (rather than the other way around). There are, for example, worker-owned cooperative theater companies, such as the "playing companies," who were active in the time of Shakespeare. In these companies, consortia of leading actors hire the venues and supporting staff, partially resolving the hold-up problem without the need for elaborate contracts.

But vertical integration and long-term contracts are not always feasible. Almost by definition, relatively few workers are in a position to purchase the company that employees them. Very few companies are organized as worker cooperatives. It is theoretically possible to envisage a labor contract that specifies the terms and conditions of the labor supply that would apply in the event of a change in the market structure (e.g., a merger or insolvency). But, in practice, such contracts are not feasible. Even where long-term contracts are feasible, theory suggests that the life of the contract must be as long as the life of the underlying sunk investment. But some sunk investments may last decades (e.g., the human capital investment by a doctor in training). Long-term labor supply contracts with a life of decades are almost completely infeasible.

In summary, although private arrangements to protect sunk investments are sometimes available, they are not always feasible and, even where feasible may not be fully effective. As a consequence, circumstances can arise where, by no fault of the investing party, that party's investment is subject to hold-up. In the absence of government intervention, this could have a chilling effect on investment. Valuable economic activity would be foregone. For example:

- Workers may be unwilling to move to a "company town" with a single employer, even though their productivity would be higher in that location, due to the threat that, once there, wages would not increase as promised.
- Individuals would be unwilling to invest in new skills or firm-specific human capital that would boost their productivity out of fear that there would be no increase in wages to justify the cost of the investment.
- (On the other side of the market) firms may be unwilling to invest in more productive equipment, out of fear that, once the investment is sunk, the workers will hold out for a bigger share of the firm's profit.

According to the transaction cost approach to competition law, a transacting party is in a *dominant position* or possesses *market power* when it is in a position to engage in hold-up–that is, when it is in a position to change the terms and conditions of trade without fear that the transacting party will go elsewhere. The economic harm from the exercise of market power is the chilling effect this has on incentives for socially valuable investment.

The transaction cost approach to competition law asserts that competition law steps in to protect, and thereby promote, the sunk investment of transacting parties. Specifically, competition law imposes two types of controls:

(a) In the case of parties in a dominant position (i.e., a firm in a position to engage in hold-up) competition law imposes strict limits on its ability to engage in hold-up–including limits on its ability to price-discriminate, to change its prices, or on its ability to withhold services; and

(b) In the case of parties which might collectively be in a dominant position, through merger or collective arrangements, competition law imposes strict limits on their ability to merge or cooperate, to put them in a position to engage in hold-up.

1. What is the benefit of the transaction cost approach to competition law?

In the previous section we noted some fundamental concerns with the total welfare standard (as it is conventionally applied): Although this approach is well grounded in conventional economic welfare principles, competition authorities and competition laws do not seem to focus on the economic harm known as deadweight loss–competition authorities do not seem to encourage price discrimination and they do not approve mergers that would increase prices, even if the elasticity of demand is low.

The transactions cost approach to competition resolves these concerns. The transactions cost approach is also founded in welfare principles (including the total welfare and total surplus concepts). The primary difference is that the transaction cost approach allows for the possibility for transacting parties to make sunk investments that shift their supply or demand curves. The resulting change in welfare can easily exceed (by many orders of magnitude) the economic harm due to the deadweight loss. In this sense the transaction cost approach allows for a more dynamic framework compared to the "static" model within which the total welfare concept is usually applied.

As we have seen, under the conventional total welfare standard, we should expect to see competition authorities approve mergers that enhance the ability of parties to price-discriminate. In contrast, under the transaction cost approach, price discrimination–by allowing the dominant firm to charge different prices depending on the degree of reliance by its customers on its services–may allow the dominant firm to expropriate some of the value of the sunk investment, reducing the incentive to invest. For this reason, the transaction cost approach to competition policy suggests that we should expect to see competition authorities taking a dim view of price discrimination–consistent with what we observe in practice.

Similarly, we have seen that, under the conventional total welfare standard, competition authorities should turn a blind eye to mergers or cartels where demand is inelastic (downstream) or supply is inelastic (upstream). In contrast, the transactions cost approach to competition law suggests that it is precisely when demand or supply is inelastic that the sunk investments of trading partners are most exposed to the risk of being expropriated. The transaction cost approach says that we should particularly be concerned about the threat of anticompetitive behavior in such circumstances–which we believe is consistent with the decisions of competition authorities in practice.

In the same way, it is common for competition authorities to take action to control the behavior of firms in a dominant position–whether in a dominant position in an output market, or in an input market (such as a labor market). Under the conventional total welfare approach, the justification for such intervention is limited–provided there is no exclusion of rivals in an upstream or downstream market, it is presumed that economic welfare is promoted by allowing the dominant firm to charge whatever it likes.[44] But this seems directly counter to the observed approach of competition authorities, who routinely place limits on the power of dominant firms, such as imposing an obligation to deal (as under the essential facilities doctrine), or requirements for licensing under Fair, Reasonable and Non-Discriminatory (FRAND) principles, in the case of standard essential patents.

Again, we see the transaction cost approach to competition law can resolve this conflict. Under the transaction cost approach, actions by a dominant firm to expropriate the sunk investment of trading partners should be prohibited. This might include engaging in price discrimination, or increasing prices to longstanding trading partners. We consider that the predictions of the transaction cost approach are broadly consistent with the decisions of courts and competition authorities in this area.

In the same way, we consider that the transaction cost approach offers benefits over the consumer welfare standard. As noted earlier, a strict application of the consumer welfare standard might require a competition authority to ignore anticompetitive behavior upstream (such as in the labor market), when such behavior might allow the firm to lower prices to consumers downstream. Under the transaction cost approach, however, as long as the upstream suppliers have made material sunk investments, competition authorities should prevent firms from taking advantage of their position to expropriate the value of investments upstream. This might include, for example, both the case of a dominant employer lowering wages to employees, or a firm in a bottleneck position (perhaps Amazon?) taking advantage of its position to exploit the sunk investment of its suppliers.

---

44 Here we are putting aside the "exploitative" abuse of a dominant position that is present in EU, but not US or Australian, competition law. But even in the case of an exploitative abuse, the total welfare standard says that the dominant firm should be able to charge what it likes provided it does not reduce total sales volumes.

The transaction cost approach also provides an economic standard of harm. A practice should be prohibited if it would lead to expropriation of relationship-specific investment sufficient to make the sunk investment unprofitable. (So that, had the expropriation been foreseen in advance, the other party to the transaction would not have undertaken a significant part of that investment in the first place.)

Finally, we consider that the transaction cost approach offers benefits over the protection-of-the-competitive-process standard. The transaction cost approach, being based in conventional economic welfare notions, allows for economic welfare trade-offs between different desirable objectives. For example, there could arise trade-offs between the need to protect sunk investment by trading partners, or sunk investment by the dominant firm itself. Such trade-offs have no resolution under a protection-of-the-competitive-process standard. The transaction cost approach allows us to continue to view competition not as an end in itself, but as a means to an end–an end that we can continue to assess through a conventional economic welfare lens.

In summary, we suggest that the transaction cost approach is a useful foundation for competition policy, particularly in those areas where the total welfare or consumer welfare standards are weakest.

What are the implications of the transaction cost approach for labor markets? A full elaboration of a competition policy for labor markets based on the transaction cost approach is beyond the scope of this short paper. We merely make some brief observations.

2. Competition policy and dominant labor-hirers

Let's consider first the competition policy issues that arise when the threat of labor market power is on the labor-hirer side of the market. As Hovenkamp observes: "nearly the full range of restraints that antitrust law has traditionally condemned in product markets can also be actionable in labor markets. These include mergers, collusion of various kinds, information exchanges, and vertical exclusionary restraints analogized to exclusive dealing."[45]

The transaction cost approach sheds light on the correct definition of market power in the context of labor markets. Under the approach to competition law, a labor-hirer has market power over labor-suppliers if and only if the labor-hirer is in a position to engage in hold-up (that is, to unilaterally change the terms and conditions of labor supply). In the light of the sunk investments noted earlier (in firm-specific human capital, in relationships, and in the costs associated with job search) most employers are likely to have some degree of market power. Some employers (particularly employers that require specialized skills, such as in antitrust economics) may have a substantial degree of market power.

---

45   Hovenkamp, *supra* note 1, at 6.

When assessing mergers of labor-hirers, competition authorities should examine whether or not there are subgroups of labor-suppliers whose sunk investment is specific to the merging firms and who, therefore, would be subject to the threat of hold-up. For example, a merger of the only two hospitals in a town may pose a threat to the sunk investments of, say, nurses in that town. The merger of the only two app developers in a town may pose a threat to the sunk investment of, say, software engineers.

As Hovenkamp emphasizes, the scope of the relevant geographic market on the input (labor market) side of two merging firms can be much smaller than the scope of the geographic market for their output or product:

> It seems clear that most labor markets are geographically quite small, many of them no larger than the commuting range of employees. One consequence of this is that labor market concentration is in fact quite high, often significantly higher than product market concentration. Often the shipping range of manufactured products is considerably larger than the commuting or job search range of actual or prospective employees.[46]

Similarly, competition authorities should be concerned about agreements between competing labor-hirers that limit the wages or terms and conditions they offer to labor-suppliers, particularly when those agreements cover a material proportion of the potential employers for any subgroup of labor-suppliers, and who therefore would be collectively in a position to engage in hold-up. One of the clearest examples is anti-poaching agreements:

> Anti-poaching agreements among two or more competitors are increasingly common and just as dangerous to competition as product price-fixing. No-poaching agreements among independent firms are analogous to market division, which, if naked, is unlawful per se. The equivalent would be if two firms agreed not to attempt to steal away each other's established customers.[47]

In recent years antitrust authorities have successfully prosecuted a number of "no-poaching" agreements. For example, in the *State of California v. eBay, Inc*, the court approved an antitrust settlement shutting down a cartel involving a no-poaching agreement between eBay and Intuit covering specialized computer engineers.[48] Given the increasing interest in competition enforcement in labor markets, we expect that labor market issues will play a greater role in competition cases in future.

---

46   *Id.* at 5.

47   *Id.* at 8.

48   *The People of the State of California v. eBay, Inc.*, No. 5:12-cv-05874-EJD (N.D. Cal 2015).

3. Competition policy and dominant labor-suppliers

Competition policy issues in labor markets are not limited to potentially adverse impacts on labor-suppliers (workers). In most countries, the desire to allow labor-suppliers a degree of countervailing power against labor-hirers has given rise to laws that allow labor-suppliers to collectively bargain with labor-hirers. Collective-bargaining arrangements allow labor-suppliers to withhold their labor as a group. Those collective-bargaining arrangements are typically exempt from antitrust scrutiny. This raises the question whether groups of labor-suppliers might be in a position to engage in hold-up of labor-hirers.

A full articulation of the competition issues associated with collective bargaining goes well beyond the scope of this paper. We merely note the following.

In principle, the development of powerful collective-bargaining associations (commonly referred to as labor unions) has the potential to lead to a degree of market power on the side of the labor-suppliers. In particular, labor-suppliers may, acting collectively, be in a position to engage in hold-up of the labor-hirer. This could reduce or eliminate the incentive for the labor-hirer to make productive investments. Specifically, the labor-hirer could fear making a productivity-improving sunk investment out of fear that, once sunk, the labor-suppliers will hold out for higher wages, eliminating the benefit of the productivity-improving investment.

There is, in fact, some evidence of this in problem. Several studies have found that highly unionized sectors experience lower levels of investment.[49] This problem can in principle be overcome through a range of controls, including labor market regulation and vertical integration. We observe instances of both.

Many countries (including Australia) have highly regulated collective-bargaining rules, which limit the market power of both unions and workplaces. In particular, in Australia, both parties have the right to seek a ruling from an independent arbitrator (the Fair Work Commission). The arbitrator plays the role of the regulator, limiting the potential for the exercise of market power by either the labor-suppliers or the labor-hirer.

In a few countries, (notably Germany) labor unions are more directly involved in the management of firms. This practice (known as "co-determination") is a form of vertical integration that allows management and workers to negotiate over the division of the benefits of major new investments before they occur, thereby eliminating the hold-up problem.

In our view, the observations set out here are just the beginning of a fuller elaboration of the implications of the transaction cost approach to competition law in the context of labor markets.

---

49 *See, e.g.,* Cameron W. Odgers & Julian R. Betts, *Do unions reduce investment? Evidence from Canada,* 51(1) ILR REV. 18 (1997); Stephen Machin & Sushil Wadhwani, *The effects of unions on organisational change and employment,* 101(407) THE ECONOMIC J. 835 (1991); Gabriele Cardullo et al., *Sunk capital, unions and the hold-up problem: Theory and evidence from cross-country sectoral data* 76 EUR. ECON. REV. 253 (2015).

IV. Conclusion

In recent years a number of papers have sought to set out principles to guide competition enforcers as they seek to promote competition in labor markets. But these papers quickly run up against a fundamental question: What, exactly, is the economic question that competition law and policy is designed to solve?

Many competition enforcers, especially in the US, have articulated their goal as the promotion of consumer welfare–that is, the promotion of welfare on the output or customer side of dominant firm. But, this standard is ill-suited to address competition concerns on the input or supplier side of the same firm. As many commentators have argued, a strict application of the consumer welfare standard would immunize anticompetitive behavior on the upstream side of the market, especially if that anticompetitive behavior resulted in lower prices to downstream consumers.

Advocates of stricter competition enforcement in labor markets argue for a rejection of the consumer welfare standard as no longer fit for purpose. We agree with this position. The consumer welfare standard, despite providing a valuable unifying framework for competition law, was always imperfect. Economic welfare considerations do not allow us to neglect the welfare of one side of the market. Perhaps more importantly, the consumer welfare standard is not consistent with the way that competition enforcers behave in practice. Competition enforcers never completely neglected anticompetitive harms on the buyer side of the market, prosecuting mergers to monopsony and buyer cartels from time to time as the need arose. The consumer welfare standard has long been in need of replacement.

But what to replace it with? The existing papers on the application of competition law to labor markets argue for some form of the total welfare standard. This is the conventional economic foundation for all public policy, found in numerous economics textbooks on competition policy. But competition authorities do not behave as though the promotion of total economic welfare is their primary concern. If competition enforcers were primarily concerned about total economic welfare, they would encourage mergers that permit parties to better price-discriminate, where doing so minimizes the deadweight loss. Mergers in industries where demand is highly inelastic would be permitted. Competition analysis would focus on the effects on output, not on price. In labor markets, where the overall supply of labor is highly inelastic, all but the most egregious forms of anticompetitive behavior could be ignored.

But, as has been recognized many times, competition enforcers do not behave in this way. If competition enforcers do not behave as though their primary concern is total economic welfare, when considering anticompetitive behavior in output or product markets, it is hard to see how we can argue for the application of a total welfare standard when considering anticompetitive behavior in labor markets.

Fortunately, in recent years a new economic foundation for competition law has emerged. This economic foundation comes out of transaction cost economics. This approach focuses on the need for parties in an ongoing economic relationship to make material sunk investments to get the most out of the transaction. In the case of labor markets there are sunk investments on both sides of the market. Labor-suppliers must invest in human capital, developing skills, knowledge, and experience, making their labor more valuable and more productive. Labor-suppliers also make a sunk investment in a location. On the other hand, almost all labor-hirers must make a substantial sunk investment in plant, equipment, and so on, in the expectation of an ongoing supply of labor at reasonable terms and conditions.

These sunk investments are subject to the threat of hold-up. A range of workplace norms, contracts, rules and regulations limit the discretion of labor-hirers to engage in hold-up by reducing the terms and conditions of employment *ex post*.[50] But these do not limit the discretion of employers entirely. The primary backstop for most employees is that offered by the competitive market–the ability to switch employers if threatened with hold-up. But not all labor suppliers can immediately find equally attractive employment. Faced with the threat of hold-up, most workers have very little bargaining power. It is for this reason that most countries have laws permitting collective bargaining by workers. Collective bargaining allows workers to exercise a degree of countervailing power against employers who are in a position to threaten hold-up. But such collective bargaining may itself become a threat to the sunk investments of the employer. Firms may be reluctant to make productive investments where they recognize that they will be forced to share the benefits of those investments with employees. A number of papers have found a link between collective bargaining and firm investment, with investment lower in firms with stronger collective-bargaining arrangements.

In our view, the transaction cost approach to competition law offers promise as a credible foundation for the development of a full competition policy for labor markets going forward.

---

50 On the other side of the market, very few labor-suppliers (acting individually, i.e., without collective bargaining) are in a position to engage in hold-up of their employer, and this is usually controlled through contractual arrangements.

The Vision for One Antitrust World

JOSEPH WILSON*
McGill University

Abstract

In 1992, some three decades ago, Professor Fox, wrote an article titled "The End of Antitrust Isolationism: The Vision of One World."[1] While proposals for a multilateral competition regime were earlier proposed, and in some cases adopted in regional settings, they had a top-down thrust aimed at establishing a common trading market. What Professor Fox has presciently seen and advocated has a bottom-up approach, necessitated by the realities of global markets, which were/are transformed though the liberalization of trade, globalization, advances in technology, and the pervasive reach of the Internet across the globe. Since 1992, Professor Fox through a large body of her work has advocated the need for a global competition order.

---

* Professor (adjunct), McGill University; former Chairman and Commissioner, Competition Commission of Pakistan.

1 Eleanor M. Fox, *The End of Antitrust Isolationism: The Vision of One World*, 1992 U. CHI. LEGAL FORUM 221 (1992).

I. Introduction

In 1992, some three decades ago, Professor Fox, wrote an article titled "The End of Antitrust Isolationism: The Vision of One World."[1] While proposals for a multilateral competition regime were earlier proposed, and in some cases adopted in regional settings, they had a top-down thrust aimed at establishing a common trading market. What Professor Fox has presciently seen and advocated has a bottom-up approach, necessitated by the realities of global markets, which were/are transformed though the liberalization of trade, globalization, advances in technology, and the pervasive reach of the Internet across the globe. Since 1992, Professor Fox through a large body of her work has advocated the need for a global competition order. Excerpts from some of her work are mentioned here:

- A minimal but unitary system for global competition: "a targeted approach to the problems raised and opportunities identified for a world competition/trading regime."[2]
- "The time has come to recognize the place of competition policy in the international arena."[3]
- Argued for establishing a common clearing house for receipt of merger filings and their dissemination to interested nation states.[4]
- "A proposal for multinational principles of cosmopolitanism with no minimum substantive rules. The proposal could be adopted in the context of the World Trade Organization (WTO). If the WTO structure currently lacks institutional capability, another forum can be found or devised."[5]
- Cosmopolitan rules and disciplines congenial to contracting countries can be adopted. These can be substantive and procedural:
  o Substantive standards need not be a code. They can be–as the EU has proposed–in the form of a framework directive allowing each nation to formulate its own rule to achieve the agreed objective (e.g., no anticompetitive closure of markets).
  o Procedural and process rules could require transparency, non-discrimination, and internalizing costs, nations could be obliged to establish a procedural system with due process so that aggrieved parties can obtain adjudication of their rights under transparent rules of law.[6]

---

1 Eleanor M. Fox, *The End of Antitrust Isolationism: The Vision of One World*, 1992 U. Chi. Legal Forum 221 (1992).

2 Eleanor M. Fox, *Competition Law And The Agenda For The WTO: Forging The Links of Competition and Trade*, 4 Pac. Rim L. & Pol'y J. 1, 29 (1995).

3 Eleanor M. Fox, *Toward World Antitrust and Market Access*, 91 Am. J. Int'l L. 1, 25 (1997) (various proposals were considered).

4 Eleanor M. Fox, *Can We Control Merger Control? – An Experiment*, in Policy Directions For Global Merger Review: Modalities For Cooperation 89 (Leonard Waverman et al. eds., 1997).

5 Eleanor M. Fox, *International antitrust: against minimum rules; for cosmopolitan principles*, Antitrust Bull. 13 (1998).

6 Eleanor M. Fox, *Global Problems in a World of National Law*, 34 New Eng. L. Rev. 11 (1999).

- There is a "need for an international economic order in which at least some players are charged with responsibility to enhance the welfare of the entire community."[7]
- "Markets are global but there is no global competition law or framework. Nations apply their own laws to conduct or transactions that hurt them, with different degrees of outreach and restraint."[8]
- "In the presence of a global economy and in the absence of a global competition law, sovereigns clash."[9]

The vision for one antitrust world rests on the pillars of: trans-border reach of anticompetitive activities, inherent limitation of national laws, greater world welfare (or global consumer welfare), and lack of dispute resolution mechanism.

Part I of this paper documents the multilateral agreement proposed and/or adopted to in establish free trading areas or common markets and thereby provide for a common competition law regime to ensure a level playing field for the member states' firms–that is, a top-down approach for establishing a common competition regime. Part II documents the rationales (reasons) and existing facts that necessitate the establishment of a common global competition regime, that is a bottom-up approach. While this part is inspired by the work of Professor Fox, it does not pretend to summarize or capture every argument made in support of a global competition regime. This paper concludes that while a number of proposals have been floated in the past that extensively discussed the substantive, procedural, and institutional setting for a global competition law regime, the first important step is to declare all national laws that allow or give exemptions to export cartels as null and void, and be de-notified.

II. Proposals for Establishing a Competition Law Regime at a Multilateral Level[10]

The idea of establishing a competition law regime at a multilateral level is not new. The first such initiative finds its origin in the interwar era when the League of Nations "commissioned a series of expert reports to explore the possibility of a system of international control on cartels."[11] Since then, many efforts have been undertaken at regional and international levels. Here is a brief review of such efforts.

---

7   Eleanor M. Fox, *Antitrust and Regulatory Federalism: Races Up, Down, and Sideways*, 75 N.Y.U. L. Rev. 1781, 1801 (2000).

8   Eleanor M. Fox, *Antitrust: Updating Extraterritoriality* (2019) https://awards.concurrences.com/IMG/pdf/4._updating_extraterritoriality.pdf?55787/361912bf66b468d8848477187d73628b861dbf86.

9   Eleanor M. Fox, *Antitrust and the Clash of Sovereigns, Bringing under one roof: Extraterritoriality, Industrial Policy, foreign sovereign compulsion, and (bad) applications of laws against my "country's" firm*, Competition L. Rev. 102 (2000).

10 Portions of this section draw upon material published in J. Wilson, Globalization and Limits National Merger Control Laws (2003).

11 Spencer Weber Waller, *The Internationalization of Antitrust Enforcement*, 77 B.U. L. Rev. 343, 349 (1997).

1. The Havana Charter

The Havana Charter was designed, in 1948, to create the International Trade Organization (ITO).[12] Although, the Charter was never adopted, it contained a complete chapter dealing with restrictive business practices. Article 46.1 reads:

> each Member shall take appropriate measures and shall co-operate with the Organization to prevent, on the part of private or public commercial enterprises, business practices affecting international trade which restrain competition, limit access to markets, or foster monopolistic control, whenever such practices have harmful effects on the expansion of production or trade and interfere with the achievement of any of the other objectives set forth in Article 1.[13]

The article encompassed three major principles of competition law: prevention against measures which: (i) restrain competition, (ii) limit access to markets, and (iii) foster monopolistic control. The framers of the Havana Charter rightly envisaged *that its objective of liberalizing trade could effectively be thwarted by private restrictive business practices.* Thus, it required the member states to take measures themselves and to "co-operate with the Organization" in preventing such restrictive practices. The Havana Charter vested the ITO with a positive duty to prevent anticompetitive conduct.

2. The European Coal and Steel Community: Treaty of Paris (1951)

In 1951, France, Germany, Italy, and the Benelux countries (Belgium, the Netherlands, and Luxembourg)[14] concluded a treaty in Paris that established the European Coal and Steel Community (the ECSC Treaty).[15] The major objective of the ECSC Treaty was to regulate the production of–and to promote free trade in–the coal, iron, and steel industries, in order to foster economic expansion and growth of employment, and to raise the standard of living in each of the member states.[16] The ECSC Treaty established a nine-member High Authority as a regulatory body for the coal and steel industries. The High Authority, composed

---

12 Havana Charter for an International Trade Organization, UN Conference on Trade & Employment, Final Act and Related Documents, UN Doc. E/ CONF. 2/78, UN Sales No. II.D.4 (1948), (held at Havana, Cuba, Nov. 21, 1947 to Mar. 24, 1948) www.wto.org/english/docs_e/legal_e/havana_e.pdf).

13 *Id.* art. 46.

14 In 1947, Belgium, Luxembourg and the Netherlands concluded the Benelux Customs Convention with the objective to establish a common trading area. Pursuant to the Convention, the member states abolished internal customs duties and established a common external tariff on all imports. In 1958, the member states formed the Benelux Union. *See* Treaty Instituting the Benelux Economic Union, Feb. 3, 1958, 381 U.N.T.S. 165. *See also* John P. Flaherty & Maureen E. Lally-Green, *The European Union: Where Is It Now?*, 34 Duq. L. Rev. 923, 928 (1996).

15 Treaty Establishing the European Coal and Steel Community, Apr. 18, 1951, 261 U.N.T.S. 140 [hereinafter ECSC Treaty]. *See also* Joseph H. H. Weiler, *The Transformation of Europe*, 100 Yale L.J. 2403, 2405 (1991).

16 ECSC Treaty, art 2.

of independent persons nominated by the member states, was responsible for the oversight of prices, wages, investment, and competition in the industry.

Article 4 of the ECSC Treaty proscribed measures or practices that (i) discriminate between producers, purchasers or consumers in terms of prices or delivery terms, (ii) interfere with the purchaser's free choice of supplier, and (iii) tend toward the sharing or exploiting of markets.[17] Article 60 prohibited anticompetitive pricing practices, more specifically, "unfair competitive practices, especially purely temporary or purely local price reductions tending toward the acquisition of a monopoly position within the Common Market."[18]

Article 65 embodied the main competition law provisions. It read in relevant part as follows:

> 1. All agreements between undertakings, decisions by associations of undertakings and concerted practices tending directly or indirectly to prevent, restrict or distort normal competition within the Common Market shall be prohibited, and in particular those tending:
>
>   a) to fix or determine prices;
>
>   b) to restrict or control production, technical development or investment;
>
>   c) to share markets, products, customers or sources of supply.[19]

Article 66 dealt with concentrations ("mergers and acquisitions") and required premerger notification before the transaction could be consummated.[20] The creation of the ECSC was the first major step toward the increased economic cooperation among European states.[21] The ECSC Treaty expired on July 23, 2002.[22]

3. The Treaty of Rome (1958)

In early 1955, the Benelux countries proposed the creation of a common market, a common transportation infrastructure, and coordination of energy resources among ECSC member states. The proposal–after being approved by France, Italy, and Germany–led to the conclusion of the Treaty Establishing the European Economic Community (the EEC Treaty or the Treaty of Rome).[23] The EEC

---

17   *Id.* art. 4.

18   *Id.* art. 60.

19   *Id.* art. 65.

20   *Id.* art. 66.

21   James J. Friedberg, The Convergence of the Law in an Era of Political Integration: The Wood Pulp Case and the Alcoa Effects Doctrine, 52 U. PITT. L. Rev. 289, 293 (1991).

22   1997 O.J. (C 340) 183.

23   *See* Flaherty & Lally-Green, *supra* note 4, at 933–34; Treaty Establishing the European Economic Community, Mar. 25, 1957, 298 U.N.T.S. 11. (EEC Treaty). The EEC Treaty was amended by the Treaty on European Union in 1992 (Maastricht Treaty) ((31 I.L.M. 247) and called the Treaty Establishing the European Community (TEC). The TEC was later amended by the Lisbon Treaty of 2007, which came into force in 2009, and the amended treaty was titled the Treaty on the Functioning of European Union (TFEU).

Treaty, signed in Rome on March 25, 1957, became effective on January 1, 1958. Its stated objectives were: "coordination of economic and monetary policies, *creation of free and fair competition* and harmonization of the fiscal and social policies and the laws of all the Member States."[24]

Like the ECSC Treaty, the Treaty of Rome embodied provisions to protect competition within the common market. Article 101(1) (originally Art. 85) prohibits agreements that have the effect of preventing, restricting, or distorting competition within the common market. In particular, it prohibits agreements relating to price-fixing, tied selling, and market-sharing.[25] Any agreement found in violation of Article 101 is automatically rendered void.[26]

Article 102 (originally Art. 86) protects against the abuse of a dominant position by one or more undertakings within the common market, or in a substantial part thereof, insofar as the abuse may affect trade between Member States.[27]

The Treaty of Rome, although regional in scope, is by far the most successful effort to establish competition law regime at a multilateral level.

Article 12 of the Treaty of Amsterdam, which came into force on May 1, 1999, (1997 O.J. (C 340) 1), renumbered the articles of the TEC; competition provisions, originally numbered as Articles 85 and 86 of the EEC Treaty, were renumbered as Articles 81 and 82, respectively. The Treaty of Lisbon, effective on December 1, 2009, again renumbered the articles. Articles 81 and 82 were now Articles 101 and 102, respectively.

24   Flaherty & Lally-Green, *supra* note 4.

25   TFEU, Art. 101 reads as follows:
1. The following shall be prohibited as incompatible with the Common Market: all agreements between undertakings, decisions by associations of undertakings and concerted practices which may affect trade between Member States and which have as their object or effect the prevention, restriction or distortion of competition within the Common Market, and in particular those which:
    a) directly or indirectly fix purchase or selling prices or any other trading conditions;
    b) limit or control production, markets, technical development, or investment;
    c) share markets or sources of supply;
    d) apply dissimilar conditions to equivalent transactions with other trading parties, thereby placing them at a competitive disadvantage;
    e) make the conclusion of contracts subject to acceptance by the other parties of supplementary obligations which, by their nature or according to commercial usage, have no connection with the subject of such contracts.
2. Any agreements or decisions prohibited pursuant to this Article shall be automatically void.
3. The provision of paragraph 1 may, however, be declared inapplicable in the case of:
any agreement or category of agreement between undertakings;
any decision or category of decisions by associations of undertakings;
any concerted practice or category of concerted practices;
which contributes to improving the production or distribution of goods or to promoting technical or economic progress, while allowing consumers a fair share of the resulting benefit, and which does not:
    a) impose on the undertakings concerned restrictions which are not indispensable to the attainment of these objectives;
    b) afford such undertakings the possibility of eliminating competition in respect of a substantial part of the products in question.

26   *Id.* Art. 101(2).

27   Article 102 reads as follows:
Any abuse by one or more undertakings of a dominant position within the Common Market or in a substantial part of it shall be prohibited as incompatible with the Common Market in so far as it may affect trade between member states. Such abuse may, in particular, consist in:
    a) directly or indirectly imposing unfair purchase or selling prices or other unfair trading conditions;
    b) limiting production, markets or technical development to the prejudice of consumers;
    c) applying dissimilar conditions to equivalent transactions with other trading parties, thereby placing them at a competitive disadvantage;
    d) making the conclusion of contracts subject to acceptance by the other parties of supplementary obligations which, by their nature or according to commercial usage, have no connection with the subject of such contracts.

4. United Nations Conference on Trade and Development

After the Havana Charter, another effort by the UN to establish competition law principles at a multilateral level was made in 1973 under the aegis of the United Nations Conference on Trade and Development (UNCTAD), when UN members tabled a proposal to negotiate a Restrictive Business Practices Code. After protracted negotiations, the members reached an agreement in 1980 on a Set of Multilaterally Agreed Equitable Principles and Rules for the Control of Restrictive Business Practices (the Set).[28] The Set encourages member nations to improve and enforce their national competition laws. It requires multinational enterprises to conform to the competition laws of the nations in which they operate. In addition, it recommends cooperation among competition law enforcing agencies of member states. In October 2000, the Fourth Review Conference to review and revise the Set adopted a resolution which, inter alia, recommended to the General Assembly to subtitle the Set for reference as the "UN Set of Principles and Rules on Competition."[29] The Set is, however, not binding on member states.[30]

The UNCTAD, through its Intergovernmental Group of Expert Meeting on Competition Law and Policy, also publishes a Model Competition Law.[31] In February 2000, UNCTAD held the UNCTAD-X Conference in Bangkok, which focused on the importance of competition policy vis-à-vis globalization and liberalization. The Declaration approved at the conference stressed that in dealing with global interdependence and development, there is a need for effective coordination and cooperation among governments, and among international institutions in the fields of trade, investment, competition, and finance.[32]

5. Organisation for Economic Co-operation and Development

The Organisation for Economic Co-operation and Development was formed in 1961 with the objective of building strong economies in its member states.[33] In 1976, the OECD adopted Guidelines for Multinational Enterprises (MNEs) that bind the member states to accord national treatment to MNEs, and direct MNEs to refrain from abusing their dominant position, for example, by means of predatory behavior or discriminatory pricing.[34] In 1995, the OECD issued recommendations

---

28   UN Doc. T.D.-RBP-CONF-10 (1980), *reprinted in* 19 I.L.M. 813 (1980), https://unctad.org/system/files/official-document/tdrbpconf10r2.en.pdf.

29   TD/RBP/CONF.5/15 of Oct. 4 ,2000, https://unctad.org/system/files/official-document/tdrbpconf5d15.en.pdf.

30   *See* Waller, *supra* note 11, at 351; Fox, *supra* note 2, at 4.

31   UNCTAD, Model Law on Competition, TD/RBP/CONF.5/7, www.unctad.org/en/docs/ tdrbpconf5d7.en.pdf.

32   Report of the United Nations Conference on Trade and Development on Its Tenth Session (Feb. 12–19, 2000), ¶ 1, https://unctad.org/system/files/official-document/ux_td390.en.pdf.

33   As of October 2021, there are 38 members of the OECD: www.oecd.org/about/members-and-partners.

34   Annex to the OECD Declaration on International Investment and Multinational Enterprises, OECD Doc. 21 (76) 04/1 (1976), *reprinted in* 75 Dep't St. Bull. 83 (1976). *See also* Barry E. Hawk, *The OECD Guidelines for Multinational Enterprises*, 46 Fordham L. Rev. 241 (1977); Claes Hägg, *The OECD Guidelines for Multinational Enterprises*, 3 J. Bus. Ethics 71 (1984).

to "strengthen co-operation and to minimize conflicts in the enforcement of competition laws."[35]

Through its Committee on Competition Law and Policy, the OECD has been active in the development of recommendations for best practices in domestic competition law.[36] On March 25, 1998, the Council approved a Recommendation Concerning Effective Action against Hard Core Cartels.[37] The Council Recommendation applies not only to all OECD countries, but also invites non-member countries to associate with the Recommendation.

6. Australia–New Zealand Closer Economic Relations Trade Agreement

On January 1, 1983, Australia and New Zealand entered into the Australia–New Zealand Closer Economic Relations Trade Agreement (ANZCERTA), which superseded existing treaties regulating trade arrangements between the two countries.[38] Article 1 of ANZCERTA, which enumerate its objectives, states in sub-article (d) that the trade between New Zealand and Australia be developed "under *conditions of fair competition.*"[39]

Since ANZCERTA came into force, Australia and New Zealand had substantially harmonized their national competition laws.[40] Before ANZCERTA, the two countries had different competition law regimes. Australian competition law was modeled upon US law with a focus on private enforcement, whereas New Zealand's competition law followed the UK model with emphasis on administrative remedies. In an effort to harmonize the two different competition law regimes, in 1986 New Zealand enacted the Commerce Act, which in large measure mimicked Australian competition law provisions.[41] The countries further amended their competition laws to facilitate trans-Tasman competition enforcement,[42] even allowing the courts of one country to sit, for certain prescribed purposes,

---

35 Revised Recommendation of the Council Concerning Co-operation between Member Countries on Anticompetitive Practices Affecting International Trade (C(95)130/FINAL, Sept. 21, 1995), www.oecd.org/daf/competition/21570317.pdf.

36 *See* www.oecd.org/competition/.

37 Recommendation of the Council Concerning Effective Action Against Hard Core Cartels (C(98)35/FINAL, July 2, 2019) https://legalinstruments.oecd.org/en/instruments/OECD-LEGAL-0452.

38 Australia–New Zealand Closer Economic Relations Trade Agreement 22 I.L.M. 945 (1983).

39 *Id.* art. 1.

40 *See, e.g.,* Tony Dellow & John Feil, *Competition Law and Trans-Tasman Trade, in* COMPETITION LAW AND POLICY IN NEW ZEALAND 24, 28 (Rex J. Ahdar ed., 1991) (describing efforts at harmonization in the trans-Tasman trade area); Rex J. Ahdar, *The Role of Antitrust Policy in the Development of Australia–New Zealand Free Trade,* 12 NW. J. INT'L L. & BUS. 317, 321–22 (1991) (analyzing the trade area's first five years); Richard O. Cunningham & Anthony J. LaRocca, *Harmonization of Competition Policies in a Regional Economic Integration,* 27 LAW & POL'Y INT'L BUS. 879, 900 (1996).

41 Commerce Act of 1986, N.Z. Stat. 5, §§ 4, 36a, 98h, 99a.

42 *Id.*

in the other country, and to have powers to proscribe contempt of court in the other country's territory.[43]

7. North American Free Trade Agreement

On January 1, 1994, the three North American countries–the United States, Canada and Mexico–entered into the North American Free Trade Agreement (NAFTA).[44] The agreement calls for abolition of virtually all existing restrictions on trade and investment by the end of 2003.[45] It also seeks to harmonize the competition polices of the three signatory states. Articles 1501–1505 of Chapter 15 of NAFTA address anticompetitive practices.[46] Article 1501 requires member states to "adopt or maintain measures to proscribe anti-competitive business conduct and take appropriate actions with respect thereto."[47] The article also emphasizes the importance of cooperation on issues of competition law enforcement policy, including mutual legal assistance, notification, consultation, and exchange of relevant information.[48]

Both the US and Canada had strong competition laws before NAFTA came into force. However, Mexico did not have a strong competition law but adopted one, Ley Federal de Competencia Economica, in mid-1993. Upon adhering to NAFTA, both Mexico and Canada have made deliberate efforts to harmonize their competition laws with those of the US.[49] In August 1995, the US and Canada, in order "to promote cooperation and coordination between the competition authorities of the Parties, [and] to avoid conflicts arising from the application of the Parties' competition laws," entered into a NAFTA supplemental agreement.[50]

8. MERCOSUR: The southern cone

In 1991, Argentina, Brazil, Paraguay, and Uruguay created a common market among themselves by signing the Asuncion Treaty.[51] One of the objectives of the Treaty is to harmonize competition policies of the member states. Article 1

---

43 *See* Cunningham & LaRocca, *supra* note 40, at 900.
44 NAFTA, Dec. 17, 1992, Can.-Mex.-US, 32 I.L.M. 289 (1993).
45 *Id. at* 309–10 (presenting a schedule for tariff elimination to be completed by Jan. 1, 2008).
46 *Id.* ch. 15.
47 *Id.* art. 1501.
48 *Id.*
49 *See* Kathleen Murtaugh Collins, *Harmonizing the Antitrust Laws of NAFTA Signatories*, 17 LOY. L.A. INT'L & COMP. L.J. 157 (1994).
50 Agreement Between the Government of the United States of America and the Government of Canada Regarding the Application of Their Competition and Deceptive Marketing Practices Laws, art. 1 (Aug. 1995); 1995 WL 522861 (NAFTA).
51 Treaty Establishing a Common Market Between the Argentine Republic, the Federative Republic of Brazil, the Republic of Paraguay, and the Eastern Republic of Uruguay (Mar. 26, 1991), 30 I.L.M. 1041 (MERCOSUR).

of the Treaty provides for "the coordination of macroeconomic and sectoral policies between the States Parties in the areas of foreign trade, ... in order to ensure proper competition between the States Parties."[52] To strengthen the integration process, member states have committed to harmonize their legislation in relevant areas.[53]

In December 1996, the MERCOSUR countries signed a protocol that provides for the harmonization and strengthening of competition policy in the region. The protocol provides for an autonomous supranational competition law enforcement agency.[54]

9. WTO Fourth Protocol's Reference Paper on Procompetitive Regulatory Principles

At the conclusion of the Uruguay Round of negotiations in 1994, which established the WTO, participants were unable to resolve the issues pertaining to basic telecommunications, and therefore agreed to negotiate a protocol to address those issues at a later time. A Negotiating Group on Basic Telecommunications (NGBT) was established by a ministerial decision.[55]

Early in the negotiations, the NGBT recognized the need to develop a set of procompetitive regulatory principles so as to prevent monopolies or former monopolies in the telecommunications industry from engaging in trade restricting anticompetitive practices.[56] In addition, the negotiators recognized the need for an independent regulatory body to settle disputes between telecommunications service providers.[57] In December 1994, US delegates initiated a dialogue on regulatory principles among selected delegates, which resulted in the drafting of the Reference Paper on Pro-Competitive Regulatory Principles (the Reference Paper).[58]

The Reference Paper embodies definitions and principles for effective implementation of the commitments filed by WTO member states with respect to basic telecommunications services. It contains six articles that deal with: (i) competitive safeguards, (ii) carrier interconnection, (iii) universal service, (iv) public availability of licensing criteria, (v) the establishment of an independent regulator, and (vi) the allocation and use of scarce resources.

---

52 *Id.* at 1045.

53 *Id.*

54 Protocolo de Defesa da Concorrencia no Mercosul, Decision 18/96 (Dec. 17, 1996), *reprinted in* 19 BOLETIM DE INTEGRACAO LATINO-AMERICANA 73 (1996). *See also* Jose Tavares De Araujo, Jr., & Luis Tineo, *Harmonization of Competition Policies Among Mercosur Countries*, 24 BROOK. J. INT'L L. 441, 442–43 (1998).

55 Decision on Negotiations on Basic Telecommunications, The Results of the Uruguay Round of Multilateral Trade Negotiations: The Legal Texts 461 (GATT Secretariat 1994).

56 GATS, Negotiating Group on Basic Telecommunications, Review of Outstanding Issues, Note by Secretariat (TS/NGBT/W/2) ¶ 15 (July 8, 1994).

57 *Id.* ¶ 16.

58 *See* Reference Paper, Fourth Protocol to the General Agreement on Trade in Services 436 (WTO 1997), 36 I.L.M. 354, 367 (1997) [hereinafter Reference Paper]. The Reference Paper was never formally issued as a WTO document.

Recognizing the difference in political and legal frameworks, market structures, and level of development among various member states, the drafter of the Reference Paper focused only on effective outcomes–for example, a level playing field for new entrants–and declined to propose any single regulatory system for adoption.[59]

In order to make the regulatory principles of the Reference Paper binding on a WTO member state, the member state must commit to "additional commitments"[60] in its schedule of commitments, pursuant to Article XVIII of GATS. Once a member adheres to the Reference Paper, violation of its principles becomes subject to the Dispute Settlement System of the WTO. For example, in 2000, the United States filed a request for consultations with the government of Mexico regarding Mexico's commitments and obligations under the GATS with respect to basic and value-added telecommunications services.[61] When consultations failed for two times, the US requested the establishment of a panel.[62] On August 26, 2002, the Director General composed a panel, which presented its report on April 2, 2004.[63]

10. Comments

The Havana Charter framers instituted restraints against private restrictive business practices because that would impede the Charter's objective of liberalizing trade. The ECSC Treaty contained provisions against anticompetitive practices as those would impede the Treaty's objective of fostering economic expansion and employment growth, and raising the standard of living in the member states by promoting free trade in the coal, iron, and steel industries. The Treaty of Rome has the objective of "establishing a common market" through the promotion of "a harmonious development of economic activities,"[64] and its promoters recognized "that the removal of existing obstacles calls for concerted action in order to guarantee steady expansion, *balanced trade, and fair competition*."[65] The UNCTAD Set encourages member nations to improve and enforce their national competition laws. The Set is, however, not binding

---

59 See Laura B. Sherman, *"Wildly Enthusiastic" About the First Multilateral Agreement on Trade in Telecommunications Services*, 51 FED. COMM. L.J. 61, 73 (1998).

60 General Agreement on Trade in Services, Apr. 15, 1994; Marrakesh Agreement Establishing the World Trade Organization, Annex 1B; The Results of the Uruguay Round of Multilateral Trade Negotiations: The Legal Texts 325 (1994), 33 I.L.M. 1167 (1994). Art. XVIII allows members to file additional commitments. Art. XVIII reads: "Members may negotiate commitments with respect to measures affecting trade in services not subject to scheduling under Articles XVI or XVII, including those regarding qualifications, standards or licensing matters."

61 WTO, Request for Consultations by the United States, Mexico–Measures Affecting Telecommunications Services (WT/DS204/1, Aug. 29, 2000); S/L/88; 2000 WL 1225266 (WTO) www.wto.org/english/tratop_e/dispu_e/cases_e/ds204_e.htm (request for Consultation filed pursuant to Article 4 of the Understanding on Rules and Procedures Governing the Settlement of Disputes and Art. XXIII of GATS).

62 WTO, Request for the Establishment of a Panel by the United States, Mexico–Measures Affecting Telecommunications Services (WT/ DS204/3, Feb. 18, 2002).

63 *See* WTO, Report of the Panel, Mexico–Measures Affecting Telecommunications Services (Apr. 2, 2004), WT/ DS204/R https://docs.wto.org/dol2fe/Pages/SS/directdoc.aspx?filename=Q:/WT/DS/204R.pdf&Open=True.

64 Art 2, TFEU.

65 TEC, Preamble, ¶ 4,

on member states.⁶⁶ However, in 2000, UNCTAD recognized the importance of competition policy vis-à-vis globalization and liberalization, and therefore the need for effective coordination and cooperation among governments in the fields of trade, investment, competition, and finance. The OECD Guidelines bind member states to accord national treatment to MNEs, and direct MNEs to not abuse their dominant position and not to engage in discriminatory pricing with their affiliates. While the Guidelines are binding on governments, they are not binding on the MNEs.⁶⁷ ANZCERTA, NAFTA, and MERCOSUR are regional free trade agreements and require member states to harmonize competition laws to ensure any loopholes are closed. The WTO's Reference Paper was needed to ensure that the liberalization in basic telecommunication services is not impeded by monopolies or former monopolies.

All multilateral efforts to establish common competition law regimes were aimed at either facilitating trade or establishing a single trading market.

III. Factors Dictating a Global Competition Regime

This section attempts to document some factual realities that point toward the establishment of a global competition regime.

1. Globalization and the limits of national competition laws

There is vast contemporary literature on the subject of globalization.⁶⁸ Globalization has been quite accurately defined as the "intensification of worldwide social relations which link distant localities in such a way that local happenings are shaped by events occurring many miles away and vice versa."⁶⁹

Professor Alfred Aman describes globalization as "complex, dynamic legal and social processes that take place within an integrated whole, without regard to geographical boundaries."⁷⁰ In other words, geographical boundaries are

---

66 *See* Waller, *supra* note 11, at 351; Fox, *supra* note 2, at 4.

67 Hägg, *supra* note 34.

68 As early as 1943, Wendell Willkie touched upon the notion of globalization in a farsighted book. WENDELL L. WILLKIE, ONE WORLD (1943). However, the term has become "common coin" after influential institutions such as the Club of Rome called attention to the global challenges posed by the ecological crisis. *See, e.g.*, Dennis L. Meadows et al., *The Limits to Growth; A Report for the Club of Rome's Project on the Predicament of Mankind* (1972); Gerald O. Barney, *Council On Environmental Quality and the Department of State, The Global 2000 Report to the President* (1981). For a perceptive analysis of processes of globalization of international policies, *see* DIETER SENGHAAS, WELTINNENPOLITIK–ANSATZE FÜR EIN KONZEPT, 47 EUROPA ARCHIV 643, 643–52 (1992). *Id.* fn. 3. *See* Jost Delbruck, *Globalization of Law, Politics, and Markets–Implications for Domestic Law–A European Perspective*, 1 IND. J. GLOBAL LEGAL STUD. 9 (1993).

69 ANTHONY GIDDENS, THE CONSEQUENCES OF MODERNITY: SELF AND SOCIETY IN THE LATE MODERN AGE 64 (1990).

70 Alfred C. Aman, Jr., *The Globalizing State: A Future-Oriented Perspective on the Public/Private Distinction, Federalism, and Democracy*, 31 VAND. J. TRANSNAT'L L. 769, 780 (1998) [hereinafter Aman, *The Globalizing State*]. *See also* Delbruck, *supra* note 68; PETER DICKEN, GLOBAL SHIFT: THE INTERNATIONALIZATION OF ECONOMIC ACTIVITY 1–8 (2d ed. 1992). Analyzing the process of globalization resulting from the interactions

becoming less and less relevant to relationships between "cause" and "effect." This is true, inter alia, of economic, social, cultural, and political relationships.

Globalization is an offshoot of internationalization, which for more than a century has affected matters that were domestic or national, and were made subject to bilateral or multilateral cooperation in an institutionalized framework. Global activities differ from international activities in that the latter occur between and among states. By contrast, global activities occur in an "integrated whole," where the "area of integration involved might be the entire globe or it might be a region or portions of regions around the world."[71] The major distinguishing characteristic of global activities (from international activities) "is that the areas of integration are largely oblivious to state boundaries, and that the processes of globalization usually occur without or with little direct agency of the state."[72] Environmental threats caused by, e.g., ozone layer depletion, which affects mankind everywhere irrespective of national boundaries, is an example of a global activity.

Embedded in the process of globalization is the idea that it is forging global population. If globalization is to serve the common good of humankind, the "global consumer welfare" standard should replace "national consumer welfare." "Consumer" used here is narrow in meaning and does not include producer, as included in the Bork's definition of "consumer welfare". Global consumer welfare, or what Professor Fox would call "global welfare," is a global public good.[73,74]

Global players acting in global markets are challenging the reach and effectiveness of the national competition regimes, which call for cooperation among competition agencies and, where possible, a common global competition order. The following examples are illustrations of the limits of national competition laws, and therefore the need for a global competition law regime.

---

between states and corporations: WILLIAM GREIDER, ONE WORLD, READY OR NOT (1997); KENICHI OHMAE, THE BORDERLESS WORLD: POWER AND STRATEGY IN THE INTERLINKED ECONOMY (1990); SASKIA SASSEN, CITIES IN A WORLD ECONOMY (1994); SASKIA SASSEN, THE GLOBAL CITY: NEW YORK, LONDON, TOKYO (1991); Alfred C. Aman, Jr., *The Earth as Eggshell Victim: A Global Perspective on Domestic Regulation*, 102 YALE L.J. 2107 (1993); Alfred C. Aman, Jr., *Introduction to Symposium, The Globalization of Law, Politics and Markets*, 1 IND. J. GLOBAL LEGAL STUD. 1 (1993); Saskia Sassen, *Towards a Feminist Analytics of the Global Economy*, 4 IND. J. GLOBAL LEGAL STUD. 7 (1996).

71 Aman, *The Globalizing State*, at 780.

72 *Id.*

73 *See* Eleanor M. Fox & Lawrence A. Sullivan, *Antitrust-Retrospective and Prospective: Where are We Coming From? Where are We Going?*, 62 N.Y.U. L. REV. 936, 946–47 (1987) *citing* R. BORK, THE ANTITRUST PARADOX 90–106 (1978). The "public good" has been excised as the generalized goal of antitrust. In its place is a goal called "consumer welfare," which is not consumer welfare at all. Consumer welfare is defined as the sum of producer and consumer welfare. According to the Chicagoans, if consumers lose but producers win more than consumers lose, "consumer welfare" has been increased.

74 Professor Eleanor Fox is an ardent supporter of welfare of consumers globally and not just national consumers. *See, e.g.,* Fox, *Clash of Sovereigns*, *supra* note 9; Fox, *Can We Control Merger Control?*, *supra* note 4; Eleanor M. Fox & Janusz A. Ordover, *The Harmonization of Competition and Trade Law, The case of Modest Linkages of Law and the Limits of Parochial State Action*, *in* COMPETITION POLICY IN THE GLOBAL ECONOMY: MODALITIES FOR COOPERATION 407 (Leonard Waverman et al. eds., 1997); Fox, *International Antitrust*, *supra* note 5; Eleanor M. Fox, *Extraterritoriality and Merger Law: Can All Nations Rule the World*, ANTITRUST REPORT 2 (Dec. 1999).

A. *Export cartels*

Canada, among other developed countries, explicitly allows export cartels.[75] A multi-country export cartel, of which two were Canadian corporations, was implicated in re *Minn-Chem, Inc. v. Agrium, Inc.* before the US courts.[76] The plaintiffs/purchasers' alleged that the world's potash reserves are confined to a handful of areas, with over half of global capacity located in Canada and Russia. The industry was dominated by a small group of companies that market, sell, and distribute potash. The key actors named were: Potash Corporation of Saskatchewan (Canada) Inc., the world's largest producer of potash; Mosaic Company, a Delaware company headquartered in Minnesota, number three globally; Agrium Inc., another Canadian corporation; three Russian companies; and one Belarusian company. The foreign producers that produced 71% of world's potash restrained the global output of potash by restricting supply during a period of especially difficult price negotiations with China, and by first negotiating prices in Brazil, India, and China, then using those prices for sales to US customers. The United States is dependent on imports for potash–85% of US potash came from overseas. The cartel initiated a sustained and successful effort to drive prices up beginning in mid-2003; by 2008 potash prices had increased at least 600%. The plaintiffs asserted that this increase cannot be explained by a significant increase in demand, changes in the cost of production, or other changes in input costs. The court noted that the trade involving only foreign sellers and domestic buyers is not subject to Foreign Trade Antitrust Improvements Act's extra layer of protection against Sherman Act claims implicating foreign activities. The Sherman Act covers foreign conduct producing substantial intended effect in the United States:

> The host country for the cartel will often have no incentive to prosecute it. Canada and Russia, here (just like California in *Parker*), would logically be pleased to reap economic rents from other countries; their losses from higher prices for the potash used in their own fertilizers are more than made up by the gains from the cartel price their exporters collect. Export cartels are often exempt from a country's antitrust laws: the United States does just that, through its Webb–Pomerene Associations ... and Export Trading Companies ... It is the US authorities or private plaintiffs

---

75 Section 45, Competition Act, 1985 (R.S.C., 1985, c. C-34). For detailed discussions on export cartel exemptions, *see* Margaret C. Levenstein & Valerie Y. Suslow, *The Changing International Status of Export Cartel Exemptions*, 20 Am. Uni. Int'l L.R. 785 (2005).

(5) No person shall be convicted of an offence under subsection (1) in respect of a conspiracy, agreement or arrangement that relates only to the export of products from Canada, unless the conspiracy, agreement or arrangement
  a) has resulted in or is likely to result in a reduction or limitation of the real value of exports of a product;
  b) has restricted or is likely to restrict any person from entering into or expanding the business of exporting products from Canada; or
  c) is in respect only of the supply of services that facilitate the export of products from Canada.

76 683 F.3d 845 (2012).

who have the incentive–and the right–to complain about overcharges paid as a result of the potash cartel, and whose interests will be sacrificed if the law is interpreted not to permit this kind of case.[77]

The court noted that the cartel not only raised prices for consumers in the US, but also for consumers in Canada and elsewhere, thus harming consumers globally. At the core of the problem are explicit exemptions for export cartels both in Canada and the US.[78] Michael Trebilcock, a leading Canadian competition law scholar, called this "cartel hypocrisy."[79] Canada on the one hand opposes export cartels, but, on the other, gave protection to the potash cartel.[80] "Potash, which is a key fertilizer for many agricultural crops, has the effect of raising food prices in many developing countries, hence further impoverishing some of the poorest citizens on the planet."[81] An egregious transfer of wealth mechanism, export cartels not only affect consumers abroad but also at home. The elimination of export cartel exemption, noted Professor Trebilcock, "would remove a discreditable blight on our competition laws." Commenting on the potash cartel case, Professor Fox notes that the "world welfare interest is clearly on the side of the US enforcement."

B. *Market allocation at global level*

An OECD report noted a rare example of cartelization, that is, a continent-wide allocation of market that was simply beyond the reach of national competition laws. In the beer market in Africa, "large beer producers effectively agreed to divide the continent up, with each given a near-monopoly in its own set of countries." A representative for a cartel member beer company talking about the deal noted: "There may be antitrust laws at the national level, but none covering the continent. I don't see what the problem is."[82]

Large corporations are dealing at a global or regional level. In a market allocation case, it is essential for a competition agency to have effective jurisdiction over the territory that is subject of allocation. In Africa, the Economic Community of West African States (ECOWAS), comprising 15 countries, has adopted a Regional Competition Policy Framework and created ECOWAS Regional Competition Authority (ERCA).[83] However, ERCA only covers 15 countries of

---

77   *Id.* at 860.(citations omitted).

78   The US exempts export cartels through its Webb–Pomerene Associations (*see* 15 U.S.C. §§ 61), and Export Trading Companies (*see* 15 U.S.C. §§ 4001) programs.

79   Michael Trebilcock, *Cartel Hypocrisy*, Financial Post, Sept, 30, 2010, https://financialpost.com/opinion/cartel-hypocrisy.

80   *Id.*

81   *Id.*

82   OECD, International Cooperation in Competition Law Enforcement, Meeting of the Council at Ministerial Level, ¶ 106 (May 6–7, 2014), www.oecd.org/mcm/C-MIN(2014)17-ENG.pdf.

83   www.arcc-erca.org/.

the 55 African countries. There is also the Common Market for Eastern and Southern Africa (COMESA), comprising 21 African states.[84] To take a meaningful action against such a continent-wide cartel, a supranational agency similar to that of the EU may be created under the auspices of the African Union (AU). The Constitutive Act of the African Union in Article 3 lays down the objective of the AU. Article 3(i) empowers the AU to "establish the necessary conditions, which enable the continent to play its rightful role in the global economy."[85] Establishing a continent-wide level playing field through a supranational competition law regime is a "necessary condition" for the continent to play its rightful role in the global economy.

C. *Transnational mergers*

The 1997 merger between two US-based aerospace companies, Boeing and McDonnell Douglas, was the first transnational merger that brought to fore the need for cooperation between competition agencies in the disparate review of a single merger transaction. In this case, the EU assumed jurisdiction over the merger because the merger met a European effects test, and the merging parties met the EU's premerger notification thresholds. The merger was approved by US antitrust authorities but faced fierce opposition from the European Commission. Americans perceived the Commission's opposition as rooted in an attempt to protect the merging parties' chief competitor, government-subsidized Airbus, rather than to preserve competition and protect consumer welfare. During the bitter merger review process, each side accused the other of playing the national favorite.[86] The review process became highly politicized and the possibility of a trade war between the Europeans and the Americans loomed. American politicians, including the president, waged a war to save the merger from the Europeans.[87] The Commission eventually allowed the merger, after imposing conditions far short of what had been thought necessary in Europe.

The Boeing case also highlighted global governance gaps in the international trading regime. Following the row over the Boeing–McDonnell Douglas merger, Sir Leon Brittan, former EU Trade Commissioner, stated that in order to avoid such clashes in the future, an antitrust division must be established within the

---

84   www.comesa.int/.

85   Constitutive Act of the African Union, https://au.int/sites/default/files/pages/34873-file-constitutiveact_en.pdf.

86   Evelyn Iritani, *Global Mergers Pushing the Boundaries of Antitrust Law Regulation*, LOS ANGELES TIMES, Nov.5 2000, at C1; 2000 WL 25915626

87   ICPAC, Final Report, International Competition Policy Advisory Committee, Antitrust Division, US Department of Justice, Final Report, at 56 (2000), < https://www.justice.gov/atr/final-report >, 4 Oct. 2021 at 56; *see also* Eleanor M. Fox, *Lessons from Boeing: A Modest Proposal to Keep Politics Out of Antitrust*, ANTITRUST REP., 19 (Nov. 1997).

WTO to deal with the growing number of transnational mergers.[88] He stressed the need for an international agreement on competition rules and smoother cooperation between national competition authorities.[89]

Four years later, in July 2001, the European Commission for the first time blocked a merger between two US-based companies–General Electric Co. (GE) and Honeywell International Inc. – which was approved by the US Department of Justice.[90] The different conclusions reached by the Commission and the DOJ once again gave rise to political furor and threats of trade war.[91]

The GE–Honeywell merger acted as a catalyst to speed up the work on harmonizing international antitrust law. In October 2001, top antitrust officials from at least 13 nations decided at a conference on international antitrust law and policy, held at Fordham University, New York, to launch a new International Competition Network (ICN).[92] The ICN has brought senior antitrust officials from developed and developing countries to work together to form consensus on proposals for procedural and substantive harmonization of antitrust enforcement. It initially focused on the transnational merger review process and on the competition advocacy role of antitrust agencies, particularly in emerging economies.[93] Over the last two decades, the ICN has been successful in promoting cooperation among its members.

Disparate national merger control regimes, while taking care of domestic markets and national consumers, promote national champions in the global market and exhibit a free-rider problem that undercuts the provision of global welfare. For example, the Boeing–McDonnell Douglas merger was seen as crucial to the competitiveness of Boeing by the US and as detrimental to the competitiveness of Airbus by the EU. Indeed, one of the lead economic advisers of the Clinton administration was quoted as saying: "From a national point of view, it is preferable to have a single producer [Boeing] earning generous profits competing

---

88   *EC Tells US to Heed Future European Antitrust Concerns; Start Up WTO Division*, BNA ANTITRUST & TRADE REGULATION DAILY, July 25, 1997, at d6.

89   *Id.*

90   General Electric/Honeywell (Case No. Comp./M.2220), Commission Decision of July 3, 2001; both GE and Honeywell on Sept. 12, 2001 appealed the decision of the Commission before the Court of First Instance. *See* Case T-210/01, General Electric Company v. Comm'n, 2001 O.J. (C 331) 24, and Case T-209/01, Honeywell International Inc. v. Comm'n, 2001 O.J. (C 331) 23; *see also* Press Release, Eur. Comm'n, The Commission Prohibits GE's Acquisition of Honeywell (July 21, 2001),; Michael A. Taverna, *Failed Mega-Merger Causing Shock Waves*, 155(2) AVIATION WK. & SPACE TECH., 27 (July 9, 2001); *see also* Brian M. Carney, *Loggerheads: Mario Monti, Central Planner*, ASIAN WALL ST. J., July 9, 2001, at 6.

91   *See, e.g.*, William Drozdiak, *EU Blocks Merger of GE, Honeywell; Trade Tension Rises*, HOUS. CHRON., July 4, 2001, at 1; John R. Wilke, *Drumbeat Persists Over Denial of Merger*, ASIAN WALL ST. J., July 6, 2001, at 5; Taverna, *supra* note 90; *Trans-Atlantic Differences Hurt GE Deal, O'Neill Says*, WALL ST. J., July 6, 2001, at A2.

92   The countries whose officials were present at the conference were: Australia, Canada, the EU, France, Germany, Israel, Italy, Japan, Korea, Mexico, South Africa, the UK, the USA, and Zambia.

93   Press Release, US DOJ, US and Foreign Antitrust Officials Launch International Competition Network (Oct. 30, 2001). At the time of writing, ICN has produced quite a number of reports. *See* www.internationalcompetitionnetwork.org.

with a subsidized foreign supplier [Airbus]. The US economy is better off even if consumers of airplane seats [around the globe] are somewhat worse off."[94]

Professor Fox calls this "blindered national vision." She noted that "the national-only concern of national law is out of step with the reality that even local transactions have global impacts."[95] The blindered national vision of competition agencies is also encouraged by the fact that the information provided to them in merger filing mostly pertain to the relevant markets in the agency's jurisdiction. However, informal and formal cooperation among competition agency officials forged through the ICN has helped remove the blinders of agency officials. The preceding statement is based on the personal experience of the author, in the acquisition of Pfizer Nutrition by Nestle S.A, a transnational merger reviewed by multiple jurisdictions, including Pakistan and Australia.[96] Acting for the Competition Commission of Pakistan (CCP), the author had the opportunity to review the transaction, and used the occasion to share competition concerns with Australia's ACCC. It was only through this exchange it was revealed that the parties were offering two drastically different objectives for acquisition in the two jurisdictions, thus trying to procure clearance by providing asymmetric information. The broader information received by the CCP through cooperation helped remove its blinders and granted approval with a condition, which it may not have imposed had it relied on the information supplied. The cooperation helped protect a set of the global population and thus increased global welfare.

D. *Global platforms*

The omnipresence of global technology platforms like Google, Apple, Facebook, and Amazon, and their dominance in ever-expanding relevant markets require no footnotes. The pattern of abuse pervades across the countries. For example, Google has been investigated and fined for its abuse of dominance in licensing its mobile applications to device manufacturers using Google's Android operating system in a single bundle in the EU,[97] South Korea,[98] and India.[99] When an anticompetitive practice is undertaken by a firm operating at a global level, the practice permeates across national borders and requires a global solution.

---

[94] Laura D'Andrea Tyson, *"McBoeing" Should be Cleared for Takeoff*, WALL ST. J., July 22, 1997, at A14.

[95] *Id.*

[96] *In re* Acquisition of Pfizer Nutrition (a business unit of Pfizer Inc.) by Nestle S.A, File No.493 /MERGER-CCP/2012.

[97] Google Android (AT.40099) (July 18, 2018).

[98] Reuters, *South Korean antitrust agency fines Google $177 million for abusing market dominance*, HINDU TIMES Sept. 14, 2021, www.thehindu.com/news/international/south-korean-antitrust-agency-fines-google-177-million-for-abusing-market-dominance/article36445571.ece.

[99] Reuters, *Google abused android dominance, Competition Commission of India report finds*, HINDU TIMES Sept. 18, 2021www.thehindu.com/sci-tech/technology/google-abused-android-dominance-competition-commission-of-india-report-finds/article36535148.ece

2. Abuse of competition law by nation states

A. *Glencore/Xstrata*

Professor Fox in her paper, "Antitrust and the Clash of Sovereigns," highlighted instances of abuse of competition law by nation states. In the acquisition by Glencore International plc (Glencore) of all of the remaining shares of Xstrata plc (Xstrata), in which Glencore already held a minority equity interest, China's Ministry of Commerce (MOFCOM) gave conditional clearance.[100] In the relevant markets in China, neither Glencore nor Xstrata owned or operated productive assets. In the global market for the production and supply of copper concentrate, Glencore and Xstrata had a market share of 1.5% and 6.1% respectively, with a combined share of 7.6%, which MOFCOM found would give the merged entity market power, and therefore imposed structural and conduct remedies. MOFCOM required that the Xstrata's Las Bambas copper mine project in Peru be divested to a firm approved by MOFCOM (read, a Chinese firm), and the merged entity to continue to sell a specified amount of copper to China. The relief, noted Professor Fox, "on its face is excessively intrusive. It has no relation to competition and it appears that China is simply using competition law as a hook to extract what it wants ... The strategy should be recognized as an illegitimate use of antitrust law."[101]

B. *Bayer/Monsanto*

In September 2016, Bayer AG's made a US$66 billion all-cash bid to acquire Monsanto Co. The acquisition was notified in around 30 jurisdictions, including Russia.[102] The acquisition was cleared in early 2018 subject to certain conditions by competition agencies of the EU, USA, Australia, Brazil, Canada, China, and India, among others. Russia, however, cleared the acquisition on the condition that the German-based Bayer share its plant-breeding technology with the local (Russian) agricultural sector, and give access to digital farming data. According to Bayer's statement, it "agreed to enable the transfer of defined technologies to Russian recipients in the area of seeds breeding and digital farming for a period of five years."[103]

---

100 Mayer Brown, *MOFCOM Orders Extraterritorial Divestiture of Key Mining Asset in Glencore/Xstrata Merger: Lessons for Future Notifications* (May 6, 2013), www.mayerbrown.com/-/media/files/perspectives-events/publications/2013/05/mofcom-orders-extraterritorial-divestiture-of-key/files/get-the-full-update/fileattachment/130506-prc-antitrustcompetition-ma-mining.pdf.

101 Fox, *Clash of Sovereigns*, supra note 9, at 21–22.

102 Diane Bartz and Greg Roumeliotis, *Bayer's Monsanto acquisition to face politically charged scrutiny*, REUTERS, Sept. 14, 2016, www.reuters.com/article/us-monsanto-m-a-bayer-antitrust/bayers-monsanto-acquisition-to-facepolitically-charged-scrutiny-idUSKCN11K2LG.

103 Ludwig Berger, *Russian nod moves Bayer closer to wrapping up Monsanto deal*, REUTERS, Apr. 20, 2018, www.reuters.com/article/us-monsanto-m-a-bayer-clearance-idUSKBN1HR13N.

IV. Conclusion

This paper canvassed the proposed and put in force efforts to establish competition law regime at a multilateral level as a means to support the primary objective of liberalization of free trade in member states. This is what I call a top-down approach. Then there is a bottom-up approach, which recognizes the "facts on the ground" that dictate the establishment of a global competition regime and argue for such regime. Professor Fox, with her foresight, proposed such one regime some 30 years ago. Since then the process of globalization progressed in leaps and bounds. We noted that globalization promotes global welfare, a public good that does not distinguish among people on the basis of nationality. Globalization has transformed national markets into one global market, in which trade requires global competition law principles. For any multilateral solution, countries closely guard their sovereignty. In this regard, the Convention on International Civil Aviation of 1944, commonly known as the Chicago Convention, is instructive.[104] The Chicago Convention requires "uniformity" in rules and regulations governing international civil aviation, not as a social idea, but as a "necessity" required for safe navigation,[105] while recognizing the "sovereignty" of every member over their airspace.[106] It established International Civil Aviation Organization (ICAO), whose council has the power to issue Standard and Recommended Practices (SARPs). While Standards are mandatory for member states, recommended practices are to be followed as closely as possible.[107] In an inclusive world trading regime, global consumer welfare is more of a necessity than a social norm. An ICAO-style SARPs may be considered by WTO for competition matters. The very first Standard to be issued should require all member states to repeal their national laws that protect or give exemptions to export cartels; the second Standard should direct member states to not abuse their competitions laws for purposes other than ensuring competition in the markets. Such a Standard is necessary to prevent remedies of the sort we saw in Glencore/Xstrata by China, or Bayer/Monsanto by Russia. Recommended practices may be issued pertaining to transnational mergers and abusive conduct by technology platforms. The mechanism has the flexibility to address emerging issues/problems in the realm of antitrust.

Through free-trade agreements and other arrangements, such as ASEAN, NAFTA, SAFTA, the EU, the AU, ECOWAS, COMESA, CARICOM, among others, nations are forming regional blocks, wherein competition assessment and enforcement take into account "regional consumer welfare" rather than just national consume welfare. Consumers of weak or underdeveloped country

---

104 Convention on International Civil Aviation 1944, www.icao.int/publications/documents/7300_orig.pdf.
105 *Id.*, Art 12.
106 *Id.*, Art. 1.
107 *See id.*, Art. 37.

members of regional blocks get added protection with their membership in the blocks. Formation of newer trading blocks is reckoning of the "facts on the ground" and thus the need for coming together.[108] The time is not far when Professor Fox's vision of one antitrust world will become a reality. Her vision reflects her compassion for the consumers of developing and poor countries, and the author being one such consumer is particularly thankful to Professor Fox for being the leading voice in advocating inclusive approach in antitrust enforcement.

I would like to take this space to thank Concurrences for giving me the opportunity and honor to contribute a piece in the *liber amicorum* in honor of Professor Fox.

---

108 See generally, WTO's Regional Trade Agreement page for new RTAs notified, https://www.wto.org/english/tratop_e/region_e/region_e.htm; *RCEP Forms the World's Largest Trading Bloc. What Does This Mean for Global Trade?*, rand.org/blog/2020/12/rcep-forms-the-worlds-largest-trading-bloc-what-does.html (The Regional Comprehensive Economic Partnership (RCEP) includes the 10 nations of the ASEAN, Australia, Japan, New Zealand, South Korea, and China. – In the long term, the agreement has the potential to influence international competition and future trade rules.)

PART III
Emerging Economies: Challenges and Opportunities

The Quest for Relevant and Inclusive Competition Laws in Small Vulnerable Economies

TAIMOON STEWART[*]
University of the West Indies

Abstract

Three issues are examined in this paper: the appropriateness of the standards of efficiency and consumer welfare for developing countries; the consequences of importing laws into developing countries from advanced economies; and the imperative of developing countries including equity and public interest into their enforcement methodology to foster inclusiveness of the marginalized masses. The economies of Jamaica and Trinidad and Tobago are examined to empirically test the appropriateness of the standards of efficiency and consumer welfare as stand-alone goals of competition law. Findings were that these goals emerged in the US out of the evangelical Christian epistemology that informs individualism, limited government, and free market, all appropriate for the American landscape and experience, but not for Caribbean economies.

The conditions under which laws were imported into Jamaica and Trinidad and Tobago are described, and findings are that introduction of competition laws was a requirement of World Bank Structural Adjustment Programs. The societies into which the laws were introduced had little understanding of the law and its purpose, and there was no attempt to link provisions of the law to the specific concerns of the economies in these countries. An examination of the experience of enforcement

---

[*] Taimoon Stewart is associate senior fellow at the Sir Arthur Lewis Institute of Social and Economic Studies, the University of the West Indies, and consultant in competition policy and law. Thanks to Marc Jones and Rajan Dhanjee for their very insightful and useful comments on this paper.

by the Jamaica Fair Trading Commission revealed serious problems that were a direct result of flaws in the drafting of the law, serving a serious blow to the work of the Commission. Yet, despite the constraints placed on the Commission, it has been able to focus on very productive advocacy and consent agreements, and to wrest some legal successes through the courts. The Trinidad and Tobago Fair Competition Act is critiqued, and many areas of concern in the drafting were found that need to be addressed.

The paper then focuses on the issue of inclusiveness, and draws on the empirical evidence of the economic conditions in Jamaica and Trinidad and Tobago. The most powerful firms have entrenched market power gained in colonial times when the masses of the population had not been long emancipated from slavery or were still indentured servants. They were excluded from economic opportunities, scratching a living out of subsistence farming, and racially discriminated against. Today, these firms control the import, distribution, and retail trades, have expanded into other sectors, goods and services, and are investing across the region, leaving little room for newcomers. It is suggested that the Caribbean takes example from the enforcement practices of South Africa, where the law is crafted to include equity and public interest, and enforcement methodology is aligned with the goals of the law.

I. Introduction

1. Concerns

For laws to be inclusive and relevant, they must address real issues in a society, and must be crafted in consultation with key stakeholders in society. Yet, from the 1990s onwards, several developing countries were required to adopt competition law as part of the neo-liberal market liberalization project. As a result, laws that were crafted in the industrialized countries to address internal market problems in their economies were transposed to the developing world through World Bank Structural Adjustment Programs (SAP). Similarly, plurilateral and bilateral trade agreements included the requirement to adopt competition law. Therefore, many developing countries imported the form of the law without interrogating and adapting to local conditions and drawing in social partners into the process, in order to link functionality and purpose to form. Several scholars, but particularly Eleanor Fox and Michal Gal, have expressed concern that competition law provisions are imported into developing countries from developed jurisdictions, and caution that one size does not fit all. Rather, countries should tailor their laws to address the specific competition concerns of the receiving economy.[1]

Few developing countries drafted their laws through an organic process that first identified the main competition problems in the economy, as the US did when drafting the Sherman Act, for instance, directly responding to the damage to

---

1   Michal Gal & Eleanor Fox, *Drafting competition law for developing jurisdictions: learning from experience* (N.Y.U. Sch. of Law, Law & Econ. Research Paper Series, Working Paper No. 14-11, Apr. 2014).

small businesses and consumers from big trust corporations wielding their power. While Germany and Japan were required to introduce antitrust law as part of the peace settlement after WWII, they have managed to adapt the law to their economic conditions. Their economies were not shaped and distorted by colonialism and imperialism, and therefore had internal authenticity and resilience. Europe also introduced competition law as part of the post-WWII reconstruction package provided by the US through the Marshall Plan, and so, yes, it was externally propelled. However, Europe took into consideration their primary purpose of creating an internal market as a way of avoiding a repeat of European tribal wars that wrecked the first half of the twentieth century. As such, the goals of the EU competition law and subsequent enforcement are clear in adhering to this intention. They recognized that market power of dominant firms in Europe originated from privatized state-owned enterprises (SOEs), that therefore government sponsorship was pivotal in securing the market power, which was transferred to private firms, and this inherited privilege merits special responsibility by these firms to behave fairly. In a proper order of process, a society should first design a competition policy to address identified market and competition problems, and, drawing from this policy, draft relevant provisions of a competition law. Instead, governments in developing countries, for the most part, hired competition experts from mature jurisdictions to draft their laws. With little understanding of the local economy, and few if any local experts to guide them on appropriate competition provisions, the consultants largely transplanted what they knew.

By contrast, South Africa went through an organic process in designing its competition law (1998), with full public engagement and support. This was because the law was seen by key stakeholders, such as the powerful union that fought for freedom, as a tool by which to address the injustices of apartheid and provide for economic protection and advancement of the masses. It was a confluence of events that married the design and drafting of South Africa's competition law as an integral part of the struggle for democracy, with the dominant narrative being the racially assigned privilege that marked every sphere of life.[2] According to David Lewis, the South African Competition Act is rooted in the concentration of ownership of private wealth in the hands of a small number of large corporations owned by a select group of white families, with the counterpoint being the dispossession, poverty, and unequal and unfair treatment of the majority Black population. There was widespread public support for introducing competition law, which was *not part of a market liberalization process*, but a central feature of the post-apartheid democratic project.[3] Therein lies an important factor that explains the success of the South African competition regime. It was a homegrown organic process of designing the law, fully supported by the majority, and part of a more fundamental revolutionary change

---

2   DAVID LEWIS, THIEVES AT THE DINNER TABLE: ENFORCING THE COMPETITION ACT 5 (2012).

3   *Id.* at 10.

in society for the benefit of the masses. Moreover, South Africa deliberately constructed into their law provisions to address issues of equity and public interest, so that the historically disadvantaged could be given windows of opportunity to advance themselves economically.

The COVID-19 crisis has laid bare shortcomings in the enforcement of competition law in many developed countries because the laws explicitly exclude equity and public interest goals. Many competition authorities had to respond to the crisis by accepting public interest considerations to allow collaboration of firms in critical sectors such as food and medical supplies. There is a growing literature challenging the Chicago school–driven economic assumption of efficiency as a basis for analyzing cases in competition law, particularly in developing countries. The new challenges posed by COVID-19 have intensified the debate in mature jurisdictions on the need to integrate equity and inclusive markets into competition analysis. Some opponents, particularly the US, argue that pure economic analysis, with efficiency and consumer welfare goals, has a long history and jurisprudence, and gives legal certainty to stakeholders. Introducing other measurements and policy issues will blur the procedures and lead to legal uncertainty. Their view is that other agencies exist to deal with public interest, particularly issues related to small enterprises. The US holds fast to the view that the market will correct failures and this will lead to efficiency.[4]

Others support inclusion of equity and public interest goals, arguing that certainty and predictability are important, but that is not why these laws exist. Rather, the wider social goals should inform the law, and then the enforcers should move toward predictability, as South Africa did, by publishing guidance on public interest.[5] Quite astonishingly, a partnership between world business and public sector leaders and the Pope has been formed, and the Council for Inclusive Capitalism established, with the objective of reviving a global approach to capitalism that promises inclusive growth and solutions to enduring issues like climate change and wealth inequality.[6] These firms are taking deliberate steps to make choices that advance the objectives of inclusive and sustainable economic practice.

Eleanor Fox has written provocatively and extensively, challenging efficiency-based analysis that excludes equity, and argues the case for competition analysis that focuses on inclusive market analysis to open opportunities for the impoverished masses. This paper will explore the main postulates of Fox, for she is foremost among antitrust scholars in challenging the inappropriateness of adopting competition laws designed for mature jurisdictions, and having the goal of efficiency and consumer welfare as the basis for competition analysis in developing

---

[4] Christine Wilson, US Fed. Trade Comm'n, Comments during the panel discussion at the OECD Global Forum (Dec. 7, 2020).

[5] Thando Vilakazi, Executive Director of CCRED, South Africa, Comments during the panel discussion at the OECD Global Forum (Dec. 7, 2020). Frederic Jenny also expressed this view at the same webinar.

[6] *See*, COUNCIL FOR INCLUSIVE CAPITALISM, www.inclusivecapitalism.com.

countries, because of the radically different economic realities. She advocates passionately for inclusion of equity issues and public interest as an integral part of competition analysis. Her views are taken into account in the paper.

I address the following questions, specifically focusing on selected countries in the Caribbean Community (CARICOM).[7] First, how are economies and markets different in these countries compared with industrialized ones, and therefore how relevant are the efficiency and consumer welfare standards in enforcement of competition law in these economies? Secondly, were their competition laws organically grown or were they transplanted from mature jurisdictions, and to what extent was there an attempt to interrogate imported provisions for relevance in the receiving economy? Are there provisions that incorporate equity and public interest into enforcement, to open market opportunities for the disadvantaged? Thirdly, did difficulties arise in enforcement due to inadequately drafted laws, and, given the market conditions described, have the commissions attempted clever interpretations of the law to get around difficulties arising from ill-fitting provisions to gain benefits for the masses?

For clarity, the current international debate on competition policy and industrial policy will not be addressed in this paper. This topic has become important in Europe because of market failure due to COVID-19 lockdowns, such as disruption of supply chains, dependence on China for critical inputs to industry, and political-economy concerns about takeover of their weakened industries by Chinese firms that are subsidized by their government. These specific issues are not what has occupied CARICOM. Rather, industrial policy was always important to developing countries, particularly small economies, as a policy instrument to deal with chronic market failure, but their arguments were given little credence by industrialized countries. Another issue that is currently on the discussion table is the need for international rules on competition policy. Both these issues are not addressed here because they require full enquiry and will constitute a forthcoming paper.

2. Perspective and methodology

In this paper, I use the term, "small economies," and more specifically, "small vulnerable economies," in keeping with international usage and usage by CARICOM countries to describe themselves.[8] These are small economies because

---

[7] CARICOM consists of includes the following countries: Antigua & Barbuda, the Bahamas, Barbados, Belize, Dominica, Grenada, Guyana, Haiti, Jamaica, Montserrat, St. Lucia, St. Kitts & Nevis, St. Vincent and the Grenadines, Suriname and Trinidad & Tobago. Of these, only three are mainland territories (Belize, Guyana, and Suriname), and the rest are small island states. The most populous territory is Haiti (11.4 million) followed by Jamaica (2.9 million), Trinidad & Tobago (1.4 million), Guyana (786,552) and Suriname (586,632). The rest of the territories have population under 400,000. CARICOM Countries 2020, WORLD POPULATION REVIEW, https://worldpopulationreview.com/country-rankings/caricom-countries.

[8] I posit here that extending the usage of the term "small economies" to refer to economies that are much larger, such as Singapore, Israel, Canada, Australia, as Michal Gal does in her work, erodes the political-economy meaning and significance that CARICOM economies and similar small economies. Indeed, these countries are now requesting in international forums that they are referred to as "small vulnerable economies" because of their extreme exposure to both economic and environmental disasters. Small physical size is not

of not only small market size/population, and gross domestic product (GDP), but, importantly, they are characterized by a lack internal resilience, with little backward and forward linkages within the economies. Concentrated markets in these small economies are not purely because of small size of market and the need for economies of scale. Rather, they have historical antecedents by which markets were captured by the privileged elites during the colonial period, while market opportunities were closed to the underprivileged, leaving footprints of barriers to entry that persist today.

Further, they are vulnerable to external shocks such as drastic decline in export earnings because their economies continue to be heavily dependent on export of commodity products, including tourism. Their exports are subject to international pricing, and highly susceptible to drastic drops in demand and prices, both externally triggered. To compound this vulnerability, environmental disasters can wipe out the mainstay economic activity in agriculture and tourism in particular. UNCTAD reported that small island developing states (SIDS) experience the world's highest frequency of natural disasters, among them hurricanes, cyclones, and other violent storms that lead to severe flooding and, in the worst cases, the loss of life, homes, and infrastructure. In terms of economic impact, the most severe storm ever, calculated on a per capita basis, hit Dominica in 2017, causing damage equivalent to 280% of the island's GDP, according to the Emergency Events Database (EM-DAT).[9] For small countries, the costs of post-disaster reconstruction can be exorbitant. On average, natural disasters cause damage equivalent to 2.1% of GDP every year in SIDS.[10] Yet they depend on these export earnings to import the majority of what they consume, with declining terms of trade creating a proverbial margin squeeze.

A brief look at the impact of COVID-19 on exports of goods and services illustrates the dependence on exports, particularly tourism services, in most of these economies. In Antigua & Barbuda, the Bahamas, Dominica, Grenada, St. Kitts & Nevis, and St. Lucia, the percentage drop of exports compared with 2019 is over 50%, with the Bahamas losing 63.8% of exports, that is, their tourism economy.[11] Barbados, Belize and Jamaica fared better, with percentage drops in the thirties, but this is because they opened up to tourism early in the COVID-19

---

the critical criteria, since the continental countries of CARICOM (Guyana, Belize, and Suriname) are far bigger than Singapore, for instance, but Singapore has an annual GDP of US$324 billion and GDP per capita of US$56,746, while Suriname has a GDP of US$3 billion and GDP per capita of US$5,251. Singapore has a population of 5.7 million, while Suriname's population is 570,496. (World Bank Country Data (2017), WORLDOMETER, www.worldometers.info/gdp/gdp-by-country/). Population size is not the critical factor either, since Haiti's population is 10,982,366, more than double that of Singapore, but its GDP per capita is US$766 and purchasing power of the majority of the population is minimal. The critical factors are the characteristics of the economy, the extent to which it is internally resilient, and the distribution of wealth and power in the country.

9 EMERGENCY EVENTS DATABASE (EM-DAT), www.emdat.be.

10 UNCTAD, *For heavily indebted small islands, resilience building is the best antidote*, UNCTAD NEWS, (Jan. 7, 2021), https://mailchi.mp/unctad/unctad-news-creative-economy-year-launch-15-jan-2021?e=d07e2a313c.

11 IMF, *World Economic Outlook Database: Country Statistics* (Oct. 2020).

crisis. A new variant of the virus is causing shutdowns in source markets as well, so that another blow has been struck to the barely surviving tourism industry in the Caribbean. Note that employment in the tourism and tourism related sector exceeds 50% of the employable population in many of these countries, and is as high as 78% in St. Lucia.[12] Interestingly, remittances, a very important source of support to lower Jamaicans and other Caribbean peoples, increased during 2020 by 25%, giving support to the poor in these dire circumstances.[13]

Jamaica had bauxite exports to prop the economy, but Trinidad and Tobago felt the effects of COVID-19 shutdowns on the petroleum sector, with the price of oil plummeting. Export earnings fell by 22.4%. In most of the countries, volume of imports dropped by over 20% due to scarcity of foreign currency.[14] There is a high level of food insecurity in the region, given that over 80% of food imports are from extra-regional sources requiring hard currency.[15] Moreover, these countries do not have the money to inject stimulus packages into the economy like the US or EU. All the economies in CARICOM are price-takers of single commodity exports, vulnerable to external shocks, whether it be bauxite in Jamaica and Guyana, or petroleum in Trinidad and Tobago, or tourism in all the other islands. To compound these problems, these countries are now carrying a heavy external debt burden. Dependence on export earnings is the most critical economic factor. What factors shaped these economies to be so vulnerable? Can these economies be characterized as workable market economies?

In Section II, I examine the economies of Jamaica and Trinidad & Tobago (to illustrate features in CARICOM economies), providing a historical explanation of why these economies are different from industrialized economies. I ask what are the real barriers to opportunities for the masses, and whether these economies can qualify as "workable market economies." I critique the Chicago school ideology that informed policies in the region, and compare the findings of the empirical exploration of these two economies with the economic conditions expected in mainstream ideology, showing disjuncture and inappropriateness. In that context, I question the appropriateness of the efficiency and consumer welfare standards. CARICOM economies were created by global capitalism to accumulate and transfer wealth to the metropole, and continue to be so reliant on the global economy for its survival that it is unrealistic to consider how these economies are structured and function without interrogating its international trade relations in a historical context. Concentrated markets in these small

---

12   WTTC, *Global Data 2019 Annual Research: Key Highlights* (2020).

13   David Rose, *Remittances–Jamaica's Economic Lynchpin*, JAMAICA OBSERVER, Jan. 17, 2020, www.jamaicaobserver.com/sunday-finance/remittances-jamaica-s-economic-lynchpin-jamaica-national-money-services-sees-significant-uptick-in-transactions-during-covid-19-period_212328.

14   IMF, *supra* note 11.

15   Inter-American Development Bank, *Agricultural Policy Reports: Analysis of Agricultural Policies in Trinidad and Tobago* (Jan. 2018), https://publications.iadb.org/publications/english/document/Analysis-of-Agricultural-Policies-in-Trinidad-and-Tobago.pdf.

economies are not purely because of small size of market and the need for economies of scale. Rather, they have historical antecedents by which markets were captured by the privileged elites, while market opportunities were closed to the underprivileged, leaving footprints of barriers to entry that persist today.

Section III examines the consequences of transplanting laws from industrialized countries. I explore the process by which competition laws were introduced into Jamaica and Trinidad and Tobago, in order to determine whether the laws were homegrown or imported, whether the actual economic realities were taken into account in drafting the laws, and whether provisions in the laws give room for inclusive and pro-poor outcomes in enforcement. This exploration will provide a grid for examining whether the domestic law addresses the real competition issues in the domestic economy, and whether enforcement has been agile enough to overcome constraints inherent in the laws to gain outcomes for the benefit of the masses. We shall see that, in both cases, introduction of the law was externally propelled, the result of succumbing to policy prescriptions from the International Monetary Fund (IMF) and World Bank. Since Trinidad and Tobago's law was only fully proclaimed in February 2020, and there are as yet are no cases to evaluate, the enforcement experience of the Jamaica Fair Trading Commission (JFTC) is examined for any problems created by import of the law, and whether the JFTCs decisions were beneficial to the masses.

Section IV provides a critique of the Trinidad and Tobago law, pointing to defects in the drafting, and provisions that are flawed and which opens the way for enforcement problems for the Commission. Section V examines the enforcement experience of the JFTC in order to discern whether there were any negative consequences due to the way the law was drafted, and to examine failures and successes in enforcement. Section VI explores the question of inclusiveness, bringing the human factor into competition law enforcement, using equity and public interest in arriving at determinations.

II. Workable Market Economies or Dependent Capitalism?

1. Historical antecedents

One cannot understand the economies of CARICOM without knowing the historical antecedents that shaped the productive sector, the ethnic composition of the population, and the landscape and transportation linkages, all in response to the colonial imperative of extractive production and export back to the metropole. The story is a complex one of enslavement and decimation of the indigenous population (Arawak and Caribs), repopulating the territories and creating dependent capitalist economies (relentless accumulation of capital and its outflow to the metropole). Profit-seeking colonizers arrived from Europe and Britain in waves, as islands changed hands during European wars fought in and over Caribbean islands, indigenous populations were wiped out, and labor transported from Africa forcibly (slaves) and from India (indentured laborers) to work on sugar plantations.[16] The processes of colonialism and imperialism shaped these economies from the beginning to be extractive commodity production, export-oriented, and reliant on imports for consumption, all to the benefit of the metropole and the local colonizers.[17]

Until the 1960s, British economists explained West Indian economies, coming from a world view shaped by their own experiences and understanding of the evolution of England's economy. Knowledge developed in the metropole informed colonial policy and seeped into all aspects of colonial life, so that West Indians saw themselves, their economies, and their societies through the eyes of the British, that is, they were backward undeveloped economies and societies that must be transformed by taking the same development path as Western Europe. From the early 1960s, a group of scholars at the University of the West Indies rejected this dominant interpretation, and an intellectual revolution flourished as they began explaining these economies through the eyes and experiences of its peoples, debunking the domination knowledge. This group, The New World Group, produced a body of intellectual knowledge that unveiled the ways in which colonial policies with imperialist intent shaped exploitative extractive economies with concentrated market structure and social inequality to support the plantation economy.[18] They explained social stratification along racial lines to support the system by which wealth was concentrated in the hands of the very small white[19] population. Lloyd Best, a member of The New World Group, published a seminal paper in which he describes a "plantation economy" as an economy that is structurally part of the overseas economy, thus making the balance of payments (BOP) account the critical one in economic analysis. The "overseas economy" consists of two parts, which constitute a system: the metropole and the hinterlands. The metropole is the "brain" of the system; it makes the decisions for the hinterland on what is produced, and provides the

---

16   One may ask, how is this different from the colonization of North America, or Australia. According to Acemoglu and Robinson, the colonizers of North America (and Australia) met empty spaces of land and a decentralized native population. The settlers were poor or middle class. The process of colonization was therefore a contest among equals, and out of this evolved institution of property rights, creation of a level playing field, and investments in new technologies, accompanied by development of skills conducive to economic growth, and distribution of political power widely in a pluralistic manner. By contrast, the elites colonized the developing world, and the institutions that emerged facilitated extraction of resources from the many to the few. There was a failure to protect property rights (indeed, deprivation of rights to property and freedom), failure to promote incentives for economic activity for the many (instead, institutional barriers to economic activity for the masses), and power concentrated in a few hands, with use of resources to cement their hold on political institutions. DARON ACEMOGLU & JAMES A. ROBINSON, WHY NATIONS FAIL: THE ORIGINS OF POWER, PROSPERITY AND POVERTY 429–30 (2012).

17   For a more detailed accounting of this history, *see* Taimoon Stewart, *Competition Regimes in the Caribbean Community and Sub-Saharan Africa: A Comparison*, 1 AFR. J INT'L ECON. L., 84–159 (Fall 2020).

18   Publications by The New World Group can be found at https://newworldjournal.org. See Trinidad and Tobago Central Statistical Office, *The Balance of Payments of Trinidad and Tobago*, 7 (T&T CSO BOP 1951–1959) as illustration of an extractive, export-oriented economy with constant negative BOP.

19   For clarity, there are no poor white people in Trinidad and Tobago. If you are white, you are part of the elite wealthy social group that keeps exclusively to its own community. There is little social intermingling with the non-white people, except at golf clubs and elite gatherings.

system with capital, technical, and managerial skill, and other ancillary services needed for production.[20]

Douglas Hall encapsulate the experience of Jamaica as follows:

> ... for nearly two centuries, we were kept as a slave-worked plantation colony producing sugar and other tropical staples for export. With our small resources devoted to production for export, we became dependent on imports. The siting of our important towns on the coastlines had nothing to do with aesthetic values or even with comfort. It reflected the dominant importance of the overseas connection. The ships brought governors, soldiers, imperial instructions, and essential supplies for the support of the plantation system; they took away the produce of the estates. Confined, for the most part, to the small transactions of unpaid slave-laborers whose chief efforts lay in estate-production, the domestic sector scarcely grew and the economic pre-occupation with exports and imports bred its social consequences. The eyes of those who conducted affairs were focused abroad where the markets lay. Moreover, because we were British and were tied by regulation, and then by association, primarily to the British market, our economic as well as our political welfare depended on conditions prevailing in the all-powerful metropolis. Even now, with political independence, we still look to "the ship" with subservience. Because we live by exports we tend to ask questions about what people abroad will buy. Because of our dependence on imports we tend to look abroad for the necessities and the comforts we want. In short, we have not been taught by experience to begin with questions about our own needs, and our own means of supplying them. We have learned to be first curious about the needs and the products of others.[21]

Despite great changes in the physical manifestation of the plantation economy as a result of significant changes in technology affecting forms of production, and changes in demand, the logic of "plantation" production responsive to the needs of the metropole persists. Production priority is still export-oriented and still responsive to the needs of the giant multinational corporations, with the highest value added accruing to the metropole. This development model persisted post-independence (1963), and was present in 1990 when the SAP required introduction of competition law in Jamaica and Trinidad and Tobago. I argue that the metaphorical "plantation economy" still describes these economies today, with dominant knowledge being imbibed, informing policy choices for

---

[20] Lloyd Best, The Mechanism of Plantation-Type Economies: Outline of *A Model of Pure Plantation Economy*, 17(3) Soc. & Econ. Stud. 283 (1968), www.jstor.org/stable/27856339.

[21] Douglas Hall, *Articles: The Colonial Legacy of Jamaica*, IV(3) New World J., 7 (undated–between 1963 and 1972).

"development," that social mobility is still skewed in favor of those having lighter skin,[22] and that concentration of wealth in the hands of white and near-white people persists in most Caribbean territories. Deep racial divides between Afro and Indo populations in Guyana and Trinidad, a product of colonialism,[23] steer policies away from what would be most beneficial for the national struggle for state resources, with politics divided along racial lines and policies skewed to the benefit of whichever racial group has political power.

An examination of the economic conditions allows us to later enquire into whether these economies are "workable market economies" or ones in which market failures are the norm, an expected outcome of "development" policies, rather than aberrations. If so, are the assumptions upon which the concepts of efficiency and consumer welfare are based in accord with the economic reality in these countries?

A. *The shaping of the Jamaican and Trinidad and Tobago economies: origins*

Spain was the first to colonize Jamaica (1509) and Trinidad (1530), but the Spanish government paid little attention to its Caribbean colonies, being much more interested in the gold and silver that it could extract from Central and South America.[24] The economies of Jamaica and Trinidad lay undeveloped, and the population was very small. The British in 1655 captured Jamaica and introduced sugar plantations and slaves from Africa, transforming the colony into a plantation economy. In Jamaica, the planter class had little interest in the island beyond extracting surpluses and exporting to Britain, and were largely absentee planters with overseers left to manage estates. The level of brutality and expendability of slaves required constant replenishing of new "stock" from Africa. This in turn led to a very defiant and rebellious Black population, causing fearful white elites to petition the British government after the abolition of slavery to resume full control of government (crown colony government).[25]

---

22   There is the unfortunate practice of skin bleaching among Afro-Caribbean women in Jamaica in particular, in order to appear fairer-skinned so as to open up opportunities for social mobility.

23   The British imported Indian indentured laborers into the larger territories (Guyana, Trinidad & Tobago) to work on the sugar plantations, because the ex-slaves were able to survive on subsistence farming on crown lands and many refused to continue to work on the plantations, or bargained for higher wages. Arrival of the Indians caused great resentment since they took away the negotiating power of the Africans. Planters were able to keep wages very low. Indentured laborers were paid very low wages. The planter class was thus able to continue to extract labor at minimal cost. In smaller territories, ex-slaves had no option but to continue working on the plantations, because there was no unoccupied land on which they could squat. Again, the planter class weas able to continue to extract labor at minimal cost.

24   Tobago was fought over by several European powers and changed hands multiple times. The British finally gained control of the island by the Treaty of Paris in 1814, after the end of Napoleonic wars, and converted the colony to a plantation economy using African slave labor. It was united with Trinidad as a single colony in 1889.

25   Orlando Patterson, The Confounding Island: Jamaica and its Post-Colonial Predicaments (2019). Patterson traces current development trajectories, institutional outcomes, and social stability to the colonial experiences of Jamaica and Barbados. Black people were never given the opportunity in Jamaica to participate in government or the economy except at the lowest levels. By contrast, in Barbados, the planter class was resident, invested in the success of not just the economy but also the society, and with emancipation

In Trinidad, the Spanish government, in order to encourage economic development, issued a special invitation by cedula in 1783 to French planters from Martinique and Guadeloupe to relocate to Trinidad. They came in droves with their slaves, frightened by the Haitian revolution. Within a few decades, the society was completely transformed, with French planters controlling the economy and society, completely outnumbering the Spanish colonizers. British colonizers arrived in the early 1800s after Britain captured the territory in the Napoleonic wars, and the economy was fully converted into a plantation economy, with production of mainly sugar, but also tobacco and later cocoa. Slave labor and, later, indentured labor worked the plantations. A complex society resulted, with British colonial administrators, the French planter class controlling the economy, a white mercantile class of British and French controlling trade, and African and Indian laborers with a sprinkling of Portuguese-Madeirans and Chinese, brought as indentured laborers early on, soon abandoned in favor of Indians.

After emancipation of slaves and end of indentureship, the Afro and Indo populations in Jamaica and Trinidad were barred from economic opportunities both by legislation and by racial discrimination. In both the 1880s and in the 1930s there were riots all over the West Indies, protesting the poverty and social conditions of the non-white population. On both occasions, the British parliament was forced to commission enquiries into the social conditions in the West Indies; the reports produced by the royal commissions revealed appalling health, housing, and economic conditions. The 1897 report revealed that workers were barely able to survive on their wages, that disease caused by malnutrition was rampant, and that access to land for the workers was severely restricted to tiny garden plots.[26] According to the Moyne report of 1939, in parts of the Caribbean pay had not increased above the shilling-a-day introduced after emancipation (1838). Conditions in housing, education, and health services were abysmally poor.[27]

It was precisely during the 1880s that the white elite mercantile class gained control of the import and export sectors of the economies in the colonies (later to merge into powerful conglomerates).[28] It is clear that in the conditions

---

asked the British government to allow them to retain their colonial assembly. Blacks were educated, integrated into the public service over time and, indeed, the entire pre-emancipation police force was disbanded and a Black police force constituted after emancipation of slaves. This is not to say that Black people were not treated with brutality in Barbados, but much less severely because they were considered valuable economic assets. They were encouraged to procreate so that the slave stock was replenished from within. Retention of African culture receded in Barbados, and British culture inculcated, while in Jamaica new arrivals from Africa nourished the cultural retentions.

26 Bonham C. Richardson, *Depression, Riots and the Calling of the 1897 West India Royal Commission*, 66(3/4) NEW WEST INDIAN GUIDE/NIEUWE WEST-INDISCHE GIDS, 6, 169–91 (1992).

27 BEN BOUSQUET & COLIN DOUGLAS, WEST INDIAN WOMEN AT WAR: BRITISH RACISM IN WORLD WAR II 29–30 (1991).

28 For details of the origins and evolution of these conglomerates, *see* Stewart, *supra* note 17, Appendix 1: 156–59. Black people sought opportunities through education, primarily through missionary schools. However, Indo-Trinidadians were despised and treated with contempt because of their dress, food, religion, and culture, and parents were reluctant to send their children, particularly girls, to schools because of the alien culture being taught. This began to change in the 1950s, and Indo-Trinidadians embraced education, excelled, and gained social mobility through education, eventually dominating the professional class.

described in the two reports of the two royal commissions, that opportunities for capital accumulation and savings for investment were closed to the non-white population. To compound this, access to loans from banks were blocked except for the well-established white businesses. The lending policies of British banks that were established overseas in the nineteenth and early twentieth centuries were highly selective and restrictive, engaging in a certain amount of discrimination, and their assessment of risk and creditworthiness were based on assumptions about ethnicity, including that people of non-European ancestry in general lacked sufficient monetary and commercial responsibility.[29] Blocked from formal channels of banking, the non-white population developed an informal savings-credit arrangement (called "sou-sou") by which a core group of participants made regular contributions to a fund, which is given in whole or in part, to each contributor in rotation.[30]

The two largest conglomerates in Trinidad and Tobago are amalgamations of family-owned white companies, started as far back as 1881, engaging mainly in import of consumer goods and export of sugar, cocoa, tobacco, and other agricultural products. They operated as agents of British companies. At that time (1881), the Black population had been emancipated from slavery just 40 years earlier, and was barely scratching out an existence through subsistence farming and informal trade of surplus products. The Indo population, brought as indentured laborers to work on sugar plantations, were the lowest in the social strata, mocked and excluded because of their alien culture, language and religion. Indentureship continued until 1917.

B. *Old wine in new bottles: mineral extraction as "plantation economy"*

The Jamaican economy was transformed in the 1950s during colonial rule from a sugar plantation economy to one dominated by multinational bauxite companies. Initially, Alcan was invited by the British government to mine bauxite, but in the immediate aftermath of WWII, several US companies began operations in Jamaica, encouraged by the US government because of the strategic location of Jamaica in the Cold War years; Canadian companies also began operations. There was a growing need for aluminum products for industry (airplanes, cars, appliances, household items, construction industry, etc. all needed aluminum).

---

29 Kathleen Monteith, *Financing Agriculture and Trade: Barclays Bank (DCO) in the West Indies, 1926–1945*, *in* WEST INDIAN BUSINESS HISTORY: ENTERPRISE AND ENTREPRENEURSHIP. JAMAICA: THE UNIVERSITY OF THE WEST INDIES 125 (B.W. Higman & Kathleen E.A. Monteith eds., 2010).

30 Shirley Ardener, *The Comparative Study of Rotating Credit Associations*, 94(2) J. ROYAL ANTHROPOLOGICAL INST. OF GR. BRIT. & IR. 201 (1964). *Quoted in* Aviston Downs, *Black Economic Empowerment in Barbados, 1937–1970 The role of Non-Bank Financial Intermediaries*, *in* WEST INDIAN BUSINESS HISTORY: ENTERPRISE AND ENTREPRENEURSHIP. JAMAICA: THE UNIVERSITY OF THE WEST INDIES 152 (B.W. Higman & Kathleen E.A. Monteith eds., 2010).

Bauxite extraction and export dominated the economy thereafter, from non-existent in 1950 growing to accounting for 10% of GDP and 47% of domestic exports by 1965. However, according to Jefferson,[31] these figures tend to overstate the contribution of the industry to the Jamaican economy, since because of foreign ownership and its capital-intensive nature, only about 50% of the value of its output accrued to Jamaican residents. Furthermore, it provided employment for less than 1% of the labor force. Yet, trade deficit continued, as imports of consumables outweighed earnings from exports. While 50% of the labor force was employed in agriculture, and agricultural exports constituted 50% of effective export earnings (outflow of investment income deducted from total exports), the contribution of agriculture to GDP declined from 27 to 12% from 1950 to 1965, and income distribution was skewed in favor of the elites. Jefferson referred to a study of income distribution in Jamaica in 1958 that indicated that the upper 5% of households accounted for 30% of total income and the upper 10% of households for 43% of income while the bottom 60% had to share 19% of the total.[32] Poverty increased because of serious dislocation of the peasantry who lived on the land needed for mining, and forests that covered the land were cleared. Peasants received small compensation for their land, and many migrated to Kingston in search of work, thus creating the slums in the capital and a significant informal economy. Others went to Britain seeking work and expecting to be embraced by the "mother country," only to face racial discrimination that persists today.[33]

Similarly, in Trinidad, the economy was further transformed during the colonial period from primarily agricultural export (sugar) to oil production, starting in 1913 when Shell began operations (invited by the colonial government, Britain), and exports of petroleum constituted 81.1% of total exports earnings in 1959.[34] As in Jamaica, the petroleum sector absorbed little of the labor force, and agriculture declined.

The post-colonial governments of Jamaica and Trinidad and Tobago sought to address the problems created by dependent development in the colonial period in order to bring greater autonomous economic development and equitable distribution. Diversification into manufacturing through invitation of foreign

---

31 Owen Jefferson, *Some Aspects of Post-War Economic Development of Jamaica*, III(3) NEW WORLD J., § II (undated–between 1963 and 1972), https://newworldjournal.org/independence/some-aspects-of-the-post-war-economic-development-of-jamaica/.

32 *Id.*, § I. The Agricultural Census of 1961/62 indicated that 71% of the country's farms were smaller than 5 acres each and occupied only 12% of the total farm acreage. On the other hand, 0.2% of the farms were over 500 acres in size and accounted for 45% of total acreage. Larger farms tend to contain land of superior quality.

33 *See* GEORGE BECKFORD, PERSISTENT POVERTY: UNDERDEVELOPMENT IN PLANTATION ECONOMIES IN THE THIRD WORLD (1972). Two centuries of deforestation of lands to give access for sugar plantations and, later, to bauxite companies, has led to major environmental problems such as flooding, soil erosion, destruction of wildlife habitat, deterioration of watersheds, and drying up of rivers and streams. *See* Owen Evelyn & R. Camirand, *Forest cover and deforestation in Jamaica: An analysis of forest cover estimates over time*, 5(4) INT'L FOREST REV., 354 (Dec. 2003).

34 T&T CSO BOP, *supra* note 18, at 7.

investors was the fashionable policy directive of intellectuals from the North.[35] Operation Bootstrap in Puerto Rico provided the model for other Caribbean countries. Incentive legislation invited foreign investment to start manufacturing, granting tax holidays, accelerated depreciation allowances, duty-free importation of raw materials, a protected domestic market, subsidized factory space, and non-interference with exports of profits. It was expected that this would absorb labor and generate value added for the country.[36] Both Jamaica and Trinidad and Tobago followed this model in the 1960s, but the expected gains never materialized. Instead, foreign investors established turnkey industries: capital intensive and dependent on imports of intermediate materials for production. There were no backward and forward linkages in the economies, and little labor demand; instead, production involved feeding inputs into machines to produce finished products, as value added in import of machinery and intermediate goods reverted to the industrialized countries.

In 1971–72, income distribution in Trinidad and Tobago was worse than it had been in 1957–58. Rather than effecting redistribution, the economic strategy of the industrialization model had instead allowed the old commercial elite to retain, spread, and deepen its control over some [the most lucrative] areas of the economy.[37] Market concentration derived from privileges available to colonial elites was entrenched, and competition and socioeconomic issues persisted in both countries. In Trinidad and Tobago, disillusionment with the post-colonial economic program led to a "Black Power Revolution" in 1970. Between February 6 and April 2, 1970, Trinidad and Tobago experienced a state of upheaval and crisis unique in its intensity and significance. Thousands of people, mainly young Black youth, marched, demanding that political, social and economic power should pass to the people and a segment of the army revolted. Key issues raised by the revolutionaries were the exclusion of Black people from economic opportunities and the stranglehold white people had on the domestic economy: the exclusive hiring practices of banks and larger firms in the economy whereby only white and near-white people were employed.[38] Overt racism was institutionalized, with white people operating exclusively in their own tight-knit circle, regarding Indian and Black people with contempt, and discriminating against Indians because of their religious and cultural differences, starkly distinct from the dominant Anglo-Saxon culture.

---

35 Granted, the initial idea was that of St. Lucian Nobel laureate, Sir Arthur Lewis, who wrote a seminal piece on industrialization by invitation as a way to absorb excess labor in the Caribbean. However, his proposal included strengthening the agricultural sector, thereby boosting employment in that sector, and only absorbing excess labor in the manufacturing sector. His vision was implemented only partially, in that agriculture was ignored and wage increases in other sectors meant that it was difficult to recruit labor for agriculture at economic wages, and the manufacturing potential was emasculated by the capital-intensive nature of manufacturing that was implemented by foreign investors.

36 Jefferson, *supra* note 31, § III.

37 Jack Harewood and Ralph Henry, *Inequality in Post-Colonial Society: Trinidad and Tobago, 1956–1981*, 76 (Occasional papers (University of West Indies (St. Augustine, Trinidad & Tobago), Inst. of Soc. & Econ. Research) Human resources 6, 1985). Recall the Black Power Revolution in Trinidad & Tobago in 1970.

38 James Millette, *Towards the Black Power Revolt of 1970*, in THE BLACK POWER REVOLUTION 1970: A RETROSPECTIVE, 59 (Selwyn D. Ryan & Taimoon Stewart eds., 1996).

Jamaica took a different path to address the socioeconomic inequalities. In 1974, the Manley government, in defiance of the international political and economic order created to benefit the industrialized countries and their multinational companies, imposed a bauxite production levy on the multinational bauxite companies, in a quest for more equitable share of the bauxite earnings. This alarmed both the bauxite companies and their home governments (UK and US), and local elites. In retaliation, bauxite companies shifted their production to bauxite-rich Australia and Guinea, reducing production in Jamaica. Further, Manley nationalized key industries in Jamaica. Economic elites fled the country and external pressures were placed on the country by the Western powers, particularly the US, to fall in line with the needs of the multinational corporations. An economic crisis arising from a backlash from the US and local elites to Manley's "democratic socialist" policies in the 1970s caused the Manley government to fall in 1980. A conservative and compliant government was ushered in headed by Edward Seaga, who submitted to international pressures to reverse the Manley policies, and the IMF/World Bank were brought in to reform the economy. The bundle of policies under the SAP all supported liberalization of the economy and included devaluation of the currency, removal of many trade barriers, privatization of SOEs, introduction of regulatory reform, and legislating competition law. The Washington Consensus took hold.

The experience of Trinidad and Tobago differed from Jamaica from 1974 onwards. Whereas Manley used nationalistic and socialist policies to wrest gains derived from foreign investment for the benefit of the people of Jamaica, Trinidad and Tobago had an unexpected windfall from oil rents because of the oil shock in 1973. The government was able to pay off the majority of its external debt and embark on another development plan. The government had a twofold strategy: take control of key sectors in the economy to reduce foreign control, and diversify the economic base to be less dependent on petroleum for foreign exchange earnings. It nationalized industries in the petroleum, sugar, and construction sectors, among others, by purchase of Shell (Trinidad) Ltd., Tate & Lyle Caroni Ltd. (sugar), and Trinidad Cement Ltd.

A conception of development still rooted in the experience of industrialized countries led to diversification through mega projects in heavy industries in the petrochemical sector (ammonia, urea, and methanol), and iron and steel production with minimal employment opportunities, rather than into agriculture to improve food security and create employment. In addition, it allowed wanton consumption from abroad, distributed through expanding the public sector, and developing disempowering largesse projects that encouraged expectations of handouts, rather than training people to be productive. These failures continue to have repercussions even today, with a significant section of the population feeling entitled to handouts from the government. From 1977 onwards, the government borrowed heavily from the Eurocurrency market as well as other commercial sources to finance these mega projects, so that by 1990 central government external debt and guaranteed external debt of SOE and statutory bodies was US$2.52 billion.[39]

These policies were accompanied by a complex array of subsidies, price controls, import protection, and expansion of the public sector, undermining agriculture, manufacturing, and tourism. As a result, the share of non-oil GDP declined from 21% in 1970 to 16% in 1980. Import substitution in the manufacturing sector morphed from foreign direct investment during the 1960s and 70s to local private investment in assembly manufacturing, with similar demand on foreign exchange. Thus, development policies, including private sector investment, relied upon the foreign currency earnings from the petroleum export sector. According to a UNIDO report, Trinidad and Tobago's light manufacturing sector largely consisted of break of bulk, packing and bottling operations, with some subsidized assembly of imported kits of consumer durables.[40]

The decline began in 1983 when falling oil price was compounded by a domestic trend of falling petroleum output from depleted oil wells. Since 40% of government revenues derived from oil, and since public sector spending underpinned growth in the non-oil economy, there was dramatic decline in economic performance. This was exacerbated by a severe decline in net terms of trade.[41] The government responded by introducing extensive import restrictions and foreign exchange controls in 1983. This in turn limited the availability of imported inputs and raw materials for manufacturing. In December 1985, the government devalued the currency. By 1986, with the collapse in oil prices, the economy was in deep recession and unemployment reached 18%.[42] A BOP crisis and inability to service debt obligations by 1989 forced the state to access funding from the IMF and World Bank, and the SAP started the process of liberalization of the economy, untangling the myriad controls introduced in the previous decade. Trinidad and Tobago accessed a short-term IMF structural adjustment facility (1989 and 1990), and a

---

[39] Central Bank of Trinidad and Tobago, *Handbook of Key Economic and Financial Statistics*, Selected Macroeconomic Indicators, www.central-bank.org.tt/statistics/handbook-key-economic-and-financial-statistics. This debt accumulation occurred despite massive earnings from the export of petroleum and petroleum products (less UPA Petroleum), 1974–1986, to the tune of US$13.9 billion and total export earnings of US$18.9 billion. According to the World Bank report upon which the loan was granted, in a population of only 1.1 million, *nearly half the windfall ended up in consumption, which grew at a faster rate than GDP throughout the decade.* There was a massive construction boom, both government projects and private homes, requiring large imports of construction vehicles and materials. SOEs and other government agencies mushroomed in the economy and government transfers to these institutions grew from 3% of GDP in 1977 to 16% of GDP by 1983 (US$110 million to US$1,285 million). World Bank Staff Report, *Report and Recommendation of the President of the International Bank for Reconstruction and Development to the Executive Directors on the Proposed Structural Adjustment Loan in an amount equivalent to US$40 million to Republic of Trinidad and Tobago*, 2–4 (Nov. 21 1989).

[40] U. N. Indus. Dev. Org., *Industrial Development Review Series: The Caribbean Region*, 103 (1987). M.P. Dookeran, former central bank governor, commented that there is an underlying problem that crops up every so often, that is, the ability of the private sector to supply its own foreign reserves has always been limited. They use more foreign reserves than they earn in the non-energy sector. Trinidad & Tobago Parliament, H. Rep. Deb., 410 (July 20, 2005), www.ttparliament.org/publications.php?mid=28&id=153.

[41] With base year at 1974=100, the terms of trade was 121 in 1981, and steadily declined, so that by 1984 it was 100.9, and by 1987 it was 71.0. Ronald Ramkissoon, *Trinidad and Tobago: the issues and the evidence*, 119 THE COURIER, 35 (Jan. – Feb. 1990).

[42] World Bank Staff Report, *supra* note 39, at 4.

World Bank 15-year loan accompanied by an SAP in 1990, because of severe economic contraction, a substantial external debt, and depleted foreign reserves.

The government's attempt to take control of key sectors of the economy was derailed precisely because the new sectors (petrochemicals and iron and steel) were subject to externally determined prices, which declined just when the plants came on-stream.[43] The industries had to be subsidized, leading to a hemorrhaging from the national treasury. To compound that, mismanagement and corruption in the 88 SOEs drained the treasury. *The economic crisis was homegrown:* the result of misguided development policies and squandering of the windfall that accrued to the country from the two surges in the price of oil between 1974 and 1982. The SAP required market liberalization, privatization, regulatory reform, and development of an investment-friendly policy framework, including introduction of competition policy and law.

Akerlof and Shiller examined the role of prevailing dominant thinking (the stories people tell) in decision-making.[44] In their view, the stories that people tell are also stories of how the economy works: stories change over time, and with them theoretical postulations and policies.[45] In Trinidad and Tobago, one can argue that the stories that policymakers told were not in sync with how the economy actually worked, and that the stories were the ones that industrialized countries told to explain their own economies, and imported into developing economies. Any attempt by these peripheral economies to tell their own stories resulted in severe backlash from the North, as Jamaica experienced in the 1970s and 1980s.

2. What were real barriers to opportunities for the masses?

The real barriers to entry for the majority of the population of brown and Black people were rooted in the history of slavery, indentureship, and the plantation economy.

All societies that came under Western European colonization developed ethnic economic divisions of labor which were used to

---

[43] It is also worth noting that the government of Trinidad and Tobago and other oil-producing nations (e.g., Nigeria, Indonesia) focused on increasingly sunset industries that were capital intensive and rooted in the old paradigm of iron and steel, and commodity petrochemicals. Singapore also used a foreign investment strategy to develop industries in the 1960s, but coupled that with a targeted human resource development strategy. The country set up many technical schools and paid international corporations to train their unskilled workers in information technology, petrochemicals, and electronics. For those who could not get industrial jobs, the government enrolled them in labor-intensive untradable services, such as tourism and transportation. The strategy of having multinationals educate their workforce paid great dividends for the country. In the 1970s, Singapore was primarily exporting textiles, garments, and basic electronics. By the 1990s, they were engaging in wafer fabrication, logistics, biotech research, pharmaceuticals, integrated circuit design, and aerospace engineering. Ping Zhou, *The History of Singapore's Economic Development*, THOUGHT CO. (July 10, 2019) www.thoughtco.com/singapores-economic-development-1434565.

[44] "The human mind is built to think in terms of narratives, of sequences of events with an internal logic and dynamic that appear as a unified whole." GEORGE A. AKERLOF & ROBERT J. SHILLER, ANIMAL SPIRITS: HOW HUMAN PSYCHOLOGY DRIVES THE ECONOMY, AND WHY IT MATTERS FOR GLOBAL CAPITALISM, 51 (2010).

[45] *Id.* at x & xiii.

control and limit the role and power of the subordinate and the intermediary ethnic groups, to perpetuate the power and privilege of the dominant whites, and to entrench a rigid ethnic hierarchy that limit and regulate competition between groups. Order in colonial society was maintained by each ethnic group's knowing its place and its limits and by social and ideological doctrines which were used to legitimize ethnic inequality. Racism was therefore an integral part of all such colonial societies. The colonial state was used to maintain this racial hierarchy.[46]

Findings of an investigation into the conditions in the social sectors in Trinidad and Tobago in the early 1990s were that there was an increase in poverty over the period 1988–1992, with the new poverty rate estimated at 22.53% of households surveyed. There was also a severe deterioration in the distribution of income and expenditure between households. Spending per capita in the health sector fell by more than half, and per capita payments to beneficiaries in the social security sector were severely reduced. Unemployment had risen to 22% by 1992, and there was a rapid expansion of the informal sector.[47]

The few government projects during the oil boom years to give economic opportunities to the poor were ill-conceived and inadequately supported by sound policies. Twelve thousand acres of Crown Land were provided for small-scale farming, but this project was an abysmal failure: low productivity, under-cultivation, unacceptably low incomes from the farms and frustrated farmers plagued the project. Critical infrastructural support was not given, resulting in farms being subject to repeated flooding, and there were poor access roads, lack of potable water, and inadequate marketing arrangements. Several farms were not cultivated, and many others were under-cultivated.[48] Meanwhile, oil rents were squandered or invested in mega projects.

The government also developed a program creating a "People's Sector" resulted in 335 cooperatives being formed, but only 119 of the 335 cooperatives which existed in 1984 were still in existence in 1990. With the redecorating of the main thoroughfare in the center of the downtown area, the artisans were moved to the outskirts of the business area, and numbers dwindled to only a few who produced little else but leather sandals.[49] While the government's policy to redistribute wealth to the Black low-income groups through the unemployment program was successful in its intent, it destroyed the work ethic of the beneficiaries, while

---

46 Carl Stone, *Race and Economic Power in Jamaica*, in GARVEY: HIS WORK AND IMPACT, 247 (Rupert Lewis & Patrick Bryan eds., 1988).

47 Karl Theodore, *An Overview of the Social Sector Conditions in Trinidad and Tobago*, i–ii (St. Augustine: UWI, July 1993).

48 Michaeline Crichlow, *State, Class and Agricultural Entrepreneurship in Trinidad and Tobago*, in ENTREPRENEURSHIP IN THE CARIBBEAN: CULTURE, STRUCTURE, CONJUNCTURE, 53–91 (Selwyn Ryan & Taimoon Stewart eds., 1994).

49 SELWYN RYAN & LOU ANN BARCLAY, SHARKS AND SARDINES: BLACKS IN BUSINESS IN TRINIDAD AND TOBAGO, 58 (1992).

creating an expectation that they were entitled to handouts from the state, regardless of the economic circumstances. This program has gone through several renaming but remains entrenched still, as the state dares not remove it. It seems that crumbs were handed out to the poor with little follow-up support and supervision, while government's economic policies were skewed in favor of the elite white businesses and the middle-income groups who were represented by trade unions.

A major complaint of the revolutionaries in 1970 was the control of the economy by white people, and discriminatory employment practices, particularly in banks and larger firms. A study on employment practices in 1994 showed that while changes were evident in that there were more non-white persons interfacing with the public in banks, there were still residues of overrepresentation of white and near-white people at the top level of banks. The study found that the old creole white people,[50] that is, descendants of colonizers, were still entrenched as management elites of the conglomerates, even though they were by then publicly listed firms after the old white family companies went through a series of amalgamations.[51]

In the World Bank report of 1989 that accompanied the rationale for assistance, the most pressing social issue was the high level of unemployment at the time of the imposition of the SAP, being 23% of the labor force, with more than 40% of the unemployed aged 15–24. The majority of job losses were in the private sector, and wages, salaries and cost of living in the public sector were frozen in 1987 and subsequently cut by 10% across the board. Overall spending in health and education had been cut by two-thirds. The welfare programs (old age pension, food subsidies, and school feeding programs) remained at about 5% of expenditure, representing a halving in real terms.[52] By the time the Fair Trading Bill was being debated in parliament in 2005–2006, there was sufficient economic recovery due to the increase in the price of oil, the mainstay of the economy. Unemployment was at 3.12% in 2005. Youth unemployment had dropped to 6.4%. Therefore, the social pain of the 1990s was not as present in 2005 and memories were short.[53] Mighty oil once more buoyed the economy. What was clear then, and is still clear now, is that multinational corporations control the major export

---

[50] The term "creole white" emerged in colonial times to differentiate between white people who were born in the colony (creoles) and those from the metropole.

[51] Centre for Ethnic Studies, Ethnicity and Employment Practices in Trinidad and Tobago, St. Augustine: The University of the West Indies, Centre for Ethnic Studies, 1994:275.

[52] World Bank Staff Report, *supra* note 39, at 23.

[53] One can trace the fortunes of Trinidad and Tobago's economy to the rise and fall of the price of oil. In 1972, crude oil sold at US$3.60. With the oil shock, prices steadily increased to US$14.95 by 1978, and jumped to US$25.10 and US$37.42 in 1979 and 80, respectively. Hence the oil boom, and the massive inflow of money to the country. From then, there was a steady decline to $26.94 in 1985 and a collapse of price to $14.44 in 1986. In 1989, when the country went to the IMF, the price was US$18.33. When the government initiated the process of developing a competition policy, it was back down to US$15.66. In 2005 and 2006, when the Bill was being debated, the price had rebounded to US$50.40 and 58.30 respectively. The government of the day came into power in October 2002, and were beneficiaries of the increases in the price of oil.

sector of the economy in the petroleum and petrochemical sectors, and some of the manufacturing and service sectors in the domestic economy,[54] while the white and now Syrian/Lebanese elites control the domestic import, distribution/retail, and services sectors (the 1% minority).[55] Other ethnic groups resent the 1% minority that controlled the economy with their entrenched market power. During the 1970 Black Power Revolution, and the 1990 coup attempt in Trinidad and Tobago, rioters burned down many of the businesses owned by these groups.[56] In 1987, one of the two conglomerates, Ansa McAl, had an injection of TT$30 million by a wealthy Syrian, Anthony Sabga[57] (when the price of oil collapsed). Today, Syrians control the company.

The oil boom opened opportunities for small businesses because there was so much liquidity in the domestic economy, leading to the emergence of many small businesses owned by Indo-Trinidadians in particular (small local groceries, hardware stores, general retail shops etc., relying in many cases on purchases of stock from big importers, the entrenched elites). Barriers to entry therefore included

---

54 Foreign companies are present in the domestic economy, in the food and beverage sector (e.g., Nestle controls the dairy sector), and Unilever produces household cleansing products, security services, pest control, appliances and miscellaneous products, among others.

55 ANSA McAL, https://ansamcal.com/about-us/group-history/. *See Capital Investment Rooted in Privilege and Power in Colonial Times: The Making of Two of the Biggest Conglomerates in CARICOM*, in Stewart, *supra* note 17, Appendix 1: 156.

56 In defense of the Syrian-Lebanese people, they started arriving penniless in Trinidad and Tobago in 1901, fleeing religious persecution and poverty, and through their hard work, entrepreneurial acumen, and strong support from family members in this tight-knit community, they built their businesses and wealth. Their cultural resources, including the willingness to sacrifice and pool resources, account in large measure for their success. The fact that they were very fair-skinned, and married within the group to preserve ethnicity, gave them easier passage into the upper echelons of the society, and acceptance by the white elites. Black and brown people did not have this ease of passage, and still do not. The fact that the Syrians had not been enslaved and had their indigenous culture outlawed and beaten out of them, or scorned and vilified, made a big difference. They were able to preserve what expertise and cultural strengths that they brought with them. Black people did not have this privilege, and Indian people clung to their culture in the face of ostracization and being relegated to the bottom rung of society. For Indian people, the only road to social advancement was to become Christian, and a small percentage did. The rest only managed to gain social mobility post-1960s through education of their children, who eventually dominated the professional services, and through developing small businesses taking advantage of the liquidity generated by the oil boom.

57 Sabga was a Syrian immigrant entrepreneur who rose from poverty in the 1940s to wealth by drawing on his knowledge of textiles derived from his cultural background (Syria was a part of the silk trade for centuries). He and other Syrian-Lebanese took stock on consignment, and peddled cloth and dry goods from door to door, giving financial credit to the middle income and poor when white firms shunned them. Lacking access to credit or bank loans, these lower income groups pooled their savings into a sou sou, and each member was able to draw from the capital in turns. They were able to finance purchases in this way. Sabga went on the sell appliances in the same way, and tapped into this group by developing a hire-purchase program by which purchases were paid over time. He had the acumen to identify a group that was ignored by white firms, and built his business by providing credit. Other Syrian families followed his example, and soon they controlled the textile trade in Trinidad and Tobago, and subsequently expanded to other Caribbean countries. In the 1960s, Syrians entered manufacturing, and by 1970, owned at least 20% of the domestic garment industry (the women brought sewing skills with them from their home country). They got involved in the assembly of electrical appliances, in the paper industry, food manufacturing, the fast food industry and real estate. (Lou Ann Barclay, *The Syrian-Lebanese Community in Trinidad & Tobago: A Preliminary Study of a Commercial Ethnic Group*, *in* THE BLACK POWER REVOLUTION 1970: A RETROSPECTIVE, 217 (Selwyn D. Ryan & Taimoon Stewart eds., 1996)). Today, they control the high-end restaurants in Trinidad and Tobago. Indeed, a wealthy member of the community hosted the famous late Anthony Bourdain, and the event was aired on CNN on June 28, 2017. During conversation, Mario Sabga boasted that though they were less than 1% of the population, they controlled the food business. He described himself as the "Starbucks of the Caribbean." Indeed, this ethic group now controls major parts of the economy, and their wealth was enhanced through lucrative contracts from the government. His comments sparked outrage in the population. Selwyn R. Cudjoe, *State Capture: Syrian/Lebanese Style*, TRINIDAD GUARDIAN, July 2, 2017, www.trinidadandtobagonews.com/blog/?p=10146.

racial discrimination that limited upward mobility, and tight control of the import, distribution, and dominant retail sectors, and, increasingly, services, by elite white and Syrian people. Access to financing is still very much controlled and limited by the banks' policies requiring equivalent security in the form of property or other assets, thus barring a significant part of the population.

Similarly, structural barriers to entry in Jamaica, created in colonial times, persist. Access to finance is still a problem. The Jamaica Manufacturer's Association complained about the lack of affordable and accessible financing, as well as unfair banking practices. They reported that base lending rates are in double digits, and manufacturers and consumers alike experience difficulties servicing loans and gaining access to credit due to the high interest rates. Yet, when the Bank of Jamaica, the regulator, adjusts interest rates, a decline in rates is not applied by commercial banks at the same pace as an increase. Bank charges and fees are prohibitive. Collateral requirements are twice or more what is being borrowed, blocking access to small and medium enterprise (SMEs), and banks do not have the appropriate human resources to properly evaluate SME risks. Instead, banks channel their resources toward a few large companies that are relatively risk-free and placing money in government instruments. Instead of building capacity to evaluate risks, they compensate for loan defaults by establishing more hurdles for smaller borrowers.[58]

Findings of recent study in Jamaica revealed, "… access to household amenities and years of schooling are starkly structured by racial category, and even more robustly by skin color, across all dimensions. The findings challenge long-held assumptions that marginalize race [as a factor] with regard to social inequality in Jamaica."[59] An IADB study calculated the informal sector in Jamaica to be 43% of official GDP in 2001, and attributes the decrease in poverty during the 1990s (from its peak of 44% in 1991 to 17% in 2001) to the informal survival strategies.[60] Loayza argued that people make a rational choice of being in the formal or informal sector, and that they are dissuaded by the price of formality, which includes costs to access the formal sector (time and monetary costs for obtaining licenses and registrations), and costs to remain in it (taxes, regulations and bureaucratic requirements).[61] The informal sector is complex, and while there are those who simply choose to operate informally to escape onerous government requirements, there is a large part of the informal sector that is simply poor people engaging in survival strategies. Informal activities include small-farm workers, retail salespeople, street vendors, domestic helpers, taxi

---

58 Jamaica Manufacturers' Ass'n, *Effect of the structure of the banking sector on manufacturers*, XV COMPETITION MATTERS, 10–11 (Jan. 2011).

59 Monique D.A. Kelly, *Examining Race in Jamaica: How Racial Category and Skin Color Structure Social Inequality*, 12 RACE SOC. PROB 300 (2020).

60 Inter-American Development Bank, *The Informal Sector in Jamaica*, 1 (Economic and Sector Studies Series, RE3-06-010, Dec. 2006).

61 Norman Loayza, *The Economics of the Informal Sector: A Simple Model and Some Empirical Evidence from Latin America* (World Bank Policy Research Working Paper 1727, 1996), quoted in Inter-American Development Bank, *supra* note 60, at 11.

drivers and owners of small businesses and microenterprises. There are low entry barriers into the informal sector in terms of skill, capital, and organization.[62]

Remittances to Jamaican families from Jamaican diasporic communities in the global North are an important source of foreign currency for the economy, and an important source of financing for small entrepreneurs in the formal and, in particular, the informal sector. The link between the informal sector and remittances is strong, as the latter often provide the seed capital for the former. Family in the global North will send money so that their relations in Jamaica can start businesses or engage in higher levels of consumption than would otherwise be possible in the domestic context: a positive form of dependent capitalism. The *Jamaica Observer* reported that although the World Bank predicted global remittances would fall by 22%, with the Latin America and Caribbean region expected to record a 19.3% drop, Jamaica has defied this as remittance inflows grew by 25% to US$1.53 billion, and net remittances went up by 30% to US $1.41 billion from April to September 2020.[63]

Can one equate the economies described above with those of industrial countries? Are these economies experiencing market failures in an otherwise workable market economy, or are they chronic and arise from the very characteristics of the economies? Can market forces correct these problems?

3. Workable market economies or persistent market failure?

A. *Critique of neo-liberal capitalist ideology*

Competition law, in mainstream thinking, is meant to protect competition in *workable market economies*,[64] where competition is assumed to be present and market failures are few. The assumption upon which the Chicago school base their non-intervention approach to antitrust enforcement, is that markets work themselves pure without any assistance from government, i.e., they will be self-correcting.[65] The Chicago school's perspective on market power is that business

---

62   *From the Womb to the Tomb via Jamaica's $800 million Informal Economy*, THE GLEANER, Jan. 12, 2021. The article elaborated on the sector as follows: Workers on small farms are generally self-employed or unremunerated employees of family farm operations; their produce is used for personal and family consumption, or sold in local marketplaces. Retail salespersons purchase goods wholesale in markets, import them into Jamaica as personal property, and sell these products in unregistered shops, market stalls, or to tourists directly on the streets and beaches; their activities, and their revenues, are unreported, unregulated and untaxed. Domestic helpers, including housekeepers, cooks, and gardeners are commonly paid in cash with no income taxes deducted from their pay. Finally, drug dealers, producers and transporters must be included in consideration of informal economy revenues. Hyman feels if all of these are accounted for, then everyone would benefit.

63   Remittances–Jamaica's Economic Lynchpin, JAMAICA OBSERVER, Jan. 17, 2021.

64   Emmert defined "workable market economies" as ones in which competition is not perfect, but it is working sufficiently to secure the general push for producers and sellers to offer the highest quality at the lowest possible price today and in the foreseeable future. Frank Emmert, *How To and How Not To Introduce Competition Law and Policy in Transitional and Developing Economies*, 1 DEVELOPING WORLD REV. TRADE & COMPETITION, 87 (2011).

65   Herbert Hovenkamp & Fiona Scott Morton, *Framing the Chicago School of Antitrust Analysis*, 4–5 (U. Penn. Law Sch., Inst. for Law & Econ., Research Paper No. 19-44, Nov. 2019).

power is fleeting and unsustainable; in enforcing antitrust law, the US has applied strong rules against hard core cartels, but the standards to identify anticompetitive mergers are such that few are found to be anticompetitive and even fewer are enjoined, and monopoly conduct is seldom found to be anticompetitive.[66] The businessperson will make rational decisions based on self-interest, and benefits will redound to society as a whole.

In Fox's view, the Chicago school economists placed a "religious" trust in the market to correct failures.[67] Indeed, we get insights into the religious roots of economic thinking from Friedman's *Religion and the Rise of Capitalism*.[68] He reminds us that Enlightenment economists developed their world view from the conditions in their own societies at the time they wrote, and that the prevailing beliefs reflect ideas that had long-standing roots in religious thinking. He argued that the American non-interventionist approached is rooted in evangelical protestant epistemology, that human choice and not predestination allowed anyone to achieve spiritual salvation and, by extension, anyone can get ahead economically thorough talent and hard work, so government should leave the economy to the people's efforts. They acknowledged that some may be left behind, but believe that the vacuum left by limiting government's involvement in the market economy should be filled by the church and charitable organizations.

An important view expressed by Wilson[69] on the evolution of perspectives on US antitrust enforcement, is that the Sherman Act is very brief, simply prohibiting unreasonable restraint of trade, and left to courts to determine. The US Supreme Court developed the narrow focus on efficiency and, in doing so, compromised the intent of antitrust law, which was to curb the threat to the economy and democracy by unchecked monopoly. Moreover, in 1979, the Supreme Court defined the goal of antitrust as consumer welfare. Economic analysis became a tool to measure consumer welfare. However, there is asymmetry between the competitive effects and efficiency claims, in that it is very difficult to prove. Courts need to balance efficiencies with competitive effects, and so defendants need to show or verify efficiencies and proof that the benefits would be passed on to consumers.

There are significant differences between the American and European approaches to antitrust, one being that whereas the US goal in antitrust is efficiency and consumer welfare, Europe's goal is economic democracy.[70] Indeed, the EU Advocate General

---

66   Eleanor Fox, *Competition Policy: The Comparative Advantage of Developing Countries*, 69 (N.Y.U. Sch. of Law, Law & Econ. Research Paper Series, Working Paper No. 17-04, Feb. 2017).

67   Eleanor Fox, *Competition Policy at the Intersection of Equity and Efficiency: The Developed and the Developing Worlds*, 63(1) ANTITRUST BULL., 3, 4 (2018).

68   BENJAMIN M. FRIEDMAN, RELIGION AND THE RISE OF CAPITALISM (2021).

69   Christine Wilson, US Fed. Trade Comm'n, Comments at the OECD Global Forum on Competition (Dec. 7, 2020).

70   Frédéric Jenny, Comments at the OECD Global Forum on Competition (Dec. 7, 2020).

Kokott cautioned that in the mounting call for more economic approach, EU courts should not allow themselves to be influenced by the thinking, but should stay faithful to the intent of the EU law.[71] Drawing on Friedman's insights, these differences in perspectives may have originated in the different conditions and experiences in Europe as opposed to America in the eighteenth and nineteenth centuries. In Europe, overpopulation and inability to feed the population in a very inegalitarian society contrasted with the vast uninhabited areas to be filled in America, the need to expand population, and the fact that settlers were on a level playing field and had the means to improve material living standards generation upon generation. The concept of "progress" was validated by the American experience.

The tide is turning in the debate in the North, and the neo-liberal views of the Chicago are under attack, with the most ardent proponents such as Alan Greenspan and Paul Krugman acknowledging their mistakes. Conversely, works of resistance against the dominating knowledge, such as Dani Rodrick, express concern for the rising poverty and inequality as a result of globalization, and are becoming mainstream.[72] Interestingly, there has been a vibrant body of indigenous analyses by scholars and NGOs, including feminist groups and activists in developing countries, that have analyzed neoliberalism and the Washington Consensus, while the policymakers in these countries studiously ignored these voices and followed the directives of the Washington Consensus. There is always a lag in applying new thinking from paradigm shifts as policy-makers in developing countries, being risk averse, wait for perspectives to become accepted knowledge before adopting them.

This analysis of CARICOM economies show a very different reality from the evolution of the UK economy, where economic theories developed in the eighteenth and nineteenth centuries. Moreover, the history of economic development in the Caribbean is diametrically different from that of Britain and the US. The epistemological roots of non-intervention in the US economy were sown in very different conditions, and the opportunities that the free market presented to American settlers were not available to colonizers in the Caribbean, and certainly not to the vast majority of the population. The evangelical Christian world view of limited government and market forces promoting individual progress is not mainstream thinking in the Caribbean. While the majority of the population is Christian, the traditional Anglican and Catholic versions are dominant. Mixed into the medley

---

71 Julianne Kokott's opinion to the European Court of Justice in the Post Denmark case (21 May 2015 Case C-23/14 referred to by Frédéric Jenny at the OECD Global Forum on Competition (Dec. 7, 2020). Jenny further elaborated that the added value of expensive economic analyses is not always apparent and can lead to the disproportionate use of the resources of the competition authorities and the courts, which are then unavailable for the purposes of effectively enforcing the competition rules in other areas. The methodology applied can (as the submissions made before the Court by Post Danmark, Bring Citymail and the Danish Government amply demonstrate) prompt considerable differences of opinion. What is more, the data available for use as a basis for such analyses are not always reliable and presuppose that the dominant undertaking is genuinely ready to cooperate with the competition authorities and the courts, which, as the German Government has pointed out, is not always necessarily the case. (Elaboration provided via email to author).

72 Michael Hirsh, *Economists on the Run*, OTHER NEWS: VOICES AGAINST THE TIDE, 1–2 (Oct. 28, 2020). *See also*, Fox, *supra* note 67.

of religious influences are remnants of and full-bloom African religious beliefs and practices, some branches of Christianity that infuse their practices with African rituals, and in Trinidad and Tobago, Guyana, and Suriname, a sizable number of Hindus and Muslims. The idea that individuals, left free to make their economic choices, will prosper, is not prevalent. The Western paramountcy of self-interest is mixed with African community values. This is borne out by the surprising increase in remittances to Jamaica during 2020. "When the Jamaican economy gets tough and people are out of work, then friends and family in the USA, London and Canada will send money home," said Group CEO of GraceKennedy Limited, Don Wehby.[73]

The underprivileged look to government to create economic opportunities, but at the same time is distrustful of government doing so. Indeed, this may be explained by the fact that government in the independence period inherited many of the features of colonial government, which never had the wellbeing of the masses as a priority. Finally, the level of poverty and unemployment, the barriers to economic progress faced by the underprivileged, and the size of the informal sector, all speak to an entirely different reality and to different aspirations of the masses. As Martin Luther King Jr. said, "It's all right to tell a man to lift himself by his own bootstraps, but it is cruel jest to say to a bootless man that he ought to lift himself by his own bootstraps."

B. *Differences in small peripheral markets*

A national market economy is presumed to consist of a group of economic units that are within a defined geographic area, and that are substantially integrated with some activities of other units. Further, the activities of all the units can be influenced swiftly and effectively in a desired direction and to an appropriate extent through monetary, fiscal, or direct measures by the government.[74] These conditions are presumed to exist in industrialized economies, *but do they exist in the small vulnerable economies of the Caribbean?* The foregoing description of the evolution of the economies in Jamaica and Trinidad and Tobago provides a clear picture of these economies being appendages of capitalist market economies in the metropole, not workable market economies. Foreign ownership of the most important export sectors persists, and even locally owned manufacturing enterprises continue to depend on imports of capital and intermediate goods. The level of backward and forward linkages of units of production and cross-linkages are minimal.[75] The imperative of earning foreign currency in order

---

73 Steven Jackson, *Remittances rebound in June*, The Gleaner, Sept. 2, 2020, http://jamaica-gleaner.com/article/business/20200902/remittances-rebound-june

74 Owen Jefferson, *Is the Jamaican Economy Developing?*, 5(4) New World J. (undated–between 1963 and 1972)

75 There are some positive changes, as, according to the president of the Jamaica Manufacturers Association, there is a trend towards vertical linkages, citing the example of a major supplier of chicken being involved in feed production, chicken rearing, preparation, and distribution, and its competitor that is also involved in egg distribution. Another example is a food distributor that is involved in farming and also has a chain of supermarkets. Brian Pengelley, *Emerging Business Strategies and Implication for Competition*, 14th Annual Shirley Playfair Lecture, Vol. XVIII, 10 (Jan. 2014).

to import essential inputs to manufacturing and consumables continues, and the exchange rate of the local currency to the US dollar is fragile and can trigger capital flight in a wink. Further, state involvement in these economies is still significant, which is inconsistent with the Chicago school perspective.

The view of the Chicago school that business power is fleeting is not validated in the experiences of these two economies, where market power in import and retail accrued to the privileged colonizers during the colonial period, and was consolidated over time through mergers and acquisitions, blocking out the underprivileged then and now. It is clear that the markets described above, in their historical context, are very different from industrialized markets, and the theories developed in those markets are inappropriate.

Fox succinctly captures the differences in market functioning in industrialized countries, in particular the US, as compared with many developing countries with young competition regimes. In the US, capital markets and venture capital work well, while in developing countries there is poor operation of capital markets. There is no history of statism and privilege in the US, while developing economies are controlled by statism and privilege. There is robust entry in the US, while there are high barriers to entry linked to privileged monopolies in developing countries. There are few monopolies in the US, while there are persistent privileged monopolies in developing economies. Given these characteristics, the US does not take into account inequality in antitrust analysis, but Fox argues that developing economies require a different approach because severe poverty and inequality in wealth, power, and economic opportunity persist.[76]

Having a workable market economy, the US uses efficiency as a standard for assessing competition cases. However, the efficiency standard is based on the assumption that markets are generally robust and work well, that market power is hard to get and keep, and that firms act to please consumers, which in turn stimulates competition. By contrast, in developing countries, markets are not robust, and there is entrenched dominance and high barriers to entry.[77] For these reasons, the standards of proof that apply in the US may not be suitable for many developing countries. For instance, the equally efficient competitor standard may be inappropriate in some developing economies where there may be no competitor "as efficient" as the dominant firm.[78] Price changes may not impact on demand and supply as they do in industrialized countries, as they depend on elasticity of demand and supply. In small import-dependent economies, increased demand may not trigger increased supply because of the time lag for import. Prices will go up. Similarly, a decrease in prices would not increase consumption

---

76 Fox, *supra* note 66, at 71–72.

77 *Id.* at 74.

78 *Id.* at 77.

where incomes are low.[79] In Jamaica and Trinidad and Tobago, there is a significant informal sector, as people struggle to earn an income for survival. Even standard notions of supply substitutability may be limited because of import dependence, rather than producers/manufacturers responding to signals. Using a standard of efficiency and consumer welfare alone is inappropriate since they are not workable market economies. Rather, they are small peripheral economies, with severe structural rigidities, dependent on the export economy, with little internal resilience, and with market failure being the norm rather than an anomaly, and not self-correcting. Chicago school economics does not transplant well from big industrial economies to small commodity extraction/service-oriented markets.

According to Emmert,[80] the worst type of economy for correcting mistakes made by investors or market failures is one dominated by a small number of private individuals via monopolies, dominance, or cartels. In such markets, private individuals will pursue short-term private benefit at the expense of public good: charging higher prices, offering less choice, and not upgrading technology because of lack of competitive pressure. This author also weighed the possibility of governments making bad investment decisions, which could be worse than investment mistakes made in the private sector because civil servants will not personally pay the consequences. We saw that a small number of firms that gained market power through privilege dominate the economy in Trinidad and Tobago: private individuals, families, and firms control the domestic economy. We saw the ill-conceived mega projects that the government prioritized during the oil boom years, with bad results that the market could not correct. Conglomerates in Trinidad and Tobago operate with great confidence, integrated upstream and downstream in the import, distribution, and retail sectors, with subsidiaries in Miami to manage orders; shipping services are covered by other subsidiaries, insurance by another; they wholesale and retail. It is very difficult to compete with these established businesses. They are upgrading technology to facilitate operations because of their long reach within the region.

One can conclude from the insights into the evolution and workings of the economies in Trinidad and Tobago and Jamaica, that they are not "workable market economies" in the way that industrialized economies are. The assumptions of efficiency and consumer welfare rest on markets being workable capitalist markets in which market failures are few, and self-correcting. The economies in Trinidad and Tobago and Jamaica were, and are, dependent economies by design. An elite mercantile capitalist class controls the domestic economy, and has more in common with the capitalist class of the industrialized countries than with the poorer classes in their country. While there has been some reshuffling of ownership

---

79 Ministry of Trade and Labor (Barbados), *Preliminary Survey of the Distribution Systems and Markets*, 7–8 (1965), *quoted in* Alan A. Ransom, *The Fair Competition Act, 1993 (Jamaica): Analysis and Comment*, 4(1) *Caribbean L. Rev.*, 124 (1994).

80 Emmert, *supra* note 64, at 79.

in Jamaica, the divide between the haves and have-nots, and the conditions in which the poor live remain dire, making Jamaica only marginally different from Trinidad and Tobago. The taste patterns, aspirations, ideology, and knowledge-construct of the elites are all imported from the North. Risk averse, their savings easily take flight to northern banks. Increasingly, to hedge against devaluation, investments are being made abroad to get capital out. Crime, security, low productivity, and high cost of doing business all contribute to the weak performance in investment. Furthermore, the weak economic environment creates an incentive for businesses and households to hold investments abroad in hard currency.[81] Technocrats, educated in the dominant knowledge of the metropole, automatically accept prescriptions and policy directives from the center, so that development policies are stuck in reacting to the global economy rather than crafting policies that would create a level of internal resilience. Bob Marley's advice to the people in 1980 to emancipate themselves from mental slavery is still very relevant. Poets and authors of lyrics and literary works are the seers of society, with deep understanding of the social condition of the people and the ability to distill the real problems. Their stories explain the social condition because they are homegrown stories, not imported, like the ones told by technocrats.

III. Transplanting of Laws: Square Pegs into Round Holes?

Transplanting competition laws from mature jurisdictions to developing ones has both benefits and limitations, according to Gal and Fox.[82] Benefits are that there is a model to follow, which brings certainty to interpretations and enforcement, hence adopting the jurisprudence of other jurisdictions. Trade is facilitated, as external actors will more easily understand the rules.[83] Limitations far outweigh the benefits of such legal transplants, however, including stakeholders questioning the legitimacy of a law adopted through external pressure. The authors cautioned that transplanting a model could be unsuccessful or even harmful if they do not take into account the special characteristics of the jurisdiction adopting the law, including socioeconomic conditions, institutional conditions and capacity to enforce the law, and the risk of political influences on the decision-maker.[84]

In the CARICOM, Jamaica was the first to adopt competition law, in 1993: the Fair Competition Act, as part of an SAP that accompanied an IMF/World Bank package of fiscal support and a loan. Barbados followed, passing the Fair Trading

---

81 Marla Dukharan, *Trinidad and Tobago Balance of Payments Risk: Why T&T could be heading to default and a balance of payments crisis by end-2022*, WWW.MARLADUKHARAN.COM (2020).

82 Gal & Fox, *supra* note 1.

83 *Id.* at 7.

84 *Id.* at 9.

Commission Act and the Fair Competition Act in 2002. The Barbados Fair Trading Commission was established in 2002, bringing under one roof utilities regulation, consumer protection, and competition law enforcement. Guyana and Trinidad and Tobago followed, passing their laws in 2006, and establishing their institutions in 2011 and 2014 respectively.[85] There is also a regional competition policy, Chapter VIII of the Revised Treaty of Chaguaramas (RTC), signed in 2001. The RTC provided the legal instruments for deepening the regional integration process by establishing the CARICOM Single Market and Economy (CSME).[86] A regional competition commission, the CARICOM Competition Commission (CCC), was established in January 2008. Chapter VIII of the RTC requires all CSME member states to enact competition law and to establish an enforcement institution. As at February 2021, only four member states have complied. All other member states have draft competition bills but advancing the process has been challenging because of concerns about funding, and because of urgent demands for attention to other critical issues in these economies. The experiences of Jamaica and Trinidad and Tobago are explored here.

1. Drafting of the Jamaica Fair Competition Act (1993)

According to Allan Ransom, the drafters of the Jamaica Fair Competition Act (JFCA) drew upon provisions from the statues of New Zealand, Australia, and Canada for its language and drafting technique, while US concepts are prominent in the substance, but not in the form. Language is drawn primarily from the Australian Trade Practices Act (TPA) of 1974, and Ransom sounded a warning that arguments that the new commission would have to deal with will be hyper-technical, judging from the experience of enforcing the TPA.[87]

McKoy acknowledged that local business experience did not contribute to the JFCA's antitrust provisions that are not reflective of Jamaica's economic history. Rather, the JFCA illustrates a desire to make a radical break from the past and to make Jamaica's economy competitive in the twenty-first century. It was a deliberate attempt to engineer Jamaica's passage into a market-driven economy rather than to ameliorate deficiencies in Jamaican law. McKoy focuses in his analysis on the influences of US antitrust law, with the Green Paper being prepared by a US consultant, and pointed to the similarities between the purpose of the Sherman Act and the JFCA, that is, to encourage competition. The Green Paper describes the purpose of the law as "for the maintenance and encouragement of

---

[85] The colonial history and experiences in Guyana, Trinidad, and Tobago were different from Barbados and Jamaica, shaping the societies, economies, and political trajectory in different directions. For clarity, Guyana was colonized by the Dutch, but captured by the British during Napoleonic wars; Trinidad was colonized by the Spanish, experienced an influx of French planters, and was captured by the British during the Napoleonic Wars. Tobago was colonized by the French and remained so until capture during the Napoleonic wars. All three territories were ceded to Britain by treaty in 1802.

[86] Only 12 of the 15 members of CARICOM are signatories to the RTC (Haiti, the Bahamas, and Montserrat are not members).

[87] Ransom, *supra* note 79, at 111.

competition in the conduct of trade, business and in the supply of services in Jamaica with a view to provide consumers with competitive prices and product choices."[88] Interestingly, this is not in the text of the law.

McKoy identified one of the most significant flaws in the way laws are developed in the Commonwealth Caribbean, which he characterized as a black box: "one knows what goes in, but one is never sure about what will come out." This referred to the practice of using expert consultants, who import provisions from other statutes, then the draft is then passed on to local legislators/drafters of the law who lack expertise and understanding of the provisions, often producing strange results. The JFCA is a mismatch of provisions from Australian, New Zealand, and Canadian laws, with the legislature inadvertently codifying some "inarticulate language" that had lost much of its substantive meaning in the translation. For instance, the inclusion of the word "unduly" limit and "unduly" prevent, "unduly" lessen competition, etc., into the language of the JFCA was imported from Canadian law, but there is no legislative history to clarify the meaning of "unduly."[89] The JFCA differs from US antitrust in that there is no criminal sanction, but it does allow for private action like the US, and includes a pecuniary penalty, a civil fine, which is in the TPA. However, while Australia does not restrict sanction to pecuniary penalty, New Zealand copied the core provision from the TPA, but differed in this regard, restricting sanction to pecuniary penalty, and Jamaica seemingly copied New Zealand.[90]

Ransom did an exhaustive analysis of the JFCA, identifying areas that replicated the TPA, and pointing to some of the obstacles encountered in the enforcing of this law in Australia, sounding warnings for the JFTC. For instance, he pointed to the difficulty that arises from the fact that the courts apply traditional concepts of contract law to rapidly developing and constantly varying economic conduct of firms. He pointed to the unfortunate judicial tendency to require traditional contractual analysis both with respect to the level of collusion required to be proven and with respect to the type of proof required, rather than analysis of mutual economic effects, benefits or detriments of the conduct at issue.[91]

McKoy pointed out that the power to declare the law is part of the inherent equitable powers of the court, thus the Supreme Court has to declare that the respondent has broken the law. He felt, though, that the fact that the JFCA is more specific with detailed provisions, rather than the vagueness of the Sherman Act, gives Jamaican courts less room to define and develop the law.[92] Another important distinction

---

88   Derek McKoy, *Antitrust Law in Jamaica: The Fair Competition Act of 1993*, Transnational L. & Pol'y 183, 185 (1995–96).

89   *Id.* at 186.

90   *Id.* at 192.

91   Ransom, *supra* note 79, at 115.

92   McKoy, *supra* note 88, at 194.

in the JFCA is that it binds the crown, subject to contrary statutory provisions, which opens the way for disputes over issues of exemptions from the JFCA.[93]

Because the JFCA has been substantively revised and will soon be sent to parliament, there is no attempt in this paper to comment on the provisions of the existing law.

2. Drafting the Trinidad and Tobago Fair Trading Bill and taking it through parliament

A new government was elected in 1991 in Trinidad and Tobago, and policymakers embraced the liberalization program with enthusiasm. The process of introducing a competition law was started in 1994 as part of the World Bank–initiated program of liberalization of the economy linked to an SAP. In February 1994, the government engaged the UK-based Adam Smith Institute to develop regulatory frameworks for electricity and telecommunications and to develop a competition policy for Trinidad and Tobago to accompany the regulatory framework.[94] In 1997, Maxwell Stamp PLC, a British consulting firm, was appointed to assist in finalizing and implementing the competition policy framework for Trinidad and Tobago. Out of this consultancy, a Green Paper, "Competition Law for Trinidad and Tobago: A Proposal for a Fair Trading Act," was published in 1998/1999.

According to the minister, the Green Paper outlined the market structure and business culture in Trinidad and Tobago, and how those impact on competition in the market.[95] However, a perusal of the Green Paper revealed no such analysis of market structure and business culture. Instead, tailoring to the specificity of the small economy was limited in the Green Paper to ensuring that competition law enforcement should not require elaborate administration or burdensome compliance procedures and that its processes must focus only on real abuses, which are actually found in Trinidad and Tobago. There was no elaboration of "real abuses found in Trinidad and Tobago" in the Green Paper. Instead, it explained that the liberalization of markets would bring international competition through trade and inward foreign investment. It cautioned that competition policy must not freeze Trinidad and Tobago's industrial structure into a pattern of small businesses. The concern, according to the minister, must not be the number of producers situated in Trinidad and Tobago, but the competitive functioning of the market. He acknowledged that other competition issues would arise because privatized state enterprises will enjoy extensive monopoly power.

---

93   *Id.* at 195.

94   Trinidad & Tobago Parliament, *supra* note 40, at 397. Interestingly, initially, it was proposed that the scope of competition policy should go beyond restrictive business practices, cartels, mergers, and monopoly power, to include consumer protection, intellectual property rights, *utility regulation, industrial or development policy,* and general barriers to entry and exits, and that SOPs and locally based foreign firms should be included. Unfortunately, most of these aspirations did not materialize.

95   Trinidad & Tobago Parliament, *supra* note 40, at 397.

There was no mention of the existing entrenched monopoly power of the elite white firms in the domestic economy. Against this background, the Green Paper advised that government's proposals would have a single clear aim–to promote and maintain effective competition throughout the economy, and to ensure that competition is not distorted, restricted or prevented, either by private business conduct or by public policy.[96]

Maxwell Stamp's draft legislation was available in 1999 and circulated for comment to the private sector and international experts, and revisions were done based on these comments, according to the minister.[97] The bill was laid in parliament in July 2005, presented by the Minister of Trade and Industry, who stated that the objective of the government's competition policy was to strengthen Trinidad and Tobago's ongoing trade liberalization and economic reform program, which could be undermined by the anticompetitive business practices of firms operating in the domestic market. The minister spoke of the new paradigm of openness, which he claimed was now a reality, and the need to have the appropriate regulatory framework to encourage investment and industry. He clarified that that initiative complemented other initiatives the government was taking at the time such as antidumping legislation, liberalization of the exchange rate, and removal of the negative list, which all formed part of that period of the early 1990s.[98] In short, competition policy was introduced as part of a package of legislation and reforms liberalizing the economy under the directive of the World Bank, and with government technocrats fully subscribing to the "wisdom" of the Washington Consensus.

An examination of the minister's presentation of the bill to parliament reveals language using the jargon of mature jurisdictions to explain and promote competition law, but little is said about how the proposed law will directly impact on issues that affect the masses or resolve high barriers to entry that blocked access to economic opportunities. He actually said, "I know of no mainstream, as it were, thinking that is different from the competition policy that is advanced, other than at the margins," therefore admitting to a quest to be as mainstream as possible.[99] The contributions of the minister and his defense of the bill were valiant but rooted in imported mainstream thinking, with total buy-in of the liberalization process. In a defense of the bill at a subsequent parliamentary hearing, he said, "I want to make the point also that as we move more and more into liberalization and globalization, international competition, as a fact, would

---

96 Trinidad & Tobago Ministry of Trade and Industry, *Competition Law for Trinidad and Tobago: A Proposal for a Fair Trading Act*, 3 (1998).

97 Trinidad & Tobago Parliament, *supra* note 40, at 397.

98 Trinidad & Tobago Parliament, *supra* note 40, 398–99.

99 Trinidad & Tobago Parliament, *supra* note 40, 420. At the time that the minister made that statement, the US DOJ had discovered and sanctioned several worldwide cartels that had harmed Trinidad & Tobago's economy (Vitamin Cartel, Lysine Cartel, Citric Acid Cartel). The Graphite Electrodes Cartel, with a price increase of 50%, cost the mini steel mill in Trinidad & Tobago approximately US$21 million during the period of the cartel's operation (1992–1997).

minimize the need for legislation of this type. We have not, however, reached to the point as yet where it is not necessary."[100] Square peg into round hole?

Parliamentarians expressed concerns that the law would inhibit domestic firms by making them less competitive internationally, particularly the merger control provisions.[101] One senator queried the exclusion of the telecommunication and financial sectors from the competition law, pointing to the issues that most affect the average lower income consumer, such as the price of cable TV, telephone rates, and banking fees.[102] The minister's response was that these sectors are already governed by their specific laws and regulators and are best left to them. There was no comment by parliamentarians on the existing concentrated market structure of domestic firms in Trinidad and Tobago, but they questioned the market power of multinational corporations operating in the market, and whether the law will apply to them. Few in the country understood the underlying meaning and relevance of this law.[103] In fact, several contributors prefaced their remarks by acknowledging little understanding of the law: this was natural and expected, given that the law was being imposed top-down, and grafted into a package of liberalization policies.

Questioned on whether the ministry had consulted with the labor movement, with workers, with farmers, the minister responded that the Green Paper was put out for public comment, and that "… the business community requested a meeting and we facilitated. Let me say clearly, if the unions had requested a meeting, if the farmers had requested a meeting, if Tom, Dick or Joe had requested a meeting, we would have done the same thing because we considered it extremely important legislation and therefore we wanted consensus."[104] The ministry therefore placed the burden on stakeholders to come to the ministry with questions on a bill that few understood. The senator responded, "I get the impression that the hon. (sic) minister is simply transplanting a foreign culture, a foreign value system, a foreign way of life on an environment that he ought to study more properly."[105] Consultations were minimal.

---

100 Trinidad & Tobago Parliament, *supra* note 40, 555–56.

101 Trinidad & Tobago Parliament, *supra* note 40, at 408.

102 Trinidad & Tobago Parliament, Senate Hearing (May 2, 2006), 196.

103 By contrast, a homegrown public procurement law was developed and passed in the country in 2018 because of indigenous recognition of a problem by a group of concerned citizens that there was not transparency in public procurement and no oversight on the public purse in that regard. This collation of civil society and professional groups researched the issues and took the initiative to draft the law and submit to the government in December 2010. The law, Public Procurement and Disposal of Public Property Act, 2015, retained some 95% of the draft submitted by civil society. The part of the Act that establishes an independent institution to oversee procurement was proclaimed and the institution set up. However, there has been a significant reversal, as the present parliament has gutted the bill: (i) government to government, (ii) special purpose companies, (iii) internationally funded projects via loan arrangements (iv) a range of minister-of-finance-determined exemptions, in addition to (v) law, health and finance–all not subject to the procurement regulator, this rendering it impotent. Civil society is fighting to retain them. Government pushback on these clauses shows the culture of secrecy under which the government prefers to operate, and this institutionalizes corruption.

104 Trinidad & Tobago Parliament, *supra* note 102, at 186. Indeed, this author was part of a panel at a public consultation at the town hall in Port of Spain in 2000. The hall has a capacity of over 500. Three persons appeared, and they had walked off the street, curious as to what was being discussed.

105 Trinidad & Tobago Parliament, *supra* note 102, at 188.

3. Competition conditions when laws were introduced

Gal and Fox questioned how appropriate is the assumption of a functioning market system in a developing country and whether there is a culture of competition.[106] We saw from the discussion in parliament that there was little understanding of competition law in Trinidad and Tobago. These authors pose a series of questions that should be investigated before a country adopts a competition law. These include an enquiry of the level of government control, how liberalized the economy is and the degree to which free market principles have been assimilated, the condition of physical infrastructure, how wealth is distributed in the economy, the level of economic vulnerability, and institutional capacity to enforce the law.[107] They also posed questions on the level of political stability in the country, the level of corruption, and what is the culture of competition among businesses, as these conditions can impact on the success of law enforcement.[108] Fox further stated that legislation should respond to contextual problems that need to be solved.[109] What then was the situation in Trinidad and Tobago at the time of the drafting of the law?

In both Jamaica and Trinidad and Tobago, government control of the economy was significant prior to the SAP, and in both, SOEs were reduced through privatization. In Trinidad and Tobago, 40 of the 87 SOEs were privatized by 1995. Import restrictions and foreign currency controls were removed, and the central banks devalued the local currency against the US dollar, to which it is pegged. Similarly, there was devaluation in Jamaica, with the Jamaican dollar going into freefall.[110] The economies were liberalized and the governments were in a hurry to meet all the demands of the industrialized countries and the IMF/World Bank.

The rest of the questions posed by Fox and Gal require answers that are more complex. Was there political stability, with parliamentary elections and peaceful transfer of power? Yes, in both countries. Was there corruption? Yes, the level of corruption was high, and in the case of Trinidad and Tobago, this was fueled by the oil rents flowing through the country, and the many SOEs and statutory bodies provided opportunities to raid the treasury. Yet, there is pushback from civil society demanding accountability. The condition of physical infrastructure? In both Jamaica and Trinidad and Tobago, physical infrastructure development has been skewed toward the needs of the city and ports to support the export sector, and

---

106   Gal & Fox, *supra* note 1, at 10.

107   *Id.* at 12–14.

108   *Id.* at 16–17.

109   Eleanor Fox, Economic Development, Poverty, and Antitrust; The Other Path, 221 (N.Y.U. Sch. of Law, Law & Econ. Research Paper Series, Working Paper No. 07-26, 2007).

110   The significance of currency valuation is twofold, in that foreign currency paid for imports, and so immediately this dampened imports, including production inputs, and increased costs of imported goods in countries extremely dependent on imports for consumables, including food, so that inflation was inevitable. The dependence on imports for inputs to manufacturing negates the expected gains in boosting exports because of lower prices to foreigners. The theory is all wrong for these economies.

not toward critical rural infrastructure needed to support agriculture, for instance, such as access roads and flood defenses. This is particularly the case in Trinidad and Tobago. How wealth is distributed in the economy? There is still a very uneven distribution of wealth in the economy and society, in favor of the elites and a significant level of poverty, with the burden falling primarily on women, since there is a significant number of female-headed households in the Caribbean.

The major problem was, and is, economic vulnerability, and this problem persists in Trinidad and Tobago because each new government, lured by the oil rents, did not have the political will to diversify the economy to more sustainable and internally resilient sectors, away from petroleum and petrochemicals. The country declined into very difficult economic circumstances during 2020 because of continued dependence on a single commodity sector, and the price of oil plummeted. In Jamaica, efforts at diversification into tourism were very successful, but the strategy was equally problematic, with tourism dependent on foreign investment and extremely vulnerable to external shocks, with even more immediate effects than mineral extraction. A government travel advisory, a shocking international event like 9/11, a hurricane, and now, the virtual stoppage of tourism amidst the COVID-19 flu pandemic, can wipe out the main economic sector, creating massive unemployment. A similar story can be told about the majority of the other CARICOM countries, whether it be tourism or other extractive industries. This lack of resources spills over into an inability to build institutional capacity to enforce competition law. All the commissions in the region, including the regional commission, operate on a shoestring with minimal staff. Despite this, there have been good enforcements in Jamaica (within its constraints, as will be discussed), and Barbados, and with Guyana and Trinidad and Tobago just starting to build capacity and enforce the law. However, the Trinidad and Tobago Fair Trading Act (TTFTA) may prove to be problematic because of the way it was drafted. These concerns are fleshed out next.

IV. Some Comments on the TTFTA

1. Goals

Like the JFCA, the TTFTA has no stated goals in the text of the law. The preamble simply states "An Act to provide for the establishment of a Fair Trading Commission, to promote and maintain fair competition in the economy, and related matters." It is important to state goals upfront because it sets a guide for interpreting the provisions that follow, and it is important that the goals reflect the key competition issues in the specific economy, such as in the South African competition law.

2. Exclusions and exemptions

The TTFTA excludes the telecommunication and financial sectors from the competition law. This raises concerns about accessibility to credit to would-be entrepreneurs that are not privileged with property holdings that could be used as security equivalent to a loan. While the telecommunication and financial sectors are regulated, the laws that govern these sectors do not address competition issues, and anticompetitive conduct of firms in these sectors may fall through the cracks, with barriers to entry being erected and maintained. Fox cautioned that the financial sector should not be exempt because this would choke off credit.[111] There is also another concern: enforcement of cross-border conduct by the CCC involving a Trinidad and Tobago financial firm. The CCC is required to cooperate with the national commission in investigation. However, the Trinidad and Tobago Fair Trade Commission (TTFTC) has no jurisdiction to investigate the financial sector, and the financial regulator has no legal basis upon which to cooperate with the CCC. Yet the largest financial firms are in Trinidad and Tobago and they are spreading throughout CARICOM.[112]

While the regulated sector is subject to the TTFTA, jurisdiction to enforce the law resides not with the TTFTC but with the Regulated Industries Commission (RIC). The RIC on required to consult with the TTFTC in merger cases. Once again, the burden of training officials is increased by this provision, since RIC staff will have to be trained in the provisions of the TTFTA and enforcement methodology, including the economics of competition.

3. Legal provisions that raise concerns

There are several drafting errors in the TTFTA that need revision and some are significant as they could cause problems when enforcing the law. It therefore requires the TTFTC to issue guidance on interpretation of the law to avoid pitfalls. Some of the problematic areas are clearly the responsibility of the consultants who drafted the law, others are the responsibility of the legislative drafters who may not have understood the meaning of the provisions and the legal implications of the errors. Yet other problematic areas are written suspiciously in favor of domestic firms, and raise concerns as to the extent to which the private sector influenced the final version of the draft law that was passed in parliament.[113] The areas of concern are too numerous to itemize here, but the following are some examples:

> Section 7.2 The Commission shall serve on all relevant parties written notice of its intention to initiate an investigation under this Act in the form prescribed in the Schedule.

---

111 Gal & Fox, *supra* note 1, at 30.

112 For instance, Republic Bank, a T&T bank, and formerly Barclays Bank of the UK, is now present in Guyana, Suriname, Grenada, St. Vincent and the Grenadines, Barbados, St. Lucia, Dominica, and Anguilla. T&T insurance companies have expanded regionally.

113 Trinidad and Tobago Parliament, *supra* note 102, at 176. The minister stated that the private sector, specifically the Manufacturers Association and the Chamber of Commerce, asked to be allowed to give further input into the draft, and so another year intervened before the bill was brought back to the parliament for the third reading. In addition, some of these provisions identified were not present in the original bill.

Does this mean that if the TTFTC is about to investigate a cartel, it *must* inform the cartel members before initiating the investigation, and thereby give them the opportunity to destroy evidence before a dawn raid, authorized by section 9.1?

Other issues are the threshold for merger notification being assets exceeding TT$50 million (section 14(1)*(b)(i)*) and *(ii)*, at least one of the enterprises carries on or intends to carry on business in Trinidad and Tobago). An asset-based threshold is not indicative of the actual business activity on the market and would be better as turnover, which would be easier to measure. In addition, if only one enterprise is present in the market, then there will be no change in market share with a merger.[114]

Fines provided in the TTFTA are much too low and would not be a disincentive. For example, failure to keep an undertaking in a merger case is liable upon summary conviction to a fine of TT$25,000 (US$3,714.71 at current conversion of US$1=TT$6.71) and an additional further TT$1,000 (US$149) a day for each day the offense continues (section 16.4). By contrast, the Barbados Fair Competition Act's (BFCA's) fine for the same offense is B$500,000 (US$250,000) or 10% of turnover of the enterprise for the financial year preceding the date of the commission of the offense, whichever is greater (BFCA section 20.7(9)).

If a firm has been found to have abused its dominant position, there is no fine if the firm complies with the TTFTC's order to cease the abusive practice. The procedure outlined in sections 23, 24, and 25 of the TTFTA are as follows: the TTFTC prepares a report, submits it to the firm with a request for it to cease the abusive practice within six months. The firm is required to submit to the TTFTC the measures it would take and the timetable for giving effect to measures to remove *the monopoly power it has on the market*. There is no penalty for the firm if it complies within six months. Only if the firm does not comply, the TTFTC may apply to the High Court for an order under section 44(1), which requires the court to determine whether there has been a contravention of the law, and the court can impose a fine not exceeding 10% of annual turnover (section 44.2). There are several issues with these provisions. Firstly, since abuse of dominance is not penalized if the firm complies with the order to cease the practice within six months, it sends a signal to dominant firms that they will get away with abusing their dominance until caught, and then will not face a penalty if they cease the conduct within six months. This raises suspicion of private sector influence in the drafting of the law. Secondly, there must be an error in drafting to require the firm to *remove the monopoly power it has on the market*, since all the preceding provisions speak to "abuse of monopoly power," not to having monopoly power in itself being abusive.

---

114 Prof. Jenny also made this point in his comments on the bill. Rajan Dhanjee commented that while it is true that market share would not change, it does capture a situation in which a foreign firm takes over a domestic firm, and allows the Commission to investigate the proposed acquisition. This author submitted the bill to the following experts and received comments, which were then submitted to the Ministry of Trade in Trinidad and Tobago: Professor Frédéric Jenny, Mr. Rajan Dhanjee of UNCTAD, Mr. Steve Ryan of the European Commission, and the Director of the Federal Competition Commission of Mexico. The ministry did not adopt many of the comments made, with flaws thus retained in the final act.

Another issue is that section 3(1)(c) of the TTFTA exempts an agreement insofar as it contains a provision relating to the use, license, or assignment of rights under or existing by virtue of any copyright, patent (other than patent rings) or trade mark. This provision gives carte blanche to IP owners to abuse their monopoly power without fear of sanction (except for patent *rings*). Yet, developing countries are targets of many abuses by IP holders in industrialized countries, where the vast majority of patent owners reside.[115] Licensing agreements often contain grantbacks of patents to the IP holder if the licensee improves the patent, tie-ins for purchases of products not connected with the patent, continued licensing fees after patents have expired, among others.

Regarding the provision that "patent rings" are caught by the law, it is puzzling what this means, as there is no such thing as patent rings in intellectual property discourse. Is it a drafting error and meant to be patent pools, with collaborators using cross-licensing as cover for anticompetitive agreements? While patent pools can be anticompetitive, they can also be used for procompetitive purposes, and so should not be prohibited outright. In addition, why prohibit this single conduct while ignoring all other anticompetitive ways in which intellectual property monopoly can be abused?

What is even more interesting is that the Barbados Fair Trading Commission (BFTC) has a very good provision on IP, by which it is exempt except "… where the Commission is satisfied that the exercise of those rights (i) has the effect of lessening competition substantially in the market; and (ii) impedes the transfer and dissemination of technology." This law was passed in 2002. The TTFTA was debated in parliament in 2005–2006 and passed in 2006. Yet, the drafters of the TTFTA and the government ministry overseeing its introduction did not think to learn from the example of Barbados. Guyana did, including the same provision in its Competition and Fair Trading Act (section 24(3)), also passed in 2006. While the JFCA, like the TTFTA, gives full exemption to IP holders, this will be corrected in the revised bill, if enacted. The RTC, Chapter VIII, also exempts IP agreements, but does give leeway to investigate for anticompetitive conduct, as it states in Article 179.3, an enterprise shall not be treated as abusing its dominant position if it establishes that *"(b)* it *reasonably* enforces or seeks to enforce a right under or existing by virtue of copyright, patent, registered trade mark, or design" [emphasis mine]. The inclusion of "reasonably" allows room for investigating the conduct.

Finally, it is very puzzling that the TTFTA includes exports in calculation of market share that will trigger an investigation into abuse of monopoly power

---

115 Findings of the World Intellectual Property Report are that, before 2000, Japan, the US and Western European economies accounted for 90% of patenting and more than 70% of scientific publishing activity worldwide. These shares have fallen to 70% and 50%, respectively, for the 2015–2017 period amid increased activity in China, India, Israel, Singapore, South Korea, among others. WIPO, World Intellectual Property Report 2019–Local Hotspots, Global Networks: Innovative Activity Is Increasingly Collaborative and International (PR/2019/839, Nov. 12 2019).

(section 22(2) requires 40% or more of market share or such percentage as the minister may by order prescribe). There is a danger in giving the minister the power to vary the percentage of market share threshold for dominance, as this could be subject to regulatory capture.

> Section 22(3) For the purposes of subsection (2), an enterprise controls more than forty per cent of a market if–
>
> *(b)* where the market relates to the export of goods of any description from Trinidad and Tobago–
>
> i. forty per cent (or the percentage prescribed) of all the goods of that description which are produced in Trinidad and Tobago are produced by that enterprise; or
>
> ii. forty per cent (or the percentage prescribed) of all the goods of that description which are produced in Trinidad and Tobago are produced by a group of interconnected bodies corporate and the enterprise is part of that group,
>
> and in those cases monopoly power shall be taken to exist both in relation to exports of goods of that description from Trinidad and Tobago generally and in relation to the exports of goods of that description from Trinidad and Tobago to each country taken separately.

Anticompetitive practices on export markets do not affect competition on domestic markets. Moreover, it is standard practice now that countries exempt exports from their competition laws, following the practice of the USA. Does this mean that a firm producing in Trinidad and Tobago and exporting all its products could be considered to have a dominant position in the market? In addition, is this extra-territorial application of the law?[116] While Fox has argued for abolishing exemption for export cartels, this is because of the harm they cause to developing countries.[117] Until the US, EU and other industrialized countries abolish this exemption, developing countries should retain them, and not pave the way without gaining benefits.

While the institutional frameworks of other commissions in the region are a mixture of administrative and jurisdictional models, the TTFTA follows the jurisdictional model. As stated earlier, the power to declare the law is part of the inherent equitable powers of the court. This applies in the Commonwealth

---

116 Questions posed by Frédéric Jenny in his evaluation of the draft law in the early 2000s at my request. Rajan Dhanjee, another of the experts who commented on the bill, also raised similar concerns. There were several other comments made by Prof. Jenny, and other experts, most of which were not taken into account by the legislative drafters, even though they were provided with the comments. Note that the minister in his submission to Parliament said that expert comments were taken into account but the final act does not bear this out.

117 ELEANOR M. FOX & MOR BAKHOUM, MAKING MARKETS WORK FOR AFRICA: MARKETS, DEVELOPMENT, AND COMPETITION LAW IN SUB-SAHARAN AFRICA, 208 (2019).

Caribbean, and so, ultimately, any case referred to the court in Jamaica, Barbados, Guyana, or Trinidad and Tobago will require the judge to determine breach of the TTFTA. The competition laws of Jamaica, Barbados, and Guyana give the Board of Commissioners power to decide in the first instance whether there is a breach. The court would have the opinion and reasoning of the Board of Commissioners (with their cumulative knowledge and experience in adjudicating competition issues) as a guide. The TTFTA, however, requires the Board of Commissioners to submit the investigative report to the court for determination. The onus is on the judge to evaluate the investigative report and give judgment.

The issue here is that the 25 judges of the Supreme Court of Trinidad and Tobago are untrained in competition law, and are burdened with case overload and backlog that goes back years. It is very worrying that competition cases would have to rely on judges who are not aware of the specialized methodology involved in investigating and determining competition cases and have little or no knowledge of the economics of competition law. Moreover, cases are randomly assigned to judges, and so there is not even the opportunity to appoint a few judges who could be intensely trained to handle competition cases. Certainly, in CARICOM, there is great danger in having well-reasoned recommendations based on rigorous methodology required by competition law investigations overturned or dismissed in courts simply because the judge had little understanding or ability to assess the methodology through which the TTFTC arrived at its conclusion. This is a big problem for CARICOM national commissions, given that all final determinations rests with judges, and only designating dedicated judges who are properly trained could resolve the issue. It is a bigger problem for the TTFTC because of reliance on courts to make all determinations, not just ones challenged in court. Indeed, studies have revealed that where courts are weak, the integrated or bifurcated tribunal institutional model is more appropriate. On the other hand, where courts are strong, independent, honest, and efficient, as in the US, the judicial model has significant advantage.[118]

The second issue is the wording of the prohibition against price-fixing. Whereas it is universally agreed that price-fixing is the most nefarious of anticompetitive conducts and per se illegal, the TTFTA provides a defense of price-fixing:

> Section 17(1) An Agreement which–
>
> a) Fixes prices directly or indirectly other than in circumstances where the agreement is reasonably necessary to protect the interests of the parties concerned and not detrimental to the interests of the public;

---

[118] Eleanor M. Fox & Michael J. Trebilcock, *The Design of Competition Law Institutions and the Global Convergence of Process Norms: The GAL Competition Project*, 10 (N.Y.U. Center for Law, Econ. and Org., Law and Econ. Research Paper Series, No. 12-20, 2012).

One can imagine firms and their lawyers using this provision as a first line of defense, creating great difficulty for the TTFTC. One assumes that the burden of proof will be on the defendants, but it still places more work on the very small staff of the TTFTC to evaluate the arguments brought by firms on the basis of the provision. The TTFTC must then submit its findings to the High Court, where a judge must interpret section 17(1)(a), and may not be familiar with the legal reasoning that makes this offense per se illegal in other jurisdictions. The TTFTC will have to try to produce guidelines on interpretation in order to temper its use. It is also interesting that this proviso to price-fixing was not present in the Fair Trading Bill 1999 that was submitted to experts for comment, leading to suspicion of private sector influence.

The TTFTC has only just started enforcing its law and so there is no enforcement experience to draw upon. We therefore look at the JFTC's record of enforcement, and make two points: the negative consequences that arose from the way the law was drafted, echoing the caution by Gal and Fox that transplanting law from other countries could be harmful, but also, the clever ways in which the JFTC has worked around the hurdles to the benefit of the people and the economy.

V. Enforcing the JFCA: Successes, Pitfalls, and Hurdles

1. Successes

The JFTC encountered some crippling blows during the first decade of its existence, but out of those experiences and the constraints placed on its powers by court judgments, the JFTC deftly redirected its focus to market studies leading to very successful advocacy to government and the private sector, and bringing firms to heel by using consent orders and consent agreements. In addition, cases were taken to court and, despite the problems arising from inexperienced and untrained judges, have wrested some significant successes. Most important, the beginnings of a culture of competition have been fostered in Jamaica through its advocacy and enforcement efforts. Firm conducts that were prevalent two decades ago are no longer commonplace, such as limiting production or restrictive sharing of markets, bid-rigging, double ticketing, sale above advertised price, and price-fixing.[119] While it is undeniable that some of these practices may have gone underground, the mere fact that firms may be finding ways to hide such practices is indicative that they are now conversant with the law, and recognize that they could be sanctioned. Aiding this progress is the fact that the JFTC has very successfully built in-house expertise, despite its very small staff. This cumulative capacity-building has been helped by the fact that for more than a decade there has been very low staff turnover, and with the assistance of several international developmental agencies, staff obtained over time specialized training in competition policy.[120]

---

119   Derrick McKoy, *Message from the Chairman*, XXIII COMPETE, 11 (Dec. 2018).

120   David Miller, *FTC at 25: The Future is Bright*, XXIII COMPETE, 14 (Dec. 2018).

From 2005 to 2018, the JFTC made over 48 advocacy efforts geared toward introducing, preserving, or enhancing competition in several markets in Jamaica, including influencing government policy, thus signifying acceptance by policymakers of the institution's expertise in competition matters.[121] Moreover, the JFTC based its advocacy on findings of market studies, market enquiries, and investigations into complaints. In August 2018, the JFTC engaged LEAR Lab of Italy, funded by a World Bank project on "Enhancing Competitiveness in Jamaica." The remit of the project was to evaluate the JFTC's advocacy efforts and recommend improvements. As a result of that project, the JFTC is now conducting one-on-one discussions with government agencies and regulators, and is formalizing relationships with these agencies through Memorandums of Understanding.[122]

There are many examples of successful interventions, ranging from gaining the cooperation of firms and trade associations, to influencing government agencies and regulators. For instance, following research into the conduct of banks, the JFTC collaborated with the Jamaica Bankers Association to ensure that information such as the posting of exchange rates, advertising of interest rates, and computation of interest charges for credit card purchases are clearly disclosed to customers. Advocacy to the utility regulator led to policy change and revision of law in the telecommunication sector. The JFTC investigated the telecommunications provider, Digicel, for its pricing strategy regarding calls terminated on its mobile network. It concluded that Digicel's pricing strategy was likely to substantially lessen competition and harm subscribers of the fixed and mobile services, and that a lax regulatory environment facilitated this anticompetitive conduct.

The JFTC successfully advocated to the Office of Utilities Regulation for the regulation of mobile termination rates and that all mobile networks should be subjected to cost-oriented regulation of mobile termination, as it would yield substantial long-term benefits to subscribers. As a result, the Telecommunications Act was amended in 2012, setting an interim termination rate of J$5[123] per minute. A spillover effect of this was that the dominant provider, LIME, also reduced its retail price for prepaid mobile service from J$12 to J$6.99 per minute and Digicel reduced its retail price from J$14 to J$6.99 per minute.[124] There are other success stories of advocacy leading to changes in firms' behavior and promoting a culture of competition. Another area of achievement is in conducting market studies and market inquiries. There are 14 market studies published on the JFTC website, with subjects including supply of gasoline and price of petroleum, cement, pharmaceuticals, telecommunications, tourism, education, commercial banking, the grocery sector, credit union sector, and money-lending services. These market studies informed and reinforced advocacy efforts with hard data.

---

121 *Id.* at 14.

122 JFTC, *FTC Sharpens Competition Advocacy Tools*, XXIV COMPETE, 7 (Jan. 2020).

123 In 2012, US$1=J$90 on average (Bank of Jamaica historical rates).

124 JFTC, *FTC contributes to lowering of mobile call rates*, VIII COMPETE, 13 (Jan. 2014).

2. Pitfalls

However, pitfalls were in no short supply in the early years, resulting from a failure to strategically target winnable cases in the first instance, to a huge blow from the court, a result of a drafting error in the JFCA. The JFTC attempted to discipline the Bar Association for breach of the JFCA, because of the restrictions on advertising in the canons of professional ethics (*General Legal Council v. Fair Trading Commission*, November 1995). It was ill-advised of the JFTC, in its infancy, to target the association most well equipped to defend itself. The JFTC had written to the Jamaican Bar Association to express its view that some of the canons of professional ethics that govern the legal profession are inconsistent with the JFCA, citing section 35, which deals with conspiracy, combination, agreement or arrangement to, inter alia, restrain or injure competition. The General Legal Council (GLC) took a case to court declaring that it operated under rules made under the Legal Professions Act, and was not governed by the JFCA. The court ruled in favor of the GLC and exempted the legal profession from the JFCA.[125] It is interesting that in Australia there were some constitutional difficulties with applying the TPA to the professions, and the National Competition Policy Review (the Hilmer Report, August 25, 1993) and the JFCA's Draft Report on the Legal Profession (October 7, 1993) called for radical changes in the regulation of the legal profession. It is possible that the JFTC could have been influenced by this debate?[126]

The other major problem encountered by the JFTC was in the Jamaica Stock Exchange (JSE) case (*Jamaica Stock Exchange v. Fair Trading Commission*, January 2001). The JFTC sought to intervene in a conduct engaged in by the JSE in response to a complaint, but was immediately brought before the Supreme Court by the JSE. The JSE requested a declaration that the JSE is governed by the provisions of the Securities Act, and not the JFCA, and that the JFTC had acted ultra vires. It requested a further declaration that the JFTC was in breach of natural justice since there was no clear firewall between its investigative and adjudicative arms (though, de facto, the JFTC operated with a firewall). *The flaw was in the drafting of the law.* The Supreme Court ruled in favor of the JFTC, but the Securities Commission appealed the ruling. The Appeal Court came back with a ruling in favor of the JSE and directed the JFTC to address the issue of breach of natural justice by revising its law and reforming its institutional structure.[127]

This error in drafting by the consultant proved to be very costly, constraining the Board of Commissioners to fully utilize the powers given to it in the JFCA. Since 2001, the Commissioners have not conducted hearings, even though

---

125   Barbara Lee, *Competition Policy in the Caribbean: Some Emerging Trends and Developments*, X Competition Matters, 12–13 (Dec. 2005).

126   Ransom, *supra* note 79, footnote 21, 116.

127   Judgment available at https://jftc.gov.jm/wp-content/uploads/2017/08/Jamaica-Stock-Exchange-vs.-The-Fair-Trading-Commission-January-2001.pdf.

empowered by section 7 of the JFCA. The JFTC continued its work by using consent agreements and the courts where necessary to tackle anticompetitive conduct. Between 1993 and 2018, the JFTC entered into consent agreements with 28 businesses, usually requiring the respondent to commit to not repeating the offensive conduct, issuing a public apology, and providing redress to the informants as well as pay the JFTC's costs. Sectors include the telecommunications, education, household furniture, live entertainment, automobile, and hotel services.[128] There were 12 judgments during the same period. The vast majority of these cases were brought under section 37(1) of the JFCA, which deals with consumer protection. While there was concern that the focus has been mostly directed toward the consumer protection provisions of the JFCA, and not the competition provisions,[129] there is a positive to this, that is, the JFTC made its presence known to the average consumer, built a reputation for defending consumers, and thus gained confidence in the public sphere. That in itself is an achievement over its 27 years of existence, and with the blow that it received from the judgment in the JSE case.

Initially, sectors that were regulated under specific sectoral laws were defiant in maintaining their independence from the JFCA and JFTC. We have seen that the JFTC has been able to claim jurisdiction through using the softer approach of research-based advocacy. This next significant case illustrates how the JFTC used its legal acumen and the language of the law to pave an innovative path to interpretation of the provisions prohibiting anticompetitive agreements (section 17(1)), and to bring to heel the defiant regulatory authorities. In *Digicel Jamaica Ltd. v. Fair Trading Commission*, the issue was the acquisition by Digicel Jamaica Limited (Digicel) of Oceanic Digital Jamaica Limited (Claro) through a stock purchase agreement and transfer of Claro's license to Digicel. The Telecommunications Authority approved the merger. Note that the minister responsible was the prime minister, and so approval came from him. The JFTC objected, stating that this acquisition could substantially reduce competition in the market, and asserted its right to investigate the merger for anticompetitive effects, citing the provision in its law prohibiting anticompetitive agreements (section 17(1)) This section applies to agreements that contain provisions that have as their purpose the substantial lessening of competition, or have or *are likely to have* the effect of substantially lessening competition in a market.

A. *Wresting success from failure*

Digicel and Claro took the case to the Supreme Court questioning the JFTC's jurisdiction to examine and rule on this acquisition. The High Court ruled in favor of the JFTC, but the two firms appealed the decision. The Jamaican Court of

---

128 JFTC, *On the Record: 1993.11.01–2018.09.30*, XXIII Compete, 24 (Dec. 2018).

129 Lee, *supra* note 125, at 12.

Appeal, in 2014, held that while the JFTC has jurisdiction in the telecommunications industry, it did not have jurisdiction over the acquisition by Digicel of Claro, which was approved by the relevant minister under the Telecommunications Act. Not to be stopped, the JFTC took the case to the highest court of appeal for this jurisdiction, the Privy Council in the UK, and, in a major victory for the JFTC, in August 2017 the Privy Council agreed with the decision, stating that:

- even *without a merger control regulation* provision as part of its law; and
- notwithstanding the *regulator's decision* (Telecommunication Authority) regarding the merger;
- the Competition Commission *has the authority of overseeing any sector or issue that can negatively impact competition in the relevant market*; and
- that the *provisions on anticompetitive agreements in the law can be applied* to acquisition agreements even in sectors overseen by a regulator.

It is important to note that in this case, as in others, the legal staff of the JFTC represented the JFTC, developing the legal argument and arguing the case before the Supreme Court, the Appeal Court, and the Privy Council. This gives testimony to the legal expertise that the JFTC has grown over the last two decades. It also shows the confidence that the Commissioners had in the legal department, as they were adamant that the JFTC should not hire British barristers to argue the case before the Privy Council.[130] Despite the drawbacks arising from the law being a hodgepodge of legal imports, the JFTC has deftly used its acumen to overcome the initial hurdles encountered. By this Privy Council decision, the issue of the scope of jurisdiction of the JFTC over regulated sectors has been firmly resolved. Yet, despite this valiant effort and success story, one must consider that the ineptitude of the drafters of the law (foreign consultants paid at a considerable fee, no doubt) led to the partial crippling of the JFTC for the last two decades, and cost the JFTC time, money, and opportunities to develop its institution robustly.

B. *Another hurdle to cross: design of institutional structure*

The Supreme Court judge's remark that a tribunal be established separate from the JFTC to correct the breach of natural justice has led to intense debate and disagreements on how to reform the institution. Some advocate the establishment of a tribunal, others propose a jurisdictional model whereby all cases are sent to the courts, and yet others argue for retaining the existing institution, but with legal language to ensure separation of investigative and adjudicative powers. B. St. Michael Hylton, former solicitor general of Jamaica, argued the case for

---

130   Michelle Brown, *A Remarkable Institutional Architecture*, XXIII COMPETE, 12 (Dec. 2018).

an independent tribunal. He pointed out that regardless of arguments for maximizing efficiency and expertise, or against increased cost, ultimately the court will only examine procedural fairness. Even if in the law the separation of investigative and adjudicative functions is made explicit, the court may not be convinced of conformity to the rule against ex parte communication between the two arms of the JFTC. In his view, in a small organization with a small number of staff, and in a small society, a court is less likely to accept that there will be no private contact. He also pointed to a significant cultural difference between Jamaican (and Caribbean) society and larger, more developed societies. Jamaicans (including Jamaican judges) are more cynical and suspicious when it comes to public officials. A Jamaican judge may be less likely than his American or New Zealand counterparts to accept that a rule against ex parte communication has been or is likely to be scrupulously followed.[131] Small size would also have an impact on the performance of commissioners, since the one who has taken part in an investigation would be more invested in the outcome than in large jurisdictions, and colleagues may be less willing to reject the claim or criticize the work and professional judgment.[132] Finally, Hylton argued against adjudication of all matters by the courts because competition law is a specialist area and there is an advantage to having a dedicated tribunal develop the expertise. He also pointed out that the court system is notoriously overburdened and that claims filed in the Supreme Court take years to come to trial.[133]

Peter Gordon argued the case for adjusting the JFCA to assign investigative and adjudicative functions to different entities within the JFTC with appropriate provisions and regulations, and with the court acting as an appellant body.[134] He pointed to the fact that competition law codifies economic structures and conduct, requiring lawyers to have good understanding of economic concepts, and that adjudicating panels are best having persons of different skills, as in the Board of Commissioners.[135] This option would be both effective and economic. Bringing together an occasional tribunal may not meet these critical requirements, and could prove ineffective by bringing together once or twice a year persons unconnected with competition matters to adjudicate on competition matters. He further argued that, in a small society like Jamaica, there is not a wide pool of expertise in this area of law. He pointed to the findings of an UNCTAD review of the JFTC in 2006 and a study commissioned by the government to examine the Jamaica regulatory impact. Both reports raised concerns about the

---

131 B. St. Michael Hylton QC, *An Independent Tribunal as an Alternative Avenue for Adjudication*, 35(1) WEST INDIAN L.J. 241, 245 (2010).

132 *Id.* at 246.

133 *Id.* at 247. For clarity, note that in Jamaica the court of first instance is called the Supreme Court, while in Trinidad and Tobago it is called the High Court.

134 Peter Gordon, *The Case for Maintaining a Single Competition Agency for Investigation and Adjudication in all Competition Matters*, 35(1) WEST INDIAN L.J. 256, 272 (2010).

135 *Id.* at 257.

excessive cost of having separate institutions for investigation and adjudication.[136] A decision has been made since the JFCA was extensively revised, but is yet not publicly available.

In sum, while the JFCA has fundamental flaws arising out of a medley of provisions imported from the laws of New Zealand, Australia, and Canada, and with overtures of US antitrust, the JFTC has demonstrated that it has been able to overcome the pitfalls it encountered and develop institutional strength. It learned lessons from the experience, and was still able to work with the law and successfully grow a culture of competition, changing business behavior through consent agreements and court judgments. Once its power of adjudication was in question, it moved to a pure jurisdictional model, taking cases directly to the courts. This has resulted in a growing body of jurisprudence based on indigenous conditions. Yes, there were problems arising from court decisions that demonstrated a lack of understanding of the law and economics, but this has occurred in other countries, including in decisions of the US FTC, the EU Commission and the South African Competition Tribunal, where the commissions had their arguments overturned by courts. The problems are many, but the path to overcome these problems has been well defined by the JFTC. It is interesting that the BFTC is following a sure-footed, steady path of informed advocacy to change firm conduct and to build a culture of compliance, with resort to courts when necessary.

VI. The Human Factor: The Quest for Inclusion of Equity and Public Interest

1. Do the laws integrate equity and public interest?

In economies where there are entrenched privileged companies dominating key sectors that affect the population at large, particularly the vulnerable, such as import, distribution and retail in the externally propelled economies of CARICOM, it is of paramount importance to have provisions in the law to constrain the abuse of power by the privileged. A perusal of the TTFTA does not reveal any provisions that directly take into account the underprivileged or disadvantaged. Instead, the TTFTA is very lenient toward dominant firms, allowing them to abuse their dominance for six months before stopping the abusive conduct, and once they do so within the time limit, there is no sanction. It allows price-fixing cartels a defense where the agreement is in the interest of the parties (are they not always in the interest of the cartel members?), and does not harm public interest. The provision is not pro public interest, but takes a negative approach. This and other provisions in the TTFTA raise concerns about the extent of influence the private sector wielded in the drafting of the law, given the lenient approach to sanctions, including fines that are abysmally low and

---

136 *Id.* at 265.

petty cash for dominant firms. The broad exemption to IP holders is in the interest of foreign companies, as the number if IP holders in Trinidad and Tobago is minuscule, and more in music copyrights than patents. In addition, the inclusion of exports in market power analysis is a reversal of the possible benefits to local firms of export cartels. It is true that Fox advocated for industrialized countries to remove exemption of export cartels because they harm developing countries.[137] However, until industrialized countries stop exempting export cartels, developing countries should continue to exempt them and gain whatever little benefit they can from the practice.

The laws in CARICOM do not contain provisions for directly addressing equity and public interest concerns in enforcement. The BFCA states: *"(c)* to ensure that all enterprises, irrespective of size, have the opportunity to participate equitably in the market," opening the way for inclusion of equity considerations. However, this provision is not threaded throughout the BFCA to reinforce the need to safeguard market opportunity for all firms regardless of size, and to keep this in focus in enforcement. A methodology for including fairness and equity in competition law enforcement directs enforcers to always ask who gains by a decision, how the poor will be affected, and are there avenues to skew decisions in favor of the disadvantaged, and not dominant firms? It means moving away from "competition law protects competition" and nothing else.

The other three competition laws in CARICOM include a section on authorizations that permits application to the commission for its opinion on whether an intended agreement or practice would contravene the law, and the commission may take into account public interest in its evaluation (JFCA section 29.2*(a)*; BFCA section 29.2; Guyana Competition and Fair Trading Act section 35.2 *(a)*). The TTFTA does not include authorization, and there is nothing codified that speaks to public interest except a defense of price-fixing in section 17(1)*(a)*, that it is not detrimental to the interests of the public. Yet, according to Jenny, more than half of OECD countries have public interest goals in their competition law, including the EU, and not just consumer welfare standard. He refuted the claim that inclusion of public interest would lead to uncertainty in enforcement, but cautioned that the provision must be explicit and transparent, and that guidelines should be published on how the commission will apply the provision to cases (as South Africa's commission has done).[138] The experience of South Africa shows that having explicit public interest goals paves the way for stakeholders' support of the law.

---

137 Fox & Bakhoum, *supra* note 117, at 208. Fox and Bakhoum suggest that the "wise international regime would at least require nations to prohibit from doing to foreigners what they would not do to themselves": to prohibit hard core cartel activity that would harm anyone in the world, including export cartels, and offending countries should aid in discovery of evidence in their jurisdictions. This would require amending their laws to provide jurisdiction for the discovery of documents and testimony from suspects and others privy to the facts of the outbound cartels and provide for subpoena power.

138 Frédéric Jenny, Comments at Concurrences Webinar #2: "Big Data, Platforms and Internet of Things: A Challenge for Developing Countries," (Oct. 29, 2020).

2. In search of equity

Akerlof and Shiller posited that economists define equity to include only monetary value of exchange being equal on both sides, while sociologists include bargaining power on either side of the equation, and the tendency of individuals and groups to only bargain with equivalent power rather than higher power. This disempowers the group with less power in society, and, in their view, may explain subservience of women in traditional societies.[139] They argue for inclusion of a broader interpretation of equity and fairness in economic decisions, and inclusion of the role of norms in perceptions of how to achieve fairness. Norms describe how people think they and others should and should not behave.[140] For instance, the economic rationale of increasing prices substantially for masks and alcohol gel in the circumstance of increased demand and shortage of supply is economically rational. Yet consumers perceived such increases as unacceptable or unfair. It is precisely because the South African competition regime was perceived as promoting and defending fairness and equity that it gained popular support. "Fairness then involves bringing into economics these concepts of how people think they and others should or should not behave."[141] They make a case for equity in that it is important for workers and citizens to feel that they live in a just society.[142] They critique the demotion of fairness to marginal reference in the quest to keep economics "pure."[143]

This view is in sync with Fox's critique of the view of the Chicago school economists that in the efficiency–equity trade-off, equity undermines efficiency. She considers this a false dichotomy, and cited research by IMF staff that showed a radical shift in understanding of the economics of inequality by empirical evidence that greater inequality in society retards economic growth.[144] Rather, she argues that equity in antitrust means tilting the scales away from powerful business and toward powerless people, away from protecting the (freedom of) the incumbent and toward protecting the access and opportunity of young challengers. In developing countries, both efficiency and equity must work hand in hand.[145]

> ... where barriers to markets are high, where most of the population has been excluded from the economic life of the country, where

---

139 Akerlof & Shiller, *supra* note 44, at 25.

140 The importance of norms in preserving democratic institutions was starkly revealed to the world by the ways in which former President Trump eschewed all expectations of how a president should behave, and the importance of norms in keeping a society's social fabric intact.

141 Akerlof & Shiller, *supra* note 44, at 25. (For example, many were dismayed at President Trump's violation of well-established norms of presidential behavior and institutional function.)

142 *Id.* at xviii.

143 *Id.* at 21.

144 Fox, *supra* note 67, at 4. Intuitively, one can posit that increasing equality will lead to more economic activity, therefore increasing competition, and therefore a drive to increase efficiency.

145 Fox, *supra* note 67, at 5.

oligarchs and their families control the cream of the economic opportunities, and where powerful state-owned enterprises occupy the lion's share of trade, efficient moves to bring competition to the market and equitable moves to help people engage in the market coincide.[146]

We have confirmed the existence of most of these conditions in the empirical analysis of the economies of Jamaica and Trinidad and Tobago, and by extension, the rest of CARICOM economies. For a large segment of the population, (i) barriers to markets are high, with a high percentage of the population operating in the informal sector, primarily in retail and services, while (ii) a few families control the cream of economic opportunities, which control came from privileged access during the colonial period. In addition to these characteristics, we established vulnerability to economic shocks; markets that are not "workable" but rather, are structurally shaped to chronic market failure. We have seen that footprints of colonialism are imprinted on the economy, and on social stratification and race relations, while racism still informs employment practices, access to financial capital, and sense of self, penetrating deeply into social relations. The legal transplants and suboptimal institutions under them do not address these market conditions in any significant way, so that the efficiency-centric ethos of the resultant competition regimes does not begin to ameliorate the real economic ailments of the societies.

3. Some considerations for incorporating inclusiveness

How do we address these issues in proactive ways? Transferring wealth from the rich to the poor is an endemic social problem, which has to be handled delicately. In Venezuela, Chavez and Maduro pursued radical policies to wrest economic power from multinationals and wealthy elites, and in so doing unraveled society, leaving the masses to starve or flee the borders into neighboring countries. Revolution is not an option, though we saw that the scare caused by the Black Power Revolution and the Manley socialist policies did lead to changes in ownership and changes in discriminatory policies.[147] Even when government has funds that could be used to better the condition of the poor, we saw very misguided policies in Trinidad and Tobago, a squandering of opportunity that is now probably lost because of the decline of oil. Any attempt at reform has to address the mindset of public officials, away from being mimic men, to responding to the real social needs created by the society's own stories. Competition law cannot solve all the deep-rooted problems in these societies, but it could play its part in "marking markets work for the poor," that is, removing blockages to market entry.

---

146 *Id.*

147 While there is a more dispersed ownership of businesses in Jamaica, this arose out of the social disruption caused by Manley as elite white, and Chinese people fled Jamaica, selling their homes and businesses to those with the means to purchase. However, this only replaced one elite class with another, leaving the masses as deprived as they were before.

It is important that CARICOM countries explicitly include public interest and equity goals in their laws, and to thread those provisions throughout their laws in relevant places, so as to keep attention focused on the poor, and to the objective of opening up market access to the disadvantaged. A positive example has been set by the JFTC and BFTC to conduct market studies as a basis for advocacy, successfully effecting change through their intervention to the benefit of wider society. Given the level of elitist privilege and racial discrimination that is historically entrenched in these societies, these countries may consider taking example from South Africa, who is forging ahead in finding ways to defend the poor and disadvantaged. Moreover, Akerlof and Shiller posited the sociologist view that the weak in society are not empowered to bargain with the strong. It is then even more important that the commissions stand up for the poor and bargain with or sanction firms that exploit the weak and poor. Competition law has many very positive instruments to bring justice and fairness to economic practices in the interest of the dispossessed and the disadvantaged. It is a matter of not imbibing the rhetoric and ideologies of the North that emanate from their social reality, but of refocusing internally, and keeping what is important and relevant to your economy and your social reality.

Many aspects of the existing laws in CARICOM adequately cover competition issues in these markets and seek the interest of consumers. The BFCA provides examples of clear and relevant provisions in many areas. The key is to enforce the laws with an eye to the effects on the poor, as in South Africa. Market definition should not just measure existing market power, but consider how entrenched is that market power, and what barriers to entry exist for newcomers, particularly small firms. Market studies should be done by commissions that trace the historical evolution of the entrenched dominant firms, to be taken into account when investigating dominance or in a merger case. Commissions can then consider the historical record going a long way back and the accompanying socioeconomic issues created by that entrenched dominance.[148] Technical and financial resources are very scarce in the commissions in this region, and so collaboration with regional universities may be needed to conduct such studies.

The TTFTA (section 15) includes interlocking directorates, and this is an important issue in these small economies and societies with close-knit commercial elites. This should be explicitly included in other laws in the region. Enforcement of this provision could reduce opportunities for collusion. In non-tradeable sectors, merger regulation is very necessary because of the danger of increasing concentration already concentrated markets. The consensus in the region now

---

148 In the *Wheat Cartel* case in South Africa, the commission decided to do an in-depth investigation of the history of the relations between the firms involved and their entrenched power, despite the fact that there was evidence on cartelization and per se illegality could have been invoked without further investigation. This provided insights into the history and practices of these firms going back to the period before the new competition law, in the time of apartheid. Similarly, in the case on collusion of oil companies, the Commission went back to the 1950s to trace the power of these companies, the legal provisions that facilitated their collusion, and the continuance of those practices once they because illegal.

is that merger control regulation is needed in both national and regional laws. At the moment, Barbados has a track record of enforcing merger control. However, Jamaica has started investigating mergers, having been given the green light in the Privy Council decision in *Digicel/Claro*. As such, the JFTC has been advising entities on proposed mergers. Moreover, the staff of the JFTC has been trained in enforcing merger controls.

Given the infancy of this aspect of competition law in the region, it is opportune for these commissions to consider how enforcement of merger control regulation could be inclusive of considerations that affect socioeconomic issues, such as in South Africa, given the peculiarities in these economies and that the equity provisions are threaded into law.

The challenge is in the methodology used in investigating and determining cases, and in market studies that inform advocacy. Further work is needed to scrutinize in detail the provisions in the laws in the region, and the draft laws, the published guidance provided by the various commissions, and the reasoning used in determining cases, to discern where methodology and reasoning could be made more relevant to the circumstances of the economies, and to point to a way forward.

All laws undergo revisions, and so the commissions in CARICOM, and the governments with draft laws under consideration, may want to consider some of the recommendations made by Fox and Bakhoum.[149] They advised that developing countries consider the following:

1. They should not use technical and complex rules and regulations, opting rather for simple rules and standards fit for the capabilities of the commissions and the context of the markets.

2. They should not adopt complexity-creating statutory language, as this exposes reversal of decisions of the competition authorities by judges, as was the case against Mittal in South Africa, in which the court interpreted the statutory language as requiring a more complex enquiry (proving effects).

3. They should use a simple approach to enforcement, rather than adopt the complex standards of proof in the US or EU, particularly proving effects, which makes a great demand on the resources and expertise of small commissions.

4. Enforcement should be strong against exclusionary and exploitative practices by which dominant firms exercise market power. Resale price maintenance should be presumptively illegal, and hard core cartels should be per se illegal or at least presumptively illegal.

---

149 Fox & Bakhoum, *supra* note 117, at 242–46.

5. They should not adopt the "as efficient as" standard of proof, which can be quite demanding on small commissions. Moreover, there may not be any "as efficient" challengers to the monopolist in these small concentrated markets.

6. Market definition should lean toward pro-poor outcomes, as in South Africa. There is the danger that market definition may be applied too economistic and mechanistically, without taking into account public interest in where the chips fall.

7. They should question Western standards and consider sympathetically standards that will open markets, while giving due regard to dominant firms' acts that bring new or better products to market. In this regard, one has to interrogate the recommendations of the ICN and OECD, which are largely fashioned after the laws and enforcement practices in developed countries.

8. The financial sector and regulated industries should not be exempt from the competition law.

Referring to research conducted by the Centre for Competition, Regulation and Economic Development (CCRED), the director of CCRED similarly advised that competition authorities in developing countries could use their tools to achieve far more pro-development outcomes. They could provide *ex ante* procompetitive regulations. They could rethink the standards they use. For instance, mergers are supposed to lead to efficiencies, but there is little evidence that this would happen, so they need to be more cautious about efficiency claims since inefficiencies could have a direct and indirect link to poverty, in that where there is inefficiency, households cannot easily recover. They must not assume that markets can work by themselves in developing countries. Free markets care not about distribution. Because of entrenched vested interests in these economies, one cannot assume the ease of entry and exit that exists in industrialized countries. Enforcers have to ensure that power is balanced with responsibility. He advised developing countries to challenge existing knowledge and create new thinking and theories of how competition law should be framed.[150] A suggestion for future work is to conduct research into the CCRED publications for lessons that are applicable to the region, such as the methodology applied in empirical research (thinking outside the box), and the specific recommendations in enforcement of competition law to overcome inequity in the societies in South Africa.

The empirical evidence provided above on the peculiarities of CARICOM economies point to the inappropriateness of taking guidance from US perspectives and their

---

150 Thando Vilakazi, Director of CCRED, Comments at webinar "Antitrust and Developing Economies in an Era of Crisis: Gouging, Opportunism, Access, Industrial Policy, and the Challenge to First Principles of Competition," jointly presented by Concurrences and N.Y.U. Law Sch., (Oct. 30, 2020). CCRED has a wealth of research that developing countries would do well to study for guidance, or emulate similar studies in their economies.

enforcement practices in antitrust law. US enforcers trust that markets work, are blind to issues of inequality, do not want to muddy the waters by including public interest, are wedded to efficiency and consumer welfare standards for enforcement, require proving effects on the market and harm to competitors and consumers, and have tied themselves up in jurisprudence that makes it difficult to prove monopolization. For these reasons, the US is lenient on dominant firms, trusting that their actions will be constrained by the market and that, left to their own devices, they will produce benefits not only to themselves but also to consumers. The EU, by contrast, still balances enforcement by taking into account the form of the law, but economic analysis on effects on rivals and consumers is creeping into the jurisprudence. As we saw above, Advocate General Kokott cautioned against being seduced by economic analyses[151]. The EU prosecutes abuses of dominance with as much fervor as they do cartels, unlike the US, and are sensitive to public interest issues, with many incorporating such provisions in their laws. The EU makes the preservation of free flow of goods and services in the single market its primary goal. For these reasons among others, the EU provides a far more relevant guide to CARICOM countries, where such guidance is sought, than does the US.

The challenge is for competition authorities in CARICOM to apply the methodology advanced by Fox[152] and CCRED to investigations and analyses, and to integrate this interpretation of their laws into their published guidance to ensure transparency and certainty on the thinking that will inform enforcement of the law. Fox further provided the insight that developing countries actually have a competitive advantage over developed ones in crafting new and innovative ways to draft and enforce relevant competition law. She pointed out that mature competition jurisdictions have the baggage of an entrenched path, which is sometimes inflexible even in this time of global change. However, new and young competition commissions do not have this baggage, and can forge a path of their own, unencumbered by a long history of jurisprudence that hems in enforcement options (as in the US) and creates reluctance in enforcers to consider change, fearing legal uncertainty. Fox's advice for developing countries is that they are free to address their own needs and need not be seduced by transplanted law tailored to markets very different from their own.[153] Bob Marley would approve.

---

151 Kokott, *supra* note 71.

152 Fox, *supra* note 67, at 5. According to Fox, "Equity in antitrust means tilting the scales away from powerful business and for powerless people; away from protecting the (freedom of) incumbent and towards protecting the access and opportunity of young challengers."

153 Fox, *supra* note 66, at 84, 83.

After Convergence: Competition Law in Emerging Markets

DAVID J. GERBER[*]
Chicago-Kent College of Law

Abstract

The digital economy and the power and size of the big data firms that dominate it have undermined the global convergence ideal that so recently seemed to be the path of the future for competition law. That ideal has been based on the belief that the economics-based model developed in the US would lead convergence, but Big Tech issues call this assumption into question. This creates a fundamentally new situation for countries that have assumed they should be guided by the convergence ideal. This essay explores some of the dilemmas they face and some of the consequences of the new situation for the future of competition law.

---

[*] David J. Gerber is University Distinguished Professor, Emeritus, and Distinguished Professor of Law, Emeritus, at Chicago-Kent College of Law. I presented an earlier version of this paper at a conference in New Delhi, India, on Dec. 1, 2019. The conference was organized by CUTS International. I am deeply indebted to the participants for their comments and reactions. I am also very grateful to my researcher, Jacob Aleknavicius, for valuable research assistance.

Since the 1990s, thought and discussion in competition law circles has often centered on the issue of convergence. The central idea has been that competition laws around the world are becoming increasingly similar to each other and will necessarily become more similar in the future. The growing importance of global markets seemed to call for reducing state-based distortions in these markets and to increased similarity among competition laws. At this general level the idea has been attractive–so attractive, in fact, that few have stopped to ask what it actually means.[1] Is there a central model to which all are expected to move? If so, what is it? If not, how will similarity be achieved? Moreover, what consequences would increased similarity have for individual countries and groups of countries? The attraction of the general idea has led most to brush these questions aside–at least in public. As a result, the convergence image has remained a bit hollow.

The digital economy and the power and size of the Big Data firms (BD) that dominate it have now cracked–perhaps even shattered–this convergence image. Views of how competition law should be applied to the platform economy have diverged. US antitrust representatives have generally held to the position that existing tools of economic analysis are adequate for dealing with BD. In Europe, however, there has been noticeably less confidence that the tools of economic analysis are appropriate for dealing with BD. Leading competition law institutions have looked beyond them to identify different concepts for use in these contexts. Many other countries have been ambivalent in the face of this divergence.

This creates a fundamentally new situation for competition laws in emerging markets. As long as the convergence idea reigned, emerging market markets were told that they should just follow the orthodoxy that had been shaped by US antitrust law and had become increasingly influential in Europe. In some ways, it was a convenient position for these newer institutions. If all states were moving toward a common model, the new competition law regimes could simply learn from those in the lead and try to move toward what they were doing. They didn't have to develop their own responses to the problems. Divergence radically changes the situation.

This contribution to the *liber amicorum* for Eleanor Fox examines this new context for developing country competition laws and identifies some of its potential implications. It identifies key factors that shaped convergence thinking and others that now threaten to undermine it. This provides insights into the forces that influence competition law decision-makers in these countries.

---

[1] I have examined the convergence concept in DAVID J. GERBER, GLOBAL COMPETITION: LAW, MARKETS AND GLOBALIZATION 79–120 & 273–292 (2010).

I. Convergence as Context
1. Different paths: Before the 1990s

In order to recognize more clearly the forces that shape the divergence context, we need to identify historical context that generated the convergence orthodoxy. Prior to 1990, competition law played a significant role in the legal and economic systems of very few jurisdictions–basically, the United States, the Federal Republic of Germany and that of the European Union. There were a few dozen other competition laws on the books, but they rarely played significant roles in either the economic or legal life of those countries. This has given these three jurisdictions exceptional influence. They have enjoyed a kind of "first mover advantage" with regard to all other regimes.

The US antitrust law regime was well positioned to take advantage of the situation. Often seen as the father of competition law regimes,[2] it was created in 1890 and gradually increased importance in the US during the following decades, especially after the Second World War. This has led many in newer regimes to rely on and follow the US model because it has "the most experience." This view has been bolstered by the myth that all competition law regimes derived from US antitrust after the Second World War. I and others have shown that this is simply wrong.[3] Europe had its own conceptions of competition law that date back to roughly the same period during which US antitrust law sprouted. Nevertheless, many are invested in the myth, and it persists in some circles. Others have followed the US model because of the dominant role of the US in global commerce.

The US regime is unique in two ways that are specifically relevant here. First, it is court-based. Nonspecialized federal judges control the content of the law. The basic substantive provisions of the law enacted in 1890 are still the primary source of legislative guidance, but they are so spare and vague that judges are constrained only by other judicial decisions that are seen as "law" in the US legal system. No other major competition law relies on courts in the same way, making US antitrust a somewhat difficult model to follow, particularly by competition law decision-makers in emerging market countries. Second, the substantive law has changed dramatically since the 1970s. Until then, the courts considered a range of goals and methods, including fairness and economic freedom, in reaching antitrust decisions.[4] During that decade, however, judges began to view antitrust law quite differently, focusing almost entirely on the economic effects of conduct, specifically, price-based effects equated with "consumer welfare." As a result of this change of direction, others are often uncertain about its content.

---

2   For discussion of foreign views of US antitrust, *see* David J. Gerber, *Prisms of Distance and Power*, 93 Bus. Hist. Rev. 781 (2019).

3   *See* David J. Gerber, Law and Competition in Twentieth Century Europe (1998).

4   For discussion, *see* Eleanor M. Fox, *The Battle for the Soul of Antitrust*, 75 Cal. L. Rev. 917 (1987).

Competition law in Europe during this period differed both procedurally and substantively from US antitrust law.[5] The basic ideas were initially developed in the 1890s independently of US influence and often in outright rejection of that influence. They gradually extended their influence until the 1990s at both the national and European levels. Two ideas were central. One was substantive: competition law was intended to control the power of economically powerful firms–its focus was on constraining the use of their power. I refer to this as the "power-constraint perspective." The other was a reliance on administrative officials to protect the competitive system from distortion and harm. The courts were assumed to be too weak and to have too few enforcement tools effectively to wield state power against powerful economic opponents.

Each model of competition law was important, and they differed from each other in fundamental ways.

2. The competition law turn: The 1990s

The competition law turn of the 1990s set the stage for the emergence of convergence thinking.[6] This "turn" involved an explosion of interest in competition law around the world. The collapse of the Soviet Union and the precipitous fall of confidence in state control of the economy led to the enactment of many new competition laws (more than 100) by the early 2000s, and to the strengthening of many others. Often these laws were initially aimed at controlling the power of telecommunications firms that acquired monopoly or near-monopoly status as a result of the privatization of telecommunication technology.

These new regimes faced many obstacles. Often the decision-makers had little experience of competition and knew nothing of competition law; many, especially those in emerging market countries, had limited support from both their governments and the firms and individuals in the society. This led the United States and Europe (and a few other countries, such as Japan) to try to influence developing country decisions. They offered incentives for developing countries to follow their lead. The new jurisdictions now had to make decisions, and they often had much to gain by following foreign models rather than trying to address new issues and embrace new approaches.

3. Convergence emerges

Convergence promised to simplify their task. If there were only one model toward which all were expected to move, decision-makers in new and poorly supported competition law regimes could just copy what the leaders did–perhaps with some modifications for their own political and economic circumstances. Convergence

---

5   Much of the material in this section is based on my detailed study of the evolution of competition law in Europe. For details and copious references, *see* Gerber, *supra* note 3.

6   For discussion, *see* Gerber, *supra* note 1, at 79–120.

began to move to center stage. Developments in Europe made the idea even more attractive. Beginning in the late 1990s, the European Commission and some other independent European competition law regimes began to move toward an economic effects-based model that promised to reduce burdens on their domestic firms. The move did not influence all areas of competition law equally. Many states resisted the move for unilateral conduct issues, and even where economic effects and price-based consumer welfare approaches were followed, application of the principles was often far more structured than the US version. Nevertheless, Europe was seen as moving toward the US approach, and for many this confirmed the convergence orthodoxy.

II. Big Data: Undermining Convergence?

Enter Big Data; exit confidence in convergence as an all-embracing process. BD issues became the focus of concern in competition law in the mid-2010s.[7] Fines and lawsuits involving Amazon, Google, and Facebook moved to the center of the competition law stage. Differences between the US and European responses to BD issues surfaced, and the convergence model lost its grip on the imagination of decision-makers.

Digital technology presents a challenge for competition law. It modifies existing forms of competition and creates new ones. In traditional markets, firms generally compete by making better products or providing more valuable services at more attractive prices. In this context, a firm or group of firms can subvert competition by acquiring sufficient power over price (or related factors) to be able to act without regard to the constraints of other firms. This power has been the focus of competition law for decades. In the digital economy, however, competitive advantage is not always based on this type of power, but on other forms of power that may have similar consequences for competition. The capacity of computers to acquire, aggregate, encode, manipulate, and strategically deploy very large amounts of information, and to perform these functions very quickly, is the primary source of change. It enables those who employ the technology to finds new forms of market advantage. The combination of digital technology and concentration of control presents decision-makers with choices regarding how to respond to the threats it poses.

Control of this technology is the new prize, and concentrated control is the primary threat. Concerns have focused on two main areas, and these have been central to divergence. One issue is privacy and its relation to competition law; the other is the potential harm from control of platforms.

Competition law regimes have responded to these concerns in three distinct ways. US commentators and decision-makers have generally argued that there is no

---

7   *See, e.g.*, D. Daniel Sokol & Roisin Comerford, *Antitrust and Regulating Big Data*, 23 GEO. MASON L. REV. 1129, 1151–61 (2016).

need for a change of course–i.e., that existing tools of competition law economics should continue to be applied to BD–perhaps with some modifications.[8] Privacy issues are not easily amenable to this form of economic analysis, and, as a result, they argue that privacy does not belong in competition law. With regard to digital platforms, they also express confidence that existing tools are adequate and appropriate for identifying the harm that might arise.[9] Most agree that the tools will have to be honed over time to deal with these issues. In general, this approach has so far led to limited enforcement against BD firms.

Responses in Europe have shown less confidence in these claims. Willingness to consider privacy issues within the framework of competition law has been more prominent in Europe. The well-known Facebook case in Germany is the most visible example.[10] The EU Commission and Member State competition law regimes have also identified competition harms in the conduct of BD firms and taken steps to limit perceived harms. For example, the European Commission has issued fines against BD firms for abusive of a dominant position in digital markets.[11] The Commission based its decision on factors other than short-term, price-based consumer welfare effects. The decisions reflect the power-constraint perspective long central to European competition law.[12]

The third response has been to "wait and see." Some competition officials have expressed concern about the perceived harms from BD firms, but most have remained generally silent on both the privacy and platform analysis issues.

III. Divergence and Development

The cracking of confidence in convergence places developing countries in a fundamentally new situation. Whereas the convergence paradigm beckoned with the message of orthodoxy ("There is one basic path. You just have to decide how much effort and resources to invest in getting there"), the new situation confronts them with three basic choices: 1) follow the US; 2) move toward a power-constraint orientation akin to European responses; or 3) wait to see what happens before addressing the new BD issues.

---

8   *See, e.g.*, Keith N. Hylton, *Digital Platforms and Antitrust Law*, 98 NEB. L. REV. 272, 274 (2019).

9   *See* Law360, *FTC's Phillips Says Privacy Breaches Not An Antitrust Issue* (May 8, 2019, 7:34 PM), law360.com/articles/1157328/ftc-s-phillips-says-privacy-breaches-not-an-antitrust-issue.

10 Bundeskartellamt [Federal Cartel Office, FCO], Case B6-22/16 (Feb. 6, 2019), bundeskartellamt.de/SharedDocs/Entscheidung/EN/Fallberichte/Missbrauchsaufsicht/2019/B6-22-16.pdf?_blob=publictionFile&v=4. *See also* Thomas Höppner, *The German Competition Authority rules that a social network abused its dominant position by improperly combining the user data that is collected (*Facebook*)*, E-COMPETITIONS FEBRUARY 2019, ART. N° 96456 (Feb. 7, 2019).

11 *See* Press Release, European Commission, Antitrust: Commission fines Google €1.49 billion for abusive practices in online advertising (IP/19/1170, Mar. 19, 2019).

12 The seeds of this focus were planted around the turn of the twentieth century. For discussion, *see* Gerber, *supra* note 3, at 53–68.

Several basic issues loom large in considering responses to this situation. First, what kind of development does the decision-maker want–i.e., what goals are they pursuing? "Development" can, of course, mean many things, and vagueness about the development goal may obscure paths toward that goal. BD firms provide information and services that are valuable for economic development. Few would dispute that. But competition law asks a different question: What kinds of harms may accompany these benefits in the context of developing countries? The focus of concern here is whether the activities of BD firms also constrain economic and social development in a country or region. Market forces in many countries are very different from those prominent in the US or Europe, and competition law decisions regarding BD should take these differences into account.

Second, competition law experience–or the lack thereof–is often a significant factor in discussions of competition law in the developing world. Developing countries have had relatively limited experience with competition law. This often leads them to rely on the experience of competition regimes that have more experience. In the context of BD, however, this reliance may be less justified than in more traditional areas of competition law. Yes, the US and Europe have had more experience with competition law, and developing countries can learn much from them, but they have as yet had very limited and divergent experience with BD issues, so in the context of development the experience they do have may be of more limited value.

The third key issue is the impact of BD on support for competition law. Competition law confronts powerful economic and political institutions everywhere, and political support is critical to its effectiveness in these confrontations. BD firms have enormous wealth, and this inevitably presents challenges for those seeking to enforcing law against them. Few developing country competition law institutions, if any, have had the kinds of political support often enjoyed by their colleagues in the US, Europe or Japan. Moreover, BD is often perceived primarily as a benefit to consumers, and this perception tends to impede support for enforcing competition law against them. Moreover, the extensive resources of BD firms can sometimes be used to influence those who make and enforce the laws in poorer countries.

Finally, and not unrelatedly, competition law institutions generally need law-based discipline in order to draw popular support as well as to be effective in enforcing or negotiating with competition law violators. Where they are viewed primarily as politically motivated, and without a firm anchoring in legal institutions and methods, they tend to be less effective. Without such legitimacy, domestic stakeholders have less incentive to support them, popular opinion is more likely to consider them corrupt, and firms may expect to gain more from bribing officials than contesting decisions on legal grounds. This is likely to be particularly true of those with exceptional wealth, such as BD firms. They may see little incentive to respect competition law norms where they can simply "buy" (in one form or another) the decisions they want.

IV. Big Data Issues: Big Data and Power

The core issue in competition law responses is how to think about "power." The economists' conception of power centers on "market power," a concept based on market structures. All competition laws have at times employed broader views of power. In the context of digital markets, the question for competition law is which images of power to employ in making decisions.

1. Privacy issues and development

Those who control the data of others have a form of power which they can use to influence those whose data they control. Awareness of this power has led to fast-growing support for competition law enforcement to protect privacy in the US and Europe, so there are reasons to believe that it will also develop rapidly in developing countries. Privacy concerns may be exacerbated there, because the power is foreign–primarily in the hands of companies in the US. Popular sensitivity to privacy may provide support for competition law enforcement in developed countries, but there is too little evidence to gauge how strong privacy concerns are now or how they may develop.[13] If development is seen as a process of increasing the capacities of individuals and societies, concentrated foreign control over data poses obvious risks. The related view, that it is a process of enhancing individual and societal freedoms, highlights the risks even more.[14] Some governments may respond to these threats with greater support for competition law, but this is likely to require support from either inside or outside of the society–perhaps both.

2. Mergers

The concentration and location of economic power shapes markets and influences economic development. This focuses attention on mergers. In the development context, the central issue involves acquisitions by BD firms of smaller indigenous firms. Such mergers foreclose opportunities for the indigenous firms to grow and perhaps to compete with BD firms on local and regional markets. On the other hand, the acquisition may represent an infusion of capital into the country. Even if it does, however, these resources are in private hands and may be moved outside the country, so they may contribute little, if anything, to development within the country. In addition, opportunities for those in control of indigenous firms to sell the firms to BD giants may indirectly benefit development by encouraging indigenous firms to develop to a point where BD firms wish to purchase them. Competition authorities need to balance these market-based benefits against the potential development harms posed by the power and resources of foreign BD firms. In

---

13 See, e.g., Maggie Fick & Alexis Akwagyiram, *In Africa, scant data protection leaves internet users exposed*, REUTERS: TECHNOLOGY NEWS (Apr. 2018), www.reuters.com/article/us-facebook-africa/in-africa-scant-data-protection-leaves-internet-users-exposed-idUSKCN1HB1SZ.

14 For the core view of this issue, *see* AMARTYA SEN, DEVELOPMENT AS FREEDOM (1999).

many cases, they can do this by conditioning approval of a proposed merger on the fulfillment of conditions that minimize harm to competition, and respect the privacy demands of the society that may underlie and support development.

3. Unilateral conduct: Dominant firms

Unilateral conduct by BD firms can also pose a significant threat to development. Where a BD firm has a dominant position in a market, it can restrict the competitive opportunities of others–competitors, firms in other markets, and consumers. It may be in a position, for example, to foreclose supply opportunities to competitors, pressure purchasers into accepting development-restricting conditions, or raise prices to consumers far higher than competition would allow. Each of these actions can restrict economic and social development, and the dominant position of BD firms in many markets make such conduct likely. Identifying the conduct and assessing its consequences is, however, difficult and costly, even for well-funded competition authorities. It is often impossible for smaller and poorer competition authorities. Much of the conduct can be accomplished "under the hood" of algorithms, for example, and extensive computer expertise is often necessary to identify it. Sharing data as well as detection resources may, therefore, be the most effective–perhaps the only–way to deter such conduct.

Most current competition laws deal with unilateral conduct in provisions relating to market dominance and control. In the US and some other countries, the concept of monopolization is applied to the conduct; in most competition regimes, principles relating to the abuse of dominance are used. The two approaches are, in practice, similar. Both become applicable to conduct only where a firm has a dominant market position. This type of dominance is often difficult to assess and prove, because markets (particularly digital markets) are often complex, and market relations are often opaque.

The competition laws of some countries, especially in Europe and Latin America, also contain provisions that identify abusive conduct without market dominance. Here the basic idea is that small and medium-sized firms are often dependent on larger firms for inputs (e.g., supplies) or sales opportunities and that the controlling firm can use the dependency of the smaller firm to impose conditions on it that harm competition. These provisions may be helpful to competition authorities in developing countries, because these relationships of dependence can often be more easily identified and proven, rather than traditional violations based on market power. These provisions do not exist in the US and some other countries.

V. Concluding Comments

This brief review of the impact of competition law divergence on competition law in developing countries reveals some of the new opportunities created by a weakening of the convergence model. It also makes clear, however, that divergence brings not only opportunities for developing countries, but also burdens and challenges. Decision-makers can no longer comfortably assume the convenient posture of following a particular orthodoxy emanating from other regimes. The new situation opens the field for decisions. It induces decision-makers to choose their goals carefully and devise their own paths for moving toward their goals. They may choose to follow one of the approaches and strategies being pursued in other countries, revise and add to them for their own needs–or face the consequences of closing their eyes.

Digital Platforms and Competition Policy in Developing Countries

HARRY FIRST[*]

New York University School of Law

Abstract

Big tech platforms have become a subject of intense antitrust scrutiny in developed economies, most recently in the United States. The thesis of this paper is that the power of platforms is not just a first-world problem, however, but is also an issue of importance for competition policy in developing countries. These platforms present different costs and benefits for developing countries than for developed countries; in particular, the major big tech platforms have become important tools for further digital platform innovation in developing economies. The paper begins with a discussion of the connection between competition law, innovation, and development. The paper then discusses how digital platform technologies are employed in Africa in four areas–online retail sales, value chains, financial technology products (fintech), and sharing platforms. The paper concludes with a discussion of the lessons these developments have for competition policy in developing countries.

---

[*] Charles L. Denison Professor of Law, New York University School of Law; harry.first@nyu.edu.
I thank Michael Kalman for his outstanding research assistance. A research grant from the Filomen D'Agostino and Max E. Greenberg Research Fund at New York University School of Law provided financial assistance for this paper. This paper is part of a book dedicated to my colleague Eleanor Fox. It should be obvious that her pathbreaking work on competition policy in developing countries, particularly in Africa, as well as her work on how antitrust can be used to control the power of the major digital platforms, is this paper's inspiration.

I. Introduction

It was just a few years ago–I date it from 2017–that concern for the power of the "big tech" platforms moved from the pages of the law reviews to the pages of major US newspapers. "We are, all of us, in inescapable thrall to one of the handful of American technology companies that now dominate much of the global economy," wrote the *New York Times*'s technology columnist Farhad Manjoo.[1] In that same year, after Amazon acquired US food retailer Whole Foods, the *Wall Street Journal*'s technology columnist, Christopher Mims, wrote that "America's biggest tech companies are spreading their tentacles ... [P]ower and wealth will be concentrated in the hands of a few companies in a way not seen since the Gilded Age."[2]

Manjoo dubbed these tech companies "the Frightful Five": Amazon, Apple, Facebook, Microsoft, and Alphabet. Sometimes these companies are listed in size order (by market capitalization in the United States): Apple, Microsoft, Alphabet, Amazon, and Facebook.[3] Sometimes by convenient mnemonic: "GAFAM" (Google instead of its parent, Alphabet), or "GAFA" (minus Microsoft, which often seems to be overlooked in the public debate, despite its continued dominance on desktop computers around the world[4]), or, even more descriptive, "FANGs" (Facebook, Amazon, Netflix, and Google[5]).

US antitrust enforcement agencies and Congress have responded to this public concern. In 2019 the US Department of Justice (DOJ) and the Federal Trade Commission (FTC) announced investigations into GAFA; state antitrust enforcers put together multistate teams to investigate whether to bring antitrust suits against Facebook and/or Google.[6] On July 29, 2020, the Antitrust Subcommittee of the US House Judiciary Committee called the CEOs of Google, Apple, Facebook, and Amazon to testify for more than five hours. Throughout this hearing, the four companies were broadly criticized by both Democrats and Republicans, although the Congress members' concerns were varied and sometimes reflected their different political perspectives.[7] The Committee's Majority Staff subsequently issued a report, taking nearly 350 pages to describe

---

1 Farhad Manjoo, *Tech's Frightful Five: They've Got Us*, N.Y. TIMES, May 10, 2017.

2 Christopher Mims, *Tech Companies Spread Their Tentacles*, WALL ST. J., June 17–18, 2017, at A1.

3 *See* Bloomberg Finance (Jan. 17, 2020), https://ext-marketing.com/wp-content/uploads/2020/01/AAPL-US-Equity-Apple-Inc-Dail-2020-01-17-10-08-12_v2.jpg.

4 *See* Microsoft Corp., Annual Report Form 10-K, 40–42 (June 30, 2020) (detailing revenue and margin increases over previous two years in Windows segment), https://c.s-microsoft.com/en-us/CMSFiles/MSFT_FY20Q4_10K.docx?version=71873a68-d431-e887-124f-4d24b9ade60c.

5 *See* Nicolas Petit, *Are "FANGs" Monopolies? A Theory of Competition Under Uncertainty* (Oct. 10, 2019), https://ssrn.com/abstract=3414386.

6 *See*, e.g., Cecilia Kang, David Streitfeld, & Annie Karni, *Tech Titans Face Tough Scrutiny From All Sides*, N.Y. TIMES, June 4, 2019, at A1; Cecilia Kang, Katie Benner, & Jack Nicas, *Justice Dept. Explores Google Antitrust Case*, N.Y. TIMES, May 31, 2019.

7 *See, e.g.*, Cecilia Kang & David McCabe, *Lawmakers Give Tech "Emperors" Jabs From 2 Sides*, N.Y. TIMES, July 30, 2020, at A1.

the GAFA's anticompetitive conduct and devoting nearly 30 pages to possible legislative remedies.[8] On October 20, 2020, the DOJ and 11 state attorneys general filed a monopolization suit against Google, the first such suit since the monopolization case against Microsoft more than two decades before.[9] The US suit against Google was then followed by two more suits against Google filed by two different groups of states.[10] Facebook was then sued by the FTC and by another large group of states.[11] The *Wall Street Journal*'s Christopher Mims reported, *"Tech's Antitrust Reckoning is Near."*[12]

Concern for the power of big tech platforms has not been limited to the United States, of course. If anything, the United States has been a lagging jurisdiction. The European Union, along with Germany and the United Kingdom, have been pressing ahead with enforcement actions and proposals for imposing significant restrictions on the competitive behavior of the GAFA. The European Commission has brought three separate cases against Google for abuse of dominance, imposing fines of more than $5 billion;[13] Germany has sued Facebook, linking competition law with privacy protections;[14] the UK's Competition and Markets Authority has published a final report of its market study on online platforms and digital advertising.[15]

This debate over high-tech platforms has taken place with a decidedly first-world perspective. In the United States and EU, the focus never seems to move beyond GAFA's impact on the citizens, consumers, and economies of the United States and Europe. Particularly in the United States, mention is almost never made of platforms elsewhere (except when they pose a perceived national security threat to the United States[16]).

The question that this paper addresses is whether antitrust's focus on big tech platforms is appropriately centered in the developed world. Does the concern

---

8   *See* MAJORITY STAFF OF SUBCOMM. ON ANTITRUST, COMMERCIAL, AND ADMIN. LAW, 116TH CONG., INVESTIGATION OF COMPETITION IN DIGITAL MARKETS (2020), https://judiciary.house.gov/uploadedfiles/competition_in_digital_markets.pdf.

9   *See* United States v. Google LLC, Case No. 1-20-cv-03010 (D.D.C. Oct. 20, 2020).

10 *See* Colorado v. Google LLC, Case No. 1:20-cv-03715 (D.D.C., Dec. 17, 2020) (35 states, Puerto Rico, District of Columbia, and Guam); Texas v. Google LLC, Case No. 4:20-cv-00957 (E.D. Texas, Dec. 16, 2020) (10 states).

11 *See* FTC v. Facebook, Inc., Case No. 1:20-cv-03590 (D.D.C., Dec. 9, 2020); New York v. Facebook, Inc., Case No. 1:20-cv-03589: (D.D.C., Dec. 9, 2020) (46 states, District of Columbia, and Guam).

12 Christopher Mims, *Tech's Antitrust Reckoning Is Near*, WALL ST. J., Oct. 20, 2020, at B1.

13 *See* Aurelien Portuese, *Google AdSense for Search: Fines Always Come in Threes*, COMPETITION POL'Y INT'L (Apr. 2019) (discussing cases).

14 *See* Bundeskartellamt, *Case Summary: Facebook, Exploitative business terms pursuant to Section 19(1) GWB for inadequate data processing* (Feb. 15, 2019), www.bundeskartellamt.de/SharedDocs/Entscheidung/EN/Fallberichte/Missbrauchsaufsicht/2019/B6-22-16.pdf?__blob=publicationFile&v=4.

15 *See* CMA, ONLINE PLATFORMS AND DIGITAL ADVERTISING: MARKET STUDY FINAL REPORT (July 1, 2020), https://assets.publishing.service.gov.uk/media/5efc57ed3a6f4023d242ed56/Final_report_1_July_2020.pdf. *See also* Australia ACCC Report (Dec. 12, 2019), https://treasury.gov.au/publication/p2019-41708.

16 *See* G. Wells, M. C. Bender, K. O'Keeffe & C. Lombardo, *Microsoft Aims for a Deal on TikTok*, WALL ST. J., Aug. 3, 2020, at A1 (reporting that TikTok sees itself as a potential equal rival to Facebook).

for the competitive effects of tech platforms have any relevance to competition law enforcement in the developing world?

The thesis of this paper is that the power of platforms is not just a first-world problem, but is also an issue of importance in developing countries. Even so, these platforms present different costs and benefits for developing countries than for developed countries. For developing countries, the US big tech platforms have become basic tools for digital platform commerce and development. They open the possibility of providing a market presence and access for small and medium businesses that might otherwise find it difficult to reach consumers in domestic and international markets. This is an important enough phenomenon that competition policy in developing countries should be particularly attuned to problems of platform access and fair competitive practices, without regard to whether antitrust in developed countries ends up reflecting these goals.

To develop the thesis that digital platform competition matters in developing countries, this paper examines two broad areas. First, the paper places the development and use of digital platforms in the context of competition policy and innovation generally. Can competition policy in developing countries help drive innovation in those countries, specifically, innovations involving the use of platform technology? Second, the paper describes some of the ways that digital platforms are now being used in developing countries and how that use may affect development. The focus will mainly be on Africa, but Africa provides sufficient heterogeneity that it can show why competition law is important for the growth of platforms in developing countries more generally.[17]

The paper begins with a discussion of the connection between competition law, innovation, and development. The next section discusses how digital platform technologies are employed in Africa in four areas–online retail sales, value chains, financial technology products (fintech), and sharing platforms. The paper concludes with a discussion of the lessons these developments have for competition policy in developing countries.

II. Competition Law, Innovation, and Development
1. What counts as innovation?

When trying to assess the connection between innovation and competition law, commentators often have a particular idea of what counts as innovation. Innovation is often thought of as a technological advance. As a former head of the DOJ Antitrust Division put it, "let's not forget what drives the hopes and dreams of so many innovators: the hope of making a technology that will improve

---

17 For a fuller exploration of competition policy in Africa, as well as the need for using competition law to advance the goal of inclusive development, *see* Eleanor M. Fox & Mor Bakhoum, MAKING MARKETS WORK FOR AFRICA: MARKETS, DEVELOPMENT, AND COMPETITION LAW IN SUB-SAHARAN AFRICA (2019).

the way people live."[18] This technology-centric view of innovation is further skewed by distinctions between different kinds of innovations. Thus, economists often distinguish between fundamental innovations and process innovations (or disruptive innovations and incremental innovations), assessing how incentives may vary depending on which type of innovation is involved.[19]

These prior assumptions about what counts as innovation tend to affect economic studies and theories about innovation, as well as competition law enforcement dealing with innovation. Empirical studies often focus on R&D expenditures or rates of patenting;[20] theoretical discussions model the incentives for and efficiencies from new product introductions.[21] Competition law enforcers focus on licensing of intellectual property rights or on the potential suppression of disruptive technologies through exclusionary practices or "killer" acquisitions.[22]

In looking at innovation from the viewpoint of competition policy in developing economies, however, it is helpful to have a broader view of innovation. Christensen, Ojomo, Gay, and Auerswald (COGA, for ease of exposition), drawing on the work of Joseph Schumpeter, define innovation as "a change in the process by which an organization transforms labor, capital, materials, or information into products and services of greater value."[23] This broader approach moves beyond the idea/invention focus to take more of an innovation process approach. "Innovation," they write, "is not necessarily high tech, overly advanced, or even entirely new." Innovation, they conclude, "is different from invention."

COGA's non-high-tech approach leads to a somewhat different categorization of innovations than an exclusive tech-centric approach provides. They posit three

---

18 Makan Delrahim, Assistant Att'y Gen., Antitrust Div., *Take It to the Limit: Respecting Innovation Incentives in the Application of Antitrust Law*, Remarks as Prepared for Delivery at USC Gould School of Law, 1 (Nov. 10, 2017), www.justice.gov/opa/speech/file/1010746/download.

19 *See, e.g.*, Wesley M. Cohen, *Fifty Years of Empirical Studies of Innovative Activity and Performance*, in 1 HANDBOOK OF THE ECONOMICS OF INNOVATION 129 (Bronwyn H. Hall & Nathan Rosenberg eds., 2010) (surveying literature explaining how a monopolized market may lead to greater process innovations because a monopolist can apply cost-cutting measures across their existing, broad scope of production); Giulio Federico et al., *Horizontal Mergers and Product Innovation*, 59 INT'L J. INDUS. ORG. 1 (2018) (presenting an economic model for product innovations where competitive markets lead to higher innovation).

20 *See, e.g.*, Federico et al., *supra* note 19; Richard J. Gilbert, *Competition, Mergers, and R&D Diversity*, 54 REV. INDUS. ORG. 465 (2019).

21 For a thorough discussion of models of innovation incentives, *see* RICHARD J. GILBERT, INNOVATION MATTERS: COMPETITION POLICY FOR THE HIGH-TECHNOLOGY ECONOMY (2020), at ch. 4.

22 *See* US DEP'T OF JUST. & FED. TRADE COMM'N, ANTITRUST GUIDELINES FOR THE LICENSING OF INTELLECTUAL PROPERTY 2 (2017) ("The intellectual property laws provide incentives for innovation … The antitrust laws promote innovation and consumer welfare by prohibiting certain actions that may harm competition with respect to either existing or new ways of serving consumers"); United States v. Microsoft, 84 F. Supp. 2d 9, 112 (D.D.C. 1999) (discussing effect of Microsoft's effort to stifle innovation) (Finding of Fact ¶ 412), *vacated and remanded on other grounds*, 253 F.3d 34 (D.C. Cir. 2001); Dep't of Justice, Antitrust Div., Press Release, Visa and Plaid Abandon Merger After Antitrust Division's Suit to Block ("In a victory for American consumers and small businesses, Visa has abandoned its efforts to acquire an innovative and nascent competitor") (Jan. 12, 2021), www.justice.gov/opa/pr/visa-and-plaid-abandon-merger-after-antitrust-divisions-suit-block.

23 Clayton M. Christensen et al., *The Third Answer: How Market-Creating Innovation Drives Economic Growth and Development*, 12 INNOVATIONS: TECH., GOVERNANCE, GLOBALIZATION 10 (2019), at 12. *See also* EDWIN MANSFIELD ET AL., RESEARCH AND INNOVATION IN THE MODERN CORPORATION (1971) (innovation process).

types of innovations: market creating, market sustaining, and efficiency producing.[24] Market-creating innovations create new markets that serve people for whom there either were no products or for whom existing products were "not accessible" because of cost or "a lack of the expertise required to use them." Market-sustaining innovations improve solutions already on the market. Their economic impact on jobs, profits, or economic climate is less than market-creating innovations because they generally use "established channels to sell to an existing customer base." Efficiency innovations are generally process innovations that allow firms to be more productively efficient. COGA views these innovations as more likely to be the result of competitive pressures on firms that are trying to stay viable.

COGA's definition of innovation, and their three-part categorization, allows us to see innovation in a way that is more useful for competition policy and enforcement in developing countries. Their examples illustrate the point. For market-creating innovation, they cite Sudanese entrepreneur Mo Ibrahim's creation of a market for mobile phones in Africa in the late 1990s and the growth of "Nollywood," Nigeria's motion picture industry. Ibrahim's company, within six years of its founding, covered 13 African countries and gained 5.2 million customers. This growth led to the spread of mobile phone networks more generally, now covering more than 950 million subscriptions and providing a platform for payments transfers and loans in many African countries.[25] Nollywood produces 1,500 movies annually, second only to India's Bollywood, with revenues that exceed $1 billion annually and employment of more than one million people.[26] Ibrahim did not invent cellphones; Nollywood did not invent motion pictures. What both did was to recognize local needs and create markets for bringing these products to local users in ways that they found useful (mobile phones) or attractive (movies that reflected the lives of average Africans).

COGA contrast their argument for markets with what they say are the two dominant theories for what drives development–ideas and institutions. COGA's argument is that ideas, in themselves, still need to be accepted and diffused; markets do this. Institutions–financial, legal, political–are needed if ideas are to be protected from appropriation but these institutions grow up in response to the markets they protect and advance.

Whether markets drive innovation and development more so than ideas or institutions is a debate that does not have to be resolved here. The critical point is to see the connection between market-advancing innovation and development, without regard to other factors that may also affect development. This puts

---

24   Christensen et al., *supra* note 23, at 12. These categories are not completely dissimilar to the distinctions that economists have often made among different types of innovation, *see supra* note 19.

25   *Id.* at 14–15. For background information on Ibrahim, *see* Lucy Handley, *Mo Ibrahim, The accidental businessman*, CNBC (May 15, 2019), www.cnbc.com/mo-ibrahim-african-entrepreneur-and-founder-of-the-ibrahim-index.

26   *See* Christensen et al., *supra* note 23, at 18–19.

competition law front and center for insuring innovation. If there is anything that competition law should be able to achieve it is making markets work.

2. Competition and innovation

If markets are necessary for producing innovation (whether broadly or narrowly defined), what is the optimal market structure that will achieve that result? Is monopoly best? Or is the "constant stress" of rivalry in competitive markets the way to insure "industrial progress," as Judge Hand wrote in *Alcoa*?[27]

Whether monopoly is necessary for innovation is a long-running debate in industrial organization economics and in antitrust. The debate is often cast as a debate between two schools, those who follow Joseph Schumpeter and those who follow Kenneth Arrow. Put simply, the Schumpeter school focuses on the "size of the prize." As Schumpeter wrote, high profits are "the baits that lure capital on to untried trails."[28] The Arrow school takes a contrary view. Monopolists will not be good innovators because if they bring out a new product, it will only take sales away from the old. This cannibalization of sales (the "replacement effect") will act as a disincentive to innovate.[29] Small firms (upstarts) will be better innovators because they have little to lose and much to gain.

Economists have continued to debate and refine Schumpeter's and Arrow's ideas. Although each approach has a plausible core, neither approach sets out a complete picture of the incentives for innovation or the optimal market conditions to produce innovation.[30] More recent economic writing thus offers a blend of the two approaches that accounts for the two cross-cutting incentives: competitive rivalry and monopoly profits.[31]

These newer approaches suggest three principles that can help developing countries to assess the relationship between the conduct subject to competition law and the desire for innovation: contestability, appropriability, and synergies.

Contestability focuses (Arrow-like) on "the extent to which a firm can gain profitable sales from its rivals by offering greater value to customers."[32] This factor puts more stress on rivalry among firms than on market concentration

---

27   United States v. Aluminum Co. of America, 148 F.2d 416, 427 (1945).

28   Joseph A. Schumpeter, Capitalism, Socialism, and Democracy 78 (Routledge Classics, 2010) (1942).

29   Kenneth Arrow, *Economic Welfare and the Allocation of Resources to Invention, in* The Rate and Direction of Inventive Activity: Economic and Social Factors 609, 620 (1962) ("The preinvention monopoly power acts as a strong disincentive to further innovation"). The phrase "replacement effect" is attributed to Jean Tirole, The Theory of Industrial Organization 392 (1988).

30   Empirical evidence with regard to the relation between concentration and innovation is also mixed. *See* Gilbert, *supra* note 21, at 116–17 table 6.1.

31   *See id.* at 108 (recent studies show "a more nuanced relationship between innovation and firm and industry characteristics").

32   Carl Shapiro, *Competition and Innovation: Did Arrow Hit the Bull's Eye?, in* The Rate and Direction of Inventive Activity Revisited 361, 364 (Josh Lerner & Scott Stern, eds., 2012).

per se, that is, on factors (including efficiencies) that lead to a robust competitive process for winning the patronage of customers.[33]

The second principle is appropriability, which focuses (Schumpeter-like) on the ability of the firm to benefit from the social value of its innovation.[34] Appropriability can be enhanced by collaborative conduct (or mergers) that enable innovators to capture spillover effects or by conduct that increases scale and allows the benefits of process innovations to be spread over more output.[35] Appropriability benefits, though, need careful assessment. In particular, the need for appropriability does not necessarily justify anticompetitive tactics that exclude rivals and increase the innovator's profits. Such tactics might add little to appropriability where appropriability is already high (say for a dominant firm), but stopping exclusionary conduct might enhance the innovation incentives of smaller rivals and force the dominant firm to substitute more costly (but more socially valuable) innovation for cheaper exclusion (which might only slightly increase the gains to the monopolist from its past innovations).[36]

The third principle is synergies, that is, combining complementary assets to enhance innovation capabilities. Synergies focus on the ability to innovate, in contrast to contestability and appropriability, which focus on the incentives to innovate.[37] That said, as with appropriability, care must be used in assessing whether synergies could be achieved in a way that is less restrictive to contestability, thus achieving gains from innovation at a lower cost.[38]

3. Does competition law matter for innovation in developing countries?

There are many factors that might lead one to be skeptical about whether competition law provides much value added when it comes to increasing innovation in developing countries. Infrastructure support for innovation generally, and for digital products and services specifically, may be more of a hurdle for innovation than weak competition law enforcement. Competition law enforcement agencies have had difficulty incorporating innovation into antitrust policy even in major developed economies; how much more so for resource-starved agencies in developing countries? Perhaps it would be better to let the major enforcement agencies take the lead, particularly when the major digital platforms are involved, on the assumption that changes in structure or business practices will likely spill over to developing countries in any event.

---

33 *See id.* at 382–83.

34 *See id.* at 364.

35 *See id.* at 388–89; Cohen, *supra* note 19, at 138.

36 *See* JONATHAN B. BAKER, THE ANTITRUST PARADIGM: RESTORING A COMPETITIVE ECONOMY 173–174 (2019).

37 For discussion of the distinctions, *see* Shapiro, *supra* note 32, at 364–65.

38 *Cf. id.* at 397–98 (discussing *Genzyme/Novazyme* merger).

Despite these caveats, it would be unwise for agencies in developing countries to ignore innovation issues in competition law enforcement. Developing countries have particular policy concerns that may seem less important to developed countries. One major concern, of course, is economic development, for which innovation may be a critical driver, particularly if we view innovation in a less technology-centric way. Another major concern is inclusive economic growth, making certain that the gains from markets are distributed more widely rather than less, particularly when it comes to groups that have faced discrimination or have not adequately participated in the economy. A third concern is sovereignty, to make sure that a developing economy is not dominated by outside economic interests. Competition enforcement that increases innovation, particularly through an emphasis on competitive rivalry in dynamic markets, offers the possibility of advancing all three goals.

III. Digital Platform Use in Developing Countries

1. An overview

Digital platforms are in widespread use in developing countries. The major US digital platforms tend to be ubiquitous–in South Africa, for example, nearly half of all Internet users use Facebook, YouTube, and WhatsApp[39]–but there are also more local platforms in developing countries that are of significant size.[40]

Digital platforms can be categorized in different ways. Most common is to categorize them by the type of service they offer; the proposed EU Digital Markets Act, for example, has eight categories of "core platform service," such as search engines, social networks, and operating systems.[41] This type of categorization is similar to product markets as analyzed under competition law. A more functional approach divides digital platforms into transaction platforms and innovation platforms.[42] Transaction platforms are generally multisided and "support exchanges between a number of different parties," Amazon and Uber

---

39 *See* Thembalethu Buthelezi & James Hodge, *Competition Policy in the Digital Economy: A Developing Country Perspective*, 15 COMPETITION L. INT'L 201, 202 (2019); *see also* Competition Comm'n of S. Afr., *Competition in the Digital Economy* (Sept. 2020) [hereinafter Competition in the Digital Economy], at 20–21 tbl. 3 (listing active digital platforms in South Africa, most of which are US- and China-based), www.compcom.co.za/wp-content/uploads/2020/09/Competition-in-the-digital-economy_7-September-2020.pdf; NICOLAS FRIEDERICI AT AL., DIGITAL ENTREPRENEURSHIP IN AFRICA: HOW A CONTINENT IS ESCAPING SILICON VALLEY'S LONG SHADOW 41 (2020) (YouTube, WhatsApp, and Facebook have continent-wide reach in Africa).

40 Examples of developing country platforms are Flipkart in India, Mercado Libre in Latin America, Jumia and Konga in Nigeria, and Takealot in South Africa. A number of these companies, however, have been acquired in whole or in part by major platform companies from developed countries. *See* UN CONFERENCE ON TRADE AND DEVELOPMENT, DIGITAL ECONOMY REPORT 2019, 109–12 (UNCTAD/DER/2019) [hereinafter UNCTAD Digital Economy Report], https://unctad.org/en/PublicationsLibrary/der2019_en.pdf.

41 *See* Proposal for a Regulation of the European Parliament and of the Council on Contestable and Fair Markets in the Digital Sector (Digital Markets Act), COM(2020) 842 final (Dec. 15, 2020), at 2, 34–35 (https://eur-lex.europa.eu/legal-content/en/TXT/?uri=COM%3A2020%3A842%3AFIN).

42 UNCTAD Digital Economy Report, *supra* note 40, at 25–27; *see also* Friederici et al., *supra* note 39, at 16–18 (distinguishing between digital production, information processing, user interconnection, and market intermediation as different forms of digital value creation by platforms).

being good examples. Innovation platforms (sometimes called technology or engineering platforms) provide components that firms in a sector can use in common for their interactions. Computer operating systems and technology standards are good examples of these platforms.[43]

Entrepreneurs in developing countries have generally not created innovation platforms.[44] Rather, they have used platform technologies created elsewhere to offer products that are distributed digitally, mostly on a relatively localized basis, that is, within the home country of the entrepreneur. Platform technologies are thus tools for these enterprises, allowing them to create new products and distribute them more efficiently. Even if entrepreneurs in developing countries do not create the tools, however, their use of platform technologies can still be market-creating or sustaining, and thereby qualify as innovation that can drive economic growth.

As the following examples will show, whether platforms are successful depends on many factors beyond competition law enforcement. Indeed, at the moment, competition law violations may not have emerged as yet. The question, though, is whether competition policy can play a role in keeping digital platform tools accessible and digital product markets competitive.

2. Mapping platform use in Africa: Four areas

A. *Online retail sales*

Online retail sale of physical products and services is developing in Africa, but slowly. In South Africa, for example, ecommerce is estimated to have only approximately 1–2% of total retail sales, in comparison with 18% in the UK, with customers generally being higher-income earners mostly concentrated in metropolitan areas.[45] Nevertheless, throughout Africa a wide range of products are sold through online retail platforms, including food, consumer electronics, fashion, and apparel.[46]

Retailers use platforms in three ways. First, traditional brick-and-mortar stores use Internet sales to complement their sales in physical stores; this has given major retailers a strong presence in online retail selling.[47] Second, some sellers have an online presence only, selling their products at retail on various digital platforms. The "most ubiquitous" digital enterprises in Africa are ecommerce

---

43 UNCTAD Digital Economy Report, *supra* note 40, at 25–26.

44 *See id.* at 109–22; Friederici et al., *supra* note 39, at 63–67 (finding that market intermediation was the most common form of value creation among African platforms).

45 *See* Shaista Goga, et al., *Online Retailing in South Africa: An Overview* 3–5 (CCRED Working Paper No. 2/2019, Mar. 2019), https://papers.ssrn.com/sol3/papers.cfm?abstract_id=3386008.

46 *Id.* at 5–6 (South Africa); Adheesh Budree, Policy Considerations for E-Commerce in South Africa and Other African Countries, 3 (GEGAfrica Policy Briefing, June 2017) (Tanzania and Kenya).

47 *See* Shaista Goga & Anthea Paelo, *Strategies for Adapting to Online Entry: The Case of Retailers in South Africa* 2–3, 19 (CCRED Working Paper No. 3/2019, Mar. 2019).

sites that present their products on Facebook.[48] Third, Africa-based platforms offer marketplace services for other retailers. Takealot in South Africa, for example, has become the largest online retail marketplace in South Africa, with more traffic than international competitors such as Amazon or eBay.[49] It has also begun integrating into offering its own exclusive brands in competition with other retailers on the platform, raising potential concerns for self-preferencing.[50]

Online retail sellers in Africa, particularly small and medium business enterprises, face a set of challenges that make it difficult to compete successfully. Online advertising is critical for these enterprises, but the two main advertising channels are Facebook and Google, and their use is expensive and complex for smaller businesses.[51] Most ecommerce payment transactions are made by credit card, but fees can be high, payments can be slow, and concern for fraud has been high.[52] Delivery may require investments in expensive assets (trucks, motorcycles, warehouses), particularly where the postal service is unreliable.[53] On the other hand, the expense of drop-shipping international packages, the unreliability of the postal service, and the relatively small size and geographical isolation of many African countries can make it difficult for international platforms like Amazon to compete successfully with local ecommerce sites.[54]

B. *Value chains*

Companies in Africa use digital platforms to participate in "value chains," that is, as intermediate transactors in the production and sale of goods and services. The ultimate consumer in the chain may be located outside the country or inside. For many African countries, participation in global value chains has been seen as an important way to stimulate economic growth, particularly if small and medium-size businesses are the beneficiaries of such participation.[55]

---

48 Friederici et al., *supra* note 39, ch. 2 at 61.

49 Goga et al., *supra* note 45, at 13–14.

50 *See* Shaista Goga & Anthea Paelo, *Issues in the Regulation and Policy Surrounding E-Commerce in South Africa* 5 (CCRED Working Paper No. 6/2019, Apr. 2019); *Menu Page for Takealot's Exclusive Product Line*, TAKEALOT.COM, www.takealot.com/promotion/exclusivetotakealot (last visited Mar. 12, 2021).

51 *See* Goga & Paelo, *supra* note 47, at 16–17; Friederici et al., *supra* note 39, at 48 (surveyed African digital entrepreneurs report they primarily use Facebook for digital advertising).

52 *See* Goga et al., *supra* note 45, at 17–18 (75% of payments by credit card); *id.* at 20–21 (use of mobile payment systems comparable to PayPal). *See also* Friederici et al., *supra* note 39, at 61 (for surveyed digital entrepreneurs, cash is the predominant method of payment).

53 *See* Goga et al., *supra* note 45, at 21 (theft prevalent in South Africa postal service); Friederici et al., *supra* note 39, at 109–13 (costliness of "last mile" delivery systems).

54 *See* Goga et al., *supra* note 45, at 29–32.

55 *See* Harry First & Eleanor M. Fox, Philadelphia National Bank, *Globalization, and the Public Interest*, 80 ANTITRUST L. J. 307, 344–46 (2015) (importance of inclusion in global supply chain as part of remedy in *Walmart/Massmart* merger); Competition in the Digital Economy, *supra* note 39, at 51.

The extent to which digital platforms have increased such participation by African firms is unclear. A study of value chains in Kenya and Rwanda examined how tourism firms integrated with international tourism sites to provide booking availability and service information, but found that their participation was often limited by a lack of technical skills and by the platforms' managerial requirements.[56] A study of small-scale fresh fruit and vegetable farmers in Tanzania and Kenya focused on the use of certain basic platform technologies (mobile phones, the Internet, and Facebook) to access payment systems, get pricing and production information, and reach export markets. Such usage was actually rather small (only 11% of farmers surveyed). Although the use of cellphones was helpful to small farmers in many local markets, reaching export markets required the use of the Internet more than the use of basic cellphones, a step that excluded farmers who lacked sophistication (technical and linguistic).[57]

The difficulties of establishing digital value chains is not just limited by access to technology. Existing market structures and entrenched competitors may stand in the way as well.

A good example is the effort to create an online tea auction market in Mombasa, Kenya. The Mombasa Tea Auction provides the link between East African tea processors and international buyers.[58] Kenya is the world's leading exporter of tea, and tea is Kenya's number one foreign exchange earner.[59] Tea is transported from highland areas in Africa to storage warehouses in Mombasa, where it is subsequently auctioned. Two groups have been the main intermediaries between growers and buyers in this process–tea brokers and storage warehouses–and only tea brokers could negotiate with buyers in the auction. Sellers made payments to the auction and then collected the tea from the warehouses for export. About 95% of tea exported from Kenya was sold through the Mombasa Tea Auction.

Asian competitors had been using online auctions, but the Mombasa Tea Auction was done in person. Recognizing the auction's inefficiencies, in 2012 an effort was made by the East African Tea Trade Association (EATTA) to introduce an online auction system. EATTA has 200 members from 10 African countries (mostly in East Africa) and includes all groups in the industry (producers, buyers, brokers, warehouses, and packers). Intermediaries were most opposed to an

---

[56] See Christopher Foster et al., *Digital Control in Value Chains: Challenges of Connectivity for East African Firms*, 94 Econ. Geography 68, 78–79 (2018).

[57] See Madlen Krone & Peter Dannenberg, *Development or Divide? Information and Communication Technologies in Commercial Small-Scale Farming in East Africa*, in Digital Economies at Global Margins 79, 88–97 (Mark Graham ed., 2019).

[58] The detail about the tea auction is from Christopher Foster et al., *Making Sense of Digital Disintermediation and Development: The Case of the Mombasa Tea Auction*, in Digital Economies at Global Margins 55, 63–66 (Mark Graham ed., 2019).

[59] East African Tea Trade Ass'n v. Competition Auth. of Kenya, Case No. CT/001 of 2017 ¶ 84 (Apr. 24, 2020) (Competition Tribunal), http://kenyalaw.org/caselaw/cases/view/194950. Kenya is not the world's largest producer of tea, but it frequently ranks as the top exporter in part because domestic consumption is low. See Kaison Chang, Food & Agric. Org. of the United Nations, *World Tea Production and Trade: Current and Future Development* (2015), at 4–5 tables. 1 & 2, www.fao.org/3/i4480e/i4480e.pdf.

online auction, particularly the brokers, who were believed to have controlled the in-person auction and feared disintermediation.[60] Interestingly, the brokers also feared that buyers would find it easier to collude when they did not have to place bids in an open auction, perhaps a not misplaced worry given a later antitrust suit against EATTA for fixing brokers' and warehouse owners' fees in the tea auction.[61]

After a trial run of an online auction, the EATTA members voted against its continuation. Apparently, the brokers were able to convince smaller producers, whose only link to these markets was through the brokers, that an online auction would harm the brokers and thereby harm them.[62] It was not until 2019 that an online tea auction became operational.[63]

C. *Fintech*

Financial technology products (fintech) operate as multisided platforms connecting buyers and sellers of financial services using the Internet, mobile devices, software technology, and/or cloud services.[64] Fintech products can cover aspects of banking, digital currencies, insurance, lending, money transfers, and payments. They can be deeply disruptive of existing banking and financial services, but can also offer platform infrastructure for many businesses. As such, fintech products are widely used throughout Africa.

Probably the most widely lauded fintech product in Africa is M-Pesa, the payments service that runs on mobile phones.[65] M-Pesa was launched in 2007 by Vodafone, the UK-based telecom company, in partnership with two African mobile phone system operators, Safaricom in Kenya and Vodacom in Tanzania.[66] M-Pesa "allows users to deposit money into an account stored on their cell phones, to send balances using SMS technology to other users (including sellers of goods and services), and to redeem deposits for regular money."[67] There is no charge for depositing the cash

---

60   See Foster et al., *supra* note 58, at 66.

61   See *East African Tea Trade Ass'n*, *supra* note 59 (upholding finding of violation of Competition Act, but exempting brokerage fees from the Act for two years).

62   See Foster et al., *supra* note 58, at 67.

63   See Agatha Ngotho, *Mombasa tea auction goes digital, switch in final stages*, THE STAR, Jan. 20, 2021, www.the-star.co.ke/counties/coast/2021-01-21-mombasa-tea-auction-goes-digital-switch-in-final-stages. The difficulties of establishing digital trading facilities for agricultural goods are not limited to developing countries. *See* Julia-Ambra Verlaine, *Poultry Trading Enters Digital Age*, WALL ST. J., Mar. 9, 2021, at B2 (detailing the effort to create a US marketplace for trading chicken parts; Tyson moves "millions of pounds daily of meat and poultry products from farmers to vendors," with consequent high brokerage fees).

64   See Competition in the Digital Economy, *supra* note 39, at 23.

65   Pesa is Kiswahili for "money," hence mobile money. *See* William Jack & Tavneet Suri, *Mobile Money: The Economics of M-PESA*, (NBER Working Paper 16721, Jan. 2011), at 6 note 10, www.nber.org/papers/w16721.

66   David Yermack, *FinTech in Sub-Saharan Africa: What Has Worked Well, and What Hasn't* 6 (NBER Working Paper 25007, Sept. 2018), www.nber.org/papers/w25007.

67   Jack & Suri, *supra* note 65, at 6.

with the mobile phone company; charges are deducted when "e-float" or "e-money" is sent to recipients or when cash is withdrawn.[68]

M-Pesa spread quickly following its introduction, with 10,000 new registrations by the end of its first year; two years later there were 7.7 million M-Pesa registered accounts.[69] In its first 10 years, the service expanded to 10 countries, including one in Eastern Europe. By that time 21% of all adults in Sub-Saharan Africa had a mobile money account; 73% of the population of Kenya and more than 50% of the populations of Uganda and Zimbabwe used mobile money.

For all of M-Pesa's important success, its growth has actually been fairly limited, as has been the growth of fintech firms generally, which "have been slow to penetrate other sectors and other countries."[70] M-Pesa has been limited by the fact that it operates a low-tech service, using basic cellphones and text technology but not relying on more advanced smartphones.[71] Thus it has proved less attractive in countries like South Africa that already had more advanced smartphone use and a "much more advanced banking network," able to meet the needs that M-Pesa met.[72] M-Pesa's technological limits also made it less attractive for integrating its mobile payments API into other software applications.[73]

Whether the slow diffusion of fintech in Africa is a result of technological impediments or competitor resistance is unclear. One author concludes that the "largest impediment to more rapid FinTech growth appears to be the electrical and communications infrastructure in many developing countries, which have only limited, unreliable access to broadband Internet connections and smartphone handsets."[74] There is little doubt that these infrastructure issues affect the ability of digital platforms to thrive in Africa, but it may also be the case that the powerful financial companies can create legal roadblocks to fintech entry, as well as trying to preempt that entry by offering products similar to those offered by potentially disruptive fintech entrants. Indeed, this may be the case in South Africa. As the South Africa Competition Commission points out, one approach is for incumbents to accommodate the competitive threat by partnering with the upstart fintech firm: "the Fintech firm commits to remain small, providing the incumbent with its offerings whilst being able to ride on the scale, distribution channels and licenses of the traditional bank."[75] Another possibility is for the

---

68   *Id.*

69   *Id.*

70   Yermack, *supra* note 66, at 18 ("success of M-Pesa in Kenya appears to be an outlier").

71   *Id.* at 1.

72   *Id.* at 2.

73   *See* Friederici et al., *supra* note 39, ch. 2 at 30 (describing mobile payment APIs as "clunky and unreliable").

74   Yermack, *supra* note 66, at 2.

75   Competition in the Digital Economy, *supra* at note 39, at 25.

incumbent to acquire the fintech firm outright. A third is for the incumbent firm to compete with the fintech's offerings, potentially leading to anticompetitive actions such as denying the fintech firm needed access to infrastructure assets.[76]

D. *Sharing platforms*

Sharing platforms are used by a wide variety of businesses in Africa. The Competition Commission of South Africa defines these platforms as offering "short-term peer-to-peer transactions to share the use of idle assets and services or to facilitate collaboration."[77] Sharing platforms include not only firms that allow owners of vehicles and accommodation to "share" them with users, but also those that allow the sharing of workspaces, money (loans), clothing, and freelance services.[78]

Sharing platforms are an area in which the major international companies face competition with local enterprises. In the ride-hailing segment, for example, Uber's entry into African markets triggered the spread of mobile mapping technology for collecting location data from mobile vehicles. This allowed local companies to develop their own products suited to the needs of customers in different cities and countries, "giving themselves an edge over foreign services."[79] In South Africa, for example, Taxi Live and Mr D Foods (both South African firms) compete with Uber for taxi ride-hailing and food delivery; Afri Ride, a South African company, competes by allowing commuters or drivers to offer unoccupied seats on their trips.[80] In Kenya, Little Cab competed with Uber by accepting M-Pesa payments.[81]

Even with the existence of local companies, international firms appear to be the major competitors in most of these sharing platform markets. In a survey of users in Nairobi, Little Cab, four years after its entry, was running a distant third to the international platforms, Uber and Bolt.[82] A 2020 survey in South Africa showed that 3 of the 15 most popular apps in South Africa were international ride-sharing platforms; none of the platforms in the survey was South African or African.[83]

---

76   *See id.* (noting how South Africa's "big four" firms have "embraced fintech as part of their strategic direction for the future").

77   *Id.* at 21.

78   *See id.*

79   Eleni Mourdoukoutas, *Africa's app-based taxis battle Uber over market share*, AFR. RENEWAL (Aug. – Nov. 2017), at 2, www.un.org/africarenewal/magazine/august-november-2017/africa%E2%80%99s-app-based-taxis-battle-uber-over-market-share.

80   *See* www.mrdfood.com/mr-delivery-is-now-mr-d-food#our-story; www.afri-ride.com/about.html (accessed Mar. 12, 2021).

81   *See* Mourdoukoutas, *supra* note 79, at 2 (Little Cab service launched by Safaricom).

82   Benson Weru & Jane Mugo, *Ride Hailing Survey: Usage of App-Based Mobility Services in Nairobi, Kenya*, 37–38 (2020) (Uber 69%, Bolt 21%, Little Cab 10%), www.changing-transport.org/wp-content/uploads/2020_Ride_Hailing_Survey.pdf.

83   *See* Statista, *Most popular mobile apps used in South Africa as of February 2020* (ride-share apps Uber, Bolt, and InDriver), www.statista.com/statistics/1103151/most-popular-mobile-apps-south-africa (accessed Mar. 12, 2021).

The competitive problems that firms in sharing platform markets face do not appear to be the result of the exercise of anticompetitive conduct by dominant firms. Of course, as in developed countries, these platform companies do face opposition from the traditional operators in the fields that the platforms challenge. In the ride-sharing market, for example, the metered taxi industry has responded to Uber's entry in ways that are similar to the responses in developed countries. Taxi drivers have tried to physically block Uber drivers;[84] they have also tried to invoke government action to stop Uber from engaging in certain business practices.[85] But they have also tried to meet the challenge with the more competitive response of developing their own apps to connect passengers to metered taxis.[86]

3. Conclusion

The mapping of digital platforms use in Africa is by no means complete. Digital platforms are being developed in many other areas. In agriculture, for example, Kenya-based mobile apps have been launched to help farmers better manage crops such as cassava, maize, and potatoes.[87] In health care, there is a long list of available apps: Hello Doctor provides free essential medical information in 10 African countries; FD-Detector (developed by five teenage girls from Nigeria) detects fake drugs by using bar codes; mTrac allows healthcare workers in Uganda to submit weekly health data via SMS; Omomi provides women in Nigeria with maternal and child health information and connects them to doctors.[88]

Even though the overview is necessarily incomplete, the picture that does emerge shows that digital platforms do hold out the promise not just of extending traditional industries into new means of distribution, but also of dealing with certain problems that are more acute in developing countries (although not absent in developed countries). Access to capital can be increased through fintech applications; business transactions can be facilitated if payment systems are more secure; small enterprises can reach markets more efficiently if digital platforms are available and open; healthcare information and data can be shared more easily where mobile applications are available. Many of these improvements are more incremental than fundamental, but they all lead to better market-driven outcomes.

---

84   *See* Mourdoukoutas, *supra* note 79, at 3 (South Africa).

85   *See* Competition in the Digital Economy, *supra* note 39, at 44–45 (filing complaint alleging below-cost pricing and other unfair competitive practices; Commission declines to pursue case).

86   *See* Mourdoukoutas, *supra* note 79, at 2 (development of Yookoo Ride in South Africa).

87   *See* Duncan Mboyah, *Kenya launches 14 mobile apps to transform agriculture*, SciDev.Net (June 18, 2018), www.scidev.net/sub-saharan-africa/news/kenya-mobile-apps-transform-agriculture. *See also* Shannon McCrocklin, *Mobile Phone Apps for Farmers in Sub-Saharan Africa*, GeoPoll (Nov. 14, 2019), www.geopoll.com/blog/mobile-apps-farmers-africa.

88   *See* Zoe Engels, *Digital Health Apps in Africa Aim to Revolutionize Medical Care*, Borgen Project Blog (Sept. 20, 2020), https://borgenproject.org/digital-health-apps-in-africa; *10 Most Successful mHealth Apps in Africa*, Dr Hempel Digital Health Network (Apr. 16, 2018), www.dr-hempel-network.com/digital-health-startups/10-most-successful-mhealth-apps-in-africa. I thank Frédéric Jenny for these examples.

IV. Lessons for Competition Policy for Digital Platforms

It is not surprising that even a brief survey of the adoption of digital platforms in Africa shows that their use is both important and spreading. To a large degree, these platform technologies are tools for a variety of improvements in the production and distribution of old and new products. The ability to use these tools to create new offerings is an important aspect of innovation.

Developed countries now seem obsessed with the power of the major platforms over many aspects of our economy and life. Developing countries seem less obsessed but, in a significant way, more dependent. Mobile technology is a key tool for delivering new digital products, but this technology often comes with a hidden "tax" imposed by developed world patent-holders, who control the standards on which these devices (now smartphones) are based and set the fees for licensing those standards.[89] Developed world competition law enforcers seem powerless to control this pricing power; we would not expect developing world enforcers to do better. This tax, however, may be more critical in economies where the incomes are lower and smartphone use more limited.

What about the power of the GAFA? Although the use of Google and Facebook products is clearly ubiquitous, Apple and Amazon seem less powerful. In particular, Amazon's business model puts it at a disadvantage in many developing economies, where shipping costs, tariffs, and delivery systems give local online sellers an edge.

Facebook and Google, but especially Facebook, loom larger. Search is important for delivering advertising, but Facebook, combined with WhatsApp, is vital not only for digital advertising but for digital presence. Sellers have come to rely on Facebook for connecting to consumers and establishing a network of users with whom to communicate and from whom to get information and data. Entrepreneurs in the developing world have complained about Facebook and Google's high advertising rates, but with Facebook the problem goes deeper. Should Facebook or WhatsApp change their terms of use in some way, there would be little that developing countries could do. If Australia is having trouble controlling Facebook, what would we expect from countries with fewer users and smaller economies?[90]

---

[89] *See* FTC v. Qualcomm Inc., 2017 U.S. Dist. LEXIS 98632 *20 (N.D. Cal. 2017) (FTC allegation that Qualcomm's "no license, no chips" policy raised price of royalties on Qualcomm's SEPs above "fair, reasonable, and non-discriminatory" rates, thereby constituting a "tax" that handset makers had to pay), *rv'sd*, 969 F.3d 974, 987 n.13 (9th Cir. 2020) (disregarding allegation of "tax"; FTC complaint "only alleged antitrust violations").

[90] *See* Mike Cherney, *Facebook's Australia Blackout Sparks Ire*, WALL ST. J., Feb. 20, 2021, at B1 (reporting on reaction to Facebook's withdrawal of news from its platform in Australia in response to proposed legislation to require Facebook to pay media companies for content that Facebook publishes on its platform); Erich Schwartzel, *When Facebook Slows the News Flow*, WALL ST. J., Feb. 27, 2021, at B2 (reporting impact on remote Australian island from Facebook's decision to not publish news; experience of those in a "tiny town on a tiny island" revealed how the world's largest social-media platform could be "blunt and brutal when challenged in a negotiation"; quoting a local business owner, "We are very much reliant on giants like Facebook").

This means that the first lesson for competition policy involving digital platforms in developing countries is actually aimed at developed countries. If antitrust authorities in the US are successful in their litigation against Facebook and Google, at least some thought should be given to how the remedies sought will affect developing countries.[91] Although consideration of extraterritorial effects is not part of the case against these companies, remedy is broader. Positive spillovers should be part of the governments' calculus.

The second lesson is that competition law enforcement may not be the most critical driver of platform innovation in developing countries. Many commentators have pointed out that basic physical infrastructure is primary–better Internet access, more broadband service, less expensive smartphones–as is better managerial training and even better ability to use English. Competition law enforcement is a good tool to keep things from getting worse, but not necessarily the best tool to make things better.[92]

The third lesson is that the hope that digital platforms will allow local small and medium-sized businesses more access to global value chains remains just that, a hope. Local marketplace platforms do not yet have a global reach and key international platforms have proven difficult to access, but not because of any anticompetitive conduct. Developing country competition law enforcers should still be alert to anticompetitive practices, like self-preferencing, but not for the purpose of driving exports. Impact on local markets and local business should be reason enough to act.

The fourth lesson is that there appears to be little evidence so far of exclusionary conduct aimed at digital platforms of the type with which competition law is tasked to deal. This does not mean that such conduct is unlikely. In some jurisdictions with active merger enforcement, attention should be paid to the possibility of acquisitions done to quash nascent competitors (as in the fintech sector in South Africa). Economic theory counsels that rivalry from upstart competitors is a key driver of innovation.

Even if there is no indication of competition law violations, however, competition agencies still have an important role to play in articulating competition policy. A good example is the entry of international platforms in a way that disrupts local incumbent firms. Even if these international firms end up leading their markets (as has been the case with ride-sharing apps), competition law enforcers should be speaking up for how competitive rivalry benefits consumers in terms of new products and, hopefully, lower prices and increased opportunity for workers. This is another way in which making markets work fosters innovation and produces a dynamic society.

---

91 Eleanor Fox has frequently pointed out this problem. *See, e.g.*, Eleanor M. Fox, *Remedies and the Courage of Convictions in a Globalized World: How Globalization Corrupts Relief*, 80 TUL. L. REV. 571 (2005).

92 See Verizon Comm'ns., Inc. v. Law Offices of Curtis V. Trinko, LLP, 540 U.S. 398, 415–16 (2004) (Sherman Act section 2 "seeks merely to prevent unlawful monopolization"; it does not give judges power "to insist that a monopolist alter its way of doing business whenever some other approach might yield greater competition").

V. Conclusion

There is a good case to be made that the surest way to incentivize innovations in the economy is through competitive rivalry, along with competition law enforcement to maintain it. Whether transformative or incremental, whether through new technology or simply through recognition of a new way to produce a product or service, innovation is important for social advancement and economic growth.

Digital platforms are an important aspect of innovative activity today both in developed and developing countries. This paper's survey of their use in four different areas shows the promise these platforms hold for local entrepreneurs and for consumers, but also shows the dependency of developing countries on the major platforms from developed countries, particularly from the United States.

In developing countries, competition law enforcement involving digital platforms may be less pressing at the moment. Enforcement against the major platforms is now the job of agencies in developed countries who will be responsible for crafting remedies in the cases being litigated, remedies that could have spillover effects in the developing world. The hope is that that these agencies will pay attention to this aspect of their enforcement.

For now, competition policy in developing countries may be more important than competition law enforcement. The goal should be competition policy that stresses the importance of rivalry and innovation, and articulates the benefits that competition can bring to consumers and the opportunities competitive markets can provide for entrepreneurs and workers. Infrastructure is important, but infrastructure is not just physical. Infrastructure also involves markets. Competition policy makes those markets work better.

PART IV
Intersection with Social Policies: Race, Inequality, and Fairness

Reasonable Expectations

OWEN FISS[*]

Yale University

Abstract

This essay seeks to assess the social consequences of the unique approach to antitrust pioneered by Eleanor Fox and to determine what contribution her approach to antitrust might make to the achievement of equality in racially stratified societies such as the United States and South Africa.

---

[*] Sterling Professor Emeritus of Law, Yale University.

We have been friends forever. I first met Eleanor Fox in the summer of 1964. She was practicing law with Simpson Thacher and I worked for a month in her firm as a summer intern, just before beginning a clerkship on the Second Circuit.

Now we are both law teachers, though our areas of specialization are markedly different. Eleanor is an expert on antitrust, and properly honored for all her achievements in that field. I claim civil rights as my field of expertise. Throughout my career, I have focused on the plight of Blacks in America and dedicated my career to studying the ways the law can be used to end their subordination and oppression. At the moment, I teach a seminar at the Yale Law School called "A Community of Equals."

Eleanor is an extremely curious person and her academic interests know no bounds. Over the years, we have talked about each other's work and in all those conversations, her commitment–not just intellectual, but also moral–to the achievement of racial equality has been manifest. Indeed, it is one of the foundations of our friendship. Our relationship began in the early 1960s and naturally, given the protests and demonstrations that marked that era, our initial conversations focused on the condition of civil rights in the United States. Yet over the years, these conversations took on a more global dimension, as Eleanor became increasingly interested in Africa, particularly South Africa.

Starting in the late 1940s, and continuing for many years afterward, South Africa was governed by a system of racial control – apartheid–that the white settlers had imposed on the African majority. This system was predicated on denying Blacks the right to vote or otherwise participate in the governance of the country. Apartheid also entailed herding Blacks into distinct residential zones known as "homelands," and tightly controlling their movement throughout the country. On top of that, rules and regulations were enacted that segregated Blacks from whites in public arenas, and precluded Blacks from competing on equal footing with whites for jobs and admission to the best schools and universities in the country. Taken as a whole, apartheid fostered and perpetuated a racial hierarchy in which the white settlers occupied positions of power and privilege and Blacks were relegated to the lower ranks.

In time, resistance to apartheid grew, and in the early 1990s, in the face of increasing violence and a global movement that condemned and isolated the country, apartheid was formally abolished. Blacks were allowed to vote, and the rules that had the effect of segregating and subordinating them were repealed–no small matter. Nevertheless, the social and economic stratification set in place by apartheid was left intact, and, for the most part, continues to this very day. Over the last 25 years, a small number of Black South Africans have prospered economically and politically, and they, along with most white South Africans, might rightly be seen as having become part of the country's ruling elite. The vast majority of Black South Africans, however, still live impoverished lives, most often in the very homelands that were created under apartheid. The question now facing the country is how the legacy of apartheid might be eradicated, and true equality achieved.

In addressing this question, Eleanor has naturally drawn on her expertise in antitrust and her own special view of that body of legal regulation. Wisely, she rejects the prevailing view of antitrust in the United States, which gives free rein to dominant firms and allows them to engage in predatory pricing and other practices that might well prevent would-be challengers from entering their markets and effectively competing with them. For Eleanor, antitrust is an instrument for promoting openness, or, as she put it, "protecting the access and opportunity for young challengers."[1]

Eleanor has defended this view of antitrust on its own terms, based on a proper reading of the governing statutes and their legislative history as well as on an assessment of the economic needs of society as a whole. Her emphasis on openness and the enhancement of access for "young challengers" is premised on a desire "to create or preserve an economy of dynamic, competitive, and innovative firms."[2] In addition, Eleanor has presented this version of antitrust as an instrument for the achievement of equality, even racial equality, in both South Africa and the United States. She set forth this view in an important article of hers in the October 2017 issue of the Antitrust Chronicle, entitled "Antitrust: Tracing Inequality–From the United States to South Africa."[3]

Eleanor begins this article in a disarming fashion. "Antitrust," she writes, "cannot produce equality." On this point I wholeheartedly agree, for it is difficult to know what legal strategy might "produce" equality, particularly racial equality, either in the United States or South Africa. Eleanor does not, however, stop with this disclaimer, but goes on to suggest that antitrust, once it is seen as a means of enhancing access for would-be entrepreneurs, can make a significant, important, or meaningful contribution to the achievement of racial equality. On this point, I am more doubtful.

I embrace her conception of antitrust and even more emphatically embrace the ends she hopes to achieve. I also believe that Eleanor's inclusive model of antitrust is likely to increase the number of Blacks, either in the United States or South Africa, who might enter the entrepreneurial class and, for that reason, contribute to the achievement of racial equality. Yet, I fear that given the legacy of racism in both countries, the number of Blacks who are likely to benefit from opening competitive markets in that way would be small–indeed, trivial–and that the principal threat to the achievement of racial equality–a system of racial stratification that assigns Blacks to the lowest ranks–will persist. Openness is not enough. As the American experience teaches, more robust remedies are required.

---

1   Eleanor M. Fox, *Competition Policy at the Intersection of Equity and Efficiency: The Developed and Developing Worlds*, 63 ANTITRUST BULL. 3, 5 (2018).

2   *Id. See also* ELEANOR M. FOX & MOR BAKHOUM, MAKING MARKETS WORK FOR AFRICA 197–98 (2019).

3   Published in COMPETITION POLICY INT'L, 1 (Oct. 14, 2017), www.competitionpolicyinternational.com/antitrust-tracing-inequality-from-the-united-states-to-south-africa/.

Much like in South Africa, the system of disadvantage in the United States imposed on Blacks has deep historical roots. It began in the seventeenth century, as Africans, either captured or already enslaved, were transported to the New World and a racially defined slave system was established in the American colonies. In the middle of the nineteenth century, following a bloody civil war, slavery was abolished and constitutional amendments were then adopted to prohibit slavery and to afford a measure of equality to the newly freed slaves. The nation also confronted the vestiges of the slave system and for that purpose launched a broad program of reconstruction, largely consisting of congressional enactments. But this path forward was abandoned in 1875, only to be superseded by yet another system of racial control–Jim Crow. Under Jim Crow, Blacks were segregated or otherwise disadvantaged in all spheres of human interaction. They were provided with inadequate public facilities, including schools, denied the right to vote, excluded from the workforce, or relegated to the most menial and low-paying jobs, systematically denied any protection by the criminal justice system, and, in fact, treated unfairly within it.

In 1954, the tide began to turn. The Supreme Court then handed down its decision in *Brown v. Board of Education*, declaring segregation inherently unequal and in so doing set in motion the Second Reconstruction, a broad reform movement in the United States aimed at the eradication of the racial caste system. This movement included mass demonstrations, which not only endowed the Supreme Court's decision with a special legitimacy, but also spurred executive and legislative action that reinforced and supplemented the Court's decision. One of the most important of these measures was Title VII of the Civil Rights Act of 1964. It guaranteed, in terms similar to Eleanor's understanding of antitrust law, equality of economic opportunity, though the focus was on employment, not entrepreneurship.

In the political struggles leading to the enactment of the Civil Rights Act, Title VII was defended on the ground that it only sought to prohibit the use of an irrelevant criterion–race–as the basis of allocating scarce employment opportunities. From this perspective, Title VII appeared, much like Eleanor's antitrust strategy, as an instrument for perfecting the market, though adjustments, often deemed minor, had to be made to stop businesses, eager to enlarge their profits, from adopting practices that would cater to the discriminatory tastes of their customers. By the end of the decade, however, the judiciary came to understand that the goal of the law should be viewed not in transactional, but structural terms–that it should be viewed not as a means of ensuring the integrity of the market, but as a device to eradicate the social stratification produced by America's racial caste system.

From the transactional perspective, the wrong to be eradicated by Title VII was individualized and presented as a species of unfair treatment. Individuals were being judged, according to this view, on the basis of race, a criterion that was unrelated to productivity and over which they had no control. In time, however, attention shifted from the quality or fairness of the allocative process itself to the history of racism in the United States–first slavery, then Jim Crow–and the consequences of that history upon the status of Blacks as a group. Although denying jobs to Blacks or limiting their employment opportunities on the basis of race may indeed be unfair, this was, in truth, only one device among many that perpetuated the subordination of Blacks and sustained the racial caste system. Allocating jobs on the basis of seemingly relevant criteria–performance on a standardized test, for example–might have the same effect.

The pernicious impact of using such seemingly innocent criteria as educational achievement to allocate jobs derived in part from the comprehensive and multi-generational nature of the system of disadvantage to which Blacks had been subjected. In slave times, it was a crime punishable by state law to teach Blacks to read or to write. Under Jim Crow, Blacks were educated, but only in segregated schools, and this system of student assignment impaired their educational opportunities. Even today these inequalities persist, for students are assigned to schools on the basis of neighborhood school policies, even though residential patterns are racially segregated. As a result of these inequalities, the allocation of jobs on the basis of educational achievement would inevitably have the effect of perpetuating the subordination of Blacks.

Admittedly, the Second Reconstruction was a multifaceted reform program that sought to curb inequalities in education as well as employment. But the vestiges of slavery and Jim Crow endure and are all-pervasive, and, on top of that, interact with and amplify each other. Accordingly, eliminating the inequalities Blacks have suffered in the employment sphere requires accounting for educational inequalities, and eliminating educational inequalities must account for the inequalities Blacks have suffered in employment. Of course, education and employment are not the only two spheres of human interaction responsible for the subordination of Blacks; consideration must also be given to the disparate impact on Blacks of seemingly innocent housing policies, police practices, and even voting requirements, for they, too, are responsible for the maintenance of our caste structure.

A fuller appreciation of the systematic character of the wrong done to Blacks was soon reflected in the law. In 1971, the Supreme Court construed Title VII to put pressure on employers to use hiring criteria that minimized the risk that Blacks, as a group, would be disproportionally disadvantaged by them.[4] For example, if a standardized test–a seemingly innocuous gatekeeper–were shown to have a disproportionately adverse impact on Blacks, the firm would have to prove in a court of law that it was job-related. Even if that burden were met, the aggrieved job applicants would have a chance to show in that very same court that there are ways to reduce the adverse impact without jeopardizing business needs.

---

4   Griggs v. Duke Power Co., 401 U.S. 424 (1971). See Owen Fiss, *The Accumulation of Disadvantages*, 106 CALIF. L. REV. 1945, 1946–50 (2018).

In 1976, soon after the most dynamic phase of the Second Reconstruction ended, a newly constituted and more conservative Supreme Court downgraded disparate impact liability from a constitutional to a statutory rule, though employers remained subject to it. In 1991, Congress responded to what it regarded as an errant Supreme Court decision interpreting the statutory rule and enacted a statute codifying–and thus reaffirming–disparate impact doctrine as originally conceived. In 2009, the Supreme Court applied that doctrine in the context of public employment (a municipal fire department) despite protest from Justice Antonin Scalia, who sought to place a constitutional cloud over it. In 2015, the Court, rather than take the route Scalia urged, went on to extend disparate impact doctrine to housing policies, including those that might disadvantage Blacks by banning multifamily housing in the suburbs. At the same time, lower federal courts and executive regulations also extended disparate impact liability to the application of voting requirements and to police practices.

In the late 1960s and early 1970s, roughly at the same time that disparate impact liability emerged, the federal government instituted another policy that had structural ambitions–affirmative action. The term has its roots in a longstanding executive order that required government contractors to "take affirmative action to ensure that applicants are employed and that employees are treated during employment without regard to their race, creed, color, or national origin."[5] Initially, the term "affirmative action" was thought to govern only recruitment policies; government contractors had to publicly assure the community, say through advertisements, that Blacks would be welcome to apply for jobs and that they would be judged on equal terms. In time, however, affirmative action was construed to require government contractors and then all employers to give Black applicants an indeterminate (but not overwhelming) plus in the competitive process.[6]

As the Supreme Court adopted a more conservative stance, limits were placed on preferential treatment in the employment context. Affirmative action was not required by Title VII, and was then deemed permissible only if the firm or employer had engaged in racial discrimination. The Supreme Court also balked when universities and professional schools used preferential treatment or affirmative action to increase the enrollment of Blacks. In the late 1970s, the Supreme Court accepted preferential treatment for Blacks in higher education on the theory that all students benefited educationally from having a diverse student body.[7] In truth, however, in all settings, education as well as employment, the aim of affirmative action is to eradicate the social stratification produced by the caste system and to disrupt the self-sustaining cycle of disadvantage it entails.[8]

---

5   Exec. Order No. 10,925, 26 Fed. Reg. 1977 (Mar. 8, 1961).

6   *See, e.g.*, Robert P. Schuwerk, Comment, *The Philadelphia Plan: A Study in the Dynamics of Executive Power*, 39 U. CHI. L. REV. 723 (1972).

7   *See* Regents of the Univ. of Cal. v. Bakke, 438 U.S. 265 (1978); Grutter v. Bollinger, 539 U.S. 306 (2003).

8   *See generally* Owen Fiss, *Affirmative Action as a Strategy of Justice*, 17 PHIL. & PUB. POL'Y 37 (1997).

In the context of education, affirmative action gives Blacks a leg-up in the competitive process governing admissions to elite universities, which would, in turn, enhance their employment opportunities and upgrade their status more generally. In this way, a new Black middle class has been created in the United States, although the challenge of achieving racial equality persists for the great numbers of the Black community who have been left behind.

It is of course conceivable that a fair employment law that did no more than ban the use of race as a hiring criterion might make *some* contribution toward the goal of ending the subordination of Blacks in the employment sphere. Those few Blacks who transcended the system of disadvantage that had been imposed on their forebears by slavery and Jim Crow might get a job, and that job might be one that is high paying and prestigious. But it was quite properly assumed that the corrective processes set in motion by such a limited understanding of Title VII would take far longer to effect this change than justice would allow. I fear a similar point may be made about the measure of racial justice that might be achieved by the equality of entrepreneurial opportunity–fair access – provided to "young challengers" under Eleanor's version of antitrust. Although there might be an upward trickle, and a few more Blacks might become members of the elite, eradicating in the here-and-now the racial stratification produced by apartheid or the American caste system would require more direct and more robust remedies.

In contemporary societies, inequalities take many different forms, even if the concern be with caste or social stratification. Justice requires that we attend not just to a racial hierarchy, but also to those hierarchies that may be defined in terms of gender or income and wealth. The structural remedies that emerged through the enforcement of Title VII–disparate impact liability and affirmative action–are race specific. Starting in the late 1970s, these remedies were extended to deal with gender hierarchy. However, these remedies do not make and should not be expected to make any appreciable contribution to the eradication of hierarchies in society based on income or wealth. In a similar vein, we should not expect that any remedies designed to eliminate economic inequalities will contribute significantly to the eradication of the racial hierarchy that mars the social fabric of the United States and South Africa.

Remedies to alleviate the plight of the poor may take many different forms. In fact, antitrust may be seen as such a remedy when it is used to vitiate price-fixing cartels among firms that supply essentials such as food.[9] Such an enforcement measure will have the effect of lowering the price of essentials. That reduction in price would be a benefit to all consumers, rich or poor, but it would be of special importance to the poor because a larger portion of their income or wealth is allocated to purchasing essentials. For the most part, however, price-fixing cartels that control essentials are likely to be exceptional and thus

---

9   Fox & Bakhoum, *supra* note 2, at 97–99 (discussing the bread cartel in South Africa).

the role of antitrust in ameliorating poverty is limited. In truth, the prosecution of a full-scale and effective war on poverty, though it may entail a limited role for antitrust, will require a broader and more direct panoply of remedies. These may include exempting meager salaries from income taxes and granting income supplements, as well as housing and food subsidies, providing public services, such as health and education, and a leveling-out of the democratic playing field through the public financing of elections. None of these remedies should be seen as a substitute–as opposed to a supplement–to the structural remedies designed to end caste or the subordination of Blacks as a group.

Remedial strategies designed to alleviate poverty will, of course, give some benefit to individual Blacks. Although this improvement in their wellbeing might be grounded on a concern for economic justice, it can also be seen as responsive to a concern for racial justice, for the impoverishment of Blacks, in both the United States and South Africa, might well be the result of racial policies that have long disadvantaged them. In South Africa, the racial implications of antipoverty measures–though no substitute for policies explicitly designed to increase the representation of Blacks in the higher social ranks–may indeed take on a very special significance. There, not only are the vast majority of the Blacks poor, but also, unlike in the United States, the vast majority of the poor–in fact, nine out of ten–are Black. Still, it is important not to confuse policies that seek to eradicate poverty with those that seek to eradicate racial hierarchy. We need both.

In the closing passage of her essay, Eleanor laments the absence in South Africa of the "radical economic transformation" that had been hoped for when, a quarter of a century earlier, apartheid was abandoned. Looking to the future, she points to the amendments to the country's antitrust laws that then-president Jacob Zuma and his Minister of Economic Development, Ebrahim Patel, had proposed in March 2017 to eliminate structural impediments to entry by "historically disadvantaged South Africans" and to ensure "that more enjoy substantive economic citizenship."

Although these amendments are not described with any specificity, Eleanor, eager to embrace them, assures the reader that there is "no trade off" between equity and efficiency and that "efficiency and equity can work together."[10] Yet the American experience in fashioning structural remedies to achieve racial justice–that is, ending caste or the subordination of Blacks as a group–teaches me to be wary of this proclamation. We must also be realistic about the sacrifice entailed in structural remedies, whether their purpose be the achievement of racial or economic justice.

Efficiency can be, as Eleanor emphasizes in other writing, an elusive concept. One very familiar form of efficiency–she calls it "productive efficiency"[11]

---

10   Id.

11   Eleanor M. Fox, *The Efficiency Paradox*, in How the Chicago School Overshot the Mark: The Effect of Conservative Economic Analysis on U.S. Antitrust 77, 78 (R. Pitofsky ed., 2008).

– requires firms to employ the most productive workers on the theory that they would maximize the production of goods and services at the lowest cost. While I affirm the need for structural remedies to achieve equality, as I do in the context of achieving racial justice, I also acknowledge that such remedies might well entail a sacrifice of productive efficiency.

Some defenders of disparate impact liability have emphasized that it does not compromise the right of employers to hire people who can perform the job. This is true, but account must be taken of (a) the cost of developing tests that could be proven in a court of law as job-related and (b) the administrative cost of using employment criteria that might reduce the disparate impact on Blacks. These costs might be limited but are nonetheless real and interfere with productive efficiency.

Similarly, in the evolution of affirmative action, advocates of preferences for the historically disadvantaged have insisted that all those who might receive the preference are qualified to perform the job or that the preferences would be given within a universe of applicants that are roughly equal in their ability. What such a defense of affirmative action ignores, however, is that such a remedy denies the employers the right to hire the best workers, where "best" is defined from a productive perspective, at least as understood by the firm. Once again, although the cost imposed by a system of racial preferences is limited (since any individual who receives such a preference is qualified to perform the job), such costs should not be ignored or wished away.

Ignoring these productive inefficiencies, especially in the effort to achieve racial justice, is a perilous strategy of argumentation. Those who bear the cost of structural remedies–not only the employers, but also those who do not get the job–are acutely aware of them. These individuals will complain and eventually the truth will emerge. Admittedly, at that point, one can defend such sacrifices in terms of justice, but the failure to acknowledge these sacrifices in the first place compounds the nature of the grievance: the aggrieved can complain that the sacrifices entailed in such remedies have been misrepresented or underestimated. Moreover, advocates of structural remedies may then rightly be faulted, not just for compounding the grievance against these remedies in this way, but also for squandering earlier and perhaps more propitious opportunities to defend these sacrifices as required by justice.

Structural remedies do not necessarily introduce inefficiencies. There is, however, a good chance that they will, and as a result lead to higher prices for goods and services. We must acknowledge that contingency and defend such sacrifices as the price that must be paid to achieve justice–to eradicate the vestiges of caste or of apartheid. Eleanor fully understands the difference between a just society and a prosperous one: I trust, once pressed, that she would acknowledge that justice cannot await prosperity and, furthermore, that we must sometimes moderate our demand for prosperity in order to achieve justice.

Competition Policy and Access to Healthcare

PRADEEP S. MEHTA AND UJJWAL KUMAR[*]
CUTS International

Abstract

This focuses on the role of competition policy and law in enhancing access to healthcare, understanding that access to healthcare is largely dependent on its "availability" and "affordability." In countries where the free or subsidized public health systems are not so robust, out-of-pocket expenditure has the potential to further push people below poverty line. The paper analyses the ex ante competition policy and then ex post competition law enforcement as tools to enhance access to healthcare.

---

[*] The authors work for CUTS International, a global policy think tank situated in India, US, Switzerland, Ghana, Kenya, Zambia, and Vietnam. Pradeep S Mehta is founder and Secretary General of CUTS, established in 1983. Mehta, a prolific writer, gifted speaker, and skilled trainer and organizer, has been a member of several national and international committees and other policymaking bodies. Mehta has been named as one of the 30 most famous columnists in India by a leading newspaper in India and has published/ edited several books and papers on trade, investment, competition, and development. Ujjwal Kumar is policy analyst at CUTS and has been working on issues related competition, regulation, and intellectual property rights across sectors for more than 20 years.

I. Background

The coronavirus (COVID-19) pandemic has put healthcare as the top policy priority the world over. Public health interests prevailed over national economic interests when widescale lockdowns were announced that had severe adverse effects on economic activities, including loss of livelihood for millions. The global economic slowdown due to the pandemic is not only shrinking gross domestic products (GDPs) of economies of the world, but is also severely hitting international trade. It is believed that economies may further spiral down before showing signs of recovery. All these have resulted (or resulting) in pushing millions below the poverty line, dwarfing several gains from liberalization and globalization in the last three decades.

Like many other policy tools, competition policy also responded on the extraordinary situation created by the pandemic lockdown. Several articles and reports dealt with how competition policy reacted or how it should react.[1] This also include a discussion paper by Andrew Tyrie, chair of the UK Competition and Markets Authority (CMA).[2]

In general, competition policy (suggested) responses are two-pronged–one for smooth supply of essential items like healthcare and food items, and the other with respect to post-lockdown economic recovery. For the first, the most prominent approach has been to ensure that competition enforcement does not pose a hurdle for business cooperation necessary for the supply of essential items. However, for the second (i.e. to address economic recovery) the matter is complex, owing to the continued economic uncertainties due to emergency pandemic measures. Nonetheless the approach suggested in this regard, inter alia includes measures to curtail likely increase in market concentrations and to check policy-induced market distortions.

In sum, the post-pandemic policy interventions would need to address increased poverty while simultaneously ensuring economic recovery. Here a decade-old competition policy prescription by Eleanor Fox could be the guiding *mantra*. According to her, "If policy is to be friendly to economic development, it must look dire poverty in the eye: it must harness market forces to keep prices competitive; it must build a ladder of mobility from the lowest rung up, to enable mobility centered entrepreneurship and stimulate innovation."[3]

---

[1] For instance, *see*, Frédéric Jenny, *Economic resilience, globalisation and market governance: Facing the COVID-19 test* (OECD, Apr. 2020); Udai S. Mehta & Sakhi Shah, *Competition Enforcement for Business Collaborations during COVID-19–A Global Perspective* (CUTS International Discussion Paper, July 2020), https://cuts-ccier.org/pdf/competition-enforcement-for-business-collaborations-during-covid-19.pdf.

[2] Andrew Tyrie, *How Should Competition Policy React to Coronavirus?* (CMA Discussion Paper, 2020), www.ippr.org/files/2020-07/how-should-competition-policy-react-to-coronavirus-july20.pdf.

[3] Pradeep S. Mehta & Taimoon Stewart, Should Competition Policy & Law be Blind to Equity? The Great Debate 96–97 (2013).

According to Fox, competition is in fact a market system with handful of sister systems and efforts, the success of each being a necessary condition for enabling the disempowered. This includes education, healthcare, infrastructure, job opportunities, and availability of capital for good ideas, all in a context of good governance, which must include the absence of pervasive corruption. The house of opportunity, participation, and ultimately growth is built one small brick at a time. The entire system, if it pulls together, can improve the lot of the half of the world that is living in poverty. All of the efforts together can help to close the gap.[4]

In this backdrop, this paper focuses on the role of competition policy and law in enhancing access to healthcare, understanding that access to healthcare is largely dependent on its availability and affordability. In countries where free or subsidized public health systems are not so robust, out-of-pocket expenditure has the potential to further push people below poverty line. This paper analyses the *ex ante* competition policy and *ex post* competition law enforcement as tools to enhance access to healthcare. The final section includes a conclusion and a few suggestions for policymakers and competition agencies around the world. In looking at the healthcare, the scope of this paper is largely confined to healthcare services and pharmaceuticals.

II. Competition Policy Approach

To keep markets competitive, competition law enforcement alone may not be sufficient. The first thing that is needed is an enabling policy environment that promotes competition in the market, including removing entry barriers, removing market distortions, and inducing ease of doing and running businesses.

1. Patent and competition policy

Competition in the pharmaceuticals market depends more on intellectual property (mainly patent) policy than on the enforcement of competition law. Access to medicines significantly increases when generic competition is present, which in turn is highly dependent on the kind of domestic patent law applicable.

For instance, change in patents law of India in 1970 are attributed to the development of domestic pharmaceutical industry and consequent high level of generic competition. It recognized process patents only and not product patents. This allowed Indian manufacturers to reverse-engineer patented pharmaceuticals and use a different process to manufacture the same at a much lower cost. This has significantly helped access to drugs not only for the poor population in India, where out-of-pocket healthcare expenditure is more prevalent, but also poor

---

4   OECD, *Global Forum on Competition–Competition and Poverty Reduction: Contribution from Ms. Eleanor Fox* (DAF/COMP/GF(2013)4, Feb. 14, 2013), at 2–3.

populations in many parts of the world. In addition, export of generic drugs from India significantly contributes to its economy. In fact, India has the largest generic pharmaceutical industry in the world.

In 2005, when the clause on product patents under the Agreement on Trade-Related Aspects of Intellectual Property Rights (TRIPs) of the World Trade Organizationcame into force, India fully incorporated the same along with its procompetition provisions (TRIPs flexibilities) in its patents law i.e. the Patents Act, 1970. This approach helped India maintain its level of generic competition to significant extent. Bangladesh has also developed a domestic manufacturing base with good level of generic competition using the mandated transition period for least developing countries (LDCs) under the TRIPs agreement.

One of the identified issues having adverse effect on competition in pharmaceutical market is "evergreening" of patents.[5] To overcome this menace, the Indian patents law has stricter patentability criteria to ensure the quality of patents.[6] The constitutionality of this unique provision has already been established by the Supreme Court of India in the famous *Gleevec* case, where the Court upheld the rejection of patents and observed that the substance sought to be patented was a modification of a known drug and there was no evidence of any enhanced therapeutic efficacy.[7] There is no ambiguity in the Indian law, which was postulated by one of these two authors.[8]

There are many flexibilities in the TRIPs agreement, such as compulsory license for domestic production as well as exports, Bolar exception, exhaustion of IPRs, data protection under article 39.3, etc., which if incorporated in domestic IP laws will have procompetition effects on the market. International instruments like the Doha Declaration on the TRIPs Agreement and Public Health, 2001 and the Global Strategy and Plan of Action on Public Health, Innovation and Intellectual Property, 2008 (GSPA-PHI) mandates countries to use such flexibilities to enhance access to medicines. However, there are bilateral, regional, or plurilateral trade agreements, particularly involving the USA, that tend to mitigate available TRIPs flexibilities. Developing countries and LDCs need to be careful in signing such TRIPs+ deals. Competition agencies can, accordingly, advocate this to their respective governments.

---

5   Evergreening of patents is a strategy to extend the life of patents by applying for secondary patents over related or derivative technologies, often for trivial changes to the invention.

6   According to section 3(d) of the Patents Act, 1970, "the mere discovery of a new form of a known substance which does not result in the enhancement of the known efficacy of that substance or the mere discovery of any new property or new use for a known substance or of the mere use of a known process, machine or apparatus unless such known process results in a new product or employs at least one new reactant" are not inventions, and hence, are not patentable.

7   Novartis AG v. Union of India (Civil Appeal Nos. 2706-2716, 2013); https://docs.google.com/file/d/0Bxi2T zVXul5ZQ1BMeFNJbnV1Mkk/edit.

8   www.financialexpress.com/archive/there-is-no-ambiguity-in-indian-legislation/211334/.

2. Regulation and competition policy

The pharmaceutical sector is one of the most regulated sectors in most jurisdictions. Two of them *viz.*, market approval regulation and price regulation, need to be optimal–not more restrictive than needed. The regulation of biosimilar drugs (generic version of biological drugs) have been flagged as overregulation in most jurisdictions, which creates barriers on generic competition.[9] Similarly, price regulation of drugs is also included in the list where generic competition is available in large volume, which kills market contestability. Price regulation needs to be used as last resort in case of market failure.

Another hurdle is with respect to the prescription practices of doctors, who generally prescribe in the form of brand names. Their main argument for such practice is "trust" of quality, however, a nexus between prescribers and pharma companies also cannot be ruled out.[10] Therefore, in order to engender confidence of doctors in available generic substitutes, it would be wise to invest in regulation and make it trustworthy. Once doctors and consumers perceive available generics to be of same quality, it will have procompetition outcomes. Having standard treatment guides would also contribute to transparency by removing information asymmetries, and hence would be procompetitive.

Similarly, policymakers need to remove entry barriers for the establishment of new hospitals and medical colleges. These have high initial establishment costs and a long gestation period to break even, which discourages investors. If government policies can facilitate land requirements, import of medical equipment and devices, penetration of health insurance, etc., coupled with optimal regulation of medical education, it will significantly contribute to competition in healthcare market as well as accessibility.

III. Competition Enforcement

There are several anticompetitive practices in the healthcare and pharmaceutical sector that have been dealt with by competition agencies around the world. Following are some of such examples.

1. Pay-for-delay

Pay-for-delay (also called as reverse payment settlements) is a practice in the pharmaceutical industry whereby the originator firms compensate their generic counterparts for delaying the introduction of their generic versions in market.

---

9 *See, e.g.*, Amit Sengupta, Biological Drugs: Challenges to Access (2018).

10 *See, e.g.*, CUTS, Unholy Alliances in Healthcare–Collusive Behaviour in Healthcare and Impact on Consumers: Evidences from Assam & Chhattisgarh (2011), https://cuts-ccier.org/pdf/Research_Report-Unholy_Alliances_in_Healthcare_Services-COHED.pdf.

Generally, such deals are in form of patent dispute settlements in which generic manufacturers acknowledge the patent of the originator company and agree to refrain from marketing their generic versions. In return, generic firms are compensated by the originator firms. Such arrangements can be anticompetitive since they prevent generic competition that could bring the prices down significantly.

In 2013, in the *Lundbeck* case, the European Commission found the presence of a pay-for-delay arrangement and imposed fines on all the parties involved—€93.8 million on Lundbeck and a total of €52.2 million on the generics companies.[11] In 2016, the General Court upheld this decision.[12] In 2014, the Commission decided another pay-for-delay case and fined Servier and five other generic drug manufacturers with €427.7 million.[13] The US Supreme Court, in *FTC v. Actavis* (2013), has also held that a pay-for-delay agreement can face an antitrust challenge under rule of reason.[14]

2. Frivolous litigation

The pharmaceuticals sector is heavily regulated mainly to ensure "unavoidably unsafe products," which offer desired benefits but are not without risk. However, these regulations provide several windows giving rise to litigation, which sometimes could be frivolous with the intention to impose hurdles on generic competition.

In the case *Biocon v. Roche* (2016) before the Competition Commission of India (CCI), it was alleged that the Roche Group started indulging in frivolous litigation with the intention of preventing the entry of the generic version (biosimilar) of the biologic drug Trastuzumab. The CCI, finding a prima facie case of abuse of dominance, ordered an in-depth inquiry.[15]

In 2005, the European Commission had fined AstraZeneca €60 million for abusing its dominance, where it made misleading representations before patent offices and national courts of several European countries and had also taken steps to delay the marketing of generic versions, including by preventing parallel imports by exploiting loopholes in the legal system.[16] The Commission's decision was

---

11 Case AT.39226 Lundbeck (Commission decision C(2013) 3803), https://ec.europa.eu/competition/elojade/isef/case_details.cfm?proc_code=1_39226. *See also* Johan Van Acker & Dina Ansari, *The EU Commission imposes fines totaling up to €145 million on a Danish pharmaceutical group over pay-for-delay agreements (*Lundbeck*)*, e-Competitions June 2013, Art. N° 53996 (June 19, 2013).

12 European Commission, Press Release, Antitrust: Commission welcomes General Court judgments upholding its Lundbeck decision in first pharma pay-for-delay case (MEMO/16/2994, Sept. 8, 2016), https://ec.europa.eu/commission/presscorner/detail/en/MEMO_16_2994.

13 European Commission, Press Release, Antitrust: Commission fines Servier and five generic companies for curbing entry of cheaper versions of cardiovascular medicine (IP.14.799, July 9, 2014), http://europa.eu/rapid/press-release_IP-14-799_en.htm.

14 FTC v. Actavis, Inc., 570 U.S. 136 (2013). *See also* Tim Frazer et al., *The US Supreme Court holds that "reverse payment" patent settlements between brand-name drug manufacturers and would-be generic competitors should be reviewed under the antitrust rule of reason (*Actavis*)*, e-Competitions June 2013, Art. N° 52994 (June 17, 2013).

15 Biocon v. Roche (Case No. 68, 2016), www.cci.gov.in/sites/default/files/68%20of%202016_0.pdf.

16 Case AT.37507 Generics/Astra Zeneca https://ec.europa.eu/competition/elojade/isef/case_details.cfm?proc_code=1_37507.

later upheld by the General Court in 2010 and an appeal to the European Court of Justice was rejected in 2012.[17]

3. Cartels

Cartels are arrangements between competing firms designed to limit or eliminate competition between them, with the objective of maximizing their profits and without resulting in any objective countervailing benefits. In practice, this is generally done by fixing prices, limiting output, sharing markets, allocating customers or territories, bid-rigging or a combination of these. Cartels are harmful to consumers and society as a whole. Pharmaceuticals and healthcare sectors are also marred by such anticompetitive agreements, facing competition enforcement.

The Fiscalía Nacional Económica (FNE), Chile, filed a complaint in December 2008 against three retail pharmacies accusing them of concerted action resulting in increases in the prices of 206 drugs between December 2007 and March 2008. In April 2009, a settlement agreement was reached between FNE and Farmacias Ahumada, which agreed to pay a fine of USD 1 million. In January 2012, Tribunal for the Defense of Free Competition (TDLC) imposed a maximum applicable fine of approximately USD 20 million on each of the two remaining retail pharmacy chains. In September 2012, the Supreme Court upheld TDLC's decision, flagging that economic interest was placed before human dignity, life and individual health.[18]

In 2008, the Competition Commission of South Africa published a press release having prosecuted three pharmaceutical companies that were involved in bid-rigging and market allocation arrangements. One of the cartel members applied for leniency and cooperated with the Commission. In the same year, the Peruvian Competition Authority sanctioned certain suppliers of medical oxygen to Peru's public health system who were found to be in cartel. These suppliers had distributed the procurement bids geographically between 1999 and 2004.[19]

A primary study by CUTS International in 2011 had found the presence of collusive behavior and vertical relationships between doctors/hospitals and pharmacies/ diagnostic centers. An extremely high frequency of referrals combined with the prevalence of "cuts" for referring doctors was noted.[20]

---

17 Case T-321/05 AstraZeneca v. Eur. Comm'n, EU:T:2010:266; Case C-457/10 P AstraZeneca v. Eur. Comm'n, EU:C:2012:770.

18 UNCTAD, Intergovernmental Group of Experts on Competition Law and Policy: The impact of cartels on the poor (13th session, Geneva, July 8–12, 2013), https://unctad.org/meetings/en/SessionalDocuments/ciclpd24rev1_en.pdf.

19 *Id.*

20 *See, e.g.*, CUTS, *supra* note 10.

4. Vertical restraints

Vertical agreements (i.e. between undertakings operating at different levels of the production chain) are a common feature in the market as a substitute for vertical integration. Since vertical arrangements exert mixed effects on the competitive process, it has to be judged on the basis of the reasonableness of any restraint that they pose. Generally, vertical agreements include exclusive or selective distribution agreements, exclusive supply agreements and tying agreements. Such agreements may result in foreclosure of the market to competitors and elimination of interbrand competition.

The CCI has dealt with a number of cases where the pan-India and/or state-level chemist and druggists associations tried to control the appointment of stockists, sales of pharmaceutical products, and wholesale and retail margins. In most such cases the practices of mandating a "No Objection Certificate" (NOC) as a prerequisite for the appointment of stockists and also to refrain from fixing "trade margins" for retailers and wholesalers were involved.[21]

The CCI, in October 2018, published a policy note titled "Making Markets Work for Affordable Healthcare," wherein it made the following observation about trade associations:

> The cases before the Commission have shown that the entire supply chain of drugs is self-regulated by the trade associations who regulate entry by mandating a NOC prior to the appointment of stockists, control distribution by restricting/controlling the number of stockists and influence price by deciding the wholesale and retail margins of drugs. The Commission's past interventions have led to some positive outcomes and businesses and business associations have revised their policies and practices to bring them in alignment with the principles of competition.[22]

In 2011, the National Development and Reform Commission (NDRC), China found that two pharmaceutical companies (Shuntong and Huaxin) had signed exclusive distribution agreements with the only two domestic producers of active pharmaceutical ingredients, allowing them to control the supply of a key raw material for a commonly used compound in high blood pressure treatments. These agreements required the producers to obtain approval from both companies before selling the product to any other party, in order to eliminate competition. The NDRC fined these companies RMB 7 million (c. USD 1.1 million).[23]

---

21   *See, e.g.*, Rupin Chopra & Chanakya Sharma, CCI–Chemists and Druggists Associations Warned to Refrain from Indulging into Anti-Competitive Practices (2016), www.lexology.com/library/detail.aspx?g=eef58c14-38da-446f-ae71-cb592d51fd8b.

22   CCI, *Policy Note: Making Markets Work for Affordable Healthcare* 6 (Oct. 2018), www.cci.gov.in/sites/default/files/event%20document/POLICY_NOTE_0.pdf?download=1

23   James Quinney et al., NDRC imposes high fines on two pharmaceutical companies for antitrust infringements (2011), www.lexology.com/library/detail.aspx?g=dc6b7cf6-1923-48b5-8307-353a9d9024b9.

5. Excessive pricing

There are instances where unilateral conduct of companies has been found to result in excessive prices of drugs. The famous *Aspen* case in Italy is a good example. In 2016, the Italian Competition Authority (AGCM) fined the Aspen pharmaceutical group for abuse of dominance in form of excessive prices concerning some essential off-patent drugs. The price increase ranged between 300 to 1500%. The AGCM found both the lack of effective competition (Aspen was the only supplier in each of the relevant markets) and potential competition. Despite being off-patent, new generic producers lacked the incentive to enter in the market given the scarce volume of the market.[24]

6. Mergers and acquisitions (M&As)

There are instances where M&As can also pose competition concerns in one or more therapeutic segments. In such cases the general trend has been to put specific divestment conditionality for allowing such M&As.

Very recently (in 2020) the European Commission approved the acquisition of Pfizer's Consumer Health Business by GlaxoSmithKline (GSK). During the review it was found that the acquisition would reduce the competition in topical pain management products in countries like Austria, Germany, Ireland, Italy, and Netherlands. The products of GSK and Pfizer were broadly substitutable in the market for topical pain management. Therefore, the acquisition was allowed, subject to a condition for the global divestment of Pfizer's topical pain management business under the *ThermaCare* brand.[25]

In 2019, the US Federal Trade Commission (FTC) reviewed the merger of Bristol-Myers Squibb (BMS) and Celgene Corporation. The FTC observed that if this acquisition would take place, it would lessen competition in the relevant market and create a monopoly by eliminating any future competition between Celgene and BMS in development of drugs for treatment of psoriasis. Consequently, any new competitors in the market would face delays for drug development and obtaining marketing approval. The merger was allowed when Celgene consented to divested Otezla, a popular skin ailment drug, to Amgen, a California-based pharmaceutical company. This was the largest divestiture ever made in a merger enforcement matter, valued at USD 13.4 billion.[26]

---

24 OECD, Excessive Pricing in Pharmaceutical Markets–Note by Italy (DAF/COMP/WD(2018)106, Nov. 28, 2018). https://one.oecd.org/document/DAF/COMP/WD(2018)106/en/pdf.

25 European Commission, Press Release, Mergers: Commission approves GlaxoSmithKline's acquisition of Pfizer's Consumer Health Business, subject to conditions (IP/19/4030, July 10, 2019), https://ec.europa.eu/commission/presscorner/detail/sv/ip_19_4030.

26 Fed. Trade Comm'n, Press Release, FTC Requires Bristol-Myers Squibb Company and Celgene Corporation to Divest Psoriasis Drug Otezla as a Condition of Acquisition (Nov. 15, 2019), www.ftc.gov/news-events/press-releases/2019/11/ftc-requires-bristol-myers-squibb-company-celgene-corporation.

In 2015, the CCI approved the Sun Pharma and Ranbaxy merger only when the parties agreed to divest certain products to a third party.[27]

IV. Conclusion and Policy Suggestions

As far as access to healthcare is concerned, competition can play a significant role. In order to have a competitive market, both *ex ante* competition policy and *ex post* competition enforcement are important tools.

Looking at the patent policy through the lens of competition policy is very important for engendering generic competition in the pharmaceutical market, which significantly reduces the price of drugs and hence enhances accessibility. Therefore, incorporating TRIPs flexibilities into domestic laws is crucial. India can serve as an example in this regard. Competition agencies around the world can advocate the incorporation of TRIPs flexibilities and cautioning their governments against agreeing to TRIPs+ provisions in bilateral or regional agreements.

Similarly, removing regulatory and policy barriers for private sector entry into healthcare services assumes importance if governments are unable to provide free universal public healthcare. Optimal regulation, i.e. regulation that is not more restrictive that to achieve the desired objective, needs to be the mantra.

Furthermore, competition agencies need to prioritize enforcement in the healthcare space because it hits the poor the most. Market studies may also be conducted in the sector to understand modern nuances. Most importantly, agencies have to play a proactive role as far as advocacy is concerned.

The ensuing pandemic, where many countries, particularly developing countries and LDCs, have felt the need to strengthen their healthcare systems with a domestic base for pharmaceutical production, means that adhering to the competition policy approach would be very helpful.

---

27   CCI, Order in Combination Registration No. C-2014/05/170 of Dec. 5, 2014, www.cci.gov.in/sites/default/files/C-2014-05-170_0.pdf.

Antitrust and Healthcare Inequity

LISL J. DUNLOP[*]
Axinn, Veltrop & Harkrider

Abstract

Eleanor Fox's recent scholarship addressing the development of antitrust policy in South Africa–and its efforts to recalibrate markets to address years of racial bias and suppression of Black, colored and Indian businesses–has inspired a dialog around the role of antitrust in addressing racism. This paper takes the debate to the US healthcare system and discusses how inequities in access to quality healthcare in the US can be unwittingly reinforced by antitrust policy. In the healthcare context, current antitrust enforcement emphasizes the impact of provider mergers on prices paid by private insurers. But does this narrow focus on the direct impact on a segment of customers ignore the complex economics of the US healthcare system and miss important implications for vulnerable communities? Should the "consumer welfare" standard contemplate a broader range of factors, including the need for significant resources to address healthcare inequities?

---

[*] Lisl J. Dunlop is a partner at Axinn, Veltrop & Harkrider LLP in New York, where she represents clients in antitrust transactions, litigations and counseling, in particular in the healthcare industry. The author is grateful for helpful comments and suggestions from her colleagues Leslie Overton and Peter Herrick. All of the opinions expressed are those of the author alone and not of any partner or client of the firm.

"Does antitrust perpetuate structural racism?" After an intense year of racial turmoil amidst a global pandemic, this was the question addressed by Professor Fox and others at an antitrust bar event in January 2021.[1] The panel debated how the application of antitrust laws had reinforced or contributed to racial inequities, and how antitrust laws could potentially be reoriented to address these concerns. Professor Fox argued that the assumptions inherent in US antitrust law–that markets work well, and that competition is vibrant and keeps even dominant firms responsive to consumers–do not reflect reality and have created a hostile environment for small firms and new entrants, which are comprised in large measure by poorer people and people of color.[2]

The question of "antitrust racism" is one facet of the ongoing debate over the proper focus of the antitrust laws in the United States. The question has often been framed as whether we should continue to hew to a principled but narrow Chicago-school economic model, interpreting "consumer welfare" as limited to direct effects on customers and markets, or whether the antitrust laws should be interpreted more broadly to encompass the wider impact on the economy and society, including addressing social and racial inequities.[3] These questions are being discussed in the halls of academia, the chambers of Congress, and in numerous small and large conversations in the antitrust world.

This paper considers the impact of this debate on an area in which significant social and racial inequities persist today: the US healthcare system. Explanations abound for how the current lack of access to quality healthcare for socially and economically disadvantaged communities has arisen, and there are as many suggestions for ways to address it. But has antitrust enforcement exacerbated–or ameliorated–social and racial disparities in our healthcare system? Going forward, is there a role for antitrust in addressing these inequities?

I. Public Interest Considerations in Antitrust Enforcement

The security of current antitrust enforcement policy is in an analytical framework based on established economic principles. The underpinning of modern antitrust is a confidence in the ability of well-functioning markets to deliver benefits to all

---

[1] *Does Antitrust Perpetuate Structural Racism?*, NYSBA Antitrust Section Annual Meeting (Jan. 22, 2021): Professor Eleanor M. Fox, NYU School of Law; Commissioner Rebecca Slaughter, FTC; Sandeep Vaheesan, Open Markets Institute; Leslie Overton, Axinn, Veltrop & Harkrider LLP; Deona Kalala, Alston & Bird; and Jay Himes, Labaton Sucharow (moderator).

[2] *Id.*

[3] There is a wide range of views on this topic, including some who argue that the consumer welfare standard already is capable of taking social issues into account, and others who advocate for a new formulation. *See* AM. BAR ASS'N ANTITRUST LAW SECTION, REPORT ON THE TASK FORCE ON THE FUTURE OF COMPETITION LAW STANDARDS (2020), www.americanbar.org/content/dam/aba/administrative/antitrust_law/aba-antitrust-standards-task-force-report.pdf [hereinafter COMPETITION STANDARDS REPORT]; Sandeep Vaheesan, *How Antitrust Perpetuates Structural Racism*, THE APPEAL (Sept. 16, 2020), https://theappeal.org/how-antitrust-perpetuates-structural-racism/.

consumers. Such benefits are typically defined in terms of prices, quality, innovation, and occasionally access to product range or diversity. While some may criticize this formulation of the consumer welfare approach as too narrow (in particular its emphasis on price effects), it is relatively well understood and provides a measure of predictability in how the antitrust agencies will approach any transaction.

There has been significant criticism of the notion that antitrust is an appropriate mechanism for addressing social and racial inequities.[4] Critics argue that there are other, better avenues through which the government can pursue such policy goals, and that it is not the role of competition policy to pursue social aims over economic goals.[5] Among OECD countries, the practice of most antitrust regulators is to stay close to the core economic goals in competition law—allocative efficiency and consumer welfare.[6] Regulators generally avoid use of so-called "public interest" factors that risk the transparency and predictability of their merger control systems, and that would jeopardize consistency of cross-border merger reviews.[7]

The economic rationality of the current approach is attractive and comfortable. It appears to follow an objective application of principles that do not incorporate value judgments or consciously nest social and racial biases. But does adherence to such "neutral" economic principles that consider consumer welfare only in these terms unwittingly harm society, in particular vulnerable communities? Should our focus on direct economic impacts and harms to customers require that we ignore the broader effects of enforcement decisions, which may also have more indirect impacts on the economy? Is the consumer welfare standard being properly enforced if it does not account for inequality? In insisting on apparent neutrality, are we actually supporting an inequitable status quo?

Professor Fox has challenged the notion that bringing "non-market discourse" into antitrust analysis challenges the limits and predictability of antitrust rules. She notes:

> We do have to confront the question of the relevance of non-market factors. We can confront it more cleanly if we don't insist: "stick with consumer welfare, or lose the legitimacy of antitrust." ... To the

---

4 Elyse Dorsey et al., *Hipster Antitrust Meets Public Choice Economics: The Consumer Welfare Standard, Rule of Law, and Rent-Seeking*, COMPETITION POL'Y INT'L ANTITRUST CHRONICLE (Apr. 2018). Joshua D. Wright & Douglas H. Ginsburg, *The Goals of Antitrust: Welfare Trumps Choice*, 81 FORDHAM L. REV. 2405, 2405–09 (2013); Christine S. Wilson, Commissioner, Fed. Trade Comm'n, Address at the British Institute of International and Comparative Law, Remembering Regulatory Misadventures: Taking a Page from Edmund Burke to Inform Our Approach to Big Tech 13–18 (June 28, 2019), www.ftc.gov/system/files/documents/public_statements/1531816/wilson_remarks_biicl_6-28-19.pdf; A. Douglas Melamed, *Antitrust Law and Its Critics*, 83(1) ANTITRUST L.J. 14–17 (2020).

5 *See* Dorsey et al., *supra* note 4; COMPETITION STANDARDS REPORT at 18–19.

6 OECD, Working Party No. 3 on Co-operation and Enforcement, Executive Summary of the Roundtable on Public Interest Considerations in Merger Control (DAF/COMP/WP3/M(2016)1, June 14, 2016), https://one.oecd.org/document/DAF/COMP/WP3/M(2016)1/ANN5/FINAL/en/pdf.

7 *Id.*

extent that the competition laws of various nations incorporate non-market goals, the systems will have to work hard to make the laws administrable and predictable.[8]

This debate is taking practical form in South Africa, which has included in its antitrust laws express provisions aimed at promoting the country's post-apartheid social and economic goals.[9] These laws stand in stark contrast to US antitrust laws. In fact, aspects of current US competition policy could arguably be defined as the inverse of South African competition law. Where South African law would facilitate a small business's prima facie case of the existence of discrimination or excessive pricing, and shift the onus of proof to an incumbent defendant (which likely gained its status in an environment where competition from Black, colored or Indian companies was suppressed), US law would require allegations and proof of broader harms to markets beyond the ability of that individual enterprise to participate. Even the somewhat outdated US laws prohibiting price discrimination–enacted expressly to protect small businesses–generally require proof of harm to competition across an entire market, not to an individual affected company.

The prevailing approach to antitrust enforcement in the US may be changing. The current debate around the future of the antitrust laws in the US consistently identifies concerns broader than simply price effects. The Committee on the Judiciary investigation into the state of competition online sought to identify how actors in the digital economy "affect[] our economy and our democracy."[10] In addition to examining price, quality and innovation effects, the investigation also looked at impacts on non-economic goals, such as a free and diverse press and privacy.[11] There are several recent legislative proposals to amend the US antitrust law that seek to introduce new presumptions and burden-shifting to address the perceived imbalance between large enterprises and society at large.[12] While the current focus is mainly on antitrust and digital platforms, similar considerations could apply when considering antitrust enforcement in healthcare markets.

---

8   CPI, *South Africa, CPI Talks ... Eleanor Fox*, 2 COMPETITION POL'Y INT'L ANTITRUST CHRONICLE (Nov. 7, 2019), www.competitionpolicyinternational.com/cpi-talks-eleanor-fox/.

9   Eleanor Fox, *South Africa, Competition Law and Equality: Restoring Equity by Antitrust in a Land Where Markets Were Brutally Skewed*, 3 COMPETITION POL'Y INT'L ANTITRUST CHRONICLE (Dec. 9, 2019).

10 MAJORITY STAFF OF SUBCOMM. ON ANTITRUST, COMM. AND ADMIN. LAW, 116TH CONG., INVESTIGATION OF COMPETITION IN DIGITAL MARKETS 6 (2020), https://judiciary.house.gov/uploadedfiles/competition_in_digital_markets.pdf?utm_campaign=4493-519.

11 *Id.* at 57–73. Similarly, other commentators such as Joseph Stiglitz advocate for expanding antitrust law to advance "the public interest" – specifically to protect consumer interests in privacy and legal recourse for dispute resolution, prevent excessive risk-taking by firms, improve workers' bargaining power, and bolster the "marketplace of ideas" in media. Joseph E. Stiglitz, *Towards a Broader View of Competition Policy*, 12–13, 18–19 (Roosevelt Inst. Working Paper, June 2017) (on file with the Roosevelt Institute), https://rooseveltinstitute.org/wp-content/uploads/2020/07/RI-Broader-View-of-Competition-Policy-201703.pdf; Joseph E. Stiglitz, Professor, Columbia Business School, The Graduate School of Arts and Sciences, Columbia University, Remarks at Fed. Trade Comm'n Hearings on Competition and Consumer Protection in the 21st Century 23–25 (Sept. 21, 2018), www8.gsb.columbia.edu/faculty/jstiglitz/sites/jstiglitz/files/Stiglitz%20FTC%20Hearing%20PPT%20FINAL.pdf.

12 *See, e.g.*, Competition and Antitrust Law Enforcement Reform Act of 2021, S. 225, 117th Cong. (2021), www.congress.gov/117/bills/s225/BILLS-117s225is.pdf.

II. Healthcare Economics and Inequity in Healthcare Access

There is no question that there are significant disparities and inequities in access to quality healthcare by economically and socially disadvantaged communities in the United States.[13] The consequences of these disparities are manifest–higher infant mortality for Black babies than for White babies; lower life expectancy for Black men and women than for their White counterparts; higher diabetes rates among Native Americans and Latinos; higher rates of death from heart disease, stroke, and prostate and breast cancers in Black populations.[14] As well as having adverse impacts on the economy, the situation raises serious moral and ethical dilemmas–how can a nation with such world-class healthcare facilities, technologies, and pharmacotherapeutics tolerate such poor access to those assets by underprivileged segments of its own population?

These disparities have their roots in the development of the healthcare economy over the last century against a backdrop of racial and social bias. They are reflected in the complex structures and economics of the current US healthcare system, involving multiple private and public actors, a wide range of providers, and myriad communities, all with varying interests and priorities. While the ultimate goal is for all Americans to have access to the best possible care and live healthy lives, the routes to that goal are at best circuitous.

The difficulties of US healthcare are in part due to the complexity of payment flows in the healthcare delivery system. A significant portion of healthcare in the US is accessed through private insurance.[15] Because healthcare is a semi-free-market economy, bargaining leverage matters. Depending on market structure, the size of the payor or provider dictates how much private payors will pay for healthcare services to be accessed by their subscribers. Individuals of course have no leverage: Ironically, those who are uninsured and therefore not receiving care at payor-negotiated rates are typically the least able to pay higher rates, resulting in "healthcare bankruptcies" and a significant volume of care for which providers ultimately remain uncompensated.

There also is a significant aspect of the healthcare system not subject to such market forces–Medicare and Medicaid programs–where rates are dictated by, rather than

---

13 *See* Margaret M. Heckler, US Dep't of Health and Human Serv., Report of the Secretary's Task Force on Black and Minority Health, Vol. 1: Exec. Summary (1985); Nat'l Research Council, Unequal Treatment: Confronting Racial and Ethnic Disparities in Health Care (Brian D. Smedley et al. eds., 2003.).

14 Wayne J. Riley, *Health Disparities: Gaps in Access, Quality and Affordability of Medical Care* 123 Transactions of the Am. Clinical and Climatological Ass'n 167, 167–68 (2012).

15 CDC data on personal healthcare expenditures by source of funds provides the breakdown: 35% private health insurance; 23% Medicare; 17% Medicaid; 12% out of pocket; and 13% other (including Children's Health Insurance Program, Veterans Affairs programs, and a variety of other third party payors and programs, such as worksite health care, vocational rehabilitation, and school health programs). *See* Nat'l Ctr. for Health Statistics, Ctr. for Disease Control and Prevention, Personal Health Care Expenditures, by Source of Funds and Type of Expenditure: United States 2008–2018 (2019), www.cdc.gov/nchs/data/hus/2019/fig18-508.pdf.

negotiated with, a government payor.[16] These rates are often below the cost of providing care: on an average basis, even the most efficient hospitals operate at a negative margin on Medicare rates,[17] and Medicaid rates are even lower. This complex and variable web of different payments for the same services leaves providers balancing the books with private payor rates: private insurance often buoys up the ship when public-pay and uncompensated care would threaten to sink it.[18]

The efforts to reform healthcare have sought to create a more equitable healthcare system by addressing three closely related goals–access, quality and cost. The inability to access quality healthcare (often due to its cost) creates and exacerbates inequities. There is a plethora of healthcare literature documenting racial and ethnic disparities in healthcare and how these disparities may be addressed.[19]

Healthcare reform advocates identify a wide range of strategies for ensuring access to quality healthcare for vulnerable communities.[20] Each of these strategies, however, requires a significant commitment and investment of resources to be realized. For example, a key element for supporting the health of disadvantaged communities is addressing the "social determinants" of health–factors such as economic stability (food security, housing, and employment), environment (such as clean air and water), and social and community support. In order to incorporate and address these concerns into their provision of healthcare services, providers need to devote energy and resources to identify systematically what specific issues face their patient population, and to develop partnerships with other providers and community stakeholders. Similarly, adopting new virtual care strategies, such as telehealth, to expand access to underserved communities also requires a significant investment in technology.[21] These investments

---

16 *Id.*

17 Susan Morse, *Efficient Hospitals Operate on -2% Margins in Medicare Payments, MedPAC Reports*, HEALTHCARE FINANCE (Mar. 15, 2019), www.healthcarefinancenews.com/news/efficient-hospitals-operate-2-margins-medicare-payments-medpac-reports. Another commonly cited metric of hospital profitability is the payment-to-cost ratio, which represents average payment relative to average cost by payer, accounting for both patient-specific clinical costs and fixed costs such as equipment, buildings, or administrators' salaries. "According to the American Hospital Association (AHA), private insurance payments average 144.8% of cost, while payments from Medicaid and Medicare are 88.1% and 86.8% of cost, respectively." Emily Gee, *The High Price of Hospital Care*, CTR. FOR AM. PROGRESS (June 26, 2019), www.americanprogress.org/issues/healthcare/reports/2019/06/26/471464/high-price-hospital-care/#fn-471464-30.

18 Rick Mayes & Jason S. Lee, *Medicare Payment Policy and the Controversy Over Hospital Cost Shifting*, 3 APPLIED HEALTH ECON. AND HEALTH POL'Y 153 (2004); Roger Feldman, et al., *Medicare's Role in Determining Prices Throughout the Health Care System* (Mercatus Ctr. Working Paper, 2015), www.mercatus.org/system/files/Feldman-Medicare-Role-Prices-oct.pdf.

19 *See* Kevin Fiscella, *Health Care Reform and Equity: Promise, Pitfalls, and Prescriptions* 9 ANN. OF FAM. MED. 78, www.ncbi.nlm.nih.gov/pmc/articles/PMC3022050/ and articles cited therein.

20 *See, e.g.*, AM. HOSP. ASS'N, REPORT OF AMERICAN HOSPITAL ASSOCIATION TASK FORCE ON ENSURING ACCESS IN VULNERABLE COMMUNITIES (2016), www.aha.org/system/files/content/16/ensuring-access-taskforce-report.pdf; Jay Bhatt & Priya Bathija, *Ensuring Access to Quality Health Care in Vulnerable Communities*, 93 ACAD. MED. 1271 (2018) and articles cited therein; DEBORAH BACHRACH ET AL., THE COMMONWEALTH FUND, HIGH-PERFORMANCE HEALTH CARE FOR VULNERABLE POPULATIONS: A POLICY FRAMEWORK FOR PROMOTING ACCOUNTABLE CARE IN MEDICAID (2012), www.commonwealthfund.org/publications/fund-reports/2012/nov/high-performance-health-care-vulnerable-populations-policy.

21 One recent study investigating the use of telehealth during the COVID-19 pandemic found that Black respondents are most likely to report using telehealth because of the COVID-19 pandemic (particularly when they perceive the pandemic as a minor health threat), concluding that opportunities to leverage a broadly defined set of telehealth tools help to reduce healthcare disparities post-pandemic. Celeste Campos-Castillo

are unlikely to generate any return on investment as understood in direct economic terms, but rather address underlying inequities and serve to support the overall health of the community, which ultimately will have benefits for the economy writ large.

The healthcare policy literature rarely cites competition as an element through which healthcare inequities can be managed for the better. In fact, many of the efforts being made to address disparities run counter to current competition policy. Take the rules imposed on health insurers by the Mental Health Parity and Addiction Equity Act–they prohibit imposing deductibles, co-pays, and OOP limits on mental health and substance abuse coverage that are higher than those imposed for medical-surgical coverage, and make similar parity mandates for hospital stays. Left to itself, the market is unlikely to have reached that result. But, from a policy perspective, such constraints on the market are necessary to achieve equitable results for a vulnerable segment of the population.

The financial pressures on the healthcare system, in particular on hospitals and physician practices, are likely to become more intense following the COVID-19 pandemic, particularly if the volume of uninsured or Medicaid patients increases due to higher unemployment. The federal government has allocated funds through a variety of programs to support healthcare providers in the wake of the crisis.[22] But Kaiser Foundation analysis questions whether the infusion of funds will be sufficient to stabilize providers who are least equipped to weather this revenue decline.[23] These factors will place even more limitations on providers' ability to fund programs specifically designed to address social disparities in healthcare delivery.

III. Antitrust Enforcement in Healthcare Markets

The US antitrust agencies–the Federal Trade Commission (FTC) and US Department of Justice Antitrust Division (DOJ) – have given significant thought to the role of antitrust enforcement in the healthcare industry over at least the last 25 years, holding several sets of hearings and publishing statements of enforcement policy,[24] influential reports,[25] and numerous advisory opinions.

& Denise Anthony, *Racial and Ethnic Differences in Self-Reported Telehealth Use During the COVID-19 Pandemic: A Secondary Analysis of a US Survey of Internet Users from Late March*, 28 J. AM. MED. INFORMATICS ASS'N 119, 122–24 (2020), https://academic.oup.com/jamia/article/28/1/119/5902454.

22 *E.g.*, the Coronavirus Aid, Relief, and Economic Security Act, 15 U.S.C. §§ 9001–9080 (2020); the Paycheck Protection Program and Health Care Enhancement Act, 15 U.S.C. §§ 636, 9006, 9009 (2020).

23 Karyn Schwartz & Anthony Damico, *Distribution of CARES Act Funding Among Hospitals*, KAISER FAMILY FOUNDATION (May 13, 2020), www.kff.org/coronavirus-covid-19/issue-brief/distribution-of-cares-act-funding-among-hospitals/.

24 *See, e.g.*, US DEP'T OF JUSTICE & FED. TRADE COMM'N, STATEMENTS OF ANTITRUST ENFORCEMENT POLICY IN HEALTH CARE (1996), www.justice.gov/atr/page/file/1197731/download; US DEP'T OF JUSTICE & FED. TRADE COMM'N, STATEMENT OF ANTITRUST ENFORCEMENT POLICY REGARDING ACCOUNTABLE CARE ORGANIZATIONS PARTICIPATING IN THE MEDICARE SHARED SAVINGS PROGRAM (2011), www.justice.gov/sites/default/files/atr/legacy/2011/10/20/276458.pdf.

25 *See, e.g.*, US DEP'T OF JUSTICE & FED. TRADE COMM'N, IMPROVING HEALTH CARE: A DOSE OF COMPETITION (2014), www.justice.gov/sites/default/files/atr/legacy/2006/04/27/204694.pdf [hereinafter IMPROVING HEALTH CARE].

The work of the antitrust agencies has been consistent with a great deal of ongoing economic and policy work in the healthcare area. Many of the recommendations for improving competition in healthcare markets identified in the 2004 *Improving Health Care* report[26]–such as tying payments to results; lowering barriers to competitor access through telehealth and relaxation of licensing requirements; improving efficiency through expanded use of technology (particularly electronic medical records systems); and encouraging pricing transparency–echo those of other policymakers and have made their way into our current system through a variety of healthcare reform efforts.

While recognizing the complex and market-distorting features of healthcare delivery markets, the bottom-line conclusion of the agencies' efforts is that antitrust should apply to healthcare markets just as it does to other industries. In the 2004 report, the drafters concluded: "The fundamental premise of the American free-market system is that consumer welfare is maximized by open competition and consumer sovereignty–even when complex products and services such as health care are involved."[27]

But viewing transactions and conduct in healthcare markets through the current antitrust lens typically results in a process that considers only private insurer prices. This can have inequitable results: When dealing with facilities serving disadvantaged communities, ignoring or deemphasizing considerations of access and impacts on the local community arguably perpetuates the status quo. A focus on price, rather than quality, may overlook those factors most likely to impact patients who are on Medicare or Medicaid, or who are uninsured. Without the increased access to capital and other advantages that come with participating in a larger organization, the hospital is left to continue on, in many cases efficiently using their current resources, but without the capacity to make transformative improvements in operations or to invest in the local community.

Making such arguments in response to competitive concerns around price effects face significant difficulties under the agencies' Horizontal Merger Guidelines. The Guidelines set a very high bar for giving weight to transaction efficiencies and the economic condition of merging firms.[28] To be cognizable, efficiencies have to be quantifiable and verifiable. Quality enhancement rarely meets this requirement, and enhanced access or impacts on disadvantaged communities never will. Similarly, the agencies will permit an acquisition of a "failing firm," but the standards by which a firm is to be considered "failing" are again very high–the financial condition of the hospital must be so dire that it is in danger of closing and there can be no alternative purchaser that would have maintained

---

26 *See id.* at 21–24.

27 *Id.* at 28–29.

28 *See* US Dep't of Justice & Fed. Trade Comm'n, Horizontal Merger Guidelines §§ 10–11 (2010), www.justice.gov/sites/default/files/atr/legacy/2010/08/19/hmg-2010.pdf.

the facility as a competitor.[29] The criteria for invoking these justifications for a transaction are rarely achieved.

Since at least 2000, these elements of US merger antitrust enforcement have played out in several successful court challenges by the FTC against mergers of competing hospitals, and the abandonment of many others in the face of FTC pre-complaint opposition.[30] Those cases have focused on the impact on the negotiating dynamic between hospital providers and private insurers, and rarely the (usually unquantifiable) benefits that such transactions may bring to their surrounding communities, in particular vulnerable and otherwise disadvantaged populations. Most merger antitrust enforcement is based around a concern that allowing hospital systems to get bigger can result in higher rates to private payors.[31] But assessing a merger by its impact on private payor pricing does not consider the overall economic impact on a provider with significant public-pay and uncompensated care. It also does not consider the potential collateral damage that rejecting certain transactions may have on their communities, those considerations being well outside the scope of current interpretations of the antitrust laws. These concerns may be exacerbated by the financial pressures faced by hospitals coming out of the COVID-19 pandemic.

In response to the narrow focus of federal antitrust enforcement, several states have adopted the approach of shielding hospital mergers and other conduct that may violate the antitrust laws as interpreted by the federal antitrust agencies. Such "Certificate of Public Advantage" (COPA) laws displace federal antitrust enforcement in favor of a state assessment (typically conducted by a state health department) of the public benefits of permitting a transaction that may outweigh any potential anticompetitive effects.[32] The FTC has vehemently opposed COPA laws–and the transactions approved under them–and has been active in regulatory proceedings leading to the grant of a COPA. However, in many instances, states have elected to grant a COPA and permit a merger to proceed, subject to stringent conditions that often include long-term price regulation to protect against

---

29 *See, e.g.*, Richard Feinstein, Bureau of Competition Director, Fed. Trade Comm'n, Statement on the FTC's Closure of its Investigation of Consummated Hospital Merger in Temple, Texas (Dec. 23, 2009), www.ftc.gov/sites/default/files/documents/public_statements/ftcs-closure-its-investigation-consummated-hospital-merger-temple-texas/091223scottwhitestmt.pdf.

30 *See* MARKUS H. MEIER ET AL., HEALTH CARE DIVISION, FED. TRADE COMM'N, OVERVIEW OF FTC ACTIONS IN HEALTH CARE SERVICES AND PRODUCTS 51–72 (2019), www.ftc.gov/system/files/attachments/competition-policy-guidance/overview_health_care_june_2019.pdf.

31 Whether this will be true in any particular case depends on the structure of the specific market, however, there is a significant body of economics literature that supports this view. *See* Zack Cooper et al., *The Price Ain't Right? Hospital Prices and Health Spending on the Privately Insured* (Nat'l Bureau of Econ. Research, Working Paper No. 21815, 2015), https://doi.org/10.3386/w21815; MEDICARE PAYMENT ADVISORY COMM'N, MARCH 2020 REPORT TO THE CONGRESS: MEDICARE PAYMENT POLICY xxv–xxvi (Mar. 13, 2020), www.medpac.gov/docs/default-source/reports/mar20_entirereport_rev_sec.pdf?sfvrsn=0.

32 COPA laws can also insulate certain conduct, such as collaborations between competing entities to organize the treatment of Medicaid beneficiaries between them. *See, e.g.*, N.Y. Pub. Health Law Art. 29–F § 2999-A, www.nysenate.gov/legislation/laws/PBH/2999-AA.

anticipated price increases to payors as a result of the increased bargaining leverage.[33]

In other instances, states have acted independently without COPA laws in obtaining commitments and conditions for permitting a transaction to proceed even while the FTC was investigating or in the midst of a formal challenge. In these instances, in the interests of comity, the FTC has stepped back from its enforcement action and permitted the transaction to close under the aegis of the state regulator.[34] But this is not the agency's preferred approach:

> The resolution of hospital merger challenges through community commitments should be generally disfavored. The Agencies do not accept community commitments as a resolution to likely anticompetitive effects from a hospital (or any other) merger. The Agencies believe community commitments are an ineffective, short-term regulatory approach to what is ultimately a problem of competition. Nevertheless, the Agencies realize that in some circumstances, State Attorneys General may agree to community commitments in light of the resource and other constraints they face.[35]

In the cases in which COPAs have been granted or conditions otherwise agreed, the states elected to take on a regulatory role to realize community benefits rather than a strict economic approach that would leave competition and the free market to determine commercial insurance rates. While expressing opposition to the displacement of the benefits of competition by local interests, both as a matter of principle and in relation to specific transactions, the FTC's forbearance in these matters suggests an acknowledgment of the complexity of healthcare policy concerns and the inability of current antitrust enforcement paradigms to address these concerns. As the 2004 report notes:

> Competition is not a panacea for all of the problems with American health care. Competition cannot provide its full benefits to consumers without good information and properly aligned incentives. Moreover, competition cannot eliminate the inherent uncertainties in health

---

33 *See, e.g.*, 2017–18 COPAs granted to Wellmont and Mountain States healthcare organizations to form Ballad Health in Tennessee and Virginia. *Certificate of Public Advantage (Tennessee) & Cooperative Agreement (Virginia)*, BALLAD HEALTH, www.balladhealth.org/copa; 2020 COPAs granted to Shannon Health for the acquisition of San Angelo Community Medical Center and to Hendrick Health System for its acquisition of Abilene Regional Medical Center. *Certificate of Public Advantage*, TEXAS HEALTH AND HUMAN SERV., https://hhs.texas.gov/doing-business-hhs/provider-portals/health-care-facilities-regulation/certificate-public-advantage.

34 *See, e.g.*, Fed. Trade Comm'n, Statement Concerning the Proposed Affiliation of CareGroup, Inc.; Lahey Health System, Inc.; Seacoast Regional Health System, Inc.; BIDCO Hospital LLC; and BIDCO Physician LLC (Nov. 29, 2018), www.ftc.gov/system/files/documents/closing_letters/nid/1710118_bidmc_commission_closing_statement.pdf; Harold Brubaker, *Pa. Attorney General drops opposition to Jefferson-Einstein deal*, PHILA. INQUIRER, Jan. 12, 2021, www.inquirer.com/business/health/pennsylvania-attorney-general-drops-opposition-jefferson-einstein-merger-20210112.html; *Einstein Healthcare Network and Jefferson Health Merger Clears Final Hurdle*, JEFFERSON HEALTH (Mar. 1, 2021), https://hospitals.jefferson.edu/news/2021/03/einstein-jefferson-health-merger.html.

35 IMPROVING HEALTH CARE, *supra* note 25 at 27.

care, or the informational asymmetries among consumers, providers, and payors. Competition also will not shift resources to those who do not have them.[36]

In many ways, state efforts in healthcare transactions that displace antitrust enforcement are an experiment. Will they actually deliver on the promises of advancement of local healthcare objectives and actively improve healthcare access for vulnerable communities? Has the elimination of inter-hospital competition actually resulted in higher commercial prices and lower quality? The agencies and policymakers are standing by ready to assess the results. The FTC has held workshops and has been studying the impact of mergers consummated under COPAs since 2019.[37] It also is studying the impact of physician group and hospital mergers.[38] This work will inform both future enforcement as well as help healthcare policymakers identify ways to ensure the potential benefits of consolidation reach disadvantaged communities, or take a different approach.

The complex US healthcare system itself is not standing still. Proposals abound for expanding access for vulnerable communities through a variety of means, including expanding existing public programs, strengthening policies around private insurance, implementing quality and other incentive programs, encouraging collaborations between different providers and community organizations, and many others.[39] Several of these will clash with the traditional application of the antitrust laws. As existing healthcare structures develop and change, antitrust will need to adjust and continue to be part of the debate.

---

36 *Id.* at 4.

37 *A Health Check on COPAs: Assessing the Impact of Certificates of Public Advantage in Healthcare Markets*, FED. TRADE COMM'N, www.ftc.gov/news-events/events-calendar/health-check-copas-assessing-impact-certificates-public-advantage; Press Release, Fed. Trade Comm'n, FTC to Study the Impact of COPAs (Oct. 21, 2019), www.ftc.gov/news-events/press-releases/2019/10/ftc-study-impact-copas.

38 Press Release, Fed. Trade Comm'n, FTC to Study the Impact of Physician Group and Healthcare Facility Mergers (Jan. 14, 2021), www.ftc.gov/news-events/press-releases/2021/01/ftc-study-impact-physician-group-healthcare-facility-mergers.

39 *See, e.g.,* Melinda Dutton et al., *Investing in Health: Seven Strategies for States Looking to Buy Health, Not Just Health Care* THE COMMONWEALTH FUND (Feb. 2021), www.manatt.com/Manatt/media/Documents/Articles/Investing-in-Health-Seven-Strategies-for-States_e.pdf.

Fairness as a Counterpoint to Efficiency in Competition Policy?

EDWARD IACOBUCCI AND MICHAEL TREBILCOCK[*]
University of Toronto

Abstract

In this paper we first briefly review the elusive role of fairness issues in competition law and policy generally. We then illustrate the problematic nature of fairness concerns in this context with a brief case study of merger review in Canada where these issues have become central.

---

[*] Edward Iacobucci is Professor and Toronto Stock Exchange Chair in Capital Markets at the Faculty of Law, University of Toronto. Michael Trebilcock is University Professor Emeritus, University of Toronto Faculty of Law.

I. The Resurgence of Fairness Concerns in Competition Policy[1]

Fairness concerns in competition policy are not new but have animated the development of the field since its inception. The economic and social dislocations occurring in the nineteenth century, especially in the US, as a result of improved transportation and communication technologies that led to large-scale production and a substantial increase in the efficient scale of manufacturing enterprises, provoked concerns among small producers, farmers, and consumers. While historians are not agreed on the ultimate intention of the US Congress in passing the Sherman Act in 1889, fairness concerns have often blended together the protection of small businesses against larger rivals; issues of wealth and income inequality; high prices for consumers; and corruption of the political process by concentrations of economic power. Even today the goals of many competition policy regimes are often stated in general or ambiguous terms, implying the simultaneous pursuit of several, often conflicting, goals.

A prominent example is the preamble to the Canadian Competition Act 1986, which explicitly identifies in section 1.1 four explicit goals that are theoretically pursued simultaneously: enhancing economic efficiency, participation in global markets, fairness toward small and medium-size businesses, and consumer welfare. South Africa's competition laws set as goals promoting participation of all citizens in the economy and promoting the fair distribution of ownership and control of markets among different racial groups, and balancing the interests of workers, owners, and consumers. The objectives of China's relatively recent antimonopoly law include promoting efficiency while safeguarding the healthy development of a socialist market economy and the public interest, protecting the state-owned economy and small business, encouraging the expansion of domestic enterprises, and scrutinizing foreign takeovers. Japan's competition law regime espouses consumer welfare as an objective, but also seeks to protect small and medium-size businesses and devotes significant resources to policing low prices in the Japanese economy. The European Union places particular emphasis on distortions within the internal common market and has historically devoted particular attention to the protection of small competitors as well as the maximization of consumer welfare and the efficiency of markets.[2]

Historical preoccupations with various fairness concerns in competition policy were relegated to second-order importance in most mature competition law regimes from the 1970s onwards under the influence of the Chicago school of antitrust, which emphasized economic efficiency as the single goal of antitrust

---

1   This section draws on a paper by Francesco Ducci & Michael Trebilcock, *The Revival of Fairness Discourse in Competition Policy*, 64 ANTITRUST BULL. 79 (2019).

2   *See* THE DESIGN OF COMPETITION LAW INSTITUTIONS: GLOBAL NORMS, LOCAL CHOICES, ch. 1 (Eleanor Fox & Michael Trebilcock eds., 2013).

law. However, fairness concerns are regaining prominence in competition policy debates, paralleling a revival or reinvigoration of debates in international trade policy of free trade versus fair trade. In domestic markets, especially the US, the resurgence of fairness concerns is closely linked to the perceived decrease in levels of market competition, manifested in three specific forms: a) evidence of increasing levels of market concentration in many markets; b) decreasing levels of new business entry; and c) increasing importance of winner-take-all markets, especially the so-called "tech titans," as a result of technological innovations.[3] These trends have been detailed in recent books by Philippon and Tepper.[4]

In response to these trends an increasing number of scholars and commentators have advocated stronger incorporation of equity concerns into competition policy in order to address problems of economic inequality, and, more generally, inequities of market outcomes through the enforcement of competition laws. These scholars include Anthony Atkinson, who has argued that competition policy should embody explicit distributional concerns;[5] Joseph Stiglitz, who has called for stronger and more effective enforcement of competition laws to address inequalities created by market power;[6] and Paul Krugman, who has blamed the collapse of antitrust enforcement in the US as a potentially important factor in the stagnating demand for labor as a result of increasing prevalence of monopsonies in many input markets and increasing inequality more generally. Similarly, the current European Commissioner for Competition, Margrethe Vestager, has repeatedly stressed the importance of fairness considerations in competition policy. To this illustrious list, we might add the equally illustrious name of Professor Eleanor Fox, who with her customary eloquence has expressed skepticism about the claim that in competition law we can pursue either efficiency or equity, but not both: if we pursue equity, we would undermine efficiency, as a result of which we would all be worse off. She states bluntly, "I never believed it."[7]

However, arguments in favor of more equity-oriented competition laws risk being based on extremely vague notions of fairness, or as George Stigler put it long ago, "a suitcase full of bottled ethics from which one freely chooses to blend his own type of justice."[8]

In a recent paper by one of us and Francesco Ducci,[9] we argued for the disaggregation of the concept of fairness into four distinct notions of fairness that are

---

[3] *See, e.g.*, Francesco Ducci, Natural Monopolies in Digital Platform Markets (2020).

[4] Thomas Philippon, The Great Reversal: How America Gave Up on Free Markets (2019); Jonathan Tepper with Denise Hearn, The Myth of Competition: Monopolies and the Death of Competition (2019).

[5] Anthony Atkinson, Inequality: What Can Be Done? (2015).

[6] Joseph Stiglitz, The Price of Inequality: How Today's Divided Society Endangers Our Future (2012).

[7] *See* Eleanor Fox, *Competition Policy at the Intersection of Equity and Efficiency: The Developed and Developing Worlds*, 63 Antitrust Bull. 3 (2018).

[8] George Stigler, *The Law and Economics of Public Policy: A Plea to the Scholars*, 1 J. Legal Stud. 4 (1972).

[9] Ducci & Trebilcock, *supra* note 1.

pertinent to market power in domestic markets: vertical fairness (between producers and consumers); horizontal fairness on the demand side (between consumers); horizontal fairness on the supply side (between producers); and procedural fairness (due process and effective remedies to redress anticompetitive harms). Not only can the different dimensions of fairness be distinguished using the categories of supply and demand, they also relate to different notions of justice: distributive justice (e.g., choosing a social welfare standard), procedural justice (due process and institutional design), and corrective justice (private rights of access to enforcement procedures for injured parties); and different notions of equity concerned with outcomes (e.g., between consumers and producers), opportunity (between producers), and procedures (due process and private remedies).

1. Vertical fairness

With respect to vertical fairness, competition policy scholarship and jurisprudence have devoted particular attention to the vertical dimension of fairness between consumers and producers, reflected in the well-known debate over the choice of welfare standard between consumer welfare and total welfare. While many developed competition law regimes have over time converged toward consumer welfare as the predominant objective of their competition laws–reflecting some notion of distributive justice and fairness toward consumers–the normative force of the consumer welfare standard is not robust. Under a distributive justice perspective, the relationship between market power and distributional fairness between consumers and producers is complex, and highly contingent on the facts of individual cases. It is often complex to calculate the incidence of price increases, especially given the fact that in many cases consumers are intermediate purchasers, and even if their claims are vindicated this may or may not do justice to final consumers.

However, even if one assumes that on average consumers are less wealthy than shareholders, the jurisdiction that has most unambiguously committed itself to the consumer welfare standard in recent decades–the US–is the jurisdiction where concerns over increasing levels of concentration in many markets, decreasing levels of new business entries, and increasing importance of winner-take-all markets, are perhaps most acute. This suggests that the choice of welfare standard, consumer welfare or total welfare, is not of central importance in explaining these trends, and rather they may be better explained, as Philippon and Tepper argue, as either the collapse in recent decades of vigorous antitrust enforcement in the US, or by a complex range of factors lying outside the direct ambit of competition policies, such as the impact of technological innovation and international trade on domestic markets.

2. Horizontal fairness on the demand side

On the demand side, consumers are often heterogeneous in their preferences for similar goods and services, and possible fairness and distributional issues can emerge in various contexts when different consumers can be affected in different ways by a given conduct. The most prominent example can be found in cases of price discrimination, greatly facilitated in recent years by information technology. Price discrimination has disparate impacts on consumers. It shifts consumer surplus of those who are already in the market to producer surplus, but also may increase surplus by allowing some consumers to be served who would not otherwise be in the market. In some cases, price discrimination that favors lower prices for senior citizens, students, and children, whose demand for the goods or services in question may be relatively elastic, may serve distributive justice ends, although in other cases the most inelastic demanders may also be the least well-endowed citizens with few choices in purchasing the necessities of life. Again, distributional impacts would need to be evaluated case by case. Many jurisdictions in recent years have abolished price discrimination prohibitions in their competition law regimes (as Canada did in 2009, at least as a specific offense), or devoted minimal attention and resources to their enforcement.

3. Horizontal fairness on the supply side

On the supply side, fairness considerations that have animated the origin of many competition law regimes, in particular in regard to small producers, are reemerging as a result of decreasing levels of competition in many sectors of the economy. However, we are generally skeptical about fairness considerations favoring less efficient or smaller competitors, which in many cases imply a tax on consumers through higher prices. Nevertheless, we recognize a narrow dimension of horizontal fairness at play on the supply side as implicit in ensuring equal competitive conditions over access to markets, and in targeting exclusionary or discriminatory forms of conduct and barriers to entry that deter entry of equally or more efficient competitors. This narrower form of horizontal fairness on the supply side may perhaps provide a normative basis for some forms of competition policy enforcement, but exclusionary practices that deter equally or more efficient competitors from participating in markets also generate efficiency losses. We note, in this respect, that Eleanor Fox observed in a brief comment in "Competition Policy at the Intersection of Equity and Efficiency: The Developed and Developing Worlds,"[10] that equity and efficiency often move together, ensuring equality of opportunity, and that often in developing countries the state itself is the source of major barriers to entry. A study by Ostry, Berg, and Tsangarides of the International Monetary Fund[11] finds that greater inequality in society strongly retards economic growth. Recent widely noted books in economic history, Acemoglu and Robinson, *Why Nations Fail*,[12] and

---

10   Fox, *supra* note 7.

11   Jonathan D. Ostry, Andrew Berg, & Charalambos G. Tsangarides, *Redistribution, Inequality and Growth* (IMF Staff Discussion Note, Feb. 2014).

12   DARON ACEMOGLU & JAMES A. ROBINSON, WHY NATIONS FAIL: THE ORIGINS OF POWER, PROSPERITY, AND POVERTY (2012). *See also*, DARON ACEMOGLU & JAMES A. ROBINSON, THE NARROW CORRIDOR: STATES, SOCIETIES AND THE FATE OF LIBERTY (2019).

North, Wallis, and Weingast, *Violence and Social Orders*,[13] find that, historically, societies that are more inclusive economically and politically tend to perform better economically in the long run than societies that are exclusionary. There is some ambiguity in the implications for competition policy enforcement from these studies. On the one hand, since the anticompetitive exclusion of efficient competitors creates efficiency losses, the finding that inclusive societies fare better economically supports a conclusion that antitrust should focus on inefficient exclusion. On the other hand, it could also be that the studies suggest that long-run, economically beneficial inclusion is encouraged by a focus on horizontal equity that would facilitate even inefficient entry. US antitrust policy historically accepts the first conclusion; EU policy, with its focus on the competitive process, rather than immediate efficiency considerations, the latter.

4. Procedural fairness

Another dimension of fairness in the competition law context is procedural fairness, including due process guarantees, transparent and predictable proceedings, and relevant legal and economic expertise–again, a dimension of fairness that Professor Fox has emphasized in much of her writing on competition law.[14] An important implication of an emphasis on procedural fairness as implicit in a commitment to the rule of law is that, as in other domains of the law, competition law should be reasonably predictable in its enforcement, interpretation, and application. Obviously, there is a serious danger that incorporating ill-defined notions of standards of fairness into competition law regimes may compromise procedural fairness in important ways by leading to more protracted and ill-disciplined proceedings, and idiosyncratic or subjective value judgments by enforcers or adjudicators.

In the next section, we illustrate these dangers through a Canadian case study focusing on the interpretation and application of the so-called efficiencies defense in Canadian merger review.

II. *Superior Propane* and Fairness

An obviously attractive approach to the decision whether to pursue conventional efficiency goals or some alternative fairness goal is to deny that they are contradictory, and pursue both simultaneously. And indeed, as Professor Fox has emphasized, there is no question that in many contexts both fairness and efficiency will rise and fall together. Low prices, for example, often promote efficiency, and also have desirable distributive properties (assuming shareholders are wealthier than consumers). But what does competition policy do when the objectives

---

13 Douglass C. North et al., Violence and Social Orders: A Conceptual Framework for Interpreting Recorded Human History (2012).

14 *See, e.g.*, Fox & Trebilcock, *supra* note 2.

conflict? This question lay at the core of *Superior Propane*, a foundational case in Canadian merger policy.[15] This section reviews the issues in that case, and points to it as an example of how policy can become muddled and indeterminate in a well-intentioned attempt to be fairer.

1. Statutory background

Before reviewing the facts of the case, it is helpful to outline the key statutory provisions at stake. As noted above, Canada's Competition Act contains a statement of the legislation's basic objectives in section 1.1:

> The purpose of this Act is to maintain and encourage competition in Canada in order to promote the efficiency and adaptability of the Canadian economy, in order to expand opportunities for Canadian participation in world markets while at the same time recognizing the role of foreign competition in Canada, in order to ensure that small and medium-sized enterprises have an equitable opportunity to participate in the Canadian economy and in order to provide consumers with competitive prices and product choices.

The provision sets out a variety of benefits from promoting competition, including efficiency on the one hand, and competitive prices to consumers on the other. It is obvious how these two objectives will be simultaneously met in many, probably most, areas of competition law enforcement. Prohibiting an exclusionary practice by a dominant firm, for example, may both promote lower prices to consumers by inviting competitive entry, and may promote efficiency by reducing deadweight losses. Similarly, prohibiting an anticompetitive merger will, all things being equal, drive prices lower (or at least keep prices low), while avoiding deadweight losses from inefficiently high prices.

But there are instances where the objectives in section 1.1 may conflict. It is clear, for example, that allowing aggressive but competitive pricing by a larger firm may limit the ability of higher-cost, small enterprises to compete. Moreover, as Oliver Williamson famously pointed out, a merger may simultaneously promote efficiency by lowering costs, and lead to higher prices by reducing competition.[16] The trade-off between efficiency and higher prices in mergers policy is at the heart of the *Superior Propane* decision.

The other key statutory provision is section 96 of the Competition Act. Section 92 of the Act sets out the authority of the Competition Tribunal to make an order

---

[15] Canada (Comm'r of Competition) v. Superior Propane Inc., [2000] C.C.T.D. No. 15 (Can. Competition Tribunal); Canada (Comm'r of Competition) v. Superior Propane Inc., [2001] F.C.J. No. 455 (Can. Fed. Ct. App.); Canada (Comm'r of Competition) v. Superior Propane Inc., [2002] C.C.T.C. No. 10 (Can. Competition Tribunal); Canada (Comm'r of Competition) v. Superior Propane, Inc., [2003] 3 F.C. 529 (Can. Fed. Ct. App.).

[16] Oliver Williamson, *Economies as an Antitrust Defense: The Welfare Tradeoffs*, 58 Am. Econ. Rev. 18 (1968).

against a merger if the merger is likely to lessen competition substantially. Section 96 provides a defense:

> The Tribunal shall not make an order under section 92 if it finds that the merger or proposed merger in respect of which the application is made has brought about or is likely to bring about gains in efficiency that will be greater than, and will offset, the effects of any prevention or lessening of competition that will result or is likely to result from the merger or proposed merger and that the gains in efficiency would not likely be attained if the order were made.

Section 96 invites the Tribunal to weigh the gains in efficiency that would result from the merger against "the effects of any prevention or lessening of competition" from the merger. Section 96, however, does not define what the "effects" of a lessening of competition are: are the effects under section 96 efficiency-related only, or does a negative distributional effect matter? The answer to this question may have a profound impact on any given case. Like section 1.1, section 96 fails to articulate clearly what objective the Act pursues when there is a trade-off between two competing possibilities. In the efficiencies defense to mergers context generally, and in *Superior Propane* in particular, however, the purported adoption of both efficiency and competitive prices as objectives is exposed as impossible, at least in some circumstances. *Superior Propane* therefore put pressure on Canadian competition law to acknowledge the potential inconsistency between efficiency on the one hand, and distributive conceptions of fairness on the other, and to pick one or the other.

2. The policy trade-off

To clarify the discussion of *Superior Propane*, it is helpful to review the familiar Williamson framework for considering efficiency gains in the merger context.

Figure 1

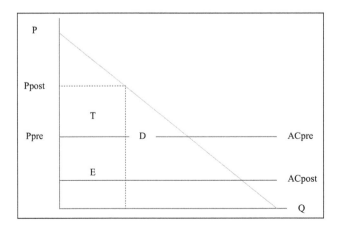

Figure 1 represents the impact of a merger that has two effects. First, the merger creates efficiency gains such that average costs fall relative to the premerger state. Second, the merger creates market power such that prices rise relative both to post-merger costs, and to premerger prices. The three effects of the merger are represented by areas T, D, and E. E reflects efficiency gains from the merger: these are social welfare gains relative to the premerger situation. D reflects the social deadweight loss from the emergence of market power that the merger causes. Finally, T is a transfer of surplus from consumers to shareholders, but does not reflect any efficiency losses.

From an economic efficiency perspective, the authorities ought to compare the efficiency losses of the merger, D, with the gains, E. If E > D, approve the merger; if E < D, reject the merger. T is irrelevant to the analysis.

There is a question, however, whether T ought to be considered out of fairness concerns. Specifically, the transfer may reflect a shift from relatively less-well-off consumers to better off shareholders and, on certain conceptions of fairness, could be considered a negative effect of the merger. *Superior Propane* compelled Canadian competition law to make a decision on the significance of T to the efficiencies defense.

3. The approach to section 96 in *Superior Propane*

Superior Propane was the subject of extensive litigation, with a hearing before the Competition Tribunal, an appeal to the Federal Court of Appeal, a rehearing before the Tribunal and another appeal before the Federal Court of Appeal. It is a rich case with many nuances.[17] We will set aside most of the subtleties and focus on the basic question. The Tribunal found as a fact that a proposed merger of propane and propane services suppliers would lessen competition substantially, and would generate cost savings and efficiency gains. The Tribunal also found that the size of the efficiency gains was larger than the deadweight losses from market power and higher prices. The significance of those factual findings turns importantly on the interpretive question at the heart of the case: does section 96, in enumerating the "effects of a ... lessening of competition," contemplate only economic efficiency effects (E v. D), or will it also account for distributional effects (E v. some combination of D and T)?

The Tribunal in the first instance concluded that section 96 considers only efficiency effects. The Tribunal compared E to D, concluded that E > D, and therefore approved the merger.

The Competition Bureau appealed the Tribunal's decision, arguing that distributional consequences of the merger, T, matter under section 96, and that it was an error of law for the Tribunal to have ignored these effects.

---

[17] *See* Edward Iacobucci, *The* Superior Propane *Saga in* Landmark Cases in Competition Law: Around the World in Fourteen Stories (Barry Rodger ed., 2012).

The Federal Court of Appeal, noting the multi-objective nature of section 1.1, did not accept the Tribunal's conclusion that section 96 was exclusively about economic efficiency. Pointing to the objective set out in section 1.1 of providing consumers with competitive prices, the Federal Court of Appeal accepted the submission of the Competition Bureau that distributional considerations could play a role under section 96.

While the Federal Court of Appeal was clear on what section 96 did not require, namely, it did not require an exclusive focus on efficiency, it was much less clear on what section 96 did require of the Tribunal. Nor did the Competition Bureau provide much guidance. The Bureau submitted that an appropriate approach to section 96 would be to adopt a balancing weights analysis. Under this approach, the Tribunal should calculate the welfare impact on both consumers and producers, and ask how many more times would consumer welfare have to count in some social calculus for the impacts of the merger on consumers and producers to be equal. Specifically, what is the balancing weight, b, such that $b(D+T) = E+T$? The balancing weight, b, would have to be greater than 1 where, as in *Superior Propane* itself, $E > D$. That is, society would have to weight consumer welfare more heavily than producer welfare for an efficient but anticompetitive merger to be considered neutral.

The balancing weights approach is not a test for the authorities to apply. There is no magic threshold for "b" that indicates a thumbs up or down on the merger. Rather the approach provides a framework for analyzing the welfare trade-offs in an efficiencies defense case. The Federal Court of Appeal acknowledged that it was not prepared to dictate to the Tribunal what threshold levels should be set for b, and further suggested that the optimal approach could vary case by case. The Tribunal were called on to exercise their judgment to assess what would be fair in any given case.

4. Fairness, indeterminacy, and *Superior Propane*

Following the adoption of the balancing weights approach, there was a rehearing before the Tribunal, who approved the merger under section 96, concluding that the efficiencies were such that the merger could go ahead even accepting that some propane purchasers were end-user consumers for whom there might reasonably be distributional concerns. The Federal Court accepted the Tribunal's reconsideration on appeal.

Both the Tribunal and the Federal Court of Appeal criticized the other's opinions in the rehearing and appeals, which made for much interesting discussion that is outside the scope of this paper. But one point came up that is central for present purposes. The Federal Court of Appeal accepted that the balancing weights approach might be unpredictable in that not only did the Court not provide or even hint at appropriate thresholds for the balancing weight, b, but it opined that the right approach may vary case to case. It acknowledged that the approach would create some uncertainty in its application, but also stated that the effects of such uncertainty ought not to be exaggerated. Even if the pure efficiency test adopted initially by the Tribunal were adopted, there would be an unpredictability about its application, with different views possibly emerging about the application of the test in any given case.

The Court of Appeal was surely correct to observe that the application of the efficiencies defense would come with some unpredictability even if focused only on efficiencies. It is easy to draw a graph that sets out values of E, T, and D in an imaginary example, but actually determining those values in an actual merger case is hard. Indeed, there could be disagreement and controversy about the values in an after-the-fact, retrospective analysis of a merger, let alone about the future, conjectural market effects of a proposed merger.

Yet there is a critical difference between the unpredictability associated with the efficiency approach and that with the balancing weight fairness approach. In the former, all parties are aware of the conceptual test that section 96 requires, although there may be disagreement over the empirical application of the test to a given case. In the latter, there is not just empirical uncertainty, but conceptual uncertainty. This is not a trivial distinction. It is one thing if all parties understand the law in an area and will work to persuade each other and an adjudicator of how to apply it in a given case. It is another thing if there is no clear law in an area, and each party has to work to persuade each other and/or an adjudicator that its suggested approach to the law is best in any given case, and then persuade each other and/or an adjudicator of how the test ought to be applied to facts in any given case. For one thing, the criteria for persuading the adjudicator are not clear, but rather the case-by-case approach confers on the Tribunal wide latitude to decide on the basis of the personal preferences of its members. Indeed, the holding by the Federal Court of Appeal that the approach may vary case to case also indicates that precedent in a given case may not have any influence on a future case; that is, the conceptual uncertainty the fairness requirement creates would not necessarily be resolved by case law. Put another way, empirical uncertainty about the application of a known legal test does not raise doubts about the rule of law, while uncertainty about the legal test itself does. The personal preferences of the adjudicator do not provide an adequate foundation for a legal test.

5. Distributional fairness and indeterminacy

The failure of *Superior Propane* to provide legal guidance provides a cautionary tale about incorporating fairness into competition policy analysis. But doubts about the rule of law that emerged in that case were not inevitable. It would have been clearly possible for the Court of Appeal to have accounted for distributional fairness between sellers and buyers, vertical fairness in the parlance we have adopted, while delineating a clear legal test. Europe provides an example. Under section 101 of the Treaty on the Functioning of the European Union, technical progress may be taken into account in assessing a possibly anticompetitive act, so long as a fair share of the benefits of that progress are passed along to consumers. This suggests that prices must fall or quality must improve for the efficiencies defense to succeed. Similarly, the US might accept efficiencies as a defense to a merger if they would result in lower prices post-merger.

There are other approaches to fairness that would be clear and coherent. For example, the rule could be that the transfer, T, counts equally as a negative effect of the merger as deadweight losses, D, such that the efficiencies defense can only succeed if $E > T+D$. Similarly, the transfer could count as some fixed proportion of the harm of D, such that the efficiencies defense will succeed if $E > xT+D$, where x is set as some fraction, $0 < x < 1$. Rather than adopting such clear rules, the Court of Appeal concluded that x could vary without apparent bounds on a case-by-case basis, which provides little guidance or clarity.

The problem for distributional fairness advocates, then, is not unpredictability in the application of a rule per se. Rather, the problem is that if the courts move to a fairness-oriented, "all-things-considered-in-any-given-case" approach to a legal test, there is no legal rule and the law will essentially turn on the personal preferences of the adjudicators. The fundamental problem in the *Superior Propane* is that the Court of Appeal asks competition adjudicators to weigh incommensurable considerations of fairness and efficiency on a case-by-case basis.

It is possible to create clear, concrete rules that are not case-by-case, and that take account of both considerations, as noted (e.g., if $E > T+D$, the defense is successful), but critics would be able to claim with justification that any such rules lack a coherent basis, even if clear (e.g., why should the transfer be treated as equally harmful as the deadweight loss?). If the rule is clear, however, the complaint about arbitrary line-drawing in establishing the rule loses much of its force. The political process will often involve a range of incommensurable values; the fairness-efficiency combination is no different. But better to "muddle through" with a clear law that rests on a contestable accounting of incommensurable factors than to weaken the rule of law by leaving everything up for grabs on a case-by-case basis.

There is another familiar and important consideration. Even assuming that two or more incommensurable values may be at stake in a given context, it is not at all clear that the law should rely on a single policy tool to vindicate those values. If fairness in distribution and efficiency both matter, it might well make sense to rely, say, on competition policy to promote efficiency, and other, better targeted instruments, such as progressive taxation and expenditures, to promote fairness. That is, an exclusive focus on efficiency in competition law and policy does not mean an exclusive focus on efficiency in the law writ large. We are not stating definitively that it is optimal to focus only on efficiency in competition policy, but are stating that such a focus would not reject fairness in distribution as a valuable societal objective. And, to reiterate, treating all values as possibly in play in every case would sit uncomfortably with the rule of law.

III. Beyond Vertical Fairness

Recent years have seen the emergence of strong challenges to the hegemony of conventional economic analysis that has provided the foundation of antitrust policy for decades. While concerns about distribution that motivated the Court in *Superior Propane* exist and are perhaps growing in prominence along with concerns about economic inequality generally, other considerations are surfacing and gaining traction in policy discussions. There are different strains of argument.[18] For example, some advocates object to the size of certain entities, rather than their market power per se. The rise of large tech platforms, such as Google, Facebook, and Amazon, has invited objections that they have become too politically powerful, with elections themselves potentially turning on their output. Often these large platforms are described loosely as "monopolies," without close attention to the specific market(s) that they supposedly monopolize.[19] There are also concerns about privacy, with significant technology platforms harboring reams of data that allow them deep insight into our personal lives, something that is seen as jarring on its own, and in addition carries the risk of harmful security breaches. There are increasing calls for antitrust policy to account for such concerns.

Experience in Canada provides support for those who object to the incorporation of various fairness considerations into bedrock antitrust foundations. In its attempt to account for distributional concerns in mergers policy, the Federal Court of Appeal in *Superior Propane* blended efficiency and fairness together in a manner that provided the adjudicator, the Competition Tribunal, with wide latitude to make decisions that turn significantly on their personal views of the relative importance of efficiency and distribution. The risk of arbitrariness grows dramatically with the more kinds of considerations we expect antitrust to incorporate. If antitrust were called upon to balance efficiency, distributional fairness, political power, privacy etc. into the analysis of every case, the challenges to the rule of law would be overwhelming. Again, *ex ante*, clear rules could be constructed that attempt to account for these considerations (e.g., no mergers if an acquiring entity is worth more than $50 billion), but these would inevitably be arbitrary and highly contestable. And *ex post* reliance on adjudicators to trade off various considerations essentially cedes authority to the personal preferences of the adjudicators.

The concerns about uncertainty or arbitrariness follow from the addition of incommensurable factors to consider into a single policy instrument, antitrust. An alternative approach that promises greater coherence is to ask antitrust to continue to rely on economic analysis as its lodestar, while ceding authority over other considerations to other policy instruments such as tax and transfer policies, data privacy laws, and campaign financing laws, that focus directly on the fairness concerns at issue.

---

18   *See, e.g.*, discussion in Daniel Crane, *Antitrust's Unconventional Politics*, 104 Va. L. Rev. Online 118 (2018).

19   For a careful discussion of tech platforms and monopoly, *see* Ducci, *supra* note 3.

A Perspective on Privatization: Whatever Happened to the 1960s New Towns Movement?

ALBERT A. FOER[*]

American Antitrust Institute

Abstract

A half-century later, the author revisits his first law review article, which presented a conflict between public law and private law in the context of the 1960s New Town Movement. His concerns in the mid-'60s about a democracy deficit in the New Towns, where municipal government would be replaced by private contract, turned out not to have the constitutional basis he had predicted. Nor did the New Town Movement grow as he expected. Rather, a new scaled-down era in land-use planning learned from the New Towns, adopting their homeowners' association feature, to a newly coined concept of Common Interest Developments, in which government by private contract occurs in about 30% of all new residential construction. The analysis considers the emergence of a privatization movement which gained dominance in the 1980s, in the course of emphasizing the range of factors beyond economic theory that help account for any given mix of public and private.

---

[*] Founder, former president, and now senior fellow of the American Antitrust Institute. The author benefited from information and comments from a number of colleagues and experts on new towns, including Carlos Campbell, Kenneth Glazer, Miriam Gusevich, David Hensler, Julius Levine, Robert Nelson, Patty Nicoson, Uriel Reichman, and Richard Stillson. Any errors are of course his own, and the paper does not purport to speak for the American Antitrust Institute.

A Perspective on Privatization:
Whatever Happened to the 1960s New Towns Movement?

I. Introduction

Professor Eleanor Fox's professional career has largely involved analysis of competition policy, broadly conceived.[1] She and I were both skeptical of the role of economic theory and its core belief in efficiency as the single-minded focus for competition theory.[2] We both began our professional lives in the 1960s, when the attitudes toward collective activities and government itself were more favorable in the US than they are today. We lived through the turbulent times, when competition policy–which includes designing the relationship between what should be public and what should be private–moved toward a mix that gave heavier weight to the private model.[3] We were both part of that movement, but always with open skepticism about where it was headed. In this paper, in homage to Professor Fox, I will return to an early interest of mine, the New Town Movement of the 1960s, using the perspective of half a century to examine what happened to this movement in the light of the complicated, dynamic relationship between our notions of the public and the private realms.

Let me stipulate some assumptions about what we mean by "public" and "private." If one were to visualize a continuum with extremes of *public* at one end and *private* at the other, the public end would be marked by such characteristics as a very large role for large-scale collective activities, especially the state, and strong emphasis on the common interests of the society. Words like "community," "public law," and "cooperation" would often be applied. The private end of the spectrum would be marked by individualism, a desire for privacy, contracts, and strong emphasis on competition and markets. Distrust of the state and its institutions would often be implicated. But the real world is far more complicated than extreme models. As we will see in this review of the history of New Towns and land-use governance, the distinction between public and private can be elusive and ever-changing, reflecting changing cultures, ideologies, technologies, economic facts, and political realities.

In 1969 I published a law review article, "Democracy in the New Towns: The Limits of Private Government."[4] It was apparently the first analysis suggesting that the US Constitution should apply in the context of privately owned property, where property ownership rather than citizenship would determine a resident's right to vote within a homeowners' association. (Free speech was also at stake

---

1   For relevant citations to the writings of Professor Fox, *see* Albert Allen Foer, *Competition Culture and the Cultural Dimensions of Competition*, *in* BALANCING EFFICIENCY AND EQUITY 295–96 (Damien Gerard & Ioannis Lianos eds., 2019).

2   Albert Foer, *On the Inefficiencies of Efficiency as the Single-Minded Goal of Antitrust Policy*, 60 ANTITRUST BULL. 103 (2015).

3   *See, e.g.*, MARC ALLEN EISNER, ANTITRUST AND THE TRIUMPH OF ECONOMICS (1991) and REGULATORY POLITICS IN TRANSITION (1993); BINYAMIN APPELBAUM, THE ECONOMISTS' HOUR: FALSE PROPHETS, FREE MARKETS, AND THE FRACTURE OF SOCIETY (2019).

4   Albert A. Foer, *Democracy in the New Towns: The Limits of Private Government*, 36 U. CHI. L. REV. 379 (1969).

on privately owned property that functioned as if it were public, but there were some cases throwing light on that topic, while I was more or less wandering in the dark on voting rights.) In returning to this subject after some 50 years, I discovered that the impetus to build New Towns, which in the mid-1960s appeared to be an auspicious sign of the future, had morphed into a focus on what is now called in land-use circles the "Common Interest Development." The engine of this evolution would not be the liberal application of public law that I had foreseen, but rather a conservative commitment to privatization that had not yet manifested itself in the mid-'60s.

After Reston in Virginia and Columbia in Maryland, the two New Towns that were the principal subjects of my article, plus a third, Irvine in California, there would be no more New Towns, as such. Instead there would be much less ambitious planned unit developments (PUDs), condominiums, and cooperative apartments, together now known as Common Interest Developments (CIDs) because of the large portion of the development reserved for common use. With the need to manage common areas, virtually all CIDs would be subject to the rule by property contract through private homeowners' associations, similar to the New Towns, but on a smaller scale. In the America of 1964 there had been only 500 CIDs, mostly in small, wealthy suburban subdivisions. Neither condominiums nor a "privatization" campaign had a noticeable presence. By 2009, there were over 300,000 CIDs, providing homes to nearly 20% of the US population.[5]

This is the story of how a regime of private contract won out over public law in the context of a complicated, dynamic mixture of public and private features. Section II provides historic background, leading up to the 1960s, in section III, when a movement seemed underway that could transform the planning of large-scale new communities. Section IV explores the particular institutions of governance in the three principal New Towns of Reston, Columbia, and Irvine. Section V attempts to explain what happened to the movement in terms of successes and failures. Section VI tracks the evolving mix of public and private elements as the movement to smaller scale CIDs became the successor to New Towns. A final section provides concluding notes on the dynamic relationship between what is public and what is private.

II. From 1890 to the 1960s

Before we can talk about the particularities of the 1960s and the half-century that followed, it is worthwhile to skim over relevant historic developments in land-use planning, noticing the ways in which different generations of community planning dealt with the public/private mix.

---

5   EVAN MCKENZIE, BEYOND PRIVATOPIA, RETHINKING RESIDENTIAL PRIVATE GOVERNMENT, 2 (2011).

A Perspective on Privatization:
Whatever Happened to the 1960s New Towns Movement?

There is usually a good reason why cities grow in their particular locations, typically involving a linkage to the principal transportation systems of their time. Most modern cities are founded on rivers or harbors, on railroad lines, or at market junctions where people traditionally came together to buy and sell or trade agricultural and other goods. Technology is clearly an important factor. After trains and streetcars became available, new suburbs were formed along rail and streetcar routes, and later along subway lines and automobile highways, with a relatively dense downtown at the urban center. In the twentieth century cars, trucks, and airplanes expanded the flexibility of locating urban centers and facilitated the geographic expansion of cities. The cities themselves had from early times gained their critics, especially in response to the industrial revolution of the nineteenth century. As the cities–so often unhealthy, air-polluted, sprawling with slums and overcrowded industrial districts, and politically corrupt–spawned suburbs that became subject to many of the same shortcomings, the absence of careful planning became part of the critique. Wasn't there a better way for communities to grow than full reliance on the market?

The first *planned* suburban residential community in America was probably Roland Park, now part of Baltimore. This was largely the work of the Olmsted architectural brothers in the 1890s. A landmark in the search for a more radical alternative came in 1898 when an Englishman named Ebenezer Howard wrote an influential book, eventually titled *Garden Cities of To-Morrow*, that offered an alternative to either city or suburb.[6] He argued that the size and character of towns is a proper subject of conscious control. Planning could replace sprawl. His concept of an ideal town was essentially a socialist community. It was to have a green belt of rural land around it. A short definition that Howard helped write stated:

> A Garden City is a Town designed for healthy living and industry; of a size that makes possible a full measure of social life, but not larger; surrounded by a rural belt; the whole of the land being in public ownership or held in trust for the community.[7]

A number of New Towns were constructed in Great Britain based more or less on Howard's ideas. In the US, the so-called company towns and mill villages provided early experience with suburban planning, as did, in a sense, Thomas Jefferson's well-designed University of Virginia. A later noted example was J.C. Nichols' Country Club Plaza, begun in 1922 just outside the borders of Kansas City. But these did not amount to Garden Cities or to what would later be called New Towns.

---

6 EBENEZER HOWARD, GARDEN CITIES OF TO-MORROW (1898) (1965 edition).

7 *Id.*, quoted in preface by F.J. Osborn at 26. *See* S. GIEDION, SPACE, TIME AND ARCHITECTURE, 782 (5th ed. 1967): ("The sense of [Howard's] plan was that the community should control the ground, and that all profits through increases in the value of the land should be returned to the community in order to discourage speculation of any sort.")

An important American Howardian was Clarence Stein, who designed Radburn, New Jersey. This opened in 1929, just as the stock market was crashing, and the construction was consequently left incomplete. However, the Radburn Idea gained a life of its own. Going beyond Howard's Garden City, it demonstrated several influential design elements: the superblock in place of the characteristic narrow, rectangular grid block, making it possible for houses to be turned around so that living and sleeping quarters faced toward gardens and parks; instead of streets, specialized roads planned and built for one use rather than for all uses; complete separation of pedestrian and automobile; and parks as the backbone of the neighborhood.[8] Radburn, like Roland Park or Country Club Plaza, but unlike Howard's Garden City or the government-sponsored New Towns that followed in England,[9] was thoroughly private in conception and execution.

During the Great Depression, the Roosevelt administration, led by Rexford Guy Tugwell,[10] built several "greenbelt towns," including Greenbelt, Maryland, which was to serve as a home for modestly paid government employees who would commute to downtown Washington, and also, explicitly, as a model for planned development and cooperative living. Greenbelt largely followed the Radburn Idea and it is still there today, hard by the Capital Beltway, a living community. Greenbelt was originally built and owned by the federal government, and all the town's businesses were owned cooperatively by the residents. When the government sold the town in 1952, the residents formed a cooperative to buy the houses. Now many of the businesses are privately owned.

The British New Towns Act of 1946 was a landmark in urban planning. Until then, there were local regulations relating to building and planning, but

> the key characteristics of the city emerged from decisions of the private developers, the policies and practices of private landlords, of private builders, industrialists, traders, and property owners guided largely by markets, prices, and profits ... The new legislation relied on a different set of premises. Local and national policy was to decide the essential character of the community in advance. Private decisions were to be made within the framework of an overall plan which embodied these social goals. The position, in short, was to be reversed.[11]

---

8 C.S. STEIN, TOWARD NEW TOWNS FOR AMERICA 43–4 (1957).

9 *See* LLOYD RODWIN, THE BRITISH NEW TOWNS POLICY (1956). ("New towns have been built and old ones renewed since the earliest times. But a national policy of building within a few years complete communities to serve new needs and to help recast our urban environment is something unique in urban history. Only in 1946 in Britain did this first become official government policy... [The post-war socialist Labour government created the framework for planning to] "attack in one stroke a whole group of problems, including reconstruction, housing, and dispersal.")

10 On Tugwell and the Greenbelt experiments, *see* OTIS L. GRAHAM, JR., TOWARD A PLANNED SOCIETY: FROM ROOSEVELT TO NIXON (1976).

11 Rodwin, *supra* note 9, at 39.

A Perspective on Privatization:
Whatever Happened to the 1960s New Towns Movement?

By the end of World War II, the American experience already included a variety of planned suburban communities, either for the wealthy or the middle class, varying in the different ways in which they combined public and private aspects. Some, like Country Club Plaza or company towns, were almost entirely private in ownership and operation; others like Radburn, had privately run common-interest functions; Greenbelt was federally owned and organized along principles of cooperatives. The British experiment pointed the way to a larger role for government.

What I am capitalizing as the New Town Movement of the 1960s learned from these precedents. It learned, for example, to protect greenery, to separate vehicles from pedestrians, to use superblocks, to maximize the potential for walking and bicycling to daily destinations, to protect the environment more generally, and to emphasize a sense of community. But first, we had to get through the 1940s and 1950s. During those years, the suburban fringe of cities grew rapidly, with the return to a post-Depression peacetime economy, mass production of housing construction, and federal subsidies of home mortgages and highways.[12] Post-war legislation helped veterans prepare for jobs through education. As new transportation allowed cities to spread into metropolitan areas, the way was opened up for working- and middle-class Americans to relocate to better housing than they could afford within the city, providing a physically healthier but often less socially and economically diverse environment.

As we entered the 1960s, the suburbs were still largely unplanned, often put together by small-scale developers who purchased farmland on the fringe of an urban center and convinced a local government to build out, subsidize, or maintain some infrastructure, such as streets, utility connections, and new public schools to support the intended residents. Typically, the individual developments congealed into suburbs that were bedroom communities for commuters with jobs in the central cities. Government services were through the city, the county, or by municipal incorporation. Suburban residents generally tended to be homogeneous in sociological and economic terms, most particularly when it came to race. An unfortunate side-effect of new civil rights legislation was that it often led to white flight, encouraged by the real estate industry and federal housing policies. In the absence of large-scale community planning, suburban developments tended to be formatted into rectangular blocks, with similar houses at standardized distances apart. Pete Seeger sang sarcastically of subdivision houses as little boxes: "they were all made out of ticky-tacky and they all looked just the same."[13]

12　NICHOLAS DAGEN BLOOM, SUBURBAN ALCHEMY: 1960S NEW TOWNS AND THE TRANSFORMATION OF THE AMERICAN DREAM 9 (2002).

13　"Little Boxes" is a song written and composed by Malvina Reynolds in 1962. It became a hit for her friend Pete Seeger in 1963.

III. The 1960s New Town Movement

The 1960s was a time characterized by big ideas, idealism, and visionary plans, both by private entrepreneurs and by governments. There then prevailed a sense that both private and public forces could work jointly to promote the common good. The concept of a public interest was not sneered at then; the libertarian "public choice" philosophy had not yet taken hold.[14] The word "privatization" would not be "proposed as a deliberate public policy to improve government performance" until 1969.[15] The civil rights movement was in full swing, preparing to overcome long-standing conservative opposition. A youthful President John F. Kennedy was asking what you can do for your country rather than what your country can do for you, challenging America to go to the moon in short order via a major new government initiative. Bob Dylan's "Blowin' in the Wind" was released in 1963: A thirst for change was in the air. After the assassinations of Kennedy and Martin Luther King, President Lyndon Johnson's war on poverty and unprecedented federal legislation using large-scale government programs to build a "Great Society" implemented the spirit of expansive public interests.

Two entrepreneurs of this period with large visionary ideas were Robert E. Simon and James Rouse. Each was planning to build a totally new city from scratch, within a one-hour car ride from the US Capitol. Reston, Virginia, would be located near the just-born Dulles International Airport. Columbia, Maryland, would be near the expanding Friendship Airport, soon to be the Baltimore/Washington International Airport,[16] on the highway from Washington to Baltimore. Some 47 other large-scale new communities were in various stages of planning.[17] New Towns seemed to be part of what's blowin' in the wind, which we will see involved complex and changing attitudes toward what should be public and what should be private.

The planning and execution of a new community intended to become as large as Reston (70,000 residents) or Columbia (110,000) requires, in addition to vision, large amounts of patient money, willing and able to endure the decades-long unfolding of a master plan from conceptualization to completion. In an economy susceptible to cycles, there will be good years and bad. The rise in value of the

---

14 Public choice, also known as rational choice theory, champions the application of the conventional methodology of economics to political science subjects. *See, e.g.,* JERRY L. MASHAW, GREED, CHAOS & GOVERNANCE, USING PUBLIC CHOICE TO IMPROVE PUBLIC LAW (1997); THE CAUSES AND CONSEQUENCES OF ANTITRUST, THE PUBLIC-CHOICE PERSPECTIVE (Fred S. McChesney & William F. Shughart II eds., 1995).

15 E.S. SAVAS, PRIVATIZATION, THE KEY TO BETTER GOVERNMENT 291 (1990), *citing* PETER F. DRUCKER, THE AGE OF DISCONTINUITY (1969).

16 Now named after the late Supreme Court Justice Thurgood Marshall.

17 Foer, *supra* note 4, *citing* the ADVISORY COMMISSION ON INTERGOVERNMENTAL RELATIONS, URBAN AND RURAL AMERICA: POLICIES FOR FUTURE GROWTH 77–8 (1968). For descriptions in the 1970s of life in Reston, Columbia, Irvine, and four other communities in the US (Soul City, North Carolina; Park Forest South, Illinois; Jonathan, Minnesota; and Cedar-Riverside, Minnesota), *see* CARLOS C. CAMPBELL, NEW TOWNS, ANOTHER WAY TO LIVE (1976).

land may depend not only on the general economy, but on changes in consumer demand or political realities. Less obviously, they require a reasonably stable public attitude toward concepts of what should be public and what should be private, whether more dependence should be on collective activity or on rivalrous activity by self-interested units.

The idea of the New Town that evolved in the 1960s held that the final product should be a complete community, able to flourish independently of an existing central city. It must be balanced, self-contained, and include not only jobs but culture and recreation. Not least, the New Town was to be racially integrated. William H. Whyte, not exactly a fan of the New Town idea, nevertheless called it "the last best chance of the metropolis."[18]

1. The entrepreneurs: Robert Simon and James Rouse

Robert E. Simon's father, Robert E. Simon, Sr., ran a real estate business whose assets included New York City's Carnegie Hall and an interest in Radburn, the New Jersey garden city. Robert, Jr., ran the family business after his father's death in 1935. In 1961 he was able to purchase a major piece of property, nearly 7,000 acres, in a rapidly growing part of Fairfax County, Virginia. The initial acquisition was financed by sale of his family's ownership of Carnegie Hall. Simon was a man of the arts, and he envisioned a great step-up from the Radburn model, naming his project Reston, thereby memorializing the initials of both father and son. He initially hired a group of consultants who helped select the mix of educational, cultural, residential, and industrial facilities that would define Reston, but his primary interest seemed to be in the architectural attractiveness of the New Town. If you asked Bob Simon what it was about planning a New Town that excited him the most, I imagine that he would have answered, "the modernistic appearance of a well-planned, diverse city."

One can compare this to the background of James Rouse, whose chosen location for Columbia would be in a slow-growth rural county. Jim Rouse came from a small town on the eastern shore of Maryland. He trained as a lawyer, and was successful first in mortgage banking and then in the pioneering development of regional enclosed shopping malls. Putting land deals together was second nature by the time he envisioned Columbia. Unlike Fairfax County, Maryland's Howard County had no sufficiently large parcel of land available, so Rouse had to aggregate a large number of small separate properties, something he would do secretly through agents so as not to raise the price of the land. The result was a bit of a Swiss cheese, approximately 30,000 acres in all, with privately owned parcels outside of his control dotting what became the Columbia landscape.

---

18   WILLIAM H. WHYTE, THE LAST LANDSCAPE 253 (1970).

Rouse, like Simon, was more than a real estate maven. As he gained experience in the field of land use, he became a civic activist, committed to urban renewal and racial integration. If one asked Jim Rouse what turned him on about developing a New Town, his answer would likely have been, "creating a successful, diverse modern American community." To a larger extent than Simon, Rouse would rely on the brainstorming of a group of noted experts from a wide range of specialties, whom he directed to consider the whole of social organization. The topic of education, for example, was carefully and creatively examined and made a basis for much of the planning.

Both men were experienced in business and in real estate development; both intended their New Town project to be profitable in the long run but while neither had any known animosity toward capitalism, profit was less the motivator than a necessary component for creating a model for community life. Reston and Columbia would diverge as they reflected the different geopolitical and philosophical starting points and fulfilled their founders' separate but closely related visions.

2. Reston, Virginia

The plan for Reston was approved by the Fairfax County Board of Supervisors in 1962, for seven villages of 10,000–12,000 residents each. The goal was to have a mix of residences in which approximately 70% would be townhouses, 15% single-family homes, and 15% apartments.[19] Although a Reston town center was planned, in fact it would not open until the 1990s, a generation later, with what is today a popular mix of stores, entertainment, and offices. It has been described as a picturesque downtown in a grid surrounded by parking lots hidden from the interior of the complex.[20]

The public's initial view of Reston was at its first village, Lake Anne, which opened in 1965. Architecturally, it was highly praised. Situated in a U-shape around the narrow end of an oblong artificial lake, the village center contained a tall, modernistic apartment building at one end of the village center and two- or three-storied buildings around the rest, with shopping on the first level and residences above. Parking was behind the buildings. Townhouses and single-family homes were located further away, linked to the village center by pathways for pedestrians and bicycles. The look was fresh, sleekly innovative at the time and even today. Multitudes of visitors saw Lake Anne, and more than a few chose to move there.

Unfortunately, they didn't move there in the anticipated numbers soon enough. What went wrong? First, Reston was relatively difficult to access. Although the

---

19 One might note that what were not so long ago called "rowhouses" would henceforth be "townhouses."

20 Bloom, *supra* note 12, at 29.

A Perspective on Privatization:
Whatever Happened to the 1960s New Towns Movement?

federal highway to Dulles goes through Reston, the federal planners would not allow it to be used by anyone not going to the airport. No entry or exit for Reston! No timely cooperation from government, so commuting to work from Reston would be unappealing, and the planned local jobs were still years in the future. Second, because of its infant status, the physical and ideological appeal of Reston, including its policy of racial integration in what was then still a very southern state, was only to a limited number of people. Not everyone wants to live in a start-up town in the middle of nowhere, and not everyone whose eye is attracted by exciting architecture wants to actually live in it. The slow start was bad news for Robert Simon personally, and nearly killed Reston in the cradle.

The main financial backer of the project at the outset was Gulf Oil Company. The economic game plan for a New Town is for the developer to buy up a large area of relatively inexpensive (often agricultural) land; to develop or otherwise arrange for infrastructure (streets, water, sewers, schools, shops, and other amenities) for housing, commerce, and industry–and eventually to generate a whole city, whose promise and eventual fulfillment will dramatically increase the value of the land; to finance this development through debt; and to pay off the interest, curtail the debt, and meet other obligations through cashflow generated by selling off parcels with the improved infrastructure or even unimproved parcels made more valuable by what has been accomplished and by the promised future.

The money behind this must be very patient, but even with patience there are loan covenants to meet. Simon could not meet them, and in 1967 Gulf Oil pushed out Simon and put its own man in charge. Gulf explained that it would maintain the master plan but would "pay more attention to the market," primarily through more conservative architecture. In 1978 Gulf sold the project to Reston Land Corp., a subsidiary of Mobil Oil. The project eventually began to turn a profit–in the 1980s.

As best I can tell, the master plan was largely followed, although some of the details have been modified from time to time, sometimes in noticeable ways. Several of the newer villages have a different layout or more conservative look from the earlier ones, and the architecture became more suburban mundane than modernistic. The village centers tend to be less like Lake Anne and more like strip malls found in any other suburb. Village governance is by cluster associations that just control the individual groupings of townhouses or apartment houses, and single-family detached houses have no groupings and are simply part of the central Reston Homeowners' Association. This lack of decentralized governance is said to be one of Bob Simon's biggest disappointments.[21]

Despite these factors, there seems to be a current consensus that Reston is a success. There are now more than 60,000 residents and there are approximately

---

21 Interview with Richard Stillson, Reston "pioneer" resident (Aug. 7, 2019), and email to author (Aug. 22, 2019). Homeowner associations are discussed in the text, section IV(2).

60,000 jobs within Reston. This balance, which sounds like what was intended, has implications for evaluating whether Reston has reduced urban sprawl, one of the standard goals of New Town designers. Since only a portion of residents are of working age and there are roughly equal numbers of residents and employees in Reston, this alone implies that many outsiders are commuting into Reston to work–primarily in its many office buildings. The propinquity of what is now a major international airport probably has an influence on the types of businesses that locate in and nearby Reston. There is now a high-speed toll road parallel to the Dulles access highway, with exits in Reston. Of perhaps great significance, a recently opened Metro station has brought new demand for housing and offices both within Reston and nearby. With ingress and egress no longer a problem, it is also clear that many residents are commuting outward to work. It seems clear that Reston has not solved the problem of the automobile or of urban sprawl.

The very success of Reston casts some doubt on Ebenezer Howard's conviction that the size of a city can be controlled by a master plan. A recent article in *Washingtonian* magazine reports on growing competition between residents who share the original plan's suburban character, many of whom are aging "pioneers" who were originally attracted by Simon's vision, and other residents (as well as county planners) who see the need for a more urban-type expansion, claiming that there is too much traffic, that Reston is already too crowded, that escalated housing prices are squeezing out middle-class residents, and that more housing is needed to reduce prices and accommodate the demand brought on by the new Metro service.[22] According to a long-time resident and Reston activist, the coming of the Metro has:

> ... fundamentally changed Reston ... [It] has created two Restons: an older, primarily homeowner, suburban area with residents very invested in maintaining the kind of community described in Simon's master plan; and a newer, younger, primarily rental, urban area with residents attracted to Reston primarily because of the Metro and having no commitment to, or even interest in, the original ideals. The older suburban area has several rental units but they tend to be low cost housing and to a great extent African American, Latino, and low-income Asians; the newer urban areas with high rise apartments is predominantly high-income whites and Asians. Although Simon's plan envisaged the town center, I don't think he foresaw or would approve of the bifurcation of the society that is in large part caused by the Metro.[23]

Although economic and racial diversity are substantial in Reston, there is obvious concern that many things have changed both in and around the New Town.

---

22 Benjamin Wofford, *What's Eating Reston?* WASHINGTONIAN, Dec. 2019 at 50 *et seq.*

23 Email from a Reston resident, to the author (Feb. 16, 2020) (on file with author).

The *Washingtonian* reports that since 2000 the number of children in Reston has fallen by nearly 10%, and Reston is now 17% whiter than Fairfax County, whereas in 1980 it was more racially diverse than Fairfax County. Since 2010, the number of household incomes of $200,000 or greater jumped by 59%, and the median home sales price rose about 25%. The mature city is whiter and wealthier than Simon envisioned.[24]

While the basic plan has been executed with much success, the enlarged role for market values, with all of its dynamism but comparatively less commitment to the values that Simon hoped would characterize the community, shaped the result in important ways.

3. Columbia, Maryland

Jim Rouse's biographer notes that Rouse was subject to three primary influences: devotion to the goals, though not necessarily the strategies, of urban renewal; the social gospel of his Christian religion; and the moral strength of his wife.[25] Rouse set out to build a city of 110,000 with four principal stated goals: (1) to respect the land; (2) to create a place to encourage human growth; (3) to create a whole city; and (4) to make a profit.[26] This was to occur through a setting of a city center and 12 villages of 10,000–15,000 people each. Each village was intended to support a middle school, a high school, a supermarket, and recreational facilities. The villages would be broken down into neighborhoods, each supporting an elementary school. Education was central to Rouse's vision for community life. Each village was given distinctive features that were intended to draw visitors from Columbia's other villages, an idea intended to encourage cross-village communication.

Along with education, racial integration was a high priority for Columbia. Today, schools in Columbia are only 18–30% white, with high concentrations of African Americans and a growing number of Latinos. The public education system does not seem to be having outstanding results, and there are ongoing controversies involving such race-central issues as school busing within Howard County and its dominant population base, Columbia. There is much adult education now in Howard County, contributed importantly by Columbia, but higher education beyond community college level has not been achieved.

A tolerant positive view of religion was at the core of Jim Rouse's motivation; interfaith centers were a well-publicized early part of the vision. In 10 villages today, however, there are but four true interfaith centers, i.e., where two or more religions share the same facilities. Of those who worship at all, 44% worship in

---

24 Wofford, *supra* note 22.

25 JOSHUA OLSEN, BETTER PLACES BETTER LIVES: A BIOGRAPHY OF JAMES ROUSE, 141 (2003). The last part of Jim Rouse's life was not always happy. Late in life, the Rouses divorced.

26 *Id.*, 155.

an interfaith center.[27] It is hard to say whether Rouse would consider these proportions a measure of success.

Mass transit within Columbia hobbled along from the start. In 1966 Howard County took over the bus routes, which could not be sustained by the homeowners' association.[28]

Although Rouse hired the young, then-unknown, Frank Gehry for some early architectural work,[29] Rouse himself did not particularly focus on architectural style, although he gave much attention to the town center, which would eventually have the region's impressive Columbia Mall at its heart. This allowed him to control the surrounding land use and gain much of the corresponding increase in its value. He sold off land parcels for single-family homes and for industry and office structures to a variety of builders, thereby not having to fund the construction or worry about most of the architecture. This also promoted diversity in architectural approaches. Rouse would develop the downtown buildings, village centers, and other projects like apartments and townhouses that could provide cash flow. While most of the construction has been described as "mundane,"[30] one smallish innovation Rouse insisted on was clustered sets of mailboxes.

A significant number of pioneers were attracted by Rouse's vision. He enforced the objectives of color-blind housing and much economic diversity, although the extreme upper and lower rungs of the socioeconomic ladder remained largely outside of the plan.[31]

The primary source of capital for Columbia was the Connecticut General Life Insurance Company, a long-time pre-Columbian supporter of Rouse. From 1962, when Rouse began secretly acquiring land, to 2017, there were six major recessions.[32] The recession in the 1970s, caused by the Arab oil boycott, high unemployment, and high interest rates, hit the real estate industry and Rouse hard.

By 1974, Columbia had lost its race between increased value and increased indebtedness.[33] Connecticut General decided that its best alternative as the lender was to move ahead with the development. In 1975, however, seven years

---

27 Len Lazarick, Columbia at 50, at 117–18 (2017).

28 *Id.*, 134.

29 Gehry was responsible for the exhibit building, a fire station, and the music pavilion, later called the Merriweather Post Pavilion.

30 Olsen, *supra* note 25, at 200.

31 *Id.*

32 1970, 1973–75, 1980–82, 1990–91, 2001, 2008–2009, according to Kimberly Amadeo, *History of Recessions in the United States*, thebalance.com (updated June 11, 2021).

33 Olsen, *supra* note 25, at 234 *et seq.*

after Reston's turn toward a more conservative direction, the insurance company removed Jim Rouse from the chairmanship and put its own people in charge. There were 40,000 residents at the time, and the ensuing refinancing reduced the projected population to 100,000. In 1985, Connecticut General (then owned by CIGNA) sold its interest to the Rouse Company, which was no longer controlled by Jim Rouse, who had stepped down as CEO in 1979, severing all his ties to the company in 1984. Since 1985, the Rouse Company has reaped a steady profit from selling land and building new structures in a mature town. In 2004, Columbia was sold to the General Growth Properties for $12.5 billion.[34] The project is proceeding to completion under the same basic plan and guidance.[35]

Jim Rouse was eventually out of the company he founded, and went on to create other organizations devoted to festival malls and low-income housing. Jim Rouse and Bob Simon aged and died as revered residents of the communities they had created.

4. A contrasting New Town: Irvine, California

A third important New Town of the same period was in Irvine, California, owned by the Irvine Company that had long controlled a vast ranch in Orange County, in the vicinity of the small John Wayne Airport, which itself has grown steadily since 1939. Irvine had a population 212,000 in 2010.

Although I have not personally visited Irvine, it provides a contrast to Reston and Columbia in terms of the relationship between public and private. Although initiated by a family-owned land company, Irvine was constructed on a giant ranch with a nucleus of a new campus for the state-owned University of California. It immediately incorporated, unlike Reston and Columbia, and has a council/manager form of government. It is planned, but less thoroughly planned than the two New Towns I have been describing. The city is divided into villages. Much green space has been preserved, despite the enormous growth of Irvine, originally planned as a college town of 100,000, but raised in 1974 to a target of 400,000. From the beginning, Irvine was not particularly committed to racial or economic integration, but would be a relatively homogeneous well-designed suburban city with options for play, work, and study.[36] Like Reston and Columbia, Irvine is consistently selected as one of the best or most livable cities in the US. Bloom wrote in 2002 that Irvine increased rather than controlled sprawl and is a new employment center for the region rather than a balanced community.

---

34   Lazarick, *supra* note 27, at 9.
35   Olsen, *supra* note 25, at 237.
36   Bloom, *supra* note 12, at 53–65.

5. The minimal role of public governments

These three New Towns of the 1960s were the largest, best publicized, and most successful of the new community experiments that were being developed in the US at the time. Each needed the zoning approval for its plans by state or county governments, but with the exception of Irvine's agreement to work with the University of California to develop Irvine around a new branch of the university, the role of state government was minimal. Unlike the Greenbelt experiment during the New Deal, the federal government played virtually no role. There were no subsidies, grants or special tax advantages to assist these New Town developers. There was no ideology of socialism or cooperative ownership involved. On the other hand, these massive projects were built around central planning by a charismatic private entrepreneur or family-owned land company, whose influence rested on the ability to sell a large-scale vision and gain access to private rather than public funding. The intention of making a profit was necessarily present, but the time horizon was long and the profit was to derive from the benefits being offered to the public as a growing community was built and served.

Although the federal government was not much involved with Reston, Columbia, or Irvine, it liked what it saw–at first. It appreciated the benefits of decentralized new small cities as one rational strategy for a growing economy and it concluded that long-term funding was the largest problem for moving forward with more New Towns. The approach of the US therefore became–all too briefly–to guarantee funding to developers with New Town–type plans, the guarantees conditioned on the inclusion of housing for low-and middle-income residents. Such a program began in 1965 and expanded in 1968 and 1970.[37] Ultimately, the program–known as Title VII–spawned plans for 14 communities in the 1970s. But of the 14, only The Woodlands in Texas escaped bankruptcy.[38] The Title VII projects ran into administrative problems under the Nixon presidency and financial difficulties during the recessionary period of late 1974 and early 1975, about the same time that Jim Rouse was losing control over Columbia. In January 1975, the Secretary of the Department of Housing and Urban Development under President Ford announced that no additional applications for New Town guarantees would be accepted.[39] Olsen concluded in his fascinating 2003 biography of Jim Rouse, "The seeds from the Columbian plant bore no fruit in the form of additional new towns."[40]

---

37 The key provisions were in Title IV of the Housing and Urban Development Act of 1968 and Title VII of the HUD Act of 1970. *See* Campbell, *supra* note 17, at 243–53.

38 The Woodlands, located 28 miles from Houston, was conceived after the oil industry investor George P. Mitchell attended a symposium by the Rouse Company, and adopted many of the planning concepts and design consultants employed by Reston, Columbia, and Irvine. The Woodlands received a federal guarantee of $50 million in 1972, and was projected to have 500,000 residents in 20 years. Campbell, *supra* note 17, at 245. In 2018 its population was estimated at over 115,000, according to www.Wikipedia.com: The Woodlands, Texas.

39 Campbell, *supra* note 17, at 252.

40 Olsen, *supra* note 25, at 228.

IV. Governance in the New Towns

In this section I will explore the particular institutions of governance in Reston and Columbia, a topic I first considered in the previously mentioned article in 1969.[41] In the intervening years, while there were no new New Towns of consequence, the private institutions of governance have become prevalent in the residential communities where one out of every five Americans lives.[42] One might have predicted that the New Towns would be governed like any municipality, incorporated or chartered by the state or county, and therefore democratically responsive to the local citizens residing there. Something like this did happen in Irvine, but initial conditions were different for Simon and Rouse.[43]

1. Context: New Town meets the local power structure

While the solution for Irvine was incorporation as a city, it should be understood that the huge Irvine Ranch was a long-time political powerhouse within California's Orange County.[44] Rouse and Simon, on the other hand were newcomers to their counties without political clout, and their property holdings were magnitudes smaller in acreage than that of the Irvine Land Company.

The first political problem facing Reston and Columbia at the outset was place-specific. Both Virginia and Maryland had strong county governments and traditions of relatively few incorporated municipalities. Fairfax County was already urbanized and pro-growth when Simon came in as sole owner of 7,000 acres. He believed the county could and would provide satisfactory zoning and services, and in fact this was to be the case.

Howard County, on the other hand, was rural and under the political leadership of a no-growth coalition. Rouse initially entered as the secret purchaser of small tracts of land from 140 separate owners, totaling 14,000 acres, an anxiety-producing 9% of Howard County, with its then-population under 40,000.

---

41 Foer, *supra* note 4.

42 McKenzie, *supra* note 5, at 2.

43 Bloom reports that the Irvine Company and those already living on ranchland there supported incorporation as a city under California law. "Incorporation," Bloom wrote, "carried its own risk, notably citizen revolt against the plan, but the company chose to risk negotiation with the residents who had chosen to live in a planned environment. In addition, [Raymond] Watson [the architect most responsible for the planning of Irvine] genuinely believed in the value of local democracy." Bloom, *supra* note 12, at 60.

44 To say a little more about Irvine, California: James Irvine acquired control of 110,000 acres in 1878. His son, James II, incorporated it into the Irvine Company and after 1947 the grandson, Myford, began making parcels of the land available for urban development. He died in 1959, the same year the University of California purchased (for $1) its first 1,000 acres for a new university site on the ranchland. The first phases of building under the master plan of 83,000 acres (130 square miles) were completed by 1970 under the prominent architecture and city planning firm, William L. Pereira & Associates. On December 23, 1971, the residents voted to incorporate the city of Irvine, representing about 18,000 acres and some 20,000 people. In June 1974, the city had expanded to approximately 26,000 acres and over 29,000 people. By 1999 there was a population of 134,000 within a total area of 43 square miles. The city contains numerous villages, and many of these have homes associations of varying but relatively minor functions. *See* Campbell, *supra* note 17, at 180–81; www.Wikipedia.com: Irvine California.

The county had to be convinced by Rouse that the convergent growth of Washington and Baltimore toward each other made the growth of Howard County inevitable, and that controlled, planned growth was more desirable than uncontrolled sprawl. He succeeded in this, but had to assume that the county could not be counted on for the infrastructure needed to make a new city of 110,000 grow rapidly. Established politicians worried about how the residents of a self-governing city of this size would affect their own power. Moreover, incorporation was arguably not a feasible option for Columbia at the outset because it didn't meet the state's contiguity requirement; as noted, Columbia was a Swiss cheese of private parcels not acquired by Rouse.

2. The planner's democratic dilemma

For small-scale land developers, it is typically necessary to borrow for up-front developmental costs, and then to repay the lender as the houses are constructed and sold. The time frame is relatively short. For the large-scale community developer, both the magnitude of the loan and the duration of the project create a more complicated problem. The developer of a New Town can expect the project to take 30 years or more to complete, which means surviving through multiple economic cycles that can have a dramatic effect on cash flow. This requires a lot of patient money, as the federal government eventually recognized, but with insufficient patience.

Less obviously, it also means that the developer needs to maintain enough control over the land it sells to ensure that the residents don't overturn the plan before it is well-established. The reputation of the developer is at stake for building according to the plan–especially in its earliest years–and the plan itself is at stake if the lender or the public loses confidence. At the same time, the early residents ("pioneers") can be expected to be drawn to the plan and be committed to its fulfillment, but later residents are more likely to be drawn by what they see on the ground than by the developer's long-term vision. In other words, the demands of the customers can be expected to change during the course of the community's development. It would seem very likely, if not inevitable, that residents will eventually demand to have a direct say in the governance of their community. Thus, a new sort of planning dilemma: how can the New Town developer maintain adherence to the vision and the confidence of both the lender and the residents over an extended period, while also providing democratic governance to the increasing population of the New Town?

An answer was found by Simon and Rouse in modifications to the concept of the "homes association." The idea of the homes (or homeowners') association was already more than a century old and had been applied in Radburn, but it had been used frequently only since the advent of the suburban subdivision. A homeowners' association is an incorporated non-profit organization that can be created by an owner of property who intends to subdivide it, simply by recording a land agreement to the effect that anyone who comes into subsequent ownership of the property, or a part of it, automatically is subject to a "subservience" requiring membership in the homeowners' association. In effect, anyone who in the future would acquire such property would be required as part of the purchase contract to agree to be a fee-paying member of the association that will not only govern the common areas of land but whatever other aspects of private and communal life were included in the covenants or were delegated to the elected directors of the association.

This had usually worked well for small developments for the wealthy, who wanted to protect their property values by having all their neighbors bound by the same rules, perhaps including a minimum size for lots (to keep out the riff-raff), or restricting neighbors of a certain race or religion (typically African Americans and Jews). The requirements might also appeal to those who wanted such functions as street cleaning, lighting, and security under their own, rather than a possibly corrupt, incompetent, or politically unfriendly government's control. In effect, such residents would sometimes be doubly taxed for the same services, i.e. those provided by the homeowners' association and those available (but not used) from the county or city.

As described by political scientist Evan McKenzie in *Privatopia*, his essential critique of homeowners' associations and the rise of residential private government: "Until 1948, homeowners' associations, voluntary and mandatory, were the primary mechanisms developers used to enforce race restrictive covenants. After 1948, when those covenants became unenforceable in court, real estate interests invented variations on the theme of using private, contractual mechanisms to enforce segregation."[45]

Simon and Rouse would feed steroids to the old concept of a homeowners' association, at the same time ironically using it to promote both economic and racial diversity rather than exclusion. They had only one truly useful model to draw on: Radburn, New Jersey. The Radburn Association of homeowners was planned "to fix, collect, and disburse the annual charges, to maintain the necessary community services, parks and recreation facilities, and to interpret and apply the protective restrictions."[46] Radburn's designer Clarence Stein himself punctuated his description of this homeowners' association with an exclamation point: "In short, the Radburn Association was to have the power and functions of a municipal government, including taxation. An American government without public representation!"[47] The homes association was justified as serving the interests of both the developer and the residents, by protecting property values well into the future.

---

45   Evan McKenzie, Privatopia, Homeowner Associations and the Rise of Residential Private Government, 75 (1994). The 1948 case referred to in the extract is Shelley v. Kraemer, 334 U.S. 1 (1948).

46   Stein, *supra* note 8, at 61.

47   *Id.*

3. Drilling down: The governance of Reston and Columbia

Both Reston and Columbia are unincorporated subdivisions, and both would depend, though to different degrees, upon county government for zoning approval and at least some public services. Both were organized into a dual system of homeowners' associations, with a central association performing significant municipal-type functions, as I will discuss, and with the peripheral associations resembling the more traditional homeowners' associations of small subdivisions.

In Reston, the central association was originally called the Reston Home Owners Association, but is now called the Reston Association or RA. The central association is run by a nine-person board, which appoints officers, including a president who runs the RA. The board was to be elected by the developer and property owners. Notably, this originally excluded lessees (criticized in my 1969 article) but was changed a number of years ago to include renters. By a process of weighted voting, the developer was expected to retain a minimum of one-third of the votes until 1985 and, according to plan, would eventually wither away so that the residents would have control. Basically, the RA could provide any services of a typical municipality that would not otherwise be provided by the county. In practice, its purview has been limited to the property it owns, i.e., the common areas, lakes, pathways, and recreational facilities. The RA can assess dues and pass on outdoor architectural aspects of new and renewed buildings. In fact, the county government provides schools, police, and judicial powers, so one might question my article's projection, based on the planning documents, that it could be deemed a de facto municipal government, although it certainly had that potential in theory.

Each Reston village consists of several small clusters of a hundred or so homes organized as cluster associations. The cluster associations function to maintain the village's local parks, pathways, parking areas, and driveways associated with the cluster. They have a taxing power for these purposes, and are managed by a five-person board, but the village has no important political role in Reston.

Comparable to Reston's RA, the central organization in Columbia is the Columbia Association (CA). Its members are the directors who are nominated by a unit called the Columbia Council, whose members are elected for the sole purpose of nominating directors. Each property owner or tenant is automatically a member of a village-level community association and one of his (or her) rights is to vote for a village representative to the Columbia Council. The controlling principle is "one unit–one vote" rather than "ownership of one unit–one vote" and the mode of election is indirect.

As in Reston, jointly held property yields but one unanimous vote. Rouse anticipated that Howard County would provide police and fire departments, water, sewers, schools, snow removal, zoning, and other services, while the CA would provide all municipal services not offered by the county. The CA was empowered to undertake the financing, construction, maintenance, and operation of roads, walkways, parks, libraries, community service facilities, mass transportation, and energy distribution systems.

The peripheral units of organization in Columbia (as opposed to the CA) are called community associations and they serve entire villages rather than small clusters of homes. They carry on more activities than the Reston cluster associations.[48] Unlike the Reston peripheral association, which reflects the architects' grouping of houses, the Columbia village association caters to 10 thousand or more residents and is an integral part of Rouse's effort to return human scale to community life such as he experienced growing up in small-town Maryland.

My 1969 article had criticized both Reston and Columbia as having a democracy deficit. Based on the planning documents, the right to vote in the homes associations being planned would be limited to property owners and (in the case of Columbia but not originally in Reston) tenants, even after the developmental period in which the homes associations gave controlling weight to the developers. I accepted the validity of maintaining developer control in the early years, but questioned how long that period should last. I was more concerned that those residents who do not own property would become a permanent vote-less class, unless, as in Columbia, renters are specifically allowed to vote. Even then, notably excluded in both New Towns are spouses who are not recorded as joint owners, young adults living with their parents, and older people sharing their children's homes. The unanimous consent rule for jointly owned property, co-owners, or co-tenants who cannot agree on how to vote also effectively disenfranchised some residents. In Reston, owners of more than one property may cast more than one vote, thereby diluting the weight of other individuals' single votes. Would the US Constitution allow these deviations from the principle of "one person, one vote"? It is at this point that we have to examine the role of public law in a private setting as we move from the Kennedy era to the present, and confront the question of what is public and what is private.

4. Constitutional considerations a half-century ago

The first prong of the constitutional argument I offered in 1969 was that if a municipal government (instead of a homeowners' association) had voting qualifications like those in Reston and Columbia, it would be subject to two lines of attack. First, property interests as a prerequisite for voting may violate the equal protection clause. In support I cited several then-recent lower court cases and *Harper v. West Virginia Board of Elections*,[49] a 1966 Supreme Court

---

48   Although a municipality, Irvine also used homes associations primarily for architectural controls. Campbell wrote: "The Community Association of Irvine functions more like the cluster associations in Reston than like the Columbia Association." *Supra* note 17, at 190.

49   Harper v. West Virginia Board of Elections, 383 U.S. 663 (1966), holding that a poll tax was invalid because of its inconsistency with the equal protection clause.

poll tax case resting on a Supreme Court reapportionment decision three years earlier.[50] The opinion in *Harper* said, "neither homesite nor occupation affords a permissible basis for distinguishing between qualified voters within the State … We think the same must be true of requirements of wealth or affluence or payment of a fee." Close, but admittedly not precisely on point.

Secondly, I cited several lower court cases that seemed to argue that a legislature could decide that for a governmental unit that has specific rather than general governing responsibilities (such as a water district), the proper test might be whether the voting restriction is rational. Even more to the point was a 1968 Supreme Court case, *Avery v. Midland County*,[51] which held that the Constitution permits no substantial variation from equal population in drawing districts for units of local government having general governmental powers over the entire geographic area served by the body. I interpreted this to mean that no factor other than unfitness to vote is a reasonable bar to voting rights for units of local government having general governmental powers. This led me to conclude that a general municipal government cannot adopt a "one unit–one vote" scheme, because all residents would not be treated equally.

But would a private homeowners' association be subject to similar constitutional restraints?

The question of whether "one unit of property–one vote" for the directors of a homeowners' association is illegal for a New Town was still open. The answer seemed to depend on whether a large-scale homeowners' association with broad potential powers is constitutionally equal to a governmental unit with general governing responsibilities, and even if its responsibilities are too limited, then is the principle of "one unit–one vote" rational under the circumstances?

Whether or not the equal protection requirements applied to the New Towns had not been litigated, but there had been cases asking when a private area becomes "public" for First Amendment purposes. The key case was *Marsh v. Alabama*,[52] a 1946 Supreme Court holding that a company town owned by the Gulf Shipbuilding Corporation could not preclude use of its business area from the free speech rights of the public, based on the functional equivalency of the privately owned space to a publicly owned forum. In 1968 the Supreme Court, relying heavily on *Marsh*, held invalid a state injunction against peaceful non-employee picketing of a privately owned shopping center.[53] Whether the standard for free speech would be extended to the right to vote would also need

---

50 Gray v. Sanders, 372 U.S. 368 (1963).
51 Avery v. Midland County, 390 U.S. 474 (1968).
52 Marsh v. Alabama, 326 U.S. 501 (1946).
53 Amalgamated Food Employees Union v. Logan Plaza, 391 U.S. 308 (1968).

to be determined, but given the general direction of the courts in upholding fundamental rights, this step might reasonably have been assumed.

What about the old saw that "a man's home is his castle"? When can the public enter the domain of the castle to protect a resident's rights? Another line of argument was raised in *Marsh*, that "ownership does not always mean absolute dominion." Justice Black wrote for the Court: "Whether a corporation or a municipality owns or possesses the town, the public in either case has an identical interest in the functioning of the community in such manner that the channels of communication remain free."[54]

In other words, I concluded, First Amendment constitutional rights are the same in a company-owned (i.e., private) town as in any other town. What about other parts of the Constitution? Later cases developed the "public function" doctrine of state action for Fourteenth Amendment purposes.[55] Would a New Town's homeowners' association meet the public-function test?

As I was doing my research in 1968, the Supreme Court was in a liberal phase under the leadership of Chief Justice Earl Warren, pumping out opinions that seemed to augur well for applying the Constitution to both free speech and equal voting rights in many new circumstances. The general sense that such a thing as "the public interest" exists was strong; laissez-faire arguments in economics were considered extreme applications of a conservatism that was out of date and out of power; the federal government was moving forward to promote greater economic and racial equality. New Towns that were designed to promote racial and economic diversity, and environmental conservation, and to be a template for building healthy communities, seemed to be on the crest of a wave moving toward the shore of a Great Society. But other forces were gathering beneath the surface of this ocean.

5. The tide goes out

When I wrote the article published in 1969, I did not foresee the large shifts in public attitude toward competition, cooperation, public law, and private property or the rise of laissez-faire ideology, led, ironically, in part by my own alma mater, the University of Chicago. I also missed the coming recognition of the real estate industry that good suburban land for residential development was going to be increasingly scarce, hence expensive, which would drive developers to seek new

---

54 *Marsh*, 326 U.S. at 507–8.

55 The leading case was Evans v. Newton, 382 U.S. 296 (1966), holding that a public park that was being turned over to private trustees would be treated for civil rights purposes as public. "Like the streets of the company town in *Marsh v. Alabama* [cited above], the elective process of *Terry v. Adams* [345 U.S. 461], and the transit system of *Public Utilities Comm'n v. Pollak* [343 U.S. 451], the predominant character and purpose of this park are municipal." At 302. But it is important to note that Justice Black, who had written the *Marsh* opinion for the Court, now dissented, as did Justices Harlan and Stewart, whose dissent stated that the public function doctrine of *Marsh* "has not since been the basis of other decisions in this Court, and certainly it has not been extended." 321.

modes of ever-denser development, leading to PUDs much smaller than New Towns, as well as condominiums and cooperative apartments, collectively known as CIDs.[56] Nor did I foresee that the coming popularity of common area amenities would carry with it ubiquitous reliance on the institution of the homeowners' association.

Although my article has been cited from time to time in other articles, books, and a few court opinions, the context was principally to make the point that "some observers" have raised the constitutional question that I had raised.[57] But it rather quickly developed that my predictions about the law would be proved wrong, as a more conservative, private property orientation became dominant. The distance that the academic world had traveled in seven years, for example, is revealed by comparing my 1969 article with one by Uriel Reichman that appeared in the same University of Chicago Law Review in 1976.[58] Here is what he wrote:

> Homeowners' associations do not perform a public function and should not be subjected to constitutional and administrative law restraints. Unless a clear and convincing case is made that the residential private government infringes the constitutional rights of non-owners and that such a violation is so injurious as to outweigh the constitutionally protected rights of free association and property privileges of the homeowners, the public law route should not be considered. To date no such convincing case has been presented, and the courts have so far refused to apply constitutional rules to homeowners' associations. Nevertheless, several law review comments have argued that the residential private government structure should be regulated in a way that would reduce the binding force of the community's general scheme and modify its voting system. It is submitted that in these two instances, as well as in other cases, it is unwise and unnecessary to go beyond the regulation provided by state law.[59]

---

56 McKenzie, *supra* note 45, at 18–21.

57 ROBERT H. NELSON, PRIVATE NEIGHBORHOODS AND THE TRANSFORMATION OF LOCAL GOVERNMENT, 3 (2005) ("As long ago as 1969, Albert Foer contended that "a strong case can be made for the position that ... the property basis of political participation in [the private] Reston and Columbia [communities] may violate the equal protection clause" of the constitution. Foer turned out to be wrong constitutionally (thus far, at least), but many observers continue to argue that, legal or not, a system of local voting based on property ownership is wrong.) Bob Nelson, a libertarian economist, was my teammate on the Brandeis University golf team in our freshman year of college. We remained friends despite ideological differences, until his unfortunate death in 2018.

58 Uriel Reichman, *Residential Private Governments: An Introductory Survey*, 43 U. CHI. L. REV. 253 (1976). The political sentiment at the University of Chicago Law School underwent remarkable change between when I was drafted in 1968 and when I returned. Before I left for the army, I was part of a class a large part of which literally moved up to Wisconsin to campaign for the anti-war candidate, Eugene McCarthy, two weeks before our first law school exams. When I returned three years later, my new classmates tended to be laissez-faire advocates preparing for positions they would be holding in the Reagan Administration. When I returned to Chicago to complete law school after my military service, I found myself sitting at a carrel next to Uriel Reichman, a visiting law student from Israel. When we introduced ourselves, he immediately informed me that he was at that instant moment writing a critique of my article! Reichman went on to become dean of the University of Tel Aviv Law School, and then in 1994 founded the very successful Interdisciplinary Center in Israel, where he is still the president.

59 *Id.*, 301.

A Perspective on Privatization:
Whatever Happened to the 1960s New Towns Movement?

I am not aware of any relevant court decisions since my article was written that would displease Professor Reichman. The Supreme Court cases I had relied on tended to be opinions generated in a far more liberal judicial era, and my favorite case, *Marsh*, simply failed to generate a new pathway that would lead the law or politics away from the ever-expanding protection of private property, freedom of association, and the sanctity of contracts that accompanied the election of Ronald Reagan. The tide of liberal activism on which my analysis had relied was in retreat.

The most immediate example of the retreat was what happened to the Warren Court's 1968 *Logan Plaza* case, resting on *Marsh*, which had held that free speech was to be protected in a privately owned shopping center. In 1976, *Logan Plaza* was altogether abandoned by the Burger Supreme Court.[60] Under the 1980 *Pruneyard* case, only a state constitution that is interpreted more broadly than the Supreme Court's reading of the federal Constitution could still protect speech rights in a privately owned shopping center,[61] but state decisions have since taken divergent views.[62]

This is not to say that the residents of Reston and Columbia were necessarily happy that they had bought into New Towns, where so many of the important decisions were made by the developer in the early days and later by the homeowners' association. In the course of their growth, both Reston and Columbia went through stages when the residents (or at least some of them) advocated for municipal incorporation.

The question of governance rose most prominently in Reston when the New Town went through changes of ownership early in its life. Worried about whether Simon's dream would be lost, residents voluntarily created the Reston Community Association (RCA), not to be confused with the Reston [Homeowners'] Association (or RA). The RCA has focused on influencing planning but also developed some needed services, such as express bus service to Washington.[63] According to Bloom, the RCA, which based suffrage on a one person–one vote system, failed to become a governing body for Reston, but found numerous ways to influence development, for instance by forming alliances with Fairfax County leaders that could thwart Gulf Reston plans at the county level. Efforts by the RCA in the 1970s and early 1980s to establish a local government for Reston failed to obtain the necessary votes for approval.

Around 1995, the idea of incorporation was in the air at Columbia, and was extremely controversial. Rouse, for one, didn't like it. According to his biographer,

---

60 Hudgens v. National Labor Relations Board, 424 U.S. 507 (1976). *See* Harvey Rishikof & Alexander Wohl, *Private Communities or Public Governments: "The State Will Make the Call,"* 30 VALPARAISO U. L. REV. 536–41 (Spring 1996).

61 Pruneyard Shopping Center v. Robins, 447 U.S. 74 (1980).

62 Rishkof & Wohl, *supra* note 60, 543; McKenzie, *supra* note 45, 157 *et seq.*

63 Bloom, *supra* note 12, at 93.

"Rouse did admit that the voting system in Columbia was too irregular, and that it should be changed to a system of one person, one vote, instead of being based on family units. However, he also made it clear that he did not support actual incorporation."[64] Nothing more came of the municipal government idea, perhaps because by 1982 the developer no longer controlled the board of the CA and the real political power over the major institutions in Howard County had come under control of the Columbia Democrats.[65]

The legal tide that swept away so much of the legacy of the Warren Court was led by economists like Milton Freedman and advocates of the "law and economics" movement such as Robert Bork and Richard Posner, all influential professors associated with the University of Chicago.[66] But there were many other academics already writing about the failures of government and the comparative advantage of a less-regulated marketplace.[67]

A political movement to bring the New Deal and Johnsonian expansion of government institutions under some control actually began under the Democrat president Jimmy Carter, by focusing on the benefits that competition could bring to consumers, particularly in the fields of air travel and trucking.[68] Regulated businesses also lobbied for less regulation, but with a different agenda, seeking the freedom from government intervention that a shift to more self-regulation would imply. At this point in time, deregulation was not considered anti-government so much as a strategy to allow markets more space to operate in the interests of consumers. The idea was that government was necessary, but regulators didn't necessarily have to oversee so many aspects of pricing, entry, exit, and terms of trade. Competition was envisioned as a good substitute for direct government regulation to a certain degree in certain industries where government then had a particularly heavy hand, such as air transportation and telecommunications. But the goal was one of more effectively serving the public interest by reducing prices.

The urge to deregulate required a revisit to the question of what is or should be public and what is or should be private. This distinction should best be viewed as an overly simplistic bipolar model. Between the extremes are a myriad of

---

64 Olsen, *supra* note 25, at 360.

65 Lazarick, *supra* note 27, at 59.

66 For further on the history and impact of the Chicago school, *see* JOHAN VAN OVERTVELDT, THE CHICAGO SCHOOL (2007); BINYAMIN APPELBAUM, THE ECONOMISTS' HOUR (2019); MARC ALLEN EISNER, REGULATORY POLITICS IN TRANSITION (1993); KENNETH M. DAVIDSON, REALITY IGNORED (2011); and TIM WU, THE CURSE OF BIGNESS (2018). With a particular focus on antitrust, *see* MARC ALLEN EISNER, ANTITRUST AND THE TRIUMPH OF ECONOMICS (1991), and HOW THE CHICAGO SCHOOL OVERSHOT THE MARK (Robert Pitofsky ed., 2008).

67 *E.g.*, NANCY MACLEAN, DEMOCRACY IN CHAINS (2017), focusing primarily on the career of the Nobel Prize–winning conservative economist James Buchanan.

68 *See* REPORT TO THE PRESIDENT [JIMMY CARTER] AND THE ATTORNEY GENERAL OF THE NATIONAL COMMISSION FOR THE REVIEW OF ANTITRUST LAWS AND PROCEDURES (Jan. 22, 1979). One of the 22 Commissioners was Eleanor Fox, and I was the representative of another, FTC Chairman Michael Pertschuk. Part Two of the Report endorsed free market competition subject to enforcement of the antitrust laws and called for reexamination of existing antitrust immunities.

mixtures of public and private: e.g., yardstick public corporations, GSEs [government-sponsored entities, such as Fannie Mae], public–private partnerships, standard-setting organizations, private associations of publicly owned utilities, private utilities that are publicly regulated in varying degrees, publicly traded private companies in which the public is the major stockholder, financial services firms that are regulated differently according to their size and interconnectedness–to name but some of the intermediate mixtures.[69]

Plainly, there are varying ways one can be private and varying ways a government can exercise influence over private commercial behavior. Indeed, one context is featured in transaction cost economics, kicked off by a now-famous essay by Ronald Coase in 1937 on the nature of the firm,[70] and carried forward by Oliver Williamson in his 1975 book, *Markets and Hierarchies*.[71] Both Coase and Williamson eventually received Nobel Prizes for their explication of the role of transaction costs in a firm's decision whether to produce certain inputs within the firm, where hierarchy rules, or in the market, where competition rules. Advocates of privatization were particularly keen on showing how functions traditionally undertaken in-house by government (such as delivery of the mail by the Post Office) could be achieved more efficiently through contracting in the marketplace.

The word "privatization" didn't appear in a dictionary until 1983, when it was defined narrowly as "to make private, especially to change (as a business or industry) from public to private control or ownership."[72] But according to Savas, in his 1987 book on privatization, the word "has already acquired a broader meaning; it has come to symbolize a new way of looking at society's needs, and a rethinking of the role of government in fulfilling them."[73] Support for privatization–a step further in removing functions that had been part of public government–had the pragmatic support of some liberals and traditional conservatives, but seemed to have a more passionate ideological support from a growing number of anti-government Americans. The difference between deregulation and privatization was subtle and not entirely distinguishable; the early advocates of deregulation focused more on finding the right mix between government and competition, whereas the later and more libertarian version

---

69   See Albert A. Foer, *An Introduction to the American Antitrust Institute's 11th Annual National Conference: Are the Boundaries Between Public and Private in Transition?* 89 ORE. L. REV. 753 (2011), and the other articles in this symposium issue.

70   R.H. COASE, THE FIRM, THE MARKET, AND THE LAW (1988). Coase taught me price theory in law school.

71   OLIVER E. WILLIAMSON, MARKETS AND HIERARCHIES: ANALYSIS AND ANTITRUST IMPLICATIONS (1975).

72   Savas, *supra* note 15, at 3. Savas himself prefers this definition: "Privatization is the act of reducing the role of government, or increasing the role of the private sector, in an activity or in the ownership of assets."

73   *Id.* at 3. Savas generalizes that there are four forces behind privatization: "The goal of the *pragmatists* is better government, in the sense of a more cost-effective one. The goal of those who approach the matter *ideologically* is less government, one that plays a smaller role vis-à-vis private institutions. The goal of *commercial interests* is to get more business by having more of government's spending directed toward them. And the goal of the *populists* is to achieve a better society by giving people greater power to satisfy their common needs, while diminishing that of large public and private bureaucracies." *Id.* at 4 (italics added).

seemed to focus more on an ideological distaste for the institutions of government.

Although deregulation began under President Carter, from the election of President Reagan up to and including President Trump, words like *public*, *public interest*, and *government* had become ideologically suspect. A favorite new doctrine of libertarians was called "public choice," the application of the Chicago school's microeconomic dogma to political science. Essentially, the economic dogma is based on the concept of the rational economic man who acts with full knowledge and in his own self-interest. But if you take this model seriously, it must also be applied to the individuals who work within governments, and you end up denying the possibility of a "public interest" with statements like this:

> The public-choice model questions whether public policy toward business is in fact driven by the goal of promoting competition so as to enhance some vague conception of the "public interest." It suggests instead that public policy emerges from political bargains in which special-interest groups purchase protection from the forces of unfettered competition, benefiting both themselves and politician-suppliers of protectionism at the expense of other groups.[74]

Later Democratic presidents Clinton and Obama were not sold on privatization or public-choice, but did relatively little to actually restore the balance between public and private to what it had been in the 1960s.

The swing from public to private in the years after 1980 was seen throughout society, from traditionally monopolized governmental services such as postal and package delivery systems to UPS, FedEx; from publicly run to privately operated prisons; from ideas that intellectual property was subject to regulation to a sense that intellectual property (copyright and patent law) had virtually sacred status; from public K-12 schools to private and charter schools;[75] from the First Amendment as an essential freedom for the individual to its current role as a primary protector of corporations from regulation;[76] from limited regulation of guns to Second Amendment sanctuary states, where citizens declared their readiness to take up guns in opposition to any form of gun control;

---

[74] Fred S. McChesney & William F. Shughart II, *in* THE CAUSES AND CONSEQUENCES OF ANTITRUST, THE PUBLIC-CHOICE PERSPECTIVE 2 (Fred S. McChesney & William F. Shughart II eds., 1995). *Also see*, JERRY L. MASHAW, GREED, CHAOS, & GOVERNANCE, USING PUBLIC CHOICE TO IMPROVE PUBLIC LAW (1997) and MacLean, *supra* note 67, at 74–87 (2017). MacLean traces public choice doctrine back to JAMES BUCHANAN & GORDON TULLOCK, THE CALCULUS OF CONSENT (1962), the book being the influential outcome of their shared mission: "to expose the foibles of government as the best way to protect the market (and property) from popular interference (the majority)." at 77.

[75] *See* DIANE RAVITCH, SLAYING GOLIATH, THE PASSIONATE RESISTANCE TO PRIVATIZATION AND THE FIGHT TO SAVE AMERICA'S PUBLIC SCHOOLS (2020).

[76] Albert A. Foer, *Civil Liberties and Competition Policy*, 56 ANTITRUST BULL. 731 (2011); ADAM WINKLER, WE THE CORPORATIONS, HOW AMERICAN BUSINESSES WON THEIR CIVIL RIGHTS (2018); JEFFREY D. CLEMENTS, CORPORATIONS ARE NOT PEOPLE (2012).

from progressive New Towns to gated communities; and from municipal government at local level to CIDs founded on homeowners' associations with governance through private contract. The increase in CIDs from covering about 500 small communities in 1960 to well over 300,000 of all sizes today is an underrecognized reflection of the more recent priority of private over public.

V. Whatever Happened to the New Town Movement of the 1960s?

1. Did the New Towns succeed?

There were essentially no successful New Towns built after Reston, Columbia and Irvine. And yet, looking back with a perspective of half a century, these most celebrated and ambitious of New Towns all succeeded in the sense that they have grown and will likely continue to grow more or less as envisioned in the original plans. All three have received repeated national commendations as being outstanding places to live. But each has had its ups and downs as the national economy changed over time. Both Robert Simon and James Rouse were forced out of leadership by their lenders, but their basic visions prevailed and both individuals lived–and were revered–in the communities they had created. Both Reston and Columbia eventually became profitable, but many years later than initially anticipated, and not under the initial ownership.

Irvine's story was more successful in some senses, with its continuity of corporate ownership and the major increase in the population target. However, Irvine started with advantages of size (over 80,000 acres compared with Reston's 7,000 and Columbia's 14,000), the presence of a major university at its core, its local political influence as a result of the long history of the huge Irvine Ranch in Orange County, and arguably less challenging planning goals, certainly in terms of economic and racial diversity.[77]

The flight to the suburbs after the Second World War often had a large and undeniable exclusionary racial element, especially after desegregation of the public schools, beginning in 1954. At the same time, the urban renewal that was a keystone of post-war planning resulted in much displacement, and many private decisions on where to live were influenced by the desire of car-mobile people for a congenial residential environment. The civil rights movement and the Vietnam War protests also contributed to a demand for citizen participation that affected city planners. As we approached the mid-1960s, bigotry was giving way to more religious tolerance, as reflected in the election of Jack Kennedy as the first Catholic president.

---

77 Campbell, *supra* note 17, 184–91.

Against this background, the goals of diversity in terms of race, religion, and income undertaken by Reston and Columbia, with Columbia having had the more ambitious goals, were extraordinary.[78] In retrospect, racial integration was largely achieved in Columbia, with many programs directed specifically toward that goal. Racial diversity was achieved in Reston, but perhaps not as much social integration of the races. Both New Towns provided homes to low- and moderate income residents, but the extreme classes of poverty and wealth were neither desired nor attracted.

In terms of building a sense of a special community, both Reston and Columbia attracted many "pioneers" who bought into the ideology of planning, but, as was anticipated by the developers, they increasingly also drew less ideologically motivated residents more attracted by good suburban housing values. Despite the democracy deficit I have described, these New Towns nevertheless generated an active civil life including but not limited to the framework presented by the developer for decentralized communal village and cluster life. Columbia worked particularly hard and successfully to bring many aspects of cultural life to its community. All three of the leading 1960s New Towns succeeded in preserving very large amounts of greenery, with nature preserves, trails, bike paths, golf courses, lakes, and competent environmental planning that was ahead of its time.

On the whole, I think it is fair to say that the 1960s New Town Movement demonstrated that much of the conventional wisdom about suburbs had been wrong, and that a better approach was possible. But there are also important caveats to note.

One challenge unmet was taming the car and presenting a model that would stop (much less reverse) urban sprawl. By meeting the self-containment goal of having as many jobs as residents, the New Towns were destined to contribute to, rather than provide an alternative to, regional sprawl. Although it is true that vehicular traffic was improved in important ways within Reston and Columbia, mainly by separating cars from pedestrians and making it possible to accomplish many tasks on foot or by bicycle, the anticipated economic success of the New Towns could have been predicted to attract many outsiders who would commute by car to the New Towns, while many residents would commute outward by car to jobs outside of the town boundaries.

Indeed, it never made sense to think that a city of, say, 100,000 residents would be able to sustain the needs or match the occupational profiles of all of those

---

78 Writing in 1976, Campbell generalized, "While the New Towns have failed to service the poor, they have in numerous instances allowed for racial integration. Traditionally in American development, whites have fled their neighborhoods when blacks moved in. In the case of Reston, Columbia, and Park Forest South [Illinois], the integration of blacks and whites has proceeded without a repetition of past practices." *Supra* note 17, at 263. Park Forest South received a federal guarantee of $30 million in 1970 and was expected to have 110,000 residents in 15 years. The name of the Park Forest South Village was changed to University Park in 1984, a time when the village had an estimated population of only 6,500. LARRY A. MCCLELLAN, PARK FOREST SOUTH/ UNIVERSITY PARK: A GUIDE TO ITS HISTORY AND DEVELOPMENT (1986). Park Forest South unfortunately cannot stand as a successful New Town.

of working age (less than half of the residents?) within its borders. The very success of the New Towns attracted new residential and commercial developments to the unplanned surrounding region, bringing new commuters to the area. Indeed, the Rouse Company's Columbia Mall, so large, beautiful and successful, was designed from the beginning to attract shoppers and employees (and hanging-out teens) from a much larger region. The rapid growth of the airports near these communities and the extension of Metro service to Reston all had impacts on the types of businesses and residents who would be drawn to the New Towns, which reflects the dynamic nature of long-term projects whose initial assumptions will almost inevitably have to be adjusted over time.

Strategic planners like to say that no plan should be in concrete, but rather must be revisited periodically to take account of changes in the initial assumptions, as well as lived experience. This necessarily applies in spades to the planning of greenfield New Towns and cities. The New Town concept has not turned out to provide for urban growth without the downsides of automobile mobility.

Education was an important aspect of Columbia's plan, with public elementary schools at the heart of each neighborhood and middle and high schools at the heart of each village. But there seems to be nothing special about the performance of Columbia's schools and, apart from Irvine, which had a large university planned as its core from the beginning, the higher education that might have been incorporated into Reston and Columbia was limited to community colleges after various other efforts failed.

As the three New Towns grew and as experience accumulated with other large new communities, including the short-lived, unsuccessful federal loan guarantee program, a decidedly more negative literature on the reform potential of planned large-scale communities was generated. For example, Uriel Reichman concluded in his 1976 article, "from all the available evidence, it appears that the most likely fate for the new towns is eventually to 'blend into the landscape' and become indistinguishable from other suburban developments."[79]

Among the problems Reichman summarized were a failure to construct "socially balanced" communities; limited employment of household heads within the community; and limited actual participation by residents in community political life. In the light of 50 years or more, I believe this generalization from the mid-1970s unduly exaggerates the negative, but the negativity it reflects did nothing to induce further New Town developments. While accurate enough when held against the ideal vision of Ebenezer Howard, this judgment does not ask the critical question of what influence the New Town Movement would have on land development?

Perhaps it was the sheer ambition of the New Town vision that limited its success as a movement. The holding costs were large and prolonged, with the vagaries

---

79   Reichman, *supra* note 58, at 267.

of the economy posing a large and uncertain risk to private lenders. Even though the land values would almost inevitably go up as the land was developed, the art of making the cash flow meet the timing requirements of lenders proved too difficult. When the federal government recognized this, it offered loan guarantees in return for the project meeting certain standards (e.g., of racial and economic diversity of the new community), but for various reasons, including a national economic downturn, this was not enough to keep the guaranteed New Town developers from bankruptcy. The federal program was very quickly dropped by the increasingly conservative federal government.

A principal result of the New Town experience was that private land developers and their sources of capital were not willing to take the risk of such large and complicated projects as the New Towns, which required too long a commitment into the future and too much patient capital. Moreover, as the best suburban land became scarcer, they saw the benefit of using many of the architectural ideas that worked well in the New Towns, in order to group homes more densely in townhouses and apartment buildings by providing common areas and amenities such as large green areas, swimming pools, privacy, and security, and fewer large lots for individual houses. The idea of CIDs grew rapidly, carrying with them the structure of the homeowners' association. Since 1970 about one-third of all new housing units in the United States have been built within a private community association.[80]

Developers who might have wanted to try their hands at building a New Town legacy instead relied on so-called New Urbanism ideas and some of the successful ideas demonstrated in New Towns, incorporating them into smaller, dense PUDs, creating what might be considered better-planned commuter suburbs such as Kentlands outside Washington, DC, and Celebration, Florida.[81] In many cases, they built gated communities that could provide a sense of security that many people had felt was lacking not only in the central cities but in the older suburbs.[82] In addition to PUDs, the condominium, which made its first appearance in the United States only in 1960, has become ubiquitous in both cities and suburbs.[83]

---

80   Nelson, *supra* note 57, at xiii.

81   New communities come in many forms. *See, e.g.*, Sophie Alexander, *Billionaire Behind Victoria's Secret Built His Version of the American Heartland,* BLOOMBERG (May 17, 2019), www.bloomberg.com/news/features/2019-05-17/billionaire-behind-victoria-s-secret-built-his-version-of-the-american-heartland, describing New Albany, Ohio, a community of Georgian-style McMansions only for the wealthy, built by retailer Les Wexner to serve a population of 20,718, with 46 miles of leisure trails, a learning campus and a speaker series that has featured US presidents, not to mention a 27-hole Jack Nicklaus-designed golf course. The fastest growing city in the US is The Villages, a "census-designated place" in Sumter County, Florida, that shares its name with a broader master-planned age-restricted community that spreads into portions of adjacent counties. *See* www.thevillages.com. It describes itself as "an amazing, vibrant over-55 active golf cart community" with a population of over 125,000 residents.

82   In the late 1990s it was estimated that about 20% of all residents living in neighborhood associations may live in gated communities. *See* Nelson, *supra* note 57, at 30 (2005). Not all CIDs have gates or guardhouses, but they all have homes associations which keep the "wrong kinds of people" from being residents.

83   Section 234 of the Housing Act of 1961 allowed the Federal Housing Administration to insure mortgages on condominiums.

Housing cooperatives are less popular, but also can be considered examples of a CID.

While many Americans were voting with their feet for privacy, security, and a more self-controlled environment, by moving into suburbs with homes associations, another movement in the opposite direction was also taking place, what Alan Ehrenhalt called "the Great Inversion."[84] This was the growing demographic inversion as people increasingly desired to live "downtown." The people who are moving downtown, Ehrenhalt said, "are doing so in part to escape the real or virtual 'gatedness' of suburban life."[85] But much of the movement back to the city is to condominiums and cooperative housing, where the common areas are governed by private contracts.

Obviously, the American Dream about where to live has not been unidirectional or stagnant. Today, vibrant city life is more popular than ever, and Jane Jacobs' vision of unplanned hustle and bustle[86] within a city has attracted many homeowners and tenants, who in the 1960s might have been tempted by the vision of the New Towns. The heritage of private government, however, carries with it challenges to our concepts of democracy that have yet to be worked out, or may simply be ignored.

VI. Instead of New Towns, CIDs with Homeowner Associations: The Mix of Public and Private Evolves

1. An antitrust analogy: Is the homeowners' association an aftermarket monopolist?

The New Towns of the 1960s, unlike their Ebenezer Howard model or their Greenbelt predecessor, were thoroughly private in ownership, and neither socialist nor cooperative in their political or economic models. Nonetheless, they were heavily motivated by the desire of far-sighted idealistic entrepreneurs and large profit-driven corporations such as Westinghouse, General Electric, and American-Hawaiian Steamship Lines,[87] to create communities in which common interests of both the residents and the developers (i.e., the customers and the manufacturers) would be emphasized. Confidence in large-scale planning permeated the climate, whether by private or public instigation.

---

84 ALAN EHRENHALT, THE GREAT INVERSION AND THE FUTURE OF THE AMERICAN CITY (2012). During the early 70s, there had been some efforts to build "New Towns in Town," such as the Ft. Lincoln project within Washington, DC, but these were generally unsuccessful. *See* Campbell, *supra* note 17, at 24–25. Condominium development of vertically stacked apartments took off in many cities.

85 *Id.* at 19.

86 JANE JACOBS, THE DEATH AND LIFE OF GREAT AMERICAN CITIES (1961).

87 James Ridgeway, *New Cities Are Big Business*, NEW REPUBLIC, Oct. 1, 1966, at 15. As described elsewhere in this paper, most of the plans that were on the boards in 1966 were not realized.

Moreover, a combination of centralized planning and planned decentralized units, as demonstrated in the three New Towns discussed, tended to push many types of community decisions downward, i.e., closer to the individual resident, while at the same time use of the central homeowners' association with weighted influence of the developer, simultaneously protected the sanctity of the plan and removed many decisions from the individual residents, once they had made the initial decision to live in the community.

From the perspective of the individual consumer, the initial choice was to purchase or rent within the New Town or not; but once within the New Town, the resident was dealing with a de facto monopolist who constructed the framework for governance. Once embedded in the community, the individual resident (or visitor) would not be guaranteed two of the most essential rights of the US Constitution: free speech and voting in local elections. As it later developed, although a state constitution, state law, or the voluntary act of the developer were not precluded from assigning these democratic features as privileges, in practice, the basic rights found in "public" municipalities were simply not something that could be depended upon by New Town residents. How should we view this combination of monopoly with democracy?

Antitrust law faces an analogous situation when analyzing aftermarkets, such as the replacement ink cartridges for printers or razor blades for hand-held razors.[88] There may exist competing suppliers of both printers and razors, but once the consumer makes the initial purchase of a primary product, there are follow-on purchases necessarily to be made in the aftermarket if the primary product is to remain useful. If the initial seller is allowed to use contracts or technology, or intellectual property claims to monopolize the aftermarket, the buyer may find that the overall lifetime price is much higher than initially contemplated. To exit from the aftermarket, one must sell the computer or the razor at a second-hand price if possible, or simply junk the product and start all over. The sunk costs may or may not be great, depending on the product and the marketplace. Not much for a razor; overwhelming for a homeowner.

The exit option for a homeowner who is unhappy with a homeowners' association's conditions imposed on his or her residence or behavior, is obviously much more expensive and life-disrupting than junking a hand razor. Analysis of the aftermarket situation requires an understanding of how much practical transparency was present when the primary product was marketed and how competent the consumer is likely to be to be able to calculate future life-cycle costs at the time of purchase in a foremarket. The fact that there was competition in the foremarket may not be very meaningful if the exit costs are high, especially if future changes in the aftermarket could not be predicted with any certainty.

---

88 *See* Gregory T. Gundlach & Albert A. Foer, *The future of aftermarkets in systems competition: an overview of the American Antitrust Institute's invitational symposium*, 52 ANTITRUST BULL. 1 (2007), and the five articles that are also in that volume.

A Perspective on Privatization:
Whatever Happened to the 1960s New Towns Movement?

As a generalization about the economics of aftermarkets, when a supplier of a primary good monopolizes the aftermarket for its product, and in particular when a captive (i.e., locked in) installed base of consumers comprise the market for the primary good, courts are probably less likely to see potential antitrust violations than what was described in 2007 as the "emerging consensus" of post-Chicago economists.[89] Courts are typically slow to recognize the evolving views of economists, and have gone both ways on antitrust decisions involving aftermarkets. Even conservative courts can be expected to pay close attention to the facts in any given case to weigh the harm to competition and consumers.

When applied to the homeowners' association in a New Town, where the functions of the association are equivalent or potentially equivalent to functions normally provided by a democratically elected government, two observations are particularly relevant. First, the individual homeowners are substantially locked in, with the homeowners' association holding the key, because their home may literally be taken away if they fail to comply with the association's rules (read: laws) and fee requirements (read: tax). The cost of giving up by selling the house or apartment and moving outside the New Town is likely to be large in terms of money, time, convenience, and lost friends. It might also mean having to change jobs for adults and schools for the children.

A second part of the analysis deals with transparency. What did the homeowner understand about the homeowners' association when the sales contract was signed? Even if a lawyer had explained the covenants and all they implied and the putative buyer fully understood the terms, calculating what the costs might be over a long-term future would be very difficult, because it would require predicting what future directors of the association will decide in regard to many issues that will only arise in the future. In fact, disagreements between homeowners and their association have undermined the civility of many CIDs.[90]

An unhappy homeowner in a CID might argue that the requirement to join a homeowners' association as part of the sale of a home constitutes an anticompetitive tying arrangement, or an anticompetitive abuse of monopoly power. I don't think these arguments will succeed in most conservative courts. Legally, the home and the homeowners' association must be recognized as two separate but tied products: you cannot buy the house without also buying into the association. But would the homeowners' association be considered a separate product? You cannot find it in the market to purchase separately. It is probably too closely related at the outset in a CID, where the developer would argue that without the mandate of a homeowners' association as part of the sales

---

89   *Id.* at 9, citing Lorenzo Coppi, *Aftermarket monopolization: the emerging consensus in economics*, 52 ANTITRUST BULL. 53,70 (2007) ("There is an emerging consensus in economics that the potential for anticompetitive effects exists whenever customers are locked in, that is, they can purchase only those aftermarket products produced by the manufacturer of the primary product.")

90   McKenzie, *supra* note 5, at 93–96.

transaction–which, the developer would argue, is intended to protect the property values of all the future homeowners–the CID project itself would not be undertaken. This defense is reasonable at the outset, but less and less reasonable as time passes and the development phase of the project is more or less completed.[91]

In terms of whether an association's decision in an individual case might be deemed an abuse of monopoly power under a state or federal antitrust law, the same question exists of whether the court (or possibly, the arbitrator) should look at the association as a monopolist, given that the now-unhappy homeowner had choices available when he or she made the choice to sign the sales contract and join the community.

I am not sanguine that enforcement trends for the antitrust laws provide a viable tool for challenging the negative aspects of the homeowners' association, but rather am calling attention to the usefulness of thinking about the association as similar to an aftermarket, in terms of the presence of monopoly power of the developer and the harm it can do to the homeowner as consumer.

Moreover, there seems to be another likely consideration: The *Marsh* question of how closely do the particular homeowners' association's functions resemble those of a municipal government? Should the decider look at the actual functions in practice or the potential functions broadly enumerated in the underlying land documents? Do we really care about an association's architectural controls over the colors of one's front door, as compared with who owns and administers the streets (read: sanitation) and transportation functions or the policies and execution of security (read: police) functions? Where are the lines to be drawn? With constitutional and antitrust litigation unpromising, the most likely route to protecting the residential consumer in a CID is through state legislation, and there are increasing examples of relevant bills being considered in recent years, though that is not the topic for this paper.[92]

2. More on the democratic deficit

One might nevertheless argue that the democracy deficit that I have described, based on the planning documents of two New Towns, is not sufficiently important to be worrisome. After all, most residents seem relatively happy and some residential efforts to change to municipal government have failed. Moreover, the role of homeowners' associations in many if not most CIDs is quite limited, not like a municipal government at all. And at least if a withering away of the

---

91   There is some limited precedent for considering product life-cycle in an antitrust case. Jerrold Electronics developed a master community television antenna system, with a monopoly position in the emerging industry and tied sale of the antenna system to a service contract. The trial court applied a rule-of-reason test to the tying arrangement that was instituted in the launching of the new business with a highly uncertain future; but it applied a per se test and found the tie unnecessary "as the industry took root and grew." United States v. Jerrold Electronics Corp., 187 F. Supp. 545, 57 (E.D. Pa. 1960), *aff'd per curiam*, 365 U.S. 567 (1961).

92   McKenzie, *supra* note 5, at 97–106.

A Perspective on Privatization:
Whatever Happened to the 1960s New Towns Movement?

developer is promised by the covenants, the democracy deficit is reduced to a stated time until the homeowners take over control of the association. But none of this reduces the harm that may accrue to an individual resident who has no vote or who comes into serious conflict with the association about functions that are in place of municipal services.

As the New Town matures, voting power within the homeowners' association generally (by covenant or political reality) moves away from the developer to the residents, and if the planned growth occurs, the political implications of the expanding population and employment center may imply that the New Town community has gained political weight within its county and state government. One way to look at this is to consider that the residents have traded away rights to vote for a municipal government in return for becoming more politically important through the growing influence of their community. Perhaps the lost rights had little philosophical or practical value compared with the gained influence on the county or state? This seems rather hypothetical but it points to the complication that underlies all competition policy, namely that institutions combine elements of cooperation and competition in varying ways. For-profit companies try to eliminate competition within themselves through vertical integration and hierarchical control so that they might more effectively compete with other companies, and we rarely think badly of this restriction on internal competition as long as there is adequate external competition between companies. In effect, we say that competition between companies is in the public realm, subject to government oversight and potential regulation, whereas what happens within the company's hierarchy that eliminates internal competition is considered fundamentally a matter of private concern. In this sense, the prospect in the mid-1960s of potentially applying public law to large-scale homeowners' associations gave way to a different reality that confirmed a private, contract-based approach.

Another aspect of competition deserves mention. At some point, there may be competition between the New Town and the surrounding county or nearby municipal governments (if any), as to who will provide what services within the New Town and who will pay for them. The residents who are paying fees to the homeowners' association are probably also paying taxes to the public government for similar but unused services. Such residents often feel that they are unfairly doubly taxed and seek relief. The public government, however, depends on these taxes to provide services to other residents who would suffer by reduced services or increased taxes if the members of the homeowners' association gain the relief in question, i.e. the elimination of double taxation. The double taxation issue is usually resolved along the same principle that permits parents to send children to private schools if they can afford it, without relieving them of the duty to pay taxes that facilitate the education of others in the community. (Similarly, citizens without children in the school system are not relieved of contributing to the education of the citizenry.)

The absence of tax relief in these situations thus far can be seen as a victory, perhaps temporary, of public over private strategies. But in a sense it is also a mixed result, in that private citizens could have been compelled to participate in a municipal government subject to majority rule, but instead are not precluded from participating in a private development that replaces government, as long as they are able and willing to pay a premium. One could say this is a victory for freedom but a defeat for equality, given that far from everyone can afford to pay a premium. In a similar sense, the very idea of the New Town and its CID successors represents a mix of public and private, in which a private entrepreneur is permitted to develop land subject to minimal government interference, which is desired by private individuals who are willing and able to pay, where part of the payment may include some deprivation of rights that would be present in a more public setting. The tension is always present between the universal premise of the public realm and the privileged premise that prevails in the private realm.

VII. Concluding Note: What is Public and What is Private?

On the continuum of what is private and what is public, the history of building new communities has always presented a fluctuating mix. The construction of homes in the US was traditionally a private matter, subject to various degrees of zoning, supported by a governmentally-driven mortgage market and tax deductions, with land developers operating on a small but growing scale. The garden city of Ebenezer Howard was a reactive socialist dream, and the development of New Towns in the UK has long involved a leading role for government.[93] In the US, the Great Depression truncated the Radburn experiment in New Jersey, a private project that introduced the homeowners' association as a private substitute for the role of municipal government. The New Deal's Greenbelt, Maryland, the next landmark, was planned and owned by the federal government, and organized along cooperative lines. The New Towns of the 1960s were on a larger scale, but privately owned and financed, with very little governmental shaping.

The first public efforts to replicate Reston, Columbia, and Irvine as a way of decentralizing economic growth focused on federally guaranteed financing, along with requirements for economic and racial diversity. This failed rather quickly and the government withdrew from the building of New Towns. The New Town Movement of the 1960s effectively ended in the 1970s. What followed, however, was the explosion of CIDs, primarily in the form of PUDs, condominiums, and cooperatives, the vast majority using the private contract formula popularized by the New Towns for governance of privately owned common areas. It is a

---

93   Rodwin, *supra* note 9.

A Perspective on Privatization:
Whatever Happened to the 1960s New Towns Movement?

history that reflects movements in ideology and changing economic realities such as economic cycles, the price of land, consumer demand, and politics at the local and national levels. The result is fluctuation in the boundaries between what is considered public and private, what is best subjected to various forms and amounts of government influence and control, and what is best left to private ownership and market forces. No simple model of microeconomics explains this history.

PART V
Agency Actions: Mandate, Cooperation, and External Pressures

The Antitrust Agencies' Successful System of International Cooperation Being Tested in the Digital Age

DONALD I. BAKER[*]

Baker & Miller

Abstract

Antitrust enforcement agencies have strong incentives and ever more reasons to cooperate closely in investigating suspected violations and in developing effective remedies and policies. The agencies' procompetition goals are complementary, and their investigations can involve parallel efforts to uncover vital facts from common targets. From modest beginnings involving few agencies in the 1960s, these cooperative efforts have mushroomed since the 1990s, with the creation of over 100 new national competition agencies, while globalization has generated many more multi-market mergers and cartels for them to collectively investigate. This paper explains why the antitrust cooperation system has become distinct and then reviews how it has evolved, with a particular focus on coordinating agencies' merger and cartel investigations. Finally, it analyzes why the unprecedented digital monopolies (such as Google, Facebook, and Amazon), often being multinational in scope, are generating a serious need for continued expansion of the successful system of global antitrust cooperation.

---

[*] Donald I. Baker is senior counsel and a founding partner at Baker & Miller PLLC, with offices in Washington DC and San Francisco, CA. My interest in exploring this interesting subject began in 2019 when the Virginia Journal of International Law invited me to give the keynote speech at a symposium on Antitrust in the Global Economy at the University of Virginia Law School on March 4, 2020. I am most grateful to the Journal for the invitation and to my numerous friends, who are US and EU officials or former officials, for providing so many insights necessary to expand and update my initial picture as a former participant and ongoing observer. Among those whom I want to thank are Randolph Tritell, Elizabeth Kraus, and Paul O'Brien of the FTC Office of International Affairs.

The Antitrust Agencies' Successful System
of International Cooperation Being Tested in the Digital Age

I. Introduction

The long-standing system of close international cooperation among antitrust enforcement agencies turns out to be distinctive and successful.

When I served at the US Department of Justice (DOJ) in the 1970s, we worked closely with a few foreign counterparts in Brussels, Berlin, and Ottawa when running parallel investigations, while the need for cooperative enforcement efforts with remaining agencies tended to be rare. Since then, the US Federal Trade Commission (FTC) has become a very active international participant, and many new competition agencies have been created or vastly expanded by their governments around the world. Now the number of national competition agencies (NCAs) has multiplied to at least 130 around the world (compared with perhaps 10 in the 1970s).

Inter-agency cooperation among NCAs has become more continuous because antitrust enforcement against mergers (which had been a unique US experiment in the 1970s) has been gradually adopted almost everywhere since 1990; ever larger portions of each agency's workload has involved foreign enterprises, transactions, and global markets. In sum, the agencies' expanded risks of conflicting efforts and the broader need to keep their policies and procedures in general alignment have increased dramatically since the 1980s.

II. Different Types of Competition Enforcement Agencies

Antitrust enforcement can be entrusted to (i) an *administrative agency* (like the European Commission or the FTC) which undertakes investigations, determines liability, and imposes administrative fines and prohibition orders–subject to some level of judicial review; or (ii) a *prosecutorial agency* (like the DOJ) which investigates and alleges violations, but then has to persuade a judge (or a jury in a criminal case) to accept its legal theory and evidence; or (iii) a *hybrid system* in a few common law countries where civil enforcement is given to an administrative agency, while anti-cartel criminal enforcement stays with the normal criminal prosecutors (e.g. in the UK and Ireland).[1]

The initial institutional choice is so important because it defines what the agency can do procedurally and sometimes substantively. Nearly all the nations that have created competition regimes since 1980 have chosen the administrative model championed by the EU, rather than the US prosecutorial alternative.

---

[1] The administrative agency can investigate suspected antitrust crimes and make recommendations, but then it must turn its evidence over to the normal prosecutors who decide whether to bring a criminal prosecution.

This choice probably reflects the thinking and assumptions in the civil law countries, which predominate globally and where criminal prosecution responsibility belongs to specialized judicial officials. An administrative agency has broader discretion in developing rules and remedies for mergers and monopolies–all subject to sometimes detailed judicial review in appellate courts.

In fact, the DOJ appears to be a unique institution where both criminal and civil enforcement powers are combined in the same agency. This may be more of an historic accident, rather than the result of a thoughtful choice. The Sherman Act of 1890 embodied a common law tradition of prosecutorial responsibility and was enacted before the emergence of the modern administrative state. Nevertheless, this combination of powers may explain why criminal antitrust prosecutions have become a continuous reality in the United States, while remaining a rarity elsewhere.

III. Why has the System of Antitrust Cooperation Become Institutionally Distinct?

The starting point is national politics. Competition agencies turn out to be distinctive. A national government is broadly divided between *constituency-serving* agencies and *mission-oriented* agencies in meeting its economic needs. The constituency-serving agencies are almost inevitably averse to their foreign counterparts (as champions of domestic constituencies in commerce, agriculture, energy, labor, etc.). Some mission-oriented agencies are also necessarily averse to their foreign counterparts when the mission concerns how an economic pie is allocated (as in the areas of tax and foreign trade). National law enforcement ministries do cooperate closely with some of their foreign counterparts using multilateral legal assistance treaties to share evidence–but this cooperation tends to be a nuts-and-bolts process, rather than the kind of the broader efforts to promote convergence on policies and processes that the competition agencies also emphasize. Other mission-oriented agencies with broad policy mandates (e.g. the US Environmental Protection Agency) may cooperate with and support their foreign counterparts, but they have less active enforcement engagement with each other. Probably the most comparable system of multilateral cooperation is the one that exists among national securities regulators–called the International Organizations of Securities Commissions or IOSCO.[2]

NCAs have highly complementary missions. Broadly speaking, protecting competition in Germany is generally consistent with the FTC's and DOJ's efforts

---

2   IOSCO is based on a developed Multi-lateral Memorandum of Understanding ("MMOU") concerning consultation, co-operation and exchange of information. The IOSCO MMOU allows a high level of co-operation between securities or financial regulators, enabling them to effectively provide mutual assistance. In particular, under the terms of the MMOU, the securities regulators can provide information and assistance, including records. Currently, the IOSCO MMOU has about 115 signatories, and the annual number of information requests reportedly are several thousands.

in the US or internationally. In addition, promoting convergent antitrust policies also makes private compliance and cross-border enforcement simpler.

The day-to-day reality of antitrust enforcement involves digging hard for facts. Several NCAs will routinely investigate the same international merger or cartel when it appears to have multi-market effects. This means that their agency staff are seeking (i) detailed evidence of "agreement" in cartel investigations, and (ii) evidence on market definition, market effects, and potential efficiencies in merger and monopoly investigations. Thus, the different agencies' staff seem to have a more continuous need to cooperate in exchanging ideas and evidence with their foreign counterparts also investigating a recurring flow of international mergers and suspected conspiracies.

Finally, the antitrust enforcement community has also developed distinctive institutions for promoting cooperation and convergence among its members.

IV. Institutions to Facilitate International Antitrust Cooperation

The two competition-specific institutions are (i) the Competition Committee of the Organisation of Economic Co-operation and Development (OECD Committee) founded in 1961, and (ii) the much more inclusive International Competition Network (ICN) founded 40 years later. These two organizations have rather complementary missions, as I shall explain. They offer venues where NCA leaders can meet, deliberate, provide assistance to each other, and even develop personal friendships.

1. OECD Competition Committee

Since it was founded in 1961, this Committee has served as a useful forum for coordinating policies and practices among NCAs. It meets three times a year at the OECD's Paris headquarters. The Committee is responsible for enhancing the effectiveness of current competition law enforcement through measures that included the development of antitrust principles and best agency practices, as well as encouraging improved competition enforcement in other OECD member countries. Since the 1990s, the Committee has become more involved in the interface between competition policy and trade policy.

The OECD Committee has made some distinctive contributions over time. One was an influential 1998 report urging more stringent enforcement against international price-fixing and market allocation agreements. The report, appropriately entitled *Effective Action Against Hard Core Cartels*, proposed minimum standards in relation to fighting such cartels by the international community. It focused on the economic injuries caused by cartels and the effectiveness of laws prohibiting such cartels, and urged more international cooperation and comity in enforcing those laws. However, it did not recommend how agencies should conduct overlapping investigations of the same cartel. The report has clearly helped encourage NCAs to put greater emphasis on anti-cartel enforcement in the twenty-first century.

Another important modern contribution by the OECD Committee has been in developing a process for the systematic and reciprocal assessment of the performance of a member enforcer by other members (called "peer reviews"), with the goal of helping the reviewed member to improve its policymaking, enforcement techniques, and compliance with OECD standards. The OECD Committee also conducts recurring substantive reviews of competition laws and policies in a country, as well as of the structure and effectiveness of its competition institutions. All these reviews are discussed with the NCA in advance before publication. They can serve as a catalyst for strengthening domestic laws, because the newly reviewed agency can return to its legislature with an OECD report suggesting potential improvements in its domestic antitrust system.

2. International Competition Network

The ICN is a newer *network* whose over 130 members constitute nearly all of the world's competition agencies (including tiny agencies like the one for the Channel Islands). The ICN lacks a headquarters, a secretariat, or other traditional organizational features that may be less needed in the Internet age.

This new type of quasi-virtual network was created in late 2001 as a result of an initiative first formulated by the then DOJ antitrust chief Joel Klein and then amplified by EU Commissioner for Competition, Mario Monti. The forces behind the initiative were well summarized by Klein in 2000, when he said:

> the burdens on international cooperation and coordination among various national antitrust authorities will likewise increase. It follows as the night the day: as markets become more global, the number of countries having a legitimate enforcement interest in a particular merger will increase as well. This creates a whole host of problems–substantively and procedurally–about simultaneous review and the implications of one competition authority's actions for the actions of other authorities. If, for example, we block a global merger in the US, that is very likely to kill the deal worldwide, no matter what other agencies think ... Similarly, the mere proliferation of agencies looking at the same transaction can have unintended side-effects ...[3]

---

[3] Joel Klein, Assistant Attorney General, Antitrust Division, US Department of Justice, Time for a Global Competition Initiative?, Sept. 14, 2000, www.justice.gov/atr/speech/time-global-competition-initiative.

Five months later, Commissioner Monti further explained what he hoped the new network could do:

> I believe that the main mission of the forum should be to put in place an inclusive venue where those responsible for the development and management of competition policy worldwide could meet, engage in constructive dialogue and exchange their experiences on enforcement policy and practice.
>
> Competition authorities and other participants in the forum should strive to achieve a maximum of convergence and consensus on fundamental issues such as the substance and economics of competition policy, the enforcement priorities of competition authorities and other issues such as the ones raised by the new economy. Such consensus should result from a common understanding about the best approach to solving the problems. It could then lead to the definition of general guidelines or the issuing of non-binding "best practice" recommendations.[4]

The founders wanted the numerous newer, often-smaller NCAs to have ready access to friendly practical advice and public support from their well-established counterparts in Europe, North America and elsewhere. This included helping such newer NCAs to be more politically independent at home by arming them with the collective experiences and policies of older NCAs.

The ICN includes all the world's NCAs that wanted to join. The OECD, the UNCTAD and the World Bank were to be invited to participate in the work and meetings but not as voting members. A special feature of the ICN is involvement of private individuals as "non-government advisers" or "NGAs" as they are commonly referred to. Each ICN member agency is permitted to invite a limited number of NGAs, who are quite often former officials or academics.[5]

ICN work is project-based. Largely self-selected "working groups" of government officials and NGAs which do research, draft memos, and formulate proposed best practices, guidelines and recommendations for consideration at the annual meetings, as well as conducting other projects such as informal technical assistance.

Each year the ICN has a major annual conference which is hosted and staffed by a NCA member. Substantive rules and best practices for conducting investigations are discussed and recommended in the annual meetings. Between these annual meetings, the ICN's working groups continue to be active, doing research

---

[4] Mario Monti, European Commissioner for Competition Policy, The EU Views on Global Competition Forum, Mar. 29, 2001, https://ec.europa.eu/commission/presscorner/detail/en/speech_01_147. (emphasis added).

[5] As a result, I have been fortunate enough to be an active participant in ICN processes for over 10 years as an NGA, invited by the FTC and DOJ.

and having workshops and programs on specialized subjects. I have been impressed by the somewhat informal but very pragmatic way that ICN meetings and working group sessions are organized–with those from smaller countries encouraged to actively participate.

3. Complementary roles

The OECD Committee, being a smaller group, which includes the European Commission and all the leading NCAs, apparently spends a higher proportion of its time *deliberating* over substantive competition policies and seeking policy convergence.[6] Meanwhile the ICN, with its over 130 members, is more focused on communicating policies and agencies' successful experiences; it also is engaged in collective efforts to develop "best efforts" recommendations for investigations and other normal NCA activities.[7]

V. Enforcement Cooperation on Multi-Market Cartels and Mergers

A majority of a typical NCA's international investigation concerns (i) suspected cartel activity or (ii) proposed mergers. These are fact-intensive inquiries where an agency seeks evidence from those directly involved, as well as potentially helpful information from third parties and experts. Where a cartel or merger investigation involves apparent competitive effects in more than one national jurisdiction, the investigating agencies have every reason to exchange impressions, questions, evidence and ideas with each other, to the extent that they are not legally barred from doing so under their national laws. Most of this day-to-day cooperation goes on among investigating staff, without necessarily involving agency leaders.

1. Global anti-cartel enforcement–cooperation in obtaining key evidence using diverse national investigatory tools

Competition agencies all seem to agree that combating cartels should be a basic enforcement priority. The most intense public and political support for tough cartel prosecutions still seems to exist in the United States, where the whole effort takes on an almost moral flavor. By contrast, in at least some civil law countries where visible cartels may have had a long history, price-fixing among competitors

---

[6] Unlike the ICN, the OECD Committee is part of a much larger organization, the Organization of Economic Organization and Development, which includes numerous other committees concerned with deliberations and coordination over a broad range of subjects (including energy and transportation).

[7] Having had no personal involvement with the OECD Committee since 1976, I am relying on well-informed friends for my information how it now operates. By contrast, my role as an NGA has given me favorable firsthand impressions about the ICN in action.

sometimes seems to be regarded as just another "regulatory offense," deserving an ordinary corporate fine.

Diverse Legal Sanctions. The underlying anti-cartel weapons differ greatly among nations. The principal US prohibition is the amended Sherman Act, which now treats a cartel violation as a felony with a maximum 10-year jail sentences and corporate fines of up to $100,000,000 per offense. The DOJ regularly seeks jail terms for cartel participants and in recent years has been getting jail terms of several years imposed by judges after trials or based on negotiated plea bargains between DOJ and the individual defendants.[8]

A few other common law countries (including Canada, the UK and Ireland) have adopted statutes authorizing the criminal prosecution of individual cartel conspirators, with fines and jail sentences. However, incarceration for antitrust violations remains rare outside the US.

The European Commission, like other administrative NCAs, can only levy civil law administrative fines against the enterprises participating in a cartel. This is part of the Commission's much broader mission–first to investigate, then to determine whether a violation has occurred and, if so, how large a fine should be imposed.[9] In the EU, this is a serious *corporate* remedy because an enterprise can be charged with very large fines, up to 10% of its worldwide group revenues.

Still, the Commission, like other civil law administrative agencies, lacks any *individual sanction* against conspiring corporate officers and employees, even when it has found a cartel violation based on a conspiracy involving specific individuals. I strongly believe this to be a serious gap in its anti-cartel arsenal, because conspiring employees (i) often have their own personal incentives to cheat (including bigger bonuses, possible promotions, etc.); and (ii) they seldom worry about gambling with the shareholders' money when contemplating whether to enter into an illegal conspiracy.

This US emphasis on individual sanctions seems to have worked. I believe that the threat of jail sentences has made US executives and salesmen more cautious about joining cartel agreements than many of their foreign counterparts seem to have been.[10] As a result, nearly all the largest corporate cartel fines ever levied in the United States or Europe have been against non-US companies whose

---

8 This modern emphasis on imposing jail sentences on individual conspirators became possible during my time as Assistant Attorney General for Antitrust (1976–77), shortly after Congress had created the new antitrust felonies with a three-year jail sentence for individuals, plus a maximum $1 million corporate fine in 1974. Prior to then, a Sherman Act violation was a misdemeanor with only a $50,000 maximum fine for even giant corporations and a one-year maximum jail sentence, which had almost never been imposed.

9 These determinations can be subjected to detailed subsequent judicial review in the General Court and possibly by the Court of Justice.

10 A particularly striking example involved conspiracies among international airlines over the fuel surcharges that they added to freight and passenger fares. This cartel was actively prosecuted by the European Commission, DOJ, and other NGAs elsewhere–but not a single US individual or carrier was charged by any of them.

conspiracies often had broad international effects.[11] Also, a high proportion of the individuals sentenced to jail under the Sherman Act have been foreign nationals employed by foreign corporate defendants.

This reality suggests that the international antitrust cooperation system may help facilitate *complementary enforcement efforts* against cartel members and their individual employees.[12] The DOJ can indict and jail wrongdoing individuals, while their employer is also heavily fined by the European Commission and other NCAs, as well as by a US judge.

Over the years, I have become impressed by what seems to be an almost unspoken consensus among the enforcement officials that having the US actively jailing foreign conspirators is a useful deterrent to future cartel participation by others. I have never heard foreign officials even grumble, let alone publicly complain, about the US serving as global jailer when prosecuting foreign conspirators under the Sherman Act.

Enforcement mechanisms vary greatly. In the US, we have a grand jury system embodied in the Bill of Rights, which requires that DOJ obtain an indictment from a grand jury of ordinary citizens in order to charge an enterprise or individual with a Sherman Act felony.[13] The grand jury is a somewhat quaint institution which operates in camera; subpoenaed witnesses must appear without counsel and only the DOJ lawyers get to question witnesses and present evidence.[14] Based on my experience, I see the modern federal grand jury as an effective government vacuum cleaner for collecting evidence, and the resulting grand jury indictments charging violations invariably reflect the conclusions of the Antitrust Division.[15]

Since the mid-1990s, when the DOJ established a corporate amnesty program, cartel investigations have often begun with a whistleblower seeking amnesty by exposing detailed evidence against its co-conspirators. The DOJ then promptly serves grand jury subpoenas on the other co-conspirators–which sets off a prompt

---

11 It is also clearly documented that nearly all the largest ever corporate fines under the Sherman Act have been received from foreign enterprises for international restraints. See DOJ report entitled *Sherman Act Violations Resulting in Criminal Fines of $10 Million or More* (Jan. 2021). The 16 highest fines were conspiracies in what are labelled "international" markets ranging from currencies to vitamins.

12 The number of international cartel investigations being investigated by the EU is also going down, which seems evidence that the increased enforcement combined with inter-agency cooperation is having a positive effect.

13 In a plea bargain, the defendant waives the right be charged by indictment and the government files a criminal information instead.

14 When I was Assistant Attorney General, an elegant British diplomat forcefully reminded me of how uncivilized our grand jury process seemed to someone from a country that had abolished its Star Chamber centuries ago!

15 There is a nice irony in the press reporting of the indictment process. As Assistant Attorney General, I, like my predecessors, made the final choices of which enterprises and individuals were to be charged–sometimes even adding more to the list of recommended defendants–but only after seriously studying the thick file of staff recommendations for and against each possible defendant, together with a discussion of the evidence upon which it was based. A few days later, the press would then report that "the grand jury in Chicago charged" the defendants whom I had selected.

race among the suspected culprits in proffering evidence and seeking lessened punishments based on the value and timing of their cooperation. Such an investigation largely bypasses the formal grand jury process and explains why so many DOJ cartel investigations end up with plea bargains between the government and the potential defendant(s) based on filed criminal information, rather than a grand jury indictment.

When the cartel is multinational in scope, the normal DOJ whistleblower will simultaneously seek "first in" leniency from the European Commission and other NCAs, which leads to active negotiation process between the enforcement staff and the other cartel members exposed by the whistleblower–with the others then competing for "second in" or "third in" reductions in fines based on the timing and quality of their cooperation. The whistleblower's simultaneous efforts mean that the European Commission and the most interested NCAs learn about a cartel at about the same time, which facilitates cooperation among them and with the DOJ.

The resulting factual investigations are likely intense, but much assisted by an enforcer's ability to promise conspiring enterprises reduced fines in return for early submission of helpful evidence.

Interagency Cooperation. The international cooperation system becomes especially important when the agencies' enforcement targets have multinational operations, which seems to be happening regularly in big cases.[16] Access to detailed facts is essential. The agencies have a common mission–to root out and prove the extent and scope of the suspected conspiracy in the context of their diverse legal systems. Thus, their staff will normally be in regular close contact with each other–exchanging impressions, questions, and any evidence that they are not legally prohibited from sharing (e.g., by the US grand jury secrecy rules). When it comes to sanctions, more punishment is normally assumed to increase deterrence, so there seems to be less need for careful coordination over corporate fines being sought.

2. International antitrust merger enforcement benefits from close cooperation under tight time schedules

This urgent need for cooperation in merger enforcement has been created and grown greatly during the last three decades. In the 1970s and most of the 1980s, the US was the only nation systematically reviewing and prosecuting some anticompetitive mergers. The situation changed in 1989, when the EU adopted a broad Merger Regulation, after several years of debate among Member States, agencies, and policymakers.[17] It was based on a version of the premerger review

---

16   As explained above, the DOJ has received its 16 largest corporate fines for conspiracies in "international" markets.

17   *See* J. William Rowley & Donald I. Baker, Rowley & Baker, International Mergers–The Antitrust Process (2020).

process that the US had invented in the 1976 Hart-Scott-Rodino Act. Many other nations soon followed, so that anti-merger enforcement became a standard feature in many jurisdictions. Premerger clearance means that a major international merger is being simultaneously investigated in many places at once–thereby maximizing the agencies' incentives and need to coordinate their simultaneous investigations as much as possible.

Each agency wants to understand others' enforcement perspectives and any specific goals on the transaction, while arranging to cooperate over day-to-day discovery, obtaining confidentiality waivers, and evaluation of evidence. During a merger review, time pressures can be intense because of statutory deadlines for agency actions, while some relevant evidence can be elusive. More discretionary balancing of pros and cons is required than in cartel enforcement, and there is much more room for divergent agency views about whether a merger should be prohibited or allowed to go forward with or without requiring divestitures, licensing or behavioral commitments. As already noted, concerns about proliferating merger enforcement regimes helped motivate the European and American leaders to strongly support creating the ICN in 2001.

In both the US and EU systems, merging parties must (i) submit an application for clearance of any transaction whose size is above the relevant regulatory thresholds,[18] and (ii) then respond to a timely demand from the agency for supplementary information and evidence.[19] Other major agencies in countries (including the UK, Germany, and Australia tend somewhat similar two-stage systems for investigating mergers subject to their jurisdiction. These regimes impose time limits for the investigating agency to take action (even if these limits can sometimes be extended by agreement in a complicated case). Only a small minority of the initial filings generate a full-scale second-stage agency inquiry– but those that do involve intense agency search for all arguably relevant facts, a process that can take well over six months. Opponents of the transaction (e.g., customers, competitors, or suppliers) normally seek enforcement action by any investigating agency, sometimes prolonging the process and creating a need for more cooperative fact-checking.

When several NCAs are investigating the same merger, collaboration between their staff tends be close and continuous. To facilitate their efforts, the agencies will generally ask the parties and some third parties for waivers from any

---

18   The required initial filings are very different in the US and EU systems: (i) The US requires only a very short initial form with quite limited information. (ii) By contrast, in the EU, merging parties must submit an elaborate initial report (the so-called Form CO), explaining the transaction, the parties, the markets and likely effects–a draft of the CO form is often submitted to Commission staff for informal comments in advance of the formal filing. The approaches vary in other countries, thus complicating the merging parties' tasks.

19   The second stages of the two systems are somewhat parallel in approach: (i) in the US, the DOJ or FTC can make a sometimes-huge demand for additional evidence (called a "second request," as if it were just a polite inquiry). This stops the clock until "substantial compliance" has been achieved by the merging parties. (ii) In Europe, after its initial review, the Commission can open a second-stage review, when much evidence could be demanded, and additional time required for the agency staff to review it.

confidentiality provisions or rules that would prevent them from consulting with each other regarding information provided in their submissions–arguing correctly that this is likely to speed up the review process and reduce the risk of inconsistent results. These requests ae typically granted.

Merger Remedies. Having determined that a merger is anticompetitive, an antitrust agency can either (i) seek to prohibit the transaction entirely, or (ii) agree to allow the transaction to go forward if the parties agree to divest some of the acquired assets to buyer(s) acceptable to the government, and/or accept other relief (e.g., on licensing, supply agreements, firewalls).[20] Most agencies, including FTC and DOJ, prefer structural remedies whenever feasible.

The formal legal processes needed for an enforcement agency to block a merger vary substantially between common law and administrative systems. (i) In the US, having investigated a transaction thoroughly, the FTC or DOJ files a complaint in a District Court alleging a Clayton Act section 7 violation and seeking an injunction. The agency must then persuade a randomly selected District Judge to enjoin consummation based on an evidentiary hearing where some live witnesses may be called. If the government prevails, the losing defendants could appeal to the Court of Appeals. (ii) By contrast, in the EU and most administrative systems, after doing the necessary investigation and fact-finding, the agency then enters a prohibition order supported by extensive factual findings and legal analysis. This prohibition order is subject to subsequent judicial review, which can be extensive, but sometimes has come too late to save a time-sensitive transaction, even when the merging parties ultimately prevail.[21]

Settlements. Despite the formally different legal regimes, practical convergence has often been achieved between the US and the EU because most close cases are resolved by settlements (called "commitments" in the EU) rather than litigation. This is possible because enactment of the US premerger notification system essentially converted (i) what had been a post-closing *litigation system* with numerous court decisions[22] into (ii) a pre-closing *administrative system*, where most contentious investigations are resolved by settlements, because of time pressures that so many deals face. Thus, the actual investigation-and-settlement process in Washington can be reasonably paralleled with what goes on in Brussels.

---

20 Also, in the US, a formal DOJ consent order embodying the merger settlement is subject to judicial review in a District Court under a public interest standard under the Tunney Act. However, history shows that District Judges have been extremely deferential to the DOJ's explanations when reviewing merger settlements and virtually none have ever been overturned (even when I tried!).

21 This can occur because a legal action seeking judicial review does not stay the administrative decision prohibiting the transaction.

22 Prior to 1976, when defending merger cases, most defendants were very willing prolong the trials and appeals, while earning profits from the already-acquired business. After 1976, new premerger system could put intense time pressures on merging parties (especially the acquirer) to hold the deal together in the face of an ongoing investigation and resulting uncertainty.

Even when the proposed merger involves two significant competitors in the same market, the investigation will often still be resolved by a partial-divestiture settlement. This may occur in Brussels or Washington or elsewhere for at least three reasons. First, the settlement offers the agency a positive public outcome from the investigation by strengthening some competitive alternative(s) in the market, while conserving the agency's limited staff resources for the next merger investigation. Second, a prolonged merger investigation is costly for the merging parties and can generate serious concerns for them over (i) retention of key personnel in the acquired company, and (ii) maintaining valuable customer and supplier relationships. These practical pressures on the merging parties intensify when they face multiple investigations from several NCAs in different markets. Third, a settlement eliminates both sides' risks of ultimately losing its case in court[23]–especially for the US agencies, which have to persuade a generalist District Judge to (i) undertake the unfamiliar judicial task of predicting future economic realities, and (ii) conclude that sufficient predictable anticompetitive effects have been proven to justify an injunction against the transaction.

When several NCAs have cooperated on a merger investigation, convergence is likely to be particularly necessary at the settlement stage. A single transaction cannot be sensibly subjected to inconsistent settlement/commitment orders from different nations. The primary task of negotiating the final settlement with the merging parties normally falls on the agency with immediate jurisdiction over them, or the agency in the market with the biggest adverse competitive effects.

Overall, the international antitrust cooperation system seems to have worked quite well in (i) encouraging various NCAs to make their processes more consistent, and (ii) minimizing potential enforcement conflicts over the same transaction(s) and how they are resolved. The staff at different agencies and their spirit of cooperation helps to make the "system" work in this key area, as it does in others too.

VI. Dominant Digital Platforms Present Challenging New Opportunities for International Antitrust Cooperation

Today, major NCAs are facing, individually and collectively, some of the biggest challenges that I can remember during my long professional lifetime. Google, Facebook, Amazon, Apple, and a few other leaders (the Platforms) are creating new multinational markets, some apparently with some winner-takes-all characteristics. Their clear commercial success is making them the targets for mounting

---

23 However, in the EU, a third party can appeal the Commission's commitment decision, and occasionally such an appellant has prevailed. Also, in the US, a third party can theoretically challenge the consent decree settling a merger case under the Tunney Act (*see supra* note 20), but in fact such challenges have never been successful, as far as I know.

political and social concerns about their size, market power, and ability to influence users.

Thus, the DOJ, FTC, European Commission and other NCAs face escalating political pressures to *do something* about the assumed *abuses* of the digital giants–yet without any clear public consensus among nations about what that *something* should be. So now the FTC, DOJ, and the European Commission, as well as other NCAs, are developing their enforcement efforts against the Platforms and then, building on their past experience of successful international cooperation, they are actively trying to coordinate their policies and overlapping enforcement efforts in the vital new digital area, but nearly all the case-specific activity is "below the radar."

1. New political and economic realities

The Platforms are not classical monopolists. Instead, each one has obtained market dominance by using new technology to offer consumers novel and widely popular services. The widespread political ferment comes not from traditional consumer annoyance about monopolistic bullying or high prices–but from the combination of (i) the Platforms' political influence as data and information gatekeepers, (ii) their unmatched commercial ability to collect and commercially exploit large amounts of individuals' personal information,[24] and (iii) the lack of credible competitive alternatives in many markets they serve.

The Platforms fall into two distinct operational categories. The first category consists of the *information platforms*, which generally offer "free" information, content and/or messaging capability in order to attract widespread consumer use, thereby generating valuable audience information that can be monetized primarily through the sale of advertising. Google, Facebook and Twitter are the most familiar examples. The second basic category consists of the major *transaction platforms*, which enable participating buyers and sellers to complete specialized transactions for which they may pay the platform for making possible. Amazon, Airbnb, NASDAQ, Uber, and Visa are all prominent examples. Both categories are attracting global antitrust attention, while generating different competition law questions.

These two distinct platform categories are efficient in different ways. A market-making *transaction platform* (e.g., NASDAQ or a local real estate multiple listing system) is most efficient when all "buy" and "sell" bids can be aggregated on that platform. By contrast, a dominant *information platform* better serves the public when it still has to compete with other sources of newsworthy information. Here, market competition can provide incentives to (i) improve the amount of

---

24 Serious concerns about privacy have articulated in these two ominously titled books: (i) Bruce Schneier, Data and Goliath: Battles to Collect Your Data and Control Your World (2015); and (ii) Shoshana Zuboff, The Age of Surveillance Capitalism: the Fight for a Human Future at the New Frontier of Power (2020).

information being made available and (ii) offer users more price/quality choices in their service(s). This difference helps explain why effective international coordination among the competition agencies cannot be based on a one-size-fits-all antitrust response to all the Platforms.

Although Google and Facebook are often considered to be novel, they are conceptual successors to traditional media enterprises (newspapers and commercial broadcasters) that have offered information and entertainment to attract readers' and viewers' attention, which can then be profitably sold to advertisers. What makes the *information platforms* like Facebook more powerful economically (and politically) than their media predecessors is their ability to (i) offer advertising more targeted to individual users' tastes and (ii) shed the mostly geographic limits that had constrained their even monopolistic media predecessors from endlessly expanding (i.e., the limited reach of printed newspaper's circulation or a broadcaster's radio signals). As a result, no traditional newspaper chain or broadcast network ever enjoyed anything approaching a near *global* monopoly the way Google and Facebook have been able to in a very short time.

Meanwhile, some of the new digital *transaction platforms* have become truly international trading venues for securities and other assets; other retail-oriented Platforms are enabling consumers to efficiently complete some purchases directly, thus by-passing traditional intermediaries (e.g., travel agents, or brick-and-mortar retailers).

2. Changing laws and institutions

Legal responses to the perceived digital monopoly dangers are busily being proposed in major legislatures–where politicians sometimes seem to be responding on their own to domestic political concerns (as in the US) and sometimes on the basis of detailed proposals from competition agencies (as in the European Parliament). Antitrust laws are being expanded and new digital rules are being considered, while new government "digital information" agencies are being contemplated or created to deal with privacy and other broad information-related concerns. Most of this expanded effort seems directed at the Platforms, which dominate so many local, regional, and national markets around the world.

A. *New antitrust legislative proposals in the US*

At this point, there seems to be some bipartisan support to *do something* about the Platforms in Congress. Today's political excitement make me think back to what happened in the US in early 1970s–when intense public concern about the new OPEC oil cartel, inflation, and the Watergate investigations caused Congress to (i) substantially increase the DOJ and FTC budgets by much more than the Nixon administration had sought, (ii) convert Sherman Act violations from a $50,000 misdemeanor into a $1 million felony with three-year jail sentences, and

(iii) establish a brand-new merger regulatory system that required a significant merger proposal to undergo a sometimes burdensome antitrust review before it could be consummated. Both the latter two were game changers in US antitrust enforcement history.

On February 4, 2021, Senator Amy Klobuchar, Chair of the Senate's Antitrust Subcommittee, introduced her proposed "Anticompetitive Exclusionary Conduct Prevention Act." Central to the Klobuchar bill are the new legal presumptions designed to strengthen antimonopoly enforcement against the Platforms. Illegal "exclusionary conduct" is defined as anything that "materially disadvantages ... actual or potential competitors" and is a violation when undertaken by any buyer or seller that "has a market share of greater than 50%." percent The bill also introduces a new "civil penalties" remedy that would enable the FTC or DOJ for the first time to recover substantial sums of money from companies for civil antitrust violations, just as the European Commission and many foreign NCAs regularly do; but this remedy is limited to violations of Klobuchar's new exclusionary conduct rules.[25] If enacted, both these changes would substantially narrow the existing gap between antimonopoly enforcement in the US and the EU.

Two months later, on April 15, 2021, the US House Judiciary Committee approved a 450-page antitrust broadside more specifically targeting various practices of the Platforms;[26] and since introduced broad new legislation based on the report. Some of this legislation goes well beyond traditional antitrust changes and could appropriately lead new "data regulation" provisions, perhaps to be enforced by a new data regulation agency.

The most recent US proposals include the Open App Markets Act introduced in the Senate by Sens. Blumenthal (D-Conn.), Blackburn (R-Tenn.), and Klobuchar (D-Minn.). A companion version of the bill has been introduced in the House by Reps. Ken Buck (R-CO) and Johnson (D-GA). The Open App Markets Act and the companion version of the bill introduced in the House cover companies that own or control an app store with at least 50 million US users (which applies to Apple and Google). They would protect developers' rights to tell consumers about lower prices and offer competitive pricing; protect sideloading of apps; open up competitive avenues for start-up apps, third party app stores, and payment services; make it possible for developers to offer new experiences that take advantage of consumer device features; give consumers more control over their devices; prevent app stores from disadvantaging developers; and set safeguards to continue to protect privacy, security, and safety of consumers.

---

25 The proposed penalties could be substantial–up to 15% of the offending company's total US revenues for the previous calendar year or 30% of US revenues in the areas affected by the "exclusionary conduct" during the period of such conduct.

26 This had been released six months earlier, before the change of administrations, as a staff report.

B. *New legislative proposals in Europe*

On December 15, 2020, the European Commission unveiled its proposed "Digital Markets Act" (DMA), a major package of new rules intended to provide a broad regulatory oversight for sizable digital platforms and specifically curb the power and discretion of what it labels the "gatekeepers" – a category that should cover all major Platforms fulfilling a set of quantitative and qualitative criteria.[27] The DMA is now being discussed in the European Parliament and the Council of Ministers. The DMA covers both *transaction platforms* (such as Amazon) and *information platforms* (such as Google). This proposal is generally based on a February 2020 White Paper, which the Commission's president (Ursula von der Leyen) explained as, "presenting our ambition to shape Europe's digital future. It covers everything from cyber security to critical infrastructures…I want that digital Europe reflects the best of Europe–open, fair, diverse, democratic, and confident." In mid-2021, it seems likely that the DMA is likely to be enacted in more less the form that the Commission proposed; and thus the situation in Europe is more predictable than in the US, where it seems much more uncertain what, if anything, Congress might enact.

Still, the real world does not consist of *Digital Europe* and *Digital America* as separate sectors. Instead, there seems to be a *global digital* reality served by the Platforms, which are internationally dominant US enterprises. Thus, a basic question is whether US Congress comes up with its own "digital markets act" or whether it might just enact some version of the Klobuchar bill or some other expansion of US antitrust rules vis-à-vis the dominant digital platforms. Either way, the expansion of antitrust in Europe, the US, and elsewhere will surely require expanded coordination by the FTC and DOJ with the European Commission, the UK Competition & Markets Authority, and other NCAs investigating the Platforms.

C. *Possible new "digital information" institutions*

Uncertainty exists in the US and some foreign jurisdictions over *who* will be entrusted with responsibility to enforce any non-competition rules for digital platforms, concerning such subjects as information access, digital security, or privacy. Earlier expert panels created by the UK and EU had recommended that governments create a separate regulatory unit for digital information issues, but without necessarily displacing the competition agencies from the area.[28] The existence of some new information agencies would complicate the coordination processes for NCAs, both within their own countries and internationally, when

---

[27] *See* the DMA, which defines "gatekeepers" in terms of (i) size by revenue, (ii) active users, and (iii) durability measured over the last three years' performances.

[28] The so-called Furman Report in the UK is an impressive effort by a very small panel of experts chaired by a prominent Harvard professor and former Chairman of the US Council of Economic Advisers. www.gov.uk/government/consultations/a-new-pro-competition-regime-for-digital-markets.

conducting a Platform investigation with an apparent overlap between distinct competition and information issues.

In the US, a new digital information agency may or may not ever be created. If established, it could be an independent agency reporting to Congress (like the FTC) or an executive branch agency reporting to the president (like the DOJ Antitrust Division). Coordination processes would be affected by that choice.

In the EU, the Commission has already moved ahead institutionally. It is also making a helpful effort to keep *competition* regulation distinct from *digital information* regulation, while trying to assure coordination of their efforts. Thus, it has established two separate directorates general within the Commission–DG Competition for the antitrust oversight, while DG Connect administers the digital information oversight–but both report to the same executive vice president who will have to decide how to coordinate any overlapping enforcement and policy efforts.[29]

3. Recent enforcement efforts

The most important enforcement efforts in the digital area are still coming from the US agencies the European Commission and the UK Competition & Markets Authority. I understand their traditional cooperation has continued as the Commission, DOJ and FTC have each brought important antimonopoly proceedings against different Platforms in 2020–21. These efforts rest on distinct but complementary legal theories, and hence are not likely to be controversial among the agencies.

On October 20, 2020, the DOJ (joined by 12 states) charged Google with violating section 2 of the Sherman Act by (i) paying Apple billions of dollars annually for installing Google as the default search engine on iPhones, iPads, and other Apple devices, and (ii) requiring licensees of Google's Android program to include Google as a non-removeable search application in their devices.[30] Google is charged with monopolizing markets for include "general search services" and "advertising search services." Google is alleged to have 94% of search services from mobile devices and 82% from computers. The annual payments to Apple under the long-term contracts are alleged to be $8–10 billion and account for 15–20% of Apple's annual net income. The DOJ seeks injunctions against the Google contracts plus unspecified "structural relief as needed to cure anticompetitive harm."

---

29   Commission Vice President (and formerly just Competition Commissioner) Margrethe Vestager assumed this dual responsibility in 2020.

30   United States v. Google LLC, 1:20-cv-03010 (D.D.C. Oct. 20, 2020); FTC v. Facebook, Inc., 1:20-cv-03590 (D.D.C. Jan. 13, 2021). On December 12, 2020, Colorado, joined by 20 more states and territories, filed a very similar suit against Google in the same court and asked that it be consolidated with the DOJ case. Colorado et al v. Google LLC, 1:2020cv03715 (D.D.C.). These overlap to a significant degree with Europe Commission's 2018 *Google Android* decision, which resulted in substantial fines.

On January 13, 2021, the FTC charged Facebook with monopolizing "personal social networking services" and some related markets by (i) acquiring potential rivals Instagram (a photo-sharing service) in 2012 and WhatsApp (a mobile phone–sharing service) in 2014, and (ii) conditioning access to the dominant Facebook platform to third-party software providers in ways designed to prevent them from creating a broader product that could rival Facebook's monopoly.[31] The defendant's economic strength is its ability to create advertising tailored to users' individual tastes, a product going well beyond traditional media advertising based on newspaper readership or television viewing. Facebook allegedly earned $70 billion in 2019 from such sales. The alleged section 2 violations in "personal social networking" would deprive both consumers and advertisers of potential alternatives. The complaint seeks an order for "divestiture of assets, divestiture or reconstruction of businesses (including, but not limited to, Instagram and/or WhatsApp)" and "a prior approval obligation for future mergers and acquisitions." The original complaint was dismissed by the District Court on June 28, 2021 for failure to clearly define a "social network" market; and the FTC has filed an amended complaint full of statistics emphasizing Facebook's dominance in its selected market.

On November 10, 2020, the European Commission announced that it had sent Amazon a Statement of Objections based on Amazon's "dual role as a platform: (i) it provides a marketplace where independent sellers can sell products directly to consumers; and (ii) sells product as a retailer on the same marketplace, in competition with those sellers."[32] The Commission's concern is about Amazon "distorting competition in online retail markets" by "systematically relying on non-public business data of independent sellers who sell on its [platform]." Access to this data allows Amazon to "calibrate ... retail offers and strategic business decisions to the detriment of the other marketplace sellers." Amazon can thus "focus its offers in the best-selling products across product categories and to adjust its offers in view of non-public data of competing sellers." The Commission asserts that Amazon should not be able to do this under Article 102 of the Treaty.

4. Inter-agency cooperation and coordination vis-à-vis the Platforms

This is an important issue. While expanding the laws and creating new *information* institutions seems to be driven by political leaders, actual enforcement of existing and expanded *competition* laws remains in the experienced hands of competition agencies. Such efforts are actively under way.

---

31   *Federal Trade Commission v. Facebook, Inc.*, 1:20-cv-03590 (D.D.C. Jan. 13, 2021).

32   European Commission Press Release IP/20/2077, Antitrust: Commission sends Statement of Objections to Amazon for the use of non-public independent seller data and opens second investigation into its e-commerce business practices (Nov. 10, 2020).

The Antitrust Agencies' Successful System
of International Cooperation Being Tested in the Digital Age

At the highest level, the G7 group of governments is focusing on competition coordination on digital markets. G7 is led by the UK in 2021 and includes the UK, Canada, the US, Italy, Germany, Japan, France, and the European Commission. (The UK has also invited Australia, South Korea, South Africa, and India as participants this year.) On April 28, 2021, the G7 put out a "Ministerial Declaration" on *Deepening Cooperation on Digital Competition*. This included the following discussion at 4–5[33]:

> Competitive digital markets drive innovation across the global economy, enhance consumer choice and allow the sectors that rely on the digital economy to flourish. However, there is increasing international concern that participants with significant market power can abuse that power to hold back digital markets and the wider economy. We recognise it is in our shared interest to coordinate and cooperate.

> To support existing workstreams on enforcement and policy related to digital competition, we will invite the UK's Competition and Markets Authority to convene a meeting of G7 competition authorities in 2021. The purpose of the meeting will be to discuss long term coordination and cooperation to better understand enforcement approaches, market characteristics and policy initiatives related to competition in digital markets, including in existing international and multilateral fora.

> The coordination and cooperation between competition authorities should be complemented by increased coordination between policymakers. The UK will therefore also host relevant officials in 2021 to discuss the importance of promoting competition through regulatory policies for digital markets, including through further coordination with competition authorities. Both meetings will draw on expertise and evidence from G7 policymakers, competition authorities and other relevant work including from the OECD, and should subsequently report to the G7, highlighting outcomes and next steps.

> Given the borderless nature of the digital economy, it is important to promote greater international cooperation and convergence in the application of competition laws; moreover, "international cooperation helps foster a coherent competition landscape, which is also of interest for business stakeholders."

---

[33] https://assets.publishing.service.gov.uk/government/uploads/system/uploads/attachment_data/file/981567/G7_Digital_and_Technology_

Expanded agency enforcement efforts vis-à-vis the Platforms can build on the agencies' well-developed experience in closely coordinating cartel prosecutions and merger investigations with multi-market effects–with their investigating staff exchanging information to the extent legally permitted. In addition, competition agencies can use bilateral dialogues as well as the ICN and the OECD Committee processes to hold regular discussions of broader policy and procedural issues.

The OECD Competition Committee organized four interesting roundtables in 2021. These were on:

a) Data Portability, Interoperability, and Competition, www.oecd.org/daf/competition/data-portability-interoperability-and-competition.htm;

b) Competition in Digital Advertising Markets;

c) Competition Economics of Digital Ecosystems, www.oecd.org/daf/competition/competition-economics-of-digital-ecosystems.htm;

d) Abuse of Dominance in Digital Markets, www.oecd.org/daf/competition/abuse-of-dominance-in-digital-markets.htm.

I understand that an on-going discussion is also underway in ICN in about the intersection of privacy, competition, and consumer protection, but that formal guidance has been released during mid-2021. The ICN's 2020 annual conference included panels on conduct remedies involving digital markets, big data and cartelization, competition advocacy in the digital age, merger investigations in the digital sector, and competition agencies' strategies to address the challenges of the digital economy.

We can anticipate expanded enforcement against the Platforms in the US, the UK, the EU and probably elsewhere, while national legislatures also continue to study and enact some new competition rules intended to limit the clear economic power of the Platforms. All this activity will generate a necessity for leading competition agencies to coordinate their enforcement efforts and policies in various different areas.

A. *Developing remedies as a particularly important area for agency coordination*

The Platforms are dominant participants internationally and in many regional and national markets. Their economic power generally comes from their success as innovators and their control of data which flows invisibly across national frontiers. When an NCA finds a violation, it may become difficult to impose an effective remedy when other agencies are prosecuting the same Platform, unless its remedy is not in conflict with others' proposals or can be geographically limited in scope. This issue is just part of a bigger problem that goes well beyond antitrust infringements–as is illustrated by Australia's effort to make global information Platforms (especially Google and Facebook) pay local media for use of their content. The message for the international antitrust community is that (i) agencies participating in overlapping investigations of a Platform should be consulting and coordinating on potential remedies from the outset of their investigations; and (ii) collectively developing best practices for competition-focused remedies in Platform cases should be high on the agendas for the ICN and/or the OECD Committee.

B. *Expanding merger enforcement against the Platforms*

A fairly broad consensus is developing that the Platforms have been able to maintain and enhance their monopolies by making acquisitions at an early stage in the development of a potential competitor. These small acquisitions tend to get through when proposed because potential anticompetitive effects that could be proven at the time fall short of the normal standards for blocking a merger. As the internal Facebook emails extensively quoted in the FTC's *Facebook* complaint show, the Platform can be quite insightful in identifying the risks that an innovative newcomer poses for its dominance–either by de novo expansion over time or by sale to another Platform like Google that dominates different market(s). One possibility is that an enforcement agency will be allowed to do what the FTC is seeking to do in its *Facebook* case–namely, challenge a merger consummated long ago where the acquired company has since been operated by the defendant Platform.

However, political critics are unlikely to be willing to wait for several years to see whether the FTC can win its *Facebook* case and obtain successful divestiture of the old acquisitions as a remedy. Thus, we may well see legislative proposals in the US and elsewhere to use the standard premerger antitrust review process but with the burden of proof sometimes switched to the defendant Platform to show specific "public interest" benefits justifying an acquisition. What would be required are some careful definitions of (i) which Platform acquirers are subject to the special rule, and (ii) which target enterprises qualify as "potential competitors." These are technical issues on which antitrust enforcers are likely to have more insights and experience; and hence it would be very helpful if they could collectively develop some careful proposed definitions for legislators considering such a new rule.

C. *Preventing a platform from penalizing users of any competing alternative*

The issue here may be that a global Platform such as Google or Amazon may face a more serious threat from (a) local platform(s) in some national market(s). Enforcers may need to coordinate their efforts on how to prosecute a Platform's efforts to cut off use of local alternatives. Enforcement concerns go well beyond flat contractual prohibitions and may require detailed inquiry into the Platform's pricing or service terms to make sure that they do not discriminate against users of alternative sources.

D. *Improperly obtaining preferential placement on access devices*

This is precisely what the DOJ is seeking to block in *Google*, where the defendant has made large payments to Apple for "default" settings on its popular devices. Behavioral economists have established how important *defaults* may be in dictating consumers' marketplace choices, because a consumer has to make an active choice to depart from the default setting. The *Google* case involves such a blatant example of a monopolistic exclusion by a US firm that the DOJ can prosecute it unilaterally. Were the effort more subtle or involving a foreign device supplier, then inter-agency cooperation could become necessary to remedy the infringement.

E. *Regulating how a platform displays its search results*

This is something that the European Commission has been concerned about and pursued in several *Google* proceedings. The Commission's concern is that the Platform's displays do not favor (i) its own products or those offered by a corporate affiliate, (ii) products that others paid Google for prioritizing. The agency's focus is on the order in which results are displayed, because those listed first may assumed to be customers' most popular choices. This effort requires a detailed, hands-on regulatory approach,[34] for which the DOJ and FTC may lack the inclination or perhaps legal authority to undertake. However, the Commission's effort should not cause any concern for the US since its case rests on analogous concerns about *default* settings reflected in DOJ's *Google* complaint.

F. *Access to market information on transaction platforms*

Effective access to market information is essential to the fair and efficient operation of a market. Equitable access to information can become a significant competitive concern when the transactions platform operator also trades on it, rather being a neutral party (as the operator of a securities exchange normally is). The concerns are that such a dual operator may (i) deny some competing platform users full access to relevant market information, or (ii) utilize their non-public information to favor itself. This is exactly what the European Commission is attacking in its *Amazon* proceeding. Where the Platform is very international (as Amazon is)

---

[34] On December 9, 2020, the European Commission announced new guidelines requiring online platforms to (i) explain how their algorithms prioritize some results over others, and also (ii) clearly state when a featured listing was paid for. "Since businesses increasingly depend on digital solutions to reach consumers, their position in online search results can make it or break it," said Thierry Breton, the EU's commissioner for internal market. "These guidelines will increase ranking transparency and allow businesses to compete fairly online in the EU single market."

consultation between different agencies could be helpful where the Platform operator and many of those injured are in different jurisdictions. At the same time, a Platform should be allowed to charge users reasonable non-discriminatory fees for access to the platform and trading information on it.

G. *Unreasonable pricing by a transaction platform*

The DOJ and FTC have never had authority to prohibit excessive pricing or to otherwise engage in price regulation, while foreign agencies periodically used their "abuse of dominance" authority prosecute excessive pricing eases. (In the US, we have relied on sectoral regulators, such as the former Interstate Commerce Commission and the Federal Communications Commission, when pricing was contested.)

There have already been numerous orders from the European Commission and other NCAs ordering Mastercard and Visa to reduce the prices they charged merchants to process their transactions.[35] Meanwhile DOJ, as a co-plaintiff in the Supreme Court, lost a case challenging a price-enhancing rule for merchants on credit card transactions.[36] While the US result appears inconsistent with the foreign agency orders, there seems no likely conflict between DOJ or FTC enforcement efforts and foreign agencies' price caps.

5. Possible complications for international cooperation vis-à-vis the Platforms

As antitrust enforcement against the Platforms continues to expand internationally, competition agencies may face some less familiar issues in order to make their successful international cooperation work well in these new circumstances. First, there is more diversity between the US and other major countries on monopoly misconduct rules than in the cartel or merger rules (although the Klobuchar bill, if enacted, would narrow those differences).[37] Second, different countries' newly enacted or proposed statutes (like the EU DMA) may seriously increase competition agencies' need to broaden the scope of their existing cooperative efforts on both policies and investigations. Thirdly, diplomatic conflicts between the US and major allies could occur if antitrust enforcement by the EU and/or by other major foreign NCAs against the US-based Platforms

---

35   However, most of these cases involve challenges to the anticompetitive *contractual* terms imposed on the card-accepting merchants, rather than single-firm *antimonopoly conduct* by the network setting the so-called "interchange fees" that get passed on via the merchant contracts.

36   Ohio v. American Express Co., 138 2274 S. Ct. (2018)

37   The European Commission has a much more flexible antitrust toolkit (as do many NCAs enforcing similar rules). Under Article 102 TFEU, an enterprise with at least a 40% market share can be declared to be a dominant firm for antitrust purposes and subjected to a heavy administrative fine for an "abuse" of such dominance if found not to be dealing with its customers, competitors and suppliers in a "fair" manner. This mandate is a much broader than anything presently prohibited by Sherman Act section 2–which has traditionally been limited to punishing a monopolist for excluding would-be competitors from its market.

were to become much more aggressive than what the FTC and DOJ were willing or able to undertake.[38] However, given where we are in 2021, this possibility seems more theoretical than realistic.

In sum, the FTC and DOJ will likely need to further expand their past coordination efforts in order to respond to the widespread public demand that there be more active enforcement against the Platforms both in the US and abroad. The enforcement and coordination efforts would also be considerably improved if Congress were to strengthen US enforcement by seriously increasing the agencies' appropriations and staffing levels (as Senator Klobuchar has urged).

VII. Other Potential Tests for International Antitrust Cooperation

The system of interagency cooperation has survived well during a period of almost unprecedented economic and political uncertainty in which rules-based internationalism has faced populist political threats. I approach the future with cautious confidence, as I now focus on two future possibilities that may test the system further: (i) possible future inter-agency disagreement(s) over whether or not to allow a pending multi-market merger to go forward, and (ii) trying to manage potentially diverse national efforts to mitigate climate-change risks by authorizing competition-limiting agreements among enterprises.

1. Inter-agency disagreements about specific merger decisions

History clearly warns us that divergent national enforcement efforts against a high-visibility international merger could generate serious future stress for the antitrust cooperation system. Fortunately, no recent examples exist.

As I have already indicated, the administrative enforcement systems of the European Commission and numerous NCAs arm enforcers with stronger tools for blocking a global merger than FTC and DOJ have.[39] Moreover, the Commission may have been slightly less cautious than the US agencies about pulling the enforcement trigger.

With today's continuing growth of global markets, ever more mergers can have potential anticompetitive effects in different national markets.[40] A highly visible international merger can generate simultaneous political concerns and

---

38 We have already had a forewarning of such possible diplomatic risks, when France and the UK sought to tax the advertising revenues that Google and Facebook were generating in their countries, and the Trump administration treated the Platforms as national champions by responding with threatened tariffs on their major exports (whisky, camembert, etc.).

39 This procedural reality is illustrated by the 2020 *Sabre-Farelogix* decision (*infra*).

40 As I have indicated, proliferation of national antitrust merger review schemes was a key concern that led to the creation of the ICN in 2001.

enforcement attention in many places. If the merger involves two companies of the same nationality, international problems are more likely when (i) a foreign agency seeks to block the transaction extraterritorially or when (ii) the "home" market agency blesses the transaction which a foreign agency believes it should be blocking.

Each type of disagreement can be illustrated by serious conflicts between Europe and the US over aeronautical mergers 20 years ago. The affected markets were clearly global and Commission favored more aggressive enforcement than DOJ did.

In 1997, two of the world's three manufacturers of large commercial jets, Boeing and McDonnell Douglas, proposed to merge. After investigating, the DOJ decided that it had to let the transaction go forward because McDonnell Douglas was in fact a failing company–although the seriousness of its financial situation had not been disclosed publicly. The EU, which was home to the merging companies' only important competitor, Airbus, became quite concerned about the proposed approval. A lively dialogue between Washington and Brussels followed, as the US sought to persuade the Commission not to block the transaction. Senior DOJ leaders and some politicians participated in this effort, which was ultimately successful, but I understand that it left some Commission leaders feeling bullied.

The next big aviation merger, four years later, ultimately went the other way. Having the European Commission successfully block a major US merger seriously annoyed numerous US business and political leaders. General Electric's proposed acquisition of Honeywell would have combined (i) a major supplier of avionics equipment used in large aircraft with (ii) one of three global manufacturers of jet engines used in those aircraft. The Commission was concerned that GE would use its leverage from the combined company to pressure purchasers not to take avionics from Honeywell's competitors. Numerous US and foreign companies were opposed to the transaction, and those of us representing objectors found officials in Brussels much more inclined to listen to us than their counterparts in Washington were. When it became apparent that the Commission might seek to block the transaction, senior DOJ appointees from the newly installed George W. Bush administration went to Brussels to protest. Ultimately, the Commission prohibited the transaction in a decision by Commissioner Mario Monti, an impressive Italian economist.[41] This result seriously annoyed the US business and political establishments.

---

41 This was soon followed closely by another celebrated Europe vs. US dispute–where again the Commission wanted the new Bush administration DOJ to be more aggressive. This dispute concerned DOJ's famous *Microsoft* monopoly case. The DOJ had had already won an important Court of Appeals victory on the merits, but the Court of Appeals had appropriately reversed the District Court's divestiture remedy for lack of detailed findings supporting divestiture. Instead of returning to the District Court to pursue divestiture properly, the new Bush DOJ decided to settle the case with a quite modest consent decree and a chorus of objections from some US states that were DOJ's co-plaintiffs. So, the Commission went seeking additional relief it could impose against Microsoft. A lively dialogue with DOJ then ensued, and the US Department

The fact that these major conflicts have apparently not been repeated for almost two decades since 2001 shows the ongoing strength of (i) the international antitrust cooperation system and (ii) particularly the effective bilateral EU–US cooperation through a succession of agency leaders in Washington and Brussels.[42]

Extraterritorial merger enforcement by a foreign agency only becomes a problem for the cooperation system when the two national enforcers have contrary views on the same international transaction. This reality has just been so well illustrated in 2020, when the UK's Competition & Markets Authority ("CMA") prohibited a merger between two US companies offering partially-competitive airline software services–Sabre and Farelogix–shortly after the DOJ had lost its preliminary injunction case against the transaction in Delaware.[43] DOJ and CMA must have cooperated closely during their respective investigations and DOJ must not have been too unhappy with the CMA's success in the wake of its loss.[44]

2. Climate change–exempting desired cooperation among competitors

How to respond to the growing climate crisis is a huge political unknown right now–both globally and within nations. Unprecedented wildfires, extreme weather events and rising oceans could eventually create a political tidal wave for governments and enterprises to "do something big" on carbon emissions. Exactly when this might occur is hard to predict, because it may depend on numerous political leaders and citizens becoming alarmed about an ever-more-likely disaster.

The underlying reality is that "many industries [could] face a daunting task of overhauling established business models to shift to lower carbon footing."[45] In these circumstances, while some companies may be able to make adequate progress on their own, there is growing recognition that collaboration within industries could be the most effective way to bring about the long-lasting change

---

of Commerce sent a high-level representative to appear at the normal public hearing in Brussels–which some former Commission officials thought was an unnecessarily crude and heavy-handed approach. Ultimately the Commission ordered a few more tweaks to the DOJ restrictions on Microsoft's conduct, but none of them practically mattered here.

42 Anything like the *GE–Honeywell* decision would have generated a diplomatic firestorm of opposition had it occurred during the Trump administration. The DOJ and FTC leaders would have been pressured to actively weigh in even if they knew that the foreign agency's decision was entirely consistent with its merger law.

43 After an extended investigation, the CMA determined that Sabre's takeover of its much smaller rival would lead to less innovation in the airline ticketing industry and could increase the fees that passengers pay when booking flights through travel agents. Meanwhile, the US judge, after a four-week trial, found that DOJ (i) had failed to meet its burden of proving a sufficiently adverse effect in any relevant market, and (ii) because Sabre operates in a two-sided market, the DOJ had to prove harm to both sides of the market, under the Supreme Court's 2018 decision in *Ohio v. American Express*. "Only other two-sided platforms can compete with a two-sided platform for transactions." (Farelogix was a one-sided platform, selling only to airlines.)

44 The DOJ's press release following the CMA's decision suggests as much. *See* Press Release, DOJ, Statement from Assistant Attorney General Makan Delrahim on Sabre and Farelogix Decision to Abandon Merger (May 1, 2020), www.justice.gov/opa/pr/statement-assistant-attorney-general-makan-delrahim-sabre-and-farelogix-decision-abandon.

45 Nicole Kar. "Competition Rules Stymie Cooperation on Climate Change" *Financial Times*, Jan. 31, 2020.

needed to attempt to slowdown the pace of global warming.[46] In addition, we could also see mounting pressure on customers (whether enterprises or consumers) to boycott carbon-intensive enterprises, services, and products.

Such cooperation among competitors, however laudable as an environmental response, could clearly generate antitrust issues when shown to have increased prices or reduced output. Even if sympathetic NCAs were willing to desist from enforcement, some economically disadvantaged parties could be expected to bring private antitrust cases against the cooperative activity unless it had been exempted from antitrust law. This problem is especially obvious in the United States, but with the expansion of private damages remedies in numerous countries, the risk could grow elsewhere over time.

There is some parallel with what we have seen during the sudden COVID-19 virus emergency in 2020–21, with some cooperative research and development of possible vaccines among competitors being encouraged by governments and then further cooperation on their allocation among nations also needed.

In responding to climate worries, some affirmative government action seems to be needed–from enforcers and/or legislators–to provide antitrust protection for enterprises engaged in collective pro-environmental activities that governments wished to encourage. While the goal may be to facilitate *some* collaborative activities, actually defining *what* should be exempted from antitrust prohibitions appears to be another technical challenge on which enforcers could usually be better qualified than legislators.

Climate change (or "sustainability") is clearly an emerging topic among antitrust organizations and agencies. The 2021 ICN annual conference hosts (Hungary) have a "special project" on the topic that will include a panel and results of a member survey. Also, in December 2020, the OECD's Competition Committee organized a roundtable discussion on "Sustainability and competition" to explore how competition authorities might take account of sustainability issues in existing analytical frameworks.[47]

VIII. Conclusion

The international cooperation system among the world's antitrust agencies is something special. It has been smoothly expanded since 1990, as the number of NCAs has multiplied, and with it the possibility of inter-agency conflicts. The system has continued to move ahead because (i) the agencies appreciate that they have complementary missions, (ii) they need to continuously cooperate

---

46   *Id.*

47   OECD Competition Committee, Best Practice Roundtable, Sustainability and Competition (Dec. 2020), www.oecd.org/daf/competition/sustainability-and-competition.htm

in investigating the ever-more-global flow of international transactions and cartels, and (iii) avoiding international conflicts and achieving complementary enforcement results remain highly desirable goals. In sum, today's national agency leaders and key staff members are showing how well-established cooperation processes can continue to work, even at a time when populists are challenging the liberal world order of which effective competition remains such an important part.

Mandate of Competition Agency in Populist Times

MACIEJ BERNATT[*]
University of Warsaw

Abstract

This paper discusses how the mandate of competition agencies is affected by actions taken by populist governments. Poland serves as a case study in this respect. Two principal problems are addressed. The first one is the prioritization of consumer enforcement over competition law enforcement by competition agencies. The second is the broadening of the agency's mandate by new, non-competition-related competences. By studying new legislation, which broadened the agency's mandate, the paper analyses whether the coherence of objectives has been safeguarded, and whether operating capabilities have been affected. The paper concludes that the competition agency being expected to deliver in other areas lacks incentives to prioritize its activity under its competition mandate. If this process is linked with insufficient resources for the agency's competition mandate, the enforcement of competition is likely to be low.

---

[*] Dr (habil.) Maciej Bernatt, Professor of the University of Warsaw, head of the Department of European Economic Law and director of the Centre for Antitrust and Regulatory Studies, Faculty of Management, University of Warsaw; email: m.bernatt@uw.edu.pl. The paper was written during a research study visit to the University of Melbourne School of Law funded by National Agency for Academic Exchange, Poland. The author is grateful to Caron Beaton-Wells for creating a great environment for conducting this research. The opinions expressed and all errors are those of the author alone. The research presented in this paper has also been included in the Chapter 4 of author's forthcoming book: Maciej Bernatt, Populism and Antitrust: the Illiberal Influence of Populist Government on the Competition Law System (2022).

I. Introduction

Eleanor Fox played an instructive role in shaping competition law across the globe.[1] When discussing institutional design of competition laws, she advocated for shaping a competition law system that takes into account local context and the broader surroundings in which competition law functions.[2] She also cautioned against state-originating anticompetitive regulatory measures.[3] Most recently, she started worrying about the condition of competition law regimes in a time of growing illiberalism and authoritarianism,[4] a phenomenon that may be linked in the European context to the rise of populist governments.[5] Indeed, existing studies suggest that populist governments play at the edges of liberal democracies, and they dismantle checks and balances inherent to liberal democratic order.[6] Adverse effects for illiberal democracies, such as dismantling of independent judicial review, also materialize as far as institutions of competition law are concerned.[7]

The rise of populist governments can be attributed, among other things, to people's belief that they are excluded from enjoying the benefits of existing sociopolitical and economic system.[8] The feeling is that it works for elites and not for "ordinary people."[9] Therefore, populist governments implement (or at least claim to implement) policies that aim to address the frustrations of "ordinary people." Some of these policies have economic character, and potentially the legislative or executive may decide that a competition agency is well placed to implement these policies. As a result, the mandate of the competition agency may be broadened. However, the broadening of a competition agency's mandate does not have to be neutral for the traditional mission of competition agency,

---

1 *See* Philip Marsden & Spencer Weber Waller, *Citizen Fox, in* Reconciling Efficiency and Equity (Damien Geradin & Ioannis Lianos eds., 2019).

2 Eleanor M. Fox, *Antitrust and Institutions: Design and Change*, 41 Loy. U. Chi. L.J. 473, 474–75 (2010).

3 Eleanor M. Fox & Deborah Healey, *When the State Harms Competition–the Role for Competition Law*, 79 Antitrust L.J. 769 (2014).

4 Eleanor M. Fox, *Antitrust and Democracy: How Markets Protect Democracy, Democracy Protects Markets, and Illiberal Politics Threatens to Hijack Both*, 46 Legal Issues of Econ. Integration 317 (2019).

5 Maciej Bernatt, *Illiberal Populism: Competition Law at Risk?* (Working Paper, Jan. 24, 2019), https://ssrn.com/abstract=3321719.

6 *See, e.g.*: for Poland, Wojciech Sadurski, Poland's Constitutional Breakdown (2019); for Hungary, Gábor Halmai, *An Illiberal Constitutional System in the Middle of Europe*, Eur. Y.B. Hum. Rts. 497 (2014); for India: Tarunabh Khaitan, *Killing a Constitution with a Thousand Cuts: Executive Aggrandizement and Party-State Fusion in India*, Law and Ethics of Human Rights (2019, forthcoming), https://ssrn.com/abstract=3367266.

7 Maciej Bernatt, *Rule of Law Crisis, Judiciary and Competition Law*, 46 Legal Issues of Econ. Integration 345 (2019).

8 See the results of qualitative in-depth sociological studies of Polish non-metropolitan societies in Maciej Gdula, *Dobra zmiana w Miastku. Neoautorytaryzm w polskiej polityce z perspektywy małego miasta* (2017).

9 According to Mudde, populism is "a thin-centred ideology that considers society to be ultimately separated onto two homogeneous and antagonistic groups, 'the pure people' and 'the corrupt elite,' and which argues that politics should be an expression of the *volonté générale* (general will) of the people," Cas Mudde, The *Populist Zeitgeist*, 39 Gov't & Opposition 541, 543 (2004).

i.e. protection of competition. The question whether such processes indeed materialize is addressed in this paper.

In the antitrust literature, the question of whether the mandate of competition agencies should extend over other areas has been addressed. Studies concentrate on the combination in one agency of competition and consumer mandates. Both advantages of such a model, in particular the synergies created,[10] and its disadvantages have been discussed in the literature.[11] In the latter respect, it has been pointed out that non-competition-related agency competences "are likely to carry serious risks of deflecting the agency from an unambiguous commitment to this policy goal and to complicate and potentially compromise accountability for its performance against a clear set of policy goals."[12] In addition, evaluative criteria that help to decide how the competences of competition agencies should be shaped have been proposed.[13] They concern, among others, questions of coherence of objectives, agency credibility and operating capabilities, internal organization cohesion, and political implications. As for the agency's actual operations, the agent theory suggests that agencies prioritize tasks for which they are expected to be rewarded, as well as these tasks that are more easily measured than others.[14]

By using Poland, which has been ruled since late 2015 by populist government,[15] as a case study, this short paper discusses whether and how the mandate of competition agencies is affected by actions taken by populist governments. By doing so, the paper fits within the literature discussed above. The paper considers two problems: the first is the prioritization of consumer enforcement over competition law enforcement by the Polish competition agency (PCA). The paper explains the reasons behind this process. The second is the broadening of the PCA's mandate by new, non-competition-related competences. By studying new legislation that broadened the PCA's mandate, i.e. the law on abuse of bargaining power in agriculture sector and the law on combating payment gridlocks, the paper analyses whether the coherence of objectives has been safeguarded, and whether the PCA's

---

10 See Katalin J. Cseres, *Integrate or Separate–Institutional Design for the Enforcement of Competition Law and Consumer Law* (Amsterdam Law Sch. Research Paper 2013-03, 2013).

11 Michael J. Trebilcock & Edward M. Iacobucci, *Designing Competition Law Institutions: Values, Structure, and Mandate*, 41 Loy. U. Chi. L.J. 361, 465 (2010).

12 *Id.*

13 William E. Kovacic & David A. Hyman, *Competition Agencies with Complex Policy Portfolios: Divide or Conquer?*, 10–33 (G.W.U. Legal Studies Research Paper No. 2012-70, 2013).

14 Eric Biber, *Too Many Things to Do: How to Deal with the Dysfunctions of Multiple-Goal Agencies*, 33 Harv. Envtl. L. Rev. 1, 18 (2009).

15 The 2015 electoral success of the Law and Justice party can be attributed, among others reasons, to its ability to speak to those who did not believe they benefited sufficiently from the (overall successful) Polish economic and political transformation. Law and Justice politicians often contrasted the privileged elite with ordinary people, and promised to introduce new rich welfare benefits. Moreover, they exploited, or even reinforced, fears related to immigration from the Middle East (even if the inflow of immigrants was almost nonexistent in Poland in 2015). They also presented themselves as defenders of traditional, family-centered values, and contrasted them with the liberal family model of Western Europe. On top of that, they aimed to boost national pride and nation-based vision of the state.

operating capabilities and internal organization have been adversely affected. In addition, the paper refers to the recent development in Czech Republic to illustrate, with concrete example, the risks faced by agencies with broad mandate.

This paper is structured as follows. Part II discusses the prioritization of consumer enforcement over competition law enforcement. Part III addresses the problem of broadening of a competition agency's mandate to areas that are not linked to its traditional mission of protection of competition. The paper closes by offering conclusions. The paper constitutes part of the author's research project on how competition law is shaped by broader legal and socioeconomic changes. In this respect, it benefits from in-depth interviews with Polish and Czech antitrust experts conducted in late 2018 and in 2019.[16] The paper primarily discusses the developments in Poland between 2015 and 2019.

II. Prioritization of Consumer Protection

As suggested above, an agency may be inclined to focus on the part of its mandate that involves easier tasks, and for which it is expected to be rewarded, for example by having its budget increased. While intuition could suggest that agencies that have competition as their original area of competence will prioritize competition against consumer protection (a newer area of its competence), the practice in Poland shows that the contrary is true.[17] Consumer rather than competition protection is the area to which the PCA attaches greater attention.[18] Such characteristics were present before the populist government was formed and they continue to exist thereafter.[19] Both the numbers (see Table 1) and the qualitative assessment of PCA activities by interviewed experts confirm that the PCA prioritizes consumer protection. Such state of affairs is additionally confirmed by resource allocation. The number of employees of the PCA Department of Consumer Protection grew over the years, and largely surpassed the number of staff in the Department of Competition Protection. As of February 2018 the respective numbers are 46 staff and 26 staff.

---

16   The interviewees represented four categories of experts: practitioners, academics, civil servants, and judges. Their anonymity has been guaranteed.

17   The PCA (Urząd Ochrony Konkurencji i Konsumentów), also has a consumer protection portfolio. The PCA enforces broad prohibition of practices infringing collective consumer interests. Under art. 24 of the Act of 16 February 2007 on Competition and Consumer Protection, a practice infringing collective consumer interests shall mean any unlawful activity of an undertaking detrimental to these interests. The prohibition covers also such practices that are not illegal but which violate "good customs." The PCA is entitled to enforce this provision by adopting infringement or commitment decisions (*see* arts. 26–28 of the Act) and by imposing fines (art 106 of the Act).

18   Some of the interviewees went so far to state that competition protection is ignored by the post-2015 PCA's presidency. While this view is quite extreme, it reflects a common perception that consumer mandate is prioritized by the agency.

19   In Poland the prioritization of consumer cases can be dated back to at least 2015. However, the prominence of consumer mandate was gradually growing even earlier. For analysis about the evolution of the PCA's mandate since 1996 *see* Marek Martyniszyn & Maciej Bernatt, *Implementing a Competition Law System–Three Decades of Polish Experience*, 8(1) J. ANTITRUST ENFORCEMENT 165, 21–22 (2020).

Table 1: Number of infringement decisions in Poland[20]

	2009	2010	2011	2012	2013	2014	2015	2016	2017	2018
Competition Mandate	65	69	67	48	69	38	19	18	19	3
Consumer Mandate	153	160	180	193	210	135	64	43	66	34

Two major reasons explain the phenomenon, in line with Biber's perception presented above.[21] The first is that competition law cases are more complex and more resource demanding. This is particularly true for cartel cases and abuse of dominance cases. Having limited resources at its disposal, the PCA may opt to focus on easily measurable consumer activity at the expense of competition law enforcement. This is one of the explanations for the apathy in competition law enforcement in Poland.[22] Secondly, the PCA's actions under the consumer mandate receive greater public attention, particularly as far as non-specialist media coverage is concerned.[23] In parallel, politicians perceive consumer law as a good tool to address social disquiet raised by business activity.[24] In consequence, it is easier for the PCA to effectively apply for budget increases for its consumer mandate. In this sense, social and political interest in the PCA activity as well as budget increases are effectively the "rewards" the PCA receives for its consumer-related activity. They drive the PCA to focus on consumer as opposed to competition protection. In this context, it is important that the PCA's focus on consumers may be informed by its past experience. The PCA was heavily criticized in 2012 for not taking enough action to address a large Ponzi scheme,[25] what was used later by a Law and Justices MP to attack the former prime minister for lack of direct control over PCA activity.[26] In addition, the PCA's focus on consumer side of its mandate may discourage the agency from developing its expertise related to competition law enforcement,[27] as well as setting clear priorities that are necessary to build coherent competition enforcement.[28]

---

20 Source: PCA annual reports, www.uokik.gov.pl/reports_on_activities.php and information at https://decyzje.uokik.gov.pl/bp/dec_prez.nsf.

21 Cseres, *supra* note 14.

22 Source: interviews with Polish antitrust experts. See, in the same vein, Martyniszyn & Bernatt, *supra* note 19, at 22.

23 Media attention is far greater, on PCA consumer-related actions are concerned. Big cartel cases (which are very rare in Poland) and politically controversial mergers are exceptions from this rule.

24 In case of Poland, the PCA was very much expected to vigorously protect consumers on the financial market.

25 Martyniszyn & Bernatt, *supra* note 19, at 23.

26 *Przesłuchanie Donalda Tuska Przed Komisją Do Spraw Amber Gold*, TVN24 (Nov. 5, 2018) www.tvn24.pl/wiadomosci-z-kraju,3/przesluchanie-donalda-tuska-przed-komisja-do-spraw-amber-gold,881239.html.

27 Martyniszyn & Bernatt, *supra* note 19, at 23. Interviewees underline that the PCA's internal organization is counter-productive in building synergies, in particular when it comes to knowledge transfer.

28 Such view corresponds with views expressed by interviewed Polish antitrust experts.

While the preference of consumer cases over competition law can be a broader phenomenon, for example in the context of risks posed by digital markets,[29] it is likely to characterize the country ruled by populist governments. Since populists speak to "ordinary people," they may see direct state intervention to protect selected group of consumers as a good policy solution. For example, in Poland, the question of how to help mortgage borrowers who took loans denominated in foreign currencies was a big issue in the 2015 presidential campaign; the Law and Justice candidate promised far-reaching state intervention. Clearly, the PCA was expected to deliver on this front.[30] In this light, it can be argued that the PCA opted to respond to political wishes by prioritizing non-competition enforcement.[31] On top of this, preference for consumer enforcement is linked with the non-expert character of nominations for the PCA head in recent years. To put it simply, a layman is more likely to learn quickly the basics of consumer law than the basics of competition law.[32] Such personal preferences may play a greater role in cases of a single-head agency such as the PCA.

III. Spoiling the Agency's Mandate

The previous section showed that the Polish case suggests that combination of competition and consumer mandates in one agency may raise doubts as far competition law enforcement is concerned.[33] However, the idea should not be rejected out of hand, in particular if resources to pursue both goals are sufficient, the internal organization of the agency helps in creation of synergies, and safeguards exist that minimize the risks of political intrusion into decision-making on competition law side. Ultimately, both competition and consumer law are aimed at addressing market failures that are harmful to consumers.

---

29 *See* Botta & Wiedemann discussing whether consumer powers are more readily applied by the agencies than competition powers to address the market failures on digital markets, in particular as far as unilateral practices are concerned, Marco Botta & Klaus Wiedemann, *The Interaction of EU Competition, Consumer, and Data Protection Law in the Digital Economy: The Regulatory Dilemma in the Facebook Odyssey*, 64 ANTITRUST BULL. 428 (2019).

30 For examples of numerous PCA interventions *see*: *Opłaty Za Historię Spłaty Kredytu–Działania UOKiK*, UOKiK (Aug. 23, 2018), www.uokik.gov.pl/aktualnosci.php?news_id=14690; *Istotny Pogląd w Sprawie–Podsumowanie Działań UOKiK*, UOKiK (July 13, 2017), www.uokik.gov.pl/aktualnosci.php?news_id=13367.

31 Marek Niechciał, the PCA president, made it clear that other areas than competition law are more important for the PCA, political preferences being the primary reason. Talking to the Global Competition Review (GCR) he stated: "The problem is that this office stands on four legs and the magazine [GCR] is only focused on one [competition]. At the moment, one of the other three legs is most important, primarily due to the current political situation": *Interview with Marek Niechciał*, 20(1) GLOBAL COMPETITION REV. (Dec. 2016–Jan 2017), https://globalcompetitionreview-com.ezp.lib.unimelb.edu.au/insight/volume-20-issue-1-december-2016-january-2017/1080830/an-interview-with-marek-niechciał. The view that the PCA does not prioritize competition enforcement is shared by interviewed antitrust experts.

32 This observation has also been made by Polish antitrust experts who pointed out the PCA president's greater interest in consumer enforcement than competition enforcement.

33 This is not to say the enforcement of consumer law by public administrative agencies is not necessary. To the contrary, since, as argued by Cseres, "competition law is not an entirely effective tool to protect consumers," consumer law is necessary to protect consumers from market failures, such as information asymmetries, which are not necessarily addressed by competition law. *See* KATALIN J. CSERES, COMPETITION LAW AND CONSUMER PROTECTION, 330 (2005).

Greater problems arise when a competition agency is given competences going beyond consumer and competition protection, i.e. competences that do not correspond to the mentioned goal. In such a case, a risk of blurred objectives, insufficient budget and political intrusion may more readily materialize. At a minimum, the expansion of a competition agency's competences means that competition protection becomes one of many agency tasks that agency leaders may lack incentive to prioritize.

The Polish example aptly demonstrates what problems may arise when a competition agency's mandate is expanded. Such process has been on the rise since Law and Justice formed a government in Poland in 2015.[34] In late 2016 the PCA was designated as an enforcer of the Act on Counteracting the Unfair Use of Contractual Advantage in Trade in Agricultural and Food Products.[35] In 2019 it was designated as the agency responsible for combating payment gridlocks in Poland.[36]

1. Abuse of bargaining power in the agriculture sector

As to the first role, one could argue that it fits into the overall PCA mission. Both the Polish Competition Act and the Contractual Advantage Act are applied, according to their article 1, in the public interest. However, the PCA's principal aim is to protect competition as a market mechanism, as well as to protect consumers (understood as a generic category).[37] By contrast, the Contractual Advantage Act can be seen as a platform of intervention in individual, *inter partes*, contractual relations aimed at protecting the weaker side of the transaction, normally a local Polish producer of agriculture products or a food processor, against the abuses by large chain retailers (very often foreign-owned). Such character of the law is reinforced by complete elimination of turnover intervention thresholds.[38] While one could argue that interventions under the Contractual Advantage Act are overall in the public interest (e.g., protection of local food production being the goal), this public interest is of different nature than the one promoted by the Competition Act.[39] What's more, it is believed that

---

34 The formerly independent Trade Inspection, which is responsible among others for product safety, was integrated within the PCA in 2009. However, one could argue that it was not a broadening of the PCA mandate in the strict sense. Rather the PCA become the institution that supervises the Trade Inspection.

35 *See* Act of Dec. 15, 2016 on Counteracting the Unfair Use of Contractual Advantage in Trade in Agricultural and Food Products (2017) O.J. 67.

36 *See* Act of July 19, 2019 amending several acts in order to curb payment gridlocks in Poland (2019) O.J. § 1649.

37 Maciej Bernatt & Marcin Mleczko, *Poland: Public Interest and a Place for Non-Competition Considerations in Polish Competition Law*, 1 Concurrences (2018).

38 The amendment to Contractual Advantage Act passed in October 2018 abolished firm's minimal turnover thresholds, to enable PCA intervention even in very small cases, which arguably are meaningless for the functioning of market as such. *See UOKiK for Agriculture–Changes in Law*, UOKiK (Aug. 10, 2018), www.uokik.gov.pl/news.php?news_id=14642.

39 Agata Jurkowska-Gomułka, *Competition Authority in a Trap? A Few (Bitter) Words on Making Public Policy by Counteracting an Unfair Use of a Contractual Advantage in Agri-Food Sector in Poland*, 16 Cent. Eur. Pub. Admin. Rev. 51, 59 (2018).

it is possible that the PCA's intervention under the Contractual Advantage Act will be anticompetitive, for example, when the PCA intervenes to protect a supplier of apples whose long-term contract has been terminated by a supermarket chain in view of availability of alternative, cheaper sources of apples.[40] Such thesis is open for discussion, in particular for those who would not consider adverse price effect as an exclusive proxy for antitrust intervention, and who would accept antitrust intervention aimed at the protection of certain product characteristics to which consumers may attach value.[41]

In any case, the Polish context suggests that the underlying goal behind the Contractual Advantage Act was to please Polish farmers, who used to complain regularly of being exploited by large chain retailers,[42] and so possibly to contribute to building a strong support for Law and Justice in the country.[43] The PCA was asked to deliver in an area that involves the political interests of the ruling party. The statements of the PCA president suggest that he readily took this role.[44] So far, the enforcement of the Contractual Advantage Act has been moderate and the PCA picked cases where the abuse of contractual advantage was rather straightforward.[45] This, however, may change.[46] It is clear that the allocation of this new power to the PCA politicized it, and could take PCA attention away from competition enforcement. This is reflected both in the statements of the PCA,[47] and the attention the PCA wanted to attract to its actions aimed at protection of Polish farmers.[48] If one adds to it that the

---

40 *Id.* at 60.

41 For a discussion in this respect *see, e.g.*, Anna Gerbrandy, *Solving a Sustainability-Deficit in European Competition Law*, 40 WORLD COMPETITION 539 (2017). The background explanation to the Contractual Advantage Act, while considering national food safety as a value the act aims to protect, mentions that low-price food production may have an adverse effect on food quality and so harm consumers. *See Druk Nr 790* (July 25, 2016), www.sejm.gov.pl/Sejm8.nsf/druk.xsp?nr=790. National food safety is clearly not a goal with which the Competition Act is concerned.

42 *See* Statement of Jan Krzysztof Ardanowski, Law and Justice MP (and later Minister of Agriculture) involved in the legislative process, *Tylko PiS Za Projektem Ustawy o Eliminacji Nieuczciwych Praktyk Handlowych–Handel Dystrybucja* (Nov. 15, 2016), www.portalspozywczy.pl/handel/wiadomosci/tylko-pis-za-projektem-ustawy-o-eliminacji-nieuczciwych-praktyk-handlowych,136929.html.

43 For a discussion in this respect *see* Zosia Wanat, *Children, Pigs and Cows–How PiS Is Winning the Rural Vote*, POLITICO (Oct. 7, 2019), www.politico.eu/article/polish-ruling-party-seeks-a-clean-sweep-in-the-countryside/.

44 The PCA president publicly supported in July 2019 the envisaged amendment to the Contractual Advantage Act under which the UOKiK would be responsible for enforcing the prohibition of sale of agricultural products below the reference price, *UOKiK for Agriculture–Summer 2019*, UOKiK (July 25, 2019), www.uokik.gov.pl/news.php?news_id=15650. Together with Minister of Agriculture, the PCA was also an initiator of the 2018 amendment to this act, aimed at increasing the number of cases handled by the PCA under this act. The PCA president noted that changes to the law "will help the state to protect a larger number of farmers. Especially those who own small farms": *UOKiK for Agriculture–Changes in Law, supra* note 38.

45 Cases involved in particular unreasonably late payments to food producers by retail chains, *UOKiK for Agriculture–Summer 2019, supra* note 44.

46 In September 2019, the PCA opened a more complex case in which it questions the rebate policy applied by the biggest, foreign-owned retail chain in Poland in relation to their fruit suppliers, *see Biedronka's Practices–the UOKiK Procedure*, UOKiK (Sept. 29, 2019) www.uokik.gov.pl/news.php?news_id=15802.

47 *See* Niechciał, *supra* note 31.

48 *See*, inter alia, the press releases entitled *UOKiK for Agriculture*, www.uokik.gov.pl/search.php?szukaj=agriculture.

PCA, while being burdened with the new task, did not receive initially significant increase in its budget, and had to stretch its limited resources to pursue new competences,[49] the overall results for the PCA competition mandate are negative. The reputation of the PCA as an antitrust enforcer suffered.[50] Using Kovacic and Hyman criteria,[51] one can argue that Contractual Advantage Act affected the agency's credibility and brand, its operating capabilities, and the its internal organizational cohesion.

2. Combating payment gridlocks as a competition agency's task

The picture is even grimmer as far as combating payment gridlocks in Poland are concerned. Since January 1, 2020, the PCA is entitled to establish proceedings and impose fines on firms that failed to pay their contractors on time.[52] Addressing the problems with liquidity of Polish SMEs is a rationale under the new law.[53] Similar to the Contractual Advantage Act, one of the new law's goals is to protect Polish SMEs from abuse by big companies, very often Multinational Enterprises (MNEs). The PCA vice-president clearly explained this goal. He noted: "New regulations will definitely improve financial liquidity of entrepreneurs. I mean mainly medium, small and micro-enterprises whom larger contractors do not pay on time. As a result, smaller entrepreneurs often credit business run by tycoons."[54]

While the new law aims at addressing the phenomenon that may indeed be problematic, allocation of powers in the hands of the PCA is controversial.[55] In this case, the requirement of policy coherence, a crucial factor in Kovacic/Hyman typology, is missing.[56] Addressing the problems of liquidity of Polish firms has very little to do with protection of market competition and protection of consumers, at least not in the meaning of competition law or consumer law. What's more, contrary to other state institutions such as the National Tax

---

49 The enforcement of the Contractual Advantage Act was allocated to UOKiK local office in Bydgoszcz, which had a good record of antitrust interventions. Since 2017, the UOKiK Bydgoszcz local office issued only one decision concerning competition.

50 The enactment of Contractual Advantage Act and entrustment of its enforcement to the PCA has been broadly criticized by Polish antitrust academia and practitioners. For an initial account, see, e.g., articles published at http://ikar.wz.uw.edu.pl/ikar.php?ikar=47.

51 See Mudde, supra note 13.

52 *100 Days to Go before The Act on Reducing Payment Gridlocks Becomes Effective*, UOKiK (Sept. 23, 2019), www.uokik.gov.pl/news.php?news_id=15797. For a legal basis see Act of July 19, 2019, supra note 36.

53 See the background explanation to draft law aimed at curbing payment gridlock in Poland, "Druk Nr 3475" www.sejm.gov.pl/Sejm8.nsf/druk.xsp?nr=3475.

54 UOKiK, supra note 52.

55 For a criticism in this respect, see also Opinion of the PCA former vice-president, Bernadeta Kasztelan-Świetlik, *Skarbówka Powinna Karać Nierzetelnych Kontrahentów–Opinia* (Feb. 21, 2019), www.prawo.pl/biznes/skarbowka-powinna-karac-nierzetelnych-kontrahentow-opinia,374419.html.

56 See also Opinion of Marta Sendrowicz, Polish antitrust practitioner, who pointed out that "it is hardly possible to see any substantive synergies in combining the core business of President Niechciał with matters regarding debtors," (2019) LinkedIn, www.linkedin.com/in/dr-marta-sendrowicz-132b82b4/detail/recent-activity/shares/.

Administration, the PCA has not been prepared to undertake such tasks: it neither has previous expertise nor existing technical capabilities to control a firm's finances. As this suggests, the PCA is put in a position to produce outcomes that are beneficial for Polish SMEs, that do not have to always correspond with the best interest of consumers and competition as mechanism on which the market is founded. What's more, since the law applies also to late invoice payments by public authorities, the PCA may be put in difficult position to intervene vis-à-vis powerful public agencies. The new law further politicizes the PCA and limits its independence by exposing it to political pressure to show that its activity under the new law brings effects.[57]

Focus on the new area is thus likely to further detach the attention of PCA leadership from competition law enforcement. The decrease of importance of the PCA competition portfolio is obvious if one takes into account the budget. Combating payment gridlocks will be dealt with by 110 new staff within the PCA's Warsaw headquarters,[58] what is quite an impressive number if one compares it with c.26 staff of the Competition Protection Department, the PCA's competition law enforcement unit. In view of it, one could ironically argue that name of the PCA should be changed, since it does not reflect anymore the PCA competences. The observation by Kovacic and Hyman fits very well in this context. They claim that when a mismatch between commitments and capacities exists, the "agency can engage in policy triage, in the hope there will be no disasters in the ignored policy space and that no one cares enough about the tasks that are being ignored to make a fuss."[59] As far as Poland is concerned, competition law possibly becomes such marginalized policy space.[60] The perspective is that the PCA becomes the "everything agency," i.e. the agency with numerous, unrelated tasks.[61] Lastly, the allocation of enforcement powers regarding combating payment gridlocks within the PCA suggests that the PCA political standing is low, and the PCA does not have a power to oppose legislative ideas that are not beneficial for the PCA role as a competition enforcer.[62]

---

57 In the literature it has been observed that there is a link between a competition agency's mandate and more limited independence, *Giorgio Monti, Independence, Interdependence and Legitimacy: The EU Commission, National Competition Authorities, and the European Competition Network* (EUI Dept. of Law Research Paper No. 2014/01, 2014), https://ssrn.com/abstract=2379320.

58 The PCA 2020 additional budget is PLN 18.7 million. *See* Druk nr 3465, 96 (May 20, 2019), www.google.com/url?sa=t&rct=j&q=&esrc=s&source=web&cd=14&ved=2ahUKEwit4t7So8DlAhWq6XMBHSqrANQQFjANegQIBRAE&url=https%3A%2F%2Fwww.senat.gov.pl%2Fdownload%2Fgfx%2Fsenat%2Fpl%2Fsenatposiedzeniatematy%2F4456%2Fdrukisejmowe%2F3475.pdf&usg=AOvVaw20a_XqrbQ0x-aPcewJE6Db.

59 Kovacic & Hyman, *supra* note 13.

60 Such view is shared by the interviewed Polish antitrust experts.

61 *Source*: interviews with Polish antitrust experts. *See also* Sendrowicz, *supra* note 56: "there is some concern whether these new functions will impact the NCA's efficiency in dealing with competition and consumer cases, which should remain the agency's priority."

62 During the legislative process the PCA criticized the original idea of amending the Competition Act in order to include in its prohibition late payments, pointing out that a change in the catalogue of anticompetitive practices in this respect will limit the possibility of addressing payment gridlocks, since enforcement will have to remain within the framework of general clauses of anticompetitive agreements and abuse of dominant

3. Reputational risks

Broadening the competences of an agency may expose it to reputational risks on competition law side that otherwise are more limited. This case is well-represented by the corruption scandal involving the chairman of the Czech Competition Authority (CCA). Since the CCA is not only a competition agency but it also has oversight powers in public procurement proceedings, it may be captured by challenges concerning this area of economy, of which corruption and non-transparent links between politicians and private firms, are often the biggest issues.

In 2019 the CCA chairman faced accusations of taking bribes and participating in secret meetings with politicians. Allegedly they were aimed to influence an appeal decision by the CCA concerning public procurement proceedings for operation of a toll collection system in the Czech Republic.[63] The CCA's office and chairman's private premises were raided by police. Large amount of money were found in the chairman's home.[64] The case allegedly involved lobbying the CCA chairman on behalf of private firms taking part in the toll services tender by a prominent member of the ruling ANO party, whose leader, populist prime minister of Czech Republic and a billionaire, faced financial misconduct accusations related to his alleged misuse of EU funds earmarked for small businesses.[65] Despite such charges and calls to the CCA chairman to step down (among others by Amnesty International),[66] the chairman did not resign.

This scandal severely damaged the reputation of the PCA. According to interviewed antitrust experts it has reached its lowest historical levels. The case raised also questions about the CCA independence vis-à-vis private powerful firms and politicians of the ruling party.[67]

---

position. Therefore, UOKiK was aware that the eventually chosen way of regulation by means of changes to the act on payment terms in commercial transactions will go beyond its core competition protection mission. For the UOKiK opinion, *see*, *(No Title)*, (Oct. 22, 2019) https://legislacja.rcl.gov.pl/docs//2/12316 111/12535098/12535101/dokument366791.pdf. For the legislative process, *see*, *Projekt* https://legislacja.rcl. gov.pl/projekt/12316111/katalog/12535129#12535129.

63 *Czech Authority Raided by Police*, Global Competition Review (2019) https://globalcompetitionreview-com. ezp.lib.unimelb.edu.au/article/1188665/czech-authority-raided-by-police.

64 *Petr Rafaj and UOHS Investigation: Police Investigate Hundreds of Prints from Envelopes and Money*, (Oct. 25, 2019), www.novinky.cz/krimi/clanek/z-novin-policie-zkouma-stovku-otisku-z-obalek-a-penez-od-rafaje-40301027.

65 *Czech Attorney Drops Fraud Case against PM Babis: Newspaper*, Reuters (Sept. 2, 2019), www.reuters.com/article/us-czech-babis/czech-attorney-drops-fraud-case-against-pm-babis-newspaper-idUSKCN1VN0DM. Journalists believe that Babis aimed to manipulate the case by dismissing the former Minister of Justice, after he decided to file charge suits and replacing it with party's loyalist. *Can Protesters Bring down the Czech Prime Minister? – Toughing It Out*, The Economist (May 23, 2019), www.economist.com/europe/2019/05/23/can-protesters-bring-down-the-czech-prime-minister. He faces massive protests and calls to resign. *Czech Anti-Government Protesters Mark Anniversary of Revolution*, BBC News (Nov. 16, 2019), www.bbc.com/news/world-europe-50446661.

66 *Czech Authority Raided by Police*, *supra* note 63.

67 *Id.*

IV. Conclusion

Determination of appropriate scope of competition agency mandate is a difficult task any time. This task becomes even more challenging in a time of rule by populist government. In particular, the analysis of Poland has shown that the coherence of objectives and the agency's operating capabilities are affected by new legislations adopted by parliament dominated by a ruling populist party. The competition agency is equipped with new competences that are not compatible with its traditional mission, i.e. protection of competition. The agency is asked to pursue objectives that make part of populist agenda: protect small local firms or individual producers, such as farmers, against the presumed exploitation by big companies. However, these goals are not to be pursed within the existing competition law framework, for example as exploitative practices of dominant firms. Rather, the laws passed provide a space for intervention in individual relations between firms to pursue goals that are not necessarily coherent with existing competition law goals. Consumers do not have to benefit from such interventions.

In addition, the allocation of new tasks to a competition agency puts the agency's operating capabilities under pressure or leads to significant internal restructuration. The amalgamation of the competition authority's competences is combined with politicians' expectation that the agency will make a use of its consumer protection powers. The result of discussed processes is the following: the agency being expected to deliver in other areas lacks incentive to prioritize its activity under competition mandate. Once this process is linked with insufficient resources for the agency's competition mandate, the enforcement of competition is likely to be low. The challenges related to insufficient safeguards of agency independence and political pressure on courts reviewing its decision, which are characteristic for illiberal change brought by the populist government, may additionally reinforce such state of affairs. Lastly, one needs to understand the reputational risks for the agency functioning with a broad mandate. They may be not only linked to decrease in trust that the agency is an expert, law-based competition law enforcer, but also, as the Czech case shows, may suffer because of agency's failures in other areas than competition.

In short, the processes discussed have adverse effect on the functioning of agency under its competition mandate. Therefore, while not illiberal at first sight, they represent yet another representation of such effects of the rise of populist governments that mark the departure from liberal democracy and open markets Eleanor Fox supports.

PART VI
Enforcement and Judicial Review: Current Issues

Extraterritoriality: Approaches Around the World and Model Analysis

KOREN W. WONG-ERVIN & ANDREW HEIMERT[*]

Axinn, Veltrop & Harkrider | Federal Trade Commission

Abstract

Enforcement of competition laws beyond the boundaries of a jurisdiction's borders has, as a general matter, become uncontroversial. The growth of international commerce, combined with the increasingly global scope of firm conduct, has required courts and agencies to determine when and whether domestic antitrust laws may have extraterritorial application, and, relatedly, whether the traditional set of remedies remain applicable to the same degree. While extraterritorial enforcement and remedies raise modest issues when competition laws are aligned, they present greater challenges when different jurisdictions have different substantive approaches, if not ones that are diametrically opposed. Part I describes several cases in which agencies or courts considered whether extraterritorial remedies were appropriate. Part II describes the legal standards for applying competition laws, and remedies, to conduct that occurs outside the jurisdiction in several countries. Part III provides our model analysis proposing how agencies and courts might best approach these questions. Finally, we include an Appendix summarizing the legal approaches in several major jurisdictions.

---

[*] Koren W. Wong-Ervin is a Partner at Axinn, Veltrop & Harkrider LLP, a senior expert & researcher at China's University of International Business and Economics, an academic adviser at China's University of Political Law & Science, and former counsel for IP & international antitrust and attorney adviser to Commissioner Joshua D. Wright at the US Federal Trade Commission (FTC). Andrew Heimert is counsel for Asian Competition Affairs in the Office of International Affairs at the FTC. The authors thank Thu Hoang for her research assistance. The views expressed here are the authors' alone and do not necessarily represent the views of the FTC, any of its commissioners, or any other person or entity.

I. Introduction

In the last 25 years, there has been a remarkable proliferation of foreign competition laws and agencies, expanding from 23 jurisdictions with competition laws in 1990 to over 130 jurisdictions to date. Enforcement of these competition laws beyond the boundaries of a jurisdiction's borders has, as a general matter, become uncontroversial, for example when conduct outside the jurisdiction has an adverse effect on competition and consumers in the enforcing jurisdiction. The growth of international commerce, combined with the increasingly global scope of firm conduct, has required courts and agencies to determine when and whether domestic antitrust laws may have extraterritorial application. Relatedly, applying antitrust laws to conduct that occurs outside a jurisdiction can also raise the question of whether the traditional set of remedies remain applicable to the same degree. When competition laws are applied to conduct outside of the enforcing jurisdiction, how (and whether) a court or agency should craft extrajurisdictional remedies (i.e., prohibitions or requirements on foreign conduct or with respect to foreign assets, such as physical or intellectual property) becomes a more challenging question.

Among Professor Eleanor Fox's contributions to the worldwide antitrust discussion is how to reconcile differences in competition laws around the globe.[1] While extraterritorial enforcement and remedies raise modest issues when competition laws are aligned, they present greater challenges when different jurisdictions have different substantive approaches, if not ones that are diametrically opposed. How these differences might be addressed is therefore a highly suitable subject to discuss in a tribute to Professor Fox.

As introductory examples to how these issues arise, two recent high-profile cases outside the United States–one involving Intel and the other involving Qualcomm– are illustrative.

The 2017 *Intel* case is an example of extraterritorial application of a domestic competition law. The Court of Justice of the European Union (CJEU) upheld jurisdiction of EU institutions over conduct by an American company (Intel) with respect to, inter alia, chip sales to a Chinese company (Lenovo) in China, when the conduct was alleged to have harmed another American company (Advanced Micro Devices or AMD).[2] The conduct at issue was loyalty rebates and payments to original equipment manufacturers to induce them to delay,

---

[1] *See, e.g.,* Eleanor M. Fox, Rule of Law, Standards of Law, Discretion and Transparency, 67 SMU L. Rev. 795 (2014); Eleanor M. Fox, Monopolization and Abuse of Dominance: Why Europe Is Different, 59 Antitrust Bull. 129 (2014).

[2] Case C-413/14 P, Intel Corp. v. Comm'n EU:C:2017:632, ¶ 51 (Sept. 6, 2017), [hereinafter CJEU 2017 Intel Judgment]. This aspect of the ruling diverged from the (non-binding but influential) Opinion of Advocate General Wahl, who concluded that Intel's jurisdiction arguments were "well founded." Opinion EU:C:2016:788, ¶¶ 278–327 (Oct. 20, 2016). *See also* François-Charles Laprévote et al., *The EU Court of Justice modernizes abuse of dominance notion (*Intel*)*, e-Competitions September 2017, Art. N° 84980 (Sept. 6, 2017).

cancel, or restrict the marketing of certain products equipped with AMD computer processing units (CPUs). As concerns sales of CPUs to Lenovo, only a few thousand of the finished products (computers assembled by Lenovo in China) were implicated (i.e., they allegedly would potentially have included an AMD CPU had Intel not induced the breach of marketing contracts). In determining whether Intel's conduct was "capable" of having a "substantial, immediate and foreseeable effect" within the European Economic Area (EEA),[3] the CJEU held that it was sufficient to consider the "probable effects" of the conduct on competition and that "Intel's conduct vis-à-vis Lenovo formed part of an overall strategy aimed at foreclosing AMD's access to the most important sales channels."[4]

The Korea Fair Trade Commission's (KFTC's) 2017 decision against Qualcomm is an example of the use of extra-jurisdictional remedies. Specifically, the KFTC imposed global, portfolio-wide remedies, including prohibiting or requiring certain licensing conduct with respect to non-Korean foreign patents.[5] The KFTC's remedies extend to licensing agreements with all handset or modem chipset companies "headquartered" in Korea, those that sell handsets in or into Korea, and those that supply modem chipsets to companies that sell handsets in Korea.

By comparison, to resolve China's National Development and Reform Commission's 2015 decision against Qualcomm finding violations of China's Antimonopoly Law for much the same licensing conduct at issue in the KFTC case, the agency accepted a rectification plan proposed by the company that limited remedies to Qualcomm's Chinese patents (specifically, its wireless standard-essential patents (SEPs)) for the manufacture of end-user devices in China for sale and use either in China or in a country in which no relevant patents have been issued to Qualcomm.[6]

Similarly, in the European Commission's 2014 decisions against Samsung and Motorola, the Commission limited its remedies to preclude the companies from certain conduct (seeking injunctive relief for infringement of certain SEPs, for

---

[3] CJEU 2017 Intel Judgment, *supra* note 2, ¶ 18.

[4] *Id.* ¶¶ 51 and 55.

[5] Korea Fair Trade Comm'n, Case No. 2015SiGam2118, *In re* Alleged Abuse of Market Dominance of Qualcomm Inc., Decision No. 2017-0-25, Reasoning, ¶ 483. (Jan. 20, 2017), *unofficial translation available in English at* www.theamericanconsumer.org/wp-content/uploads/2017/03/2017-01-20_KFTC-Decision_2017-0-25.pdf [hereinafter KFTC Order]. In December 2019, the KFTC Order was upheld by the Seoul High Court with respect to this aspect of the KFTC's decision. Qualcomm has appealed that decision to Korea's Supreme Court.

[6] Rectification Plan Related to NDRC's Investigation of Qualcomm § I.A. (Feb. 9, 2015) ("These rectification measures apply to Qualcomm's licensing of Manufacturers under its Chinese Wireless SEPs to (i) make Devices and sell such Devices For Use in China or (ii) make Devices in China and sell such Devices For Use in a Territory."), *translated in* Qualcomm's Briefing Ex. C, www.qualcomm.com/media/documents/files/reply-in-support-of-motion-for-stay-6-18-19.pdf; *see also* Press Release, Qualcomm, Qualcomm and China's National Development and Reform Commission Reach Resolution–NDRC Accepts Qualcomm's Rectification Plan–Qualcomm Raises Midpoints of Fiscal 2015 Revenue and Non-GAAP EPS Guidance (Feb. 9, 2015), https://investor.qualcomm.com/news-events/press-releases/detail/672/qualcomm-and-chinas-national-development-and-reform. *See* Appendix I for a summary of the approved remedies.

which the companies had made a commitment to license on fair, reasonable, and nondiscriminatory (FRAND) terms) only in the EEA, and only with respect to patents granted in the EEA.[7]

This paper seeks to explore the issues raised by extraterritorial enforcement and the remedies used in those circumstances first by discussing the approaches taken in several major jurisdictions around the world, and then providing model analysis in the context of common situations that have arisen or may arise. We conclude with a chart summarizing the approaches taken in Brazil, Canada, China, the European Union, India, Japan, Korea, the United States, and Taiwan. In this way, we hope to expand upon Professor Fox's insightful and informative work in this area in order to provide guidance for courts and agencies.[8]

II. Approaches in Major Jurisdictions

Most major jurisdictions apply some sort of effects test when determining whether to apply their domestic antitrust laws to foreign conduct, as summarized in Appendix I. The approaches are comparable to that specified in the US Foreign Trade Antitrust Improvements Act (FTAIA), which provides that foreign conduct is outside the scope of the Sherman Act unless it "has a direct, substantial, and reasonably foreseeable effect" on domestic or import commerce and "such effect gives rise to a claim under" the Sherman Act.[9] Other countries take similar approaches, although in different words. For example, China's Antimonopoly Law provides that the law is "applicable to monopolistic conducts outside the territory of the People's Republic of China, which serve to eliminate or restrict competition on the domestic market of China."[10] The EU applies either a "qualified effects" test (reasonably "foreseeable" of having "immediate and

---

7   European Comm'n, Antitrust Decisions on Standard Essential Patents (SEPs) – Motorola Mobility and Samsung Electronics–Frequently Asked Questions (MEMO/14/322, Apr. 29, 2014). *See also* Case AT.39939–Samsung, Comm'n Decision (Apr. 29, 2014) (summary at 2014 O.J. (C 350) 8), https://ec.europa.eu/competition/antitrust/cases/dec_docs/39939/39939_1501_5.pdf; Case AT.39985–Motorola, Comm'n Decision (Apr. 29, 2014) (summary at 2014 O.J. (C 344) 6), https://ec.europa.eu/competition/antitrust/cases/dec_docs/39985/39985_928_16.pdf.

8   *See* Eleanor M. Fox, *Extraterritorial Jurisdiction, Antitrust, and the EU Intel Case: Implementation, Qualified Effects, and the Third Kind*, 42 FORDHAM INT'L L.J. 981 (2019); Eleanor Fox, *Antitrust: Updating Extraterritoriality*, 0/2019 ANTITRUST & PUB. POLICIES REV. (inaugural issue) (Italian Competition Authority) [hereinafter Fox, *Updating Extraterritoriality*]; Eleanor M. Fox, *Extraterritoriality and Input Cartels: Life in the Global Value Lane–The Collision Course with Empagran and How to Avert It*, CPI ANTITRUST CHRON. (Jan. 2015).

9   Foreign Trade Antitrust Improvements Act of 1982, 15 U.S.C. § 6a(1). Section 5(a)(3) of the Federal Trade Commission Act closely parallels the FTAIA. *See* 15 U.S.C. § 45(a)(3).

10 Antimonopoly Law of the People's Republic of China, promulgated by the Standing Comm. Nat'l People's Cong. (Aug. 30, 2007), art. 2, http://english.mofcom.gov.cn/article/policyrelease/Businessregulations/201303/20130300045909.shtml. A court in China held that this provision included conduct outside China that "directly ha[s] a major, substantial and reasonably foreseeable effect of impairing and restricting the domestic production activities, export opportunity and export trade of domestic enterprises." Huawei Jishu Youxian Gongsi Su Jiaohu Shuzi Tongxin Youxian Gongsi (华为技术有限公司诉交互数字通信有限公司) [Huawei Tech. Co. v. InterDigital Commc'n, Inc. (Huawei v. IDC)], Section II, 2013 Yue Gao Fa Min San Zhong Zi No. 306 (Guangdong High People's Ct. No. 306 2013) (China). Application of antitrust laws to export commerce finds a parallel in the US FTAIA. *See* 15 U.S.C. § 6a(1)(B).

substantial" effects in the EU) or an "implementation" test (focusing on where the conduct is implemented, rather than the location of the undertaking). The CJEU in *Intel* clarified that the two tests pursue the "same objective, namely preventing conduct which, while not adopted within the EU, has anticompetitive effects liable to have an impact on the EU market."[11]

Applying a country's competition law allows for the use of extra-jurisdictional remedies, at least implicitly, in certain circumstances. What those circumstances are is a matter of how expansively a country's courts and competition enforcement agencies seek to assert their authority, or are limited by either the principles of competition law or broader principles of international relations in doing so.

In addition to applying some sort of effects test, most major jurisdictions also take into consideration comity concerns, both in deciding whether to apply domestic laws to foreign conduct and whether to impose extra-jurisdictional remedies.[12] Comity refers to the "broad concept of respect among co-equal sovereign nations and plays a role in determining 'the recognition which one nation allows within its territory to the legislative, executive or judicial acts of another nation.'"[13] In applying principles of international comity, jurisdictions typically consider whether significant interests of foreign sovereigns would be affected.

By way of example, the US antitrust agencies consider and weigh the following factor when deciding whether to pursue enforcement action against foreign conduct as well as to seek remedies for that conduct:

- The existence of a purpose to affect or an actual effect on US commerce;
- The significance and foreseeability of the effects of the anticompetitive conduct on the United States;

---

11 CJEU 2017 Intel Judgment, *supra* note 2, ¶ 45. *See also id.* ¶¶ 40–44.

12 *See, e.g.*, Organisation for Economic Co-operation and Development (OECD) Roundtable on the Extraterritorial Reach of Competition Remedies–Note by the European Union ¶ 7 (DAF/COMP/WP3/WD(2017)35, Nov. 30, 2017) ("The Commission applies the principle of international comity and cooperates on competition cases on the basis of international agreements concluded between the EU and third countries and memoranda of understanding entered into with other agencies."), https://one.oecd.org/document/DAF/COMP/WP3/WD(2017)35/en/pdf; OECD Roundtable on the Extraterritorial Reach of Competition Remedies–Note by Korea ¶ 32 (DAF/COMP/WP3/WD(2017)37, Nov. 23, 2017) (stating that, in its 2017 Qualcomm decision, the KFTC "took into account facts that various countries are paying attention to this case, and there might be efforts to find different solutions due to differences in national systems"), https://one.oecd.org/document/DAF/COMP/WP3/WD(2017)37/en/pdf [hereinafter Korea 2017 OECD Note]; OECD Roundtable on the Extraterritorial Reach of Competition Remedies–Note by Chinese Taipei ¶ 10 (DAF/COMP/WP3/WD(2017)45, Nov. 22, 2017) (the TFTC "uses the principle of effect as the basis for its law enforcement in extraterritorial merger cases ... and then limits the applicability of the principle of effect while giving consideration to the comity of nations, principle of interest balancing, and principle of reasonable jurisdiction"), www.oecd.org/officialdocuments/publicdisplaydocumentpdf/?cote=DAF/COMP/WP3/WD(2017)45&docLanguage=En [hereinafter Chinese Taipei 2017 OECD Note]; OECD Roundtable on the Extraterritorial Reach of Competition Remedies–Note by Brazil ¶ 8 (the Brazilian Competition Authority's international cooperation documents allow for "the grant of negative or positive comity considerations") (DAF/COMP/WP3/WD(2017)42, Dec. 3, 2017), https://one.oecd.org/document/DAF/COMP/WP3/WD(2017)42/en/pdf.

13 US Dep't of Justice & Fed. Trade Comm'n, Antitrust Guidelines for International Enforcement and Cooperation 27 (Jan. 13, 2017) (quoting Hilton v. Guyot, 159 U.S. 113, 164 (1895)), www.justice.gov/atr/internationalguidelines/download [hereinafter US Int'l Guidelines].

- The degree of conflict with a foreign jurisdiction's law or articulated policy;
- The extent to which the enforcement activities of another jurisdiction, including remedies resulting from those enforcement activities, may be affected; and
- The effectiveness of foreign enforcement as compared with US enforcement.[14]

Additional factors that US courts have considered in a variety of circumstances in assessing whether principles of comity warrant exercising US jurisdiction over foreign conduct include:

1. The nationality or allegiance of the parties and the locations of principal places of business of corporations;
2. The extent to which enforcement by either state can be expected to achieve compliance (e.g., whether the court can make its order effective);
3. The relative significance of effects on the United States as compared with those elsewhere;
4. (The extent to which there is explicit purpose to harm or affect American commerce;
5. The foreseeability of such effect;
6. The relative importance to the violations charged of conduct within the United States as compared with conduct abroad;
7. The possible effect upon foreign relations if the court exercises jurisdiction and grants relief;
8. If relief is granted, whether a party will be placed in the position of being forced to perform an act illegal in either country;
9. Whether an order for relief would be acceptable in the United States if made by the foreign nation under similar circumstances; and
10. Whether a treaty with the affected nations has addressed the issue.[15]

---

14 *Id.* at 28.

15 *See, e.g., In re* Vitamin C Antitrust Litig., 837 F.3d 175, 193 (2d Cir. 2016) (setting forth a non-exhaustive list of factors for comity analysis), *vacated on other grounds and remanded sub nom.* Animal Sci. Prod., Inc. v. Hebei Welcome Pharm. Co., 138 S. Ct. 1865 (2018); Timberlane Lumber Co. v. Bank of Am. Nat.l Tr. & Sav. Ass'n, 749 F.2d 1378, 1384 (9th Cir. 1984) (holding that a comity determination "***requires*** that a district court consider [the] seven factors" set forth in *Timberlane I*) (emphasis added); Mannington Mills, Inc. v. Congoleum Corp., 595 F.2d 1287, 1297–98 (3d Cir. 1979) (setting forth a non-exhaustive list of factors). In *Timberlane II*, the court applied the factors as follows (749 F.2d at 1386):

All but two of the factors in *Timberlane I*'s comity analysis indicate that we should refuse to exercise jurisdiction over this antitrust case. The potential for conflict with Honduran economic policy and commercial law is great. The effect on the foreign commerce of the United States is minimal. The evidence of intent to harm American commerce is altogether lacking. The foreseeability of the anticompetitive consequences of the allegedly illegal actions is slight. Most of the conduct that must be examined occurred

Of significance, the US Supreme Court, in its 1993 decision in *Hartford Fire Ins. Co. v. California*, appeared to limit the application of these factors–or any comity analysis–to situations when there is a "true conflict" in the sense that foreign law requires conduct the Sherman Act forbids.[16]

In weighing comity considerations, many jurisdictions provide relief in the case of direct conflicts with foreign decisions. For example, in its 2017 decision against Qualcomm, the KFTC stated that comity may "be considered in cases where there is any conflict between the Corrective Order issued [against Qualcomm] by KFTC and any law enforcement of another country."[17] The KFTC Order states that Qualcomm "may request" a reconsideration of the Order "if the final and binding judgment, measure or order of a foreign court or competition authorities affirms, after the date of this Corrective Order, conflicts with this Corrective Order, making it impossible to comply with both at the same time."[18]

In 2017, the Canadian Competition Tribunal in *Commissioner of Competition v. HarperCollins Publisher LLC et al.* rejected a jurisdictional challenge where the allegations were that HarperCollins US formed an anticompetitive arrangement in the United States with other US publishers of electronic books and Apple, which ultimately led to higher prices for Canadian consumers.[19] The Tribunal held that the principle of international comity (which, in Canada "calls for the promotion of order and fairness, an attitude of respect and deference to other states, and a degree of stability and predictability in order to facilitate reciprocity") "cannot be offended when there is a 'real and substantial connection' between an offense or a conduct and Canada, even when persons or acts outside Canada are affected."[20] The Tribunal reasoned that "there is no offense to international comity in these circumstances because the exercise of jurisdiction does not primarily affect a foreign conduct or person, but a legal situation which has a significant link with Canada."[21] The Court went on to say that:

> In the current case, the US Judgment does not address the Canadian situation. It only deals with the expression of the

---

abroad. The factors that favor jurisdiction are the citizenship of the parties and, to a slight extent, the enforcement effectiveness of United States law. We do not believe that this is enough to justify the exercise of federal jurisdiction over this case.

16 Hartford Fire Ins. Co. v. California, 509 U.S. 764, 798-99 (1993); *see also In re* Vitamin C Antitrust Litigation, – F.4th –, 2021 WL 3502632, slip op. at *16-18 (2nd Cir. Aug. 10, 2021) (concluding after finding "true conflict" that other comity factors did not warrant exercising antitrust jurisdiction over foreign conduct).

17 KFTC Order, *supra* note 5, Reasoning, ¶ 483.

18 *Id.*; *see also* Korea 2017 OECD Note, *supra* note 12, ¶ 18 ("The issue of an international comity related to the enforcement of laws in other countries is a matter to be considered when the corrective measure for a case is in conflict with the law enforcement of foreign countries and is not a matter caused simply by including an act conducted overseas into the subject to the corrective measure.").

19 Comm'r of Competition v. HarperCollins Publishers LLC & HarperCollins Canada Ltd., [2017] Comp Trib 10.

20 *Id.* at ¶¶ 171–72.

21 *Id.* at ¶ 172.

Arrangement in the United States and with remedial measures affecting E-book publishers and retailers in the United States. The Tribunal's jurisdiction is anchored on the substantial connection between Canada and the activities of HarperCollins resulting in alleged anticompetitive effects in this country, not on any extraterritorial application of [Canada's Competition Act]. Recognizing the Tribunal's jurisdiction over the alleged anticompetitive effects of the Arrangement in Canada, not in the United States, does not infringe on the sovereignty of foreign states or courts. Nor could it lead to the violation of the US Judgment or of the laws of the United States.[22]

In other words, in considering international comity, the Tribunal assessed, among other considerations, whether imposition of remedial measures would create a direct conflict with a foreign judgment.

Other agencies, such as the Taiwan Fair Trade Commission (TFTC) and the US antitrust agencies, expressly consider not only direct conflicts of law, but also policy conflicts. For example, the TFTC's *Disposal Directions on Extraterritorial Mergers* states that, in determining whether to assert jurisdiction over extraterritorial mergers, the TFTC "shall" consider a number of factors including "the likelihood of creating conflicts with the laws *or policies* of the home countries of the combining enterprises."[23] Similarly, the US Department of Justice (DOJ) and US Federal Trade Commission (FTC) *Antitrust Guidelines for International Enforcement and Cooperation* state that, in performing a comity analysis, the agencies consider a number of factors, including "the degree of conflict with a foreign jurisdiction's law *or articulated policy*."[24] The Guidelines go on to say that, "in determining whether to investigate or bring an enforcement action regarding an alleged antitrust violation, the Agencies consider the extent to which a foreign sovereign encourages or discourages certain courses of conduct or leaves parties free to choose among different courses of conduct."[25]

---

22 *Id.* at ¶ 173.

23 *Fair Trade Commission Disposal Directions (Guidelines) on Extraterritorial Mergers* Point 3 (Dec. 10, 2019) (emphasis added), www.ftc.gov.tw/internet/english/doc/docDetail.aspx?uid=744&docid=2720; *see also* Chinese Taipei 2017 OECD Note, *supra* note 12, ¶ 10 ("It is clear from Subparagraphs 5, 7 and 8 of the Disposal Directions that the FTC gives consideration to potential conflicts with foreign laws *or policies* when determining jurisdiction over extraterritorial merger cases") (emphasis added).

24 US INT'L GUIDELINES, *supra* note 13, at 29 (emphasis added).

25 *Id.* at 29. One example where such policy considerations may be in the starkest relief is the degree to which a country's policies regarding intellectual property rights respect an intellectual property right holder's core right to exclude others from using its patented technology. *See, e.g.*, US DEP'T OF JUSTICE & FED. TRADE COMM'N, ANTITRUST ENFORCEMENT AND INTELLECTUAL PROPERTY RIGHTS: PROMOTING INNOVATION AND COMPETITION 6 (Apr. 2007) ("Antitrust liability for mere unilateral, unconditional refusals to license patents will not play a meaningful part in the interface between patent rights and antitrust protections. Antitrust liability for refusals to license competitors ... would restrict the patent holder's ability to exercise a core part of the patent–the right to exclude."), www.justice.gov/sites/default/files/atr/legacy/2007/07/11/222655.pdf.

The United States' 2017 OECD Note on Extraterritorial Reach of Remedies states:

> In the limited number of civil non-merger cases in which the Agencies find that the licensing of intellectual property is necessary to remedy allegedly anticompetitive conduct, the Agencies generally rely on a domestic-only licensing remedy because the license can be tailored to permit use of the intellectual property only in the domestic markets affected by the conduct. However, in rare cases, when a broader license may be necessary to provide effective relief, the Antitrust Agencies seek a remedy that is no broader than necessary.[26]

In a 2018 speech, then DOJ Deputy Assistant Attorney General Roger Alford further expanded on the US approach, stating that it is not "enough to ask whether the parties are between a rock and a hard place, unable to comply with competing commands. Comity also requires a degree of policy cooperation as to the interests of other affected jurisdictions."[27] He went on to articulate the following standard, stating that "transparency demands" that, before imposing extraterritorial remedies, antitrust enforcers must "clearly articulate the harm to its commerce and consumers and describe how the proposed remedy is necessary to address that harm" and "why that remedy is narrowly tailored to achieve the desired ends."[28]

Similarly, in a 2017 speech, then Acting FTC Chairman Maureen Ohlhausen emphasized the limits on extra-jurisdictional remedies set forth in the DOJ–FTC *International Guidelines*.[29] Specifically, she explained that the Guidelines provide that the agencies "will seek a remedy that includes conduct or assets outside the United States only to the extent that including them is needed to effectively redress harm or threatened harm to US commerce and consumers and is consistent with the Agency's international comity analysis."[30]

It should also be noted that the *International Guidelines* state that a foreign government policy alone, without sovereign compulsion, would not bar application of US antitrust law when the conduct at issue has a sufficient connection with United States. In the case of sovereign compulsion (i.e., when a foreign sovereign compels the very conduct US antitrust law would prohibit), the US

---

26 OECD Roundtable on the Extraterritorial Reach of Competition Remedies–Note by the United States ¶ 24 (DAF/COMP/WP3/WD(2017)41, Dec. 1, 2017), https://one.oecd.org/document/DAF/COMP/WP3/WD(2017)41/en/pdf.

27 Roger Alford, Antitrust Enforcement in an Interconnected World, Address Before the American Chamber of Commerce in South Korea 11 (Jan. 29, 2018), www.justice.gov/opa/speech/file/1034976/download.

28 *Id.* at 10.

29 Maureen Ohlhausen, Guidelines for Global Antitrust: The Three Cs–Cooperation, Comity, and Constraints, Address Before the IBA 21st Annual Competition Conference 5 (Sept. 8, 2017), www.ftc.gov/system/files/documents/public_statements/1252733/iba_keynote_address-international_guidelines_2017.pdf.

30 US INT'L GUIDELINES, *supra* note 13, at 47 (citations omitted).

will recognize and consider the foreign sovereign compulsion as a defense when determining whether to bring, or the appropriate scope of, an enforcement action. The defense will not apply when it is possible for a party to comply with both the foreign and US laws.[31] In such circumstances, the US antitrust agencies will still consider any policy conflicts when conducting a comity analysis.

Lastly, pursuant to a cooperation agreement, the EU and the US competition authorities have agreed to respect and cooperate pursuant to comity principles in competition cases, with the aim of safeguarding trade and investment between and consumer welfare within their respective territories, and avoiding enforcement conflicts. In addition to notifying each other of cases concerning the other's important interests, one of the authorities may request the other to investigate and remedy anticompetitive behavior that adversely affects the former's interests (so-called "positive comity"), and the authorities will consider the important interests of the other when taking measures to enforce its competition rules (so-called "traditional comity").[32] The EU also cooperates with competition authorities in other jurisdictions,[33] and may request parties to an investigation to authorize cooperation with other competition authorities beyond that provided by applicable international agreements.

III. Model Analysis to Common Situations

There are a wide range of scenarios in which comity considerations may come into play. While variations are potentially infinite, there are three basic scenarios that can arise when two competition agencies evaluate the same merger or course of conduct.[34] The following taxonomy helps to lay the foundation for how comity considerations might be evaluated. Our analysis of these scenarios assumes that the conduct at issue satisfies the relevant jurisdiction's effects test (or, in Europe, the alternative "implementation" test) as the threshold requirement for extraterritorial application of domestic competition law.[35]

---

31   *Id.* at 32–33.

32   Agreement between the Government of the United States of America and the Commission of the European Communities regarding the application of their competition laws (1991 EU/US Competition Cooperation Agreement), 27 April 1995, O.J. (L 95) 47–52, *and* Agreement between the European Communities and the Government of the United States of America on the application of positive comity principles in the enforcement of their competition laws (1998 EU/US Positive Comity Agreement), 18 June 1998, O.J. (L 173) 28–31. The antitrust cooperation agreement between the United States and Japan has some similar provisions, in particular an agreement to consider coordination of enforcement actions and take into account the important interests of the other in enforcement activities. *See* Agreement between the Government of the United States and the Government of Japan concerning cooperation on anticompetitive activities, Art. IV(4) (Oct. 7, 1999), /www.ftc.gov/system/files/agree_japan.pdf.

33   *See* European Comm'n, *Facing the challenges of globalisation*, https://ec.europa.eu/competition/international/bilateral/index.html.

34   For simplicity, we have limited the discussion to two countries (A and B), although the same scenarios could occur with three or more jurisdictions and the considerations would be similar for each scenario.

35   *See* Appendix I, identifying the standards used in various major jurisdictions.

- *First*, the competition agencies in countries A and B are both pursuing an investigation of the same or similar conduct or transaction.
- *Second*, the competition agency in country A is pursuing an investigation of conduct or a transaction, and, while the agency in country B generally holds the same views and is supportive, it is not pursuing an investigation, whether because of resource limitations or pragmatic considerations (including reliance on country A's authority to address concerns).[36]
- *Third*, the competition agency in country A is pursuing an investigation of the conduct or transaction, but the competition agency in country B has decided affirmatively not to take action.[37]

The first two scenarios present relatively uninteresting comity questions, at least at the enforcement stage (differences may arise at the remedies stage, in which case the third scenario may best describe the situation). Indeed, there is little need for resort to comity considerations in the first two scenarios, as the two jurisdictions are basically aligned in their views of the ultimate merits of the investigation, even if they may not both pursue enforcement.

The third scenario can be further divided into several variants. Variant (a) involves differences in factual circumstances, such as different degrees of market power or likely anticompetitive effects in the two jurisdictions. These cross-country differences raise minimal comity concerns in themselves. For example, if conduct or a transaction has substantial effects in country A, perhaps because the companies involved have a significant market presence, but a minimal presence in B, then there is no real conflict that calls for comity considerations.

Variant (b) involves legal or policy differences that could result in different views. These could be one (or more) of several types:

i. Disagreement on cartel policy;

ii. Disagreement on merger policy;

iii. Disagreement on unilateral conduct policy;

---

[36] This could arise in two different ways. First, relevant burdens of proof might lead one agency to conclude that, while its evidence and theories of harm are sound, it would face difficulties successfully proving its case in court or before the relevant decision-maker (or having its decision upheld on appeal). A second scenario might involve different applicable legal standards–for example the law in one country might deem the conduct under investigation presumptively unlawful or per se illegal, whereas the other might require evaluation under the rule of reason or another balancing test. As a result, an agency required to meet a more challenging burden might opt not to bring the case for prudential reasons, even if it believed the conduct to be unlawful.

Notably, however, this is distinct from a scenario in which policy differences that lead to different burdens of proof alter an agency's approach to a particular case. For example, with respect to resale price maintenance (RPM), some countries' laws call for assessment of the conduct under the rule of reason, whereas others evaluate it as a per se (or by object) offense. These differences may reflect policy determinations regarding whether RPM should generally be permitted or whether it should generally be regarded with suspicion.

[37] A fourth scenario, in which country B's enforcer is agnostic on the merits, is possible but irrelevant to the discussion here. In such a circumstance the agency likely has no views because the impact of the conduct or transaction on competition in the jurisdiction is de minimis. If the conduct or transaction has minimal if any impact, then any remedies imposed by another jurisdiction also are likely to have minimal impact on the jurisdiction.

iv. Different policy objectives, such as a greater or lesser emphasis on the importance of intellectual property rights or a different balancing of competition with industrial policy goals, such as elevating the interests of certain productive sectors through exemptions to the antitrust laws[38]; and

v. Protectionism (whether explicit or tacit) of domestic companies by not pursuing an investigation (or, when reversed, an investigation motivated by protectionism when the foreign counterpart agency does not see a basis in antitrust laws to proceed).

The first three variants (3(b)i–iii) present common issues, although they are not identical. In particular, with respect to variant 3(b)i, most jurisdictions condemn cartel conduct under their domestic competition laws. As such, only in rare instances is there likely to be a genuine conflict, such as when one country formally has a policy of promoting cartel behavior (e.g., with respect to export cartels).[39]

Variants 3(b)ii and 3(b)iii (disagreement on merger or unilateral conduct policy) present somewhat trickier situations. This arises in large part because there appear to be greater divergence in merger approaches around the world, and even more so with monopolization or abuse of dominance. Unlike for cartels, which are (nearly) universally condemned, merger policy has greater variation that may fall within reasonable policy differences. For example, Europe has placed greater emphasis on "conglomerate effects" as a theory of merger harm, whereas the United States does not recognize the theory as such.[40] Similarly, monopolization or abuse of dominance has a range of approaches that remain subject to significant international debate, including on such matters as essential facilities and excessive pricing.[41] (For purposes of this discussion, we include within abuse of dominance non-cartel vertical agreements, on which there is similar variation in approach.)

In all these circumstances (variants 3(b)i–iii), a divergence between enforcers that results from policy differences potentially can (and should, when possible) be avoided by appropriately limiting the scope of enforcement (and remedy).

---

38 *E.g.*, conduct that otherwise might constitute a cartel may be immunized from antitrust scrutiny (*e.g.*, in the agriculture industry). *See, e.g.*, Agriculture Marketing Agreement Act of 1937, 7 U.S.C. §§ 608b–608c.

39 One possible approach is to take into consideration the general consensus that cartel conduct is rightly condemned by any sound competition law. As Professor Fox argued in Fox, *Updating Extraterritoriality*, *supra* note 8, at 8:

When the subject matter of the enforcement action is one in which there is a world common interest and there is consensus as to what is harmful to competition, as in commonly desired eradication of private firm world cartels, we should recognize a global commons of competition and a world-welfare interest in its preservation. In such a case, any particular controversy before national courts is greater than the sum of the interests of the parties (or nations) in the dispute. The world-welfare interest is appropriately considered as a referent in determining appropriate reach and limits of national law.

40 It is beyond the scope of this paper to assess whether aspects of conglomerate effects theory as applied in Europe and some other jurisdictions (including China) is instead treated as a type of vertical foreclosure by US antitrust enforcement agencies.

41 *See* ABA Antitrust Law Section, *Differences and Alignment: Final Report of the Task Force on International Divergence of Dominance Standards*, ABA (Sept. 1, 2019), www.americanbar.org/content/dam/aba/administrative/antitrust_law/comments/october-2019/report-sal-dominance-divergence-10112019.pdf.

This derives from the basic comity principle that countries should, when possible, avoid taking actions that are in conflict with another co-equal sovereign's policies and laws. This can be facilitated through cooperation between the involved agencies in order to understand the basis for their potentially different outcomes. In such circumstances, for example, a merger infringement finding might be specifically confined to a given jurisdiction. When a court is involved in rendering a decision, it would be sensible for the court to consider the possible conflicts with the other jurisdiction's policy in rendering its decision and determining the scope of any remedy. Importantly, divergence in enforcement with a broad remedy, without restraint based upon comity, could lead to the most stringent law or enforcement approach, establishing the approach for the entire world.[42]

Likewise, a course of conduct that one jurisdiction determines to be anticompetitive but another considers not to violate the law (whether it is affirmatively procompetitive or just competitively ambiguous or neutral) can be addressed through agency-to-agency exchanges. When the conduct is global, developing remedies that minimize the effects in the other jurisdiction would be appropriate. For example, the European Commission's 2017 *Google Search (Shopping)* decision finding a violation of EU competition law is in substantial tension with the conclusion reached by the US FTC in its 2013 decision to close its investigation without taking action.[43] The European Commission's remedy was limited to the EEA. Specifically, the Commission ordered that corrective measures "should apply to all users of Google situated in the thirteen EEA countries in which the Conduct takes place, irrespective of the Google domain that they use (including Google. com)."[44] As a result, Google was not prohibited from continuing conduct in the US that the FTC had concluded did not on balance harm competition.[45]

Variant 3(b)iv, involving divergent policy objectives, presents more difficult challenges, yet also may be addressed by narrowing both enforcement reach and the jurisdictional scope of remedies to minimize those policy conflicts. The most significant challenge with remedies occurs when a global remedy is necessary, because a global market makes it difficult to limit the scope only to conduct in

---

42 The converse is not necessarily true. If each country limits its remedy to accord with its policies then there is no an inevitable "race to the bottom" that results in the least stringent approach becoming the one applicable globally. Only if a country promotes anticompetitive conduct and seeks to insulate that conduct outside its jurisdiction through assertion of comity in other countries might this occur. The appropriate response to such an effort would be for courts or enforcers to disregard or reject such comity assertions.

43 Case AT.39740 *Google Search (Shopping)* ¶ 700(b) (June 27, 2017), https://ec.europa.eu/competition/antitrust/cases/dec_docs/39740/39740_14996_3.pdf [hereinafter EC *Google Search (Shopping)* Decision]; In the Matter of Google Inc., FTC File Number 111-0163 (Jan. 3, 2013), www.ftc.gov/sites/default/files/documents/public_statements/statement-commission-regarding-googles-search-practices/130103brillgooglesearchstmt.pdf. Google did voluntarily change certain conduct to address concerns identified by the FTC. *See also* Tony Woodgate et al., *The EU Commission imposes a record fine on a Big Tech undertaking for abuse of dominance in the search engine market (*Google shopping*)*, E-COMPETITIONS JUNE 2017, ART. N° 84415 (June 27, 2017).

44 EC *Google Search (Shopping)* Decision, *supra* note 43, ¶ 700(b).

45 Although the remedy applied to google.com–the Google domain typically presented to US-based users–we understand that geolocation technology allows Google to provide compliant results only with respect to EU-based consumers.

a country while still crafting an effective remedy for domestic harm. Examples include situations involving global supply chains or where a company's global scale is necessary for effective competition. For instance, a global remedy may be appropriate when an agency is able to show that it is necessary to allow rivals to achieve minimum-efficient scale in order to compete effectively. That said, an important first step prior to imposing an extra-jurisdictional remedy should be a determination that a geographically narrower remedy cannot effectively address harm to domestic competition and consumers. Engaging in such careful assessment of a potential remedy helps to ensure that it is appropriately tailored to protect domestic consumers, and is not instead promoting national champions or other domestic industry.[46]

Variant 3(b)v, involving pure protectionism, is an easier case in that comity considerations should not be relevant. Comity is not appropriately considered because a purely protectionist approach to competition law is outside the bounds of legitimate competition enforcement. As Professor Fox has said, using industrial policy "as part of a strategy to impose costs on outsiders, as by extracting intellectual property or resources in the course of antitrust enforcement but without any relation to competition policy ... should be recognized as an illegitimate use of antitrust law. It violates the general cosmopolitan principles embedded in the WTO [World Trade Organization]" agreements.[47] In short, protectionism is not a legitimate basis for competition enforcement (even if it may form a basis for other policies) and thus is not properly regarded as a legitimate policy consideration worthy of deference by an enforcer.

IV. Conclusion

Determining when to apply domestic antitrust laws to foreign conduct or when and how to impose extra-jurisdictional remedies can be challenging. It is our hope that the principles and model analysis in this paper serve as useful guidance to courts and agencies in making sound decisions that allow them to protect domestic competition and consumers while respecting international comity.

---

46   Where a remedy is broader than needed to protect consumers, it may raise questions as to whether the purpose is to pursue other non-competition goals such as protecting certain industries or companies.

47   Fox, *Updating Extraterritoriality*, *supra* note 8, at 22. By way of example, the US is a party to seven trade agreements with competition chapters that generally include provisions aimed at non-discriminatory and fair treatment in antitrust proceedings of each party. For a discussion of (and links to) these agreements, *see* OECD, Competition Provisions in Trade Agreements–Contribution from the United States (DAF/COMP/GF/WD(2019)3, Dec. 5, 2019), https://one.oecd.org/document/DAF/COMP/GF/WD(2019)3/en/pdf.

Appendix I:

Approaches in Major Jurisdictions Around the World

Brazil	Article 2 of the Brazilian Competition Law states that the law "applies, without prejudice to the conventions and treaties of which Brazil is a signatory, to practices performed, in full or in part, on the national territory, or that produce or may produce effects thereon."[i] Brazil's Administrative Council for Economic Defense (CADE) has explained that, pursuant to article 2, "CADE is entitled by law with competence, within the administrative level, over practices whose effects can cause harm, at least potentially, in the Brazilian market. In these terms, the effects doctrine is adopted."[ii] With respect to remedies, CADE has required global commitments in merger cases (*e.g.*, in Dow/Dupont) that were not directly related to the concerns identified in Brazil. For a discussion of this (and other) cases, see Brazil's 2017 OECD Note at https://one.oecd.org/document/DAF/COMP/WP3/WD(2017)42/en/pdf.
Canada	In 2017, the Canadian Competition Tribunal held that jurisdiction under section 90.1 of Canada's Competition Act depends upon the existence of a "real and substantial connection" between the challenged conduct and Canada[iii]. Section 90.1 is a non-criminal provision prohibiting any person from doing anything under an existing or proposed agreement or arrangement between competitors that "prevents or lessens, or is likely to prevent or lessen, competition substantially in a market."[iv] Section 90.1 does not expressly address the Act's territorial jurisdiction. The territorial scope of section 90.1 and similar reviewable conduct provisions of the Act (including mergers and abuse of dominance) had not previously been expressly addressed in a contested Tribunal decision. Although the Tribunal took care to indicate that it was not ruling on the geographic scope of the criminal conspiracy offense, it did suggest that its analysis applies to other reviewable conduct provisions in the Act, including mergers and abuse of dominance. With respect to remedies, at the OECD 2017 Roundtable on the Extraterritorial Reach of Competition Remedies, the Canadian Competition Bureau reported on a non-competition decision of the Supreme Court of Canada (*Google Inc. v. Equustek Solutions Inc.*), in which the Court held that Canadian courts have discretion to issue injunctions with extraterritorial application.[v] Specifically, the Supreme Court held that Canadian courts may enjoin conduct anywhere in the world if necessary to ensure the injunction's effectiveness.[vi]

---

[i] Law 12,529/2011.

[ii] OECD Roundtable on the Extraterritorial Reach of Competition Remedies–Note by Brazil ¶ 2 (DAF/COMP/WP3/WD(2017)42, Dec. 3, 2017), https://one.oecd.org/document/DAF/COMP/WP3/WD(2017)42/en/pdf.

[iii] Comm'r of Competition v. HarperCollins Publishers LLC & HarperCollins Canada Ltd., [2017] Comp Trib 10. The Tribunal credited the Commissioner's claims that a "real and substantial connection" existed because: "(1) HarperCollins and the other US publishers always contemplated that the alleged Arrangement would be implemented in Canada and has indeed been implemented in this country; (2) HarperCollins US, through its affiliate HarperCollins Canada, carried on business in Canada; and (3) the alleged Arrangement caused harm in the market for the retail sale of E-books in Canada." *Id.* at ¶¶ 5, 8, 159–65.

[iv] Competition Act (R.S.C., 1985, c. C-34).

[v] OECD Summary of Discussion of the Roundtable on the Extraterritorial Reach of Competition Remedies, 5 (DAF/COMP/WP3/M(2017)2/ANN2/FINAL, Oct. 5, 2018), https://one.oecd.org/document/DAF/COMP/WP3/M(2017)2/ANN2/FINAL/en/pdf [hereinafter OECD Summary].

[vi] Google Inc. v. Equustek Solutions Inc. (2017 S.C.C. 34). The Court upheld the issuance of a worldwide interlocutory injunction prohibiting Google from indexing certain websites anywhere in the world. Google had agreed to an order on consent to de-index certain web pages from google.ca, but the court concluded that was insufficient.

Extraterritoriality: Approaches Around the World and Model Analysis

Canada — The Competition Bureau also said that the it may adopt extraterritorial remedies if necessary to ensure that the anticompetitive conduct does not substantially lessen competition in Canada. The Bureau went on to say that it "gives careful consideration to the remedies it imposes on a case-by-case basis; one of its primary concerns is to prevent conflicts that may arise when a remedy has extraterritorial effects. In their assessment, the Bureau considers other jurisdictions' interests and policies and cooperates with them."[vii]

With respect to merger remedies in particular, the Bureau's *Information Bulletin on the Communication of Confidential Information under the Competition Act* states that:

> While enforcement decisions are made on a case-by-case basis, the Bureau is more likely to formalize negotiated remedies within Canada when the matter raises Canada-specific issues, when the Canadian impact is particularly significant, when the asset(s) to be divested reside in Canada, or when it is critical to the enforcement of the terms of the settlement. In contrast, the Bureau may rely on the remedies initiated through formal proceedings by foreign jurisdictions when the asset(s) that are subject to divestiture, and/or conduct that must be carried out as part of a behavioral remedy, are primarily located outside of Canada. However, the Bureau will do so only if it is satisfied that the actions taken by foreign authorities are sufficient to resolve the competition issues in Canada.[viii]

For a discussion of important mergers involving cross-border remedies, see the 2013 Competition Bureau Submission to the OECD Competition Committee Roundtable on Remedies in Cross-Border Merger Cases at www.competitionbureau.gc.ca/eic/site/cb-bc.nsf/eng/03771.html.

China — Article 2 of China's Antimonopoly Law provides: "This law is applicable to monopolistic conduct outside the territory of the People's Republic of China which has an eliminative or restrictive impact on competition in the domestic market."[ix]

With respect to remedies, in the National Development and Reform Commission's (NDRC's) 2015 decision against Qualcomm, the agency stated that Qualcomm's "licensing of Wireless SEPs outside the territory of the People's Republic of China that does not result in significant effect on elimination or restriction of the competition in China shall not be subject to th[is] decision."[x] In connection with this decision, the NDRC approved a rectification plan proposed by Qualcomm under which:

1) Qualcomm will offer licenses to its current 3G and 4G essential Chinese patents separately from licenses to its other patents and will provide patent lists during the negotiation process;

2) If Qualcomm seeks a cross-license from a Chinese licensee as part of such offer, it will negotiate with the licensee in good faith and provide fair consideration for such rights;

---

vii   OECD Summary, *supra* note v, at 5.

viii Information Bulletin on the Communication of Confidential Information under the Competition Act, Competition Bureau ¶ 78 (Oct. 10, 2007).

ix   Antimonopoly Law of the People's Republic of China, promulgated by the Standing Comm. Nat'l People's Cong. (Aug. 30, 2007), art. 2, http://english.mofcom.gov.cn/article/policyrelease/Businessregulations/201303/20130300045909.shtml. A court in China held that this provision included conduct outside China that "directly ha[s] a major, substantial and reasonably foreseeable effect of impairing and restricting the domestic production activities, export opportunity and export trade of domestic enterprises." Huawei Jishu Youxian Gongsi Su Jiaohu Shuzi Tongxin Youxian Gongsi (华为技术有限公司诉交互数字通信有限公司) [Huawei Tech. Co. v. InterDigital Commc'n, Inc. (Huawei v. IDC)], Section II, 2013 Yue Gao Fa Min San Zhong Zi No. 306 (Guangdong High People's Ct. No. 306 2013) (China). Application of antitrust laws to export commerce finds a parallel in the US FTAIA. *See* 15 U.S.C. § 6a(1)(B).

x   Nat'l Dev. & Reform Comm'n, Administrative Penalty Decision No. [2015] 1 § III.A. (Feb. 9, 2015), *translated in* Freshfields & Fangda, Unofficial Translation, Administrative Penalty Decision: Fa Gai Ban Jia Jian Chu Fa No. [2015] 1.

China	3) For licenses of Qualcomm's 3G and 4G essential Chinese patents for branded devices sold in China for use in China (or made in China and sold for use in a country in which no patents have been issued to Qualcomm), Qualcomm will "charge a royalty equal to 5%" for 3G devices (including multimode 3G/4G devices) and 3.5% for 4G devices (including 3-mode LTE-TDD devices) that does not implement CDMA or WCDMA, in each case using a royalty base of 65% of the net selling price of the device; 4) Qualcomm will give its existing licensees an opportunity to elect to take the new terms for sales of branded devices for use in China as of January 1, 2015; and 5) Qualcomm will not condition the sale of baseband chips on the chip customer signing a license agreement with terms that the NDRC found to be unreasonable or on the chip customer not challenging unreasonable terms in its license agreement.[xi]
EU	In light of case law of the CJEU, the Treaty on the Functioning of the European Union and the EU Merger Regulation allow for extraterritorial application if an agreement is implemented within the internal market or when it is foreseeable that the conduct will have an immediate and substantial effect in the European Union.[xii] The CJEU in *Woodpulp* found that the decisive factor of the applicability of EU law is the place where the conduct is implemented, rather than the location of the undertaking.[xiii] The CJEU did not rule on whether the effects doctrine applies. Subsequently, the CJEU held in *Intel* that the "qualified effects test pursues the same objective [as the implementation test], namely preventing conduct which, while not adopted within the EU, has anticompetitive effects liable to have an impact on the EU market."[xiv] Under the qualified effects test, EU competition law can apply to conduct outside the EU "when it is foreseeable that the conduct in question will have an immediate and substantial effect in the European Union."[xv] In *Gencor*, the General Court held that EU competition law applies to concentrations of undertakings conducting operations outside the EU, consistent with the (predecessor of the) EU Merger Regulation and public international law "when it is foreseeable that a proposed concentration will have an immediate and substantial effect" in the EU.[xvi] With respect to remedies, in the European Commission's 2014 commitments decision involving Samsung, the Commission accepted that Samsung limit its commitments (which restricted Samsung's ability to seek injunctive relief on FRAND-committed SEPs) to the seeking of injunctions in the EEA, and only in respect of patents granted in the EEA.[xvii] For further discussion of the EU's approach to extra-jurisdictional remedies, see the EU's 2017 OECD Note at https://one.oecd.org/document/DAF/COMP/WP3/WD(2017)35/en/pdf.

[xi] Rectification Plan Related to NDRC's Investigation of Qualcomm (Feb. 9, 2015), *translated in* Qualcomm's Briefing Ex. C, www.qualcomm.com/media/documents/files/reply-in-support-of-motion-for-stay-6-18-19.pdf; Press Release, Qualcomm, Qualcomm and China's National Development and Reform Commission Reach Resolution–NDRC Accepts Qualcomm's Rectification Plan–Qualcomm Raises Midpoints of Fiscal 2015 Revenue and Non-GAAP EPS Guidance (Feb. 9, 2015), https://investor.qualcomm.com/news-events/press-releases/detail/672/qualcomm-and-chinas-national-development-and-reform.

[xii] *See, e.g.*, Case C-22/71, Béguelin Import Co. v. S.A.G.L. Import Exp., EU:C:1971:113, ¶ 11; and Case C-413/14 P, Intel Corp. v. Comm'n, EU:C:2017:632, ¶¶ 43–44.

[xiii] Joined cases C-89/85, C-104/85, C-114/85, C-116/85, C-117/85 and C-125/85 to C-129/85, A. Ahlström Osakeyhtiö v. Comm'n, EU:C:1988:447, ¶ 16.

[xiv] Intel Corp. *supra* note xii, ¶ 45.

[xv] *Id.* at ¶ 49.

[xvi] Case T-102/96, Gencor Ltd v. Comm'n, EU:T:1999:65, ¶ 90. *See also* Philip Owen, *The EU Court of Justice confirms the Commission's decision prohibiting a merger in the platinum and rhodium markets (*Impala Platinum/Gencor/Lonrho*)*, E-COMPETITIONS MARCH 1999, ART. N° 39345 (Mar. 25, 1999).

[xvii] Case AT.39939–Samsung, Comm'n Decision, (Apr. 29, 2014), ¶ 76, https://ec.europa.eu/competition/antitrust/cases/dec_docs/39939/39939_1501_5.pdf, and Samsung's commitments, ¶ 1 and definition of "Mobile SEP," https://ec.europa.eu/competition/antitrust/cases/dec_docs/39939/39939_1502_5.pdf.

India	Section 32 of India's Competition Act states that the Competition Commission of India (CCI) has the "power to inquire … into [an] agreement or abuse of dominant position or combination if such agreement or dominant position or combination has, or is likely to have, an appreciable adverse effect on competition in the relevant market in India," and to "pass such orders as it may deem fit in accordance with the provisions of this Act." Section 32 specifies that CCI has this power "notwithstanding that": a) An agreement referred to in section 3 has been entered into outside India; or b) Any party to such agreement is outside India; or c) Any enterprise abusing the dominant position is outside India; or d) A combination has taken place outside India; or e) Any party to combination is outside India; or f) Any other matter or practice or action arising out of such agreement or dominant position or combination is outside India.[xviii]
Japan	Japan has traditionally taken a restrictive approach toward extraterritorial application of its competition laws. Until January 1999, Japan's merger review laws applied only to transactions taking place "in Japan," i.e. one of the merging parties had to be a Japanese company to trigger the application of Japan's Antimonopoly Act. A 1998 Amendment removed the territorial nexus, making it possible to review foreign transactions.[xix] The Japan Fair Trade Commission's 1990 Study Group Report states that, when foreign firms engage in activities such as exporting to Japan and the said activities are sufficient to constitute a violation of the Antimonopoly Act, then the Act applies.[xx]
Korea	In 2004, Korea's Monopoly Regulation and Fair Trade Act (MRFTA) was modified to address "Application to Overseas Act[s]," stating: "This Act shall apply to cases where any act committed outside the country affects the domestic market." Korea interprets MRFTA to enable "not only the extraterritorial application of the MRFTA in a general meaning, but also the extraterritorial application of competition remedies."[xxi] The KFTC's 2005 *Guidelines for Remedies* set forth principles including effectiveness, correlation, clarity and specificity, possibility of implementation, and proportionality. In its 2017 OECD submission, Korea stated that "when there is an extraterritorial application of the MRFTA, the scope of remedies should be designed in accordance of the principle of proportionality within the scope of an act judged to be illegal, while ensuring the effectiveness."[xxii] In its 2017 decision against Qualcomm, the KFTC imposed global remedies, including on foreign patents.[xxiii] Specifically, the KFTC required Qualcomm to renegotiate existing license agreements upon request, including with respect to non-Korean patents, and to offer exhaustive worldwide licenses to suppliers of modem chipsets. Both remedies extend to all handset or modem chipset companies "headquartered" in Korea, that sell handsets in or into Korea, or supply modem chipsets to companies that sell handsets in Korea.

---

xviii Competition Act, 2002, § 32 (Jan. 2003), www.cci.gov.in/sites/default/files/cci_pdf/competitionact2012.pdf.

xix For discussion, *see* K. Yamaguchi, *Extra-territorial application of Japanese anti-monopoly law to pure non-Japanese M&As*, 5(4) INT'L TRADE L. & REG. 100, 100 (1999).

xx Dumping Regulations and Competition Policy, Extraterritorial Application of the Antimonopoly Act–Report of the Study Group of the Antimonopoly Act on External Affairs Issues (Summary), FTC/JAPAN VIEWS, No 9, July 1990, at 27 (on file with author).

xxi OECD Roundtable on the Extraterritorial Reach of Competition Remedies–Note by Korea ¶ 5 (DAF/COMP/WP3/WD(2017)37, Nov. 23, 2017), https://one.oecd.org/document/DAF/COMP/WP3/WD(2017)37/en/pdf.

xxii *Id.* ¶ 8; *see also* Korea Fair Trade Comm'n, Case No. 2015SiGam2118, *In re* Alleged Abuse of Market Dominance of Qualcomm Inc., Decision No. 2017-0-25, Decision and Order, ¶ 6 (Jan. 20, 2017), *unofficial translation available in English at* www.theamericanconsumer.org/wp-content/uploads/2017/03/2017-01-20_KFTC-Decision_2017-0-25.pdf [hereinafter KFTC Order].

xxiii KFTC Order, *supra* note xxii, Reasoning ¶ 483.

Korea	The order provides that Qualcomm "may request" a reconsideration of the KFTC's order "if the final and binding judgment, measure or order of a foreign court or competition authorities affirms, after the date of this Corrective Order, conflicts with this Corrective Order, making it impossible to comply with both at the same time."[xxiv] For further discussion of Korea's approach to extra-jurisdictional remedies, see Korea's 2017 OECD Note at https://one.oecd.org/document/DAF/COMP/WP3/WD(2017)37/en/pdf.
US	The Foreign Trade Antitrust Improvements Act (FTAIA) provides that foreign conduct is outside the scope of the Sherman Act unless it "has a direct, substantial, and reasonably foreseeable effect" on domestic or import commerce and "such effect gives rise to a claim under" the Sherman Act.[xxv] Section 5(a)(3) of the Federal Trade Commission Act closely parallels this provision.[xxvi] Section 3 of the DOJ–FTC 2017 *Antitrust Guidelines for International Enforcement and Cooperation* states that, "although the FTAIA clarified the reach of the Sherman Act and the FTC Act, it did not address the reach of the Clayton Act. Nevertheless, the Agencies would apply the principles outlined ... [in these Guidelines] when making enforcement decisions regarding mergers and acquisitions involving trade or commerce with foreign nations."[xxvii] In the United States, an effect is "direct" if there is a reasonably proximate causal nexus. In other words, an effect is direct if, in the natural or ordinary course of events, the alleged anticompetitive conduct would produce an effect on commerce. The substantiality requirement does not provide a minimum pecuniary threshold, nor does it require that the effects be quantified. The "reasonable foreseeability" requirement is an objective test, requiring that the effect be foreseeable to "a reasonable person making practical business judgments."[xxviii] Section 4.1 of the *International Guidelines* states that, in performing a comity analysis, the agencies consider a number of factors, including "the degree of conflict with a foreign jurisdiction's law or articulated policy."[xxix] "In determining whether to investigate or bring an enforcement action regarding an alleged antitrust violation, the Agencies consider the extent to which a foreign sovereign encourages or discourages certain courses of conduct or leaves parties free to choose among different courses of conduct."[xxx] With respect to remedies, section 5.1.5 of the *International Guidelines* states: > The Agencies seek remedies that effectively address harm or threatened harm to US commerce and consumers, while attempting to avoid conflicts with remedies contemplated by their foreign counterparts. An Agency will seek a remedy that includes conduct or assets outside the United States only to the extent that including them is needed to effectively redress harm or threatened harm to US commerce and consumers and is consistent with the Agency's international comity analysis.[xxxi]

[xxiv] *id*; *see also* Press Release, Qualcomm, Qualcomm Responds to Announcement by Korea Fair Trade Commission (Dec. 27, 2016), www.qualcomm.com/news/releases/2016/12/27/qualcomm-responds-announcement-korea-fair-trade-commission; Press Release, Qualcomm, Qualcomm Stay Appeal Denied by Seoul High Court on Absence of Irreparable Harm; Appeal to Seoul High Court on Merits of the Case to Proceed (Sept. 4, 2017), www.qualcomm.com/news/releases/2017/09/04/qualcomm-stay-appeal-denied-seoul-high-court-absence-irreparable-harm.

[xxv] 15 U.S.C. § 6a(1).

[xxvi] 15 U.S.C § 45(a)(3).

[xxvii] US Dep't of Justice & Fed. Trade Comm'n, Antitrust Guidelines for International Enforcement and Cooperation 18 (Jan. 13, 2017), www.justice.gov/atr/internationalguidelines/download.

[xxviii] *Id.* at 21–22 (internal citations omitted).

[xxix] *Id.* at 28.

[xxx] *Id.* at 29.

[xxxi] *Id.* at 47.

US	With respect to intellectual property remedies in particular, the United States' 2017 OECD Note on Extraterritorial Reach of Remedies states:
> In the limited number of civil non-merger cases in which the Agencies find that the licensing of intellectual property is necessary to remedy allegedly anticompetitive conduct, the Agencies generally rely on a domestic-only licensing remedy because the license can be tailored to permit use of the intellectual property only in the domestic markets affected by the conduct. However, in rare cases, when a broader license may be necessary to provide effective relief, the Antitrust Agencies seek a remedy that is no broader than necessary.

(referring in a footnote to the FTC's 2013 decision against Google/Motorola Mobility (MMI)).[xxxii]

In Google/MMI, the FTC prohibited the companies from seeking or enforcing "injunctive relief" on FRAND-committed SEPs, defined as "a ruling of any legal or administrative tribunal, whether in or outside of the United States,"[xxxiii] on any "patent claim" on a patent "issued or pending in the United States or anywhere else in the world."[xxxiv] |
| **Taiwan** | Point 3 of the TFTC's *Disposal Directions on Extraterritorial Mergers* states:
> The following factors shall be taken into account while determining the Fair Trade Commission's jurisdiction over extraterritorial merger cases:
> 1) Whether the merger will have a direct, substantial, and reasonably foreseeable effect on the domestic market;
> 2) The relative importance of the merger's effects on the relevant domestic and foreign markets;
> 3) The residence and main business places of the combining enterprises;
> 4) The degree of explicitness and the possibility of a foreseeable consequence on the impact of the market competition in the Republic of China;
> 5) The likelihood of creating conflicts with the laws or policies of the home countries of the combining enterprises;
> 6) The feasibility of enforcing administrative dispositions;
> 7) The impact of enforcement on the foreign enterprises;
> 8) What the rules of international conventions and treaties, or the regulations of international organizations say;
> 9) Whether any of the combining enterprises has production or service facilities, distributors, agents, or other substantive sales channels within the territory of the Republic of China;
> 10) Other factors deemed important by the Fair Trade Commission.[xxxv]

For case examples, see Chinese Taipei's 2017 OECD Note at www.oecd.org/official documents/publicdisplaydocumentpdf/?cote=DAF/COMP/WP3/WD(2017)45&docLanguage=En. |

---

xxxii OECD Roundtable on the Extraterritorial Reach of Competition Remedies–Note by the United States ¶ 24 (DAF/COMP/WP3/WD(2017)41, Dec. 1, 2017), https://one.oecd.org/document/DAF/COMP/WP3/WD(2017)41/en/pdf.

xxxiii Decision and Order, Motorola Mobility LLC & Google Inc., FTC File No. 121-0120, at 4 (July 24, 2013), www.ftc.gov/sites/default/files/documents/cases/2013/07/130724googlemotorolado.pdf.

xxxiv *Id.* at 5.

xxxv *Fair Trade Commission Disposal Directions (Guidelines) on Extraterritorial Mergers* Point 3 (Dec. 10, 2019), www.ftc.gov.tw/internet/english/doc/docDetail.aspx?uid=744&docid=2720. *See also* OECD Roundtable on the Extraterritorial Reach of Competition Remedies–Note by Chinese Taipei ¶ 10 (DAF/COMP/WP3/WD(2017)45, Nov. 22, 2017), www.oecd.org/officialdocuments/publicdisplaydocumentpdf/?cote=DAF/COMP/WP3/WD(2017)45&docLanguage=En.

The Digital Markets Act and Private Enforcement: Proposals for an Optimal System of Enforcement

ASSIMAKIS P. KOMNINOS[*]
White & Case

Abstract

The DMA Proposal is silent about private enforcement, although the general view takes this as granted. Indeed, as the Commission's Proposal currently stands, national courts would apply Articles 5 and 6 and enforce the related obligations in civil litigation. However, the prospect of unlimited private enforcement raises concerns about fragmentation, especially in view of the novel nature of the DMA rules. For this reason, the EU legislator would be well-advised to introduce certain limitations on private enforcement and provide for a rule of precedence for public enforcement. Private enforcement should be allowed in its follow-on but not in its stand-alone form. This limitation could be revisited after a number of years and once a body of precedent on the DMA has been built. The DMA should also include concrete mechanisms of co-ordination and co-operation with the European Commission, with a view to safeguarding the consistent application of its rules in the Union.

---

[*] Partner, White & Case LLP; Visiting Research Fellow, University College London (UCL); Visiting Professor, Université catholique de Louvain (2020–2021). The present views are strictly personal.

The Digital Markets Act and Private Enforcement:
Proposals for an Optimal System of Enforcement

I. Introduction

The European Commission's proposal of December 16, 2020 for an EU Digital Markets Act (DMA Proposal)[1] is going to result in a major paradigm shift in the European Union. The fact that the DMA is presented as a "regulatory" tool, as opposed to a competition law statute, should not distract from the reality that the DMA is inspired by competition law cases and relies heavily on competition law concepts and methodologies. That being said, when the DMA is adopted, there will be a change of focus for the digital markets (i) from *ex post* to *ex ante* intervention, (ii) from an effects-based analysis to a list of per se prohibitions, and (iii) from flexible prohibitions based on general clauses (Articles 101 and 102 TFEU) to a *numerus clausus* of specific but inflexible prohibitions. While mainstream competition law will still apply, it is expected that the DMA enforcement will supplant (to a degree) competition law enforcement.

The purpose of the present paper is not to critically present the DMA Proposal[2] but rather to shed light on a particular question that has received relatively little attention, the role of private enforcement. In particular, we examine whether the enforcement of the DMA will be restricted to public authorities, i.e. the European Commission (if the DMA Proposal's exclusion of decisional competence for national authorities is retained), or whether it will also be enforced by the courts in civil law disputes between private parties.

This question is addressed from two angles. First, we analyze how private enforcement will work under the current version of the DMA Proposal (*de lege lata*). We show that, as the DMA Proposal currently stands, private enforcement is clearly possible with regard to all provisions that are unconditional and grant individuals actionable rights; in other words, for all provisions that enjoy "direct effect." This is certainly the case for the prohibitions contained in Articles 5 and 6 of the DMA Proposal. Then, we examine whether this is a desired policy option

---

1   *Proposal for a Regulation of the European Parliament and of the Council on contestable and fair markets in the digital sector (Digital Markets Act)*, COM(2020) 842 final (Dec. 15, 2020).

2   Among the rather voluminous commentary, *see* Jürgen Basedow, *Das Rad neu erfunden: Zum Vorschlag für einen Digital Markets Act* (Max Planck Private Law Research Paper No. 21/2, 2021), https://ssrn.com/abstract=3773711; Alexandre De Streel & Pierre Larouche, *The European Digital Markets Act Proposal: How to Improve a Regulatory Revolution*, CONCURRENCES N° 2–2021, ART. N° 100432, 46 (2021); Jean-Louis Fourgoux et al., *Le DMA, une arme contre les abus contractuels – Dossier: DMA/DSA: l'Europe s'est-elle vraiment donné les moyens de ses ambitions?*, CONCURRENCES N° 2–2021, ART. N° 100023, 29 (2021); Florian Haus & Anna-Lena Weusthof, *The Digital Markets Act – A Gatekeeper's Nightmare?*, 71 WIRTSCHAFT UND WETTBEWERB 318 (2021); Pablo Ibáñez Colomo, *The Draft Digital Markets Act: A Legal and Institutional Analysis* (Feb. 22, 2021), https://ssrn.com/abstract=3790276; Giorgio Monti, *The Digital Markets Act: Improving its Institutional Design*, 5(2) EUR. COMPETITION & REG. REV. 90 (2021); Nicolas Petit, *The Proposed Digital Markets Act (DMA): A Legal and Policy Review* (May 11, 2021), https://ssrn.com/abstract=3843497; Rupprecht Podszun et al. *Proposals on how to Improve the Digital Markets Act* (Feb. 18, 2021), https://ssrn.com/abstract=3788571; Romina Polley & Friedrich Andreas Konrad, *Der Digital Markets Act – Brüssels neues Regulierungskonzept für Digitale Märkte*, 71(4) WIRTSCHAFT UND WETTBEWERB 198 (2021); Simonetta Vezzoso, *The Dawn of Pro-competition Data Regulation for Gatekeepers in the EU*, 17 EUR. COMPETITION J. 391 (2021). *See also* CERRE, *The European Proposal for a Digital Markets Act: A First Assessment* (Jan. 2021); CERRE, *DMA Recommendations for the Council and the Parliament* (Apr. 2021) [hereinafter CERRE, *DMA Recommendations*].

(*de lege ferenda*). We examine the fragmentation risks that an unlimited private enforcement would entail for the enforcement of the DMA and develop arguments for introducing certain limitations on it. In particular, we argue for limiting the role of private enforcement only to "follow-on" cases for a reasonable period, until the DMA comes to maturity. Finally, we advocate the introduction of appropriate cooperation and coordination mechanisms between the Commission and national courts in the EU.

II. The (Unspoken) Role of Private Enforcement in the DMA

The role of private enforcement of EU competition law is well established and well known.[3] The process was not without obstacles. It took 40 years from the recognition of the competition rules' direct effect[4] to the adoption of the EU Damages Directive.[5] And it took over 20 years from the Commission's 1999 White Paper on modernization,[6] which commenced the process of decentralization of EU competition enforcement, for private antitrust enforcement to take off.

What about the DMA? Is there space for private enforcement? The DMA Proposal itself includes no reference at all to the potential of private enforcement. There are no provisions on the role of national courts or national remedies or, indeed, on mechanisms of cooperation between the Commission and national courts.[7] However, EU officials, in their statements,[8] have stressed the "self-executing" nature of the DMA rules and seem to take private enforcement for granted. The key players in the legislative process, i.e. Member States (which together form part of the Council) and the Parliament, seem also to take private enforcement as granted and, indeed, stress the need for the DMA to expressly acknowledge the possibility of private enforcement and to provide for specific mechanisms to enhance it. For example, the joint letter of May 27, 2021, signed by the Ministers of Economy of France, Germany and the Netherlands, specifically mentioned the need to clarify that private enforcement of the DMA

---

3   *See*, for a historical analysis, ASSIMAKIS P. KOMNINOS, EC PRIVATE ANTITRUST ENFORCEMENT, DECENTRALISED APPLICATION OF EC COMPETITION LAW BY NATIONAL COURTS (2008).

4   Case 127/73, Belgische Radio en Televisie and société belge des auteurs, compositeurs et éditeurs v. SV SABAM and NV Fonior, ECLI:EU:C:1974:6.

5   Directive 2014/104/EU of the European Parliament and of the Council of 26 November 2014 on certain rules governing actions for damages under national law for infringements of the competition law provisions of the Member States and of the European Union, 2014 O.J. (L 349) 1.

6   Commission White Paper of 28 April 1999 on Modernisation of the Rules Implementing Articles 85 and 86 of the EC Treaty, Commission Programme No. 99/027, COM(1999) 101 final, 1999 O.J. (C 132) 1.

7   Unlike Regulation 1/2003, which includes numerous references to the role of national courts and cooperation mechanisms between them and the European Commission.

8   *See, e.g.*, Guillaume Loriot, ABA Panel – EU Digital Markets Act and Gatekeeper Platforms (Mar. 2, 2021).

obligations is possible.⁹ In addition, the European Parliament is unwavering in its support of private enforcement.¹⁰

The fact that the DMA Proposal mentions nothing about private enforcement is not material. Private parties can enforce the DMA rules before the national courts as an automatic consequence of the DMA taking the form of an EU Regulation. Regulations, pursuant to Article 288 TFEU, are binding in their entirety and directly applicable in all Member States. The direct applicability of regulations means that "by reason of their nature and their function in the system of the sources of [EU] law, [they] *have direct effect* and are, as such, capable of *creating individual rights which national courts must protect*."¹¹ Thus, normally, the direct applicability of regulations means that they are also directly effective, i.e. they can be "invoked before the national courts by a natural or legal person without there being any need for further implementing provisions."¹²

As a matter of EU law, there are two aspects to direct effect: a vertical and a horizontal aspect. Vertical direct effect refers to the relationship between individuals and the State. This means that individuals can invoke an EU provision against Member States. Horizontal direct effect refers to relations between individuals. This means that an individual can invoke an EU provision against another individual. Private enforcement presupposes the existence of horizontal direct effect.¹³ In the case of directly effective regulations, the distinction is irrelevant, because direct effect is horizontal always.¹⁴

However, the fact that a regulation is directly applicable does not necessarily mean that every single provision has direct effect. The provisions of a regulation will still need to be sufficiently precise and unconditional to create rights for individuals and thus to be relied upon by individuals before national courts.¹⁵ If they are conditional on the exercise of discretion by the EU or Member States, they cannot (yet) confer rights on individuals. For example, in *Monte Arcosu*, the Court of Justice (CJEU) held that certain provisions of a regulation were

---

9   "Private enforcement would further increase the effectiveness of the DMA. Therefore, it must be clarified that private enforcement of the gatekeeper obligations is legally possible."

10 *See*, European Parliament's Committee on the Internal Market and Consumer Protection (IMCO) Draft Report, Amendment 28 (June 1, 2021).

11 Case 43/71, Politi s.a.s. v. Ministero delle finanze della Repubblica Italiana, ECLI:EU:C:1971:122, ¶ 9, emphasis added. *See also* Case 93/71, Orsolina Leonesio v. Ministero dell'agricoltura e foreste, ECLI:EU:C:1972:39, ¶¶ 18, 23.

12 Case C–253/00, Antonio Muñoz y Cia SA and Superior Fruiticola SA v. Frumar Limited and Redbridge Produce Marketing Limited, Opinion of AG Geelhoed, ECLI:EU:C:2001:697, ¶ 37.

13 *See* KOMNINOS, *supra* note 4, at 178.

14 Case C-253/00, Antonio Muñoz y Cia SA and Superior Fruiticola SA v. Frumar Limited and Redbridge Produce Marketing Limited, Opinion of AG Geelhoed, ECLI:EU:C:2001:697, ¶ 39: "In the case law horizontal direct effect as a distinguishing criterion in regard to vertical direct effect plays a significant role in the case of directives but not in the case of directly applicable rules (such as regulations)."

15 *Id.*, ¶ 47.

not directly effective and did not confer rights on individuals, because Member States retained discretion in their implementation.[16]

In the case of the DMA, the substantive provisions of the future regulation are mainly in Article 3 (on the criteria for designating "gatekeepers"), and Articles 5 and 6 (which include lists of obligations). The other provisions of the DMA Proposal are mostly of a procedural nature and relate to the enforcement of the DMA by the Commission. So the question of direct effect arises for the former provisions only.

The provisions of Articles 5 and 6 rely on the notion of "gatekeepers" and Article 3 therefore is critical. Article 3 is both a substantive and a procedural rule. Paragraphs 1 and 2 relate to the qualitative and quantitative criteria/conditions that need to be fulfilled for an undertaking to be designated as a "gatekeeper." Paragraphs 3 to 8 relate to the mechanism for that designation. From the latter paragraphs, it is clear that only the European Commission would have competence to designate "gatekeepers." This is an exclusive competence. The designation of "gatekeepers" would take place by means of an individual decision by the Commission, addressed to the undertaking concerned, pursuant to Article 3(4), (6), (7). It is only after the Commission has designated a "gatekeeper" that the latter will be bound by Articles 5 and 6. Indeed, under Article 3(8), "the gatekeeper shall comply with the obligations laid down in Articles 5 and 6 within six months *after a core platform service has been included in the list pursuant to paragraph 7 of this Article.*"[17] Paragraph 7 states that "for each gatekeeper ... *the Commission shall identify the relevant undertaking to which it belongs and list the relevant core platform services* that are provided within that same undertaking and which individually serve as an important gateway for business users to reach end users ..."[18]

It follows from the above that (i) the national courts (exactly like national authorities) cannot designate "gatekeepers," since this is an exclusive competence of the Commission, and (ii) prior to the Commission's decision designating a "gatekeeper," the rules of Articles 5 and 6 do not create obligations and, therefore, cannot be invoked before the national courts. Therefore, the possibility of private enforcement of Articles 5 and 6 arises only after the Commission has designated a "gatekeeper."

As for Articles 5 and 6, there is no doubt that these are sufficiently unconditional and precise and therefore can be invoked before the national courts by individuals that base rights on them. The fact that the title of Article 6 refers to "Obligations

---

16   Case C–403/98, Azienda Agricola Monte Arcosu Srl v. Regione Autonoma della Sardegna, Organismo Comprensoriale n° 24 della Sardegna and Ente Regionale per l'Assistenza Tecnica in Agricoltura (ERSAT), ECLI:EU:C:2001:6, ¶ 28.

17   Emphasis added.

18   Emphasis added.

for gatekeepers susceptible of being further specified," has no impact on direct effect. A closer look at how "specification" works shows that the title of Article 6 should not be critical for our purposes. It becomes clear from Article 7(2)[19] and Recital 58[20] that the "specification" process is not varying or affecting the nature of each of the rules contained in Article 6 but only relates to effective compliance measures that need to be taken by the gatekeeper. In other words, the rules of Article 6 are not specifiable and adjustable in themselves; only the required compliance measures are. The content of the legal rule is not affected by the specification process. Therefore, although a Commission decision may specify the necessary compliance measures, the Article 6 obligations themselves are unconditional and precise legal rules, and to that extent they are also generally applicable and directly effective.

Indeed, the compliance measures that may be "specified" by means of a Commission decision under Article 7(2) are very different from the Article 101(3) TFEU "individual exemption decisions" that the Commission had exclusive competence to adopt prior to 2004. In that case, the "exemption" was an integral part of the legal rule: a particular practice was prohibited only if it restricted competition per Article 101(1) TFEU *and* the conditions of Article 101(3) TFEU were not fulfilled. On the other hand, the prohibitions of Article 6 of the DMA Proposal are complete and apply, irrespective of a possible "regulatory dialogue" between the Commission and the gatekeeper and a possible specification decision. Thus, in conclusion, the possible "specification" process would not make the Article 6 rules less unconditional or less susceptible of direct effect.[21]

Of course, practically speaking, when the national courts would apply Article 6 and consider imposing remedies on gatekeepers by way of an injunction, the specification process of Article 7(2) may come into play. We can think of three scenarios here:[22]

First scenario: If the Commission has already "specified" compliance measures by means of an individual decision addressed to the gatekeeper, the national court will need to respect that decision and avoid taking measures against its effectiveness. Although there is no explicit provision in the DMA Proposal to

---

19 "Where the Commission finds that the measures that the gatekeeper intends to implement pursuant to paragraph 1, or has implemented, do not ensure effective compliance with the relevant obligations laid down in Article 6, it may by decision specify the measures that the gatekeeper concerned shall implement."

20 "It may in certain cases be appropriate for the Commission, following a dialogue with the gatekeeper concerned, to further specify some of the measures that the gatekeeper concerned should adopt in order to effectively comply with those obligations that are susceptible of being further specified. This possibility of a regulatory dialogue should facilitate compliance by gatekeepers and expedite the correct implementation of the Regulation."

21 In that sense, we do not share the view expressed by some commentators that "the regulatory dialogue according to Art. 7 would shield gatekeepers from private enforcement as long as there are no clear decisions on the exact obligations"; see Podszun et al., *supra* note 3, at 9. In our view, the specification process cannot "shield" gatekeepers from private enforcement risks related to Article 6.

22 *See*, by analogy, Case C–234/89, Stergios Delimitis v. Henninger Bräu AG, ECLI:EU:C:1991:91, ¶ 50 *et seq.*; Case C–344/98, Masterfoods Ltd. v. HB Ice Cream Ltd., ECLI:EU:C:2000:689, ¶ 45 *et seq.*

that extent, a general duty to do so emanates from Article 4(3) TEU.²³ Of course, the possibility that the national court may go further than the measures "specified" by the Commission cannot be excluded. If such over-enforcement is not prejudicing the effectiveness of the Commission decision, it may be allowed under EU law.²⁴

Second scenario: If there is concurrently a pending specification process before the Commission, the national court could suspend proceedings until the Commission has taken a specification decision, especially if there is a risk of conflict between the measures specified by the Commission and those considered by the national court.²⁵

Third scenario: If there is neither a final specification decision nor a pending proceeding before the Commission, the national court retains unfettered discretion. Of course, the litigant-gatekeeper may decide to act strategically and seek to engage in a "regulatory dialogue" with the Commission by notifying it of certain measures under Article 7(2). If then the Commission decides to open proceedings under Article 18, we go back to the second scenario above. If the Commission does not open proceedings, the national court's discretion remains intact.²⁶

In conclusion, as the DMA Proposal currently stands, Articles 5 and 6 can and will definitely be invoked by individuals before national courts. Therefore, private enforcement of the DMA should be taken for granted. The fact that the DMA rules are enforced by the Commission and that the DMA provides for a particular method of public enforcement does not mean per se that private enforcement is excluded.²⁷ Public enforcement does not exclude private enforcement of the DMA.

Indeed, most commentators agree that the DMA will give rise to private enforcement, although some would prefer the introduction of special dispute resolution mechanisms that echo the P2B Regulation.²⁸ In particular, under such

---

23 *Masterfoods, supra* note 23, ¶ 49.

24 *See*, however, *infra* on the fragmentation problem.

25 *See*, by analogy, *Stergios Delimitis, supra* note 23, ¶ 52.

26 Another scenario is for the gatekeeper to invite the Commission to intervene before the national court and submit observations. The Commission retains full discretion to do so. There is no legal basis for such amicus curiae intervention in the DMA Proposal, but Art. 4(3) TEU should make this possible. *See*, by analogy, Case C-2/88 Imm, *J. J. Zwartveld and Others*, Order of the Court, ECLI:EU:C:1990:440.

27 *Compare*, Opinion of AG Geelhoed, *supra* note 13 ¶ 55: "It is not to be inferred from the regulation itself ... that enforcement by the authorities of the Member States has to be the sole method of supervision. In other words, *the regulation grants no monopoly in regard to enforcement.* Nor is any such monopoly to be inferred from the context of Regulation No 2200/96. Nor is that altered by the fact that the regulation itself solely makes provision for enforcement by means of public law. *[EU] law does not operate on the notion that enforcement by means of private law is precluded where provision is made* expressis verbis *solely for enforcement under public law.*" (emphasis added).

28 Regulation (EU) 2019/1150 of the European Parliament and of the Council of 20 June 2019 on promoting fairness and transparency for business users of online intermediation services, 2019 O.J. (L 186) 57 (P2B Regulation). *See* CERRE, *DMA Recommendations, supra* note 3; Monti, *supra* note 3, at 96. This position is also shared by the Body of European Regulators for Electronic Communications (BEREC). *See, Draft BEREC Report on the* ex ante *regulation of digital gatekeepers*, BoR (21) 34, Annex II (Mar. 11, 2021).

mechanisms gatekeepers could be asked to institute internal systems for handling complaints, and if the matter is not resolved, there should be recourse to a mediation procedure. Enforcement may also be by representative organizations or public bodies which could take action in national courts.[29]

III. Available Remedies in the Current (Default) Situation

This all means that the default situation is the following: even if the future DMA Regulation has no specific reference to private enforcement and civil litigation, as long as its provisions enjoy horizontal direct effect and the regulation itself does not exclude or limit private enforcement *expressis verbis*,[30] national courts can adjudicate disputes among individuals and grant appropriate remedies.

Indeed, a right to damages for harm sustained as a result of a violation of the DMA should exist *as a matter of EU law*, without the need to refer to national law. On that point, the CJEU's case law is quite clear. Regulations can generally qualify as basis for EU law-based tort liability claims. Indeed, soon after the seminal *Courage* ruling,[31] which introduced the right to damages for competition law violations as a matter of primary EU law,[32] the CJEU held in *Muñoz* that generally and directly applicable EU regulations, "owing to their very nature and their place in the system of sources of [EU] law ... operate to confer rights on individuals which the national courts have a duty to protect."[33] In fact, the CJEU's reasoning in *Muñoz* echoed that in *Courage*.[34] The CJEU stressed the instrumental nature of such claims and held that the availability of tort claims strengthens the effectiveness of the rules on quality standards and, in particular, the practical effect (*effet utile*) of the obligations laid down therein. Therefore, a careful reading of the CJEU's ruling leads to the conclusion that the right to damages is EU and not national law-based.[35]

29　See also BEUC, *Digital Markets Act Proposal, Position Paper*, 17 (Apr. 2021), which stresses the need to facilitate collective redress and proposes that the future DMA Regulation should be added to the annex of the Representative Actions Directive (Directive (EU) 2020/1828 of the European Parliament and of the Council of 25 November 2020 on representative actions for the protection of the collective interests of consumers and repealing Directive 2009/22/EC, 2020 O.J. (L 409) 1).

30　*Id. See*, however, further *infra* on the possibility of EU secondary law to exclude or limit private enforcement.

31　Case C–453/99, Courage Ltd v. Bernard Crehan and Bernard Crehan v. Courage Ltd and Others, ECLI:EU:C:2001:465.

32　See Komninos, *supra* note 4, at 167 for an exhaustive analysis. The EU law basis of the right to damages is now universally accepted. *See, e.g., Commission Staff Working Document on the implementation of Directive 2014/104/EU of the European Parliament and of the Council of 26 November 2014 on certain rules governing actions for damages under national law for infringements of the competition law provisions of the Member States and of the European Union*, at 1, SWD(2020) 338 final (Dec. 14, 2020).

33　Case C–253/00, Antonio Muñoz y Cia SA and Superior Fruiticola SA v. Frumar Limited and Redbridge Produce Marketing Limited, ECLI:EU:C:2002:497, ¶ 27.

34　*See* Walter Van Gerven, *Harmonization of Private Law: Do We Need It?*, 41 Common Mkt L. Rev. 505, 522 (2004).

35　*Muñoz, supra* note 34, ¶¶ 30–31. *See further*, Cees van Dam, European Tort Law 345 (2006); Folkert Wilman, Private Enforcement of EU Law before National Courts 54 (2015).

Apart from damages claims, national courts can grant other remedies as provided for by both EU[36] and national law. One particularly important remedy is permanent injunctions, i.e. court-ordered measures requiring an infringer to cease and desist from any DMA-infringing conduct. A permanent injunction can contain detailed negative and positive orders aiming at changing the defendant's conduct specifically vis-à-vis the victim of the unlawful conduct. Another available remedy is interim measures. Preliminary injunctions can generally be granted by national courts, notwithstanding the parallel competence of the Commission to order them. The former are of a civil nature and are aimed at the protection of private interests by provisionally securing civil claims, such as a claim for damages, whereas the latter are of an administrative nature and are aimed at safeguarding the public interest – at least as far as the Commission is concerned. Nothing in the current text of the DMA Proposal stands in the way of national courts adopting interim measures based on the DMA.[37]

Other remedies include restitutionary and declaratory relief. Restitution may be a more convenient remedy for claimants, particularly in cases where proving the existence of harm and of a causal link between the harm and the alleged violation is too onerous, as it is sufficient in restitution cases to prove that an infringer has enriched itself in an unjustified manner, to the detriment of the victim of that conduct. Finally, most national legal systems allow parties to seek a judicial declaration concerning the legality or illegality of certain conduct. A declaratory judgment may be quite useful for a litigant, because it clearly states the legal situation at a specific point in time and has a res judicata effect *inter partes*.

In the absence of EU law provisions on procedures and sanctions related to the enforcement of the DMA by national courts, the latter apply national procedural law and – to the extent that they are competent to do so – impose sanctions provided for under national law, under the principle of "procedural/remedial and institutional autonomy" of the Member States. The application of these national provisions must, nevertheless, be compatible with the general principles of EU law, in particular the twin principles of "equivalence" and "effectiveness."

The principle of equivalence requires that the rules on procedures and sanctions that national courts apply to enforce EU law must be no less favorable than the

---

36 The EU Damages Directive (*supra* note 6) or, to be more correct, the national laws transposing it, would not apply here, since private actions would rely on the infringement not of the EU competition rules but only of the DMA. There is, of course, a question as to which is the applicable law, if the civil action is based on the infringement of both the DMA and EU or national competition law. These are scenarios to which the Damages Directive gives no answer.

37 Article 22(2) provides that "[a] decision pursuant to paragraph 1 [ordering interim measures] may only be adopted in the context of proceedings opened in view of the possible adoption of a decision of non-compliance pursuant to Article 25(1)." This specific provision does not apply to national courts and does not impose any limitations on their powers.

rules applicable to the enforcement of equivalent national law provisions.[38] This does not, however, mean that a Member State is obliged to extend its most favorable rules governing liability under national law to all actions based on a breach of EU law.[39] Before the principle of equivalence can be relevant, it is necessary that actions based on a breach of EU law and those based on an infringement of national law be similar, i.e. comparable.[40] In the context of the DMA, the principle of equivalence may play a role, when a Member State has introduced special rules for digital gatekeepers. The fact that such rules may not represent a form of *ex ante* but only *ex post* intervention[41] is, in our view, immaterial, since the requirement of comparability seems to be satisfied.

The principle of effectiveness, which is a direct corollary of the principles of direct effect and supremacy, requires that national rules on procedures and sanctions that national courts apply to enforce EU law must not make such enforcement excessively difficult or practically impossible.[42] It reflects a more general guiding principle of EU law, namely that of full and useful effectiveness (*effet utile*).[43] Whether a national procedural provision renders the exercise of the rights conferred on individuals by the EU legal order impossible or excessively difficult must be analyzed by reference to the role of that provision in the procedure, its progress, and its special features, viewed as a whole.[44]

Some commentators[45] have proposed that the DMA should echo the P2B Regulation and include a provision that specifically requires Member States to ensure "adequate and effective enforcement" of the DMA obligations.[46] That would certainly be a welcome clarification, though the EU case law already described is clear on the duties of national courts to provide for effective enforcement of the rights that individuals base on EU law.

---

38   Case 33/76, Rewe-Zentralfinanz eG and Rewe-Zentral AG v. Landwirtschaftskammer für das Saarland, ECLI:EU:C:1976:188, ¶ 5; Case 199/82, Amministrazione delle Finanze dello Stato v. San Giorgio, ECLI:EU:C:1983:318, ¶ 12; Case C-231/96, Edilizia Industriale Siderurgica Srl (Edis) v. Ministero delle Finanze, ECLI:EU:C:1998:401, ¶¶ 36–37.

39   *Edis v. Ministero delle Finanze, supra* note 39, ¶ 36.

40   Case C-78/98, Shirley Preston and Others v. Wolverhampton Healthcare NHS Trust and Others and Dorothy Fletcher and Others v. Midland Bank plc, ECLI:EU:C:2000:247, para. 57.

41   *See, e.g.*, the new § 19a of the German Competition Act.

42   Case 45/76, Comet BV v. Produktschap voor Siergewassen, ECLI:EU:C:1976:191, ¶ 12; Case 79/83, Dorit Harz v. Deutsche Tradax GmbH, ECLI:EU:C:1984:155, ¶¶ 18 & 23; Case C-169/14, Juan Carlos Sánchez Morcillo and María del Carmen Abril García v. Banco Bilbao Vizcaya Argentaria SA, ECLI:EU:C:2014:2099, ¶ 31.

43   *See* KOEN LENAERTS ET AL., PROCEDURAL LAW OF THE EUROPEAN UNION 83 (2006).

44   Joined Cases C-222/05 to C-225/05, J. van der Weerd and Others v. Minister van Landbouw, Natuur en Voedselkwaliteit, ECLI:EU:C:2007:318, ¶ 33.

45   See CERRE, *DMA Recommendations, supra* note 3, at 72–73.

46   *See* P2B Regulation, Art. 16: "1. Each Member State shall ensure adequate and effective enforcement of this Regulation. 2. Member States shall lay down the rules setting out the measures applicable to infringements of this Regulation and shall ensure that they are implemented. The measures provided for shall be effective, proportionate and dissuasive."

IV. The Risk of Fragmentation

From the foregoing analysis it is obvious that, as the DMA Proposal currently stands, private enforcement will be a reality, notwithstanding the Proposal's silence. National courts would have full competence to apply Articles 5 and 6 and decide whether there has been an infringement of the obligations contained therein. Apart from adjudicating on claims for damages or other restitutionary or declaratory relief, they would also be competent to grant permanent or interlocutory injunctions and order the gatekeepers to take specific measures of a negative or positive nature, to the extent the applicable national procedural law gives them such powers. Such judicial pronouncements will not obviously have *erga omnes* declaratory effect, like a non-compliance decision of the Commission pursuant to Article 25 of the DMA Proposal. They would constitute res judicata *inter partes*, i.e. as between the gatekeeper and the claimant.

However, such national decisions may inevitably result in a considerable degree of fragmentation within the EU. In parallel to and notwithstanding the centralized system of enforcement by the Commission, there will be full decentralization to the level of countless national courts of a generalist nature deciding on countless cases, leading to countless "mini-regulations" with *inter partes* effects within the EU. They may not produce *erga omnes* effects and would only bind the parties to the litigation, but, from a practical point view, their disintegration and fragmentation effects are obvious.

Such disintegration and fragmentation within the internal market will be distractive and will mean increased compliance costs, since gatekeepers, instead of interacting with one centralized enforcer, or at worst with 1 + 27 enforcers (if national authorities were to be given certain competencies), will need to defend their business practices before an innumerable number of courts.[47] Especially the fragmentation of remedial outcomes would be prejudicial to the effectiveness of the whole system, detrimental to the internal market and burdensome and disproportionate for the undertakings concerned.

The ideas of harmonization and avoidance of fragmentation are central to the DMA Proposal. Indeed, its legal basis is Article 114 TFEU, since it aspires to adopt a harmonized legal regime at Union level. The DMA Proposal is quite definitive and explicit on why there should be no national competence to legislate and enforce the DMA rules. It makes significant effort to highlight the risk of fragmentation but for the adoption of the DMA, including a number of references to "regulatory initiatives by Member States," which "without action at EU level … will be further aggravated," "could lead to fragmentation," and create "a risk

---

47   The problem of fragmentation is accentuated by the parallel application (and confusion) among different policy tools, such as consumer and data protection laws, on top of competition law. *See further* S. Yakovleva et al., *Kaleidoscopic Data-related Enforcement in the Digital Age*, 57 COMMON MKT L. REV. 1461 (2020).

of divergent regulatory solutions."[48] In addition, both the DMA Proposal itself and its Impact Assessment Report spend pages highlighting the risks that a fully decentralized system of enforcement (with emphasis on the role of national authorities) would bring and defend the choice of centralization at the EU level.[49] Yet, if a risk of fragmentation exists with 27 specialist administrative authorities, surely the risk is much higher with potentially thousands of generalist courts having full decisional powers on Articles 5 and 6 of the DMA Proposal.

An unlimited private enforcement may also disrupt public enforcement. It is true that judgments of national courts cannot bind the Commission and the Commission will be entitled to adopt at any time individual decisions under Articles 7, 8, 9, 15, 16, 22, 23(1), 25, 26 and 27 of the DMA Proposal, even where a gatekeeper's conduct has already been the subject of a judgment by a national court and the decision contemplated by the Commission conflicts with that national judgment.[50] However, a degree of disruption in that case is inevitable. We can take as an example the Article 6 obligations and the "specification" process of Article 7.[51] The idea behind that process is that a "regulatory dialogue" ensues between the Commission and the gatekeepers.[52] The effectiveness of that procedure and of the "regulatory dialogue" may be reduced, if national courts systematically preempt it.[53]

Besides, there are serious risks for the uniform, consistent and effective application of the DMA rules.[54] National courts will be called upon to adjudicate on a highly

---

48   *See* Explanatory Memorandum to the DMA Proposal.

49   *See, e.g.*, Explanatory Memorandum to the DMA Proposal and Recital 9; *Commission Staff Working Document, Impact Assessment Report, Part 1*, §5, SWD(2020) 363 final (Dec. 15, 2020), *in particular* §5, ¶ 192: "Given the pan-European reach of the targeted companies, a decentralized enforcement model does not seem to be a conceivable option, including in light of the fragmentation that the initiative is supposed to address, nor would it be proportionate given the limited number of gatekeepers that would be in scope of the proposed framework."

50   *See*, by analogy, *Masterfoods*, *supra* note 23, ¶ 48.

51   *See also*, CERRE, *DMA Recommendations*, *supra* note 3, at 74, with an acknowledgment of the risk of divergent interpretations of the DMA particularly in the area of Article 6 obligations that are being "specified" ("A national court may find an infringement of Article 6 in settings where the Commission might not, or vice versa").

52   *See* Recitals 29 and 33 of the DMA Proposal.

53   The risk appears lower, if not inexistent, if the Article 7(2) "specification" decision by the Commission precedes in time the national litigation. In that case, the national courts would be bound not to take decisions running counter to a decision adopted by the Commission pursuant to Article 1(7) of the DMA Proposal. That provision refers only to "national authorities" (*see also infra*) but should be interpreted broadly. In any event, this is just a *lex specialis* to the *lex generalis* of Article 4(3) TEU.

54   Apart from being mentioned in the DMA Proposal (Recital 9), these principles have always been considered central to EU law. On the principle of uniform application of EU law, *see* Joined Cases C–453/03, C–11/04, C–12/04 and C–194/04, The Queen on the application of ABNA Ltd and Others v. Secretary of State for Health and Others, ECLI:EU:C:2005:741, ¶ 104 ("the uniform application of [EU] law, which is a fundamental requirement of the [EU] legal order"); Case C–411/17, Inter-Environnement Wallonie ASBL and Bond Beter Leefmilieu Vlaanderen ASBL v. Conseil des ministres, ECLI:EU:C:2019:622, ¶ 177. With particular reference to Regulations, *see* Case 94/77, Fratelli Zerbone Snc v. Amministrazione delle finanze dello Stato, ECLI:EU:C:1978:17, ¶ 25 ("simultaneous and uniform application of [EU] regulations throughout the whole of the [EU]"). *See also generally* F. Fines, *L'application uniforme du droit communautaire dans la jurisprudence de la Cour de justice des Communautés européennes, in* LES DYNAMIQUES DU DROIT EUROPÉEN EN DÉBUT DE SIÈCLE: ÉTUDES EN L'HONNEUR DE JEAN-CLAUDE GAUTRON 334 (2004).

complex and entirely new system of legal rules which inevitably relies on a number of nebulous concepts. Unlike the 2004 decentralization drive and the subsequent enhancement of private enforcement in the area of EU competition law, when the national courts could count on a 40-year body of precedent (1962–2004), unlimited private enforcement here would mean putting the cart before the horse. Even in the case of the application of competition law by national courts, the EU legislator recognized the risks to the consistent application of EU competition rules and introduced a number of safeguards in Articles 15 and 16 of Regulation 1/2003,[55] in particular, duties of cooperation with the Commission and a powerful supremacy clause. These were supplemented by appropriate soft law measures adopted by the Commission, in particular the 2004 Co-operation Notice.[56] The DMA Proposal, on the other hand, is entirely silent on that point. So the already-increased risks are accentuated by the complete absence of any cooperation and coordination mechanisms.

These risks cannot be brushed aside simply by counting on the role of the CJEU and of the preliminary reference proceeding, which acts as an ultimate safeguard that ensures the uniformity and consistency of application of EU law. While decentralized enforcement remains the rule in EU law and centralization is the exception, a degree of centralization and the introduction of certain rules of precedence is sometimes appropriate. We elaborate further on this in the following section. In any event, if the competition rules can be a guide, a centralized model existed in effect for 40 years (1962–2004), and even today the role of the Commission in enforcing EU competition law is paramount.[57] In addition, there are other areas of EU law in which the Commission enjoys exclusive competence.[58]

V. Arguments in Favor of Limiting Private Enforcement to Follow-on Claims

From public statements of senior officials, it seems that the European Commission does not seem too concerned about the risks of fragmentation of unlimited private enforcement.[59] The Commission seems to think that the involvement of national courts can be beneficial in terms of filling the "enforcement gap"

---

55 Council Regulation (EC) 1/2003 of 16 December 2002 on the implementation of the rules on competition laid down in Articles 81 and 82 of the Treaty, 2003 O.J. (L 1) 1.

56 Commission Notice on the co-operation between the Commission and the courts of the EU Member States in the application of Articles 81 and 82 EC, 2004 O.J. (C 101) 54. See also the older Notice of 1993: Commission Notice on co-operation between national courts and the Commission in applying Articles 85 and 86 of the EEC Treaty, 1993 O.J. (C 39) 6.

57 See Article 105 TFEU.

58 *See* CERRE, *DMA Recommendations*, *supra* note 3, at 68, with references to the Commission's exclusive competence in merger enforcement (for concentrations of an EU dimension), the European Central Bank's exclusive competence to supervise systemically significant banks, and other examples.

59 MLex, *EU "gatekeeper" law should expose Big Tech to national court suits, Guersent says* (June 10, 2021).

generated by the perceived inability of the Commission to deal with all attention-worthy cases. This line of argument sits in stark contrast with the DMA Proposal's exclusion of national authorities as enforcement organs, which is precisely premised on the need to avoid the risk of fragmentation. It is unclear why fragmentation will be avoided if a finite number of specialist national organs are excluded but the infinite number of generalist organs are included.

For the reasons explained above, we believe that the EU legislator would be well advised to introduce certain proportionate limitations on the private enforcement of the DMA rules or a "rule of precedence" for public enforcement. Private enforcement should only be allowed in its "follow-on" form, i.e. only after the Commission has taken a decision and has declared *erga omnes* that a particular gatekeeper has violated the DMA rules. In that case, there is no reason why aggrieved parties could not pursue follow-on claims against the infringer. Indeed, they should be able to bring damages claims for harm suffered as a result of the DMA infringement. They should also be able to bring other civil claims (e.g. nullity, restitutionary or declaratory claims) to the extent they have a legal interest. Such private enforcement would enhance the deterrent effect of DMA prohibitions and convey the message that a DMA infringement could result not only in administrative fines but may also give rise to damages and other civil sanctions.

However, the EU legislator should accord precedence to public enforcement and should not allow for private enforcement in its "stand-alone" form, i.e. before the Commission has had the chance to declare the infringement of a DMA rule by a gatekeeper and has also possibly ordered specific remedies. This form of litigation could be distractive and would thus bring about an intolerable degree of legal uncertainty. It would result in fragmentation in the Union and prejudice the consistent and effective application of the DMA rules.

The introduction of a rule of precedence of public over private enforcement does not have to be permanent but could be reexamined by the legislator at an appropriate time, e.g. in 10 years'time, after the Commission has had a chance to build up a body of precedent and after the EU Courts have delivered their first rulings on the interpretation of the DMA.

We can again take the example of the EU competition rules to support that proposition. Although the direct effect of those rules was recognized in 1974,[60] it took 40 years of case law (1962–2004) for the EU legislator to opt for a full decentralization of the application of the rules (of Article 101(3) TFEU), with the introduction of Regulation 1/2003. It took 10 more years for the EU legislator to introduce specific measures aimed at enhancing private antitrust enforcement in Europe and to adopt a harmonized system of civil liability for damages with

---

60   *Belgische Radio v. SABAM*, supra note 5.

the Damages Directive. If that was the case with EU competition law, *a fortiori* a degree of prudence is called for in the case of the novel regime of the DMA.

The question arises whether such a limitation would be possible and defendable from an EU law point of view. To our mind, there is no doubt that it would. The DMA is not primary law, i.e. it is not part of the Treaties. If that were the case, it would not have been open to secondary law (a regulation) to restrict the direct effect of a Treaty provision.[61] Since, however, the DMA is the product of secondary EU legislation (a regulation), it is open to EU legislation to introduce limitations on competence and, thus, on the direct effect of the legal rules it contains. In *Muñoz*, Advocate General Geelhoed considered that the provisions of an EU Regulation were directly effective and that they could be applied by national courts in private enforcement cases, relying on the following reasoning:

> It is not to be inferred from the regulation itself ... that enforcement by the authorities of the Member States has to be the sole method of supervision. In other words, the regulation grants no monopoly in regard to enforcement. Nor is any such monopoly to be inferred from the context of Regulation No. 2200/96. Nor is that altered by the fact that the regulation itself solely makes provision for enforcement by means of public law. [EU] law does not operate on the notion that enforcement by means of private law is precluded where provision is made *expressis verbis* solely for enforcement under public law.[62]

E contrario, there is nothing precluding the EU legislator to provide *expressis verbis* for a limitation on the competence of national authorities and courts to enforce the secondary EU rules it introduces. This is precisely what we advocate here, with a view to safeguarding the effective, consistent and uniform application of the DMA rules. As explained, this rule could be revisited at a time when the DMA Regulation will have produced a sufficient body of precedent.

Indeed, secondary EU law includes examples where private enforcement and thus by implication the horizontal direct effect of EU law was excluded altogether or restricted. For example, Article 3(3) of the Environmental Liability Directive[63] provides that "without prejudice to relevant national legislation, this Directive shall not give private parties a right of compensation as a consequence of environmental damage or of an imminent threat of such

---

61 With regard to EU competition rules, which are Treaty-based, *compare* Case C–819/19, Stichting Cartel Compensation and Equilib Netherlands BV v. Koninklijke Luchtvaart Maatschappij NV and Others, Opinion of AG Bobek, ECLI:EU:C:2021:373, ¶¶ 79 & 92.

62 Opinion of AG Geelhoed, *supra* note 13, ¶ 55 (emphasis added).

63 Directive 2004/35/CE of the European Parliament and of the Council of 21 April 2004 on environmental liability with regard to the prevention and remedying of environmental damage, 2004 O.J. (L 143) 56.

damage."⁶⁴ In other words, the Directive provides for the exclusive competence of administrative authorities, i.e. for public enforcement exclusively.⁶⁵

There are also examples where the CJEU restricts private enforcement, in order to protect the effectiveness of EU sectoral regulation in certain areas. For example, in *CTL Logistics*,⁶⁶ the CJEU held that the German courts could not use a national doctrine based on the German Civil Code (BGB) to perform a review based on equity of the charges levied by railway infrastructure undertakings. Such levies were already regulated by Directive 2001/14/EC⁶⁷ (later repealed by Directive 2012/34/EU⁶⁸), and there was a sectoral regulator in Germany which had competence to deal with the matter. In essence, the CJEU thought that this constituted "excessive protection" incompatible with the requirements and objectives of EU sectoral legislation. In particular, the CJEU held that the assessment of fairness of a contract, carried out by virtue of the BGB, on the one hand, and sectoral regulation flowing from Directive 2001/14, on the other hand, related to different considerations which, if applied to a single situation, could lead to contradictory results.⁶⁹

Staying in the same area, the pending *DB Station & Service* case before the CJEU is highly relevant.⁷⁰ It relates to a private action in Germany brought against a subsidiary of Deutsche Bahn (DB), a railway infrastructure undertaking which maintains 5,400 stations (traffic hubs), by a rail transport undertaking that uses the defendant's traffic hubs for passenger railway services. The civil action alleged that the charges levied for that purpose were excessive and thus constituted an abuse of a dominant position. The complication here was, however, that the Federal Network Agency, acting as the competent regulatory body, declared the DB price system to be invalid, albeit with effect from a later date than their adoption. The referring court, influenced by *CTL Logistics*, entertained doubts as to whether national civil courts are entitled and obliged to review the charges

---

64 Notwithstanding the fact that the Directive excludes private enforcement, it includes certain provisions of relevance to private enforcement based on national environmental laws (*see, e.g.*, Article 9 on rights of contribution in accordance with national law).

65 Article 11(1): "Member States shall designate the competent authority(ies) responsible for fulfilling the duties provided for in this Directive." On this Directive and the question of private enforcement, *see* Gerrit Betlem, *Environmental Liability and Private Enforcement: Lessons from International Law, the European Court of Justice, and European Mining Laws*, 4 Y.B. EUR. ENVTL. L. 117 (2004); Gerrit Betlem, *Torts, a European* ius commune *and the Private Enforcement of Community Law*, 64 CAMBRIDGE L.J. 126 (2005).

66 Case C-489/15, CTL Logistics GmbH v. DB Netz AG, ECLI:EU:C:2017:834. *See also* Francesco Martucci, *Judicial review: The Court of Justice of the European Union rules that the ordinary courts cannot provide for a review of the equity of charges for the use of railway infrastructure (*CTL Logistics*)*, CONCURRENCES N° 1–2018, ART. N° 86170, 176–78 (2017).

67 Directive 2001/14/EC of the European Parliament and of the Council of 26 February 2001 on the allocation of railway infrastructure capacity and the levying of charges for the use of railway infrastructure and safety certification, 2001 O.J. (L 75) 29.

68 Directive 2012/34/EU of the European Parliament and of the Council of 21 November 2012 establishing a single European railway area, 2012 O.J. (L 343) 32.

69 *CTL Logistics*, supra note 67, ¶¶ 74–75.

70 Case C-721/20, DB Station & Service AG v. ODEG Ostdeutsche Eisenbahn GmbH, *pending*.

levied based on Article 102 TFEU and national competition law, independently of the monitoring carried out by the regulatory authority.

The currently pending case focuses on whether the existence of EU secondary regulation should impose a rule of precedence in favor of the sectoral regulator (the Federal Network Agency), thus resulting in limiting private enforcement of EU/national competition law.[71] If such limitations were recognized by the CJEU, they would *a fortiori* be appropriate in the DMA scenario, where the regulator would not be a national authority but rather the Commission itself. Indeed, the question of whether national courts applying the DMA provisions should accord precedence to the EU regulator can be legitimately posed.

Finally, we can again use EU competition law as a guide. CJEU case law allows for some limitations on private enforcement, when there is a need to safeguard the effectiveness of public enforcement. This is notably the case in limiting the discoverability of leniency statements.[72] The Damages Directive has, indeed, introduced a rule excluding discovery of leniency statements.[73] It is also interesting that the Damages Directive has gone even further and limits the joint and several liability of immunity recipients under the leniency programs.[74] Such a limitation is not seen as interfering with the EU law-based right to damages but rather as a necessary and proportionate measure, in order to safeguard the effectiveness of the leniency programs and of public enforcement.[75]

In any event, the solution we advocate does not result in the total exclusion of private enforcement. Instead, we advocate the introduction of a limitation: a rule of precedence of public enforcement and the exclusion of private enforcement only in its stand-alone form, i.e. before the Commission has had the chance to take a decision in certain specific proceedings whereby the Commission (i) specifies compliance measures per Article 6 (Article 7(2)), (ii) adopts non-compliance decisions (Article 25(1)), (iii) imposes behavioral or structural remedies in cases of systematic infringements (Article 16(1)), and (iv) imposes interim measures (Article 22). From the point of view of EU law, such a solution

---

[71] The critical question referred to the CJEU is the following: "Is it compatible with Directive 2001/14/EC ... for national civil courts to review the charges levied based on the criteria laid down in Article 102 TFEU and/or in national competition law on a case-by-case basis independently of the monitoring carried out by the regulatory body? If Question 1 is answered in the affirmative: Are the national civil courts permitted and required to conduct an assessment of abusive practices in the light of the criteria laid down in Article 102 TFEU and/or in national competition law, even where the rail transport undertakings have the possibility to request the competent regulatory body to review the fairness of the charges paid? Must the national civil courts wait for a decision in the matter by the regulatory body and, where applicable, if it is contested before the courts, for that decision to become enforceable?"

[72] *See, e.g.*, Case C-360/09, Pfleiderer AG v. Bundeskartellamt, ECLI:EU:C:2011:389, ¶¶ 25–27, 30; Case C-536/11, Bundeswettbewerbsbehörde v. Donau Chemie AG and Others, ECLI:EU:C:2013:366, ¶¶ 33, 41–42.

[73] Article 6(6)(a).

[74] Article 11(4).

[75] *See further* Assimakis Komninos, *The Relationship between Public and Private Enforcement: Quod Dei Deo, Quod Caesaris Caesari*, in EUROPEAN COMPETITION LAW ANNUAL 2011, INTEGRATING PUBLIC AND PRIVATE ENFORCEMENT: IMPLICATIONS FOR COURTS AND AGENCIES 149 (Philip Lowe & Mel Marquis eds., 2014).

would be fully appropriate and proportionate. It would ensure the effective and consistent enforcement of the DMA in the EU while avoiding fragmentation, and would also further the undertakings' legal certainty. It could also be reexamined by the EU legislator at an appropriate time, when the DMA is sufficiently mature.

VI. The Need of Coordination and Cooperation Mechanisms

The DMA Proposal should be completed with the introduction of mechanisms of coordination and cooperation between the European Commission (acting as DMA enforcer) and national courts, following the example of Articles 15 and 16 of Regulation 1/2003.

First, the future DMA Regulation should introduce a supremacy rule modeled on Article 16 of Regulation 1/2003.[76] If no rule of precedence is adopted, as is proposed, a national court may be called to apply the DMA provisions at the same time as the Commission or even before the Commission has ever initiated proceedings. This will raise issues relating to the consistent application of the DMA in the EU. In that case, the introduction of a supremacy rule is indispensable; a supremacy rule would also be welcome even if the DMA Regulation allows only for follow-on private enforcement.

In the EU competition law area, these issues were dealt with in detail by the CJEU in its seminal ruling in *Masterfoods*[77] and this case law was subsequently codified verbatim by Article 16 of Regulation 1/2003. A similar provision should be included in the future DMA Regulation. Article 1(7) of the current DMA Proposal, which provides that "national authorities shall not take decisions which would run counter to a decision adopted by the Commission under this Regulation," is unfortunate in that it does not specifically mention national courts. Although courts could be considered "judicial authorities" and, in any event, the above provision is a *lex specialis* to the *lex generalis* of Article 4(3) TEU, a specific reference to the duty of national courts to respect the Commission's decisions seems warranted.[78]

Thus, where the national litigation takes place before the Commission has adopted a decision (if stand-alone private enforcement is allowed), there should be a rule providing that the national court must avoid adopting a decision that would conflict with a decision contemplated by the Commission. To that effect, the

---

76 *See*, CERRE, *DMA Recommendations*, *supra* note 3, at 74.

77 *Masterfoods*, *supra* note 23, ¶¶ 51–52.

78 Indeed, this is a gap that has been noticed by the European Parliament. The IMCO Draft Report (*supra* note 11) includes Amendment 32 which adds "national courts" to Article 1(7).

national court should be allowed to ask the Commission whether it has initiated proceedings regarding the same conduct and, if so, about the progress of proceedings and the likelihood of a decision.[79] The rule should also provide that the national court may, for reasons of legal certainty, consider staying its proceedings until the Commission has reached a decision.[80]

If, on the other hand, there is a follow-on litigation and the Commission has already reached a decision, the DMA Regulation should make sure that the national court cannot rule in a manner running counter to a Commission decision. The only alternative for a national court intending to rule in a manner running counter to a Commission decision, is to refer a question to the CJEU for a preliminary ruling under Article 267 TFEU.[81] The CJEU will then decide on the compatibility of the Commission's decision with EU law.[82]

The future DMA Regulation could decide to go even further than Article 16 of Regulation 1/2003 and introduce a rule conveying a "binding effect" on Commission decisions finding an infringement of the DMA rules, following the model of Article 9 of the Damages Directive. Such a far-reaching rule would enhance follow-on litigation and would facilitate claims by victims of conduct that is found to have infringed the DMA rules.

Second, like Regulation 1/2003, the future DMA Regulation should establish a number of mechanisms of cooperation between the national courts and the Commission. This should be particularly so, if our proposal to exclude stand-alone private enforcement is not followed. Such mechanisms should be built on the principle of loyal cooperation contained in Article 4(3) TEU and should aim at promoting the coherent application of the DMA rules. Again, Article 15 of Regulation 1/2003 can be used as a model. These rules could include the right of the national courts to seek the Commission's opinion on the application of the DMA Regulation. That possibility should be without prejudice to the possibility or the obligation for a national court to refer questions to the CJEU for a preliminary ruling regarding the interpretation or the validity of the DMA Regulation in accordance with Article 267 TFEU. Another possibility is to adopt a mechanism for the Commission to intervene before the national court as amicus curiae in cases that have important policy implications for the application of the

---

79 *Stergios Delimitis, supra* note 23, ¶ 53; Joined Cases C–319/93, C–40/94 and C–224/94, Hendrik Evert Dijkstra v. Friesland (Frico Domo) Coöperatie BA, Cornelis van Roessel and Others v. De coöperatieve vereniging Zuivelcoöperatie Campina Melkunie VA and Willem de Bie and Others v. De Coöperatieve Zuivelcoöperatie Campina Melkunie BA, ECLI:EU:C:1995:433, ¶ 34.

80 *Masterfoods, supra* note 23, ¶ 51.

81 Case 314/85, Foto-Frost v. Hauptzollamt Lübeck-Ost, ECLI:EU:C:1987:452, paras 12 to 20.

82 If the Commission's decision is, however, being challenged before the EU Courts pursuant to Article 263 TFEU, and the outcome of the dispute before the national court depends on the validity of the Commission's decision, the national court should stay its proceedings pending final judgment by the EU Courts unless it considers that, in the circumstances of the case, a reference to the CJEU for a preliminary ruling on the validity of the Commission decision is warranted. *See Masterfoods, supra* note 23, ¶¶ 52–59, as codified by Article 16(1) of Regulation 1/2003.

DMA.[83] This mechanism is particularly necessary in the early stages of DMA enforcement, when there is no sufficient body of precedent.

Such coordination and cooperation mechanisms are necessary and, indeed, it is surprising that they are conspicuously absent in the DMA Proposal; and yet the Commission officials seem so keen on allowing the private enforcement of the DMA rules.[84]

---

83 *Compare* Article 15(3) of Regulation 1/2003.

84 The IMCO Draft Report (*supra* note 11) includes Amendment 28 which proposes the introduction of a new Recital 77a: "National courts will have an important role in applying this Regulation and should be allowed to ask the Commission to send them information or opinions on questions concerning the application of this Regulation. At the same time, the Commission should be able to submit oral or written observations to courts of the Member States."

Still Hanging in the Balance – Judicial Assessments of Authorities' Merger Decisions

GÖNENÇ GÜRKAYNAK,[*] BERFU AKGÜN,[**] BULUT GIRGIN[***]
ELIG Gürkaynak Attorneys-at-Law

Abstract

The judicial review of decisions rendered by administrative bodies constitutes one of the most crucial aspects of any legal system, since the lack of any supervisory mechanism would deprive such administrative decisions of substantial elements that could only be achieved by filtering them through multiple levels of legal scrutiny. However, such judicial reviews may also give rise to serious consequences for all involved parties. This paper aims to discuss the consequences of the annulment of the Commission's merger control decisions by the EU courts. These consequences are reviewed initially from the perspective of the transaction parties, as well as interested third parties and the respective market. Through the analysis of the EU courts' decisional practice, this paper aims to demonstrate that the annulment of merger decisions is likely to give rise to grave consequences that cannot be completely fixed through any compensation mechanism, and, in any case, it is very difficult for the applicant to fulfill the conditions required to be awarded damages due to the Commission's erroneous conduct in practice. Finally, we will provide certain proposals relating to the possible measures that could be taken to mitigate the losses incurred by all parties involved in the process.

---

[*] Gönenç Gürkaynak is the founding partner of ELIG Gürkaynak Attorneys-at-Law, and member of faculty at Bilkent University, Faculty of Law and Bilgi University, Faculty of Law.

[**] Berfu Akgün is an associate at ELIG Gürkaynak Attorneys-at-Law.

[***] Bulut Girgin is an Attorney-at-Law, Istanbul.

Still Hanging in the Balance –
Judicial Assessments of Authorities' Merger Decisions

I. Introduction

Timely and effective review of the decisions rendered by regulatory or administrative bodies, including competition law authorities, constitutes a crucial aspect of establishing an effective judicial system and ensuring legal coherence and stability. This is because administrative decisions that are rendered in the absence of any supervisory mechanism would lack substantial elements that could only be achieved by filtering them through multiple levels of legal scrutiny. It is quite evident that multiple layers of legal examination and assessment are necessary to ensure the appropriateness of any given decision and to enhance its legal standing and authority. Especially in recent years, EU courts (i.e., the General Court and the European Court of Justice) have proved to be prominent bodies in terms of shaping EU law, acting "as an effective check on the Commission's application of the EUMR [EU Merger Regulation] and exerting discipline on its decisions in the same way as US courts discipline the US federal agencies' determinations of whether mergers should be allowed to proceed."[1] The judicial review of merger control decisions, by its very nature, comprises many uncertainties, since the Commission's decisions relating to Articles 101 and 102 of the Treaty on the Functioning of the European Union (TFEU) are rendered as a result of an *ex post* review, while merger control decisions are rendered based on an *ex ante* review by taking into account the future state of the market in question, which involves the assessment of a hypothetical market landscape that has not yet occurred at the time of the decision. This in turn brings forth the potential of further aggravating the review of the merger control decisions by the judicial body at the latter stages.

In the simplest terms, in a scenario where Company X is acquiring Company Y, if the hypothetical consequences of the acquisition are either (i) not scrutinized by the relevant competition authority via thorough concrete economic analysis, or (ii) not examined sufficiently to establish satisfactory legal grounds for rejection or clearance, the resulting decision could lead to grave consequences for the undertakings in question, as well as having adverse effects on public welfare. The lack of sufficient grounds would leave the relevant case open to the threat of further judicial review, regardless of its actual material content. As an alternative scenario, consider the rejection or clearance of the acquisition of Company Y by Company X based on inaccurate data or a faulty assessment leading to the judiciary stepping in when, simultaneously, the stock price of either company falls drastically or, even worse for consumers, an anticompetitive structure is created in the given market. Therefore, the dichotomy between the competition authority's decision and the judiciary's decision would have a major impact on the commercial path of a given company, as well as significantly affecting the competitive landscape of any given market.

---

1   Nicholas Levy, *Judicial review of merger decisions: An overview of EU and national case law* (2019), e-Competitions Mergers judicial review, Art. N° 90747 (Aug. 14, 2019).

In correlation with such hypothetical (and, based on recent jurisprudence, occasionally real and valid) concerns, it is important to highlight that the correction of a merger control case is necessary to uphold the law itself; however, it cannot be overemphasized that such reviews carry a number of uncertainties and pitfalls that are too crucial to be ignored. These elements further aggravate the judicial review of those decisions and pose various difficulties in terms of the correction of any unlawful conduct.[2]

II. A Brief Overview of the Judicial Review System in the EU

The merger control regime in the EU, fundamentally based on Articles 101 and 102 TFEU, and the EUMR, is primarily led by Europe's competition sentinel, i.e., the European Commission. The decisions of the European Commission are subject to the judicial monitoring of the General Court at first instance, followed by the Court of Justice of the European Union (ECJ). The Commission's decisions are subject to extensive substantial scrutiny, "illustrated notably by the Court's competence to review not only the legality of actions or decisions of the Commission, but also the claims for failure to act and claims for damages."[3]

Article 256 TFEU bestows competence on the General Court in terms of actions brought against the Commission's decisions in merger control transactions. Accordingly, the General Court would be tasked with assessing the compliance of the relevant action brought against a Commission decision under Articles 101 and 102 TFEU and, by doing so, "It can review the factual basis of the decision, the interpretation of the law on which it is based, the finding of a violation, the legality of any fines or of other remedies imposed, the grounds on which a merger is authorized or prohibited, etc."[4] Any action brought against the General Court's decisions would, in turn, be subject to the review of the ECJ.

Article 263(2) TFEU limits the instances in which a Commission decision may be subject to review by the appeals court to the following grounds: (i) lack of competence, (ii) infringement of an essential procedural requirement, (iii) infringement of the Treaties or of any rule of law relating to their application, or (iv) misuse of powers. The General Court, while able and authorized to review the legality of the decision, cannot act on behalf of the Commission or substitute its assessment with that of the Commission.[5]

---

2   *Id.*

3   Organisation for Economic Co-Operation and Development (OECD), *The standard of review by courts in competition cases*, DAF/COMP/WP3/WD(2019)9 (June 3, 2019).

4   *Id.*

5   *Id.*

III. Judicial Review Statistics

Official ECJ data indicates that a significant amount of judicial activity was observed in 2020 (the most recent full year in review), even though the pandemic had a vital impact on the normal functioning of the judiciary institutions.[6] "In 2020, the Court of Justice of the European Union managed to maintain a high level of activity in a context marked by working from home and travel restrictions which made it impossible to hold hearings between 16 March and 25 May 2020."[7] . The overall case statistics show that 1582 cases were brought before the institution as a whole, which is naturally lower compared to the year 2019, where 1905 cases were brought for review in total, due to the global health crisis. That said, until these exceptional circumstances, the number of new cases brought for review and number of cases completed by the institution had shown a steady increase and illustrated an upward trend throughout the years.[8]

According to the 2020 annual statistics of the ECJ, which include the annual data related to the General Court and the ECJ, the average duration of the proceedings of both courts were found to be 15.4 months.[9] Historically, there have been measures taken to accelerate the judicial process in cases where a timely review is of the utmost importance, and these naturally include merger control cases. In this respect, in 2001, the Court of First Instance (now known as the General Court) introduced a "fast-track" route, which is currently stipulated as the "expedited procedure" under Article 151 of the Rules of Procedure of the General Court.[10] This procedure is especially notable for putting greater emphasis on oral proceedings, simplifying the written exchange of pleas, and allowing a more timely evaluation.[11] In 2015, an additional provision was adopted, which allowed the General Court to employ the expedited procedure without the request of the applicant (usually the third party challenging the decision) or the defendant (usually the Commission) initiating the process, further aiming to preserve the rights of the parties. With that said, even with such measures, the judicial review of merger control decisions still takes a considerable amount of time, which could, in turn, be fatal for a transaction where timing is of the essence.

---

6   *See* Court of Justice of the European Union, *Annual Report 2020*, https://curia.europa.eu/jcms/upload/docs/application/pdf/2021-04/ra_pan_2020_en.pdf

7   *Id.*

8   *Id.*

9   *Id.*

10 *See*, Rules of Procedure of the General Court (as amended), 2015 O.J. (L 105) 1.

11 Kyriakos Fountoukakos, *Judicial review and merger control: The CFI's expedited procedure*, 3 Competition Pol'y Newsletter 7 (Oct. 2002), https://ec.europa.eu/competition/publications/cpn/2002_3_7.pdf.

IV. Prominent Merger Cases That Have Been Subject to Judicial Review

Recent years have exhibited a significant upsurge in terms of the judicial review of merger control decisions, and although the Commission's decisions are very rarely annulled outright by the EU courts, the impact of such assessments tends to have far-reaching consequences, principally for the transaction parties, as well as the third parties, the market in question, and ultimately for the consumers. The following examples and the dynamics of the Commission's assessments, followed by the evaluations of the EU courts, demonstrate the practical applications of Article 263(2) TFEU and provide insights that would constitute de facto guidelines for the annulment of decisions rendered in merger control cases.

1. *Telefónica/Hutchison*

The transaction concerned CK Hutchison Holdings Limited's (Hutchison) (operating under the brand Three in the United Kingdom) proposed acquisition of Telefónica Europe Plc (Telefónica), which operates under the brand "O2" in the United Kingdom.[12] The application, which was submitted to the Commission on September 11, 2015, was ultimately prohibited after a review of approximately one year. "According to the Commission, "that acquisition would have removed an important competitor on the United Kingdom mobile telephony market and the merged entity would have faced competition only from two mobile network operators, Everything Everywhere (EE), belonging to British Telecom, and Vodafone."[13] Therefore, the Commission considered that the presence of solely two mobile networks in the sector, would ultimately result in the increase of prices and decrease of consumer choice and quality. The decision was later on brought for the review of the General Court through Hutchison's application and the General Court annulled the Commission's said decision, on May 28, 2020.[14] In its evaluation, the General Court found that all three theories of harm (i.e. non-coordinated effects on the retail market, non-coordinated effects produced by the disruption of the network-sharing agreements and non-coordinated effects on the wholesale market) set forth by the Commission were erroneous, thereby the Commission's analysis was unable to clearly put forth that the consummation of the transaction would lead to a significant impediment of effective competition on both the retail and wholesale levels of the market. This judgement is prominent in terms of providing guidance on the cumulative conditions that must be met when assessing whether there is a significant

---

12   Telefónica/Hutchison (Case No. COMP/ M.7612) Commission Decision C(2016) 431 final (May,11, .2016)

13   General Court of the European Union,, Press Release *The General Court annuls the Commission's decision to block the proposed acquisition of Telefónica UK by Hutchison 3G UK in the sector of the mobile telephony market,* May 28, 2020, https://curia.europa.eu/jcms/upload/docs/application/pdf/2020-05/cp200065en.pdf.

14   Case T-399/16, CK Telecoms UK Investments Ltd v. Commission, Judgement of the General Court (2020).

impediment to effective competition in cases where non-coordinated affects are in question (i.e. "the concentration must involve (i) 'the elimination of important competitive constraints that the merging parties had exerted upon each other' and (ii) 'a reduction of competitive pressure on the remaining competitors"[15]), and setting the bar for standard of proof, since the decision reads that "Commission is required to produce sufficient evidence to demonstrate with a strong probability the existence of significant impediments following the concentration."[16]

On November 16, 2020, it has been published in the Official Journal of the European Union that the General Court's judgement has been appealed by the Commission[17], and the conclusion of the case is likely to constitute one of the most significant merger control decisions through the decade, since if the decision is upheld, the Commission could be required to re-evaluate its analysis relating to the significant impediment of effective competition through non-coordinated effects of mergers in oligopolistic markets.

2. *UPS/TNT Express*

The proposed acquisition of TNT Express NV (TNT) by United Parcel Service, Inc. (UPS), was concerned with the transaction between two major players in the market for international express delivery of small parcels. This transaction, which was notified to the Commission on June 15, 2012, was ultimately prohibited by the Commission following a detailed review process.[18] This decision was based on the Commission's findings that the proposed acquisition would lead to a significant impediment to effective competition within the respective markets. The Commission noted that "TNT–and to an even greater extent DHL–appear as the strongest sources of competitive constraint on UPS in the international intra-EEA express market for customers that need to ship packages to a broad range of countries of destinations."[19] The Commission further determined that the consummation of the transaction would give rise to price increases in the Swedish market, even if the transaction brought about a series of efficiencies, mainly based on cost-savings that would result in consumer benefits.

The Commission's decision, dated January 30, 2013, was subsequently appealed by UPS, primarily based on the grounds that the it was in violation of its rights

---

15   *Id.* at. para 96

16   *Id.* at. para 118

17   Official Journal of the European Union (C 390/20) Nov. 16, 2020

18   UPS/TNT Express (Case No. COMP/M.6570), Commission Decision C(2013) 431 final (Jan. 30, 2013). *See also* Ianis Girgenson, *Phase II–Prohibition: The European Commission prohibits the merger between two providers of express parcel delivery services (*UPS/TNT Express*)*, CONCURRENCES N° 3–2015, ART. N° 75077 (2013).

19   *Id.* at 1847.

of defense, since the analysis conducted by the Commission was based on a different econometric model than the one that had been set out in the Commission's statement of objections, of which the parties had been informed.[20] As a result of its assessment, the General Court found that the revisions made to the econometric model on which the Commission had based its assessment, and which led to the prohibition of the transaction, were not of a negligible nature. In this regard, affirming the right of defense as one of the cornerstones of EU law, the General Court noted that the fact that the statement of objections issued by the Commission during the review procedure solely comprised the provisional conclusions related to the assessment did not grant the Commission the right to amend the econometric model applied in its assessment, without first communicating it to the parties and thereby providing them with the opportunity to submit their own comments, observations and objections, prior to the finalization of the assessment and the rendering of the decision. Therefore, the General Court concluded that the Commission's decision should be annulled, since it was in violation of UPS's right of defense. The decision was subsequently appealed to the Court of Justice by the Commission, and the decision rendered on January 6, 2019 by the Court of Justice upheld the General Court's ruling, by setting forth that, in the absence of such irregularity, UPS might have had the opportunity to better defend itself.[21]

The annulment of the Commission's decision led UPS to bring an action against the Commission under Article 340(2) TFEU on December 29, 2017, in order to seek compensation for the losses it had incurred during the process, which amounted to €1.742 billion, according to UPS.[22] Article 340(2) TFEU regulates claims for damages regarding the non-contractual liability of the public administrations in the EU. In particular, the relevant article states that: "In the case of non-contractual liability, the Union shall, in accordance with the general principles common to the laws of the Member States, make good any damage caused by its institutions or by its servants in the performance of their duties."[23] The non-contractual liability of the said institutions arising under Article 340(2) TFEU should be read and interpreted together with Article 268 TFEU, which stipulates that "The Court of Justice of the European Union shall have jurisdiction in disputes relating to compensation for damage provided for in the second and third paragraphs of Article 340." In this respect, since Article 340(2) TFEU refers the application to the general principles common to the laws of

---

20   Case T-194/13, UPS v. Commission, EU:T:2017:144. *See also* Olivier Billard & Guillaume Fabre, *Annulment of a commission decision: The General Court of the European Union annuls a Commission's decision prohibiting a merger on the ground that the European Commission breached the notifying party's rights of defence (*UPS*)*, Concurrences N° 2–2017, Art. N° 83942 (2017).

21   Case C-265/17, United Parcel Service v. Commission, EU:C:2019:23. *See also* Alexandre Lacresse & Barbara Monti, *Access to file: The Court of Justice of the European Union confirms the annulment of the European Commission's decision prohibiting a merger because of the failure to communicate to the parties the econometric model on which that decision was based (*UPS, TNT*)*, Concurrences N° 2–2019, Art. N° 90465 (2019).

22   *See* Case T834/17, United Parcel Service v. Commission, 2018 O.J. (C 72) 41.

23   TFEU, Article 340(2).

the Member States, when read together with Article 268, the regulations leave the application principles and conditions to the jurisprudence of the General Court and the ECJ. The threshold for liability set for asserting the rights arising under such articles will be discussed further.

In UPS's case, following the Commission's decision on the prohibition of the acquisition of TNT by UPS, one of UPS's prominent competitors, FedEx, acquired TNT for approximately €4.4 billion in 2016.[24] Therefore, the losses incurred were also related to FedEx's acquisition of TNT, during the period in which the Commission's prohibition decision was subject to the General Court's review, prior to its annulment.

Going forward, even if UPS is able demonstrate (at the end of the ongoing proceedings) that the Commission indeed acted unlawfully within the meaning of the thresholds that would trigger the application of Article 340(2) TFEU, it will not be able to be compensated for the potential losses incurred in failing to acquire one of its closest competitors, and instead losing the target company to its biggest competitor, FedEx. Consequently, UPS now has the burden of proving that the Commission had erred in the application of the law, which would amount to a violation under Article 340(2) TFEU, in order to be able to recoup its losses, which would, in any case, fall far short of the actual loss inflicted by the prohibition decision.

3. *Liberty Global/Ziggo*

The transaction relating to the acquisition of Ziggo by Liberty Global was concerned with the combination of two premium pay TV channels, which was approved by the Commission on October 10, 2014 after a lengthy Phase II investigation, on the basis of a set of commitments.[25] "The European Commission identified two main vertical concerns, namely that the merged entity would (i) exclude competitors through full input foreclosure; or (ii) use its enhanced bargaining power to raise rivals' costs (either through partial input or partial customer foreclosure)."[26] In order to remedy these concerns, Liberty Global committed to divesting its Film1 channel to eliminate the vertical and horizontal competitive issues. Furthermore, in order to remove the concerns related to "over-the-top" (OTT) services, in which broadcasts are streamed through online

---

24 FedEx/TNT Express (Case No. COMP/M.7630), Commission Decision C(2015) 9826 final (Jan. 8, 2016). *See also* Ianis Girgenson, *Unconditional clearance: The European Commission clears a four to three merger between two suppliers of small package delivery services in Europe and worldwide* (FedEx/TNT Express), CONCURRENCES N° 1–2017, ART. N° 83465 (2016).

25 Liberty Global/Ziggo (Case No. COMP/M.7000), Commission Decision C(2014) 7241 final (Oct. 10, 2014). *See also* Menno Cox & Violeta Staykova, *The EU Commission clears the acquisition of a Dutch cable TV operator by a competitor, subject to conditions* (Liberty Global/Ziggo), E-COMPETITIONS OCTOBER 2014, ART. N° 72124 (Oct. 10, 2014).

26 OECD, Directorate For Financial And Enterprise Affairs Competition Committee, *Vertical Mergers in the Technology, Media And Telecom Sector, Background Note By The Secretariat*, DAF/COMP(2019)5 (May 2, 2019).

media, the parties committed to abolish any restrictions within their current and future contracts that would prevent TV broadcasters from distributing their channels via OTT services.[27]

The Commission's approval decision was then appealed by KPN, one of the parties' competitors, mainly based on claims that the Commission had violated its duty to explain and demonstrate the reasons why the transaction would not create anticompetitive vertical effects within the market for premium pay TV sports channels.[28] The General Court sided with KPN, ruling that the Commission had indeed failed to identify and set forth the grounds, even if briefly, on why there would be no vertical concerns arising from the potential market for "premium pay TV sports channels,"[29] and therefore annulled the approval decision on October 26, 2017, for procedural reasons.

In its decision, the General Court noted that:[30]

> In that regard, while it is true that the Commission is not obliged, in the statement of reasons for decisions adopted under the legislation relating to the control of concentrations, to take a position on all the information and arguments relied on before it, including those which are plainly of secondary importance to the appraisal it is required to undertake, it nonetheless remains the case that it is required to set out the facts and the legal considerations having decisive importance in the context of the decision. The reasoning must in addition be logical and must not disclose any internal contradictions (judgment of 10 July 2008, Bertelsmann and Sony Corporation of America v. Impala, C-413/06 P, EU:C:2008:392, paragraph 169).

Although the General Court annulled the Commission's decision based on a procedural error that was mostly unrelated to the substantive part of the Commission's decision, the parties were nevertheless obliged to notify the transaction anew in order to obtain a valid and enforceable clearance decision. In that regard, in 2018 (i.e., approximately four years after the Commission's initial approval decision in 2014), the parties submitted a supplementary Form CO to the Commission and obtained a conditional approval decision on May 30, 2018, incorporating a similar assessment to that which had been previously conducted for the purpose of the initial approval decision.[31]

---

27 *See* Case T-394/15, KPN v. Commission, EU:T:2017:756, 21–23. *See also* Michele Giannino, *The EU General Court sets aside the Commission's approval decision of a merger in the market for television and telecommunication services (*Liberty Global/Ziggo*)*, e-Competitions October 2017, Art. N° 85254 (Oct. 26, 2017).

28 *Id.* at 32.

29 *Id.* at 71.

30 *Id.* at 51.

31 Liberty Global/Ziggo (Case No. COMP/M.7000), Commission Decision C(2018) 3569 final (May 30, 2018).

4. Sony/BMG

The transaction relating to the merger of two prominent media and entertainment companies (Bertelsmann Music Group and Sony Corporation of America) under a joint venture was first notified on January 9, 2004, and cleared by the Commission on July 19, 2004, after a Phase II review.[32] That clearance decision was appealed by a third-party trade association of independent music companies, known as the Independent Music Publisher and Labels Association (IMPALA), and thereby became subject to the General Court's review. In its ruling, the General Court annulled the Commission's approval decision,[33] based on the grounds that the evidence presented by the Commission for declaring that the transaction would not create or strengthen a collective dominant position was far from substantiating the respective conclusion, and that the Commission had ultimately deviated from its initial findings in its statement of objections (where it had concluded that the consummation of the transaction would be incompatible with the internal market), without providing adequate justifications in its final decision.[34] Subsequently, following the General Court's annulment, the case was re-notified to the Commission on January 31, 2007, and the parties once again obtained a clearance decision on September 15, 2007,[35] three years after the joint venture was implemented and the transaction was consummated. This second clearance decision was once again appealed by IMPALA; however, Sony and BMG also submitted an appeal before the ECJ, which then reversed the General Court's decision,[36] on the grounds that "the Commission had met the standard of proof in finding that the recorded music market was not transparent enough to allow the companies to monitor deviations from tacitly collusive behavior."[37] At the end of this procedural chaos, in 2008, Sony ultimately acquired Bertelsmann's stake in the joint venture, establishing sole control over EMI Music Publishing,[38] which resulted in the termination of the appeals procedures due to the matter becoming devoid of purpose.

---

32 Sony/BMG (Case No. COMP/M.3333), Commission Decision C(2004) 2815, 2005 O.J. (L 62) 30. *See also* Peter Eberl, *The EU Commission approves after an in-depth investigation the creation of a joint venture in the music industry (*Sony/BMG*)*, e-Competitions July 2004, Art. N° 37328 (July 19, 2004).

33 Case T-464/04, Impala v. Commission, 2006 E.C.R. II-2289. *See also* Jean-Mathieu Cot, *Musical rights– Annulation of an authorisation merger decision: The CFI annuls the European decision authorising the merger between Sony and BMG (*Impala*)*, Concurrences N° 3–2006, Art. N° 1746 (2006).

34 *Id.*

35 Sony/BMG (Case No. COMP/M.3333), Commission Decision C(2007) 4507 (Oct. 3, 2007) (second approval).

36 *See* Case C-413/06 P, BMG and Sony v. Impala, 2008 E.C.R. I-4951, overturning *Impala v. Commission*, *supra* note 33. *See also* Jérôme Philippe & Aude Guyon, *Standard of proof–Annulment: The ECJ confirms the CFI ruling having annuled the EC merger clearance Sony-BMG and rules on the standard of proofs in merger proceedings (*Bertelsman–Sony/Impala*)*, Concurrences N° 4–2008, Art. N° 22257 (2008).

37 *See* Götz Drauz et al., *Recent Developments in EC Merger Control*, 1(1) J. Eur. Competition Law & Prac., 12 (2010), https://doi.org/10.1093/jeclap/lpp004.

38 Sony/EMI Music Publishing (Case No. COMP/M.8989), Commission Decision C(2018) 7293 final (Oct. 26, 2018). *See also* Olivier Billard & Guillaume Fabre, *Sole control: The European Commission clears a change from joint to sole control after assessing whether the removal of the veto rights of the outgoing shareholder on the commercial policy decided by the remaining shareholder would have any effects on the market (*Sony/EMI Music Publishing*)*, Concurrences N° 2-2019, Art. N° 90330 (2018).

5. *MyTravel/First Choice*

The transaction concerning the acquisition of First Choice plc by Airtours plc (later renamed MyTravel Group plc), a tour operator and supplier of package holidays in the United Kingdom, was notified to the Commission on April 29, 1999. Following its assessment of the case, the Commission decided to prohibit the application based on the grounds that it would give rise to a collective dominant position in the market for short-haul foreign package holidays in the United Kingdom.[39] This decision was subsequently appealed by Airtours on December 2, 1999, and brought to the General Court's review. The General Court annulled the prohibition decision in June 2002, almost three years after the transaction was initially notified, since it concluded that "... the Commission prohibited the transaction without having proved to the requisite legal standard that the concentration would give rise to a collective dominant position of the three major tour operators, of such a kind as significantly to impede effective competition in the relevant market."[40]

Having said that, the deal was ultimately not consummated and MyTravel afterwards brought claims against the Commission under Article 340(2) TFEU, seeking compensation for the losses it had incurred due to the annulled decision. However, the company was unable to demonstrate that the Commission's unlawful ruling was sufficiently serious to invoke the application of the Article and incur damages for non-contractual liability. In particular, the General Court noted that:[41]

> Because of the need to have regard to such an effect, which is contrary to the general Community interest, a failure to fulfill a legal obligation, which, regrettable though it may be, can be explained by the objective constraints to which the institution and its officials are subject in the control of concentrations, cannot be held to constitute a breach of Community law which is sufficiently serious to give rise to the non-contractual liability of the Community.

Therefore, the applicant's claims for damages were rejected.

---

39 Airtours/First Choice (Case No. COMP/IV/M.1524), Commission Decision C(1999) 3022 final (Sept. 22, 1999).

40 *See* Case T-342/99, Airtours v. Commission, 2002 E.C.R. II-2585. *See also* James Killick, *The EU Court of Justice overturns the EU Commission decision's to block a merger between two UK tour operators addressing the issue of collective dominance (*Airtours/First Choice*)*, e-Competitions June 2002, Art. N° 37057 (June 6, 2002).

41 Case T-212/03, MyTravel Group plc v. Commission, 2008 E.C.R. II-1967. *See also* Jean-Mathieu Cot, *EC non-contractual liability: The CFI holds that non-contractual liability of the European Commission can only arise in case of a manifest and grave disregard by the institutions of the limits in their discretion (*MyTravel*)*, Concurrences N° 4-2008, Art. N° 22255 (Sept. 9, 2008).

6. *Schneider Electric/Legrand*

Schneider Electric SA and Legrand SA, two undertakings that were active in the manufacture and distribution of electrical products and equipment, submitted a notification to the Commission on February 16, 2001, relating to a public exchange offer for all of Legrand's shares held by the public. The Commission harbored serious doubts by considering that the transaction could give rise to competition law concerns, and ultimately issued a prohibition decision on October 10, 2001, ordering Schneider to divest its stake in Legrand.[42] Later on, Schneider appealed the Commission's decision and brought an annulment action before the General Court on December 13, 2001.[43] The Court decided to annul the Commission's decision–along with its compulsory divestment order–mainly based on the evaluation (among other substantive errors) that Schneider's right of defense had been breached during the process, since the Commission's initial statement of objections did not include the competitive concerns laid out in its final decision to the fullest extent, particularly in terms of the problems relating to the distributor level of the French market. In that regard, the General Court noted that:[44]

> The Commission was consequently required to explain all the more clearly the competition problems raised by the proposed merger, in order to allow the notifying parties to put forward, properly and in good time, proposals for divestiture capable, if need be, of rendering the concentration compatible with the common market.

Afterwards, the Commission conducted a subsequent review of the transaction and still deemed that the transaction raised a set of competition law concerns that precluded it from rendering an approval decision, thereby requiring Schneider to demerge[45] from Legrand.[46]

Schneider was the first case in which the concerned party was awarded compensation under Article 340(2) TFEU, due to the Commission's unlawful conduct during the merger control procedure.[47] Upon its review of Schneider's damage claims, which amounted to almost €1.7 billion, the Court decided that the sole conduct of the Commission that could be deemed to satisfy the criteria sought under Article 340(2) was the breach of Schneider's right of defense, thus rejecting

---

42 Schneider/Legrand (Case No. COMP/M.2283) Commission Decision C(2002) 360 (Jan. 30, 2002).

43 Case T-310/01, Schneider v. Commission, 2002 E.C.R. II-4071.

44 *Id.* at para. 444.

45 The Commission notes in the decision that "Article 7(3) of the Merger Regulation allows a public exchange offer to be implemented provided that the acquirer does not exercise the voting rights attached to the shares in question. The public offer closed on 25 July 2001 and Schneider holds 98.1% of Legrand's capital." *Schneider/Legrand, supra* note 42, at 2.

46 *Id.*

47 *See* Ivo Van Bael, Due Process in EU Competition Proceedings, 510 (2011).

the rest of Schneider's claims for damages.[48] The decision was subsequently appealed by the Commission and brought before the ECJ, which agreed with the General Court's decision in majority; however, the ECJ partially annulled the damages awarded to Schneider, since it concluded that some of those did not occur due to the Commission's faulty behavior, but that of Schneider.[49]

V. The Evaluation of the *Ex Post* Judicial Review of Merger Decisions

The decisional practices of EU courts, as briefly outlined above, demonstrate that the erroneous or deficient aspects of Commission decisions have been meticulously detected and conveyed back to the Commission, along with comprehensive explanations and reasoning as to why the respective procedural or substantive shortcomings have led to the annulment of the decision in question. Therefore, it is safe to say that EU courts usually tend to amply fulfill their duties in terms of the review of all of the circumstances surrounding a particular decision, even if they refrain from going as far as scrutinizing the merits of the case and ultimately remedying the unlawful aspects in question. A sound and effective system of judicial review has now become more important than ever, considering the rising global trend of challenging decisions rendered by competition authorities (including the Commission), both by the parties to the relevant transactions and the interested third parties. This trend is clearly portrayed by the recent *UPS/TNT* and *Liberty Global/Ziggo* cases, demonstrating that both the transaction parties and third parties can take the initiative and pave the way for attaining a different outcome through the effective challenge and resulting judicial review of Commission decisions, thus playing a significant role in shaping the merger control regime.

Accordingly, once a decision rendered by the Commission has been reversed as the result of judicial review, this brings forth the question of where the parties to the transaction stand in the midst of all these recent developments. In other words, what happens to the commercial and financial interests of these market players, when they have to break up a marriage, or when they receive clearance for a merger that was commercially reasonable years ago but no longer is by the time of the clearance decision? Furthermore, it is worth noting that the judicial review process not only affects the parties to the transaction, but inherently

---

48 Case T-351/03, Schneider v. Commission, 2007 E.C.R. II-2237. *See also* Jean-Mathieu Cot, *Commission's liability: The CFI founds that grave and manifest failure by the Commission when reviewing a merger may constitutes a sufficiently serious breach of Community law to confer such a right to compensation of the loss (*Schneider Electric*)*, Concurrences N° 4–2007, Art. N° 14424 (2007).

49 Case C-440/07 P, Commission v. Schneider, 2009 E.C.R. I-6413. *See also* Jean-Mathieu Cot & Alice Blanchet, *Merger review–Breach of EC law – Compensation: The ECJ rules that a grave and manifest failure by the European Commission when reviewing a merger may constitutes a sufficiently serious breach of Community law to confer a right to compensation of the loss (*Schneider Electric*)*, Concurrences N° 4-2009, Art. N° 29205 (July 19, 2009).

affects the market itself, including the interested third parties and, ultimately, the consumers who could have benefited from the outcome of a certain transaction if it had been consummated, or who could be deprived of the efficiencies brought forth through a transaction, even in the form of a delay.

In terms of the transaction parties, each of the examples discussed above has shown that the annulments of prohibition decisions and the reversals of clearance decisions have had serious consequences that ultimately altered the competitive landscape in the relevant market, or resulted in a complete turnaround of commercial strategies for the parties involved. For instance, even if UPS ultimately prevails in its court battle against the Commission and is eventually awarded damages (even though the success rate in these types of cases is extremely low),[50] it will never be able to recoup the losses (from a strategic and commercial perspective) that it incurred by failing to acquire TNT, which was subsequently grabbed by one of its closest and most significant competitors.

Moreover, it should be noted that, even if the losses incurred by the transaction parties are somehow compensated, the parties still have to go through the burden of the notification process anew and become subject to the Commission's reevaluation, which then has to assess the transaction under the current market conditions, as opposed to the conditions present at the time of the initial notification. Therefore, the length and the financial burden of the process as a whole, even if the fast-track procedure is adopted (which includes the potential stock price fluctuations, legal costs, loss of faith by stockholders and declining market reputation), not only has the potential to hinder the ordinary operation of the consummation of the transaction, but also questions whether the same transaction would even have been contemplated under the market conditions at the time of the Commission's reevaluation, upon the annulment of its previous decision.

For instance, in *Sony/BMG*, the judicial process had lingered for so long that Sony eventually acquired sole control of the joint venture, rendering the ongoing appeal process moot and devoid of purpose. IMPALA, the appellant third party, did not request the suspension of the consummation of the transaction; Sony and BMG had already completed the transaction when the Commission's clearance decision was annulled by the General Court almost one-and-a-half years later,[51] which was subsequently reversed by the ECJ. Ultimately, three full years had passed from the date of the formation of the joint venture until the point where the Commission issued another clearance decision upon its reevaluation. Whether Sony would have pursued the same commercial strategy if the judicial process had not progressed the way it did, remains an unanswered and unsettling question.

---

[50] See VAN BAEL, *supra* note 47, at 510.

[51] Javier Ruiz Calzado & Eric Barbier de La Serre, *Judicial Review of Merger Control Decisions After the Impala Saga: Time for Policy Choices*, THE EUR. ANTITRUST REV. 2009 (2009).

Another inherent problem for the parties to a merger transaction is the lacuna of legal certainty that the current system engenders. This specifically becomes a visibility and planning issue, especially since the parties are unable to rely on the outcome of the Commission's review, more so in cases where the consummation of the transaction concerns the interests of certain third parties, and the decision rendered by the Commission is at odds with their respective strategies. The fundamental principle of legal certainty, which constitutes the groundwork of any sound and just legal system, aims to provide individuals and corporations with legal security through predictability. By establishing legal predictability and legal certainty, a given governance system frames itself within the context of foreseeable legal principles, thus enhancing confidence in the state and all its actions, and obliging the state to refrain from employing any means that may impair or weaken such legal security in its regulations.[52] This principle would, in turn, dictate that state administrative bodies should be consistent when rendering administrative decisions and undertaking administrative actions. Consequently, it is clear that legal certainty can *only* exist if the jurisprudence is precise, certain, understandable and timely.

In situations where the parties to a merger cannot trust or rely on the outcome of the Commission's review, which is the most competent and proficient institution for conducting the vital assessment of whether the proposed transaction would give rise to or strengthen dominance (thereby significantly impeding competition in the relevant market), it would be challenging to evaluate whether any legal certainty can be found in such cases. Therefore, in consideration of the bigger picture, when the Commission's decisions are susceptible to constant and potentially enforceable scrutiny, the legal basis of ordinary transactions becomes questionable and problematic; this state of affairs would, in turn, not only result in an artificial imbalance within the commercial market dynamics, but it would also change the perception of antitrust enforcement from a single-tiered system to a multi-tiered system, which makes sharp turnarounds and unexpected plot twists possible. Moreover, bearing in mind that time is of the essence for any merger transaction, awaiting the outcome of the appeals court's review process prior to closing a transaction (in order to ensure legal certainty) would not be a viable option either. Furthermore, the damages suffered in such cases would be very likely to significantly exceed the potential damages that could be incurred if the initial decision were to be annulled after a certain time.

The annulment of a merger decision, whether in the form of a prohibition or a clearance, also bears certain effects on the third parties who engage in commercial dealings with the transaction parties, and ultimately, on the consumers. For instance, in *UPS/TNT*, the transaction parties were not the only ones who suffered

---

52 Xavier Groussot & Timo Minssen, *Res Judicata in the ECJ Case Law: Balancing Legal Certainty with Legality?*, 3 EUR. CONST. L. REV., 385 (2007).

from Commission's alleged faulty economic analysis, which led to the prohibition of the transaction. On September 11, 2018, ASL Aviation Holdings and ASL Airlines brought an action against the Commission, in order to seek compensation for the losses they had incurred due to the cancellation of the transaction.[53] This was due to the fact that, in 2012, ASL had concluded a deal with TNT for the acquisition of its shares in TNT Airways and Pan Air, subject to the approval of the transaction between UPS and TNT. Holding the Commission liable for its initial prohibition decision, ASL claimed damages amounting to €263 million in total, in order to recoup its losses and regain the position that it would have held had the transaction not fallen through.[54]

In terms of the effects on consumers, the potential harms arising from an erroneous decision rendered by the Commission would be rather difficult to assess. This is because such an assessment would require: (i) a comparative analysis of the potential efficiencies that would be attained by the transaction, for instance, in a case it had been consummated through the approval of the Commission, but where the transaction instead fell through due to a prohibition decision by the Commission that was subsequently annulled by the appellant court, and (ii) the current state of the relevant market in the absence of the consummated transaction. The Commission's erroneous assessment in a merger case could also give rise to further negative externalities on other transactions, since:[55]

> one can easily imagine a situation in which the Commission wrongly allows a merger concerning a highly concentrated market, thereby preventing the implementation of other transactions that would have been perfectly legal in the absence of the (wrongly) cleared merger. Or it may wrongly block a merger on reasoning that, though faulty and eventually overturned, deters potentially beneficial mergers in the meantime.

Therefore, the Commission's misconduct in such cases could, in turn, lead to consequences that contradict the essential purpose of competition law, since even though different jurisdictions may have different outlooks on the operation of the market in the most efficient manner, the general consensus on the fundamental goals of competition law would be to ensure that consumers are offered a better choice of products with higher quality and lower prices.[56]

---

53 *See* Case T-540/18, SL Aviation Holdings and ASL Airlines (Ireland) v. Commission, 2018 O.J. (C 399) 49 (2018).

54 *Id.*

55 Calzado & de La Serre, *supra* note 51.

56 OECD, Policy Roundtables, *Competition Policy and Efficiency Claims in Horizontal Agreements* OCDE/GD(96)65, 5 (1995), www.oecd.org/competition/mergers/2379526.pdf.

VI. Action for Damages Under Article 340(2) TFEU

As briefly explained throughout the foregoing sections, Article 340(2) TFEU allows claimants to bring an action against EU institutions in cases of non-contractual liability. Existing case law demonstrates that there are three conditions that must be cumulatively met under Article 340(2) TFEU in order for the Commission to be held liable for its conduct:[57] (i) there must be an unlawful conduct on the Commission's part, which indicates that the Commission's said conduct must have given rise to a sufficiently serious breach of law, (ii) there must be damages incurred due to the said unlawful conduct, and (iii) there must be a causal link between the Commission's unlawful conduct and the loss incurred.

In practice, these cumulative conditions have been very difficult to satisfy, and, therefore, it is a rare occasion for applicants who bring an action for damages under Article 340(2) to be actually awarded damages for the Commission's wrongdoing.[58] More often than not, as exemplified by *MyTravel/First Choice*, such a claim is dismissed because:[59]

> ... either it is found to be inadmissible and is therefore dismissed or, it is held to be insufficiently established in terms of the facts pleaded under the applicable rules of procedure such that it does not warrant adjudication by the court. In short, the Court finds that claimant has not discharged the legal burden of proof as regards the legal elements of non-contractual liability.

Therefore, the persons and undertakings who have suffered loss due to an erroneous review by the Commission (such as a faulty or deficient decision rendered as a result of the review of a transaction, which is later annulled through judicial review) are usually unable to recover even a small portion of the said loss, due to the exceptionally stringent (and rare) application of Article 340(2) TFEU.

VII. Conclusion

The European Commission is vested with wide discretion and endowed with substantial powers in competition law proceedings, which inevitably require the existence and implementation of an efficient judicial review procedure, in order to ensure that the decisions rendered by the Commission are fully compliant

---

57   *See*, GEORGE CUMMING, MERGER DECISIONS AND THE RULES OF PROCEDURE OF THE EUROPEAN COMMUNITY COURTS (2011).

58   *See,* ALISON JONES & BRENDA SUFRIN, EU COMPETITION LAW: TEXT, CASES, AND MATERIALS, 1050 (6th ed., 2016).

59   *See*, Cumming, *supra* note 57.

with the existing legislation. That said, in cases where the Commission's merger control decisions are annulled, this judicial review process could give rise to irreversible damages for all parties involved. These consequences may also produce a spillover effect on the relevant market and the consumers, which could have the potential to create economic inefficiencies and ultimately diminish social welfare.

Therefore, the first measure that could be adopted to avert such consequences would be to efficiently ensure that the Commission's decisions set out sufficient reasoning for all of its evaluations, including a properly reasoned statement of objections (before the decision is finally rendered), as well as offering adequate details regarding any economic analysis, and be free from any procedural errors that are unrelated to the substance of the review, in order to ensure that, among other goals, the parties' right of defense is properly preserved and respected throughout the process. Considering that the rulings of EU courts annulling the Commission's decisions provide extensive insights on the legal and factual grounds for such reversals, the Commission, as the most competent and proficient administrative authority in competition law proceedings, is provided with all the necessary tools and clues (i.e. reasoned decisions) to be able to refrain from repeatedly erring on the same grounds in its evaluations. In light of the recent upwards trend in the number of applications for judicial review of merger control decisions, it would be prudent for the Commission to employ additional mechanisms, especially in order to avoid procedural errors that could result in the annulment of its decisions. Taking such precautionary steps would enable the Commission to fully preserve the trust of participants in administrative proceedings and ensure legal certainty for all the parties involved in (or affected by) the transactions that are reviewed by the Commission.

Furthermore, in cases where such errors inevitably lead to the annulment of the Commission's decision, and in which the parties incur loss due to the Commission's evaluation, such parties should be assured that the law allows for the reparation of their losses, to the greatest extent possible. This laudable objective could be achieved through the more efficient use of Article 340(2) TFEU, regulating the non-contractual liability of EU institutions. Naturally, as Advocate General Wahl succinctly stated, Article 340(2) is not a magic wand to erase all of the damages incurred, since "according to well-established case-law, Article 340 TFEU cannot be interpreted as requiring the European Union to make good every harmful consequence, even a remote one, of conduct of its institutions."[60] Nevertheless, the parties involved in a transaction should be better informed about the requirements that need to be met in order to successfully trigger the application of Article 340(2). For this purpose, it may be beneficial to issue guidelines that precisely elucidate the principles of the operation of Article 340(2)

---

60 Case C-150/17 P, European Union, represented by the Court of Justice of the European Union v. Kendrion NV, EU:C:2018:612, Opinion of A.G. Wahl.

and clarify the instances in which the parties could be entitled to compensation for non-contractual liability.

Lastly, bearing in mind that there is an upward trend of increased third-party appeals of merger decisions, the parties to a transaction could consider issuing publicly available information, and providing comprehensive explanations on the potential efficiencies that would be brought about by the consummation of the transaction. Naturally, this should only be done in a way that would avoid rendering the market transparent, in order to prevent any impediment to the competition. Even if this strategy may be unfruitful in terms of the applications submitted by the competitors of the transaction parties, it may prove to be useful in terms of mitigating and reducing the number of third-party applications (i.e. other interested third-party players in the sector) against merger control decisions, by underlining that the proposed transaction would essentially promote public welfare and that it would not give rise to any competition law concerns, when consummated.

PART VII
Reform: Focus on China

Competition Law 2.0: Amending China's Anti-Monopoly Law

WANG XIAOYE* AND ADRIAN EMCH**

Shenzhen University | Hogan Lovells

Abstract

In January 2020, the State Administration for Market Regulation–China's antitrust agency–published a draft proposal for amending the Anti-Monopoly Law (AML). The proposal's key goals are to beef up the rules against anticompetitive government conduct, tighten the merger control rules, and strengthen the sanctions regime. In this paper, we explain the key high-level issues that we believe an AML reform should address–namely, elevating the status of competition policy, as well as solving the most pressing problems that have come up in enforcement cases–and then we examine whether the proposed AML amendments address these issues.

---

*   Xiaoye Wang is Distinguished Professor at Shenzhen University and Professor at the Chinese Academy of Social Sciences.

** Adrian Emch is partner at Hogan Lovells in Beijing.

I. Introduction

Over 12 years have passed since the Anti-Monopoly Law (AML) came into force in August 2008. The law's enactment (a year earlier) and entry into force not only indicate that China has made great achievements in implementing the Reform and Opening-up policy, but also show that China has undergone a substantial transition from planned economy to market-driven economy.

China's antitrust agencies and courts have dealt with a large number of AML cases since August 2008. These cases show that the Chinese antitrust regime has come a long way, and valuable antitrust enforcement experience has been accumulated. At the same time, the cases also indicate that challenges remain.[1] Against this background, there has been a debate–first mainly among academics, then also among government officials and other stakeholders such as lawyers–as to whether it is time to update the AML.

The debate gained momentum in January 2020, as the State Administration for Market Regulation (SAMR) – China's current antitrust agency–published a draft proposal for amendment on its website (Draft AML Amendment).[2] This gave a further boost to the plan to amend the AML, which was already included in the legislative plan of the Standing Committee of the National People's Congress.[3]

In this paper, we will analyze the Draft AML Amendment and discuss the need to reform the Chinese antitrust regime more broadly. Section II will summarize the key proposals of the Draft AML Amendment. Then, in sections III and IV, we will explain the key high-level issues that we believe an AML reform should address–namely, elevating the status of competition policy and solving the most pressing problems that have come up in enforcement cases. In these sections, we will also examine whether the Draft AML Amendment addresses these issues. Section V concludes.

II. Draft AML Amendment

The declared strategy for SAMR to amend the AML was that of "minor modification" (小修). The idea behind this strategy is that the current antitrust regime is not "broken," but generally works quite well. Fine-tuning some parts of the AML is what is needed.

---

[1] See, e.g., Xiaoye Wang & Adrian Emch, *Chinese Merger Control Eight Years On*, Eur. Competition L. Rev. 53–59 (2017).

[2] SAMR, *Announcement of the State Administration for Market Supervision on Public Consultation on the Draft Amendment to the Anti-Monopoly Law* (Jan. 2, 2020), www.samr.gov.cn/hd/zjdc/202001/t20200102_310120.html.

[3] Standing Comm. of NPC, *13th NPC Standing Committee Legislative Plan* (Sept. 8, 2018), www.gov.cn/xinwen/2018-09/08/content_5320252.htm.

The main changes proposed in the Draft AML Amendment affect three areas: (1) beefing up the rules against anticompetitive government behavior; (2) tightening the merger control rules; and (3) strengthening the sanctions regime.

1. Beefing up rules against government restrictions to competition

The Draft AML Amendment proposed to strengthen the rules against anticompetitive conduct by government bodies in two ways–by incorporating the Fair Competition Review System (FCRS) into the AML, and by strengthening the procedure for investigations against "administrative monopoly" conduct by government bodies.

In terms of the FCRS, its incorporation into the AML framework is politically very significant, as it confirms or even upgrades the importance of the FCRS, and at the same time strengthens the AML framework. We will discuss the importance of the FCRS incorporation into the AML in more detail below. For now, we would like to highlight that the Draft AML Amendment proposes to include a new article 9: "The State establishes and implements a fair competition review system to regulate government administrative conduct and prevent the promulgation of policies or measures which eliminate or restrict competition."

The new article 42(2) states: "When formulating stipulations affecting the economic activities of market players, administrative authorities and organizations authorized by laws or regulations to perform public functions shall conduct a fair competition review in accordance with the relevant stipulations of the State."

In terms of "administrative monopoly" conduct, the current AML dedicates an entire chapter to it.[4] "Administrative monopoly" is the term of art used to designate abuses of administrative power to distort competition. The substantive rules–prohibitions on government bodies–are quite detailed in the current AML. However, the current procedural framework is based more on cooperation, than coercion. As such, SAMR as the antitrust agency does not have the power to aggressively investigate other government bodies and has no direct decision-making powers against them. SAMR can merely recommend actions to be taken, while the decision-making powers are with the hierarchically superior organ to the infringing government body.

Now the Draft AML Amendment attempts to strengthen the procedural mechanism, by giving SAMR more formal investigative and decision-making powers. The new article 52 would allow SAMR to conduct formal investigations and (though written in somewhat soft language) would put obligations on the investigated government bodies to cooperate with SAMR. In addition, SAMR would be able to directly order the infringing body to rectify its conduct (without

---

4   AML, chapter 5.

having to go through its superior organ). SAMR would also gain powers to supervise the infringing body's compliance with the rectification order.

2. Tightening the merger control regime

Merger control is the area where the Draft AML Amendment proposes the most far-reaching changes.

Under the current AML, the merger control regime is based on two key premises–that the transaction must amount to a "concentration between business operators," and that certain revenue-based filing thresholds must be exceeded.

The Draft AML Amendment proposes changes to both these elements, as we will discuss. However, the most significant change is that the Draft AML Amendment proposes a change to article 21, whose key tenet is that concentrations above the thresholds need to be filed–and implicitly, concentrations below the thresholds are not subject to the notification obligation.

Now, the Draft AML Amendment proposes to add language to the effect that SAMR can investigate concentrations below the thresholds if it finds them to likely have anticompetitive effects. This idea is not new–in fact, very similar language was contained in a State Council regulation.[5] However, the legal value of the provision in the State Council regulation may be questionable at present, as article 21 of the AML established the rule that (only) concentrations above the thresholds need to be filed.

Against this background, it is clear that writing the option to investigate concentrations below the thresholds into the AML represents an important shift from the previous basic merger control set-up. On the upside, updating the AML on this point removes any ambiguity as to whether there is an adequate legal basis for the current set-up.

In practical terms, the option to allow SAMR to investigate concentrations below the thresholds may have an impact on its enforcement in the Internet sector, especially against perceived "killer acquisitions" – a point we will discuss in section IV(3).

In terms of the double-premise of "concentration" and revenue thresholds, the Draft AML Amendment proposes further changes. In terms of the "concentration" concept, current article 20 essentially defines it as an acquisition of a "controlling right" by one company over another, without providing guidance on what a "controlling right" is.[6] In the past 12+ years of AML enforcement,

---

5   State Council Regulation on the Notification Thresholds for Concentrations between Business Operators, [2008] State Council Order No. 529 (Aug. 3, 2008), art 4.

6   Similar to EU competition law, article 20 also refers to the acquisition of the ability to exercise decisive influence over the target company. However, neither the AML nor any of its implementing rules explains this concept, but instead exclusively focuses on the "controlling right" concept.

the merger filing process has been shrouded in considerable uncertainty, as neither the former merger control authority (the Ministry of Commerce) nor SAMR have provided clear-cut guidance on what exactly constitutes a "controlling right." Indeed, when confronted with questions on the lack of clear guidance on the "controlling right" concept, the antitrust agencies frequently argued that such guidance should be enshrined in the AML itself, not in implementing rules.

In that sense, it would make sense that the Draft AML Amendment proposes to clarify the term "controlling right." However, the current definition proposed in the Draft AML Amendment is still too broad to provide clear-cut guidance to market players: "a controlling right refers to the right or actual condition of a business operator to directly or indirectly, alone or jointly, have or likely to have decisive influence over another business operator's production or operation activities or other major strategic decisions."

In our view, unless SAMR quickly follows up with detailed implementing rules, the relative lack of detail in this proposed definition will be a missed opportunity.

In terms of the filing thresholds, the current AML does not determine the nature (e.g., revenue-based) and amount of the threshold, but refers to State Council rules.[7] The Draft AML Amendment does not determine these points either, but proposes to shift back the power to fix and change the thresholds from the State Council to SAMR. The Draft AML Amendment does not set any procedural or substantive limits to this power. Given that SAMR is also the enforcement authority, it will be important that there are objective benchmarks and a safe procedure to be set in place.

There are other important changes to merger control rules proposed by the Draft AML Amendment. As such, it proposes to introduce a "stop the clock" option for SAMR to interrupt the merger review process, instead of strictly following the statutory timeline and deadlines. While we are aware that many antitrust regimes have similar rules, we note that the introduction of a "stop the clock" option would come at the expense of predictability of the transaction timeline.

3. Strengthening the sanctions regime

The Draft AML Amendment proposes additional, and stronger, sanctions on many fronts.

In the areas of monopoly agreements and abuse of dominance, the Draft AML Amendment does not propose a general increase of the level of sanctions on companies. However, it proposes to raise the amount of the fine for companies which concluded, but did not implement, anticompetitive agreements from RMB 500,000 to RMB 50 million, and those for industry associations from RMB

---

7   AML, art. 21.

500,000 to RMB 5 million. In addition, under the Draft AML Amendment, entities or persons assisting companies in concluding monopoly agreements would be subject to the same sanctions as the companies themselves.

More generally, even if the main sanctions on companies are not proposed to be changed, this does not mean that the provisions are without problems, as we will discuss in section IV(2).

In the merger control area, the Draft AML Amendment aims to broaden the types of conduct subject to sanctions, including failure to file, gun-jumping, non-compliance with remedies, or violation of prohibition decisions. Importantly, it also proposes to increase the level of the fines significantly–from RMB 500,000 to 10% of annual revenues. We will discuss this in section IV(2).

In the administrative monopoly area, as noted, SAMR would gain the power to adopt decisions against other government bodies, but no powers to sanction them (only to order them to rectify the objectionable conduct). Importantly, however, the Draft AML Amendment puts forward a possibility to impose of up to 1% of annual revenues on "other entities." Most likely, the idea behind this rule is to provide a possibility to fine companies which "lobby" government bodies to distort competition to their benefit.

Finally, the amended AML would also include a reference to criminal liabilities. However, since no specific criminal offenses are listed in the Draft AML Amendment, this should be understood as a general referral to the criminal law.[8]

III. Elevating the Status of Competition Policy

Compared with 2007, when the AML was enacted, China's economic policy has changed considerably. Over the past few years, the Chinese government has pointed out that fair competition is the basic principle of a market economy and, more generally, that the market plays the key role in the efficient operation of market mechanism.[9] For example, the 2018 Central Economic Work Conference proposed to strengthen the basic status of competition policies and create an institutional environment for fair competition.[10]

We believe that this shift in economic policy–upgrading the importance of competition policy–should also be reflected in the amended AML. We see four areas where this shift can be reflected in the AML: (1) limiting the role of

---

8   Xiaoye Wang, *Several Contemplations on the Modification of China's Anti-Monopoly Law*, L. Rev. 11 (2020).

9   Central Committee of the Communist Party of China & State Council, *Opinions on Accelerating the Improvement of the Socialist Market Economic System in the New Era* (May 11, 2020), www.gov.cn/zhengce/2020-05/18/content_5512696.htm.

10 Wang, *supra* note 8, at 11.

industrial policy; (2) incorporating the FCRS into the AML; (3) simplifying the AML's goals; and (4) removing deference to non-antitrust law concepts.

1. Limiting industrial policy

Several provisions of the current AML contain explicit or (more often) implicit references to industrial policies. For example, article 4 provides that "the State shall establish and implement competition rules appropriate for the socialist market economy, shall improve macroeconomic regulation and control, and shall establish a unified, open, competitive and well-ordered market system."[11]

The reference to "improving macroeconomic regulation and control" may not be incorrect as such, as the Chinese state has powers to regulate from a macro-economic perspective. However, the reference seems misplaced in an antitrust statute. The AML is not a macroeconomic regulation tool, but a law that should embody the national competition policy. In addition, article 4 contains ambiguous concepts that can be interpreted differently–for example, what competition rules are suitable for a socialist market economy, or what is a "well-ordered" market system?

We note that the Draft AML Amendment proposes to add language to article 4, namely that the state shall "strengthen the fundamental position of competition policy." However, the reference to "macroeconomic regulation and control" and the generally vague concepts remain intact.

Article 7 is a particularly complex and ambiguous provision: Its first paragraph suggests that certain conduct by companies in key industries may not fall under the AML, while the second paragraph could be interpreted in the opposite way. In our view, state-owned enterprises (SOEs) in general do not deserve special protection, and article 7 could therefore be abolished. We recognize that the provision has very rarely been used. Against this background, one could argue that it is best to "let sleeping dogs lie" and not modify article 7.[12] This would make sense, taking into account that the provision was reportedly subject to heated debate in the lead-up to the enactment of the original AML, as various factions had different perceptions of what the AML is supposed to achieve. At the same time, however, while article 7 has not been involved frequently to exempt SOEs, this could change in the future. Removing article 7 from the AML would prevent that outcome.

---

11 These provisions were added to the draft AML during the second reading by the Standing Committee of the NPC. See Central People's Government of the People's Republic of China, *Six new provisions are added to the draft of the second-reading of the Anti-Monopoly Law to promote fairness and order* (June 26, 2007), www.gov.cn/jrzg/2007-06/26/content_661765.htm.

12 *See* Jin Sun, *Economic Law Interpretation of Xi Jinping's Important Statements on Fair Market Competition*, L. Rev. 1 (2020).

2. Incorporating the FCRS into the AML

Without a doubt, the FCRS is one of the milestones in the history of Chinese competition policy. In 2016, the State Council issued rules to establish the FCRS.

The FCRS complements the existing regime against "administrative monopoly" in the AML. Article 8 and Chapter 5 of the current AML provide rules to prohibit certain types of anticompetitive conduct by government bodies. As noted, the AML contains a specific procedural mechanism for administrative monopoly conduct, whereby the hierarchically higher authority of the perpetrating body can order it to rectify the conduct. The role of the antitrust agency is limited to investigating the conduct and then issuing recommendations to the higher authority.

In turn, the FCRS goes further than the AML's administrative monopoly rules, in that it proposes a mechanism whereby each government body systematically goes through its own rules to check whether they are compatible with the principle of fair competition. If the rules are not compatible, then they need to be abolished or brought into compliance. The procedural mechanism is for government bodies to make a self-assessment of current and future rules, policies and measures.[13]

The importance of the FCRS should not be underestimated. As noted, it aims to eliminate (and prevent the adoption of) anticompetitive government rules, policies, and measures. In this way, the FCRS elevates the rank of competition policy.

The FCRS features an "exemption" system for rules that pursue certain public goals, such as national security and social security.[14] In a way, this "exemption" possibility is similar to that for agreements, under article 15 of the AML. In that way, competition policy does not always take precedence over other government policies.

However, we believe the FCRS is still very significant as it mandates that all government rules and policies need to be screened for competition compatibility, and this includes industrial policies. Unless they qualify for an exemption, industrial policies must comply with the principle of fair competition. In a way, in the notional conflict between competition policy and industrial policy, the former has received a tremendous push through the establishment of the FCRS.

Despite the obvious benefit of the FCRS, there are drawbacks. Of course, the self-assessment mechanism may lack teeth, and indeed, there is some evidence

---

[13] There is also a mechanism to enlist the assistance of third parties to do the assessment. *See* Announcement of the State Administration for Market Regulation on Issuing the Implementation Guidelines for Third-Party Evaluation of Fair Competition Review, [2019] SAMR Announcement No. 6 (Feb. 16, 2019).

[14] State Council Opinions on Establishing a Fair Competition Review System in the Construction of the Market System, [2016] State Council Order No. 34, Part III, Section 4.

that FCRS "enforcement" has been patchy.[15] For our purposes, one drawback we would like to highlight here is that the FCRS operates outside the AML framework so far. As noted, the system was set up through a State Council rules in 2016, running in parallel to the AML regime.

The Draft AML Amendment tries to bring the FCRS into the AML framework. However, the new provisions are very high-level.[16] As a result, there is an imbalance compared with the administrative monopoly rules, which occupy a full chapter in the AML. Considering that the FCRS pursues the same purpose as the administrative monopoly provisions, the parallel application of rules would continue after the AML reform and the link between the two systems (if any) is not clearly explained in the AML.

3. Simplifying the AML's goals

Article 1 of AML sets out its goals. The goals are manifold: (1) preventing and prohibiting monopolistic conduct; (2) protecting fair market competition; (3) enhancing efficiency of economic operations; (4) safeguarding consumer interests and the public interest; and (5) promoting the healthy development of the socialist market economy.

We believe that the large number of goals, and the vague nature of some of them (e.g., the promotion of the healthy development of the socialist market economy) create tension for AML enforcement, or at least risk losing the focus. We would like to comment on a specific points in relation to article 1, on the protection of "fair market competition" as a goal. In our view, "fairness" in competition is a difficult concept to handle, especially in an antitrust statute. In China, there is a specific statute tackling "unfair" commercial practices: the Anti-Unfair Competition Law (AUCL).[17]

There are important differences between the AML and the AUCL–the AUCL prohibits companies from gaining a competitive advantage relative to other businesses by unfair means. At a very high level, the benchmarks for assessing unfairness are the principles of good faith and business ethics in market behavior. In contrast, the AML aims at maintaining competition in the market, not between companies as such.[18]

---

15 See Jifeng Liu, *A Discussion on the Problems and Solutions in the Examination System of Fair Competition*, PRICE: THEORY AND PRACTICE 31–34 (2016). At the same time, according to SAMR statistics, government bodies at all levels have conducted fair competition reviews on more than 430,000 documents up to August 2019. Wang, *supra* note 8, 13.

16 Draft AML Amendment, new arts. 9 and 42(2).

17 Anti-Unfair Competition Law of the People's Republic of China, [1993] Presidential Order No. 10 (Sept. 2, 1993), as amended.

18 Meng Yanbei, *The Uneasy Relationship between Antitrust and Anti-Unfair Competition Laws in China*, in WANG XIAOYE: THE PIONEER OF COMPETITION LAW IN CHINA: LIBER AMICORUM 219–229 (Adrian Emch & Wendy Ng eds., 2019).

On a global comparative level, the ultimate goal of antitrust law is to improve the social welfare of consumers. This ensures that consumers have the right of choice in the marketplace. This in turn indicates that antitrust law mainly protects free–not fair–competition. However, "free competition" is not mentioned as a goal in the AML. The reason may be that, at the time of enactment of the original AML, the concept of "free competition" was not widely accepted in China, as it was associated too closely with neoliberalism.

Even though the AML does not explicitly mention the protection of "free competition" as a goal, the Chinese antitrust agencies often implicitly base their enforcement actions based on arguments that a company's conduct restricted "free competition" between companies. For example, in *Qihoo 360 v. Tencent*, the Supreme People's Court (SPC) recognized that the allegedly anticompetitive conduct at issue–the "from-two-choose-one" practice by Tencent–caused "inconvenience" to users and led to a visible drop in market share of Tencent's competitor, but still held that the conduct did not amount to an abuse of dominance.[19]

For the AML reform, in order to avoid overlaps with the AUCL and to clarify enforcement priorities, we propose replacing the word "fair" with "free" in article 1. More broadly, we advocate for a simplification of the AML's goals. However, the Draft AML Amendment does not reduce the complexity of article, but further increases it by adding one goal–encouraging innovation.

4. Removing deference to other legal areas

In the AML, there are certain references to other legal areas. At article 15(1)(6), there is a reference to trade law, and article 55 refers to intellectual property right (IPR) law.

According to article 15(1)(6) of the AML, anticompetitive horizontal or vertical agreements can be exempted if they "safeguard legitimate interests in foreign trade and foreign economic cooperation." This provision may be meant to allow coordination among companies hit by foreign trade remedy measures, such as anti-dumping duties. For example, the provision could be used to exempt an agreement between competitors to reduce their price so as to avoid anti-dumping duties.

At first sight, article 15(1)(6) does not seem to be overly problematic from a Chinese antitrust perspective. In particular, at article 2, the AML stipulates that its jurisdiction applies to conduct with an effect in the domestic market in China. As a result, pure export-oriented conduct would not actually fall under the AML. However, foreign antitrust laws have effects-based jurisdiction similar to the

---

19 Adrian Emch, *Effects Analysis in Abuse of Dominance Cases in China–Is* Qihoo 360 v. Tencent *a Game-Changer?*, Competition L. Int'l 11–31 (2016).

AML, so an exemption of export cartels could create conflict with foreign laws, which would end up harming Chinese exporters falsely believing in the legitimacy of their conduct.[20] More broadly, incorporating trade law policies into the AML risks bringing confusion and further mixing up the already broad aims of the AML.

Against this background, although we are not aware of actual enforcement cases where article 16(1)(6) has been relied on, we would recommend repealing the provision in the amended AML to avoid confusion.

In turn, article 55 directly refers to IP law, by stipulating that the AML does not apply if a company exercises its IPRs pursuant to the relevant IP laws and regulations. The AML only applies if the company *abuses* its IPRs. However, over the past 12 years, the Chinese antitrust agencies and courts have had enforcement cases which–one could argue–deviate from the stipulations of article 55. For example, in the *Qualcomm* and *Huawei v. IDC* cases, the antitrust agency and the courts found a violation of the AML even where the actions of the defendants complied with the Patent Law. Against this background, one could argue for a deletion or adjustment of article 55 from the AML.

At the same time, the counter-argument for retaining article 55 in the AML would be that the provision sends an important signal to the market–that China is keen to maintain a high protection of IPRs. In any event, the Draft AML Amendment published by SAMR in January 2020 does not propose to modify article 55.

IV. Solving the Key Problems in the Enforcement Practice

While there have been very considerable achievements in antitrust enforcement in China over the past 12+ years, there are equally areas where improvements are needed. In this paper, we will discuss three of them where revisions to the AML text could bring about improvements: (1) clarifying the standards for review of anticompetitive conduct; (2) adjusting the sanctions mechanisms; and (3) injecting some flexibility to allow more targeted enforcement in the Internet space.

1. Clarifying standard of review

The AML does not explicitly name the standard of review to assess the various types of anticompetitive conduct. One can attempt to identify standards of

---

20 For example, four Chinese pharmaceutical companies that produce and export vitamins encountered antitrust lawsuits in the United States in 2005 and were fined $153.3 million by for civil damages. The ruling was ultimately upheld by the US Supreme Court. Animal Science Products v. Hebei Welcome Pharmaceuticals, 585 U.S. __ (2018). *See* Mark A. Robertson et al., *The US Supreme Court rules, in relation to a class action for conspiracy to fix vitamin prices, that federal courts determining foreign law are not bound by the foreign government's own interpretation of that law (*Animal Science products/Hebei Welcome Pharmaceutical*)*, e-Competitions June 2018, Art. N° 90010 (June 14, 2008)..

review by implication. For example, in the agreements area, it would appear that the exemption reasons at article 15 can be invoked for all types of agreements (both horizontal and vertical).[21]

In the face of the perceived gap in the AML, as to clear guidance on the standard of review, the SPC has stepped in. In 2012, the SPC issued the Provisions on Several Issues Concerning the Application of Law in the Trial of Civil Disputes arising from Monopolistic Conduct.[22] There, the SPC clarified the burden of proof for horizontal agreements (and abuse of dominance cases), but not that for vertical agreements. For horizontal agreements, the defendant in a private lawsuit has the burden of proving that the agreement does not have anticompetitive effects. The absence of guidance on vertical agreements was interpreted by many Chinese courts that the standard should be different–hence, that the plaintiff has the burden of proving anticompetitive effects. *Rainbow v. Johnson & Johnson* is perhaps the best known of series of cases on this point.[23]

The string of court cases requiring proof of anticompetitive effects for vertical agreements cases–cases of alleged resale price maintenance (RPM) – stood in contrast with the public enforcement cases, in which the antitrust agencies seemingly did not find it necessary to examine anticompetitive effects. Therefore, for a number of years, there was a discrepancy between private and public enforcement, where the courts required plaintiffs to prove the anticompetitive effects of RPM arrangements, while the authorities did not have the prove those effects.[24]

At the end of 2018, the SPC stepped in again. In *Yutai v. Hainan Price Bureau*, the SPC provided clearer directions on the standard of proof for RPM cases–but also provided some guidance for horizontal agreements.[25]

---

21 Judging only based on that circumstance, agreements are arguably subject to a "rule of reason" type of standard. In addition, article 15 of the AML does not apply if the agreement "significantly restricts competition in the relevant market," which could be interpreted as requiring an effects-based analysis. A similar conclusion could be drawn for abuse of dominance, as the AML stipulates that the listed abusive conduct is only unlawful if it is done "without legitimate reasons." In the merger control area, Article 28 states that SAMR needs to prove that the merger has or is likely to have the effect of eliminating or restricting competition. If the merger's positive impact clearly outweighs its negative impact, it can still be cleared. This language suggests that an effects-based analysis is required. In contrast, there appears to be no exemption possibility in the administrative monopoly area.

22 Provisions of the Supreme People's Court on Several Issues concerning the Application of Law in the Trial of Civil Dispute Cases Arising from Monopolistic Conduct, (2012) Law Interpretation No. 5 of Supreme People's Court (June 1, 2012).

23 Shanghai High People's Court, Ruibang Yonghe Technology & Trade Co. Ltd. v. Johnson & Johnson Medical (Shanghai) Ltd. and Johnson & Johnson Medical (China) Ltd., [2012] Hu Gao Min San Zhi Zhong Zi No. 63 (Aug. 1, 2013). *See also* Susan Ning, *The Chinese Shanghai Higher Court renders final judgment in first antitrust private action (*Rainbow/Johnson & Johnson*),* e-Competitions August 2013, Art. N° 54937 (Aug. 1, 2013)

24 Xiaoye Wang & Yajie Gao, *Some thoughts on the revision of China's Anti-Monopoly Law*, Eur. Competition L. Rev. (forthcoming 2021).

25 Supreme People's Court, *Yutai v. Hainan Price Bureau*, [2018] Xing Shen No. 4675 (Dec. 18, 2018). *See* Jiang Wan, *The Chinese Supreme Court recognises the dual effects of vertical restraints and the courts will consider competitive and anti-competitive influences of a vertical restraint when judging on its legality (*Hainan Yutai Technology Feed/Hainan Provincial Price Bureau*),* e-Competitions December 2018, Art. N° 91444 (Dec. 18, 2018).

The *Yutai v. Hainan Price Bureau* judgment is significant, as the SPC introduced the distinction between "per se illegality" and "rule of reason" analysis (using the term "detailed analysis" for the latter) in Chinese antitrust law. The court basically followed international antitrust orthodoxy by pointing out that price-fixing, output-reducing and market-partitioning cartels are "by their nature unreasonable restrictive conduct, [which] has a harmful effect on competition and lacks compensatory value."[26] The SPC even mentions the "per se illegality" principle by name.

Coming back to RPM, the court stated that a "detailed analysis" is required, which looks at factors such as the market situation, the changes to the market structure before and after the agreement, and the nature and consequences of the agreement. In other words, RPM is subject to a rule-of-reason analysis, which requires a close look at the effects of the RPM arrangement.[27]

When it came to the burden of proof, the SPC was, however, reluctant to place it on the antitrust agency: if SAMR were required to conduct a complete investigation and complex economic analysis to evaluate the impact on the market of each RPM arrangement, then this would impose a high cost on enforcement, would reduce enforcement efficiency, and would not satisfy current Chinese antitrust enforcement needs.[28] Although the SPC did not explicitly say so, it might have had in mind that SAMR and its provincial offices have very limited staff available for antitrust enforcement. Requiring a lengthy and complex procedure for each RPM case would further slow down antitrust enforcement. As a result, the SPC held that SAMR does not need to prove the anticompetitive effects of the RPM arrangement, but the defendant is entitled to prove the absence of such effects. In short, although the SPC did not use this term, it basically allows SAMR to *presume* anticompetitive effects in RPM cases.

Interestingly, the SPC also confirmed that two different standards of review apply for RPM cases before SAMR and before the courts. Explicitly referring to *Rainbow v. Johnson & Johnson*, the SPC accepted that a plaintiff in a private lawsuit would bear the burden of proving the anticompetitive effects of RPM conduct, while SAMR would be able to presume these effects in an administrative procedure.

Against the background of this bifurcated approach for the standard of review for RPM cases, we think that the AML revision provides an opportunity to clarify the law.[29] However, at present, the Draft AML Amendment merely gives hints about the standards of review, but no clear-cut guidance. For example, at

---

26 *Yutai v. Hainan Price Bureau*, supra note 25 at 13.

27 Adrian Emch, *China: New Framework for Resale Price Maintenance Analysis* (IBA Antitrust Newsletter, Feb. 2020).

28 *Yutai v. Hainan Price Bureau*, supra note 25, at 14.

29 Xiaoye Wang, *A critique on how the rule on resale price maintenance in the Anti-Monopoly Law uses the "rule of reason principle"*, 1 STUD. IN L. & BUS., 52–53 (2021); and Wang & Gao, *supra* note 24, at 134–35.

current article 45, the Draft AML Amendment proposes to disqualify price-fixing, output reduction and market-partitioning agreements from the commitments procedure. This is an indication that these types of agreements are considered more harmful for competition. But it is an indication, not more.

2. Fine-tuning the sanctions regime

The AML needs improvements to its section on liabilities, in particular sanctions. SAMR appears to be quite aware of this need, and accordingly has placed considerable focus on clarifying–and strengthening–the sanctions regime.

The sanctions for violations of the monopoly agreements and abuse of dominance prohibitions are "cease-and-desist orders" (i.e., orders to stop the conduct), fines of 1–10% of the perpetrator's revenues, and confiscation of illegal gains.[30]

The Draft AML Amendment does not touch upon the main concepts in that regard. However, it is arguable that the minimum requirement of a fine of at least 1% restricts the flexibility of SAMR to impose the right level of fine. By comparison, the European Commission is subject to the same upper limit, 10% of revenues, but does not have a minimum level for the fine.[31] At the same time, one could take the opposite view that SAMR already has the option to "settle" the case by accepting commitments of the defendants,[32] so a lower limit to the fine amount is not needed.

Another point of contention is the confiscation of illegal gains. This is a concept that is very hard for SAMR to implement in practice, as it requires a complex assessment and calculation. As noted by the SPC in *Yutai v. Hainan Price Bureau* in a somewhat different context, labor-intensive cases may not be in line with the current needs of Chinese antitrust enforcement. But beyond the practical issues, there is also a theoretical question about the need to confiscate illegal gains as part of an administrative sanction.

Indeed, article 50 of the AML allows anyone harmed by anticompetitive conduct to sue the wrongdoer and request compensation for damages. This provision seems to be the main venue for disgorging the gains resulting from the illegal conduct. Under article 50, the beneficiary of the repaid gains is the person harmed by the conduct. In turn, SAMR's confiscation of illegal gains benefits the government budget, but not the persons harmed.[33]

---

30 AML, arts. 46 and 47.

31 Council Regulation 1/2003 on the implementation of the rules on competition laid down in Articles 81 and 82 of the Treaty, 2003 O.J. (L1) 1 (EC).

32 AML, art. 45.

33 Under article 41 of the Price Law, it is possible for the authority to "refund" the illegal gains confiscated in an administrative procedure to the persons harmed. See Price Law of the People's Republic of China, [1997] Presidential Order No. 92, (Dec. 29, 1997). This provision was used in the *LCD panels* case, an international cartel case. *See* NDRC, *Six Overseas Companies Implementing LCD Panel Price Monopoly were Investigated and Punished According to Law* (Jan. 4, 2013), www.ndrc.gov.cn/xwdt/xwfb/201301/t20130104_956590.html.

While the Draft AML Amendment does not address the abovementioned points, it does propose changes to another area where the AML needs improvement: the sanctions for failure to file notifiable transactions, or gun-jumping. In its current form, article 48 allows SAMR to issue cease-and-desist order, unwind the transaction, and impose a fine of up to RMB 500,000. The level of the fine was widely perceived as clearly insufficient to exert a deterrent effect.[34]

Now the Draft AML Amendment proposes to raise the fine very significantly, up to 10% of annual revenues. In our view, with this adjustment, we would face the opposite concern: the risk would be that the fine could be excessive in relation to the harm caused by failure to file or gun-jumping a single transaction, at least if there is no further guidance as to how SAMR can exercise this wide discretion (0–10% annual revenues).

3. Fine-tuning rules to facilitate digital economy enforcement

In parallel with other jurisdictions, China is in the process of adjusting its antitrust rules to allow for more effective enforcement in the Internet sector.

In this paper, we examine two issues–whether the AML needs to be amended to allow SAMR to investigate perceived "killer acquisitions" and whether changes are need to de-emphasize the importance of market shares for Internet sector investigations.

In terms of "killer acquisitions," in foreign jurisdictions, there is much discussion in the antitrust community about how to tackle this type of acquisition. By this term, commentators often refer to transactions where a large Internet company acquires a smaller company or start-up that operates in the same or adjacent market to that of the buyer. The allegation is that this type of acquisition is driven not by the wish to use the assets of the target, but to "kill" them–in other words, to eliminate a current or potential competitor from the market. In many instances, "killer acquisitions" are not notifiable under merger control rules because the target is usually at an initial phase of operations and does not meet the revenue (or other) thresholds to trigger the filing obligation.

China long stayed away from the debate of "killer acquisitions,"[35] but no longer.

As noted in section II(2), the Draft AML Amendment proposes to include language in the AML that would allow SAMR to investigate concentrations below the thresholds. This would provide a formal legal basis to pursue perceived "killer acquisitions" where the buyer is above, but the target is below, the thresholds.

---

34   Xiaoye Wang, *Comment on the "Concentration of Operators" in China's Anti-Monopoly Law*, 2–7 L. Sci. Magazine (2008).

35   Adrian Emch, *Antitrust and the internet: Is China different?*, Competition L Int'l 167, 172 (2019).

In a separate development, the Anti-Monopoly Guidelines on the Platform Economy Field (Platform Guidelines) were issued in February 2021.[36] At article 19(2), these guidelines give further guidance on what kind of transactions SAMR may wish to pursue: i.e., those where a platform acquires start-ups, emerging platforms, or companies with free or low-price models (resulting low revenue), or those in markets with high concentration and a small number of platforms present.

In terms of how to use market share to assess dominance of Internet companies, the initial debate on this topic was shaped by the SPC judgment in *Qihoo 360 v. Tencent*. There, the SPC stressed the highly dynamic nature of digital markets and the difficulties in market definition, and concluded that the importance of market share should not be overestimated.[37]

Over the past two years, SAMR pushed for additional rules to assist with the appraisal of market share for the digital economy.[38] In 2019, the Interim Regulation Prohibiting Conduct Abusing a Dominant Market Position mentions additional factors for assessing dominance for Internet players: competition characteristics, business models, number of users, network effects, lock-in effects, technical features, market innovation, the ability to control and handle data, and market power in adjacent markets.[39] The Platform Guidelines provide even more details.[40]

Now, the Draft AML Amendment proposes to add a new paragraph to current article 18 of the AML, suggesting that network effects, economies of scope, lock-in effects, and data control and processing ability should be taken into account in the determination of dominance for Internet players.

V. Conclusion

Over the past 12+ years, China's antitrust regime has made considerable and clearly visible progress. Especially in the merger control area, China has become one of the most influential antitrust regimes globally. Enforcement in the agreements and abuse of dominance areas has been steady, but interest by foreign media and observers has tended to focus around specific high-profile cases, such as *Qualcomm*, *Tetra Pak*, *Huawei v. InterDigital*, or *Qihoo 360 v. Tencent*.

---

36 State Council Anti-Monopoly Commission on the Anti-Monopoly Guidelines on the Platform Economy Field, [2021] Guofanlongduan No. 1 (Feb. 7, 2021).

37 *Qihoo 360 v. Tencent*, *supra* note 19, at 11–31. *See also* Wang & Gao, *supra* note 24.

38 The Platform Guidelines also contain high-level guidance on market definition for online platforms, mentioning the options of narrowly looking at one side of a platform market, at multiple sides, or even at the entire platform if cross-platform network effects are sufficient to constrain the given platform's competitive actions. *See* Anti-Monopoly Guidelines on the Platform Economy Field, *supra* note 36, art. 4.

39 Interim Regulation Prohibiting Conduct Abusing a Dominant Market Position, art. 11.

40 Anti-Monopoly Guidelines on the Platform Economy Field, supra note 36, arts. 4 & 19.

The Antimonopoly Law of China: Prospects for Change

DEBORAH HEALEY[*]

University of New South Wales

Abstract

China's Antimonopoly Law (AML) has unique characteristics among competition laws, with some unusual objects and substantive provisions, set against the background of its fundamental relationship with China's industrial policy. In January 2020, the government called for comment on a draft of proposed amendments to the AML (the Draft). This paper considers the Draft from the perspectives of policy and its specific provisions to consider its likely impact. It recognizes that even given China's traditional socialist market economy background, it has made substantial inroads into the global competition law and policy framework. The regulator in the main applies relatively standard economic analysis and the majority of determinations are in line with global competition law norms. In some areas, however, the regulators have taken different approaches to decision-making in applying the provisions. Several of the proposed amendments would bring the AML closer to the laws of other established competition law jurisdictions. The Draft includes amendments based on policy, amendments to rectify problem areas and those that clarify the law. This paper considers whether the Draft will assist the AML to deliver the economic and consumer benefits that are the major purpose of competition laws.

---

[*] Professor and Director, Herbert Smith Freehills China International Business and Economic Law (CIBEL) Centre, UNSW Sydney. The author thanks CIBEL for support in the development of this paper. An earlier version was presented at the Tsinghua-UNSW Joint Research Centre for International Commercial and Economic Law (JCICEL) workshop held on August 12, 2020, and the author thanks participants for their comments. Any errors are those of the author.

I. Introduction

China's Antimonopoly Law (AML) has operated since 2008, with a growing number of enforcement decisions by regulators and private actions in court. The AML has unique characteristics among competition laws, with some unusual objects and substantive provisions,[1] set against the background of its fundamental relationship with China's industrial policy. It evidences a robust role for competition policy. In January 2020, the government called for comments on a draft of proposed amendments to the AML (the Draft).

Given its traditional socialist market economy background, China has made substantial inroads into the global competition law and policy framework. Despite the substantial discretions contained in the existing provisions of the AML, the regulator in the main applies a relatively standard economic analysis and a majority of determinations are in line with global competition law norms.[2] There are, however, areas where the regulators have taken different approaches to decision-making in applying the provisions. Several of the proposed amendments would bring the AML closer to the laws of other established competition law jurisdictions.

Jurisdictions globally are struggling to reconsider competition law goals and tools, examining their suitability and, in particular, whether they deal effectively with the implications of the growth and impact of digital platforms and other digital advances on traditional norms. This paper also assesses proposed AML amendments aimed at the digital economy.

This paper places the proposed amendments into three categories and assesses their likely impact. It considers whether they demonstrate a change in legislative direction; the effectiveness of the individual provisions; and whether the amendments will assist the AML to deliver the economic and consumer benefits that are the major purpose of competition laws. It concludes that while the proposed amendments are not monumental, they contain significant policy elements that will have substantial impact going forward, others that will clarify important issues which have arisen to date, and some that assist enforcement and deterrence.

---

1   "The AML is largely consistent in form and substance with prevailing international competition law norms, particularly the European Union and Germany." Wendy Ng, The Political Economy of Competition Law in China 16 (2018). The same author emphasizes the importance of China's political economy in the drafting and interpretation of the AML and states that the drafters decided that, while it was important to learn from the experiences of other jurisdictions, "... the AML also needed to reflect and suit China's specific needs and circumstances," *id.* at 20.

2   The enforcement agencies and courts have "gradually applied economic analysis in all areas of enforcement": *see generally* Lin Ping and Yan Yu, *The use of economics in competition law enforcement in mainland China and Hong Kong*, in Research Handbook on Models and Methods of Competition Law 89, and particularly 107 (Deborah Healey et al. eds., 2020).

II. The Draft

The Draft contains the first formal reform proposals since the enactment of the AML. The proposed amendments can be grouped into three broad categories:

- The first category contains what might be described as policy amendments. These policy amendments have broader implications than just amending the wording of the AML. They signal the overall approach to be taken to the AML in its operation and interpretation.

- The second category contains amendments that update or clarify particular provisions of the law, generally reflecting the experience of its 12-year life.

- The third category is miscellaneous or consequential amendments that will not generally be discussed.

1. Category 1: policy amendments

The policy amendments contain three major statements about the philosophy and goals of the AML. The first two statements are in relation to markets and competition policy, and the third relates to the relationship between the AML and the digital economy. These are discussed below.

A. *Supporting markets and competition policy*

The Draft reinforces the commitment of the state to markets and competition policy, while retaining recognition of the strong role of government in markets in China.

At the outset it should be noted that existing article 1 sets out the express goals of the AML, which are multiple and diverse,[3] and which reflect the socialist market economy background of the AML as a law of China.[4]

---

[3] The existing goals are: preventing and restraining monopolistic conduct, protecting fair market competition, enhancing economic efficiency, safeguarding the consumer interest, and promoting the healthy development of the socialist market economy. The impact of the broad goals in the AML are discussed in Deborah Healey & Eleanor Fox, *State Restraints in China: A Different Case?*, in WANG XIAOYE LIBER AMICORUM: THE PIONEER OF COMPETITION LAW IN CHINA (Adrian Emch & Wendy Ng eds., 2019).

[4] "(A) socialist market economy ... authorizes a muscular statism and a commensurate, supporting legal system ... While the nature of 'Chinese characteristics' and socialism may have shifted dramatically, the labels and rhetorical strategies connected to them remain deceptively static." Glenn Tiffert. *Socialist Rule of Law with Chinese Characteristics*, in SOCIALIST LAW IN SOUTH EAST ASIA 72 (Fu Hualing et al. eds., 2018); "China has never had a commitment to the adoption of a full-scale capitalist economy with private ownership of production assets. This is included in the promotion of the goal of 'promoting the healthy development of the socialist market economy'." See Ping Lin & Yue Qiao *Understanding the Economic Factors that Have Affected China's Anti-monopoly Law*, in THE ECONOMIC CHARACTERISTICS OF DEVELOPING JURISDICTIONS: THEIR IMPLICATIONS FOR COMPETITION LAW 114 (Michal S. Gal, Eleanor M. Fox et al. eds., 2015). *See also* STATE CAPITALISM, INSTITUTIONAL ADAPTATION AND THE CHINESE MIRACLE 3 (Barry Naughten & Kellee S. Tsai eds., 2015).

Article 4 then talks of the state implementation of "competition rules which accord with the socialist market economy, perfect macro control, and advance a united, open, competitive and orderly market system."[5]

At the same time, article 7 contains a significant potential carve-out from the application of the AML to certain state-owned enterprises (SOEs). It provides that stated-controlled and owned industries that are important to the national economy or national security and those given exclusive or monopoly rights by the state shall be protected by the state. It further provides that these businesses must operate in accordance with the law, in good faith, and with self-discipline, while not using their controlling or exclusive position to the detriment of consumer welfare.

The Draft proposes the insertion of the words "the state strengthens the fundamental status of competition policy" at the very start of article 4. These new words strongly reinforce the government commitment to markets and the role of the AML, which is seen in China as an economic constitution.[6] A number of government statements and policies from 2014 onward made reference to markets,[7] but the *primary* importance of markets to assist economic development in China was first emphasized in 2017,[8] and has been re-emphasized in 2020.[9] So this amendment is important in confirming that approach, particularly in its placement at the very beginning of the article.

While the incorporation of industrial policy considerations into the AML gave regulators the clear right to take them into account in enforcing the AML, no guidance is given in the existing AML about how to balance competition policy goals and industrial policy goals in any given assessment. Some commentators suggested that industrial policy goals should be secondary and only applied where the conduct in question was "competition neutral."[10] This amendment, however, grants clear priority to market competition in any such contest, and for that reason is extremely significant.

Other commentators believe that the inclusion of the proposed words in article 4 will raise the status of the AML in national governance, and promote the position of competition policy in relation to other policies such as industrial policy and SOE

---

5   As well as other additions, discussed below.

6   Lin & Qiao, *supra* note 4.

7   State Council, Opinion of the State Council on Promoting Fair Market Competition and Maintaining Normal Market (Order No 20, June 4, 2014); Notice of the State Council on Ratifying and Forwarding Opinions of the NDRC on Deepening the Reform of the Economic System in 2014 [2014] No. 18.

8   Notice of State Council on Issuing the Plan for Market Regulation during the 13th Five-Year Period [2017] No. 6.

9   Communiqué of the Fifth Plenary Session of the 19th Central Committee of the Communist Party of China 20-10-29 www.gov.cn/xinwen/2020-10/content_5555877.htm, notes that China "will give full play to the decisive role of market in the allocation of resources."

10 *See* Lin and Qiao, *supra* note 4, at 146, quoting Ping Lin and Jingjing Zhao, *Merger Control Policy Under China's Anti-Monopoly Law* 41(1) REV. INDUS. ORG. 109 (2012).

reform.[11] Influential commentator Professor Wang Xiaoye has, in fact, stated that "... compared with the policy environment when the AML was legislated, competition policy has become a fundamental economic policy and industrial policy has stepped back to a second place ..."[12] Given this new focus on markets and competition, Professor Wang also suggests that a number of other articles, such as articles 5 and 7,[13] should be repealed, given the new focus on market, but this has not been proposed in the current amendments. In particular, she argues that article 28, which allows the consideration of "public interest in the society," when considering mergers, is sufficient to protect the interests of SOEs, and the other provisions are no longer needed. None of these subsequent amendments have been proposed in the Draft.

Nevertheless, this amendment and related developments indicate the growing acceptance in China of competition law as a framework for more efficient operation of markets. In the words of Professor Wang, "competition policy has played an increasingly dominant role in resource allocation in China,"[14] although always with the qualification that China is a socialist market economy, with the role of SOEs entrenched in the constitution.

B. *Fair Competition Review System*

The second strand of the policy amendments involves incorporating the Fair Competition Review System (FCRS) process, which currently exists in regulations, into the AML. New article 9 states: "The state establishes and implements fair competition review system, standardizes government administrative behaviors, prevents the introduction of policies and measures which eliminate and restrict competition."

The FCRS is made up of mandatory examination of all laws, rules, and regulations to see whether they contain anticompetitive aspects.[15] It addresses policy

---

11 See Dentons China, *A Practical Review of the Draft Amendment to the Antimonopoly Law of China: Highlighting Six Areas with Eighteen Changes*, Dentons 7 (Feb. 2020), www.dentons.com/en/insights/guides-reports-and-whitepapers/2020/february/27/a-practical-review-of-the-draft-amendment-to-the-antimonopoly-law-of-china.

12 Wang Xiaoye, *Several Thoughts on the Amendment of the Anti-Monopoly Law of China*, 220(2) Law Rev., 11-21 (2020) (in Chinese). Her view is also that article 28, which allows the consideration of 'public interest in the society' when considering mergers, is sufficient to protect the interests of SOEs and the other provisions are no longer needed.

13 Article 5 states: "undertakings may through fair competition, voluntary alliance, concentrate according to law, expand business operation scale and enhance their market competitiveness." It is focused on mergers and emphasizes the concentration.

14 *Supra* note 12. Professor Wang also states there: "... we should further promote modernization of the AML of China, besides the amendment and refinement of the AML, we should further promote the fundamental position of competition policy in the allocation of resources, improve the independence and authority of AML enforcement, and build a strong AML enforcement agency because these are the indispensable fountainhead to promote the competitiveness of the nation, increase the production efficiency of enterprises and improve the social welfare of customers."

15 *See* Opinions of the State Council on Establishing a Fair Competition Review System in the Building of the Market System 2016 [No 34.]; Provisional Rules for the Implementation of the Fair Competition Review System (Oct. 2017); Implementation Guide for Third-Party Evaluation of Fair Competition Review (Feb. 12, 2019).

measures that distort the allocation of market resources, raise transaction costs, and stifle innovation, detracting from market competition. It prevents anticompetitive measures such as local protectionism, regional exclusion, industry barriers, business monopolies, illegal granting of preferential policies, or harming the interests of market participants. It applies to national, provincial, municipal, and county-level governments.[16]

Anticompetitive provisions are allowed, even if they restrict or exclude competition, if they:

– Involve national economic or cultural security, or are related to national defense enhancement;

– Involve social security purposes, such as poverty alleviations and disaster relief and rescue;

– Are in the public interest, such as energy and resource conservation and environmental protection;

– If prescribed by law or regulation. In these cases, the policy must be essential to achieving the policy objective.

The Draft thus adds another competition policy element to the AML, which already contains provisions attacking the problem of administrative monopoly in existing articles 32–37. Articles 32–36 remain the same, (articles 37–41 following amendment). The amendment incorporating the FCRS is added to existing article 37 (article 42 after amendments). It will now read:

> No administrative organ or organization empowered by law or administrative regulation to administer public affairs may abuse its administrative power to formulate any provisions on eliminating or restricting competition.
>
> Administrative organs or organizations empowered by law or administrative regulation to administer public affairs shall conduct fair competitive review in accordance with the relevant provisions of the state when formulating regulations concerning the economic activities of market entities.

C. *Supervision of policy by enforcement authority*

In addition, both administrative monopoly and FCRS are placed under the Anti-Monopoly Enforcement Authority (AMEA). Amendment to article 9 is particularly important because it centralizes oversight and includes the

---

16   *See CPI Talks ... with DG Zhenguo Wu*, COMPETITION POL'Y INT'L (Mar. 2020), https://competitionpolicyinternational.com/cpi-talks-with-zhenguo-wu/. The Director General referred to four additional documents issued in 2019: Notice on Screening Policies and Measures that Hinder Unified Market and Fair Competition; Notice on Further Promoting Fair Competition Review Work; Implementation Guidelines for Third-Party Evaluation of Fair Competition Review; and Implementation Rules for the Fair Competition Review System (Interim), which he said would improve the enforcement system and its foundations.

competition regulator in the FCRS process. In the process of regulatory review of laws, regulations and policies for anticompetitive impact, the OECD has stated that the greater the level of competition regulator involvement in the process, more effective is the process and the outcomes.[17] This amendment brings the FCRS within that ambit, which strongly suggests that its outcomes will improve.

In relation to the existing administrative monopoly provisions this is also particularly important. Currently, legal liability for administrative monopoly is not particularly effective since agencies in breach of the administrative monopoly provisions are only referred to their supervising agency, who may order rectification the violation. There is no oversight of that process.

Under new article 52, power is given to the AMEA to investigate administrative monopoly conduct, and relevant organs, organizations or officers must assist and provide documents as requested. The AMEA may make orders and check whether rectification has been made. In addition, article 58 now provides that the AMEA may order rectification and provide suggestions to the relevant superior authority to impose punishments on those personally responsible. The administrative agencies concerned must complete the rectification and report to the AMEA on completion within specified time limits. Prohibitions against administrative monopoly were originally placed in the AML because administrative monopoly is such a source of anticompetitive conduct in China, although this placement of what is often a policy elsewhere was quite unusual. The inclusion of administrative monopoly and FCRS in the AML and the placement of both under the supervision of the AMEA and with reporting lines heightens the focus of government on these crucial competition issues and is to be commended for that reason. It should help to facilitate a more level playing field for competition in relation to the activities of government bodies at all levels.

III. The Digital Economy: Recognition of the Importance of Innovation

China is an exceptionally large user of the Internet and digital services and is home to a number of the world's largest digital companies. The second major policy area (and third policy strand) impacted by amendments is the area of digital markets, a strong area of growth and one that is the focus of attention in competition circles worldwide.

The Draft includes "encouraging innovation" as a new legislative goal in article 1. This reflects the importance of the consideration of innovation in the application

---

17 OECD Competition Committee, Experiences with Competition Assessment (2014), www.oecd.org/daf/competition/Comp-Assessment-ImplementationReport2014.pdf.

of competition laws both generally and in respect of digital markets and intellectual property. A significant representation of cases involving intellectual property issues has been decided under the AML to date. The case against Qualcomm for abuse of a dominant position, for example, resulted in the highest fine levied under the AML,[18] and issues such as standard essential patents have been commonly considered in merger review, sometimes prompting the imposition of novel conditions on a merger.[19]

But, more broadly, the issue of innovation is relevant to the ongoing global consideration of whether existing competition law tools are effective in dealing with digital platforms. The digital economy is the new frontier in competition law globally–much research and policy consideration these days involves aspects of it, including the link between competition law, digital markets, and privacy. Issues relating to digital platforms, network effects, lock-in and tipping; artificial intelligence and the possibilities of collusion; and the market power of large platforms such as Google, Facebook, Amazon, Baidu, Alibaba and a number of other corporations, exercise many academic, regulator, and practitioner minds. Competition authorities throughout the world are grappling with these issues. The proposed amendments discussed in this section recognize the growing importance of digital technology in the market and seek to address some of the contentious issues involved. They seek to address a number of the unique aspects of digital markets.

On the issue of intellectual property, existing article 55 (which will become article 62) sets out the relationship between the two areas of law. It basically says that intellectual property rights are not in themselves anticompetitive but that rights-holders should not abuse their rights. It is useful to have such a provision in the AML in a relatively new jurisdiction where there are issues about precedence of laws and their interaction. It is a contentious area, and the provision means that the mere use of intellectual property rights is not necessarily but may be in breach of the AML.[20]

1. Abuse of dominance

The issue of digital markets is also addressed in relation to abuse of dominance in article 21 (former article 18). The existing provision prohibits abuse of dominance, listing types of conduct prohibited by parties holding dominance such as selling at unfairly high prices and refusal to deal. The threshold test for the application of the provision is "dominant market position," and article 21 lists factors that will be relevant to the determination of whether an undertaking

---

18   NDRC Administrative Penalty Decision (2015). The fine was 6.08 billion Chinese yuan (approximately US $75m). *See* Ping & Yum, *supra* note 2, 93.

19   See Deborah Healey et al., *Sustaining the status quo: the use of conditions in Chinese merger clearance*, 10 TSINGHUA L. REV. 1–32 (2017).

20   *See* Wang Xianlin, *Recent Developments in China's Anti-Monopoly Regulations on Abuse of Intellectual Property Rights*, 62(4) ANTITRUST BULL. 806 (2017).

is in a dominant market position, such as market share and competitive status; the ability to control sales or raw supplies; financial and technological conditions of the company; the extent of reliance on the undertaking by other undertakings in transactions; and difficulties in market entry. These factors would be relevant to the determination of whether a party was in a position of dominance in many other jurisdictions. A new clause added to the end of the list, which focuses on digital markets, states: "To determine the dominant position of undertakings in the Internet industry shall also consider factors, such as network effects, economies of scale, lock-in effects, and the ability to master and process related data."

This new list of factors covers issues that have been identified as sources of power in recent global debates around markets and competition in the digital economy. This also mirrors to some extent the wording of the *Interim Provisions on Prohibiting Abuse of a Dominant Position* issued by the State Administration for Market Regulation (SAMR) in 2019,[21] which emphasizes that market share alone should not be determinative of market power in relation to digital (or other) markets. However, it is important to note that some of these factors such as network effects, economies of scale and lock-in effects are also relevant to other industries and would perhaps be better targeted at analysis of dominance in all circumstances rather than just those in digital markets.

It may have been a good idea to delete the general provisions in existing articles 18(1) and article 19 (amended article 22), which contain rebuttable presumptions of market power based on market share. Purists would say that they should be deleted as market share is not a true determinant of market power without evidence of other features such as high barriers to entry, but such provisions may be useful in developing jurisdictions without a history of markets and competition. In the author's view these provisions should be considered for removal at some later stage after there has been more experience and further detailed decisions have been made on the determination of dominant market position.

These amendments overall indicate, however, that the issue of the digital economy is now to be more specifically addressed by the AML going forward, in the same way that the issue is being considered in other jurisdictions. In that context, on November 10, 2020, SAMR released the draft Antimonopoly Guide for the Platform Economy for public comment.[22] The 24-article guide contains provisions that focus on the application of the AML in the context of the platform economy. The guide talks of enforcing the AML while safeguarding fair competition and encouraging innovation and quality, and invigorating creativity "in the whole society, and constructing new advantages and new motivations for economic and social development."[23] Provisions deal with market definition and all aspects of the AML

---

21 Order No. 11 of SAMR (July 2019).

22 www.samr.gov.cn/hd/zjdc/202011/t20201109_323234.html.

23 Article 2(iii) and (iv).

in the context of the platform economy. The guide is too comprehensive to outline here, with extensive consideration of the issues relevant to particular types of potentially anticompetitive conduct, giving many relevant examples. Nevertheless, it is significant as it substantially complements these proposed amendments to the AML by focusing attention on the digital economy in a practical manner.

2. Turnover for concentrations (mergers)

Finally, a new article 34 is proposed which would operate generally but is particularly relevant to the area of digital platforms. It addresses sanctions that may be imposed even where the notification thresholds are not met and states:

> Where the State Council's Anti-Monopoly Enforcement Authority, upon investigation, finds that a concentration of undertakings that fails to meet the notification thresholds has or may have the effect of excluding or restricting competition after investigation, it may make a decision in accordance with articles 32 and 33 of this law. Where the concentration is already implemented, the State Council's Anti-Monopoly Enforcement Authority may also order to cease, require disposal of shares or assets or the transfer business in certain time limits, and take other necessary relief measures to restore it to the pre-concentration status.

This provision allows the AMEA to look at mergers, including digital mergers, even when they fail to meet the concentration thresholds, and to impose remedies on such mergers even if they have previously been completed, without time limitation.

This is particularly important in a digital environment where thresholds are routinely not met because of the way these businesses are structured and carry on their business activities. This is recognized in a number of international reports and reviews on digital competition law, for example the Furman Report in the UK.[24] The turnover thresholds are generally based on sales and these digital businesses often provide many of their services free, or while growing very large and diversified, make little discernible profit. For example, Didi and Uber, two ride-sharing companies, were strong competitors undercutting prices so that they did not reach concentration thresholds when they sought to merge. However, Didi paid a very a large amount to buy Uber's business in China, with the turnover below the notification thresholds.[25]

---

24   *See, e.g.*, Unlocking Digital Competition: Report of the Digital Competition Expert Panel (Mar. 2019) (the Furman Report) https://assets.publishing.service.gov.uk/government/uploads/system/uploads/attachment_data/file/785547/unlocking_digital_competition_furman_review_web.pdf.

25   *See* Wang, *supra* note 12. This scenario was replicated in a number of Southeast Asian jurisdictions in the Grab/Uber merger–see generally Deborah Healey, *Grab–Uber Merger in Southeast Asia: the Singapore Approach*, J. ANTITRUST ENFORCEMENT (2021). In Singapore, the notification thresholds were not relevant as notification there is based on likely competitive impact and not turnover; nevertheless, the transaction itself involved the operations of the companies in Southeast Asia, and a number of jurisdictions were precluded from examining the transaction on the basis of notification turnover. As the article notes, the outcomes have been criticized for their likely long-term anticompetitive impact.

Finally, in very recent and additional policy moves related to this area but not specifically involving the AML, China has indicated that it will intervene more generally in the digital space.[26] In November 2020, market and Internet regulators reportedly convened a meeting of leading Internet platforms. China also published the abovementioned draft guidelines. It was also reported in late November 2020 that a ministerial conference system will be formed to coordinate efforts to crack down on unfair market competition in the area, "led by the [SAMR] and representatives from 17 parties and ministries, including the People's Bank of China, Cyberspace Administration China and China Banking and Insurance Regulatory Commission."[27] This also follows the suspension of the listing of the planned $34 billion IPO of Ant, financial affiliate of Alibaba Group Holding Ltd, two days before its market debut in Shanghai and Hong Kong. Alibaba is China's biggest technology company by market value.[28] At the same time, regulators published new draft laws for online lending.[29] These developments are clearly at an early stage but indicate that regulators in China are reviewing their previous light-handed approach to digital markets at a number of important levels.[30]

IV. Amendments that Update or Clarify the Law

This second category contains amendments proposed for various substantive provisions of the AML.

1. Chapter II: monopoly agreements

A number of amendments concern the provisions on monopoly agreements. Some are made to clarify issues that have arisen in relation to standards of proof in resale price maintenance (RPM) cases, some to clarify the position of trade associations and others in relation to possible contraventions.

---

26 Liza Lin, *China Targets Alibaba, Other Homegrown Tech Giants With Antimonopoly Rules*, WALL ST. J., Nov. 10, 2020, www.wsj.com/articles/chinas-regulators-prepare-to-roll-out-new-antimonopoly-rules-11605013205. The article states: "The rapid expansion of the digital economy in China has led to problems of unruly competition, fraudulent sales and personal information leaks, China's internet regulator, the Cyberspace Administration of China, said Tuesday in a separate post. Chinese tech firms should not allow consumers to be 'prisoners to algorithms' it cautioned."

27 *China Creates Conference System to Oversee Unfair Market Practices*, COMPETITION POL'Y INT'L (Nov. 22, 2020), www.competitionpolicyinternational.com/china-creates-conference-system-to-oversee-unfair-market-practices/.

28 Lin, *supra* note 26.

29 Ryan McMorrow et al., *China Draws Up first antitrust rules to curb power of tech companies*, FINANCIAL TIMES (Nov. 10, 2020), www.ft.com/content/1a4a5001-6411-45fa-967c-0fd71ba9300b?shareType=nongift.

30 In March 2020, for example, DG Zhenguo Wu (*supra* note 16) stated that the approach of SAMR was to: "adhere to the principle of 'prudent tolerance, encouragement of innovation, and specific case analysis,' supervise the Internet field in accordance with the law, maintain the competitive vitality and momentum of the Internet industry, and promote the sustainable and healthy development of the Internet industry in China."

A. *Resale price maintenance*

There has been confusion about whether the prohibitions in relation to monopoly agreements are "per se" or are subject to a competition test, particularly in relation to RPM.

Monopoly agreements are currently prohibited, with some types such as price-fixing, output restrictions, market division, and boycotts (usually called hard core cartels) being specifically named, and with capacity for other agreements to be designated. There are exemptions that mean that they may be exempted following analysis of their impact on competition or other factors, some of which do not relate to competition, contained in current article 13 (amended article 15), which focuses on horizontal agreements. Importantly, there is currently a definition of "monopoly agreements" after the list of prohibited conduct in article 13. This definition states that monopoly agreements among undertakings are prohibited and that "'monopoly agreement' refers to agreements, decisions or other concerted conducts that eliminate or restrict competition." Based on its current position in article 13, one would presume that the definition applies only to article 13 conduct. Existing article 14 (new article 16) deals with vertical agreements such as RPM.

The Draft moves the wording in existing article 13 to a completely new article 14, which is placed at the very beginning of Chapter II, and now reads: "Monopoly agreements among undertakings are prohibited. For the purposes of this law, 'monopoly agreement' refers to agreements, decisions or other concerted conducts which eliminate or restrict competition."

Theoretically one would assume that it now applies to all monopoly agreements in the Chapter: that is, both horizontal (new article 15) and vertical (new article 16), while previously it applied only to horizontal agreements. The rest of the existing article 13 is substantially the same (becoming article 15).

Existing article 14, which becomes article 16, lists vertical monopoly agreements such as fixing the price of commodities for resale to third parties (RPM); fixing the minimum price of commodities for sale to a third party; or other agreements as determined by the Antimonopoly Commission.

As in the EU, conduct under each of existing articles 13 and 14 is exempt if the parties can prove that the conduct will not substantially lessen competition, that it improves technology, upgrades product quality, improves efficiency, and adds a range of other positive attributes. The amendments also add the additional condition "as a necessary condition for realizing the relevant circumstances" to the wording of the exemption provisions contained in article 15 (now article 18). It becomes more like the EU, where the wording requires that the exemption may only apply if the nominated positive attributes are "not otherwise available," which narrows this list of exemptions somewhat.

The approach to assessment of monopoly agreements in China has been described by Chinese commentators as a "two-step prohibition-exemption approach."[31] The first step is to examine whether the conduct is prohibited and the second whether it can be exempted. This approach requires the proof of the prohibited conduct by the regulator followed by proof of factors that would allow exemption by the party to the conduct.

However, in practice these provisions have created difficulties of interpretation, particularly in relation to RPM, which is conduct whereby the supplier of a product sets the on-sale price for its acquirer. RPM is prohibited in many jurisdictions on the basis that price is arguably the most important criteria for selection by consumers and that the setting of prices by the supplier is inherently anticompetitive. The question in more established competition jurisdictions has been whether RPM should be prohibited per se or whether there should be consideration of the actual competitive impact of the conduct.

In the US, a Supreme Court case in 2007 changed the long-held approach to RPM from one of per se consideration to one of rule of reason, based on Chicago school views that vertical arrangements are almost never a competitive problem.[32] In the EU, Australia and a number of other jurisdictions, the opposite view has been taken and RPM is still per se.[33] There are advantages and disadvantages in each approach. The Chicago school view fears over-enforcement, but even in *Leegin v. PSKS*, which changed the US standard, Justice Breyer in a strong dissent in the Supreme Court stated that it is not clear that Chicago school views are correct on vertical restrictions. Economists who subscribe to the "post-Chicago" view certainly do not agree. But if the provision is not per se, it is generally costly and time-consuming to prove anticompetitive effects in court in a particular case.

The courts and enforcement authorities in China traditionally took conflicting approaches to the issue of proof of RPM. For example, in cases such as the *Moutai and Wuliangye* case (2013),[34] and other cases (*Hainan Yutai Scientific*

---

31 Hou Liyang and Li Qing, *Resale Price Maintenance and its Proof under the Anti-Monopoly Law*, in WANG XIAOYE LIBER AMICORUM: THE PIONEER OF COMPETITION LAW IN CHINA (Adrian Emch & Wendy Ng eds., 2019); Kate Peng et al., *A Brief Analysis of Standards for Resale Price maintenance under the PRC Anti-Monopoly Law*, COMPETITION POL'Y INT'L (Mar. 10, 2020), www.competitionpolicyinternational.com/a-brief-analysis-of-standards-for-resale-price-maintenance-regulations-under-the-prc-anti-monopoly-law/.

32 Leegin Creative Leather Products, Inc. v. PSKS, Inc., 551 U.S. 877 (2007).

33 Parties in Australia may seek to notify and obtain administrative permission to engage in RPM based on public benefit, but there have been very few applications. In Australia, the courts and comprehensive reviews of the Competition and Consumer Act 2010 have found that there is insufficient evidence to show that RPM is not anticompetitive in most cases, so that a change in standards is not justified.

34 Moutai Administrative Penalty Decision, Guizhou Price Bureau, Order No. 1 (Feb. 22, 2013)《行政处罚决定书》[Moutai Administrative Penalty Decision], 贵州省物价局 [Guizhou Price Bureau], 黔价处[2013]1号 [(2013) Qian Jia Chu Order No. 1], (Feb. 22, 2013); Wuliangye Administrative Penalty Decision, Sichuan Development and Reform Commission, Order No. 1 (Feb. 22, 2013)《行政处罚决定书》[Wuliangye Administrative Penalty Decision], 四川省发展和改革委员会 [Sichuan Development and Reform Commission], 川发改价检处[2013]1号 [(2013) Chuan Fa Gai Jia Jian Chu Order No. 1] (Feb. 22, 2013).

Feed Company v. Hainan Provincial Price Bureau (2018)[35] and *Toyota RPM Decision* (2019)[36]), the enforcement agency decided that the parties had breached article 14 by their conduct on a per se basis.

The rule of reason approach was applied by the courts in civil lawsuits such as *Rainbow v. Johnson and Johnson* (2013)[37] where the Shanghai No. 1 Intermediate People's Court and the Shanghai High People's Court both found that competition issues were relevant. The court required the plaintiff to prove that the conduct had anticompetitive effects in the market. In determining that issue, the court analyzed in detail "(1) whether the competition in the relevant market is sufficient; (2) whether the defendant has a strong market position; (3) the defendant's motivation to impose RPM; and (4) the anticompetitive effect and procompetitive effect of the RPM agreement."[38] The court thus found that anticompetitive effects were a necessary requirement for a finding of a monopoly agreement, and that they needed to be material and not offset by procompetitive effects. Other courts followed this approach.

More recently the Supreme People's Court of China in the *Yutai* case[39] affirmed that a per se approach should be applied in RPM cases while the market is still underdeveloped in China. A business operator may still rebut the allegations by proving that the particular agreement does not restrict competition, or by invoking an exemption.

As stated, the movement of the definition of monopoly agreement before both the provisions on horizontal and vertical agreements "can be interpreted to mean that both horizontal and vertical agreements caught by the AML need to be in fact anticompetitive, which reflects that the way that legislators have paid attention to concerns arising from practices." Despite this, the same authors state that the differences between administrative enforcement and judicial practice are still unclear. They conclude: "We expect legislators, enforcement agencies and judicial authorities to further clarify the standards by modifying the law, formulating judicial interpretations, issuing guiding cases, or issuing guidelines for enforcement against vertical agreements, so as to provide business operators with clearer guidance."[40]

---

35 《海南裕泰科技饲料有限公司诉海南省物价局再审行政裁定书》 [Hainan Yutai Scientific Feed Company v. Hainan Provincial Price Bureau], 最高人民法院 [Zui Gao Ren Min Fa Yuan, People's Republic of China], (2018) 最高法行申4675号 [(2018) Zui Gao Fa Xing Shen No. 4675] (Dec. 18, 2018).

36 《江苏省市场监督管理局行政处罚决定书》 [Administrative Penalty Decision of the State Administration for Market Supervision of Jiangsu Province] (People's Republic of China), 苏市监反垄断案[2019] 1 号 [Sushijian Fanlongduanan [2019] No.1] (Dec. 6, 2019).

37 Beijing Ruibang Yonghe Science and Technology Trade Company (Rainbow) v. Johnson & Johnson Medical (China) Ltd [2012] No 63, Shanghai People's Court (Aug. 1, 2013); 北京锐邦涌和科贸有限公司与强生（中国）医疗器材有限公司纵向垄断协议纠纷上诉案民事判决书》 [Beijing Ruibang Yonghe Science and Technology Trade Company (Rainbow) v. Johnson & Johnson Medical (China) Ltd], 上海市高级人民法院 [Shanghai Higher People's Court, People's Republic of China] （2012）沪高民三（知）终字第63号[(2012) Hu Gao Min San (Zhi) Final Order No. 63] (Aug. 1, 2013).

38 *See* Peng et al., *supra* note 31.

39 Yutai, *supra* note 35; *see* Peng et al, *supra* note 31.

40 *Id.*

Professor Wang Xiaoye has stated: "... this problem should be resolved ... by amending article 14 of the AML or by the SPC modifying its 2012 judicial explanation on the civil dispute cases of AML, to improve the stability of law and increase the predictability of the legal consequence of its behavior for the contract parties."[41]

In one further amendment, in the context of whether any monopoly agreements are in fact per se in nature, new article 50 (formerly article 45) prohibits the application of the AML investigation suspension mechanism to price-fixing, output restriction and market allocation agreements, which are prohibited in the current article 15(1) – (3).[42] These agreements are all what are known as hard core cartel provisions. The implications of this suggest that agreements of this kind are treated more severely, at least in this respect.

B. *Trade associations*

Amendments have broadened the reach of the law in respect of the conduct of trade associations and others who assist with collusion. This is important, since in the enforcement of horizontal monopoly agreements since the AML came into force "most horizontal monopoly agreement cases involve the organization, assistance and implementation of monopoly agreements by industry associations."[43] Some other conduct has involved parties, such as wholesalers, who have organized the agreements. Article 19 (formerly article 16) now says that trade associations may not organize undertakings to implement monopolistic conduct as prohibited by the Chapter–the provision was formerly limited to conduct "in its own industry" but these words have been removed. Another new provision, new article 17, also prohibits undertakings from organizing or assisting other undertakings to reach monopoly agreements. This was necessary because the earlier provisions that covered conduct of this kind limited the provision to "undertakings and their trading partners." The new provision has been characterized as providing for "hub and spoke" agreements.

2. Chapter III: abuse of a dominant position

New article 20 (formerly article 20) prohibits the abuse of a dominant position, listing conduct that will fall within the provisions. The Draft provides that in article 20(6), which talks of "applying dissimilar prices or other transaction terms to counterparties with equal standing without any justifiable cause" the words "with equal standing" are removed.

---

41 Wang, *supra* note 12.
42 This is consistent with article 22 of the Interim Regulation on Prohibition of Monopoly Agreement.
43 Dentons China, *supra* note 11.

As discussed, article 21 (formerly article 18) lists factors to be considered in determining whether an undertaking has a dominant position, and new factors specific to the "Internet industry" are added by the amendments.

3. Chapter IV: concentrations of undertakings

Article 23 (formerly article 20) refers to the conduct that will constitute a "concentration" (merger) for the purposes of the provision. A new paragraph clarifies the meaning of "control," which has proved problematic in a number of international jurisdictions. Article 23 lists the following transactions:

1. A merger of undertakings;
2. An undertaking acquires control over other undertakings by acquiring their equities or assets; or
3. An undertaking acquires control over other undertakings by contract or other means.

Paragraphs 2 and 3 currently refer to "control." The amendment deleted the words "or is able to exert a decisive influence on other undertakings" from existing paragraph 3, which will now be in the form set out above. A more detailed definition of "control" is then inserted at the end of the whole article: "The term control as mentioned in the preceding paragraph refers to an undertaking's direct or indirect, separate or collective right or actual status which have or may have a decisive influence on the production and operation activities or other major decisions of other operators."

Commentators note that the definition of "control" under the AML is different from that in the Company Law of China and the Securities Law of China, sometimes leading to confusion about the need for filing and review under the AML, particularly in relation to joint ventures and acquisitions by minority shareholders.[44] These amendments thus seek to clarify the position in the AML.

A. *Notification thresholds*

Article 24 (formerly article 21), which refers to thresholds for notification, is amended to add the following words:

> The State Council's Anti-Monopoly Enforcement Authority may formulate and modify notification thresholds based on the level of economic development and industry scale, and public in time.
>
> Where a concentration reaches the threshold, yet the undertakings fail to file, or a concentration of undertakings has not reached the

---

44   *Id.*

thresholds but has or may have the effect of excluding or restricting competition, the State Council's AMEA shall conduct investigations in accordance with the law.

This means that it will be easier for regulators to amend the thresholds but also to review concentrations in digital and other markets that fall below the thresholds.

B. *Integrity of documents*

Amendment to article 26 (formerly article 23) will make those who file notifications for mergers responsible for the integrity of the documents, by adding words which state that filers "must account for the authenticity" of documents.

C. *Stop the clock provisions in merger notification*

New article 30 clarifies timing in relation to examination of mergers. It allows for a "stop the clock" mechanism that is common in other jurisdictions and foreshadows the development of guidelines or regulations setting out more specific details. It states:

> The time required for the following circumstances shall not be included in the time limits for examination as provided in articles 28 and 29 of this law:
>
> 1. The period of examination is suspended upon required or consent by the notified parties;
> 2. Undertakings submit documents and materials submitted as requested by the State Council's AMEA;
> 3. The State Council's AMEA negotiates with the undertakings on the proposal of restrictive conditions in accordance with article 33 of this law.
>
> The specific provisions for suspension shall be formulated separately by the State Council's AMEA.

This means that parties will no longer be required to withdraw incomplete notifications until additional documents required by the regulator are included, and then resubmit them. This was previously extremely time-consuming, so the proposed amendments provide a more efficient way of handling the notification process.

D. *Investigating mergers*

In reviewing a merger, article 31 (formerly article 27) currently contains the factors to be taken into account, such as market shares, market concentration, and market access following the merger. The words "and investigating" have been added to the preliminary wording so that the regulator's role now includes both reviewing and investigating a particular merger.

E. *Broader national security review*

> Where concentration of undertakings involves national security, the national security review shall be conducted in accordance with relevant provisions of the State.

This provision has been shortened and simplified, but the main change of substance is that it is now not just aimed at foreign investors but at mergers generally.

F. *Enhanced remedies in relation to mergers*

Article 48 is deleted and replaced with new article 55, which creates additional actions available to the AMEA in relation to merger activity.

> Where undertakings are under any of the following circumstances, the AMEA shall impose a fine of 1% up to 10% of the total turnover in the previous year:
>
> 1. Failing to file a transaction that reaches the thresholds;
> 2. Implementing the transaction before obtaining an approval;
> 3. Violating restrictive conditions;
> 4. Violating of the prohibited decision.
> 5. Except the provisions in the preceding paragraph, the AMEA may, based on the specific situations, order the undertakings to cease the implementation of concentration and add restrictive conditions which would reduce anticompetitive effects of the concentration, to continue to perform the restrictive conditions, or may change restrictive conditions, instructs the disposal of shares or assets, transfer of business within certain time limits, and adopt other necessary remedy measures to restore the pre-concentration status.

This contains additional and more specific actions for the AMEA in a merger situation. The quantum of potential fines is substantially increased (from CNY 0.5 million) to the same level as for breach of other provisions. This should deter gun-jumping and act as a general deterrent for other conduct that would otherwise breach the merger provisions.

Finally, new article 51 provides that a decision permitting a merger may be revoked if documents and materials provided by the declarant prove to be untrue or inaccurate when investigated by the AMEA at the request of an interested party, or in accordance with its functions and powers. This new provision and the amendments discussed above clearly show the seriousness with which non-complying conduct of this kind is viewed by authorities. It acts as a further incentive for parties to ensure the accuracy of their submissions.

4. Chapter V: abuse of administrative power to eliminate or restrict competition (administrative monopoly)

The most important amendment in administrative monopoly is that which has been already discussed, that is, that the process of rectification will now be under the supervision of the AMEA, which will also have the power to impose punishments on people in charge and others. This is set out in amended article 58 (formerly article 51).

A small number of additional amendments are made to the administrative monopoly provisions. The most significant of these are:

- The references to "non-local" and "local" have been removed from article 39 (formerly article 34). This substantially broadens the ambit of the provision.

- Article 41 (formerly article 36) is amended to prohibit administrative bodies from compelling undertakings to engage in monopolistic activities prohibited by the AML either overtly or "in disguise," which presumably means by covert means that achieve this end, or other means that achieve that result.

- Article 44 (formerly article 39) involves investigation of suspicious monopolistic behavior and the steps AMEA can take. The Draft adds, "Where necessary, the public security organ shall assist in accordance with the law," which means the police can assist the AMEA to do its work by protecting officers investigating possible contraventions or by other means.

5. Amendments to other enforcement provisions

Changes to the enforcement provisions include:

- Article 11 (formerly article 10) now confirms that the SAMR is responsible for the enforcement of the AML. It is referred to throughout the AML as the State Council's AMEA.

- Article 46 (formerly article 41) now compels the AMEA and its officers to keep trade secrets confidential and, in an amendment highlighting the growing importance of personal privacy in China, to preserve personal privacy.

A. *Investigations*

Article 59 (formerly article 52) is about requests for cooperation and documents by the AMEA. The words "threaten personal safety" are added to the wording of the provision where it talks about refusal to supply and assist. Obligations and sanctions are also imposed in relation to the failure to cooperate by government bodies in relation to administrative monopoly. Fines are increased for breach of these provisions.

Article 50 (formerly article 45) relates to the ability of the AMEA to accept undertakings and suspend its investigations into conduct in fulfilling its duties as enforcement agency. The following words are added: "Antimonopoly law enforcement agencies shall not suspend investigations of monopoly agreements which are suspected of violating article 15(1), (2) (3) of this law."

These provisions are price-fixing, output restrictions, market sharing–the conduct that is regarded as most harmful and which are usually called "hard core cartel conduct." In many jurisdictions these provisions are per se or subject to criminal liability. This means that there is no capacity to take commitments for this conduct.

Where the AMEA chooses to suspend an investigation on the basis of commitments given by the parties, a new clause in article 50 states that those parties must give notification of performance of the commitments within the prescribed time limits.

B. *Substantial increases in fines and other orders*

The fines that may be imposed for breaches of the AML have been increased substantially to provide a far more significant deterrent in a couple of categories. Article 53 (former article 46) provides that where undertakings violate the AML, the AMEA can order them to cease the violation, shall confiscate the illegal proceeds, and may impose a fine of 1–10% of the turnover in the previous year. This remains the same. However, "where the undertakings have no turnover" (a new category) or where the monopoly agreement has not been implemented, a fine of less than CNY 50 million (up from CNY 5 million in the second category) may be imposed.

A new paragraph is also added to catch those "organizing and helping undertakings to reach a monopoly agreement," which concludes that the preceding paragraph applies, that is, a fine of less than CNY 50 million applies.

Another new paragraph on trade associations that involves situations where a trade association organizes undertakings to reach an agreement in breach of the AML provides that the AMEA can order them to "cease the violations" (new words) and the potential fine increases from less than CNY 0.5 million to CNY 5 million.

Overall, the provisions on enforcement are clarified and strengthened in a number of respects.

V. Conclusion

Competition laws differ between jurisdictions for a variety of reasons, many of which are linked to the development status or differing political economies. In addition to differently worded provisions, individual jurisdictions have always had areas of non-application, exemption, and exception. Differing market conditions, approaches to enforcement and court systems can result in dissimilar outcomes in relation to the same or similar conduct undertaken elsewhere. Most jurisdictions have applied industrial policies from time to time, often applied under separate laws, rules or policies that have overridden the usual competition law processes based on their conception of the public good.

Ultimately, the shortcomings of competition law frameworks in these environments depend upon the number and importance of the derogations from the "standard" competition law framework and the suitability to the particular jurisdiction of the alternatives that are adopted. The outcome is generally felt, however, in the particular jurisdiction: if the competition law is ineffective within the jurisdiction, the jurisdiction itself does not benefit from delivered efficiencies and consumers are not the beneficiaries. It may also impact on foreign firms doing business in that location.

The AML is important to China but also it is important globally because of China's importance as a substantial global trading nation. In relation to international mergers alone, the AML has a very significant impact globally. Other provisions also have the capacity to influence global trading decisions. This Draft is to be welcomed for its reaffirmation of the importance of the market and its consideration of the important position of digital platforms in a competition law context going forward. The legislative process in China is in three stages.[45] The first is the proposal of a draft by the relevant ministries or commissions, such as SAMR, based on past law enforcement experience. This is submitted to the legislative department of the State Council, which produces a new draft based on public comment. This new draft is submitted to the legislative department of the National People's Congress (NPC), which will here be the Economic Office under the Legislative Affairs Commission of the NPC Standing Committee. It will deliberate and produce a new version for the NPC to discuss and pass if agreed.[46]

This means that there is still some way to go before the Draft in its current or, as is more likely, an altered form is put to the NPC. But there are strong indications in the Draft that a robust approach to markets, a focus on emerging issues

---

45   Legislation Law of the People's Republic of China (Order of the President No 31) (Mar. 15, 2000).

46   *See* Ng, supra note 1, for a detailed discussion of this process as it was applied during the drafting of the AML itself.

of importance such as the digital environment, the efficiency of enforcement processes, and increased fines and other remedies will underscore the operation of the AML going forward, which is a win for increased efficiency and the competitive process in China and may be result in enhanced predictability for the global trading community.

Unpacking the Personal Information Protection Regime and its Potential Implications for Competition Law in China

WENDY NG[*]

University of Melbourne

Abstract

This paper examines whether and how personal information protection laws might shape the way in which competition laws are enforced in China's digital economy. Analyzing the principal laws that constitute China's personal information protection regime, this paper shows that it implicates, coordinates, and balances a range of personal, commercial, and public interests. This paper argues that the more that personal information protection interests and goals can be appropriately balanced and coordinated with competition concerns and interests, the more likely that China's competition laws may be used to address the personal information–handling practices of businesses, and compliance with personal information protection obligations may be considered relevant to competition law analysis.

---

[*] Senior lecturer, Melbourne Law School, University of Melbourne.

I. Introduction

The Internet, digital platforms, and technology have become ubiquitous in society. While these technological advances bring with them many benefits and conveniences, they also present challenges for governance. One such challenge lies in the regulation of data and, in particular, the personal information of consumers. The significant and broad reach of the digital economy, the Internet, and smart mobile devices into our daily social and economic lives means that vast amounts of personal information are in the hands of Internet, technology, and digital companies. The practices of these companies in collecting, sharing, using, and processing this personal information are coming under growing regulatory scrutiny. In addition to personal information protection concerns, these practices are also attracting attention under competition law. This has prompted a wider discussion on whether personal information protection concerns should be considered in competition law and, if so, how.

These issues and questions are also becoming more prominent in China. As of March 2020, there were more than 900 million Internet users, 4 million websites, and 3 million apps in China.[1] As the digital economy has expanded and developed, consumers' concerns have also grown about personal information leaks, theft, and misuse, and the practices of websites, apps, and other technologies in collecting and handling personal information. To deal with these issues, over the past few years, China has been developing a personal information protection regime that is growing in its scope, detail, and sophistication. China's competition laws are being revised and updated to deal with competition issues emerging from its burgeoning digital economy and being enforced with more frequency and rigor against China's big technology companies. Increasingly, these two spheres of regulation are likely to intersect and interact with one another. There is now a real question of whether and how China's personal information protection regime might shape the way in which its competition laws are enforced, especially in the context of its digital economy.

Professor Fox has long held a keen interest in the development and implementation of China's competition law. In particular, she is curious about the function of China's competition law in a system where the state has a high degree of involvement in the market and is generally the dominant force in the state–market relationship. This paper will explore some of the potential implications of China's personal information protection laws for competition law in a manner that shares this same interest.

This paper first sets out the views and expectations of privacy in China, the societal and cultural background against which personal information protection

---

[1] Explanation of the Personal Information Protection Law (Draft) (Standing Comm. Nat'l People's Cong. Legis. Aff. Comm'n, Oct. 31, 2020).

exists and should be understood. It then examines China's evolving personal information protection regime to understand not only the rights and obligations that it sets out, but also its nature, the array of personal, commercial, and public interests affected, and how they are balanced. Finally, some potential implications of the personal information protection regime for competition law enforcement in China will be considered. It should be noted that, while China's approach to personal information protection and competition law may have consequences beyond its national borders, such considerations, including comparisons with the approaches taken in the United States and European Union, are beyond the scope of this paper.

II. Views and Expectations of Privacy in China

It is a misconception that Chinese citizens do not care about privacy and are more willing than citizens of other countries to trade privacy for convenience. In fact, there is a growing awareness of and demand for privacy rights in China.[2] As views on and expectations of privacy are shaped by its cultural, historical, and political contexts, privacy might look a bit different in China when compared with other countries.

Traditionally, the societal notion of privacy in China was linked to the community and not to the individual. This sprung from the influence of Confucian teachings in Chinese society, which emphasize the family, community, and country over the individual, and the importance of interpersonal relationships and social order and harmony.[3] Privacy was about the nondisclosure to the public of matters that were considered to be shameful, that is, matters that would cause one to "lose face" in the community. As such, privacy was about protecting one's reputation in the community, and that of the family. Privacy is thus a consequence of the commitment to the community and its stability, not the individual.[4] This stands in contrast to, as Bennett notes, the Western philosophical root of privacy, which "tends to reinforce individuation, rather than community, sociability, trust and so on."[5] However, with the introduction of the market economy and the Internet, opening up to the outside world, economic development, and growing recognition of individual rights and interests, this community-based notion of privacy is evolving to one that is increasingly associated with the individual and

---

2 *See, e.g.*, Yuan Yang, *China's Data Privacy Outcry Fuels Case for Tighter Rules*, FINANCIAL TIMES, Oct. 2, 2018; Samm Sacks & Lorand Laskai, *China's Privacy Conundrum*, SLATE (Feb. 7, 2019), https://slate.com/technology/2019/02/china-consumer-data-protection-privacy-surveillance.html; *Public Pushback*, THE ECONOMIST (Jan. 27, 2018), 52.

3 HAO WANG, PROTECTING PRIVACY IN CHINA 35–36, 38 (2017); Tiffany Li et al., *Saving Face: Unfolding the Screen of Chinese Privacy Law*, J.L. & INFO. SCI. (Aug. 2017, forthcoming) 4.

4 WANG, *supra* note 3, 34–37, 38–40; Li et al., *supra* note 3, 9–13; Cao Jingchun, *Protecting the Right to Privacy in China*, 36(3) VICT. U. WELLINGTON L. REV. 645, 646–47 (2005).

5 Colin J Bennett, *In Defence of Privacy: The Concept and the Regime*, 8(4) SURVEILLANCE & SOC. 485, 487 (2011).

the personal matters that they do not want to be known to, or interfered with by, others.[6]

China does not have a historical legacy of forms of government where citizens have expectations of privacy from their government. For much of its history, China was ruled by emperors through dynastic, monopolistic, and authoritarian rule, with a strong state at its core (although the state was not monolithic and at various points in time it was unstable and contestable), and citizens' interests were not formally represented in the political system.[7] The Chinese Communist Party, in power since 1949, had aimed to establish a society that was focused on the community and the state, not the individual, with mechanisms to control various aspects of people's private lives. Although this has changed somewhat since China embarked on economic reform and opening up in December 1978, its one-party Leninist system and many social control measures remain in place. In this context, a notion of privacy that is focused on protecting the individual from interference by the state is not very likely or expected.[8]

III. Understanding China's Legal Framework for Personal Information Protection

In contemporary China, while privacy is increasingly understood in terms of the rights and interests of individuals, it is still largely framed as protecting citizens from other citizens, rather than the state. This view of privacy is reflected in the legal framework that is being developed to protect personal information in China.

At the time of writing, the protection of personal information is dealt with mainly in the Civil Code,[9] Cybersecurity Law,[10] Data Security Law[11] and Personal Information Protection Law.[12] Together, these laws provide the basic legal framework for personal information protection in China. A number of regulations and non-binding (but influential) documents have also been adopted

---

6   WANG, *supra* note 3, 40–43; Lu Yao-Huai, *Privacy and Data Privacy Issues in Contemporary China*, 7 ETHICS & INFO. TECH. 7, 8–9 (2005).

7   *See, e.g.*, Yu Liu, *The State with a Surname: a Dialogue with Fukuyama on the State in China*, 1(3) J. CHINESE GOVERNANCE 506 (2016).

8   Li et al., *supra* note 3, 5; Zhizheng Wang, *Systematic Government Access to Private-sector Data in China*, 2(4) INT'L DATA PRIVACY L. 220, 221 (2012).

9   Civil Code (People's Republic of China), (Nat'l People's Cong., May 28, 2020), arts. 1034–1039.

10 Cybersecurity Law (People's Republic of China), (Standing Comm. Nat'l People's Cong., Nov. 7, 2016). The protection of personal information is one of the six regulatory frameworks established pursuant to the Cybersecurity Law.

11 Data Security Law (People's Republic of China), (Standing Comm. Nat'l People's Cong., June 10, 2021).

12 Personal Information Protection Law (People's Republic of China), (Standing Comm. Nat'l People's Cong., Aug. 20, 2021).

to implement the personal information framework under the Cybersecurity Law.[13]

1. Key rights and obligations under the personal information protection regime

China's personal information protection regime provides individuals with some degree of control over and protection of their information. Unless otherwise provided by laws or administrative regulations, an individual must consent to the collection, use, and handling of their personal information,[14] which includes the provision of their personal information to third parties.[15] The Personal Information Protection Law clarifies that consent will be required where a change occurs in the purpose or method of handling personal information or in the type of personal information handled,[16] and that consent may be rescinded and withdrawn.[17] Individuals also have the right to request that their personal information be transferred to another handler,[18] access and copy their personal information,[19] request that errors in their personal information be corrected, and request that illegally obtained or handled personal information be deleted.[20] The Personal Information Protection Law further provides that, before personal information can be handled, individuals must be provided with certain information.[21]

Individuals, businesses, and organizations[22] that collect, use, and handle personal information are subject to a range of obligations under the personal information protection regime. They are required to obtain consent to collect, use, and handle personal information, to publish their rules for doing so, and to clearly state the

---

13 *See, e.g.*, Information Security Technology–Personal Information Security Specification, National Standard GB/T 35273-2020 (People's Republic of China), (St. Admin. for Market Regulation and Standardisation Admin. of China, Order No. 1, Mar. 7, 2020, effective Oct. 1, 2020); How to Identify Illegal Collection and Use of Personal Information by Apps (People's Republic of China), (Cyberspace Admin. of China, Ministry of Industry & Information Technology, Ministry of Public Security, and St. Admin. for Market Regulation, Order No. 191, Nov. 28 2019).

14 Civil Code, art. 1035; Cybersecurity Law, art. 41; Personal Information Protection Law, art. 13.

15 Cybersecurity Law, art. 42; Personal Information Protection Law, art. 23.

16 Personal Information Protection Law, art. 14.

17 *Id.*, art. 15.

18 *Id.*, art. 45.

19 *Id.*; Civil Code, art. 1037.

20 Civil Code, art. 1037; Cybersecurity Law, art. 43; Personal Information Protection Law, arts. 46, 47.

21 Personal Information Protection Law, arts. 17, 22, 23, 30, 35, 39, 57.

22 The Civil Code applies to natural and legal persons and unincorporated organizations. "Legal persons" are defined in the Civil Code and does not generally include state authorities such as government departments and Chinese Communist Party entities: *Id*, arts. 57–58 (*see also* Tingmei Fu, *Legal Person in China: Essence and Limits*, 41(2) Am. J. Comp. L. 261 (1993)). The personal information protection–related obligations under the Cybersecurity Law apply to network operators, including network owners, network managers, and network service providers: Cybersecurity Law, art. 76(3). The data protection provisions of the Data Security Law apply to organizations and individuals. The Personal Information Protection Law applies to organizations and individuals: Personal Information Protection Law, art. 2.

purpose, means, and scope for their collection, use, and handling of personal information.[23] The personal information handling activities of individuals, businesses, and organizations are also restricted. They are prohibited from stealing or otherwise illegally acquiring personal information, selling or unlawfully providing personal information to others, collecting or handling excessive personal information or personal information that is unrelated to the services provided, disclosing or tampering with personal information, and acting otherwise unlawfully with respect to the collection and handling of personal information.[24] Further, they have some positive obligations. They are required to use technological and other means to ensure information security and to prevent the unauthorized access, disclosure, theft, tampering, and loss of personal information and, if such breach does occur, to take corrective measures, notify the individuals involved, and report the incident to the relevant government authorities.[25] They are also required to conduct a personal information impact assessment in certain situations.[26] In addition, they are required to provide assistance to and cooperate with government departments carrying out personal information protection duties, public security and national security authorities (collecting data as necessary to maintain national security or investigate crimes), cybersecurity and informatization departments, and other relevant government departments that engage in supervision and inspection activities.[27]

Further, the use of automated decision-making, digital platforms, and data intermediaries are subject to some specific personal information protection obligations. In relation to automated decision-making, individuals, businesses, and organizations must not engage in unreasonable differential treatment (such as price discrimination), and where automated decision-making is used in information push delivery and commercial selling, the Personal Information Protection Law requires that non-tailored options–as well as the option to refuse–must also be provided. Additionally, where a decision that has a major effect on an individual's rights and interests is made via automated decision-making, that individual has the right to request an explanation from the business for the decision and to refuse to have that decision be made by way of automated decision-making means.[28] With respect to digital platforms, the Personal Information Protection Law requires businesses to actively supervise the handling of personal information on their platforms, by establishing compliance systems and an independent body to supervise personal information–handling activities, abiding by principles of fairness, openness, and justice, formulating relevant

---

23 Civil Code, art. 1035; Cybersecurity Law, art. 41; Personal Information Protection Law, arts. 13, 17.
24 Civil Code, arts. 1035, 1038; Cybersecurity Law, arts. 41, 42, 44; Data Security Law, art. 32; Personal Information Protection Law, arts. 5, 6, 10, 25.
25 Civil Code, art. 1038; Cybersecurity Law, art. 42; Personal Information Protection Law, arts. 51, 57.
26 Personal Information Protection Law, art. 55.
27 Cybersecurity Law, arts. 28, 49; Data Security Law, art. 35; Personal Information Protection Law, art. 63.
28 Personal Information Protection Law, art. 24.

rules and standards, stopping the provision of platform services to users that breach personal information protection laws and regulations, and releasing periodic personal information protection social responsibility reports.[29] Finally, under the Data Security Law, data intermediaries must require the party providing the data (which may include personal information) to explain the origins of the data; the data intermediary must review and verify the transacting parties' identities and retain records of such transactions and verifications.[30]

The state, on the other hand, is subject to relatively few restrictions and obligations under the personal information protection regime. State authorities[31] that collect or use personal information in carrying out their legally prescribed duties must do so within the scope of those duties and only to the extent necessary to carry out those duties.[32] They also have notification obligations under the Personal Information Protection Law and are required to maintain the confidentiality of personal information they come across in the course of carrying out their duties and to not disclose or unlawfully provide that information to third parties.[33]

Further, there are a number of exceptions that apply to state authorities or activities involving particular state functions and purposes. Under the Cybersecurity Law, where network operators collect and use personal information in situations relating to, inter alia, national security, national defense, public health and safety, significant public interests, and criminal investigations and enforcement, consent is not required.[34] Similarly, the Civil Code gives an exemption from civil liability in relation to the gathering and handling of personal information where it relates to reasonable measures taken to safeguard public interest,[35] which might be more likely demonstrated by non-state actors acting under the direction of state authorities. The Personal Information Protection Law also provides that notice is not required where a state authority is carrying out its duties and giving notice would impede the carrying out of those duties, or where laws or regulations stipulate that confidentiality must be maintained

---

29 *Id.*, art. 58.

30 Data Security Law, art. 33.

31 Under the Civil Code, state institutions, statutory bodies with administrative functions, and their staff have personal information protection obligations. Under the Cybersecurity Law, art. 45 applies to departments responsible for cybersecurity supervision and management, and art. 30 applies to departments responsible for cybersecurity and informatization and cybersecurity protection. Under the Data Security Law, art. 38 applies to state authorities and other organizations that are authorized by law to carry out public affairs management duties. Under the Personal Information Protection Law, art. 37 provides that the obligations imposed on state organs also apply to organizations that are authorized by law to carry out public affairs management duties.

32 Data Security Law, art. 38; Personal Information Protection Law, art. 34.

33 Civil Code, art. 1039; Cybersecurity Law, art. 45; Data Security Law, art. 38; Personal Information Protection Law, art. 34.

34 Information Security Technology–Personal Information Security Specification, National Standard GB/T 35273-2020, ¶ 5.6.

35 Civil Code, art. 1036.

or that notification is not required.[36] Further, prior consent and notification are not required for all parties that handle personal information where the handling of personal information is necessary to carry out statutory duties, responsibilities, and obligations, respond to public health incidents or to protect lives, health, and property in an emergency, or is reasonable to carry out news reporting, public opinion oversight, and similar activities in the public interest.[37]

2. Balancing personal, commercial, and public interests in personal information

Looking at the rights and obligations created by the personal information protection framework and the parties to which they are addressed, it appears that China's personal information protection regime is characterized by some key features.

The personal information protection regime has been developed under the auspices of laws that are very different in nature. The Civil Code deals principally with private dealings and relationships entered into by individuals with other individuals and businesses. It sets out the rights, obligations, and liabilities relating to property, contracts, personality rights, marriage, family, and succession. The protection of personal information is linked to the right to privacy and is treated as a right of personality, that is, a right that is inherent to natural persons.[38] The Personal Information Protection Law is also principally aimed at protecting the rights and interests of individuals in personal information.[39] By contrast, the Cybersecurity Law and Data Security Law are key pillars of China's national security legal framework. The development of personal information protection under the scope of cybersecurity reflects the fact that the Internet and digital economy are the now the principal sources, sites, and means of data collection, access, analysis, and control. Under the Cybersecurity Law, personal information protection is not viewed solely in terms of its value to natural persons or even to businesses, but also in terms of its value and implications for the state. Personal information protection is an important aspect of ensuring data security,[40] and could also be relevant to protecting the macro-level interests of national security, the national economy and people's livelihoods, and public interest.[41] This view of personal information is reflected and reinforced in the Data Security Law,

---

36   Personal Information Protection Law, arts. 18, 35.

37   *Id.*, arts. 13, 18.

38   Civil Code, part 4.

39   Explanation of the Personal Information Protection Law (Draft), *supra* note 1.

40   Cybersecurity Law, ch 4.

41   Personal information that poses a risk to or has implications for national security, the national economy and people's livelihoods, and public interest will be treated as "important data" under the Cybersecurity Law: Hong Yanqing, *Outbound Data Security Assessment: An Important Part of Protecting Fundamental Strategic Resources*, NEW MEDIA MAGAZINE (Aug. 7, 2017), www.cac.gov.cn/2017-08/07/c_1121443948.htm.

which treats any data that relates to national security, the lifeline of the national economy, important aspects of people's livelihoods, and major public interests as the core data of the state.[42] The Data Security Law also aims to promote the development of data and data-related industries and technologies.[43] As such, the origins of the personal information protection framework demonstrate and highlight that personal information in China is both private and public in nature, and relevant to a range of personal, commercial, and state interests.

The personal information protection regime appears to achieve two seemingly contradictory objectives. On the one hand, it responds to Chinese consumers' growing demands that their personal information be protected from being disclosed, leaked, or used against their wishes, and provides them with some rights and protections with respect to their personal information. At the same time, it ensures that the state's ability to access, control, and use personal information is not significantly constrained. This paper argues that there are two key reasons why China's personal information protection regime is able to pursue these contrary aims concurrently, and they are in keeping with societal and state views and attitudes toward privacy in China, which remain largely framed in terms of protection from non-state actors.

First, individuals, businesses, and organizations that collect, use, and handle personal information have both user-facing and state-facing obligations and are tasked with furthering the interests of both in relation to personal information. The personal information protection regime clearly addresses the risks associated with the private and commercial collection, use, and handling of personal information, as most of its obligations are imposed on individuals, businesses, and organizations. At the same time, individuals, businesses, and organizations that handle personal information are required to cooperate with state authorities, including those that are tasked with enforcing the personal information protection obligations as well as related national security, cybersecurity, public security, and data security duties. Second, while state authorities do have personal information protection obligations, there are a number of exceptions that relate to state authorities and the types of activities they carry out. This likely means that, in practice, the state's power to access, control, and use personal information to carry out its functions, most prominently those relating to national security and defense, public security, cybersecurity, and the public interest, will be maintained and the state will not be significantly constrained by its personal information protection obligations.

It is not yet clear how any tensions or conflicts between the different personal, commercial, and public interests in personal information may be resolved, how trade-offs will be made, or how the Civil Code, Cybersecurity Law, Data Security

---

42   Data Security Law, art. 21.

43   *Id.*, ch 2.

Law, and Personal Information Protection Law will be situated in relation to each other. At the same time, as Lu notes, the relationships between these different stakeholders in personal information protection and the balancing of their interests and objectives is not necessarily a zero-sum game.[44]

The balancing of these interests and their relationships are, however, made even more complicated by the regulatory arrangements underlying the personal information protection regime. The administrative enforcement responsibilities for these laws are dispersed both horizontally (that is, across ministries, departments, and party authorities responsible for different areas and functions) and vertically (that is, across various levels of government), reflecting the variety of interests that state authorities have in personal information.[45] The Cyberspace Administration of China (CAC),[46] the Ministry of Public Security (MPS),[47] and the Ministry of Industry and Information Technology (MIIT)[48] all have responsibilities under the Cybersecurity Law. The enforcement of the Data Security Law is led by the Central Leading Authority on National Security, and the regulatory departments, public and state security organs, and Internet information departments in each region are responsible for the data collected and data security in that region.[49] Similarly, the Personal Information Law provides that, while the CAC will be responsible for planning, coordinating, supervising, and managing the state's personal information protection work, as well as formulating rules and standards to implement the Personal Information Protection Law,[50] other government departments will be responsible for personal information protection, supervision, and management within their own scope of duties and responsibilities, which includes, inter alia, handling complaints and investigating breaches of the Personal Information Protection Law.[51] Not only do these various authorities not have the protection of personal information as their main concern, but the involvement of multiple authorities also brings with it the potential for conflicting interests and bureaucratic turf wars. In fact, the involvement of multiple government bodies, unclear delineation of

---

44 Lu Chuanying, *Data Security Law Must Balance the Needs of All Sides*, GLOBAL TIMES (May 27, 2020), https://3w.huanqiu.com/a/de583b/9CaKrnKr9Bz?agt=11.

45 Cybersecurity Law, art. 8; Personal Information Protection Law, arts. 60–65.

46 The CAC is the main regulator under the Cybersecurity Law. It is both a government organ (State Internet Information Office) and a Chinese Communist Party organ (Office of the Central Cyberspace Affairs Commission), and it reports directly to the Chinese Communist Party Central Committee. *See* Notice of the State Council Authorizing the State Internet Information Office to be Responsible for Internet Information Content Management (People's Republic of China) (St. Council, Order No. 33, Aug. 26, 2014).

47 The MPS is responsible for cybercrime and data security, as part of their broader remit of criminal enforcement and public security.

48 The MIIT is the information technology industry regulator. It is responsible largely for the technological development aspects of cybersecurity: *Central Committee of the Chinese Communist Party Issues "Plan to Deepen Reform of Party and State Institutions"*, XINHUA (Mar. 21, 2018), www.gov.cn/zhengce/2018-03/21/content_5276191.htm.

49 Data Security Law, arts. 5, 6.

50 Personal Information Protection Law, arts. 60, 62.

51 *Id.*, arts. 60, 61.

responsibilities, turf wars, inconsistencies, and inefficiencies have marred the implementation of the Cybersecurity Law.[52]

IV. Interface Between Personal Information Protection and Competition Law in China

The interaction of competition law and personal information protection law can be both complementary and contradictory. For example, if a large digital platform collects excessive information from its users, that conduct may be illegal under both competition law and personal information protection law; here, both laws are aligned. Conversely, while it may level the playing field between digital platforms and apps and improve interoperability if they were to share their users' information with one another, that could give rise to personal information protection concerns. The question of how to address and resolve these potential tensions between personal information protection and competition law is one with which regulators around the world are grappling.

The interaction of personal information protection laws with competition law in China takes place amidst a myriad of interlocking and overlapping interests. As discussed, China's personal information protection legal regime encompasses and balances several key interests: consumers' interest in having their personal information protected, the state's interest in being able to access, control, and use that information, and the commercial interests of the Internet, technology, and digital companies that collect and handle that information. At the same time, as I have argued elsewhere,[53] China's competition laws are guided by, serve, and further the interests of the state. The state's interests in relation to competition law are broad, ranging from conventional competition goals such as enhancing economic efficiency, maintaining competition, and promoting the interests of consumers to other objectives such as industrial policy, market supervision and regulation, and public interest. Therefore, the personal information protection laws and competition laws in China effectively act to coordinate and balance a variety of interests of consumers, businesses, and the state.

---

52 Wang Shenjun, Report of the Law Enforcement Inspection Group of the Standing Committee of the National People's Congress on its Review of the Implementation of the Cybersecurity Law and the Decision of the Standing Committee of the National People's Congress on Strengthening Network Information Protection (Report, 31st meeting of the Standing Committee of the 12th Nat'l People's Cong, Dec. 24, 2017). The creation of the CAC in 2014 and the elevation of its supervising body from being a leading small group (which was chaired by CCP Party Secretary Xi Jinping) to a commission in 2018 were attempts by the leadership to centralize authority over cyberspace and Internet activities and overcome bureaucratic turf wars; Creemers et al., *China's Cyberspace Authorities Set to Gain Clout in Reorganization*, NEW AMERICA (Mar. 26, 2018), www.newamerica.org/cybersecurity-initiative/digichina/blog/chinas-cyberspace-authorities-set-gain-clout-reorganization.

53 Wendy Ng, *State Interest and the State-Centered Approach to Competition Law in China*, 65(2) ANTITRUST BULL. 297 (2020); Wendy Ng, *Changing Global Dynamics and International Competition Law: Considering China's Potential Impact*, 30(4) EUR. J. INT'L L. 1409 (2019).

Unpacking the Personal Information Protection Regime and its Potential Implications for Competition Law in China

Moreover, these legal frameworks and interests exist against the background where the state actively controls, manages, coordinates, and guides the economy. Even though China's Internet and digital economy is dominated by private companies, the state uses various means, such as a range of legal and regulatory measures and policy incentives, as well as the political connections between private entrepreneurs and companies, to exercise control and influence over them.[54] Further, while Internet, digital, and technology companies had faced a relatively permissive regulatory environment, there has been a clear shift to strengthen the government's control and influence over these businesses to support its political goals and "prevent the disorderly expansion of capital."[55] For example, the Chinese government has embarked on a high-profile, multipronged enforcement campaign directed at Alibaba, starting with the suspension of the initial public offering of Ant Group (an affiliate of Alibaba) on the Shanghai Stock Exchange in November 2020, which has been followed by a raft of regulatory demands and ramifications, including a record RMB 18.2 billion antimonopoly fine.[56] Taking regulatory action against one of China's biggest and leading Internet conglomerate companies sends a strong and clear message to all Internet, technology, and digital companies that the time of relaxed regulation and enforcement has ended. The balancing of interests therefore occurs against this background of a significant degree of state control and influence over the economy, and it can pull various legal and regulatory levers to pursue its interests.

This paper argues that, to find out whether and how competition law might be enforced at its interface with personal information protection, we must first directly engage with the variety of consumer, commercial, and state interests that may be affected at that interface. To determine where and how the balance may be struck to resolve any conflicts or tensions between these interests, in addition to identifying and considering the relative importance of each interest to the objectives of the state, it will also likely be necessary to take into account the political power of and relationships between relevant stakeholders with an interest in the matter, such as the CAC, MIIT, MPS, and other government

---

54 *See generally* Wendy Ng, *Data Governance in China's Digital Economy: Can Competition Law Play a Meaningful Role?*, ANTITRUST L.J. (forthcoming 2021).

55 *See, e.g.*, Nationwide Deepening of "Decentralisation, Management, and Service" Reforms to Optimize the Business Environment, Video and Telephone Conference Division of Key Tasks Plan (People's Republic of China), (Gen. Office of the St. Council, Order No. 43, Nov. 1 2020, ¶ 14.3, 15.3), www.gov.cn/zhengce/content/2020-11/10/content_5560234.htm; Zheping Huang & Coco Liu, *China Clampdown on Big Tech Puts More Billionaires on Notice*, BLOOMBERGQUINT, (Nov. 10, 2020), www.bloombergquint.com/global-economics/china-turns-up-heat-on-internet-giants-with-new-antitrust-rules.

56 Administrative Penalty Decision (People's Republic of China), (St. Admin. for Market Regulation, Order No. 28, Apr. 10, 2021) (hereinafter SAMR Alibaba Abuse of Dominance Decision); *Pan Gongsheng, Deputy Governor of the People's Bank of China, Answered Reporters' Questions about the Financial Management Department's Interview with Ant Group*, THE PEOPLE'S BANK OF CHINA (Dec. 27, 2020) www.pbc.gov.cn/goutongjiaoliu/113456/113469/4153479/index.html; Raymond Zhong & Cao Li, *China Halts Ant Group's Blockbuster I.P.O.*, NEW YORK TIMES, (Nov. 3, 2020, www.nytimes.com/2020/11/03/technology/ant-ipo-jack-ma-summoned.html; Keith Zhai & Lingling Wei, *China Lays Plans to Tame Tech Giant Alibaba*, WALL STREET JOURNAL (Mar. 11, 2021), www.wsj.com/articles/china-regulators-plan-to-tame-tech-giant-alibaba-jack-ma-11615475244.

departments responsible for personal information protection, as well as China's competition regulator, the State Administration for Market Regulation (SAMR), and the broader governance and political environment. This paper contends that competition law becomes an increasingly viable and likely avenue through which to deal with the personal information–handling practices of businesses operating in the digital economy, the more that competition concerns can be appropriately balanced and coordinated with personal information protection goals and the other interests and goals of the state, and, of course, there also needs to be a justifiable case under competition law. At least where enforcement produces consistent outcomes under both competition and personal information protection laws, it would not be surprising to see competition law used as a means to deal with personal information protection matters as well as competition concerns.

As of the time of writing, the political environment is one that appears to favor the enforcement of competition law to discipline Internet, technology, and digital companies. The Chinese government has made it clear that competition law will play an important role in supporting its efforts to rein in Internet, technology, and digital companies. China's leaders have expressly called for the strengthening of competition law efforts as part of China's economic work in 2021 and, specifically in relation to digital platforms, for regulators to crack down on monopolies, promote fair competition, and strengthen antitrust supervision.[57]

This high-level political support for competition law seems to have provided the SAMR with the political capital and momentum to boldly pursue competition enforcement vis-à-vis Internet, digital, and technology companies. It has clearly and definitively stepped up its competition law enforcement efforts in this space ever since the suspension of the Ant Group's planned initial public offering in November 2020. It released draft antitrust guidelines that would apply to digital platforms in November 2020,[58] which were finalized and adopted by the Anti-Monopoly Commission in February 2021.[59] The SAMR launched a high-profile antitrust investigation into Alibaba in December 2020, and imposed a record-breaking fine of over RMB 18.2 billion on Alibaba for engaging in exclusive dealing conduct constituting an abuse of market dominance in April 2021;[60] it has also initiated an antitrust investigation into Meituan, a food delivery platform, for engaging in similar exclusive dealing conduct.[61] In December 2020, Alibaba

---

57 *See, e.g., Xi Focus: Xi Chairs Leadership Meeting on Economic Work for 2021*, XINHUA, (Dec. 11, 2020), www.xinhuanet.com/english/2020-12/11/c_139582746.htm; *Xi Jinping: Promoting the Healthy and Sustainable Development of the Platform Economy* (China Central Television, Mar. 15, 2021), https://finance.sina.com.cn/china/2021-03-15/doc-ikknscsi5370359.shtml.

58 Antitrust Guidelines on the Platform Economy (Consultation Draft) (People's Republic of China) (St. Admin. for Market Regulation, Nov. 10, 2020), www.samr.gov.cn/hd/zjdc/202011/t20201109_323234.html.

59 Antitrust Guidelines on the Platform Economy (People's Republic of China) (St. Council Anti-Monopoly Commission, Feb. 7, 2021).

60 SAMR Alibaba Abuse of Dominance Decision, *supra* note 56.

61 *SAMR Initiates Investigation into Meituan for Suspected Monopoly Conduct*, SAMR (Apr. 26, 2021) www.samr.gov.cn/xw/zj/202104/t20210426_328234.html.

and Tencent were punished for not notifying their mergers to the SAMR for antitrust review, and it was the first time that the SAMR had both punished large Chinese Internet companies for such breaches and imposed the highest fines possible.[62] Moreover, in April 2021, the SAMR, together with the CAC and the State Taxation Administration, gave digital platforms in China one month to rectify any anticompetitive conduct, and 34 Chinese digital platforms submitted commitments to the regulators in response to this call.[63] Against this background, it seems that likely that the SAMR's enforcement vigor will soon extend to addressing competition issues arising from the possession, collection, use, and handling of personal information by companies operating in the digital economy.

To date, there has been some limited consideration of personal information matters under China's two key laws that deal with different aspects of competition. The Anti-Monopoly Law[64] (AML) is China's antitrust law and prohibits monopoly agreements, abuses of market power, anticompetitive mergers, and anticompetitive abuses of administrative power. The Anti-Unfair Competition Law[65] (AUCL) covers a range of unfair competition practices and focuses on the fairness of business transactions and business ethics.[66] In particular, though not relied upon much to date (and not in relation to personal information), article 12 of the AUCL is specifically directed at Internet-related businesses and prohibits businesses from using technological means to influence user choices or to otherwise hinder or prevent the normal operations of other businesses in their lawful provision of Internet-related goods and services.[67] Since late March 2018, both laws have been enforced by the SAMR, with different bureaus within the SAMR responsible for enforcing each law. However, to date, most of the

---

62 *Head of SAMR Anti-Monopoly Bureau Answers Reporters' Questions on Sanctions for Three Cases of Failure to Notify Relating to Alibaba Investment's Acquisition of Yintai Commercial, Tencent Holdings's China Literature's Acquisition of Xinli Media, and Fengchao Network Technology's Acquisition of China Post Smart Delivery*, SAMR (Dec. 14, 2020), www.samr.gov.cn/xw/zj/202012/t20201214_324336.html.

63 *SAMR, Cyberspace Administration of China, and the State Taxation Administration Jointly Hold Administrative Guidance Meeting of Internet Platform Businesses*, SAMR (Apr. 13, 2021), www.samr.gov.cn/xw/zj/202104/t20210413_327785.html. The texts of the digital platforms' commitments are found here: *Internet Platform Businesses Disclose to the Public "Commitments to Operate in Compliance with Laws and Regulations" (First Batch)*, SAMR (Apr. 14, 2021), www.samr.gov.cn/xw/zj/202104/t20210413_327811.html; *Internet Platform Businesses Disclose to the Public "Commitments to Operate in Compliance with Laws and Regulations" (Second Batch)*, SAMR (Apr. 15, 2021) www.samr.gov.cn/xw/zj/202104/t20210414_327847.html; *Internet Platform Businesses Disclose to the Public "Commitments to Operate in Compliance with Laws and Regulations" (Third Batch)*, SAMR (Apr. 16, 2021), www.samr.gov.cn/xw/zj/202104/t20210415_327862.html.

64 Anti-Monopoly Law (People's Republic of China), (Standing Comm. of the Nat'l People's Cong., Aug. 30, 2007).

65 Anti-Unfair Competition Law (People's Republic of China), (Standing Comm. of the Nat'l People's Cong., revised Nov. 4, 2017).

66 The AUCL applies to passing off, commercial bribery, misleading advertising, infringement of trade secrets, prize promotions, commercial slander and libel, and Internet-related conduct. *See* AUCL, arts. 6–12.

67 Under art. 12 of the AUCL, businesses must not: (1) insert a URL link or force a URL redirection in an online product or service lawfully provided by another business without their consent; (2) mislead, deceive, or force users to change, shut down or uninstall an online product or service lawfully provided by another business; (3) maliciously cause incompatibility with an online product or service lawfully provided by another business; and (4) engage in other conduct that hinders or destroys the normal operation of an online product or service lawfully provided by another business.

competition law cases that have involved personal information have been private litigation cases decided by Chinese courts under the AUCL.

Under the AUCL, disputes relating to personal information have usually involved situations where a business has taken user information from another business's digital platform without authorization.[68] Courts have referred to personal information protection principles such as consent, lawfulness, and necessity when determining whether such conduct constitutes unfair competition. They recognize that there are two different types of data on digital platforms: the data resource as a whole and the data relating to a specific individual. While the overall data resource is owned by the digital platform business, the data relating to a specific individual is owned by the individual who created that data, and the digital platform only has a limited right to use that data in accordance with its user agreement and the principles of consent, lawfulness, and necessity.[69] Before a business (the third party) can take user data from another business's website or digital platform (the data controller) for its own use, it must obtain three authorizations: from the user to the data controller, the user to the third party, and the data controller to the third party.[70] Courts regard failure to obtain such authorizations as contrary to business ethics and therefore in breach of article 2 of the AUCL,[71] which is the catch-all provision that requires that businesses abide by the principles of voluntariness, equality, fairness, and trustworthiness, and to comply with laws and business ethics.

Some more recent AUCL cases have expressly considered the personal information protection regime in their decisions. For example, in *Tencent v. Sodao Network Technology*, the court found that the defendants had collected and stored the platform user data without authorization, which breached the *Cybersecurity Law* (by harming the users' data rights) and article 2 of the AUCL, as the defendants had endangered users' data security and therefore substantially harmed the competitive advantage that Tencent derived from the overall data resource, which was conduct contrary to business ethics.[72]

---

68 *See, e.g., Dianping v. Baidu; Sina Weibo v. Fuyu; Sina v. Maimai (infra note 70); Taobao v. Meijing; Tencent v. Sodao Network Technology (infra note 69).*

69 Shenzhen Tencent Computer System Co. Ltd v. Zhejiang Sodao Network Technology Co. Ltd (People's Republic of China), (Hangzhou Railway Transportation Court (2019) Zhejiang 8601 Minchu No. 1987, June 2, 2020).

70 Beijing Weimeng Chuangke Network Technology Co. Ltd. v. Beijing Taoyou Tianxia Technology Co. Ltd (People's Republic of China), (Beijing Intellectual Property Court (2016) Jing 73 Min Zhong No. 588, Dec. 30, 2016) (*Sina v. Maimai*); Shenzhen Tencent Computer System Co. Ltd v. Beijing Weibo Vision Technology Co. Ltd (People's Republic of China), (Tianjin Binhai New Area People's Court (2019) Jin 0116 Minchu No. 2091, Mar. 18, 2019) (*Tencent v. Douyin*).

71 *See, e.g., Sina v. Maimai; Tencent v. Douyin; Tencent v. Sodao Network Technology; Dianping v. Baidu.*

72 This is consistent with the courts' approach in the other AUCL cases not involving user data, where they have referred to regulations, industry customs and practices, and technical standards to interpret the notion of good faith in the digital economy: Yaotian Chai, *The New Anti-Unfair Competition Law of the People's Republic of China 2018*, 13(12) J. Intell. Prop. L. & Prac. 998, 1004 (2018).

By contrast, personal information has not been directly considered under the AML, whether by the competition authority or the courts. *Qihoo 360 v. Tencent*[73] did look very briefly at the related question of data security. In that case, when evaluating whether Tencent had engaged in tying conduct in breach of article 17(4) of the AML, the Supreme People's Court determined that it made sense for Tencent to insist that its security software be installed with its instant messaging software, because that would help to ensure the security of user accounts and thereby increase the value and performance of the instant messaging software and enhance efficiency. The court therefore viewed data security as an attribute of product and service quality or as a valid justification for having engaged in that conduct.

Although the possession, collection, use, and handling of personal information by businesses and concerns about personal information protection have not been considered in a meaningful way under the AML to date, this may change in the future as the AML is being updated to better deal with competition issues in the digital economy. The Antitrust Guidelines on the Platform Economy were adopted in February 2021. They set out the SAMR's approach to general matters such as market definition and market dominance when looking at digital platforms, and address some specific issues that have been observed in China's digital platform environment.[74] In particular, the guidelines specifically refer to some personal information matters, mostly in relation to abuse of dominance conduct and mergers. The SAMR may consider the forced collection of non-essential user information when determining whether a dominant company has engaged in tying conduct or imposed unreasonable trading conditions,[75] and the use of big data and algorithms (such as those relating to users' ability to pay, their consumption preferences, and usage habits) can be taken into account when determining whether a dominant company has engaged in differential treatment;[76] the protection of the interests of consumers and data security may also be regarded as legitimate reasons for why a dominant company restricted its transactions.[77]

The guidelines also provide that, when evaluating the potential impact of a proposed merger on competition, the SAMR can consider whether the merged firm will have the ability and incentive to misuse consumer information,[78] and possible merger remedies could include requiring the merging firms to divest

---

73 *Beijing Qihoo Technology Ltd. v. Tencent Technology (Shenzhen) Company Limited* (People's Republic of China), (Supreme People's Court (2013) Min San Zhong Zi No 4, Oct. 8, 2014).

74 Such matters include the use of exclusive dealing requirements, variable interest entities, and hub-and-spoke agreements, and acquisitions of start-up or emerging platforms that do not meet notification thresholds: Antitrust Guidelines on the Platform Economy, arts. 8, 15(1), 18, 19.

75 *Id.*, art. 16(1)(5).

76 *Id.*, art. 17(1)(1).

77 *Id.*, art. 15(2)(1), (2).

78 *Id.*, art. 20(6).

their data or provide access to their data to third parties.[79] It is also likely that personal information protection issues will be considered more expressly under the AML in the future, as Chinese competition authorities have enforced the AML to reinforce and ensure compliance with sector regulations and to support sector reforms and policies in regulated industries in the past.[80] Non-compliance with China's now more comprehensive personal information protection laws might similarly be used to justify findings of breach of the AML.

V. Conclusion

The building of a more complete personal information protection regime is an important development in China's legal and governance system and its digital economy. While China's personal information protection laws emphasize the importance of protecting personal information, they also preserve the state's ability to access, control, and use that information. Businesses operating in the digital economy have in their possession vast amounts of personal information, and they sit in amidst multiple stakeholders and interests–growing pressures from the public and government alike to provide personal information protection to consumers, requests for cooperation with state authorities that may include providing them with access to their customers' personal information, and being able to use the personal information in their possession to pursue their commercial objectives and interests. Businesses also face an increasingly tight regulatory environment in which competition law is being promoted as an important legal tool to help impose market order on companies. These dynamics are likely to work together to lead to increased competition law scrutiny and enforcement in China in relation to the Internet, technology, and digital businesses, and their collection, use, and handling of personal information, in a manner that might more expressly and materially consider compliance with personal information protection laws as being relevant to competition, fairness, and business ethics.

---

79 *Id.*, art. 21.
80 WENDY NG, THE POLITICAL ECONOMY OF COMPETITION LAW IN CHINA (2018) 270–73.

Concurrences Review

Concurrences is a print and online quarterly peer reviewed journal dedicated to EU and national competitions laws. It has been launched in 2004 as the flagship of the Institute of Competition Law in order to provide a forum for academics, practitioners and enforcers. Concurrences'influence and expertise has garnered contributions or interviews with such figures as Christine Lagarde, Bill Kovacic, Emmanuel Macron, Antonin Scalia and Magrethe Vestager.

Contents

More than 12,000 articles, print and/or online. Quarterly issues provide current coverage with contributions from the EU or national or foreign countries thanks to more than 1,500 authors in Europe and abroad.

Format

In order to balance academic contributions with opinions or legal practice notes, Concurrences provides its insight and analysis in a number of formats:
- Forewords: Opinions by leading academics or enforcers
- Interviews: Interviews of antitrust experts
- On-Topics: 4 to 6 short papers on hot issues
- Law & Economics: Short papers written by economists for a legal audience
- Articles: Long academic papers
- Case Summaries: Case commentary on EU and French case law
- Legal Practice: Short papers for in-house counsels
- International: Medium size papers on international policies
- Books Review: Summaries of recent antitrust books
- Articles Review: Summaries of leading articles published in 45 antitrust journals

Boards

The Scientific Committee is headed by Laurence Idot, Professor at Panthéon Assas University. The International Committee is headed by Frederic Jenny, OECD Competition Comitteee Chairman. Boards members include Douglas Ginsburg, Bruno Lasserre, Howard Shelanski, Richard Whish, Wouter Wils, Joshua Wright, etc.

Online version

Concurrences website provides all articles published since its inception, in addition to selected articles published online only in the electronic supplement.

Write for Concurrences

Concurrences welcome spontaneous contributions. Except in rare circumstances, the journal accepts only unpublished articles, whatever the form and nature of the contribution. The Editorial Board checks the form of the proposals, and then submits these to the Scientific Committee. Selection of the papers is conditional to a peer review by at least two members of the Committee. Within a month, the Committee assesses whether the draft article can be published and notifies the author.

e-Competitions Bulletin

CASE LAW DATABASE

e-Competitions is the only online resource that provides consistent coverage of antitrust cases from 85 jurisdictions, organized into a searchable database structure. e-Competitions concentrates on cases summaries taking into account that in the context of a continuing growing number of sources there is a need for factual information, i.e., case law.

- 18,000 case summaries
- 4,000 authors
- 85 countries covered
- 30,000 subscribers

SOPHISTICATED EDITORIAL AND IT ENRICHMENT

e-Competitions is structured as a database. The editors make a sophisticated technical and legal work on all articles by tagging these with key words, drafting abstracts and writing html code to increase Google ranking. There is a team of antitrust lawyers – PhD and judges clerks - and a team of IT experts. e-Competitions makes comparative law possible. Thanks to this expert editorial work, it is possible to search and compare cases by jurisdiction, legal topics or business sectors.

PRESTIGIOUS BOARDS

e-Competitions draws upon highly distinguished editors, all leading experts in national or international antitrust. Advisory Board Members include: Sir Christopher Bellamy, Ioanis Lianos (UCL), Eleanor Fox (NYU), Frédéric Jenny (OECD), Jacqueline Riffault-Silk (Cour de cassation), Wouter Wils (King's College London), etc.

LEADING PARTNERS

- Association of European Competition Law Judges: The AECLJ is a forum for judges of national Courts specializing in antitrust case law. Members timely feed e-Competitions with just released cases.

- Academics partners: Antitrust research centres from leading universities write regularly in e-Competitions: University College London, King's College London, Queen Mary University, etc.

- Law firms: Global law firms and antitrust niche firms write detailed cases summaries specifically for e-Competitions: Allen & Overy, Baker McKenzie, Cleary Gottlieb Steen & Hamilton, Jones Day, Norton Rose Fulbright, Skadden, White & Case, etc.

The Institute of Competition Law

The Institute of Competition Law is a publishing company, founded in 2004 by Dr. Nicolas Charbit, based in Paris, London and New York. The Institute cultivates scholarship and discussion about antitrust issues though publications and conferences. Each publication and event is supervised by editorial boards and scientific or steering committees to ensure independence, objectivity, and academic rigor. Thanks to this management, the Institute has become one of the few think tanks in Europe to have significant influence on antitrust policies.

AIM

The Institute focuses government, business and academic attention on a broad range of subjects which concern competition laws, regulations and related economics.

BOARDS

To maintain its unique focus, the Institute relies upon highly distinguished editors, all leading experts in national or international antitrust: Bill Kovacic, Mario Monti, Eleanor Fox, Laurence Idot, Frédéric Jenny, Ioannis Lianos, Richard Whish, etc.

AUTHORS

3,800 authors, from 55 jurisdictions.

PARTNERS

- Universities: University College London, King's College London, Queen Mary University, Paris Sorbonne Panthéon-Assas, etc.

- Law firms: Allen & Overy, Cleary Gottlieb Steen & Hamilton, Baker McKenzie, Hogan Lovells, Jones Day, Norton Rose Fulbright, Skadden Arps, White & Case, etc.

EVENTS

Brussels, Dusseldorf, Hong Kong, London, Milan, New York, Paris, Singapore, Warsaw and Washington, DC.

ONLINE VERSION

Concurrences website provides all articles published since its inception.

PUBLICATIONS

The Institute publishes Concurrences Review, a print and online quarterly peer-reviewed journal dedicated to EU and national competitions laws. e-Competitions is a bi-monthly antitrust news bulletin covering 85 countries. The e-Competitions database contains over 18,000 case summaries from 4,000 authors.

17 years of archives
30,000 articles

4 DATABASES

Concurrences
Access to latest issue and archives
- 12,000 articles from 2004 to the present
- European and national doctrine and case law

e-Competitions
Access to latest issue and archives
- 18,000 case summaries from 1911 to the present
- Case law of 85 jurisdictions

Books
Access to all Concurrences books
- 42 e-Books available
- PDF version

Conferences
Access to the documentation of all Concurrences events
- 500 conferences (Brussels, Hong Kong, London, New York, Paris, Singapore and Washington, DC)
- 250 PowerPoint presentations, proceedings and syntheses
- 300 videos
- Verbatim reports

NEW

New search engine
Optimized results to save time
- Search results sorted by date, jurisdiction, keyword, economic sector, author, etc.

New modes of access
IP address recognition
- No need to enter codes: immediate access
- No need to change codes when your team changes: offers increased security and saves time

Mobility
- Responsive design: site optimized for tablets and smartphones

Lightning Source UK Ltd.
Milton Keynes UK
UKHW021522151221
395598UK00002B/7/J